Exploring Our Nation's History

Exploring Our Nation's History

Sidney Schwartz
John R. O'Connor

GLOBE BOOK COMPANY, INC.
NEW YORK/CHICAGO/CLEVELAND

SIDNEY SCHWARTZ served as a social studies teacher, guidance counselor, and department chairperson of social studies and other academic subjects. He wrote social studies texts including Globe's *Inquiry: Western Civilization*, and is the author of several workbooks and teachers' manuals. For many years he was active as a member of the Association of Chairmen in the New York City Schools.

JOHN R. O'CONNOR
Mr. O'Connor taught social studies for many years before becoming a principal in the New York City school system. He is widely known for his lectures and for his articles on reading skills in the social studies. In addition to this book, Mr. O'Connor has edited the Globe social studies textbooks *Exploring the Western World, Exploring Africa South of the Sahara, The New Exploring a Changing World,* and *The New Exploring American History*. He is also the coauthor of *The New Exploring the Urban World, Exploring Urban New York,* the series *Inquiry: Western Civilization, The New Exploring World History,* and *Exploring American Citizenship*.

Photo editor: Adelaide Garvin Ungerland
Illustrations: Joseph Forté
Maps and graphs: Milton S. Venezky, Clifton O. Spurlock, Dyno Lowenstein, Pictograph Corp., and Joseph LeMonnier
Time lines: Bill Gray
Cover design: Caliber Design Planning, Inc.
Cover photograph: Robert Llewellyn

ISBN: 0-87065-615-5

© 1984, 1979, 1969 by Globe Book Company, Inc.
50 West 23 Street, New York, New York 10010
All rights reserved. No part of this book may be kept in an information storage or retrieval system, transmitted or reproduced in any form or by any means without the prior written permission of the publisher.

Published simultaneously in Canada by Globe/Modern Curriculum Press

Printed in the United States of America   9 8 7 6 5 4 3 2

CONTENTS

Introduction: The United States Today ... 3

Unit One
THE COLONIAL PERIOD 11

CHAPTER 1: THE EXPLORATION AND SETTLEMENT OF AMERICA ... 13
Section 1: Why Were Europeans Seeking a New Route to the East? ... 14
Section 2: How Did Europeans Open a New World in the Americas? ... 22

CHAPTER 2: SETTLING THE THIRTEEN COLONIES ... 29
Section 1: Why Did Europeans Come to the Thirteen Colonies? ... 30
Section 2: How Did the English Settlements Grow Into Thirteen Colonies? ... 35

CHAPTER 3: THE BEGINNINGS OF AMERICAN DEMOCRACY ... 45
Section 1: How Did Democracy Come to the Thirteen Colonies? ... 46
Section 2: How Did Democracy Develop in the Thirteen Colonies? ... 52

CHAPTER 4: THE BACKGROUND OF THE AMERICAN REVOLUTION ... 60
Section 1: Why Were the Colonists Loyal to Great Britain Before 1763? ... 61
Section 2: Why Did the Spirit of Independence Grow After 1763? ... 68

CHAPTER 5: THE AMERICAN REVOLUTION AND ITS RESULTS ... 76
Section 1: How Did the Americans Win the Revolutionary War? ... 77
Section 2: What Did the Revolution Mean in America and the World? ... 85
SUMMING UP THE UNIT: HOW DID THE UNITED STATES GET STARTED? ... 91
RECOMMENDED READING ... 94

Unit Two
OUR FEDERAL GOVERNMENT 99

CHAPTER 6: THE CRITICAL PERIOD	101
Section 1: How Was the United States Governed Under the Articles of Confederation?	102
Section 2: What Were the Problems of the New Government?	108
CHAPTER 7: MAKING THE CONSTITUTION	115
Section 1: What Is the Federal System of Government?	116
Section 2: Why Is Our Constitution "a Bundle of Compromises"?	123
CHAPTER 8: THE LEGISLATIVE BRANCH	130
Section 1: How Is the Lawmaking Branch Organized?	131
Section 2: How Does a Bill Become a Law?	137
CHAPTER 9: THE EXECUTIVE AND JUDICIAL BRANCHES	144
Section 1: How Powerful Is the President?	145
Section 2: How Do the Judicial, Executive, and Legislative Branches Work Together?	152
CHAPTER 10: OUR CHANGING GOVERNMENT	158
Section 1: How Has Our Federal Government Changed Through the Years?	159
Section 2: How Does the Constitution Protect Our Liberties?	164
SUMMING UP THE UNIT: DID THE CONSTITUTION ACHIEVE ITS PURPOSES?	171
RECOMMENDED READING	175

Unit Three
OUR NATION BECOMES STRONG 177

CHAPTER 11: BEGINNING THE NEW GOVERNMENT	179
Section 1: How Did the New Government Handle Its Problems at Home?	180
Section 2: How Did President Washington Deal With Foreign Nations?	186
Section 3: How Did Political Parties Arise?	191
CHAPTER 12: THE FIRST REPUBLICAN PRESIDENTS	199
Section 1: Did Jefferson Really Change the American Government?	200
Section 2: Why Did the United States Declare War on Great Britain?	206

CHAPTER 13: THE WAR OF 1812 212
    Section 1: Who Won the War of 1812? 213
    Section 2: What Were the Aftereffects of the War of 1812? 218

CHAPTER 14: THE RISE OF SECTIONALISM 226
    Section 1: How Did Industry and Commerce Grow in the Northeast? 228
    Section 2: How Did the Plantation System Develop in the South? 233
    Section 3: Why Did Settlers Move to the "Old West"? 240

CHAPTER 15: PRESIDENT JACKSON AND DEMOCRACY 248
    Section 1: Was Jackson Really "the People's President"? 249
    Section 2: Why Were the 1830s Called an "Era of Democracy"? 257

CHAPTER 16: A PERIOD OF EXPANSION AND PROGRESS 265
    Section 1: How Did the United States Expand to the Pacific? 266
    Section 2: How Did the United States Progress Within Its Borders? .. 272
    SUMMING UP THE UNIT: HOW DID THE UNITED STATES BECOME A
        STRONG NATION? 278

RECOMMENDED READING 282

Unit Four
THE CIVIL WAR   285

CHAPTER 17: THE PROBLEM OF SLAVERY 287
    Section 1: How Did Slavery Become Established in America? 288
    Section 2: Why Did the North and South Clash Over Slavery? 294

CHAPTER 18: THE ROAD TO CIVIL WAR 302
    Section 1: How Did Congress Deal With the Western Territories? 303
    Section 2: Why Did the North and South Go to War? 310

CHAPTER 19: THE CIVIL WAR AND ITS RESULTS 317
    Section 1: How Did the North Win the Civil War? 318
    Section 2: How Did the Civil War Change the United States? 327

CHAPTER 20: THE RECONSTRUCTION OF THE SOUTH 334
    Section 1: What Were the Opposing Plans for Reconstruction? 335
    Section 2: How Did Congress' Plan for Reconstruction Work? 342
    SUMMING UP THE UNIT: WHAT WERE THE RESULTS OF "A GENERA-
        TION OF CONFLICT"? 348

RECOMMENDED READING 350

Unit Five
THE ECONOMIC REVOLUTION 353

CHAPTER 21: THE REVOLUTION IN INDUSTRY — 355
   Section 1: How Did the United States Become a Great Industrial Nation? — 356
   Section 2: What Problems Did Big Business Create? — 363
   Section 3: What Problems Did the Workers Face? — 369

CHAPTER 22: THE AGRICULTURAL REVOLUTION — 376
   Section 1: How Was the Wild West Tamed? — 377
   Section 2: Why Were the Farmers Dissatisfied? — 384

CHAPTER 23: POLITICS AND CULTURE IN THE GILDED AGE — 391
   Section 1: What Was Wrong With Our Government in the Gilded Age? — 392
   Section 2: What Did Reformers Accomplish? — 399

CHAPTER 24: THE PROGRESSIVE ERA — 406
   Section 1: What Reforms Were Made in Local and State Governments? — 407
   Section 2: Why Was Theodore Roosevelt Considered a Progressive? — 413
   Section 3: Were Presidents Taft and Wilson Progressives? — 418
   SUMMING UP THE UNIT: How Did the United States Progress Between 1865 and 1916? — 424

RECOMMENDED READING — 428

Unit Six
OUR NEW FOREIGN POLICY 431

CHAPTER 25: AMERICA ACQUIRES AN EMPIRE — 433
   Section 1: How Did the United States Become Involved in the Far East? — 434
   Section 2: Was the Spanish-American War Justified? — 439
   Section 3: How Has the United States Governed Its Possessions? — 445

CHAPTER 26: OUR INVOLVEMENT IN LATIN AMERICA — 453
   Section 1: How Did the United States Protect Latin America? — 455
   Section 2: Why Did Latin Americans Object to Our New Policy? — 460

CHAPTER 27: THE UNITED STATES AND WORLD WAR I — 466
   Section 1: How Did the United States Become Involved in the War? — 467
   Section 2: How Did the United States Help Win the War? — 473

CHAPTER 28: THE FAILURE TO MAKE A LASTING PEACE — 481

Section 1: Why Did the United States Return to Isolationism? 482
Section 2: How Did the Policy of Isolationism Work? 488
SUMMING UP THE UNIT: HOW WAS THE UNITED STATES DRAWN INTO WORLD AFFAIRS? 494
RECOMMENDED READING 498

Unit Seven
BETWEEN TWO WORLD WARS 501

CHAPTER 29: THE UNITED STATES AFTER WORLD WAR I 503
Section 1: How Did the United States Change in the 1920s? 504
Section 2: What Were the Causes of the Great Depression? 512

CHAPTER 30: FDR AND THE NEW DEAL 519
Section 1: How Did the New Deal Provide Relief and Promote Recovery? 520
Section 2: How Did the New Deal Reform the Economy? 526

CHAPTER 31: FDR's FOREIGN POLICY 533
Section 1: How Did FDR Improve Relations With Latin America? 534
Section 2: How Did the United States Get Into World War II? 539

CHAPTER 32: THE UNITED STATES IN WORLD WAR II 546
Section 1: How Did the United States Organize for War? 547
Section 2: How Did the Allies Win the War? 554

CHAPTER 33: MAKING THE PEACE AFTER WORLD WAR II 563
Section 1: What Agreements Did the Big Three Reach? 564
Section 2: How Does the UN Work to Keep World Peace? 571
SUMMING UP THE UNIT: HOW WAS OUR NATION AFFECTED BY TWO WORLD WARS? 578
RECOMMENDED READING 582

Unit Eight
AFTER WORLD WAR II 585

CHAPTER 34: DEVELOPMENTS IN THE GENERATION AFTER WORLD WAR II 587
Section 1: How Did Presidents Handle Problems at Home in Midcentury? 588
Section 2: How Did Presidents Meet the Problems of the 1960s and 1970s? 600

CHAPTER 35: POVERTY, PREJUDICE, AND DISCRIMINATION 609

Section 1: How Have Black People Been Denied Equal Rights? — 610
Section 2: How Have Blacks Advanced Toward Equality? — 616
Section 3: What Other Groups Have Suffered From Discrimination? — 625
Section 4: What Problems Do Americans Face? — 635

CHAPTER 36: IMPROVING THE QUALITY OF AMERICAN LIFE — 643
Section 1: What Problems Do Cities Face? — 644
Section 2: How Can We Conserve Our Natural Resources? — 651
Section 3: How Can the Nation Meet Its Energy Needs? — 656
Section 4: How Can We Conserve Our Human Resources? — 661

CHAPTER 37: THE NEW AMERICAN FOREIGN POLICY — 667
Section 1: How Did a "Cold War" Develop and Deepen? — 668
Section 2: How Did Communist Expansion Lead to Wars in Asia? — 677
Section 3: How Has the United States Been Working for Peace? — 684
SUMMING UP THE UNIT: HOW HAVE CONDITIONS CHANGED SINCE WORLD WAR II? — 694

RECOMMENDED READING — 701

Appendix

Map of the United States — 702
The Presidents of the United States — 704
The Declaration of Independence — 706
The Constitution of the United States — 708
Glossary — 732
Index — 742

TIME LINES, MAPS, GRAPHS, AND PICTOGRAPHS

Unit One

Geography of the United States — 2
Unit One time line: A.D. 500-2000 — 12
Voyages of Exploration — 16
European Colonies in the Americas, 1750 — 25
The Thirteen Colonies (about 1750) — 36
Population Growth in the Thirteen Colonies — 42

Social Classes in 18th-Century Europe	48
Social Classes in 18th-Century America	52
Untitled sketch of tree	59
Triangular Trade Routes	62
Effects of French and Indian War—1763	63
The Revolutionary War	78
United States in 1783	86
Unit One summary time line	92

Unit Two

Unit Two time line: 1775-1789	100
Effects of the Northwest Ordinance	105
Division of Powers	117
Methods of Election in the Constitution	124
Unity of Powers Versus Separation of Powers	132
How a Bill Becomes a Law	139
The Close Election of 1976	146
The President's Cabinet	147
Checks and Balances	154
The Amendment Process	159
Important Provisions of the Bill of Rights	165

Unit Three

Unit Three time line: 1789-1849	178
Cause of the Whiskey Rebellion	182
Population Growth and Increase in Wealth	185
Louisiana Purchase	201
War of 1812	214
Rise of Sections of the United States	227
Growth of Manufacturing	229
Production of Raw Cotton	234
Slaveowning in the South in 1850	236
Routes to the Old West in 1840	242
Growth of Population in the Old West	242
Mexican War	268

Expansion of the United States	271
Immigration Into the United States, 1821-1860	275
Unit Three summary time line	280

Unit Four

Unit Four time line: 1849-1877	286
Blacks in the United States	295
Freedom and Slavery in the United States in 1850	309
Kansas-Nebraska Act	310
Election of 1860	312
South Versus North in 1860	319
Opposing Sides in the Civil War	320
The Civil War	322
American Casualties in Wars	327
Military Rule	339

Unit Five

Unit Five time line: 1865-1916	354
Value of American Manufactures, 1859-1919, and Railroad Mileage in the United States, 1860-1920	362
Union Membership in the United States, 1870-1920	373
Routes to the Far West	379
United States Agriculture, 1860-1920	389
Civil Service Employees in the United States, 1891-1941	394
The United States in 1916	423

Unit Six

Unit Six time line: 1789-1932	432
United States Pacific Possessions in 1900	435
Spanish-American War	441
Latin America	454
World War I	476
Rivals in the Pacific, 1921	489

Unit Seven

Unit Seven time line: 1918-1945	502
Immigration Into the United States From Europe, 1880-1930	506
The Tennessee Valley Authority	528
High Tide of Axis Conquest, 1942	543
Spending by the United States War Department, 1940-1945	553
United States Naval Construction, 1940-1945	553
Allied Offensives in the West	555
Offensives in the Pacific	558
American Casualties in Wars	561
The Division of Germany	566
Communist Gains as a Result of World War II	567

Unit Eight

Unit Eight time line: 1945-Present	586
The Federal Debt	605
Black and White Unemployment in the U.S., 1954–1982	614
The Gap Between Black and White Family Income in the U.S., 1955–1980	615
Average Income, 1981	623
Percentage, All Workers with $10,000 Yearly Income or More	623
Life Expectancy in the United States, 1900–1980	624
The Ten Leading Sources of Immigrants to the United States	634
How Education Raises Income	638
Who Are the Poor?	639
The Increasing Cost of Public Assistance	642
Giant Urban Areas of the United States	646
World Oil Production, 1981	657
Share of Total U.S. Oil Use From Imports	658
Military Alliances in 1982	670–671
U.S. Economic Aid to Foreign Nations, 1946–1981	683
The Middle East	685
Unit Eight summary time line	697

SHORT BIOGRAPHIES AND OTHER FEATURES

The Man Who Saved Jamestown: Captain John Smith	38
Roger Williams and Anne Hutchinson: Fighters for Freedom	54
The Life of Benjamin Franklin: An American Success Story	64
Samuel Adams: "Mr. Revolution"	70
Daniel Boone: Pioneer	104
George Washington: The Father of His Country	118
Alexander Hamilton: Aristocratic Commoner	192
Thomas Jefferson: Aristocrat for Democracy	193
John Marshall: Chief Justice of the Supreme Court	220
Andrew Jackson: Our First President From the West	253
Abraham Lincoln: A Successful Failure	321
Lincoln's Gettysburg Address (1863)	323
Thomas Alva Edison: The "Wizard of Menlo Park"	358
Elizabeth Blackwell and Belva Lockwood: Two Who Opened Doors	375
Franklin Delano Roosevelt: Friend of the "Forgotten Man"	521
Highlights of World War II	559
John F. Kennedy: Hero in War and Peace	593
Mary McCleod Bethune: A Black Educator	619
Martin Luther King: The Man Who Would Not Hate	621

SKILLS EXERCISES

Using This Textbook 7

Mastering the Map 8–9, 20, 28, 42, 67, 84, 89–90, 107, 150, 204, 217, 232, 246–47, 271, 309, 326, 341, 383, 423, 438, 444, 459, 479, 494, 531, 545, 562, 569–70, 650, 693

Reading the Time Line 20–21, 106–7, 184–85, 292, 361–62, 438, 510, 599, 700–701

Understanding the Sketch 28, 51, 129, 143, 197–98, 264, 405

Finding Word Meanings 34–35, 43–44, 51, 58, 75, 84

Interpreting the Graph 42–43, 185, 233, 239, 247, 277, 300–1, 327, 333, 362, 389–90, 398, 510, 552–53, 561, 614–615, 623–624, 633, 641–642, 660, 683

Finding the Main Idea 107–8, 113–14, 122, 128–29, 163, 204–5, 224–25

Making an Outline 141–43, 150–51, 163, 190, 360–61, 517–18, 538

Answering Essay Questions 205, 210–11, 217, 374

Telling Facts from Opinions 237–39, 246, 367–68, 383, 398, 444–45, 451–52, 479–80, 493–94, 576–77, 614, 676

Looking at Both Sides 256–57, 271–72, 301, 368, 404–5, 471–72, 486–87, 532, 545, 570, 599, 608, 623, 650, 666

Choosing Reliable Sources 292–93, 308–9

Getting Different Viewpoints 411–12, 417, 422–23, 459, 532

This Land Is Your Land ©

CHORUS:

This land is your land, this land is my land,
From California to the New York Island.
From the redwood forest to the Gulf Stream waters,
This land was made for you and me.

As I went walking that ribbon of highway
I saw about me that endless skyway,
I saw below me that golden valley,
This land was made for you and me.

CHORUS

I roamed and rambled, and I followed my footsteps,
To the sparkling sands of her diamond deserts,
All around me a voice was sounding,
This land was made for you and me.

CHORUS

When the sun come shining, then I was strolling,
And the wheat fields waving, and the dust clouds rolling,
A voice was chanting as the fog was lifting,
This land was made for you and me.

CHORUS

                                    Woody Guthrie

GEOGRAPHY OF THE UNITED STATES

- Atlantic Coastal Plain
- Appalachian Highlands
- Mississippi River Basin
- Far West

INTRODUCTION

The United States Today

A. A Great Nation. We Americans are a fortunate people. Four hundred years ago our land was wilderness. Over two centuries have passed since we became an independent nation. Today, our country is one of the largest in the world, both in size and in population. It is, moreover, the world's richest nation and one of its strongest military powers. Our factories produce a large portion of all the goods manufactured in the world. Our farmers raise such large crops that we are able to sell and give away millions of tons of food each year to hungry people in other lands. Thanks to this huge production, our nation is wealthier by far than any other country in history.

How did the United States become such a great nation in so short a time? There are three main reasons for our nation's success. They are our land, our people, and our high ideals.

B. Our Rich Land. 1. SIZE OF THE UNITED STATES. As the map on page 2 shows, the main part of the United States stretches some three thousand miles from the Atlantic Ocean on the east to the Pacific Ocean on the west. Its width from Canada on the north to Mexico on the south is about 1,200 miles. When we add Alaska, Hawaii, and a few small possessions, the total area of the United States comes to more than 3,600,000 square miles. It is many times the size of France, Germany, and other important European countries. Only the Soviet Union (Russia), Canada, and mainland China have a greater area than the United States. Brazil is almost as large.

2. FERTILE FARMLANDS. Other large countries have vast areas that are unfit for farming. In the Soviet Union and Canada, these areas are cold; in China, they are dry and mountainous; in Brazil, they are hot and wet. Most of the United States, on the other hand, enjoys a moderate climate, plenty of rainfall, and rich deep soils. Our country has over 2,000,000 square miles of fertile farmlands. Even the Soviet Union, which is more than twice the size of the United States, does not have as much.

3. FORESTS. The United States is also rich in other important natural resources. One-half of our entire country was once covered with thick forests. These provided the settlers with fuel for their fires and lumber for building their houses, wagons, and boats. The forests were full of wild game and the streams were full of fish. Lumbering, hunting, fishing, and fur trapping became important occupations in our country's early days. They are still important in some places today.

4. MINERAL RESOURCES. The United States has an unusually large supply of minerals. Modern industry is based in part on three mineral resources: coal, iron ore, and petroleum. Rich deposits of all three were found in the Appalachian Highlands and the Mississippi River Basin (see map, page 2). Large oil fields have been discovered in southern California and Texas, in the waters of the Gulf of Mexico and off the Pacific Coast, and in northern Alaska. Mountains of the Far West have large amounts of gold, silver, lead, zinc, and other valuable minerals.

5. WATERWAYS. Thanks to its abundant rainfall, the United States has many important rivers and lakes. Its Great Lakes are among the world's largest bodies of fresh water (see map, page 2). The Mississippi and its tributaries (rivers that run into it) form one of the greatest river systems on earth. These waterways make it easy to move people and goods from one part of the country to another. They also supply water for irrigating crops and for making electricity. In addition, our country has long coastlines with many good harbors. These have made it easy for Americans to develop a large trade with foreign lands.

A lighthouse on New England's "stern and rockbound coast."

Alaska's Mt. McKinley, the highest mountain in North America.

Brilliant, colored rock formations of Bryce Canyon in Utah.

6. **NATURAL BEAUTY.** The United States is as rich in natural beauty as it is in natural resources. It contains a great variety of scenery —broad grassy plains and towering forest-covered mountains, green river valleys and sandy deserts, wave-beaten ocean shores and calm blue lakes. The United States also has hundreds of breathtaking natural wonders like those shown on this page and the next. In fact, people in many regions of the country consider this natural beauty to be a natural resource. Millions of people, many from other countries, visit these areas each year. All of us should travel through our country to see for ourselves its great size, natural wealth, and beautiful scenery. Then we will truly understand why we are lucky to be Americans.

C. The American People. The United States is likewise rich in human resources. Our country has about 230,000,000 people, more than any other nation except mainland China, India, and the Soviet Union. The American people are a mixture of immigrants from many lands. In early days, most settlers came here from northern and western Europe. The largest number came from the parent country, England, and also from nearby Scotland and Ireland. Another large group migrated from Germany, which was suffering from wars and other troubles. Colonies settled by the Dutch, Swedes, French, and Spanish also became part of our nation. In the past hundred years or so, millions of immigrants have come here from Italy, Poland, Russia, and other countries of southern and eastern Europe.

The largest percentage of the American people are of European descent. These include not just descendants of immigrants from Europe, but also those from Canada, Mexico, and other parts of the New World. Another 11 percent are those of African descent whose ancestors were brought here as slaves. Several million Americans are descendants of people from still other areas. Many are descendants of the Native Americans or Indians (the first settlers in America). Others are the descendants of later immigrants from Asia, such as the Chinese, Japanese, and Filipinos. All—regardless of race, religion, or the nationality of their ancestors—are Americans.

Our country has been enriched by the contributions of many peoples. Our language is very rich because it contains many words from other languages. Our literature, art, music, and dancing are full of ideas from other cultures. Our industry and agriculture have developed rapidly because of the skills of immigrants from many lands.

D. Our High Ideals. Our nation's growth has also been stimulated by the high ideals and

The North Carolina countryside. These hills are located between the low coastal plains and the Blue Ridge and Great Smoky mountains.

The broad plains of Kansas with rolling fields of wheat.

The Pacific coastline of Oregon is noted for its scenic beauty.

5

The Oroville Dam on the Feather River in California. It is the highest dam in the United States. It supplies great amounts of water for irrigating dry farmland and great amounts of electric power for industry.

principles that developed in America. Here the common people freed themselves from the control of the upper class. They came to believe that all people are equal and that they are entitled to such rights as freedom of speech and the press. When the British government tried to interfere with the exercise of these beliefs, Americans fought and won a war for independence from British rule.

The new American spirit—based on liberty, equality, and democracy—encouraged progress. "In worn-out, king-ridden Europe," one observer said, "people must stay where they are born! But in America people are accounted failures unless they rise above their parents' station in life." Because Americans could improve their position in life through their own efforts, they worked very hard. In a few hundred years, they changed a vast wilderness into a great nation.

When the United States became a world power, it did not forget its high ideals. Some powerful nations have used their strength to conquer and enslave other peoples. But America has helped weaker nations to win and keep their independence. It has also helped the people of these nations to improve their ways of life.

E. Outlook for the Future. Despite its many achievements, the United States is still far from perfect. Though it is a very rich nation, millions of Americans are poor. Equality is one of our democratic ideals; yet many of our citizens suffer from discrimination. This means that other Americans refuse to treat them as equals because they are different in one way or another. You and your fellow students will soon become adults with full rights as American citizens. Correcting these weaknesses will be your responsibility.

This year you will study the history of the United States. You will see how earlier Americans built our nation and made it great. You will also learn about the mistakes they sometimes made. By studying their successes and their failures, you will become a well-informed citizen. You will then be able to help solve the many problems that our nation faces today, and so make it an even greater nation in the future.

Students learning about history. How can learning about our nation's past help us to understand present-day national problems?

USING THIS TEXTBOOK

To make learning easier, each of the chapters in this book is divided into short reading and study units, or sections. For each section that you read, follow these simple rules:
1. Look over the section first to see what it is about. Read all the headings and look at all the illustrations in it.
2. Read the entire section as you would read a story. When you have finished, ask yourself, "What have I learned so far?"
3. Do the exercises at the end of the section. Write the *title* of the section at the top of a new page in your notebook. Under it write the *numbers* of the questions and then the *answers*.
4. Read the section over again carefully. Find the answers you did not know after the first reading. Check the answers you did know and correct any mistakes you might have made.

REVIEWING THE SECTION

A. *Knowing Important Facts*

PART 1. Write "True" in your notebook if the statement is correct. Write "False" if it contains an error.
1. The United States is the largest nation in area in the world.
2. The United States is the richest nation in the world.
3. The United States has one of the strongest armed forces in the world.
4. The United States needs large amounts of food from other countries.
5. The American people are richer than the ancient Romans were.
6. Canada, China, and Brazil are all larger in area than the United States.
7. The United States has more fertile farmland than any other country in the world.
8. The United States became a rich country even though it lacked important natural resources.

PART 2. Write the *letter* of the correct choice in your notebook. Be prepared to support your answers in class.
1. All of the following countries have a larger population than the United States *except:*
   a. Canada   b. China   c. India   d. the Soviet Union
2. Large numbers of people have come to the United States from every continent *except:*
   a. Africa   b. Asia   c. Australia   d. Europe.

7

3. The contributions of many peoples enriched American life in every one of these ways *except* in:
   a. culture   b. foods   c. industries   d. natural resources
4. The American people had to fight a war to win their freedom from the:
   a. British   b. Dutch   c. French   d. Spanish.
5. After the United States won its freedom, it:
   a. tried to conquer other countries   b. kept its people from achieving more than their fathers did   c. continued to develop ideals of liberty and equality   d. followed the ideas of European kings.

B. *Understanding the Facts*

Write a sentence or two *in your own words* to answer each question.

1. What is discrimination?
2. Why is discrimination a problem in the United States today?
3. What other problems *not* mentioned in this section will you and your fellow students face as adult American citizens?

IMPROVING YOUR SKILLS

Mastering the Map

When you plan a trip, it is important to have a map. The map is like a picture of the country you will be traveling through. It will help you to find the distance from one place to another. By studying it carefully, you can also learn a good deal about conditions in each place.

We are starting a year-long trip through the United States. Study the map on page 2 carefully. Note: (1) the oceans and other bodies of water; (2) the symbols for rivers, mountains, and other special features of the land surface; and (3) the key explaining the map.

Now test your mastery of the map. Write in your notebook the names on the map that best complete these sentences. (Each dash represents one word.)

PART 1. Boundaries of the United States

1. The United States is bordered on the north by the _____ _____ River, the _____ Lakes, and the country of _____.
2. On the east, it is bordered by the _____ _____.
3. On the south, it is bordered by a large body of water called the _____ _____ _____, a river named the _____ _____, and the country of _____.
4. On the west, it is bordered by the _____ _____.

PART 2. Important Geographic Features

1. The Mississippi River rises near the border between the United States and _____. It flows southward into the _____ _____.

2. The two main tributaries flowing into the Mississippi are the _____ River on the east and the _____ River on the west.

3. The two main mountain ranges in the United States are the _____ Mountains in the east and the _____ Mountains in the west.

PART 3. Geographic Regions (Use both the map and the key to find the answers.)

1. Most early immigrants from Europe settled along the eastern seacoast in the region called the _____ _____ _____.

2. When people moved inland from the coast, they came to the mountainous region known as the _____ _____.

3. Those who crossed the mountains came into a broad river valley, the _____ _____ _____.

4. The region of the United States west of the Rocky Mountains is called the _____ _____.

5. The largest of the four regions is the _____ _____ _____.

6. The main farmlands of the United States are in the two level regions, the _____ _____ _____ and the _____ _____ _____.

7. Most of our mineral resources have been found in the two mountainous regions, the _____ _____ and the _____ _____.

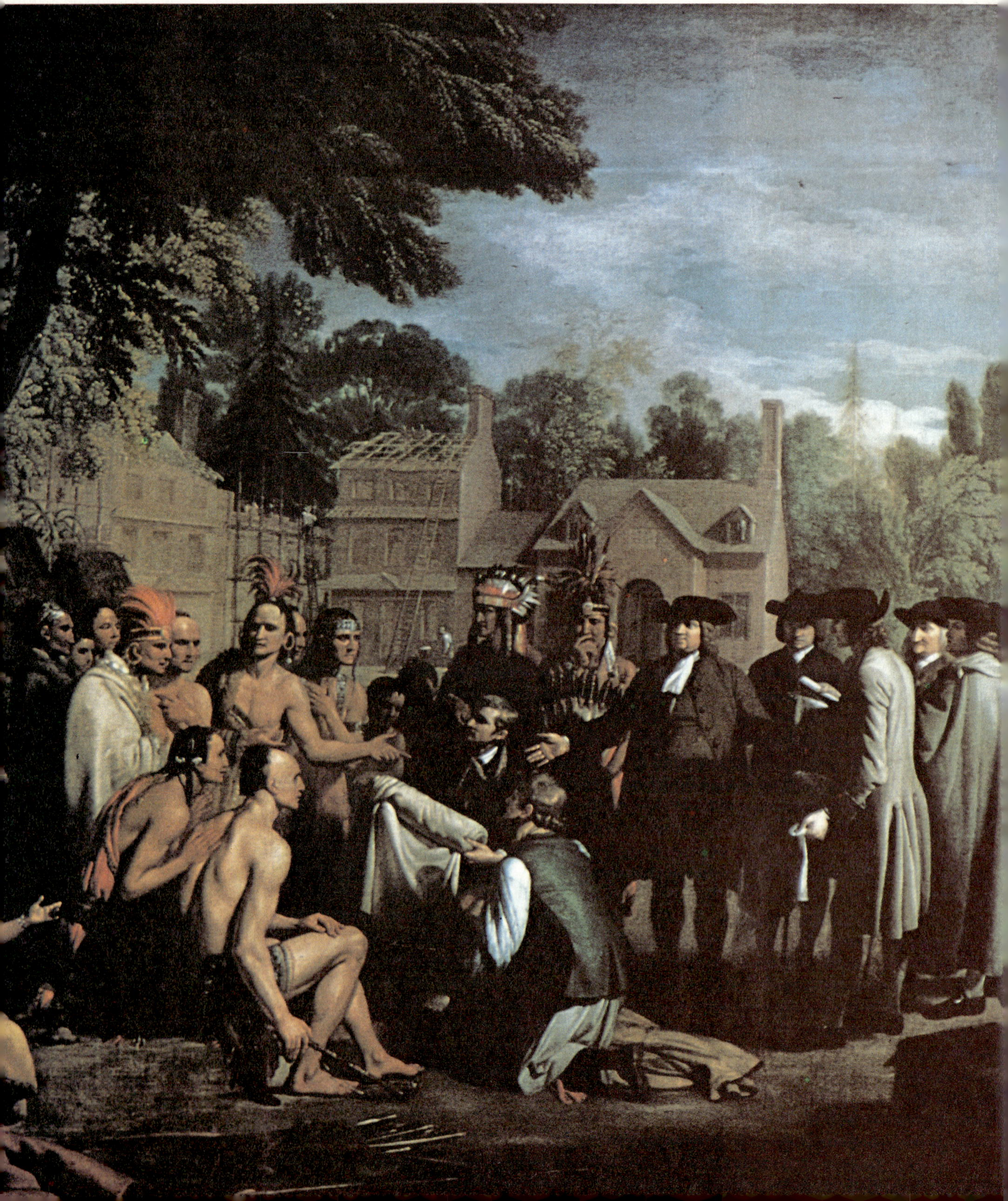

Unit One

THE COLONIAL PERIOD

Compared with Asia and Africa, Europe is not a large continent. It is divided into many countries. Except for Russia, all of these countries are rather small. Yet a few of them—Spain, Portugal, France, and England—succeeded in taking control of most of the world after the year 1500.

In this unit you will see how Europeans took possession of the two American continents and established many colonies, or settlements. You will learn the following:

1. *How America was explored, and settled*
2. *How the English settled thirteen colonies along the Atlantic coast of North America*
3. *How the thirteen English colonies became very prosperous and progressive*
4. *Why the thirteen colonies revolted against English rule*
5. *How the thirteen colonies won their independence and formed a new nation, the United States of America*

William Penn making a treaty with the Lenni-Lenape Indians. This picture was painted many years after the treaty was made.

UNIT 1: A.D. 500-2000

500	DARK AGES
1000	
1095	• Calling of the First Crusade
	CRUSADES
1300	
1492	• Columbus's first voyage to America
	VOYAGES OF EXPLORATION
1607	• Settling of Jamestown
1621	• First Thanksgiving
	COLONIAL PERIOD
1776	UNITED STATES OF AMERICA

Chapter 1

THE EXPLORATION AND SETTLEMENT OF AMERICA

You are probably familiar with the story of Christopher Columbus, the Italian sea captain who sailed to America. Columbus believed that the world was round. He thought that by sailing west across the Atlantic Ocean he would reach China, the Indies, and other rich countries of eastern Asia. In the year 1492, he boldly set sail from Spain with three small ships. After two fearful months at sea, Columbus finally reached land. Thinking that he was in Asia, he called the islands he had found the Indies and their people the Indians.

We now know that Columbus was probably not the first to sail so far west across the Atlantic. The Vikings had sailed to America from northern Europe about 500 years before Columbus. They left no permanent settlements. Columbus, however, knew nothing of these early Viking voyages.

During the ten years after 1492, Columbus made three other voyages. He explored a number of islands off the American coast and parts of the mainland (see map, pages 16-17). But he found only small villages and a people with a way of life different from his, instead of the rich cities he was looking for. He died a disappointed man. To the end, he refused to admit that he had come upon a "New World," instead of a new route to Asia.

Why Were Europeans Seeking a New Route to the East?

A. Start of the Crusades. In the fifth century A.D., barbarians overthrew the once mighty Roman Empire. The next five hundred years following the fall of the Roman Empire (about A.D. 500-1000) are known in European history as the Dark Ages. In this period governments were weak and bandit gangs roamed freely over the countryside. To travel or to carry on trade was almost impossible. Most people were poor and ignorant. Only the Christian Church and a few strong rulers kept European civilization alive.

Because of its weakness, Europe was invaded many times. The most powerful invaders were the Moslems or Mohammedans. They followed Islam, a religion founded in the seventh century A.D. by the Prophet Mohammed. The Moslems tried to conquer Europe and convert the Christians, that is, make them Moslems. They managed, however, to conquer only Spain, which they ruled for hundreds of years, and part of France.

In time the Christians became very tough fighting men. Their knights, dressed in armor and mounted on sturdy horses, were able to stop invasions. In time, also, conditions in Europe improved greatly. Eventually, Pope Urban II, the head of the Christian Church in western Europe, felt that his people were strong enough to defeat the Moslems. In the year 1095, he called on the Christian knights to drive their enemies out of the holy land of Palestine, where Jesus was born (see map, pages 16-17). Many knights answered his call. To show they fought in a holy cause, they wore on their clothes and armor the sign of the holy cross (*crux* in Latin). Their wars against the Moslems have therefore been called the Crusades, or Wars of the Cross.

B. Results of the Crusades. After overcoming many hardships, the Crusaders reached the Near East (the part of Asia near Europe). They defeated the Moslems in a series of battles and conquered Jerusalem, the capital of Palestine. But the Moslems did not admit defeat. Forming new armies, they gradually drove the Crusaders out of Palestine and the neighboring countries. The Europeans in turn sent fresh armies of Crusaders to the Near East. Altogether the Crusades lasted almost two hundred years. In the end the Moslems won. They kept control of the Holy Land.

Nevertheless, the Crusades should not be considered a failure because they had important effects on Europe's development. Europeans learned a great deal from the Moslems, who had a more advanced civilization. Educated people learned that the earth is round, not flat. Wealthy people learned to use the fine goods of the easterners—their silk and cotton cloth, rugs and tapestries, perfumes and glassware. Both rich and poor people learned to like pepper and other spices, which came from India and the Indies. Europeans had been using salt to keep meat from spoiling. Spices, they now discovered, not only preserved meat; they also gave it a much better taste.

Since the people of Europe wanted the spices and fine goods of the East, a rich trade

A Moslem market place. In Moslem bazaars, or markets, small shops and stalls lined the streets. What kinds of merchants can you see in this picture?

soon sprang up between the two regions. The Mediterranean Sea was the main route for this trade. Ships piloted by Italian sea captains were the main carriers. Italians and other Europeans also sailed out into the stormy Atlantic to bring the valuable cargoes to northwestern Europe.

C. Improvements in Navigation. As a result of their long voyages, Europeans became much better seamen and shipbuilders. They learned to build larger, stronger, and more seaworthy ships. They developed a new rudder and a new type of sail that improved their control of their ships. From the Moslems they acquired two important instruments, the compass and the astrolabe. The compass showed them the direction in which they were sailing. With the astrolabe they could determine their location by studying the positions of the heavenly bodies. They were now ready to sail long distances—across an entire ocean, if necessary.

D. Need for a New Route. The trade routes then in use presented several difficulties. Goods from the Far East (the part of Asia farthest from Europe) were transported the first part of the way by ship. Then they had to be unloaded and repacked on the backs of camels and donkeys for the overland trip to the Mediterranean Sea (see map, pages 16-17). There they were again reloaded by Italian merchants, who brought them to other parts of Europe. Each part of the journey was difficult and dangerous. The total amount of goods delivered each year was small. Because of the great risks and the costs of unloading and reloading, prices were very high.

By the fifteenth century, there were strong new nations in northern and western Europe. Their rulers were eager to find an all-water route to the Far East. If ships could carry the goods the entire distance, cargoes would

An early compass. Why was the compass often decorated with pictures of sea monsters? Did educated people think the earth was flat?

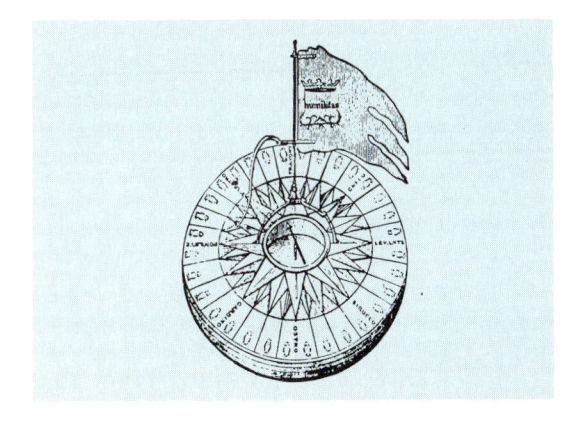

15

EXPLORERS OF THE WORLD

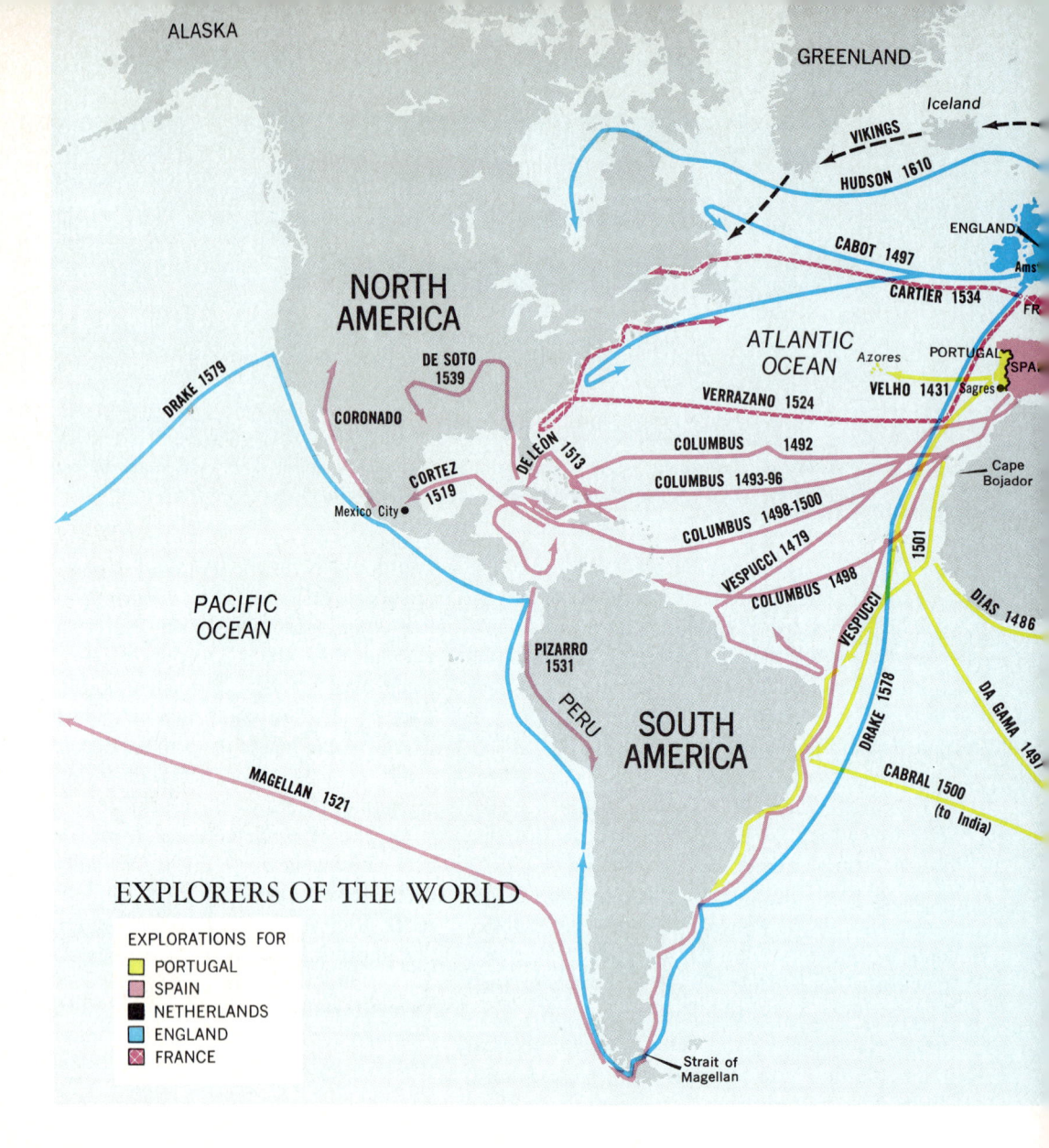

EXPLORATIONS FOR
- PORTUGAL
- SPAIN
- NETHERLANDS
- ENGLAND
- FRANCE

be larger and costs would be lower. Even if prices were reduced, profits would still be very high.

E. The Portuguese All-Water Route. The Portuguese decided to reach the Far East by sailing southward around the tip of Africa. For almost a century their sea captains gradually sailed farther and farther along the African coast. Finally, in 1498, Vasco da Gama rounded the Cape of Good Hope and sailed on to India (see map shown above). He returned with a cargo worth sixty times what his voyage cost. The Portuguese quickly developed a large and profitable trade with India, the Indies, and China by the all-water route they had discovered.

F. The Naming of America. Meanwhile Columbus had persuaded Ferdinand and Isabella,

16

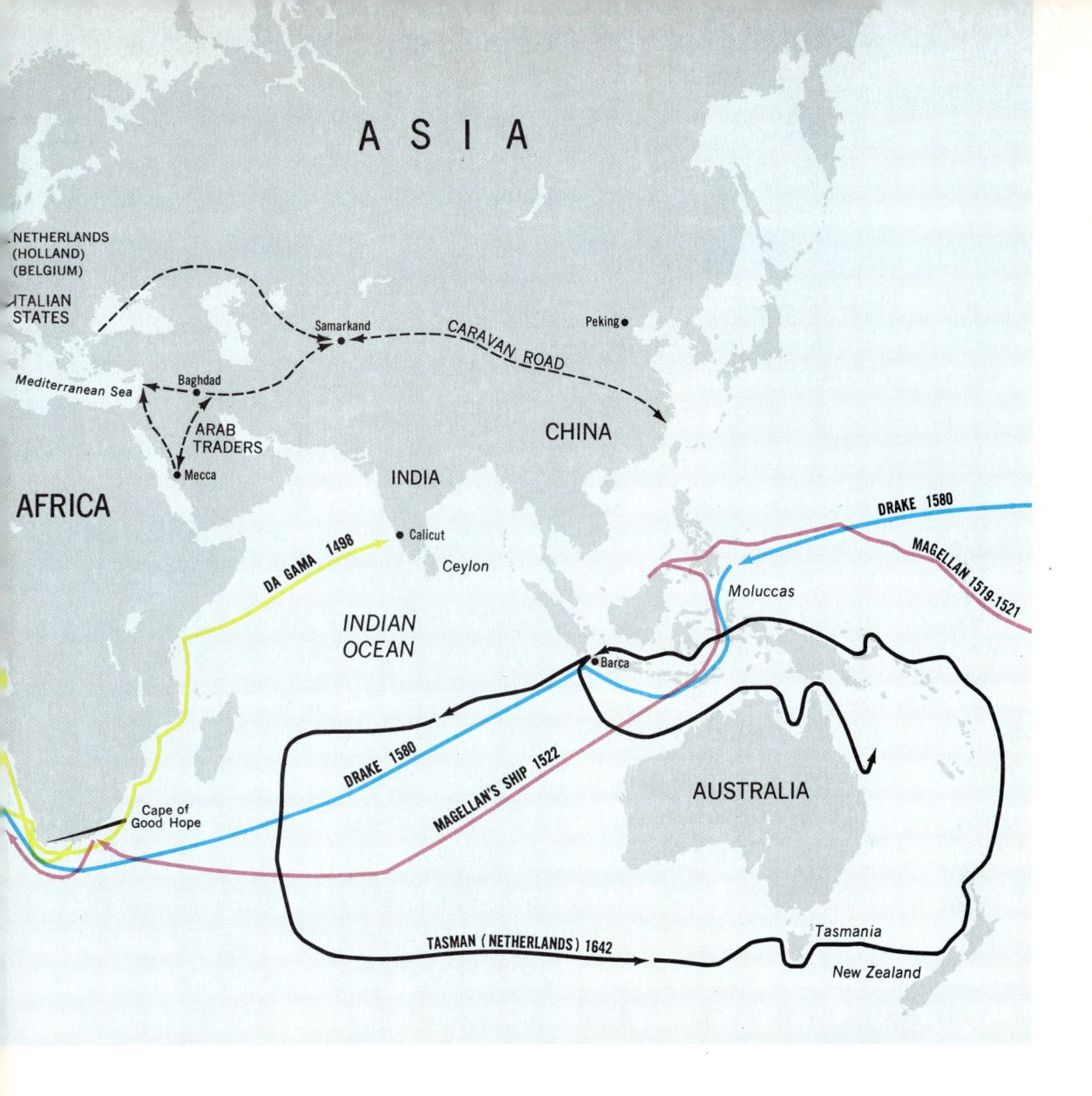

the rulers of Spain, to support his daring plan to reach the East by sailing west. His plan seemed a good one because experts in his day thought the world was much smaller than it actually is. Columbus did not expect to find other continents between Europe and Asia.

Since Columbus would not admit that he had made a mistake, he did not name the New World. It was named after another Italian, Amerigo Vespucci. Amerigo visited South America ten years after Columbus's first voyage. He wrote interesting descriptions of the strange places and people he saw. A famous map maker read his descriptions and named the new land America ("Amerigo's Land") in his honor.

G. Other Voyages of Exploration. Columbus's success in crossing the Atlantic Ocean inspired other sea captains to follow his plan. A fellow Italian, usually known by his English name of

Carib Indian homes. These present-day houses are similar to those that the early European explorers found in the West Indies. What had Columbus expected to find on his first voyage?

John Cabot, won the support of the king of England. In 1497 and 1498, Cabot made two voyages along the coast of North America. His voyages gave England the basis for a claim to a part of North America. Two years later, the Portuguese mariner Pedro Cabral explored the eastern coast of South America. He strengthened Portugal's claim to that region, which is now part of Brazil (see map, pages 16-17).

Probably the greatest of all the voyages of discovery was begun in 1519 by Ferdinand Magellan, a Portuguese nobleman sailing for the king of Spain. Magellan set out from Europe with five ships and almost 250 men. Reaching South America, Magellan sailed southward along the coast until he finally discovered the straits which now bear his name (see map, pages 16-17). He passed through the straits into the Pacific Ocean.

For fourteen long weeks, Magellan's ships sailed slowly across the broad Pacific before finally reaching land. Many of his sailors died of hunger and disease on the way. A little later Magellan himself was killed in a fight with natives of the Philippine Islands. Eighteen survivors managed to guide the one remaining ship around the Cape of Good Hope back to Europe. Their voyage had taken almost three years. They had proved that the earth is round and also much larger than the experts had thought. But they had not found a practical all-water route to the Far East.

The search for an all-water route moved northward. In 1535 the Frenchman Jacques Cartier sailed up the St. Lawrence River. He thought that it might empty into the Pacific Ocean. Many years later the English mariner Henry Hudson, sailing for the Netherlands, took up the search. He discovered the Hudson River in 1609. One year later he sailed into the Hudson Bay in northern Canada. There he perished when his crew, refusing to go farther, set him adrift in an open boat. Although the voyages of Cartier and Hudson failed to find a "northwest passage" to Asia, they were very important. They gave France and the Netherlands claims to parts of the North American continent.

REVIEWING THE SECTION

A. Knowing New Terms

In your notebook write the new terms in this section that best complete these statements.
1. The period after the fall of the Roman Empire, when civilization declined in Europe, has been named the _____ _____.

2. The followers of the Prophet Mohammed are known as Mohammedans or _____.
3. The Christian knights of Europe tried to conquer the holy land of Palestine in the Wars of the Cross or _____.
4. The part of Asia close to Europe was named the _____ _____. The part of Asia farthest from Europe was called the _____ _____.
5. The old trade routes brought goods from Asia to Europe by land and sea. Both Columbus and da Gama were looking for an _____ route.

B. Understanding the Facts

Write "True" in your notebook if the statement is correct. If the statement contains an error, rewrite it so that it is correct.
1. The Crusades failed to make Palestine a Christian country, but they brought about important changes in European civilization.
2. In trading with the East, European seamen learned to build better ships and to sail longer distances.
3. The new all-water route to the East was better than the old sea-and-land route because it was shorter.
4. In Columbus's day only a few educated Europeans knew that the earth is round.
5. Magellan's voyage proved that the earth is much larger than the experts of his time had thought.

C. Knowing Important People

For each explorer in the first column, write the *letter* of his description in the second column.

Explorers
1. Cabot
2. Cabral
3. Cartier
4. Columbus
5. Da Gama
6. Hudson
7. Magellan
8. Vespucci

Descriptions
a. Discovered America for Spain
b. Explored the St. Lawrence River for France
c. Found a practical all-water route to the Far East
d. Gave the Netherlands a claim to part of North America
e. Gave England a claim to part of North America
f. Led Moslem armies in Europe
g. Gave America its name
h. Led expedition that sailed around the globe
i. Strengthened Portugal's claim to part of South America

IMPROVING YOUR SKILLS

A. Mastering the Map

Use the names on the map on pages 16-17 to complete the following sentences:

1. The New World is now usually called the Western Hemisphere (the western half of the globe). The two continents located in the Western Hemisphere are _____ _____ and _____ _____.
2. The four continents in the Eastern Hemisphere are _____, _____, _____, and _____.
3. The four oceans shown are the _____, _____, _____, and _____.
4. In the Middle Ages, Italian sea captains sailed to the eastern end of the _____ Sea. There they picked up goods that had been brought overland from _____ or by land and sea from _____ and the _____.
5. Columbus explored a group of islands now called the _____ _____ and the coast of the continent of _____ _____.
6. Other explorers who sailed along the coast of South America were _____, _____, and _____.
7. The important sea captains who explored the eastern coast of North America were _____, _____, and _____.
8. The shortest voyage of exploration was that of _____.
9. The longest voyage of exploration was that of _____.
10. Magellan's men crossed the _____, _____, and _____ oceans.

B. Reading the Time Line

PART 1. A time line, like a map, is a kind of picture; but, unlike a map, it shows periods of time instead of places. The time line may be horizontal or vertical, straight or curved. In every case, however, it is marked with dates that show the passing of time.

Look at the time line on page 12. It is a straight vertical line. It is drawn so that half an inch represents one hundred years. Examine it carefully; then answer these questions:

1. Five important developments are shown on the time line. Which lasted longest? About how long did it last?
2. Which development took the shortest time? About how long did it take?

3. Before the United States became an independent country, it was a group of colonies ruled by England. Exactly how long did the colonial period last?
4. How long has the United States been an independent nation?

PART 2. It is also important for you to know the terms historians use to mark the passing of time. We all know such time words as *second, minute, hour, day, week, month,* and *year.* But the historian deals with much longer periods of time than the average person does. Here are some of the words he or she uses:

1. *Decade*—ten years
2. *Generation*—the time it takes for new-born children to become adults and start families of their own; about twenty-five to thirty years
3. *Century*—one hundred years
4. *Millennium*—one thousand years
5. B.C. and A.D. We use the Christian calendar, which begins with the birth of Jesus Christ. Events that took place before the birth of Jesus are marked B.C., meaning "before Christ." Events that have occurred since the birth of Jesus are marked A.D. "A.D." is an abbreviation of the Latin words *anno Domini*, meaning "in the year of our Lord." Events that happened in the years A.D. 1 to 99 happened in the first century A.D. An event that occurred sometime between the years A.D. 100 and 199 occurred in the second century; between A.D. 200 and 299, in the third century; and so on. We are now living in the 1900s, or twentieth century.

To check your understanding, choose the best answer for these questions:

1. Which of these important developments took place during the first millennium A.D.?
   a. the Dark Ages   b. the Crusades   c. the voyages of exploration   d. your birth.
2. The Crusades began in 1095. This year was near the end of the:
   a. tenth century   b. eleventh century   c. twelfth century   d. none of these.
3. Columbus set sail in 1492. This year was near the end of the: a. fifteenth century   b. sixteenth century   c. seventeenth century   d. none of these.
4. One of the last major voyages of exploration was that of Henry Hudson in 1610. This was early in the: a. fifteenth century   b. sixteenth century   c. seventeenth century   d. none of these.
5. In which decade of the twentieth century are we now living?
   a. the fifth decade   b. the sixth decade   c. the seventh decade   d. none of these.

How Did Europeans Open a New World in the Americas?

A. Spain's Leadership. At first, as we have seen, European rulers were not interested in the Americas. They looked upon the new lands as a barrier between them and the riches of the East. After a time, however, they realized that the Americas might be valuable. The question then arose, "To whom do they belong?"

The king of Spain promptly laid claim to all the newly discovered lands on the basis of Columbus's voyages. The other rulers challenged this claim because of the voyages their own explorers had made. In the end the question was decided by each nation's ability to conquer or to settle various parts of the New World.

In this effort, too, Spain led the way. The Spanish people had just finished driving the Moslems from their country after hundreds of years of wars. They were used to fighting and were not afraid to face death in battle. They were also moved by three desires—to become rich, to win glory by conquering new lands for their king, and to bring Christianity to the Indians.

B. Spanish Explorations and Conquests. Between 1500 and 1550, Spaniards explored and conquered large parts of the Americas. The most startling successes were those of Hernando Cortés and Francisco Pizarro. In 1519 Cortés managed with only a few hundred men to conquer the great empire of the Aztec Indians in Mexico. In 1531 Pizarro seized the even larger and richer empire of the Incas in South America (see map, page 25).

The Spaniards won because they had complete confidence in their cause. Believing that God was with them, they dared to advance against impossible odds. The Indians did little to oppose them. They had never before seen people with light skins and thick beards, who wore heavy armor, carried firearms, and rode on horses. They believed that the newcomers were gods. This gave the Spaniards a chance to seize the ruler of each empire and take control of his people and lands.

Spaniards were the first white people to explore large parts of what is now the southern United States. They were lured by Indian tales of great cities built of gold and other marvels. In 1513 Ponce de León found a land he called Florida ("Land of Flowers"). It is said that he was searching for the "Fountain of Youth" (waters that would keep him young). In 1540 Francisco de Coronado explored much of our Southwest, but discovered only small Indian villages. One of his lieutenants found the Grand Canyon. About the same time, Hernando de Soto marched through the lands north of the Gulf of Mexico. He discovered the mighty Mississippi River and crossed to its western bank (see map, page 25). When de Soto died of a fever, his body was buried in its waters. These expeditions uncovered no gold or other wealth. So only a few settlements were built in all the vast regions these men had explored.

C. The Spanish and Portuguese Empires. Brazil was settled by the Portuguese. The rest

The military section of Machu Picchu, a fortress city of the ancient Incas. The city was built high on a rock. It was unknown to the Spanish explorers of Peru who destroyed the Inca empire. What other great Indian empire did the Spanish conquer?

of South America, Central America, Mexico, and the West Indies were all settled by the Spaniards (see map, page 25). The entire region is known today as Latin America. For both Spanish and Portuguese, the languages chiefly spoken there, are derived from Latin, the language of the ancient Romans.

The Spanish and Portuguese empires were alike in many respects. European settlers and their descendants formed a ruling class. They divided the land into large ranches and plantations. On the ranches they raised cattle and sheep. On the plantations they grew cotton, tobacco, and corn. They also built cities and established schools where their sons could receive a good education.

The Indians, the first people to live in these lands, were treated as slaves. They were made to tend the herds, to care for the crops, and to work in the mines. Many died of overwork or of diseases their masters brought from Europe. To fill their places, the Europeans obtained blacks from Africa. Like the Indians, black slaves died in great numbers. About a third of them died on the trip across the Atlantic from Africa. About another third died during the first year of slavery. But Africa's population was very large. It seemed to the Europeans that they would never run short of slaves.

At the same time, Catholic missionaries were converting the Indians and blacks to Christianity. They also protected converts from harsh treatment by their masters. Even today, many Latin Americans have some Indian or black ancestors. Most Latin Americans also belong to the Roman Catholic Church.

Spain kept a close watch over its colonies. The king sent governors and other officials to the colonies to carry out his laws. He also controlled the colonists' trade and took a share of all they produced. Every year large fleets carried cargoes of gold, silver, and other valuable products from the New World to Spain.

Indian pueblos in Taos, New Mexico. Coronado was looking for "cities of gold" that the Indians had told him about. They probably meant pueblos (stone or adobe villages) like this one. Why was Coronado disappointed when he found them? Today, these buildings are considered masterpieces.

The first Spanish mission (religious settlement) in what is now Arizona. The Spanish built missions in many of the areas they conquered in order to spread the Roman Catholic religion.

Mariners of the sixteenth century voyaged across the oceans in caravels (ships) like these.

D. The Decline of Portugal and Spain. Portugal, on the other hand, did not watch over Brazil closely. Most of Portugal's wealth came from its empire in the Far East. So it spent most of its energy in keeping that empire. But Portugal had only a small population. As its fighting men were killed in battle or died at sea, it grew less able to defend its possessions. Before the end of the sixteenth century, stronger European powers had overrun its colonies in the East. Only then did Portugal turn its attention to Brazil, the most important colony it still possessed.

Thanks to its American colonies, Spain became the greatest power in sixteenth-century Europe. But its rulers drained their nation's wealth and strength in attempts to spread their power. While trying to govern a vast empire in the Americas, they were also waging religious wars in Europe and fighting the Moslem Turks in the Mediterranean. Their worst mistake was an attempt to invade England in 1588. The powerful and costly Spanish Armada (fleet) was defeated by the English and then wrecked by storms.

E. The French and English Colonies. Spain never regained control of the seas. Its main rivals, England and France, were now able to attack the Spanish settlements and establish colonies of their own in the Americas. They even took from Spain some of the West Indies,

EUROPEAN COLONIES IN THE AMERICAS, 1750

- Spanish
- Portuguese
- French
- British
- Unsettled territory

25

which were valuable for sugar and other tropical crops. In the long run, however, the colonies on the mainland of North America proved far more important than those in the West Indies.

The French settled along the St. Lawrence River and the Great Lakes. In this region they established the colony of New France, from which present-day Canada developed. Later French explorers sailed down the Mississippi to the Gulf of Mexico. They claimed the whole rich river basin for King Louis XIV, after whom they named it Louisiana (see map, page 25).

The French king, like the king of Spain, watched his empire very closely. He allowed only Roman Catholics from France, or from nations friendly to France, to settle there. He directed their activities and took a share of their profits. As a result, the population increased very slowly. Most of the colonists were young men. They trapped for furs until they had saved enough money to buy farms in France; then they returned home.

The English planted thirteen colonies along the Atlantic coast between New France and Florida (see map, page 25). These colonies were very different from those of the Spanish, Portuguese, and French. They were founded by private companies or individuals, and were given a good deal of freedom to govern themselves. They progressed much more rapidly than the colonies of the rival powers. We shall study the thirteen English colonies because they were the beginning of the United States.

By the year 1750, large parts of the Americas had been colonized by the four leading European powers. Settlements in these areas were still mainly along the seacoasts and waterways. Nevertheless, settlers kept pushing deeper inland. These hardy colonists were opening two large continents, each much larger than all of Europe. They were obtaining great riches for their mother countries. Most important of all, they were laying the foundations for great new nations. These would someday surpass the countries that had given them birth.

REVIEWING THE SECTION

A. *Knowing Important People*

For each explorer in the first column, write the *letter* of the region in the second column that he explored.

Explorers	*Regions*
1. Coronado	a. Aztec Empire
2. Cortés	b. Florida
3. De León	c. Inca Empire
4. De Soto	d. Southeastern part of the United States
5. Pizarro	e. Southwestern part of the United States
	f. Brazil

B. Finding the Reasons

In this exercise, one, two, or even all three answers to each question may be correct. Write the letters of *all* the correct answers in your notebook.

1. Why were the Spaniards bold explorers and conquerors?
a. They hoped to find great wealth. b. They were accustomed to wars of conquest. c. They wanted to spread the Christian religion.

2. Why were small bands of Spaniards able to conquer the large Aztec and Inca empires?
a. They were considered gods by the Indians. b. They had much better weapons than the Indians. c. They were much more intelligent than the Indians.

3. Why is the part of the Americas south of the United States called *Latin* America?
a. Its people speak the Latin language. b. Its people speak languages derived from Latin. c. Its culture is like that of the ancient Latins.

4. Why does Latin America have a large population of Indian and black descent?
a. The Spaniards and Portuguese found a large number of Indians living there. b. The Europeans brought over many blacks from Africa. c. The number of Indians and blacks increased rapidly because they were treated well.

5. Why did the power of Portugal and Spain decline in the sixteenth and seventeenth centuries?
a. They fought too many wars. b. They tried to conquer and hold too much territory. c. Their colonies were very costly to run.

6. Why did population grow slowly in the French holdings in America?
a. Europeans could not find jobs because most work was done by blacks and Indians. b. Only Catholics were allowed to settle there. c. Settlers had to obey many government regulations.

C. Summing Up the Chapter

In your notebook, arrange the following events in the proper order.

1. Conquest and settlement of the Americas
2. Crusades
3. Dark Ages
4. Large-scale trade between Italy and the East
5. Voyages of exploration

IMPROVING YOUR SKILLS

A. Mastering the Map

Study the map on page 25. Then for each part of the Americas in this list, write the *name* of the European nation to which it belonged in 1750.

1. The Atlantic coast south of the St. Lawrence River
2. Brazil
3. Central America
4. The Great Lakes region
5. Mexico
6. The Mississippi River Basin
7. The southeastern and southwestern parts of the present-day United States
8. The St. Lawrence River Valley
9. Much of South America (except Brazil)
10. Most of the West Indies

Conclusions. 1. Which of the four European countries owned the most American territory in 1750? 2. Which country owned the least territory?

B. Understanding the Picture

The picture at the beginning of each section helps you to know what the section is about. Look at the picture on page 22; then answer these questions:

1. Who are the people on the right and the left? What are they doing?
2. Who is the person in the center? What is he doing?
3. How does this picture help you to understand the title of the section, "How Did Europeans Open a New World in the Americas?"

MAKING HISTORY LIVE

1. Make a simple astrolabe and explain how it works.
2. Use a sketch or model of a caravel (a typical sixteenth-century ship) to show the improvements that made possible the voyages of discovery.
3. Read a detailed account of one of the voyages of exploration or overland explorations mentioned in this chapter. Then imagine you were there. Write a letter or a page from a diary to describe your experiences.
4. Suppose you are leaving eighteenth-century Europe. Tell whether you would prefer to settle in a Spanish, French, or English colony, and explain why.

Chapter 2

SETTLING THE THIRTEEN COLONIES

It took five or six weeks for a ship to cross the Atlantic in the seventeenth century—even longer if the weather or winds were unfavorable. The ship was crowded with people, foodstuffs, and other cargo. The living quarters below deck soon became filthy, and the food generally spoiled or ran short. Eyewitness descriptions give us a vivid picture of how bad conditions could be on a transatlantic voyage in those days:

> There is on board these ships terrible misery, stench, fumes, many kinds of seasickness, fever, dysentery, headache, boils, scurvy, cancer, mouth-rot, and the like. The lice abound so frightfully, especially on sick people, that they can be scraped off the body. We were compelled to eat the ship's biscuit which had spoiled long ago; though in a whole biscuit there was scarcely a piece the size of a dollar that had not been full of red worms and spiders' nests.
>
> . . . .
>
> Children from one to seven years rarely survive the voyage; and many a time parents are compelled to see their children miserably suffer and die from hunger, thirst, and sickness, and then to see them cast into the water. I witnessed such misery in no less than thirty-two children in our ship, all of whom were thrown into the sea.

The old and weak, as well as the very young, often died during the long voyage overseas. Those who were strong enough to live through the terrible journey still had to face many hardships in America. It took backbreaking toil to start a farm in the wilderness. Hunger, disease, Indians who did not like intruders on their lands, and wild animals killed off many settlers. Yet Europeans came to America by the thousands. In this chapter we shall discover the reasons why they came and what they accomplished.

Why Did Europeans Come to the Thirteen Colonies?

A. Desire for Economic Advancement. 1. Poverty in Europe. Most of the settlers of the thirteen colonies were poor people from England and other European countries. They hoped to improve their economic condition—that is, earn a better living—in the New World. They also hoped that America would provide a better life for their children and their children's children.

In seventeenth-century Europe, the average peasant (person of low social rank) owned a small piece of land or worked on the estate of a noble. Either way, his income was very small. Yet he had to pay heavy taxes to his noble, his king, and his church. Thus burdened, he remained poor his whole life. Moreover, his children were also destined to lead the same kind of life. As population increased, living conditions grew even worse because there was less land for each peasant family.

In England there existed a special problem. Sheep raising proved so profitable that large landowners drove out many small farmers to make room for more sheep. Thousands of these homeless people wandered about the countryside looking for work. The government showed little pity for such "sturdy beggars," as they were called. They might be sent back to the place they came from, or be thrown into prison, or be forced to work without pay for a wealthy landowner. Even the terrible dangers of the American wilderness seemed better to such people than their poverty and suffering in England.

2. Economic Opportunities in America. Since poor people could not pay for an ocean voyage, they usually became indentured servants. This meant that they promised to work without pay for a certain number of years for the person who paid their passage money. The usual term of indenture was four or five years for an adult and twice that for a young person. At the end of the agreed time, the indentured servant was set free. The master was expected to provide land and tools or money for freed male servants. About two-thirds of the indentured servants were men. The women received no land and usually were not given money.

Most colonists became independent farmers. Families cut down trees, built crude huts, and planted crops. Women had to make almost all that the family needed. Women also had to help with the farm work. Families were large. Children were valued because they could help in the house and in the fields.

With good health, hard work, and a little luck, farmers could expect to earn a good living. On the Atlantic Coastal plain, the soil was rich and deep, and the climate was mild. Here it was easy for farmers to raise a surplus—that is, an amount over what was needed for family use. By selling the surplus, more land could be bought. Perhaps a better house could be built and even some indentured servants acquired. If all went well, the farm family might be able to acquire a large estate during the parents' lifetime. The children might even become wealthy.

Skilled craft workers also prospered because their skills were in great demand. They usually opened small shops. If they saved a large sum,

A farm building in Sturbridge, Massachusetts. Old Sturbridge Village is a model of an early American village designed to show life in colonial days. What does the clothing and building tell you about these farmers?

A busy eighteenth-century kitchen. What does this picture tell you about colonial life? How does it show the progress made during the first hundred years of settlement?

they might become well-to-do merchants or bankers. These two types of business people had the best opportunities for becoming wealthy in the colonies.

A third road to wealth was to speculate in land—to buy a large plot and to resell it years later for more than it cost. The price generally went up as more settlers arrived hungry for land. Most leading families of the thirteen colonies rose to wealth from humble beginnings in one of these ways—as farmers, business people, or speculators in land.

B. To Obtain Release from Prison. Many early settlers were former convicts. A common practice in England at that time was to release prisoners from jail if they promised to sail to America. This was not a bad or foolish thing to do. Death was the usual penalty for serious crimes in seventeenth-century Europe. The prisons were mostly filled with people who were guilty of minor offenses. Men and women might be put in prison for stealing some food or for falling into debt. A debtor—that is, a person owing money—had to stay in jail until the debt was paid. The jail sentence might be for years if friends or family could not pay back the money owed. Furthermore, prisons of that day were terrible, disease-ridden places. Prisoners who were not afraid of the ocean voyage and wilderness often preferred to take their chances in America.

C. To Escape Religious Persecution. Other groups of settlers came to America to escape persecution (punishment) for their religious beliefs. Such persecution had its roots in events of the early sixteenth century. At that time, the Roman Catholic Church was shaken from within by serious disagreement. The result was that a number of new churches were formed. People belonging to them were called Protestants because they protested against many practices of the Roman Catholic Church. Thus Europe, which had been largely Catholic from early times, was now divided in its faith.

In each European country, rulers made their religion the religion of the land. If the ruler was a Protestant, for example, the Protestant faith became the official, or established, church. All subjects of the ruler—Catholics as well as Protestants—were expected to belong to the established church and pay for its support. Those who refused were punished—by torture, imprisonment, or death often by burning. Worn out by persecutions, many people from England and other European countries looked to America for the freedom to worship as they wished. They usually settled in colonies that practiced religious toleration—that is, allowed various religions.

In some European countries, fighting broke out between rival religious groups. Germany, in particular, was torn by a series of terrible religious wars during the first half of the seventeenth century. As a result, many Germans left their ruined lands and came to America.

D. To Escape Political Persecution. Still another reason for going to America was political persecution—that is, punishment for disagreeing with the government. Most European countries were ruled by one person, a monarch (king or queen), who had inherited the throne. To criticize the ruler or officials of the country was a serious crime. For doing this, a person might be beaten, thrown in jail, or forced to leave the country. Fear of unjust rulers drove many Europeans to flee to America. The number of people who migrated (moved) from England also increased as a result of a struggle for power between the monarch and the Parliament (see page 47).

E. Promoters of Settlement. England's rulers encouraged migration to the colonies for several reasons. 1. Settlements were needed to support claims to a large part of North America. 2. Rulers wanted to get rid of the unemployed. 3. Settlers would produce goods—such as ship timbers and other naval supplies, or tropical products like sugar—that England was buying from foreign countries. English monarchs also expected the settlers to buy woolens and other manufactured goods that England produced in surplus. 4. Most of England's migrants to America were Protestants. This meant that the settlers would spread the Protestant faith in America, just as the other European powers were spreading the Catholic faith.

Poster to attract settlers to the British colonies. (*Nova Britannia* means "New Britain.") What reason does this poster give for going to Virginia? What were other reasons for going to Virginia?

Because of struggles with Parliament, English monarchs did not have money and power to promote settlements themselves. Lacking these resources, they would give away a whole colony to an important person or company organized by rich merchants. The proprietor, or owner, of a colony would then promise large plots of land to anyone who would bring over a certain number of settlers. Different methods were used to get settlers for the colonies. Notices about the advantages of life in America were printed in newspapers and posted in public places. Passage money was put up for people willing to work as indentured servants. Prisoners were released from jail. Sometimes young people were kidnapped and sent off to America. One large group, the unfortunate blacks, was brought by force from Africa by slave traders. So many came that they soon made up one-fifth of the population of the colonies.

Altogether, the English colonies had some two million people by 1750. They formed an important empire, superior in many ways to the much older and larger empire of Spain.

REVIEWING THE SECTION

A. Understanding the Facts

For each bad condition in Europe, write in your notebook the *letter* of the improvement people found in the thirteen colonies.

Bad Conditions in Europe
1. Absolute monarchy
2. Established church
3. Prison for debtors and minor criminals
4. Widespread unemployment and poverty

Improvements in the Colonies
a. Control by private individuals and companies
b. Opportunities for advancement
c. Need for exconvicts and other workers
d. Raising of surplus crops
e. Religious toleration

B. Finding the Reasons

In this exercise, one, two, or even all three answers to each question may be correct. Write the letters of *all* the correct answers in your notebook.
1. Why did many poor English people go to the thirteen colonies?
   a. Sheep raising had caused widespread unemployment in England.
   b. The English government treated unemployed people very harshly.
   c. In America even indentured servants were well paid for their work.
2. Why were many colonists able to become well-to-do or wealthy?
   a. Fertile soils and a moderate climate made farming profitable.

33

  b. Skilled workers usually opened businesses of their own. c. Those who bought land benefited because land values kept going up.

 3. Why would most convicts sent to America in the seventeenth century *not* be considered criminals today?

  a. To be poor was a crime at that time. b. People were thrown into jail for owing money. c. The prisons were filled with people who had committed minor offenses.

 4. Why was there widespread religious persecution in seventeenth-century Europe?

  a. Catholic governments persecuted Protestants. b. Protestant governments persecuted Catholics. c. Protestant governments persecuted Protestants who did not belong to the established church.

 5. Why did the English government encourage migration to America?

  a. It wanted to strengthen its claim to the region discovered by Cabot. b. It hoped to drive the Spanish and French out of America. c. It wanted to obtain raw materials and increase the sale of English manufactured goods.

 6. Why were the thirteen colonies established by private individuals and trading companies, and not by the English government?

  a. This was the usual way to establish colonies. b. English business people did not want their rulers to become too powerful. c. The English monarchs could not afford to establish colonies.

IMPROVING YOUR SKILLS

Finding Word Meanings

 One of the difficulties of studying history is the large number of new words you meet. You can deal with this difficulty by becoming a kind of detective, one who is able to find and use word clues. Authors of textbooks usually explain new and difficult words the first time they use them. They also provide clues to attract your attention to the explanation.

 Here are two rules that will help you to recognize such clues.

First Rule: If the explanation is a short one, it is usually given in the same sentence as the new term.

 a. It is often introduced by punctuation marks—commas, dashes, or parentheses.

 b. It may also be introduced by "clue words" such as *or, that is, meaning that,* or *was called . . . because.*

 EXAMPLE (in A1): "They hoped to improve their economic condition—*that is,* earn a better living—in the New World." (Here we have a double clue, the dashes and the words *that is.*)

34

Second Rule: A long explanation is usually given in a separate sentence. This sentence usually follows the one containing the new term. It often begins with clue words such as *this, this was,* or *this meant that.*

> EXAMPLE (in **A2**): "Since poor people could not pay for an ocean voyage, they usually became indentured servants. *This meant that* they promised to work without pay for a certain number of years for the person who paid their passage money."

To practice finding the clues to word meanings, look up the following terms in the section you have just read. Write each term and its meaning in your notebook. Underline the clues.

(In **A**1) peasant
(In **A**2) surplus
            to speculate in land
(In **C**) persecution
            Protestants
            established church
            religious toleration

(In **D**) political persecution
            monarch
            migrated
(In **E**) proprietor

For additional practice, look through the introduction and Chapter 1 for new terms. Write the new terms and their meanings in your notebook. Underline the clues.

How Did the English Settlements Grow Into Thirteen Colonies?

A. Virginia and the Plantation System. Each of the thirteen colonies began differently; each grew in a different way. But we can group them according to their location into the southern colonies, the northern or New England colonies, and the middle colonies (see map, page 36). Because of differences in climate and natural resources, the colonists in each of these regions developed different occupations and ways of life. These differences lasted for centuries. In fact, some of them still exist today.

The oldest colony, Virginia, was founded by the London Company. This was organized by patriotic Englishmen to start English settlement in North America. King James I gave the company a permit, called a charter, to settle and govern a large section of the continent. In 1607 the London Company sent a hundred men and boys to Virginia. They named their settlement Jamestown in honor of

35

THE THIRTEEN COLONIES (about 1750)

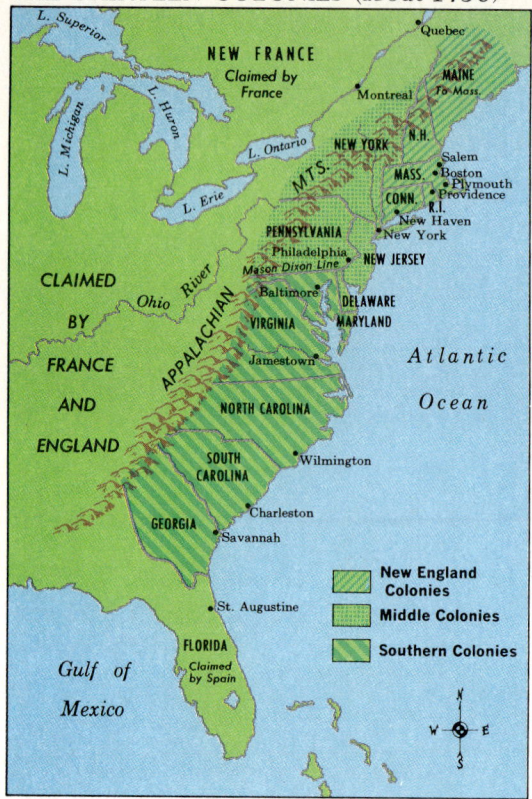

the king. It was the first successful English settlement on the North American mainland.

The earliest settlers of Jamestown were gentlemen—that is, men of rank and education. They felt that hard work like farming was neither good enough for them nor very profitable. They hoped to get rich quick by finding gold or a passage to the East. The settlement almost failed as a result. Many settlers died of hunger and disease; the rest wanted to return to England. Fortunately, one of the settlers, John Smith, proved a strong leader. He saved the colony by forcing the settlers to grow their own food and by winning the help of the Indians nearby.

Virginia became prosperous when a new crop, tobacco, was introduced from the West Indies. Tobacco smoking, an old Indian custom, was then spreading rapidly through Europe. Virginia tobacco brought a high price because it was milder and had a better flavor than West Indian tobacco. The colonists hurried to grow this valuable plant on every available foot of ground, including even the streets of Jamestown. Many became wealthy in a few years. Raising tobacco for sale abroad became Virginia's main occupation. It is still important there today.

Tobacco soon exhausts (uses up) the minerals in the soil. Wealthy farmers therefore moved inland along the rivers. They bought up large plots of land for plantations. The plantation system—in which one main crop is raised on large estates—spread through Virginia and the other southern colonies. Poor farmers had to settle farther inland, in places that were harder to reach and less fertile.

The large planters found it hard to get enough people to work their land. Indentured servants had to be set free after a few years; many even ran away before their time was up. This problem was solved when merchants began to bring in large numbers of blacks from Africa.

In the early seventeenth century blacks were treated like indentured white servants. They were given their freedom after several years. But soon the labor shortage grew worse. White colonists found it profitable to revive slavery—a practice that had almost disappeared in Europe. Slavery permitted one person to own another—as in owning a house or cattle. The slave trade could make some of the white merchants in the northern colonies rich. Slavery could provide unpaid labor for white southern planters. Some whites tried to justify slavery. They claimed that blacks were inferior and did not need or deserve human treatment. Blacks were forced into the brutal system of slavery. Next, whites passed laws in some colonies declaring that the children of slaves were to remain slaves. Thus a dark skin became the badge of slavery. Black slaves gave the southern plantations a supply of cheap labor until the Civil War, 250 years later.

B. The Other Southern Colonies. 1. MARYLAND. The colony of Maryland was begun on a stretch of land just north of Virginia (see map, page 36). King Charles I gave this property to Lord Baltimore, a wealthy Catholic nobleman, as a place for settling Roman Catholics who wanted freedom of worship. But Protestants were also permitted to settle there. They soon outnumbered Catholics. To avoid clashes between the two groups, a law was passed in 1649 called the Toleration Act. It granted equal rights to Catholics and Protestants alike.

Maryland, like Virginia, enjoyed a long growing season, fertile soil, and good water transportation. It too became a colony of plantations growing tobacco as their main crop.

2. THE CAROLINAS. Carolina, to the south of Virginia, was named after King Charles II (*Carolus* in Latin). He gave it to some nobles who had helped him in his struggle with Parliament. The colony was so large that it was later divided into two parts, North and South.

North Carolina was settled by small farmers forced out of Virginia by the large, wealthy planters. Even though tobacco was its major crop, North Carolina remained a colony of small farms. Its farmers added to their income by producing naval stores—that is, timber, pitch, turpentine, and other forest products used by England's navy and merchant ships.

The fertile lowlands of South Carolina, on the other hand, attracted wealthy planters. Rice and indigo (a plant from which a purple dye was made) were the main crops because they grew well in the warm climate. Charleston, with its excellent harbor, became the largest city in the South.

3. GEORGIA. This southernmost colony was the last to be established. King George II was anxious to settle this region because the king of Spain claimed it as his territory. In 1733 George II gave a charter to a charitable organization that promised to settle debtors and other convicts there. This organization also welcomed persecuted Protestants, especially those from Germany. At first slavery was forbidden in Georgia. But the colony grew so slowly, mainly because of Spanish attacks, that the ban on slavery was finally lifted in 1750. Georgia became prosperous after rice and indigo plantations were started.

C. Religion and Industry in New England.
1. MASSACHUSETTS. The northern colonies, located in the region called New England, were very different from those in the South. They were founded mainly to give places of shelter to various persecuted religious groups. One was a small and poor Protestant group called the Pilgrims that had separated from (left) the Church of England. The Pilgrims set sail from England for America in a ship named the *Mayflower*. They founded the first New England colony at Plymouth in 1620.

Massachusetts Bay Colony was established in March of 1629 by a much larger and richer Protestant group, the Puritans. The Puritans were members of the Church of England, but

Pilgrims going to church. What part did religious beliefs play in the Pilgrims' lives.

THE MAN WHO SAVED JAMESTOWN: CAPTAIN JOHN SMITH

Did the Indian princess Pocahontas really save Captain John Smith by throwing herself in front of the executioner? We shall never know for sure. For the only account of the incident was written by Smith himself many years afterward. Still it is an exciting story. There are many others in John Smith's writings.

According to his own accounts, John Smith became a professional soldier at the age of sixteen. He fought for several European countries. In battles against the Turks, he defeated three Turkish champions in single combat. Later, he was taken prisoner and sold as a slave. But he escaped and returned to England. There he joined the expedition that founded Jamestown in 1607.

The new colony almost failed at first because its "gentlemen" refused to work. Then Captain Smith took charge. "No work, no eat" was his order. He made the colonists build houses and a fort, dig wells, and plant corn. To keep them from starving until the corn ripened, Smith himself hunted for meat and traded with the Indians for corn. It was on one of his food-hunting expeditions that he was captured by unfriendly Indians. Whether Smith was saved by Pocahontas or not, it is a fact that he was set free. What is more, the Indians offered to help the colonists. We have accounts by other colonists to prove this part of Smith's story, as well as his work in saving Jamestown.

The next year Smith was badly burned in a gunpowder explosion. He returned to England and never went back to Virginia. A few years later, however, he explored the Atlantic coast to the north. He named it New England and predicted that the rich fisheries off its shores would some day be more valuable than gold.

Captain John Smith may not always have told the exact truth. But his exciting stories were very popular. They aroused the English people's interest in America. This "advertising" and his services in saving Jamestown entitle him to an important place in our nation's history.

they wanted to "purify" their church by making its services very plain. Their leaders quarreled bitterly with the king. He answered by threatening to persecute them if they did not change their forms of worship. Instead of giving in, however, more than 10,000 Puritans migrated to America in a few years. Their settlements surrounded Plymouth, which later became part of the Massachusetts colony (see map, page 36).

2. THE OTHER NEW ENGLAND COLONIES. The Puritans were so certain they were right that they would not tolerate (allow) any other religion. When one of their ministers, Roger Williams, spoke out for religious toleration, they drove him from Massachusetts. Roger Williams established the little colony of Rhode Island to the south of Massachusetts in 1636. There freedom of worship was granted to people of all faiths.

In the same year another Puritan minister, Thomas Hooker, led some settlers into the fertile Connecticut River Valley. Here he founded the colony of Connecticut. Still other colonists from Massachusetts moved northward into land that is now New Hampshire, Maine, and Vermont. New Hampshire became a separate colony in 1679. Maine and Vermont were still parts of other colonies when the American Revolution began.

3. NEW ENGLAND'S INDUSTRIES. New England did not have the fertile farmlands of the South. The Appalachian Mountains came down almost to the sea, so that there was little level land along the coast (see map, page 2). Winters in this region were long and cold. Except in a few fertile river valleys, farms were small and poor. The seas off the coast, on the other hand, were rich in cod and other fish. New Englanders soon became expert in fishing, and dried codfish became their main product for sale. They also learned to build sturdy ships from the timber of their hardwood forests. New England's ships and sailors carried codfish and other products to many parts

Colonial shipyard. Why did shipbuilding become an important industry in the colonies? What were other important colonial industries?

of the globe. Fishing, shipbuilding, and shipping remained New England's most important industries for some two hundred years. The region's leading port, Boston, was for a long time the largest city in the thirteen colonies.

D. Variety in the Middle Colonies. 1. NEW YORK AND NEW JERSEY. The middle colonies, as their name indicates, were situated between New England and the South (see map, page 36). The oldest of these colonies, New Netherland, was established by the Dutch in 1624. The colony grew very slowly. The Dutch were interested mainly in trading with the Indians for furs, and they did not encourage settlers. England seized the colony in 1664. King Charles II gave it to his brother James, Duke of York, after whom it was renamed New York.

New Jersey was first settled by the Swedes and Dutch. The Duke of York took it over in 1664 and gave it to two of his friends. Once New York and New Jersey came under English rule, they attracted many settlers from England and other European countries.

2. PENNSYLVANIA AND DELAWARE. Pennsylvania, meaning "Penn's Woods," was founded by William Penn in 1681. The colony

39

Philadelphia, the leading port of the thirteen colonies, in 1768. This picture shows what great progress the colonists had made in 150 years.

was given to him by Charles II as payment for a debt the king owed his father. Penn belonged to the Quakers, a Protestant group that believed in complete religious toleration, equality, and brotherhood. Penn put these advanced beliefs into effect in Pennsylvania. Settlers of every nationality and religion were welcomed there and given equal rights. Each family received fifty acres of land free and could rent additional land for only a penny an acre. Penn also treated the Indians as equals, and they rarely attacked the settlers. Despite its late start, Pennsylvania quickly became one of the leading colonies in population and in wealth.

The little colony of Delaware was originally settled by Swedes. It was taken over first by the Dutch and then by the English, who made it part of Pennsylvania. Delaware finally became an independent colony in 1704. Two surveyors, Mason and Dixon, marked off the boundary between Delaware and Maryland. The Mason and Dixon Line (see map, page 36) is still considered the dividing line between North and South today.

3. A Varied Economy. Economically—that is, in the way people made a living—the middle colonies combined the advantages of both New England and the southern colonies. In this region were a number of large estates, much like the southern plantations; there were also thousands of small and medium-sized farms. The middle colonies were called the "bread colonies" because wheat was their main crop. They also grew corn and raised cattle, both for their own use and for export (sale outside the region). In addition, they developed some important industries—especially fur trading, ironmaking, shipbuilding, and shipping. Philadelphia and New York became the main ports of the middle colonies. In time both cities became larger than Boston.

E. One Hundred and Fifty Years of Progress. In 1750, less than 150 years after the founding of Jamestown, thirteen thriving colonies lined the Atlantic coast of North America. They were larger in area than most European countries. Thanks to immigration and a high birth rate, their population already totaled two million people and was increasing rapidly. Their farms and plantations were producing great quantities of food and raw materials for export. Their fisheries were among the richest in the world. Their industries were growing in size and number. In economic development, they were far ahead of the colonies planted by other European nations in the Americas. They were also, as we shall soon see, leaders in political and social progress.

REVIEWING THE SECTION

A. Knowing Important Facts

PART 1. For each occupation listed below, write in your notebook the section or sections of the country where it was important.

1. Fishing
2. Fur trading
3. Ironmaking
4. Corn and cattle raising
5. Rice and indigo growing
6. Shipbuilding
7. Shipping
8. Tobacco planting
9. Wheat growing

PART 2. For each colony in the first column, write the *letter* of its founder in the second column.

Colonies
1. Connecticut
2. Delaware
3. Georgia
4. Maryland
5. Massachusetts
6. New Netherland (New York)
7. North and South Carolina
8. Pennsylvania
9. Rhode Island
10. Virginia

Founders
a. A charitable organization
b. The Dutch
c. Friends of Charles II
d. Captain John Smith
e. The London Company
f. Lord Baltimore
g. The Pilgrims and Puritans
h. Roger Williams
i. Thomas Hooker
j. William Penn
k. The Swedes

B. Understanding the Facts

Write "True" in your notebook if the statement is correct. If the statement contains an error, rewrite it so that it is correct.

1. Gentlemen made good settlers because they were usually willing to work hard.
2. Captain John Smith saved Jamestown by forcing the settlers to grow tobacco.
3. The plantation system brought wealth to only a small part of the population of the southern colonies.
4. Slavery took hold in America because it was widespread in Europe.
5. Only blacks became slaves in the thirteen colonies.
6. The Toleration Act was passed in Maryland to protect Protestants from Catholics, who greatly outnumbered them.
7. North Carolina was the only southern colony where small farms were more important than large plantations.
8. Georgia became prosperous when tobacco plantations were established there.

9. Though the Puritans were themselves persecuted for their religion, they persecuted people of other religions.
10. Pennsylvania's success shows that people work better when they are well treated.

IMPROVING YOUR SKILLS

A. Mastering the Map

PART 1. Locate each of the thirteen colonies on the map on page 36. Then write the name of the region in which it was situated—the South, New England, or the middle colonies.

1. Connecticut
2. Delaware
3. Georgia
4. Maryland
5. Massachusetts
6. New Hampshire
7. New Jersey
8. New York
9. North Carolina
10. Pennsylvania
11. Rhode Island
12. South Carolina
13. Virginia

PART 2. From the map on page 36, tell in which colony these cities or towns were located.

1. Boston
2. Charleston
3. Jamestown
4. New York
5. Philadelphia
6. Plymouth

POPULATION GROWTH IN THE THIRTEEN COLONIES

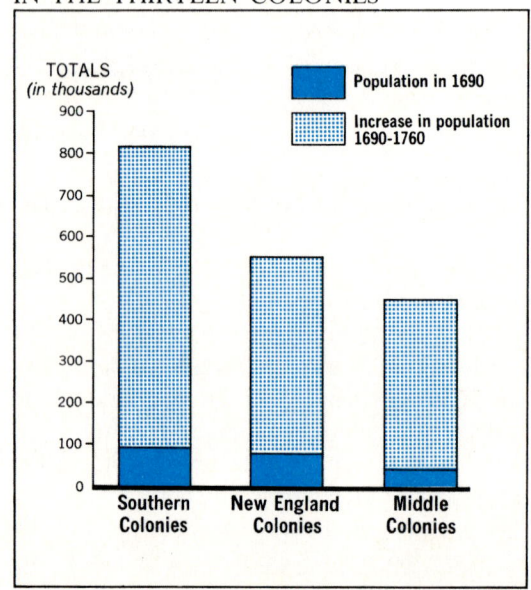

B. Interpreting the Graph

A graph, like a map or time line, is a kind of picture that gives you information in a way that is easy to understand. It usually has lines, bars, circles, or symbols that show how two or more factors are related. The graph on the opposite page has bars that show population growth in the colonies during the period described in this section. Examine it carefully; then answer these questions.

1. Which group of colonies had the largest population in 1690? In 1760?
2. Which group had the smallest population at both dates?
3. About how large was the population of the southern colonies in 1690? In 1760?
4. What was the total population of the thirteen colonies in 1690? In 1760?

C. Finding Word Meanings

PART 1. Review the clues to word meanings on pages 34-35. Practice finding them in this section. Copy each new term and its definition in your notebook; then underline the clues.

(In **A**)	charter	(In **D1**)	Middle colonies
	plantation system	(In **D2**)	Pennsylvania
(In **B1**)	Toleration Act		Quakers
(In **B2**)	naval stores	(In **D3**)	export
(In **C1**)	Pilgrims		
	Puritans		

PART 2. Sometimes a word that is new and strange to you is not explained in the text. How can you find its meaning? You can find it in the dictionary, of course. That is a sure-fire way. But more interesting, you will agree, is to work out the meaning yourself. This can best be done in three ways:

First Way: Look for familiar prefixes and suffixes. These are the small additions to the beginnings and ends of words. Also look for roots or stems. These are the main parts of words. Knowing part of a word will sometimes help you to find out what the whole word means.

> EXAMPLE: *root* re*vive*: to make *live*
> *prefix* *re*vive: to make live *again*
> meaning: to make *live again,* as the practice of slavery.

Second Way: When you meet a strange phrase or word that is made up of other words, find the meaning of each word in it; then fit the words together to make sense of the whole.

> EXAMPLE: eyewitness: from *eye* and *witness*; one who was there and saw the event with his own eyes

Third Way: Read the entire sentence in which an unfamiliar word appears. If necessary, read the sentences before and after it, or even the entire paragraph. Once you get the general idea, the meaning of the unfamiliar word or phrase will usually become clear.

> **EXAMPLE:** economic advancement (see page 30): We learn the meaning of this phrase by reading through the first paragraph in **A**1. From this context we learn that "economic" has to do with earning a living. To make a better living is to "advance" economically.

There are many words and phrases in Chapter 2 that you can apply your new skills to. Some of these are listed next. In your notebook write each word and the meaning you have given it.

First Way: Taking Words Apart
(In **B**3) southernmost (What does "northernmost" mean?)
(In **E**)   immigration (What does "emigration" mean?)

Second Way: Taking Phrases Apart
(In **A**2, page 30) term of indenture
(In **C**, page 31)   religious persecution

Third Way: Getting the Meaning From a Sentence or Paragraph
(In **B**3, page 37) ban

MAKING HISTORY LIVE

1. Suppose that you are a seventeenth-century European planning to go to the thirteen colonies. Tell in which of the three regions you would settle and why.
2. Read accounts by actual seventeenth-century immigrants. Then imagine that you have just crossed the Atlantic and settled in one of the thirteen colonies. Write a letter home describing your experiences aboard ship or on your arrival in America.
3. Imagine that you are an African who has been captured and brought to America as a slave. Describe your feelings and experiences.
4. Report on an important person in colonial America, like John Smith, the Puritan leader John Winthrop, Anne Hutchinson, or the Indian Squanto.
5. Draw pictures or make models to show how the colonists dressed and lived in *one* of the three regions of the English colonies.
6. If you have visited an old colonial mansion, a colonial museum, or a restored colonial town like Williamsburg, describe what you learned there about life in the thirteen colonies. If you have not visited such places, check your library for information.

Chapter 3

THE BEGINNINGS OF AMERICAN DEMOCRACY

W E AMERICANS are used to living in a democracy, and so we think that most other countries are democracies, too. Actually, the democracy we live under is a new form of government. It is only a little over two hundred years old. Until the eighteenth century, almost every country was ruled by an absolute monarch, a king or queen who had complete control of the government. Even today most people do not live in democracies. Most people are ruled by dictators. Dictators are much like absolute monarchs, but most have not inherited their positions and usually cannot leave them to their children.

1. What is democracy?
2. How is it different from absolutism or dictatorship?
3. How did democracy begin in England?
4. How did democracy develop in the thirteen colonies?

How Did Democracy Come to the Thirteen Colonies?

A. The Basic Features of Democracy. The word *democracy* means "government by the people." In democratic countries today, the people control the government by choosing their officials in fair and free elections. These officials are expected to carry out the people's wishes. If they fail, they can be replaced at the next election.

Whenever differences of opinion arise in a democracy, they are settled by voting. The side with a majority (more than half) of the votes wins. Its ideas are carried out by the government. The minority, the side with less than half the votes, is expected to obey the laws the majority passes. But the minority still has the right to disagree. Liberty—the freedom to express our opinions—is one of the most precious rights we have in a democracy. As long as the members of the minority are free to convince other people that their views are correct, they have a fair chance to become the majority. Then they, too, can put their ideas into effect.

Equality is another basic principle of democracy. All citizens of a democracy are equal before the law—that is, each person has the same rights as all other persons. All qualified citizens have the right, for example, to vote and run for government office.

Justice is another principle important to democracies. Great care is taken to see that persons accused of crimes receive fair trials. To be convicted, they must be found guilty "beyond a reasonable doubt." This means that a jury must be convinced that those on trial have committed the crime. Thus, it is possible for guilty persons to keep their freedom through a trial. But the people of democratic countries believe that it is better for some guilty people to go free than to have unfair trials or to have no trials at all.

B. Absolute Monarchy and Dictatorship. In an absolute monarchy or dictatorship, on the other hand, the people have no rights. The ruler can make any law he wants. He appoints and dismisses officials at will. He chooses judges and controls justice. Anyone who displeases him can be thrown into prison or be executed.

The absolute monarchies of the seventeenth and eighteenth centuries had other features we would consider unfair. There was no religious toleration. Instead, everyone was expected to belong to the ruler's church. An upper class, consisting of nobles with titles like "duke" or "count," enjoyed a number of special privileges. The nobles usually owned large estates, which they had inherited along with their titles. The king appointed them to the highest positions in the government, the armed forces, and the church. They could tax the common people—those without titles and special privileges—but they themselves did not have to pay certain heavy taxes. If a noble committed a crime, he was tried by a special court of nobles like himself. If convicted, he generally received a much lighter sentence than a commoner who had committed the same offense.

Most of the common people were peasants or serfs. They were the lowest class of society.

Though their incomes were small, they had to pay heavy taxes. Commoners living in the towns were somewhat better off. Some of them, especially merchants and bankers, were even wealthy. They formed a middle class between the nobility and the peasants. But the law still considered them commoners and the nobles looked down on them. The three social classes—the nobles (the upper class), the well-to-do commoners (the middle class), and the peasants (the lower class)—did not mix with one another. It was very difficult for a person to rise above the class into which he or she was born.

In modern dictatorships there is no class of nobles. But the dictator's supporters usually enjoy a number of special privileges, including appointment to the highest government posts.

C. Direct Democracy in Ancient Greece. The first people to overthrow absolute monarchs and dictators and to establish democratic governments were the ancient Greeks. They did this some 2,500 years ago. At that time Greece was divided into a number of small countries, called city-states. Since each city-state was small, it was a simple matter for its citizens to meet often. At their assemblies (meetings) they decided important public questions and elected officials to carry out their decisions. This type of government, in which the citizens rule the country themselves, is called direct democracy. It is a type of democracy that can work well only in small countries. It died out when the Greeks came under Roman rule.

D. Representative Government in England. Modern nations are much too large for direct democracy. A democratic nation is therefore divided into several hundred election districts. The voters of each district elect a representative to present their views. The representatives meet in an assembly to decide public questions. Their decisions are the laws by which the people are governed. A representative assembly may, or may not, be democratic. It is undemocratic if it represents only a small part of the population. It is democratic if it represents the majority of the people.

Louis XIV, king of France. How does this picture show the wealth and power of an absolute monarch? Where do you think monarchs obtained their wealth?

Representative government began in England during the later Middle Ages. In the thirteenth century, an English monarch called together representatives of the upper class from all parts of the kingdom. Their assembly was named Parliament, meaning "a place for talking." The English Parliament is one of the oldest representative assemblies in the world.

At first, Parliament only advised monarchs. Then it refused to vote for new taxes unless the king took its advice. For a long time, monarchs and Parliament struggled for power. In 1649 Parliament executed one king, Charles I. Later it drove his son, James II, from the throne and chose a new king. This event, the Glorious Revolution of 1688, proved that Parliament had become stronger than the monarch.

Since that time Parliament has made England's laws. Thus England became a limited monarchy—that is, a nation in which the rulers keep their throne, but lose some powers. The powers of the English monarchs were further limited during the next two centuries. Today, Elizabeth II still takes part in all sorts of ceremonies, but she has very little influence in the government.

SOCIAL CLASSES IN 18th-CENTURY EUROPE

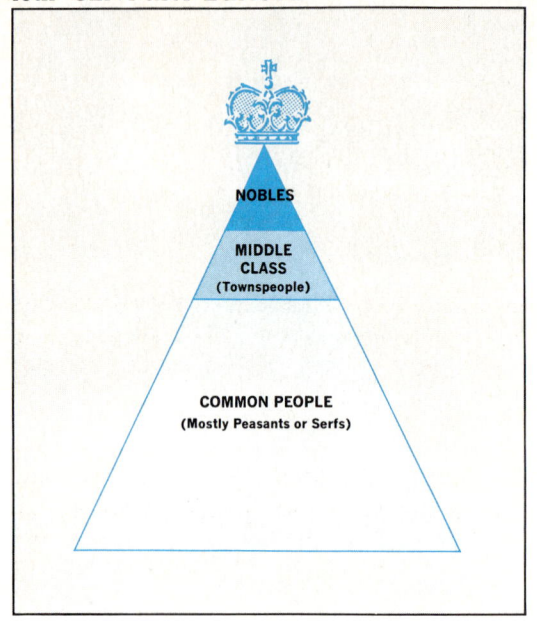

[Diagram: pyramid showing NOBLES at top, MIDDLE CLASS (Townspeople) in middle, and COMMON PEOPLE (Mostly Peasants or Serfs) at the base, with a crown above.]

How can you tell from this diagram that there were many more common people than nobles?

E. The "Rights of Englishmen." During the long struggle between the kings and Parliament, the English people made other advances in democracy. Men and women gained a number of rights to protect them from unjust rulers. Some of these protections were included in the Bill of Rights, passed by Parliament in 1689. Others were put into laws. Still others were recognized by the courts as rules.

1. Monarchs agreed not to raise new taxes unless Parliament agreed.

2. People had the right of petition—that is, the right to ask for changes in the law without fear of punishment.

3. No person's life, liberty, or property might be taken away without a fair trial or hearing. In addition, the government had to pay a fair price for any property it took away from the people.

4. Soldiers might not be sent to live in a person's house in peacetime unless the owner agreed. This ended the custom of stationing troops in private homes either to save the government money or to punish private citizens.

5. A person's home might not be searched without a special permit known as a warrant. To obtain a warrant, government officials had to prove to a judge that there was a good reason for making the search. One reason might be the possession of stolen goods.

6. It was unlawful to keep a person in jail without a trial. If this happened, a lawyer could obtain an order from a judge to either set the prisoner free or bring the prisoner to trial at once. This kept rulers from arresting persons they did not like and keeping them in prison a long time without trial.

7. Persons accused of crimes could not be forced to be witnesses against themselves. This put an end to the use of torture to obtain confessions.

8. An accused person had the right to trial by jury. A person's innocence or guilt was to be decided by other citizens, not by a judge whom the ruler had appointed. Such a jury would be freer from the ruler's control.

9. Cruel and unusual punishments, such as death by slow torture, were forbidden.

Execution of Charles I, king of England, in 1649. Charles was sentenced to death by Parliament as a traitor to England. How did his execution weaken the idea of absolute monarchy? How did Charles's death show Parliament's power?

F. Rights of the Colonists. The democratic reforms (improvements) that had taken place in England spread very quickly to the English colonies in America. In order to attract settlers there, the king promised them all the rights enjoyed by people in England.

In addition, the colonies modeled their new governments after that of the mother country. At the head of each colony was a governor. In most colonies he was appointed by the ruler and had similar powers. But the people of each colony also elected a representative assembly, much like Parliament. These assemblies, following Parliament's example, often disagreed with the governors. Like Parliament, too, they slowly succeeded in increasing their own powers and reducing those of their governors. Thus the colonists started off with all the advantages that their ancestors in England had taken hundreds of years to win.

Virginia's House of Burgesses. The first representative assembly in the colonies met in Williamsburg, the capital of Virginia, in 1619. Why are representative assemblies important? This photograph was taken in modern Williamsburg.

REVIEWING THE SECTION

A. Knowing New Terms

For each form of government in the first column, write in your notebook the *letter* of the best description in the second column.

Forms of Government
1. Absolute monarchy
2. Dictatorship
3. Direct democracy
4. Limited monarchy
5. Representative democracy

Descriptions
a. Rulers inherit the throne and have complete control of the government.
b. Rulers inherit the throne but do not have complete power.
c. Rulers have complete power, but their position is not inherited.
d. The country is governed by a few thousand nobles.
e. The citizens make the laws and choose officials to carry them out.
f. The citizens elect officials to make the laws and carry them out.

B. Knowing Important Facts

Here is a list of the way things are done in an absolute monarchy or dictatorship. For each item, tell how the same thing is done in a democracy like the United States today. Write the answers in your notebook.

Absolute Monarchy or Dictatorship	*Democracy*
1. The ruler inherits the throne or seizes power.	1.
2. The ruler makes the laws.	2.
3. The ruler appoints all important officials.	3.
4. The ruler controls justice. People may be punished without a trial.	4.
5. It is a crime to criticize the ruler or his officials.	5.
6. The ruler is supported by an upper class with special privileges.	6.

C. Understanding the Facts

All Americans still enjoy almost all the rights that used to be called "the rights of Englishmen." In your notebook write "Yes" if you think the following incidents could happen in the United States today; write "No" if you think they could not happen. Tell which of the rights listed in **E** applies to each case.

1. You go with your friends to City Hall to ask for a new ball field. You are told to sit down and wait your turn. When it comes, you are asked to come to the front of the room and explain what you want and why.
2. Your family receives a notice from the government. It says that you must move because your house is being condemned to make way for a housing project. Instead of moving, your parents hire a lawyer and bring legal action against the government.
3. The police have been told that a criminal is hiding in your neighborhood. They go from house to house looking for the criminal. One of your neighbors refuses to let them enter her home.
4. You are traveling with a group of schoolmates through the United States. In one place, two of your schoolmates disappear.
   a. Witnesses say they were taken away in a police car, but the police refuse to give out any information about them.
   b. After a few weeks, the two are brought to trial on charges of dis-

turbing the peace. Their confessions are read in court, and the judge finds them guilty.

c. They are sentenced to serve five years in jail and pay a fine of $10,000.

IMPROVING YOUR SKILLS

A. Finding Word Meanings

PART 1. In your notebook write each term and the meaning it has in the text. Underline the clue or clues that helped you find the meaning.

(In the chapter introduction) absolute monarch
(In **A**) democracy
majority
minority
liberty
(In **B**) the common people
(In **C**) direct democracy
(In **D**) limited monarchy
(In **E**) right of petition
trial by jury

PART 2. You cannot be sure that you really understand the meaning of a term until you can explain it in your own words. So this time, work out the meaning of each important term from its context; then write it down *in your own words,* not in those of the text.

(In the chapter introduction) dictator
(In **B**) middle class
(In **C**) assemblies
(In **D**) Parliament
Glorious Revolution of 1688
(In **E**) "rights of Englishmen"
English Bill of Rights
warrant.

B. Understanding the Picture

Look at the picture on page 46. Then answer these questions.

1. How can you tell that the people in the right of the picture are nobles?
2. How can you tell that the people on the left are commoners?

51

How Did Democracy Develop in the Thirteen Colonies?

A. Economic Advancement. The following words were written by a Frenchman who visited America in the eighteenth century:

"In this great American asylum [shelter], the poor of Europe have met together. Here they have become men. In Europe they were so many useless plants. They withered and were mowed down by want, hunger, and war; but now they have taken root and flourished. Formerly they were not numbered in any lists except in those of the poor; here they rank as citizens. The laws protect them as they arrive; they receive ample rewards for their labors; these rewards procure them lands; those lands confer on them the title of freemen; and to that title every benefit is affixed which men can possibly require."

This Frenchman saw that democracy could grow in America because here conditions favored the economic progress of the common people. Most immigrants were poor when they landed. But within a generation or so, they or their children could become prosperous farmers and businessmen. America was truly a land of economic opportunity. Here people could rapidly increase their income and improve their way of life.

B. Social Progress. An American could improve his position socially, as well as economically, through his own efforts. Since few English nobles came to the colonies to live, the privileged class was very small. The upper class consisted mainly of planters, merchants, bankers, and other people who had gained high position through wealth rather than birth. The lowest classes were the indentured servants, who were given their freedom after a few years, and the slaves. Most colonists formed a large middle class of well-to-do farmers and businessmen. They could advance

Compare this diagram of eighteenth-century society in America with the diagram of European society on page 48. What important differences can you find?

SOCIAL CLASSES IN 18th-CENTURY AMERICA

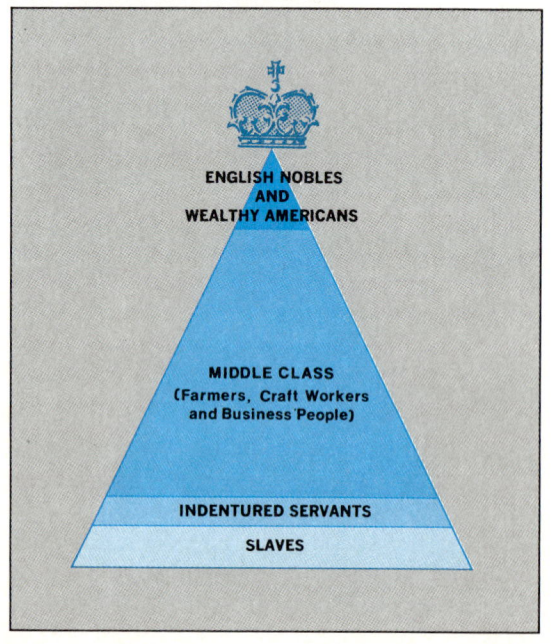

- ENGLISH NOBLES AND WEALTHY AMERICANS
- MIDDLE CLASS (Farmers, Craft Workers and Business People)
- INDENTURED SERVANTS
- SLAVES

into the upper class by becoming wealthy.

A hard worker could move to a higher social class without much difficulty. That is why Americans did not show the same respect for "their betters" that Europeans did. As Benjamin Franklin pointed out, Americans did not ask who you were, but what you could do! They respected people for their ability or wealth, instead of their family background.

C. Religious Toleration. Religious differences also began to break down in America, mainly because the colonies were settled by many kinds of Christians. Toleration of different faiths began in Rhode Island, Maryland, and Pennsylvania (see pages 37, 39, and 40). The idea soon spread throughout the middle colonies because they had the greatest mixture of different peoples. In most of New England, on the other hand, the Puritans kept their control. In the South, the Church of England remained the established church. But persecution of other religious groups came to an end in both regions long before the Revolution.

D. Political Advances. 1. A HIGH PERCENTAGE OF VOTERS. The thirteen colonies also made important political advances—that is, improvements in government. In England a man had to own property and belong to the established church in order to vote. To hold a government position, he had to own still more property. These property and religious qualifications (requirements) kept most Englishmen from taking part in politics.

In the thirteen colonies, property qualifications for voting and officeholding were lower than those in England. Most American men could meet these qualifications because they owned land or other property. Most could also meet the religious qualification. Their ancestors had usually settled in colonies where their religion was practiced or where religious toleration existed. On the whole, a much larger part of the population could vote and hold office in

Signing the Mayflower Compact. Almost one-third of the ship's passengers were women and girls. Why do you think no women signed the Mayflower Compact?

America than in England. The percentage of adult males who voted in Massachusetts colony was probably as high as it is in some states today!

2. REBIRTH OF DIRECT DEMOCRACY. When the Pilgrims arrived in Plymouth harbor in 1620, they had no royal charter giving them the right to begin a colony there. They therefore drew up an agreement, which is known as the Mayflower Compact because it was signed on board their ship, the *Mayflower*. The Pilgrims agreed to draw up such just and equal laws as they thought would be most convenient for the general good of the Colony. They then established a government of their own for their little settlement.

Other early colonists also had to set up governments for their villages and towns. The average New England community was small. The townspeople found it easy to meet in the town hall or church to decide policies and elect officials. This type of local government became known as the New England town meeting. The town meeting is an example of direct democracy like that practiced by the ancient

ROGER WILLIAMS AND ANNE HUTCHINSON: FIGHTERS FOR FREEDOM

Roger Williams in the wilderness after his flight from Massachusetts.

Anne Hutchinson presenting her religious ideas to a group in the Massachusetts Bay Colony.

Roger Williams was born in the early seventeenth century, a time of bitter religious disputes. He was educated in the best English schools. A brilliant student, he could have led a good life as a minister of the Church of England. But he became a Puritan minister instead. To escape persecution, he sailed to America.

Here too, Roger Williams found himself in trouble. He criticized the Puritans for persecuting members of other faiths. Everyone should be free to worship God in his or her own way, Williams insisted. When the Puritan leaders ordered him sent back to England, he fled into the wilderness. Fortunately, he had made friends of the neighboring Indians. They took care of him and gave him land for a settlement.

Williams's new colony, Rhode Island, was a success. It attracted many people, such as Quakers and Jews, who were persecuted elsewhere. Williams devoted the rest of his life to his colony and his ideals. He made many speeches and wrote a number of books on religious freedom. Four times he made the difficult and dangerous trip across the Atlantic to obtain a royal charter for Rhode Island. A key provision of the charter stated:

No person within said colony shall in any wise be molested, punished, disquieted, or called in question for any differences of opinion in matters of religion, but shall freely and fully have and enjoy his and their own judgments and consciences in matters of religion.

Anne Hutchinson was another fighter for freedom. She was born and educated in England. She came with her husband and family to Massachusetts Bay Colony. Very soon she got into religious arguments with some of the colony's leaders. She also held meetings of women in Boston twice a week.

After repeated warnings about her religious views and her preaching, a court tried her for being rebellious and lacking respect. She was ordered to leave the colony. Hutchinson, with her husband and family, moved to Rhode Island. There they were free to practice their religion as they saw fit.

The principle of religious freedom, for which Roger Williams and Anne Hutchinson fought so long and hard, gradually spread to other colonies. Later it was made part of our country's Constitution. It has also been adopted by many other countries. Roger Williams and Anne Hutchinson, fighters for freedom, will long be remembered as two of the great people who have made our world a better place.

Greeks (see page 47). It proved so successful that small communities in many parts of the United States today still govern themselves in this way.

3. THE WRITTEN CONSTITUTION. In 1639 the founders of Connecticut colony faced the same problem as the Pilgrims; they had no royal charter. They drew up a document called the Fundamental Orders of Connecticut. This was the first written constitution in America. (A written constitution is a document containing the rules for running a government.) Having a written constitution proved a good idea. In the United States today, we have fifty-one constitutions—one for the federal government and one for each of the fifty states. Dozens of countries all over the globe have followed the American example. Many have constitutions modeled on ours.

4. FREEDOM OF THE PRESS. The "rights of Englishmen" granted to the colonists did not include three rights we consider necessary today. They are freedom of speech, freedom of the press, and freedom of religion. We have already seen how freedom of religion began in the thirteen colonies. Now we shall see how Americans took the first step toward freedom of the press in a case tried in New York City in 1735.

John Peter Zenger printed a newspaper that often criticized the governor of New York. He was arrested and tried for seditious libel—that is, for writing statements damaging to the governor. The judge asked the jury to find Zenger guilty because he admitted printing the criticisms. But Zenger's lawyer asked the jury to consider also whether the criticisms were true. In that case, said the lawyer, his client should be acquitted (cleared of the charge).

The jury dared to clear Zenger of the charge against him. Since then, truth has been considered the best defense in a libel suit. More important, Zenger's case helped to establish freedom of the press—the idea that people should be allowed to write and publish criticisms of the government. This development led in turn to freedom of speech—the right of the people to speak freely, even against the government. It soon became clear that such criticism is desirable. Government officials are more likely to do a good job if they fear that their mistakes will be made known.

E. Cultural Progress. Another democratic idea, public education, began in Massachusetts. The Puritans and other Protestants believed that every man should know his Bible well. This meant that he had to be able to read.

The Zenger trial. Zenger's lawyer won over the jury with these famous words: "It is not the cause of a poor printer which you are now trying. It is the cause of liberty, the right of opposing arbitrary power by speaking and writing truth."

View of Harvard College during colonial times. Why was the founding of colleges in the colonies so important?

In the seventeenth century, however, most people were illiterate—that is, they could not read or write. So Massachusetts passed laws in the 1640s requiring small towns to hire schoolmasters and large ones to establish public schools. Most pupils had to pay for their schooling, but poor boys could attend free. With an education, they had a much better chance to advance economically and socially.

At first, public school pupils were taught only the three Rs (reading, 'riting, and 'rithmetic). In a few years, however, more advanced subjects were added to their studies to prepare them for college. The first American college, Harvard, was established in Massachusetts in 1636. The first printing press in the colonies was built at Harvard three years later.

Learning also flourished in the other colonies. In this regard, Pennsylvania became a rival of Massachusetts in the late seventeenth century. Its leading city, Philadelphia, had the largest number of newspapers, the first circulating library, and the first medical school in the colonies. Its most famous citizen, Benjamin Franklin, gathered together a group of educated men to discuss scientific questions. He himself conducted experiments with lightning.

F. Undemocratic Features of Colonial Life. The thirteen colonies were pioneers of progress in the eighteenth-century world. Yet they would hardly be considered democratic by modern standards. There were, for example, sharp differences among the various classes of society. These differences were greatest in the southern colonies. There the planters looked down on the small farmers. The small farmers in turn looked down on indentured servants and slaves. The revival of slavery in America, long after it had begun to disappear in Europe, was the darkest blot on American society. It created many serious problems, some of which have not been completely solved to this day.

Colonial government, too, was undemocratic in a number of ways. The governors, sent over by the monarch of England, had far too much power. They appointed officials, commanded the armed forces, and could veto (kill) bills passed by the representative assemblies. In addition, many male citizens could not meet the qualifications for voting and holding office.

In the thirteen colonies, as in Europe, women were not politically or legally equal to men. Married women could not own property. Husbands controlled any money their wives might earn. Some women did run businesses, shops, and farms. But very few women received an education or worked outside the home. On the other hand, there was usually a shortage of women in America. As a result, women were treated with more consideration and respect here than in Europe.

G. The American Spirit. Despite these shortcomings in colonial democracy, the colonists had good reason to be proud. They already spoke of America as a land of liberty. Many even boasted that the colonies would someday become a great country. Though they still thought of themselves as loyal English people, they considered themselves better than the people who had stayed at home in England. They therefore objected strongly when officials who had been sent over from England tried to treat them as inferiors. This spirit of pride and independence was to lead to one of the greatest democratic advances in history, the American Revolution.

REVIEWING THE SECTION

A. Knowing New Terms

PART 1. For each new term in the first column, write the *letter* of the best description in the second column.

Terms	Descriptions
1. Fundamental Orders of Connecticut	a. First example of direct democracy in modern times
2. Harvard	b. First agreement for self-government
3. Mayflower Compact	
4. Town meeting	c. First instance of freedom of speech
5. Zenger's trial	d. First written constitution
	e. First case won for freedom of the press
	f. First college of higher learning in the thirteen colonies

PART 2. You have been reading about economic, social, religious, political, and cultural progress in the thirteen colonies. Can you tell which is which? Write in your notebook which type of progress is shown in each of the following statements. Be prepared to explain your answer in class.

1. Americans did not ask who you were, but what you could do!
2. Connecticut and other colonies drafted (drew up) written constitutions.
3. A high percentage of adult males voted.
4. The idea of tolerating different faiths soon spread throughout the middle colonies.
5. Immigrants could become well-to-do farmers or merchants in a single generation.
6. Indentured servants became free after a few years.
7. New England towns were ruled by assemblies of citizens.
8. Philadelphia had a number of newspapers, a library, a medical school, and a scientific society.
9. The privileged class was very small in the thirteen colonies.
10. Zenger's trial established the principle of freedom of the press.

B. Understanding the Facts

Write "True" in your notebook if the statement is correct. If the statement contains an error, rewrite it so that it is correct.

1. An Englishman had to own more property to vote than to run for office.
2. The percentage of men voting in Massachusetts colony was probably as high as it is in Massachusetts today.
3. The New England town meeting was like the people's assemblies of the ancient Greek city-states.
4. Today every state of the United States has a written constitution.
5. Many foreign countries have constitutions like ours.
6. In the thirteen colonies, married women were not permitted to own property.
7. Our right to criticize public officials helps to bring about improvements in our government.
8. Public schools were a step forward in democracy because they gave poor children a better chance to advance in life.
9. There was more social progress in the southern colonies than in the middle or northern colonies.

C. Summing Up the Chapter

Examine the sketch of the tree on the next page; then answer these questions.

1. What do the roots show?
2. What do the branches represent?
3. What would be a good name for the tree?
4. Here you see only the roots and part of the trunk. What would the rest of the tree represent if it were shown?

IMPROVING YOUR SKILLS

Finding Word Meanings

Write the meanings of these new terms *in your own words*. Continue to watch for clues, but do not include them in your definitions.

(In **A**)	a land of economic opportunity	(In **E**)	illiterate
(In **B**)	social progress in America		the three Rs
(In **D**)	political advances	(In **F**)	the governor's veto
(In **D3**)	written constitution		
(In **D4**)	freedom of the press		
	freedom of speech		

MAKING HISTORY LIVE

1. Read the biography of a famous leader in the development of colonial democracy, such as Roger Williams, William Penn, or Benjamin Franklin. Explain why he was important.
2. Write a composition or a short play about one of the outstanding events in the development of colonial democracy, such as:
   a. the first meeting of Virginia's House of Burgesses in 1619   b. the drafting and signing of the Mayflower Compact   c. the Zenger Trial.
3. Join a "town meeting" held in your classroom to discuss a school matter, such as the election of school officers.
4. Imagine that you are an English nobleman visiting the colonies in 1750. Write a letter to friends in Europe describing what you see and what you think about it.

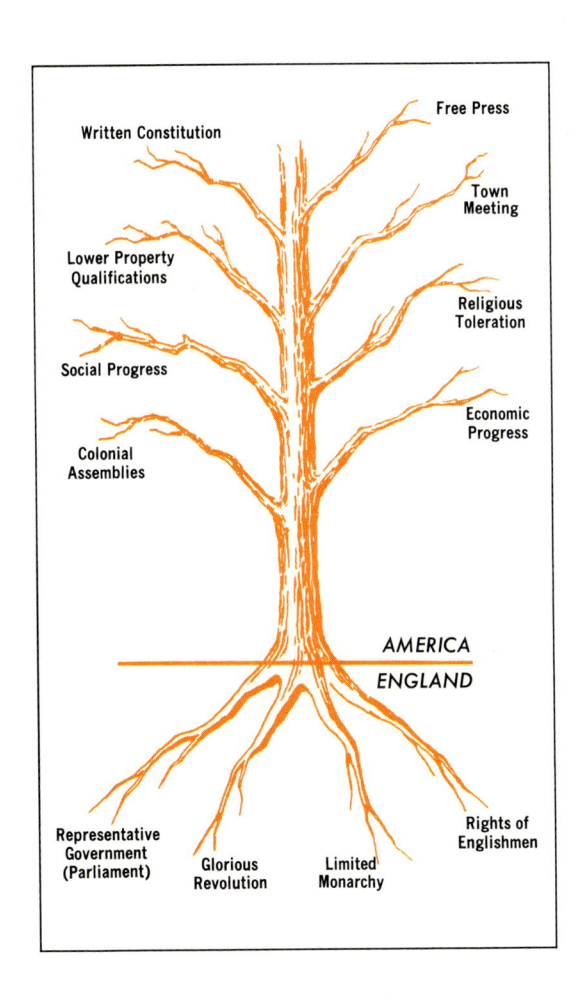

Chapter 4

THE BACKGROUND OF THE AMERICAN REVOLUTION

In 1754 a small army advanced slowly through the forests of the Appalachian Highlands in what is now western Pennsylvania. The army was made up of British redcoats and Virginia militia (colonial troops). Its goal was to capture a chain of forts built by the French along the Ohio River. But the British commander, General Braddock, knew little about forest fighting. George Washington, a young colonial officer, warned him that his men's bright uniforms and regular ranks made them an easy target for the enemy. The general would not listen. Suddenly the air was filled with the wild war-whoops of Indians and the sharp crack of musket fire. Men began to fall, shot down by the French and Indians hidden in the woods. Two-thirds of the force was wiped out. The rest retreated eastward in confusion. Young Washington fought bravely and was lucky to escape unharmed.

That was how the French and Indian War began. The war lasted nine years, from 1754 to 1763. It proved to be a turning point in the history of the thirteen colonies. Before 1763 the colonists were loyal subjects of Great Britain (the name given to England and Scotland after they were united in 1707). But only a dozen years later, the colonists were fighting against their former allies, the British redcoats.

In this chapter you will find out:

1. Why the colonists were loyal to Great Britain before the French and Indian War.

2. Why the colonists revolted against British rule after the war.

Why Were the Colonists Loyal to Great Britain Before 1763?

A. The Colonists' Ties to Great Britain. Great Britain was truly the parent country of the thirteen colonies. Ten of the colonies were started by British subjects and companies. Most of the settlers came from England or Scotland. English was their native tongue (language). Their governments, laws, and customs were all English in origin. They carried on most of their trade with British merchants. Finally, they depended on Great Britain in case of war. In the period from 1689 to 1748, Great Britain fought three wars with France and Spain. During these wars, the colonists relied on the British fleet to protect their shipping and their coast from attack. In short, the colonists were bound to their mother country by ties of family, business, and defense.

B. Sources of Trouble. Nevertheless, the colonists and the British government often quarreled. One cause of conflict was the question of self-government. Though the colonies were started by private individuals or companies, they were taken over, one after another, by the British government. This meant that the English monarch appointed their governors. These men had important powers (see page 56). Quarrels often broke out between them and the colonial assemblies.

Trade was a second source of trouble. In the seventeenth and eighteenth centuries, European governments believed that colonies should be controlled in ways that benefited the mother countries. Great Britain was no different from other European countries in this respect. Before 1763 Parliament had passed a series of laws known as the Trade Acts. 1. The people of the thirteen colonies were required to sell their main exports, such as tobacco and naval stores, to British merchants. 2. The colonists were forbidden to make and sell woolen cloth, iron wares, and other products manufactured in the parent country. They were expected to buy such products from the British. 3. Colonial trade had to be carried in British ships, manned by British sailors. 4. If the colonists did business with foreign countries, their ships were supposed to stop at British ports to pay taxes on their cargoes.

C. Effects of the Trade Acts. The colonists gained some benefits from the Trade Acts. First, they did not have to worry about selling their products. They knew that the British would buy all they could export. Secondly, their ships and sailors were considered British under the law. They were allowed therefore to carry cargoes to and from Great Britain or any other part of the British Empire. In 1750 one-seventh of Britain's large trade was being carried by colonial ships.

In other ways, however, the Trade Acts threatened colonial prosperity. The colonists often had to sell their goods to British merchants at prices lower than they might have gotten elsewhere. Planters in the southern colonies had special cause for anger. The British paid lower and lower prices for their tobacco. Even rich plantation owners fell into debt. The

TRIANGULAR TRADE ROUTES

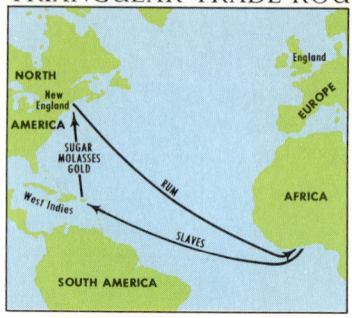

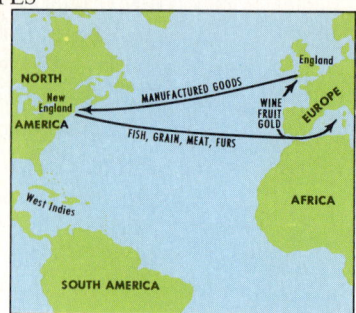

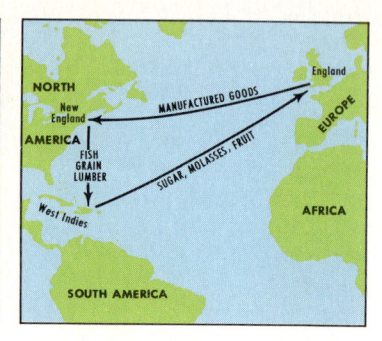

New England and middle colonies also had good reason to be unhappy with the regulations. They had succeeded in building up a profitable trade with the French and Spanish West Indies (see the maps above). If their ships had to sail to faraway British ports to pay taxes, this trade would be crippled.

Fortunately for the colonists, the British government was too busy with other problems to enforce the Trade Acts. Only a few British officials were sent to the colonies to watch over their trade. Colonial merchants found it easy to avoid the regulations. Many bribed the officials—that is, paid them not to enforce the law. Others took part in smuggling (illegal trade). They unloaded their cargoes secretly outside the ports at night. Even if caught and brought to trial, they could expect to be freed by a jury of their fellow colonists.

D. Basic Cause of the French and Indian War. Until 1763 the colonists were helped more than they were hindered by Great Britain. They especially needed British help against the French. As population increased, the colonists moved westward. Fur traders began to cross the Appalachian Mountains into the rich Mississippi River Valley. Wealthy men formed land companies and made plans to bring settlers into the region. English monarchs had promised some colonies in their charters "all the land from sea to sea." Therefore the colonists expected the British government to support and protect their settlements.

The French felt, however, that the British colonists had no right to cross the Appalachian Mountains. They claimed the entire Mississippi River Valley because French explorers were the first Europeans to sail down the river. Moreover, the French had established settlements and built up a profitable fur trade with the Indians in the Mississippi Valley. To keep out the British, they built a chain of forts along the Ohio River. As we have seen, a British attempt to capture these forts started the French and Indian War. Thus the rival claims of the two European powers to the land between the Appalachian Mountains and the Mississippi River were the basic cause of the war.

E. Defeat and Victory. At first the war went badly for the British. Braddock's defeat showed them that they knew little about fighting in the American wilderness. Moreover, they had to fight against three enemies, not just one—the French, the Indians, and the Spanish. Most Indian tribes in the Appalachian Highlands joined the French side because they preferred French fur traders to British settlers. The French lived among them and gave them valuable goods in exchange for their furs. The British colonists, on the other hand, wanted to take away their hunting grounds to start farms. Spain joined with France in order to regain a part of Florida that the colony of Georgia had taken.

After Braddock's defeat, the British government sent several small forces to America. They failed to win any important victories. Meanwhile the settlers in the northern and western parts of the thirteen colonies were being wiped out by Indian raids. Finally, in 1758, the British government decided to send over stronger forces. With some help from the colonists, the British captured the French forts in the Ohio Valley. They also attacked the main French settlements in New France (now Canada). Their most important victory was the capture of Quebec. This town controlled the St. Lawrence River. Since the river was the only highway the French had for sending supplies into the interior, they had to surrender.

F. Results of the French and Indian War. The French and Indian War had three important results. 1. Great Britain gained a great deal of territory. It won the region between the Appalachian Mountains and the Mississippi River over which the war had started. It also took New France and Florida. France gave its holdings west of the Mississippi to Spain to make up for Spain's loss of Florida (see map on this page). 2. The war strengthened the colonists' spirit of independence. It showed them that they could fight better than the famous British redcoats in the forests. Even more important, they no longer needed Britain to protect them against France

EFFECTS OF FRENCH AND INDIAN WAR—1763

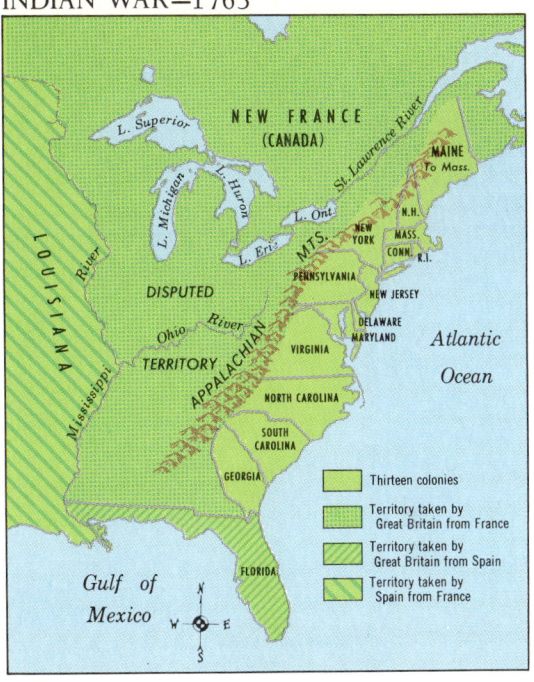

and Spain. France, their most powerful enemy, had lost almost all its holdings in America. Spain's new holdings were too far away to be a source of trouble. The Indians were now the colonists' only important enemy. 3. The war created a serious problem for Great Britain. The fighting in America was part of a worldwide struggle that included fighting in Europe and India. Though Great Britain won, it was left with very large debts. The British govern-

Braddock's defeat. This painting is neither lifelike nor accurate. But what can you learn about the battle by examining it? Can you find Braddock? Washington?

THE LIFE OF BENJAMIN FRANKLIN: AN AMERICAN SUCCESS STORY

Early to bed and early to rise,
Makes a man healthy, wealthy, and wise.

Wise sayings like this, together with humorous stories and good common-sense advice, made *Poor Richard's Almanack* the most widely read book in eighteenth-century America (except, of course, for the Bible). Its author was Benjamin Franklin, a Philadelphia printer. Franklin also published a popular newspaper, the *Pennsylvania Gazette*. His income from his printing business permitted him to retire at the age of forty-two.

Franklin was not only a writer, publisher, and printer; he was also a scientist, inventor, and statesman (wise government official). As a scientist, he was known in Europe as well as America for his experiments with lightning and electricity. His inventions included the lightning rod, an efficient stove, and improved eyeglasses. His greatest achievements, however, were as a statesman working for his city, colony, and country.

Thanks to Franklin, Philadelphia became the most advanced city in the thirteen colonies. It was the first to have policemen and firemen, paved streets and street cleaners, and an efficient postal service. Franklin also started two learned societies and a new type of high school in Philadelphia. In 1757, when he was fifty-one years old, Franklin began a new career as a government official. He was sent to England to represent Pennsylvania in its dealings with the British government. He remained there for fifteen years. His knowledge, wit, and good judgment won him the respect of the British nobility.

When the colonies were about to revolt against Great Britain, Franklin returned to America. He helped to write the Declaration of Independence and to set up a new government for Pennsylvania. Then he went to France to obtain aid for the United States. He quickly won the admiration of the French nobility and succeeded in making France an ally of the United States. When the Revolution ended, Franklin helped to write the peace treaty. Then he returned to the United States and became president (governor) of Pennsylvania. Finally, at the age of eighty-one, he helped to write the Constitution under which our country is still governed.

This list of Franklin's achievements, though long, is incomplete. It is enough, however, to show that he was a great man. What makes his story even more remarkable is the fact that he was the son of a poor Boston candlemaker. The fifteenth of seventeen children, he had to leave school at an early age and go to work. When he was seventeen, he ran away from Boston and went to Philadelphia. Though poor and unknown, he rose quickly to fame and fortune because of his ability. Benjamin Franklin's life is truly an American success story.

ment decided that the thirteen colonies, which had benefited from the war, should pay part of the cost. They also wanted the colonies to share the expense of keeping troops in America in case of another war. We shall soon see how this new British policy (plan) to make the colonists pay led to the American Revolution.

REVIEWING THE SECTION

A. Knowing New Terms

In your notebook write the new terms in this section that best complete these statements.

1. Troops of the colonies were called the _____.
2. The name of the country resulting from the union of England and Scotland was _____ _____.
3. The fighting in America between 1754 and 1763 is known as the _____ _____ _____ War.
4. Because British soldiers wore red uniforms, they were often called _____.
5. The thirteen colonies were mostly started and settled by British subjects. Great Britain was therefore known as their _____ _____.
6. The British laws that regulated the colonies' trade with other countries were known as the _____ _____.
7. Landing goods secretly to avoid government regulations and taxes is known as _____.

B. Knowing the Facts

PART 1. In your notebook complete this chart on the effects of the Trade Acts on the thirteen colonies.

Provisions of the Trade Acts	Benefits	Harmful Effects
1. Colonists had to sell their main products to British merchants.	1.	1.
2. Colonists were forbidden to export certain manufactured goods.	2.	2.
3. British goods had to be carried on British ships, manned by British sailors.	3.	3.

65

Provisions of the Trade Acts	Benefits	Harmful Effects
4. Colonial ships carrying foreign goods had to stop at British ports to pay taxes.	4.	4.

Conclusion. On the whole, were the Trade Acts good or bad for the thirteen colonies? What did the colonists do to avoid the Trade Acts?

PART 2. Complete this chart on the results of the French and Indian War.

Country	Gains	Losses
1. Great Britain	1.	1.
2. Thirteen colonies	2.	2.
3. France	3.	3.
4. Spain	4.	4.

Conclusion. Which of the four gained most from the war?

C. Finding the Reasons

In this exercise, one, two, or even all three answers to each question may be correct. Write the letters of *all* the correct answers in your notebook.

1. Why was Great Britain considered the parent country of the thirteen colonies?
   a. The colonies were all started and settled by British citizens. b. Their people spoke the English language. c. Their governments, laws, and customs came from England.
2. Why did the British government often quarrel with the thirteen colonies before 1763?
   a. British governors took actions that the colonial assemblies opposed. b. The British government tried to control the colonists' trade for its own benefit. c. The British refused to protect the colonies.
3. Why did the French and Indian War begin?
   a. France and Great Britain were always fighting. b. Both nations claimed the same territory in America. c. The colonists wanted to defeat the Indians west of the Appalachian Mountains.
4. Why did France claim the entire Mississippi River Valley?
   a. French explorers were the first Europeans to sail down the Mississippi. b. French people had settled in the Mississippi Valley. 2. French fur traders had built up a large trade with the Indians.

5. Why did the British capture of Quebec decide the French and Indian War?
   a. The French grew tired of fighting. b. The Indians went over to the British side. c. The British gained control of the St. Lawrence River, by which the French sent supplies to their settlements in the interior.
6. Why was winning the French and Indian War important to Great Britain?
   a. It defeated its rivals, France and Spain. b. It gained large territories in America. c. It greatly improved its relations with the thirteen colonies.
7. Why did the British government begin a new policy in the thirteen colonies after 1763?
   a. It needed money to pay the heavy costs of the French and Indian War. b. It needed military aid to put down the French and Indians. c. It now felt strong enough to crush the colonists' spirit of independence.

IMPROVING YOUR SKILLS

Mastering the Map

PART 1. Look at the map on page 62. Then for each of the following statements, write "True" in your notebook if the map shows it to be true. If the map shows the statement to be false, rewrite it so that it is true.

1. The three trade routes shown on this map are called the triangular trade routes because they form triangles.
2. The colonists shipped out raw materials and brought back manufactured goods on all three routes.
3. The West Indies were stopping places on all three routes.
4. An important part of the triangular trade included bringing slaves from Africa to the New World.
5. Trade on all three routes would become unprofitable if colonial shippers had to sail to England every time they took on new cargo.

PART 2. Look at the map on page 63. Then write in your notebook the names on the map that best complete these sentences.

1. As a result of the French and Indian War, Great Britain gained two territories from France. They were _____ _____ and the disputed territory between the _____ _____ and the _____ _____.
2. Great Britain took the territory of Florida from _____.
3. The name "Louisiana" was now used only for the territory, west of the _____ River, that _____ gave to _____.

67

Why Did the Spirit of Independence Grow After 1763?

A. Enforcing the Trade Acts. In 1763 the people of the thirteen colonies thought of themselves as being loyal English subjects of King George III. They were grateful to the British government for defeating their enemies. Yet in 1776, only thirteen years later, they turned against the British and declared themselves independent. Why did so great a change occur in so short a time?

The direct cause of trouble was the new British policy resulting from the French and Indian War. The first feature of this policy was the British government's enforcing of the old Trade Acts. It sent a large fleet and hundreds of new officials to the colonies to hunt down smugglers. These officials could enter any place of business or home without a warrant to search for smuggled goods. Colonists arrested for smuggling were to be tried by special courts with a single judge and no jury. If they were found guilty, their ships and cargoes could be sold. One-third of the money from such a sale went to the officials who had made the arrests.

These British actions aroused anger in the colonies. Merchants complained that they could not do business under such conditions. Other colonists protested that the new regulations violated their rights as English people. To make matters worse, dishonest British officials sometimes arrested innocent merchants in order to profit from the sale of these merchants' ships and cargoes.

B. "Protecting" the Colonies. 1. CLOSING THE WESTERN LANDS. A second feature of the new British policy was the desire to avoid the expense of new wars. In 1763 Indian tribes west of the Appalachians started a war to keep settlers from their hunting grounds. To calm the Indians, George III closed the newly won lands to settlers, fur trappers, and traders from the thirteen colonies. A few years later, he turned over the northern part of the region to the governor of Quebec in Canada.

To the colonists, these actions were clearly violations of their rights. Hadn't the royal charters promised them "all the land from sea to sea"? Hadn't they fought the French in order to open the region west of the Appalachians to settlement? But now the king himself had shut them out. He seemed to be siding with Indians and French fur trappers against his own people!

2. BRITISH TROOPS IN THE COLONIES. The British government also decided to keep 10,000 redcoats in the colonies as a defense against future attacks. It required the colonies to pay one-third of the cost of keeping these troops. Colonial leaders objected. They declared that the colonies did not need British protection now that their most powerful enemies had been defeated. They were also afraid that the redcoats would be used against them if they dared to oppose the new British policy.

C. New Taxes. 1. THE STAMP TAX. The strongest objections of all were raised against the third feature of the new British policy—

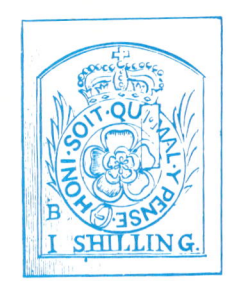

British tax stamps. American businessmen were supposed to buy these stamps and put them on the articles that were taxed.

more and higher taxes. In 1765 Parliament put into effect in the colonies a type of tax long used in Great Britain. This was the Stamp Tax. Colonial business people were required to buy special stamps from British officials. They had to put them on dozens of different articles such as newspapers, pamphlets, legal documents, and playing cards. The articles cost more as a result.

The colonists considered the Stamp Tax still another violation of their rights. They insisted that Parliament did not represent them and that only their own colonial assemblies could pass new taxes. "No taxation without representation!" became their battle cry.

The colonists supported their views with action. Nine colonies sent delegates (special representatives) to a meeting in New York. The Stamp Act Congress, as this meeting was called, sent a strong protest to the British government. New groups calling themselves the Sons of Liberty and the Daughters of Liberty were formed. Their members pledged themselves to protect colonial rights. Angry mobs led by the Sons of Liberty attacked stamp sellers and burned bundles of tax stamps. Most effective of all, colonial merchants boycotted (refused to buy) British goods. Faced with heavy losses, British merchants persuaded Parliament to repeal (end) the Stamp Tax.

2. NEW CUSTOMS DUTIES. The British government then tried to raise income from the colonies in other ways. Parliament voted several new customs duties (taxes on goods coming into the colonies). Income from these duties was to help pay for the many customs officials in the colonies. One item on which a duty now had to be paid was tea—a very popular drink at the time.

Once again the colonists protested. Once again they organized a boycott of British goods. The New York, Massachusetts, and Virginia assemblies declared that the new taxes violated their citizens' rights. The British governors of all three colonies replied by dismissing the assemblies. Britain sent additional troops. In Boston, a crowd attacked a small group of redcoats with sticks and stones. The soldiers fired into the crowd, killing five persons.

The Sons of Liberty called this incident the Boston Massacre (cruel, needless killing of a number of people). The story they spread about it through the colonies aroused hatred of the British everywhere. Again the British government gave in. It ended all customs duties except one, the tax on tea.

D. The Last Round. 1. THE BOSTON TEA PARTY. The next three years, 1770 to 1773, were prosperous and peaceful ones. Most of the British and colonists thought that the conflict between them had ended. But the Sons of Liberty still kept their boycott on British tea. They insisted that patriotic colonists should drink tea smuggled from the Dutch East Indies.

The American boycott hurt the British East India Company, which sold all the tea raised in the British Empire. To help the company, Parliament gave it permission to sell tea in the thirteen colonies at a very low price. Even with the duty, it would be cheaper than smuggled tea. The British expected that only a handful of colonists, mainly tea merchants, would protest.

The Sons of Liberty, however, again raised the cry of "No taxation without representation!" They refused to pay any tax that had not

SAMUEL ADAMS: "MR. REVOLUTION"

Did one man cause the American Revolution? Of course not. But many historians believe that the revolution might not have started if it had not been for Samuel Adams of Massachusetts. Sam Adams was, strangely enough, a member of the colonial upper class. The son of a wealthy merchant, he graduated from Harvard College as a lawyer. But he went into business instead and lost his entire fortune. His loss resulted, in large part, from an unfair law passed by the British Parliament. His bitterness over this loss may have made Adams a revolutionary. But it is more likely that his experience showed him, earlier than most Americans, that the British could not rule wisely over a large empire far from their shores.

Adams's work as a revolutionary increased in 1765, when Parliament passed the Stamp Act. If the Stamp Act was legal, he said, why could not the British tax the colonists' lands, "the produce of our lands, and everything we possess or make use of? If taxes are laid upon us in any shape without our having a legal representative where they are laid, are we not reduced from free subjects to the miserable state of slaves?"

Adams not only spoke and wrote against the Stamp Act; he also formed the Sons of Liberty, an organization that played an important part in getting the law repealed. After that, he led the protests against British customs duties, the stationing of British troops in Massachusetts, and the Boston Massacre. But it was during the quiet period from 1770 to 1773 that Adams did his most important work. He formed the Committees of Correspondence, groups of important men in every colony who wrote often to one another about what the British were doing. The Committees of Correspondence kept the colonists informed and ready for action. When the British sent tea ships to America, it was Sam Adams who organized the Boston Tea Party. And it was Adams the British troops were looking for when they clashed with the Minutemen at Lexington and Concord.

Adams did not play an important part in the Revolutionary War or in the events that followed. But he certainly deserves to be remembered as "Mr. Revolution." For Samuel Adams did more than any other American to bring on our nation's war for independence.

been voted by the colonial assemblies. Ships bringing in the tea were not permitted to unload. In Boston, a small band dressed up like Indians dumped two shiploads of tea into the ocean. The Boston Tea Party, as this incident was called, reopened the conflict between the colonists and the British government.

2. THE INTOLERABLE ACTS. King George III insisted that this time the colonists must be taught a lesson. They had to be shown that they could not disobey British laws. Parliament therefore closed the port of Boston until the dumped tea was paid for in full. Still more British troops were sent to Boston, and their commander was appointed governor of Massachusetts. To cut costs, he was allowed to keep his troops in private homes. The powers of the Massachusetts assembly were sharply reduced, and town meetings were forbidden. If a British official broke a law of the colony, he was to be tried in England. There he would stand a much better chance of being freed by a friendly judge and jury. These laws violated so many of the colonists' rights that they were called the Intolerable Acts—that is, laws impossible to bear.

E. Start of the War. Aroused by the threat to American liberties, the other colonies came to the aid of Massachusetts. They sent supplies to Boston to feed people thrown out of work by the closing of the port. In 1774 representatives from all the colonies except faraway Georgia met in Philadelphia. Their meeting was called the First Continental Congress—that is, the first meeting of delegates from different parts of the American continent. The Continental Congress sent a strong protest to the British government and ordered a new boycott of British goods. A citizens' army named the Minutemen was organized. As their name indicates, the Minutemen were ready to act at once in case of trouble.

The British government replied by sending more troops to Massachusetts. It also ordered

The Boston Massacre. Crispus Attucks, a former slave, was the first victim of British bullets. He has been called "the first casualty of the Revolution."

the commander there to crush all opposition. One night in April, 1775, a British force secretly left Boston. Its mission was to find hidden supplies of colonial arms and to arrest two colonial leaders, Samuel Adams and John Hancock. But the colonists had been warned by "the midnight ride of Paul Revere." When the British came to Lexington, they found the Minutemen waiting for them. Someone fired a shot, and a battle followed. The redcoats quickly scattered the small band of Minutemen, then advanced to Concord. There they were met by a much stronger force of Minutemen. They retreated to Boston, under heavy fire all the way. The Battle of Lexington and Concord opened the conflict known in history as the American Revolution or Revolutionary War.

F. Fundamental Causes of the War. We have examined the chain of events that led to

Patrick Henry addressing the House of Burgesses in 1775. In calling on the Virginia assembly to prepare for war, Henry said: "Is life so dear or peace so sweet as to be purchased at the price of chains and slavery? Forbid it, almighty God. I know not what course others may take, but as for me, give me liberty or give me death!"

the Revolutionary War. These events were a result of the new British policy toward the colonies after the French and Indian War. This policy was the *immediate,* or direct, cause of the Revolution. But what were the *fundamental* causes—that is, the conditions or attitudes which made each side act as it did? Historians give three fundamental causes for the conflict between the colonies and Great Britain.

1. THE INFLUENCE OF GEOGRAPHY. Three thousand miles of ocean separated the colonies from Great Britain. This was a very great distance in the age of slow sailing ships. Because the colonies were so far away, it was hard for the British government to understand their problems and to govern them wisely. For a long time Britain did not really try to do so. As a result, the colonists became used to running their own affairs themselves.

2. A BASIC DIFFERENCE IN VIEWPOINT. When the British government decided to tax the colonies and control their trade, the colonists resisted. They objected because the British regulations would hurt their business. They also protested that the British were taking away rights that they had enjoyed for more than 150 years. The British, on the other hand, believed they had the right to rule the colonies they had founded. They regarded the colonies as ungrateful children, unwilling to help their parent country in a time of need. Because of this difference in viewpoint, each side failed to understand the actions of the other. With each misunderstanding, bad feeling grew on both sides.

3. THE AMERICAN SPIRIT OF INDEPENDENCE. After governing themselves for 150 years, the colonists were ready for independence. Their spirit is clearly shown in this interview, held many years later, with an old veteran of the Battle of Concord.

"Did you take up arms against intolerable oppressions?" the old man was asked.

"Oppressions?" he replied. "I didn't feel them."

"What, were you not oppressed by the Stamp Act?"

"I never saw one of those stamps. I certainly never paid a penny for one of them."

"Well, what then about the tea tax?"

"I never drank a drop of the stuff; the boys threw it all overboard."

"Well, then, what was the matter? And what did you mean in going to the fight?"

"Young man, what we meant in going for those redcoats was this: We always had governed ourselves, and we always meant to. They didn't mean that we should."

REVIEWING THE SECTION

A. Knowing New Terms

PART 1. In your notebook write the *letter* of the word or phrase that best explains each italicized new term.

1. *Exports* are goods shipped: a. into a country   b. from one place to another within a country   c. out of a country.
2. *Imports* are goods shipped: a. into a country   b. from one place to another within a country   c. out of a country.
3. *Customs duties* are taxes on: a. lands   b. imports   c. sales
4. A *boycott* is a refusal to: a. make certain goods   b. buy from certain people   c. sell to certain people.
5. *Intolerable* means: a. unbearable   b. unfair   c. unwise.
6. A *congress* is: a. a court for special cases   b. a group of lawyers   c. a meeting of delegates.
7. The *fundamental causes* of a war are: a. the opening battles of the war   b. the events that led to the fighting   c. the conditions that caused the events to happen.

PART 2. For each new term in the first column, write the *letter* of the best description in the second column.

Terms	*Descriptions*
1. Battle of Lexington and Concord	a. Attempt by Parliament to tax business within the colonies
2. Boston Massacre	b. British laws controlling the colonies' imports and exports
3. Boston Tea Party	c. Army of colonists formed to fight the British on short notice
4. Continental Congress	d. Destruction of British property by the colonists
5. Intolerable Acts	e. First fighting of the Revolutionary War
6. Minutemen	f. Measures to punish the people of Massachusetts Colony
7. Sons of Liberty	g. Meeting of delegates from the various colonies to protest British policy
8. Stamp Tax	h. Organization formed by colonists to protect their rights without fighting
	i. Shooting of several colonists by British soldiers

B. Knowing Important Facts

Turn to the list of English rights on page 48. Write in your notebook the right violated by each of the following British policies:

1. British customs officials could search for smuggled goods wherever they wished.
2. Smugglers were to be tried by a judge only.
3. Parliament put into effect in the colonies the Stamp Tax and customs duties.
4. Troops in Boston were stationed in the people's homes.
5. Boston harbor was closed to trade.

C. Finding the Reasons

In this exercise, one, two, or even all three answers to each question may be correct. Write the letters of *all* the correct answers in your notebook.

1. Why did the British government keep troops in the colonies after the end of the French and Indian War?
a. To force the colonists to pay taxes. b. To prevent future attacks by the Indians or other enemies. c. To reduce the number of unemployed in England.
2. Why did Parliament repeal the Stamp Tax?
a. It was surprised by the colonists' violent attacks on tax collectors. b. It thought there would be less opposition to customs duties. c. British trade was hurt by the colonial boycott.
3. Why did the Sons of Liberty dump British tea into the ocean?
a. It was less tasty and more expensive than Dutch tea. b. The use of British tea would seriously damage colonial trade. c. They did not want to pay a tax for which their representatives had not voted.
4. Why did the American Revolution occur?
a. The British government decided to teach the colonists to obey its laws. b. The colonists wanted to keep their rights as English people. c. The colonists made up their minds to win their independence.
5. Why do the British and Americans have different views of the American Revolution even today?
a. Both sides have good reasons to prove that they are right. b. Patriotic persons should see only their own country's side of the story. c. We Americans have been taught the truth in our history classes; the English have not.

IMPROVING YOUR SKILLS

Finding Word Meanings

Write in your notebook the *clues* given in the text to help you find the meaning of these new terms.

> EXAMPLE: (In **C**1) Stamp Tax—"This was" and the following sentences

(In **C**1) delegates
Stamp Act Congress
Daughters of Liberty
boycott
repeal
(In **C**2) customs duties
Boston Massacre

(In **D**1) Boston Tea Party
(In **D**2) Intolerable Acts
(In **E**) First Continental Congress
Minutemen
(In **F**) fundamental causes

MAKING HISTORY LIVE

1. Bring in the tax stamps for cigarettes, playing cards, liquor, and other such articles we use today. Explain why Americans do not object to paying these stamp taxes now.
2. Read the biography of a colonial leader like Samuel Adams, John Hancock, or Patrick Henry. Tell the class about the part he played in causing the Revolution.
3. Write views supporting each side in a debate on one of these:
   a. Were the British customs duties on colonial imports really a case of "taxation without representation"?
   b. Were the British or the colonists more to blame for the Revolution?
   c. Could the Revolution have been prevented?
4. Draw a cartoon to show one of the following:
   a. The steps by which the British government and the thirteen colonies fell from friendship after the French and Indian War to fighting in the Revolution;
   b. The ties that bound the colonies to Great Britain and how they were broken;
   c. How the actions of each side looked to the other side.
5. Read and explain passages from "The Midnight Ride of Paul Revere," "The Concord Hymn," or other poems about the events leading to the Revolution.

Chapter 5

THE AMERICAN REVOLUTION AND ITS RESULTS

How did the colonies dare to revolt against Great Britain? Many Europeans were asking this question and wondering when the Revolution began. Great Britain was one of the strongest powers in the world. It had a large population, well-developed industries, a strong government, a well-trained army, and a powerful navy. The thirteen colonies, on the other hand, had only two million people, few industries, and no regular army. They were also weak, as we shall soon see, in several other ways. How then did Americans succeed in winning the war against Great Britain? What effects did their victory have on them, on the British, and on other countries? You will find the answers in this chapter.

How Did the Americans Win the Revolutionary War?

A. American Weaknesses. The thirteen colonies were strung out along a thousand miles of Atlantic coast. For this reason, they needed a strong government to keep them working together. They had all sent delegates to the Second Continental Congress, which met in Philadelphia just before the Battle of Lexington. The Continental Congress was only supposed to plan ways to change the British policy. But it soon found itself serving as the American government to carry on the war. Unfortunately, the Congress did not have all the powers a government needs. It could not, for example, tax the American people. As a result, it did not have enough money to conduct the war effectively.

The Congress decided to raise its own army, which it called the Continental Army. It chose George Washington as the commander and ordered him to enlist troops. But it was never able to supply his men with enough arms and ammunition, uniforms and blankets, or even food and shoes. Washington could also call on the militia of each colony for help. But men enlisted in the militia for only a few months. Many left ahead of time to take care of the planting and harvesting on their farms.

To make matters worse, the colonists were divided in their feeling about the Revolution. A great many, including most of the wealthy upper class, remained loyal to the king and the British government. These Americans were known as Loyalists or Tories (the name of the king's party in Great Britain). Supporters of the Revolution called themselves Patriots. The number of Patriots was small at the start of the war. Though it grew larger as the war continued, less than half the American people actively supported the war at any time.

B. Spread of the Fighting. Few Americans wanted independence when the fighting started. Most only wanted the king to recognize their rights as British subjects. The Continental Congress sent a petition (formal request) to George III. The petition asked him to repeal the Intolerable Acts as a step toward peace. A number of the British, including important members of Parliament, supported the American petition. But George III would not even read it. He insisted that the rebellion had to be crushed and that the rebels should be treated as traitors.

So the fighting continued. After the Battle of Lexington, American troops occupied the hills around Boston. The British decided to drive them from their position on top of one hill. A force of redcoats was ordered to charge straight up the hill. The redcoats were mowed down by heavy American fire and had to retreat. Again they were ordered to advance, and again they were forced to retreat. The third time the redcoats charged, the Americans ran out of ammunition. The British took the hill. But the Battle of Bunker Hill (#1 on the map on page 78) is usually considered an American victory. It proved that untrained American troops could fight the famous British redcoats and cause them heavy losses.

As the months passed, the fighting spread. The British fleet blockaded the American coast—that is, it kept ships from going into or out of the country. It also seized a number of American ships. A small American force marched into Canada but soon had to pull back. In Maine, a British commander ordered a town burned because its Minutemen had attacked his ship. In North Carolina, fighting broke out between Loyalists and Patriots.

THE REVOLUTIONARY WAR

- Main British Advances
- Main American Advances

BATTLES
1. Bunker Hill
2. Long Island
3. Trenton and Princeton
4. Battles for Philadelphia
5. Oriskany and Saratoga
6. Clark's conquest of the West
7. British offensives in the South
8. Yorktown

With each fight, bad feeling between Americans and British grew. It reached a high point when the British government, unable to get volunteers, hired 12,000 German soldiers. Many Americans could no longer feel loyal to a king who hired foreigners to shoot them down. A majority of the Continental Congress now decided that the quarrel with Great Britain could not be settled peacefully. The time had come for the thirteen colonies to declare their independence.

C. The Declaration of Independence. In July 1776, the Continental Congress issued the Declaration of Independence. This great document was prepared by Thomas Jefferson and four other delegates. It told the world that the thirteen colonies had become a new nation, the United States of America. It set forth in unforgettable words the democratic principles on which the new nation was founded. It also listed more than twenty-five ways in which the king of England had violated American rights. It ended with a bold promise: "And for the support of this Declaration, with a firm Reliance on the Protection of divine Providence, we mutually pledge to each other our Lives, our Fortunes, and our sacred Honor." (For the full text of the Declaration of Independence, see pages 706-707.)

At this time, the Declaration of Independence was mainly a war measure. It raised the morale (spirit) of the American people by giving them a better reason for fighting than the "rights of Englishmen." As an independent nation, moreover, the United States could ask foreign nations for money and supplies. It got help from the French government, which still wanted revenge for its defeat in the French and Indian War. France began to send the United States much-needed military equipment. A number of liberty-loving Europeans—like Lafayette from France, Pulaski from Poland, and von Steuben from Germany—crossed the Atlantic to help the American cause.

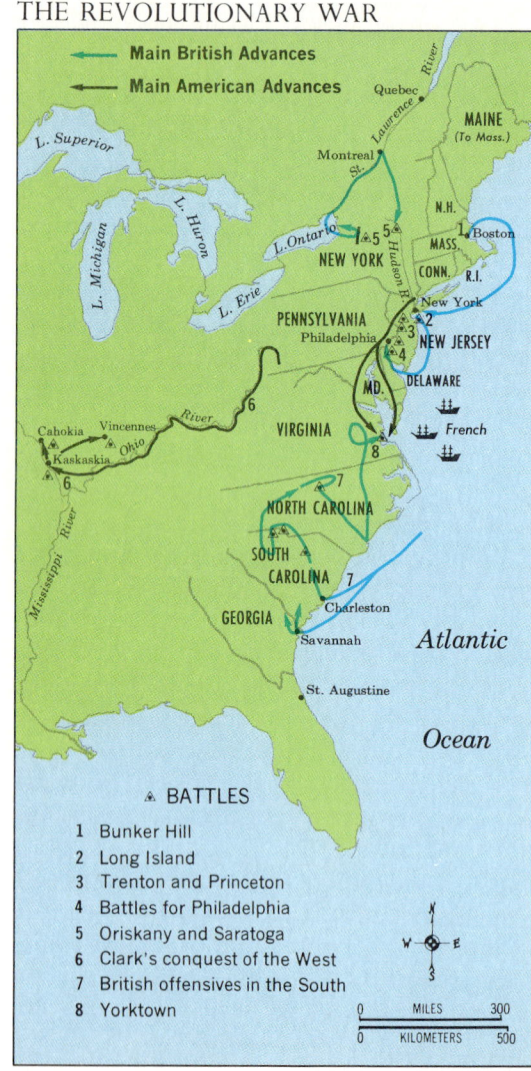

Mary Katherine Goddard, printer of the Declaration of Independence.

Marquis de Lafayette, French general who led American troops.

Baron von Steuben, German general who trained American troops.

D. Close to Defeat (1776). It proved much easier to declare independence than to win it. In the spring of 1776, General Washington succeeded in driving the British from Boston. But the British fleet carried the redcoats to New York. To keep them from taking that important city, Washington marched his army there. The two forces met in the Battle of Long Island (#2 on the map). This clash almost spelled the end of the war for the Americans. The British under General William Howe routed the Continental Army. They pursued it for months—first northward to White Plains, then southward to New Jersey. The Americans were saved only when cold weather began. Following the custom in those days, General Howe stopped fighting for the winter.

By this time, thousands of Americans had been killed or taken prisoner. Many more had deserted or were waiting for the day when their time of service would end. Late in December 1776, Washington wrote sadly to the Congress, "Ten more days will put an end to the existence of our army."

The American commander hoped that the Revolution might still be saved. On Christmas night, he led what was left of his small army across the icy Delaware River and marched toward Trenton, New Jersey. There he found the king's hired soldiers, the Hessians, sleeping soundly after their Christmas celebrations. Catching them by surprise, he took a thousand prisoners.

The British promptly sent a large force to destroy the Americans. But Washington again managed to take the enemy by surprise near Princeton, New Jersey. Here he won his second victory of the war. The Battles of Trenton and Princeton (#3 on the map) came just in time to save the United States. Morale rose, more men joined the army, and the war went on.

E. The Tide Turns (1777). When warm weather came, the British worked out a plan to split the United States in two by taking New York State. General Howe's army was to advance northward from New York City along the Hudson River. A second force was to move eastward from Canada by way of Lake Ontario and the Mohawk River Valley. A third was to march southward from Canada by way of Lake Champlain. The three British armies were to meet near Albany.

Luckily for the Americans, General Howe's orders were not clear. Instead of Albany, he moved on Philadelphia. He took that city after twice beating Washington's weak army (#4 on the map). Meanwhile the second British army was turned back by the brave attacks of small bands of American fighters. The third British army, led by General John Burgoyne, was heavily loaded with cannon and other equipment. It advanced very slowly southward through the forests and swamps of the Lake Champlain region. This gave thousands of patriotic farmers time to join the American forces. Outnumbered and surrounded, Burgoyne was forced to surrender near Saratoga (#5 on the map).

The Battle of Saratoga was the turning point of the Revolutionary War. The French government now saw that the Americans had a chance to win. It therefore joined in a military alliance with the United States—that is, an agreement to fight on the American side. As an ally, France declared war on Great Britain and greatly increased its aid to the United States. Spain and the Netherlands soon joined France in fighting against their old enemy, Great Britain.

The Americans won another important victory in the territory west of the Appalachians. George Rogers Clark led a small force of Virginia militia across the mountains into land that is now Indiana and Illinois. There he defeated the British and their Indian allies and took several important settlements (#6 on the map).

F. The Final Victory. After failing to take New York, the British decided on a new plan. They landed large forces in Georgia and South Carolina (#7 on the map). The plan was for the redcoats to march northward and conquer one southern state after another. Because the South was thinly settled, the British advanced easily. They also won a few battles. But after a while they were beaten back by a combination of regular army units and cunning backwoods fighters.

Next the British landed a force in Virginia. From here they could advance either north or south. These new troops were joined by most of the army that had been fighting in the South. The British commander, General Cornwallis, led these forces to Yorktown (#8 on the map). There he began to build a strong base for future operations.

Meanwhile General Washington had been struggling to keep his army together. Since Trenton and Princeton, he had not won a single complete victory. His troops had already gone through two bad winters, first at Valley Forge in Pennsylvania and then at Morristown in New Jersey. Now his men faced still another winter of suffering. Washington could neither pay them nor supply them with proper food and clothing.

Once again, the American commander worked out a plan that saved the American cause. When he learned that the British had withdrawn to Yorktown, he saw at once that they could be trapped there. He marched his forces swiftly southward to meet a French force led by General Lafayette. At the same time, he sent a call for help to a French fleet sailing off the American coast. The French ships arrived in time to drive off a British fleet bringing aid to Cornwallis. On land, the Americans and French surrounded the British and forced them to surrender.

The Battle of Yorktown was the last major battle of the Revolutionary War. The British people were tired of the long and unsuccessful war against their "American cousins." One group in Parliament had been trying for years to weaken King George's power. This group now made the king appoint a new government

The American navy, though small, fought well in the Revolutionary War. Captain John Paul Jones was especially famous. Though his ship, the *Bonhomme Richard*, was badly damaged, he refused to surrender. "I have not yet begun to fight," he told the British captain, and went on to win the battle.

Washington's army at Valley Forge, Pennsylvania, in the winter of 1777-1778. The soldiers suffered greatly because the Congress did not have money to feed and clothe them. Do you think that the British government provided better supplies for its troops? Why?

to open peace talks with the Americans. In 1783, the Treaty of Paris was signed and the war formally came to an end.

G. Reasons for the American Victory. At the start of the war, the Americans had seemed to be fighting against impossible odds. How were they able to win the war? Historians agree on four main reasons for the American victory.

1. GEOGRAPHY. The map was on the American side. The British found it difficult and costly to carry troops and supplies across three thousand miles of ocean. They found it even more difficult to take and hold thirteen large states that were mostly farmland and wilderness. Most of their victories were won along the seacoast and rivers. When they fought inland, they were usually defeated.

2. FIGHTING IN SELF-DEFENSE. The Americans, on the other hand, were fighting on their own soil. Even Americans who were not interested in politics often decided to fight when British and German troops overran their neighborhoods. They joined either the state militia or small bands using hit-and-run tactics. These bands made sudden raids on the British, much like Indians or modern guerrilla fighters. The British never learned how to deal with this kind of fighting.

3. GENERAL WASHINGTON. The Americans had a great commander in George Washington. His basic plan was sound. He could not hope to beat the British in a few big battles. So he wore them down in many small ones. He managed to win some surprising victories; but he also knew how and when to retreat after some serious defeats. Above all, Washington refused to give up. No matter how hopeless the situation seemed, he continued the war.

4. THE ALLIES. The United States was greatly helped by its ally, France. Spain and the Netherlands also joined in the war against Great Britain. Set upon by old enemies and worn out by years of fighting, Britain finally agreed to the independence of its colonies.

REVIEWING THE SECTION

A. Knowing New Terms

In your notebook write the new terms in this section that best complete these statements.

1. Americans who sided with the British were known as _____ or _____.

2. Americans who wanted independence called themselves _____.
3. The government that conducted the war for the thirteen colonies was called the _____ _____ _____. Its army was called the _____ Army.
4. The thirteen colonies became an independent country when they issued a famous document, the _____ _____ _____.
5. The new nation was named the _____ _____ _____ _____.

B. Knowing Important People

For each important person in the first column, write the *letter* of the best description in the second column.

Important People
1. Burgoyne
2. Clark
3. Cornwallis
4. Jefferson
5. Lafayette
6. Goddard

Descriptions
a. American who won victories in the West
b. Author of the Declaration of Independence
c. British commander in the South
d. British commander who defeated Washington
e. Commander of the British forces at Saratoga
f. Printer of the Declaration of Independence
g. Commander of the French forces

C. Knowing Important Facts

For each battle in the first column, write the *letter* of the best description in the second column.

Battles
1. Bunker Hill
2. Long Island
3. Saratoga
4. Trenton and Princeton
5. Yorktown

Descriptions
a. The Americans almost lost the war.
b. The British government decided to give up.
c. Victory brought France into an alliance with the United States.
d. Raw American troops showed that they could stand up against veteran redcoats.
e. This was the first battle of the Revolutionary War.
f. Washington's victory encouraged Americans to keep fighting.

D. Understanding the Facts

Write "True" in your notebook if the statement is correct. If the statement contains an error, rewrite it so that it is correct.

1. Members of the militia signed up for longer periods of time than soldiers in the Continental Army.
2. Few Americans remained loyal to the king of England after the Battle of Lexington and Concord.
3. George III's policies were an important reason for the Declaration of Independence.
4. The Battle of Bunker Hill was considered an American victory even though the British took the hill.
5. The French deserve much of the credit for the British defeat at Yorktown.
6. Unlike the Americans, the British people were united behind their government during the Revolutionary War.
7. The British found it easy to conquer and hold large areas of the South.
8. Geography was an important reason for the American victory in the Revolutionary War.
9. Small bands of Patriots played an important part in winning the Revolutionary War.
10. George Washington was a great general even though he lost more battles than he won.

E. Finding the Reasons

One, two, or even all three answers to each question may be correct. Write *all* the correct answers in your notebook.

1. Why did the British government expect to crush the American revolt quickly and easily?
a. Great Britain had a much larger population than the thirteen colonies. b. Britain was a great industrial power; the colonies had few industries. c. The British government was more democratic than the colonial assemblies.
2. Why was the Declaration of Independence important?
a. It explained why the thirteen colonies had revolted against their mother country. b. It encouraged Americans to fight harder. c. It enabled the United States to get more help from European countries.
3. Why did George Washington lose most of the battles he fought?
a. His army was small, poorly trained, and poorly equipped. b. He did not have the skill the British commanders had. c. His troops had low morale because they were not paid regularly.
4. Why did the Americans win the Battle of Saratoga?
a. They knew the country better than the British. b. Their army, in-

cluding volunteers, greatly outnumbered the British forces. c. The British army was poorly equipped.
5. Why did the Americans win the Revolutionary War?
a. They were fighting for their lands and freedom. b. The Continental Congress was a strong and effective government. c. Poor roads made it hard for the British to take and hold large areas.

IMPROVING YOUR SKILLS

A. Finding Word Meanings

PART 1. Write in your notebook the clue or clues the text gives to the meaning of these terms.

- (In **A**) Loyalists
  Tories
  Patriots
- (In **B**) blockaded
- (In **E**) military alliance

PART 2. Work out the meanings of these terms from their contexts. Write them *in your own words*.

- (In **A**) Second Continental Congress
  Continental Army

B. Mastering the Map

After studying the map on page 78, fill in the blanks in these statements.

1. The Revolutionary War began near the city of _____.
2. The next major battles were fought near the cities of _____ _____ and _____.
3. The first great British offensive of the war was intended to capture the state of _____ _____. It ended in British defeats at _____ and _____.
4. George Rogers Clark captured British forts near the _____ and _____ rivers.
5. To invade the South, the British landed troops in the ports of _____ and _____.
6. The final battle was fought at Yorktown, in the state of _____.

What Did the Revolution Mean in America and the World?

A. Boundaries of the New Nation. In the Treaty of Paris, Great Britain officially recognized the United States of America as an independent nation. The new nation stretched from Canada to Florida, and from the Atlantic Ocean to the Mississippi River (see map, page 86). The western boundary proved the most difficult to agree on. The British wanted the United States to end at the Appalachian Mountains. They wanted to keep control of the profitable fur trade with the Indians in the region between the Appalachians and the Mississippi. The Americans, on the other hand, insisted that the territory was theirs. It had been promised them in the royal charters and had been conquered by George Rogers Clark. The British finally gave in to the American demands.

This decision proved important to our country's future in several ways. 1. The United States gained a very valuable territory in the fertile Mississippi River Valley (see map, page 86). 2. The United States became a very large nation. With almost a million square miles of territory, it was much larger than any European country except Russia. 3. The way was opened for our country's westward expansion, which was to bring it to the Pacific Ocean seventy years later.

B. Progress in Democracy. 1. ADVANCES IN GOVERNMENT. The Revolutionary War, as its name shows, was both a war and a revolution (a sudden, great change). By winning the war, the American people gained their independence. Their new nation was a republic, a country without a king. It did not, however, have the strong national government that it has today. Instead, it was a loose union of thirteen self-governing states, each with its own government.

Each state wrote its own constitution—the set of rules by which it was to be governed. These constitutions were usually much more democratic than the old royal charters. The governors, formerly appointed by the monarch, were now chosen by the representative assemblies or elected directly by the voters. Property qualifications were reduced so that even small farmers and businessmen could vote. Every state added a bill of rights to its constitution. This generally listed the old "rights of Englishmen," such as the right to trial by jury and the right to resist search with-

The British surrender to Clark. George Rogers Clark led his little force hundreds of miles through the wilderness in bad weather to catch the British by surprise. Why were his victories important?

UNITED STATES IN 1783

During the war, thousands of blacks had managed to join the American armed forces. As a reward, several states, including Virginia, granted these black soldiers freedom. In 1781 Massachusetts became the first state to abolish (do away with) slavery. One by one, the other northern states followed its example. In the southern states, too, there was a strong feeling that slavery should be ended. Even wealthy planters condemned the system.

C. Ideals of the Declaration of Independence. The United States was the first nation to proclaim the democratic ideals of liberty and equality. These ideals were clearly expressed in the second paragraph of the Declaration of Independence. Its words should be read, studied, and memorized by every American.

We hold these truths to be self-evident, that all men are created equal, that they are endowed by their Creator with certain unalienable Rights, that among these are Life, Liberty and the pursuit of Happiness.—That to secure these rights, Governments are instituted among Men, deriving their just powers from the consent of the governed,—That whenever any Form of Government becomes destructive of these ends, it is the Right of the People to alter or to abolish it, and to institute new Government.

out a warrant. It also usually included the new freedoms of speech, press, and religion. Only a few states still had an established church, but even in these states its power was limited.

2. SOCIAL AND ECONOMIC PROGRESS. The war also brought about other advances in democracy. With the British gone, Americans did away with all titles of nobility. The wealthy upper class was weakened because many of its members had been Loyalists during the war. Thousands of Loyalists fled this country for Canada or England. Their estates were seized by the state governments, broken up, and sold. As a result, the number of small farms increased. In five of the thirteen states, small farmers gained control of the government.

This paragraph contains four main ideas: 1. "... all men are created equal." People should therefore be treated as equals by the law—that is, the laws should be the same for all Americans, rich or poor. This belief in equality helped, as we shall see later, to shake the power of the upper class and to weaken the system of slavery. In our own day it has inspired the struggles for women's rights and against poverty and racial discrimination.

2. "... among these [rights] are Life, Liberty and the pursuit of Happiness." Every individual has certain rights that the government may not take away. When we study the Constitution of the United States, we shall see how it protects

lives and liberties. The phrase "pursuit of Happiness" is more difficult to explain. It does *not* mean that the government has to make every American happy. That would be impossible. It does mean that it should allow Americans the opportunity to work for the things that will make them happy. For most people, this means the chance to earn a good living, to advance in life, and to provide for their children's future.

3. "... Governments are instituted among Men, deriving their just powers from the consent of the governed." This states a basic principle of democracy: that the government should be run by the people and should carry out their wishes.

4. "... whenever any Form of Government becomes destructive of these ends, it is the Right of the people to alter or to abolish it." In other words, people have the right to revolt against an unjust government, just as the thirteen colonies revolted against the British. The Declaration of Independence has been called, with good reason, "the most revolutionary document in history." In an age of absolute monarchies, it told the common people they had the right to overthrow their rulers and establish democratic governments.

D. Influence of the American Revolution. The influence of the American Revolution and American ideals has spread far beyond our borders during the past two centuries. In Great Britain, George III had tried to increase the power of the monarchy. His defeat in America ended the attempt. His opponents were able to reestablish Parliament's leadership of the British government. During the next century, the royal power was further reduced. Though Great Britain still had a monarch, it became a democracy.

Democratic ideas from the United States also spread to France. They stirred the French people to revolt against their absolute monarchy in 1789. French armies then spread revolutionary ideas throughout Western Europe. Though the monarchs managed to regain control for a time, France and most other countries of Western Europe eventually became democracies.

During the early nineteenth century, the peoples of Latin America followed the example of their neighbor to the north. They revolted against their mother countries, Spain and Portugal, and won their independence. Almost all of them became republics and modeled their governments after ours.

In recent years, many peoples in Asia and Africa have fought to gain their independence from European rule. Interestingly enough, their leaders often quote the words of the Declaration of Independence or of great Americans like Washington and Jefferson. Thus the United States has served as a pioneer in the development of modern democracy. Its democratic government and ideals have opened a path of progress for the rest of the world to follow.

Presenting the Declaration of Independence. John Hancock, president of the Continental Congress, is shown accepting the Declaration from the committee that wrote it. The tall man holding the document is Thomas Jefferson. Can you recognize other members of the committee? Why did they have to be brave to sign the document?

The Liberty Bell. This famous bell, once in the tower of Independence Hall (see page 171), rang out the news that the Declaration of Independence had been signed. It bears these words from the Bible: "Proclaim liberty throughout the land unto all the inhabitants thereof."

REVIEWING THE SECTION

A. Understanding the Facts

Write the *letter* of the correct choice in your notebook.

1. The official name of our nation is:
   a. America   b. the United States   c. the United States of America   d. the United States of North America.
2. The western boundary of the new nation, set by the Treaty of Paris, was the:
   a. Appalachian Mountains   b. Mississippi River   c. Rocky Mountains   d. Pacific Ocean.
3. The American claim to the lands between the Appalachians and the Mississippi was based mainly on:
   a. conquest   b. exploration   c. settlement   d. treaties with the Indians.
4. As a result of the Revolutionary War:
   a. the thirteen colonies became an independent republic, the United States   b. each colony became a self-governing state   c. the new state governments were more democratic than the old colonial governments   d. all these changes took place.
5. The new state constitution guaranteed (pledged) to American men and women some new rights that had been among the old "rights of Englishmen." These included the following:
   a. freedom of speech and press   b. no search without a warrant   c. trial by jury   d. all of them.
6. In the period after the Revolution, the practice of slavery was:
   a. ended in both the North and South   b. ended in the North and weakened in the South   c. ended in the North, but strengthened

in the South   d. hardly affected in either the North or South.
7. To the signers of the Declaration of Independence, equality meant that everyone had:
a. equal abilities   b. equal rights under the law   c. the right to the same income   d. the same standing in society.
8. The Declaration of Independence states that a government's powers come from:
a. its army and navy   b. its ruler and nobility   c. its middle class   d. the people it governs.
9. The Declaration of Independence said that the people had a right to revolt against a government that:
a. fights too many wars   b. takes away their rights   c. taxes them too heavily   d. is too far away to know their needs.
10. The ideals and example of the United States have been followed by people in:
a. Africa and Asia   b. Latin America   c. Western Europe   d. all these places.

B. Summing Up the Chapter

In your notebook, arrange the events in each group in the correct order.

EXAMPLE: a. Boston Massacre   b. enforcement of the Trade Acts   c. French and Indian War.

The correct order of these events is: c. French and Indian War   b. enforcement of the Trade Acts   a. Boston Massacre.

1. a. Battle of Lexington and Concord   b. Boston Tea Party   c. Intolerable Acts.
2. a. Battle of Bunker Hill   b. Battles of Trenton and Princeton   c. Declaration of Independence.
3. a. alliance with France   b. Battle of Saratoga   c. Battle of Yorktown.
4. a. Treaty of Paris   b. Clark's capture of the western settlements   c. American plans to settle west of the Appalachians.
5. a. revolutions in Latin America   b. the French Revolution   c. the American Revolution.

IMPROVING YOUR SKILLS

Mastering the Map

Study the map on page 86. Then write in your notebook the names on the map that best fill in the blank spaces.
1. By the Treaty of Paris, the United States was bordered on the north

by the Great Lakes, the _____ _____ River, and the British colony of _____.

2. The eastern boundary of the United States was formed by the _____ _____.

3. To the south of the United States was the territory of _____, which Great Britain had returned to the country of _____.

4. The western boundary was the _____ River. It separated the United States from the territory of _____, owned by _____.

5. Disputes arose because some parts of the western lands were claimed by two or more governments.
   a. The northwest was claimed by Virginia, but parts were also claimed by the states of _____ and _____.
   b. The western part of New York was also claimed by _____.
   c. In the southwest, one region was claimed by two states, _____ _____ and _____.
   d. Another region was claimed by both the state of _____ and a foreign country, _____.

MAKING HISTORY LIVE

1. Suppose you could hear three "Americans of 1776" discussing what policy to follow toward Great Britain. The first speaker is a Patriot, the second a Loyalist, and the third a neutral (someone who does not take sides). Write the position each of them might take. Be sure to include the reasons each might give to support his or her position.
2. Write a report on George Rogers Clark's conquest of the West, the southern hit-and-run fighters led by Francis Marion, the heroic deeds of Molly Pitcher, the sufferings of Washington's army at Valley Forge, or some other dramatic events in the Revolutionary War.
3. People from many different kinds of backgrounds helped to make the American Revolution successful. Read accounts of the part played by three of the following individuals in gaining American independence: Johann Kalb, Marquis de Lafayette, Casimir Pulaski, Deborah Sampson, and Haym Salomon. Write up your findings for the class.
4. Make drawings or models of a redcoat and a typical Continental Army soldier. Explain how their dress and equipment differed.
5. After reading actual accounts by soldiers in the Continental Army, imagine that you are one of them. Write an account in diary form of your good and bad experiences.
6. Study the Declaration of Independence at home and state at least ten of its complaints against the king of England.

SUMMING UP THE UNIT

How Did the United States Get Started?

A. European Conquest of America. Columbus discovered America at just the right time. Europe had recovered from centuries of barbarian invasions. Its people were eager to sail across the seas to unknown lands. They were ready to conquer other people for "God, gold, and glory." At first the Spaniards and Portuguese were the great conquerors. They seized most of the newly discovered lands in America and the Far East. In the seventeenth century, however, the French and English became the leaders in conquest. These two powers divided most of North America between them.

B. Settlement of the Thirteen Colonies. The thirteen colonies planted by the English along the Atlantic coast were especially successful. They were started by private individuals or trading companies, and their people enjoyed a great deal of freedom. As a result, the thirteen colonies attracted thousands of people from England, Scotland, Ireland, Germany, and other European countries. Most of the colonists were poor, but they were willing to work hard. They succeeded in starting plantations, farms, and industries. By 1750 the thirteen colonies had about 2,000,000 people and were very prosperous.

C. Development of Democracy. The people of the thirteen colonies also made progress in developing democratic government. They brought with them from England some knowledge of self-government and the "rights of Englishmen." In America, they carried these beginnings of democracy much further. Ordinary people rose rapidly to positions of wealth and power. As a result, social classes became less important in America than in Europe. The colonists practiced self-government through their representative assemblies and town meetings. They wrote their own constitutions. They developed freedom of speech, press, and religion.

D. The American Revolution. The colonists' spirit of independence led to a conflict with the mother country after the French and Indian War. The colonists refused to pay taxes voted by the British Parliament. They objected to violations of their rights by British officials. The British government gave in at first. When it decided to enforce its policies, the Revolutionary War resulted.

To the world's surprise, the colonists won the war. A new nation, the United States of America, was born. It was the first democratic republic in modern history. In its Declaration of Independence, it set forth democratic ideals that stirred the common people everywhere. Its success, together with the ideals it announced, made the United States an important nation from the start. For over two hundred years now, it has inspired oppressed peoples all over the world.

REVIEWING THE UNIT

A. Knowing Where Things Happened

To show our country in 1783, mark an outline map of the United States as follows:

1. Use a light blue crayon or a pencil to shade in these large bodies of water: the Atlantic Ocean, the Gulf of Mexico, and the Great Lakes. Label all three.
2. Find the following important rivers: the Mississippi, Ohio, St. Lawrence, and Hudson. Write the name of each river on the line that shows its course.
3. Draw a series of cones (AAA) to show the Appalachian Mountains. Label them.
4. Label Canada, Florida, and the West Indies.
5. Label the thirteen states, using the following abbreviations:

   Connecticut—Conn.   New York—N.Y.
   Delaware—Del.   North Carolina—N.C.
   Georgia—Ga.   Pennsylvania—Pa.
   Maryland—Md.   Rhode Island—R.I.
   Massachusetts—Mass.   South Carolina—S.C.
   New Hampshire—N.H.   Virginia—Va.
   New Jersey—N.J.

6. Use four different colors or markings to show (1) New England; (2) the middle states; (3) the South; and (4) the western lands acquired by the United States in 1783. Make a key to explain your colors or markings.

B. Knowing When Things Happened

In Chapter 1 of this unit (page 20), you learned that a time line is a kind of picture showing periods of time. It is marked with dates that indicate the passing of time. The following time line is a straight, horizontal line. Examine it carefully.

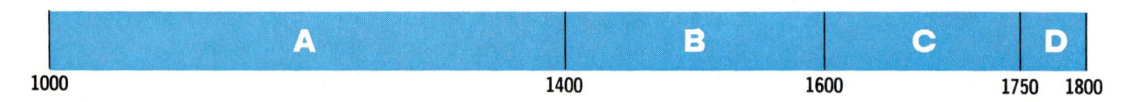

A	B	C	D
1000 1400	1600	1750	1800

PART 1. Fill in the blanks with the correct dates. Write in your notebook.

1. This time line covers the period from the year _____ to the year _____.
2. The time line is divided into four parts. A, the longest part, is the period from the year _____ to _____.
3. B is the period from _____ to _____.
4. C is the period from _____ to _____.
5. D, the shortest period, begins in _____ and ends in _____.

92

PART 2. Locate each of the following events in the correct period (A, B, C, or D).

1. Crusades
2. Founding of the French and English empires
3. Founding of the Spanish and Portuguese empires
4. French and Indian War
5. Revolutionary War
6. Voyages of discovery

Write the *numbers* of the six events above in the order they occurred.

PART 3. Here are three dates every American should know. Tell what important event happened on each date.

1. 1492 2. 1607 3. July 4, 1776

C. *Knowing Important People*

For each important person in the first column, write the *letter* of his or her description in your notebook.

Important People
1. John Cabot
2. John Smith
3. Anne Hutchinson
4. Lord Baltimore
5. William Penn
6. John Peter Zenger
7. Samuel Adams
8. George III
9. George Washington
10. Thomas Jefferson
11. Crispus Attucks

Descriptions
a. Able organizer who saved the Jamestown settlement
b. Author of the Declaration of Independence
c. Commander of the Continental Army
d. Sea captain who discovered North America for England
e. Scientist, author, and ambassador
f. Religious leader banished from Massachusetts
g. First casualty of the Revolution
h. Revolutionary who formed the Sons of Liberty
i. Printer who won the first case for freedom of the press
j. Proprietor of a colony established as a refuge for Catholics
k. Quaker proprietor of a large, prosperous, and tolerant colony
l. Ruler of Great Britain during the Revolution

D. Knowing Important Terms

PART 1. For each undemocratic feature of eighteenth-century Europe, write in your notebook the *letter* of the democratic advance made in the United States.

Eighteenth-Century Europe
1. Absolute monarchy
2. Established church
3. Illiteracy
4. Privileged classes
5. Royal charters

United States
a. Democratic republic
b. Equality
c. Strong central government
d. Religious toleration
e. Public education
f. State constitutions

PART 2. In your notebook write the new terms in this unit that best complete these statements.

1. In the sixteenth century, the Protestants broke away from the _____ _____ Church.
2. Two groups of Protestants who settled in the thirteen colonies were the _____ and the _____.
3. People forced to work without pay for a master for a certain number of years were called _____ _____.
4. Those who remained the property of a master for life, and whose children also remained as property, were known as _____.
5. The first written constitution in the thirteen colonies was the _____ _____ _____ _____.
6. Under English law, a home could not be searched without a _____.
7. English people could not be held in jail without a _____.
8. If they were brought to trial, their innocence or guilt was determined by a group of men called a _____.
9. Parliament's tax on newspapers, legal documents, and playing cards was the _____ Tax.
10. As punishment for the Boston Tea Party, Parliament passed the so-called _____ Acts.

RECOMMENDED READING

An important benefit of your study of history is your reading and enjoyment of historical books. These are of various types. Some are factual accounts by historians, news writers, or other experts. Others are accounts by ordinary people who happened to witness important events. Often a historian collects a number of such eyewitness stories in a single book. This is called a source book, because it serves as a source or supply of firsthand information for other historians and students. Biographies and autobiographies of important people are another type of historical book. So are historical novels by famous writers. These books often appear on best-seller lists. They are popular because most people like to read true stories about real people, or novels based on real events.

For you this outside reading will have an additional value. A textbook covers such a large amount of material that it can give you a little more than the dry bones of history. Your outside reading, however, provides the colorful, flesh-and-blood details that make history come alive.

In choosing a book for your outside reading, follow the recommendations in this textbook and also those of your teachers, librarians, and fellow students. But you must be the final judge of what you will read. You should select books that you will find interesting and enjoyable as well as informative.

Have you ever learned to *browse*? Look over the shelves where the various kinds of historical books are kept. When you find a book with a title or by an author that interests you, take it down. It isn't always true that you can't judge a book by its cover. The blurb (the short description on the book jacket) can give you an idea of what the book is about. So can the table of contents and preface. The final test is to dip into the book. Turn the pages; look at the headings and illustrations; stop occasionally to read a paragraph or two. This is browsing. When you have found a book that really awakens your interest, take it home and enjoy it. When you have finished, and while the book is still fresh in your memory, write a short report about it. This report should include the following information:

1. Author, title, pages read
2. Setting (time and place)
3. Main characters, with a brief description of each
4. Theme—that is, what the book is about
5. Your opinion of the book. Do you recommend it to other people? Why or why not?

You should follow the same steps even if you read only a few chapters of a book, or a short biography, or a short story. Save your reports. You will find them useful in reviewing for examinations. You can also keep them as historical material of your own, to remind you of your school days.

A. *Reference Books* (*useful throughout the year*)

   1. HISTORY BOOKS

      American Heritage. American Heritage Magazine. A series of illustrated books.

      BUTTERFIELD, R. P., ed. *The American Past.* 2d ed. New York: Simon & Schuster, 1966.

      CALKINS, C. C., ed. *The Story of America.* New York: Reader's Digest, 1975.

      DAVIDSON, M. B. *Life in America.* 2d ed. 2 vols. Boston: Houghton Mifflin, 1974.

2. GEOGRAPHY BOOKS
   ADAMS, J. T. *Atlas of American History*. rev. ed. Ed. K. T. Jackson. New York: Scribner, 1978.
   LORD, C. L., and LORD, E. H. *Historical Atlas of the United States*. New York: Holt, Rinehart & Winston, 1953.

3. BIOGRAPHIES
   BOLTON, S. K. *Lives of Poor Boys Who Became Famous*. rev. ed. Ed. M. Wilson. New York: Harper & Row, 1962.
   JAMES, E. T., and JAMES, J. W., eds. *Notable American Women 1607–1950: A Biographical Dictionary*. 3 vols. Cambridge, Mass.: Harvard Univ. Press, 1980.
   Webster's Biographical Dictionary. Springfield, Mass.: Merriam, 1980. Many short biographies.

4. MISCELLANEOUS BOOKS
   BONI, M. B., and LLOYD, N., eds. *Fireside Book of Folk Songs*. 2d ed. New York: Simon & Schuster, 1966. Includes chords for the guitar.
   HOLBROOK, S. *Story of American Railroads*. New York: Crown, 1981.
   JOHNSON, J. J. *A Pictorial History of the Black Soldier in the United States (1619–1969) in Peace & War*. Hampton, Va.: Carver, 1976.
   MAGINLEY, C. J. *Historic Models of America and How to Make Them*. New York: Harcourt Brace Jovanovich, 1947.
   TUNIS, E. *Oars, Sails & Steam: A Picture Book of Ships*. New York: Harper & Row, 1977.
   WHITNEY, A. *Sports and Games the Indians Gave Us*. New York: McKay, 1977.

B. Historical Books (*by historians, popular writers, and eyewitnesses*)

ASIMOV, I. *The Shaping of North America*. Boston: Houghton Mifflin, 1975.
BENNETT, L. *Before the Mayflower: A History of Black America*. Chicago: Johnson, 1982.
BLIVEN, B., JR. *The American Revolution*. New York: Random House, 1981.
BRANDON, W. *American Heritage Book of the Indians*. New York: Dell, 1964.
FARR, N., and DOSTERT, D. *The New World: 1500–1750*. West Haven, Conn.: Pendulum Press, 1976.
LANCASTER, B., and PLUMB, J. *American Heritage Book of the Revolution*. New York: Dell, 1965.
LANGDON, W. C. *Everyday Things in American Life*. Vol. 1, *How Americans Lived from 1607–1776*. New York: Scribner, 1937.
LECKIE, R. *The World Turned Upside Down*. New York: Putnam, 1973.
MARTIN, J. P. *Private Yankee Doodle*. Boston: Little, Brown, 1962.
MURRAY, H. *Adventures in the Wilderness*. Ed. William K. Verner. Syracuse, N.Y.: Syracuse Union Press, 1970.
PERL, L. *Slumps, Grunts & Snickerdoodles: What Colonial America Ate and Why*. Boston: Houghton Mifflin, 1975.
WRONG, G. M. *Washington and His Comrades in Arms*. Chronicles of America, vol. 12. New York: U. S. Pubs.

C. Biographies and Autobiographies (*the lives of famous people*)

BOWEN, C. D. *The Most Dangerous Man in America: Scenes from the Life of Benjamin Franklin*. Boston: Little, Brown, 1974.
BRODIE, F. M. *Thomas Jefferson: An Intimate History*. New York: Norton, 1974.
CAMPBELL, N. D. *Patrick Henry*. Old Greenwich, Conn.: Devin-Adair, 1969.
CRAWFORD, D. *Four Women in a Violent Time*. New York: Crown, 1970. Fighting against intolerance in the 1640s.

Davis, B. *Black Heroes of the American Revol*
vich, 1976.

DePauw, L. G. *Founding Mothers*. Boston:
Revolutionary Era.

Donovan, F. *The Many Worlds of Benjamin*
York: American Heritage, 1963.

Fritz, J. *Cast for a Revolution: Some Amer*
Boston: Houghton Mifflin, 1972.

———. *Traitor*. New York: Putnam, 1981.

Havighurst, W. *George Rogers Clark, Soldi*
1952.

Lloyd, A. *The King Who Lost America*. Gard
times of King George III.

Morris, R. B. *Seven Who Shaped Our Destin*
ies. New York: Harper & Row, 1976.

D. Historical Fiction (stories based on re

Boyce, B. *Morning of a Hero*. New York:
French and Indian War.

Bristow, G. *Celia Garth*. New York: Crowell
tion.

Clapp, P. *Constance: A Story of Early Plymo*
1968.

Cooper, J. F. *The Last of the Mohicans*. Vario
girl.

Fleming, T. J. *Beat the Last Drum*. New Yc
town.

Forbes, E. *Johnny Tremain*. Various eds./pu

Lancaster, B. *The Big Knives*. Boston: Little
ture of the West.

Peck, R. N. *Hang for Treason*. Garden City,
the war's tragedies.

Petry, A. *Tituba of Salem Village*. New York
ferings during the witch trials.

Richter, C. *Light in the Forest*. New York:

"The Spirit of '76"

apitol, and Supreme Court.

Unit Two

OUR FEDERAL GOVERNMENT

In 1783, when the Revolutionary War came to an end, it was hard to tell what lay ahead for the United States of America. On the one hand, there were good reasons to be hopeful about the new nation. It had large territories, rich natural resources, and a fast-growing population. On the other hand, its type of government—a democratic republic made up of thirteen separate states—had never been tried before. Many Europeans, especially among the upper class, were sure that such a government would fail. They believed that every nation needed a ruler to guide it. They thought that democracy, which they called "mob rule," could not possibly succeed. They were also sure that the thirteen states would not be able to work together peacefully.

For the first few years after the Revolution, it looked as though they might be right. The new nation had so many problems that it seemed to be falling apart. But then some leading Americans met to draw up plans for a new government. The Constitution they drafted still governs our nation today. Under its rules the United States has grown into the richest and most powerful country in the world.

In this unit you will learn the following:

1. *What was wrong with the government in the years after the Revolution*
2. *What kind of government the new Constitution created*
3. *How our government works*
4. *How our government has changed to keep up with the growth of the United States*

UNIT 2: 1775-1789

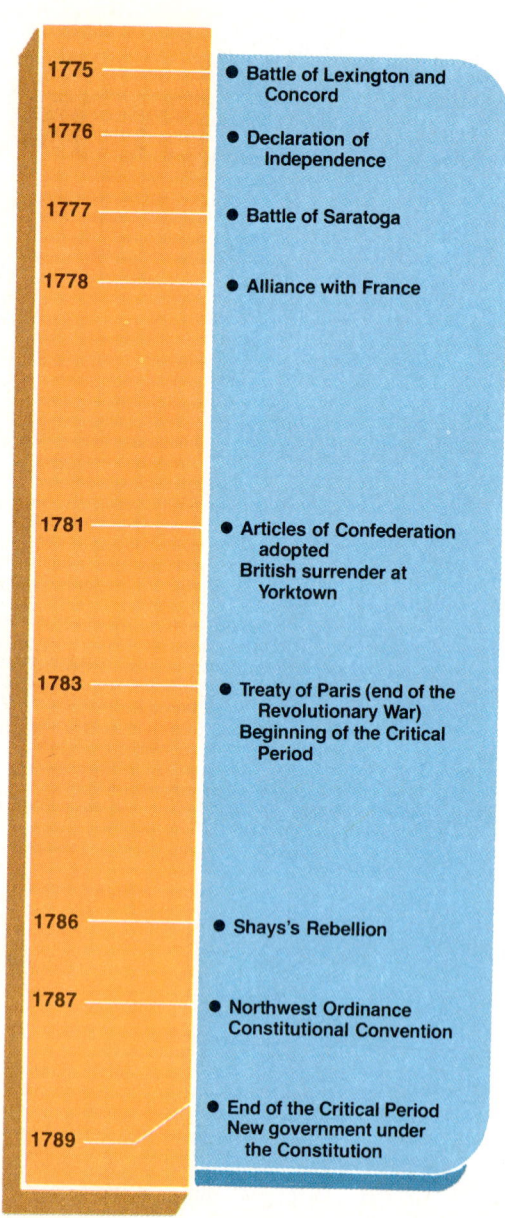

1775	Battle of Lexington and Concord
1776	Declaration of Independence
1777	Battle of Saratoga
1778	Alliance with France
1781	Articles of Confederation adopted / British surrender at Yorktown
1783	Treaty of Paris (end of the Revolutionary War) / Beginning of the Critical Period
1786	Shays's Rebellion
1787	Northwest Ordinance / Constitutional Convention
1789	End of the Critical Period / New government under the Constitution

Chapter 6

THE CRITICAL PERIOD

THE WORDS "crisis" and "critical" indicate great danger. When a hospital tells us, for example, that a person is "on the critical list," we know that he or she is very ill. If the doctor says, "The patient is passing through the crisis," then the next few hours will probably decide whether the patient will live or die. In the same way, historians speak of the years after the Revolutionary War, from 1783 to 1789, as the "Critical Period." The United States had so many troubles during these years that its existence was in danger.

In this chapter you will find answers to two important questions: What kind of government did the United States have after the Revolutionary War? Why did this government fail to solve the nation's problems?

How Was the United States Governed Under the Articles of Confederation?

A. Our First Government. Many Americans think that the United States has had the same central government (government for the entire nation) since it gained its independence from Great Britain. This is not true. Actually, our nation has had two different governments and two different constitutions. Our first government was the Continental Congress. As we have seen, the Congress met in 1775 to protest against British policies, but soon found itself conducting the Revolutionary War. To strengthen its position, it decided to draw up a constitution. This document, called the Articles of Confederation, was finished and ratified (approved) by all the states in 1781. It was the first constitution of the United States.

The Articles kept the Continental Congress with only a few changes. The Congress was given the powers it was already using—to raise an army and navy, carry on the war, and make treaties (formal agreements) with foreign nations. It was also given a few other powers. Most important were the powers to coin money, establish a system of post offices, and deal with the Indian tribes.

B. Weaknesses of the Confederation. A *confederation,* says the dictionary, is a "league or alliance of independent countries." Under the Articles of Confederation, each of the thirteen states was like an independent country. Each had its own constitution, its own armed force or militia, and its own money. It had complete control over affairs within its own borders. It could also make treaties with the Indian tribes, other states, and foreign nations. Many states, for example, signed agreements to return escaped criminals and runaway slaves to one another.

The Continental Congress was completely controlled by the states. Each state government chose its delegates to the Congress, paid their salaries, and could remove them at will. Voting in the Congress was by states. Each state, regardless of its size or population, had one vote. The votes of nine of the thirteen states—much harder to get than a simple majority—were needed to decide any important question. Amending (changing) the Articles required a unanimous vote—that is, the consent of every single state.

The Articles of Confederation failed to give the Congress certain powers that a government usually has. It could not tax the people. So it had to ask the states for money or borrow it. It also lacked the power to control the states' trade with one another or with foreign countries. What is more, it had no president or courts to carry out its decisions. It could only beg the states to do what it asked. These weaknesses led George Washington to call the Confederation a "rope of sand."

C. Reasons for a Weak Central Government. The men who drafted the Articles of Confederation were aware of these weaknesses. Why then did they fail to create a stronger central government? To answer this question, we need to know how Americans thought and felt about their country two hundred years ago. They had grown up in thirteen separate colonies, not in the United States. From the start, each colony had been like a separate country. Each had its own government and its own way of running its affairs. Most colonies were large by eighteenth-century standards. Roads were poor; travel was slow and dangerous. Most people never visited another colony during their entire lives. So the colonists naturally thought of themselves as Georgians or Virginians or New Yorkers rather than as Americans. Loyalty to the colony became loyalty to the state when our nation became independent. This feeling hindered the development of a strong central government.

A second obstacle to a strong central government was the colonists' unhappy experience with Great Britain. The British government had tried to make regulations for all the colonies. These had often proved harmful to the colonists' interests. British efforts to enforce these regulations had led to the Revolution. Many American leaders were afraid to set up a strong central government that might repeat the mistakes the British had made.

D. The Western Lands. Despite its weaknesses, the Congress scored a few successes under the Articles of Confederation. As we have seen, it made a favorable peace treaty with Great Britain. It also made wise rules for the new lands west of the Appalachian Mountains. The central government gained title to these lands because of a quarrel among the states. Seven states had claims to them under their old royal charters (see map, page 86). Other states also demanded a share. To settle the dispute, the states finally agreed that the entire territory should be given to the central government.

The Congress wished to encourage the settlement of the new western lands. In the Land Ordinance (law) of 1785, it ordered the new lands to be divided into sections, each a square mile (640 acres) in size. A section was to sell for $640, or only a dollar an acre. Since this was a large sum in those days, the sections were later divided and sold in smaller pieces. The Land Ordinance also provided that one section in every thirty-six should be used for education. The money raised by selling this section would be used to build and support schools.

E. The Northwest Ordinance. Two years later the Congress passed another important law, the Northwest Ordinance. The law set up a government for the Northwest Territory. This area consisted of the western lands north of the Ohio River (see map, page 105). Congress appointed a governor, a secretary, and three judges for the territory. As soon as the popula-

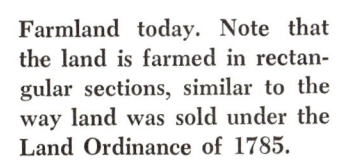

Farmland today. Note that the land is farmed in rectangular sections, similar to the way land was sold under the Land Ordinance of 1785.

DANIEL BOONE: PIONEER

Daniel Boone lived to the ripe old age of eighty-six. This fact becomes remarkable when you learn that he spent much of his life fighting Indians. For Boone was a pioneer, a man who explored Indian country and opened it to settlement by white farmers.

Boone was born in Pennsylvania in 1734. Since his father was well-to-do, he received a good education. But young Daniel was interested in hunting and the outdoor life. At the age of seventeen, he moved into the wilderness of North Carolina. There he heard of a region west of the Appalachian Mountains where large herds of game animals fed on rich blue grass. Boone explored the region (now a part of Kentucky) and decided to settle there. But his early attempts were failures. Three times he fought—and lost—battles with the Indians. Once they captured him; another time they killed one of his sons. Finally, in 1775, Boone was hired to develop a tract of land that a wealthy North Carolinian had bought from the Cherokee Indians. As part of this work, Boone laid out the Wilderness Trail, which thousands of Americans were to use in the next half-century. He also started the fort and settlement of Boonesborough.

Soon afterward the Revolutionary War began. The Shawnee Indians, who sided with the British, made many raids on the little settlement. Boone and his men beat them off each time. But in 1778 he was again captured by the Shawnees. According to his own account, he overheard them planning to attack Boonesborough again. To save his people, he escaped and ran 160 miles in four days, outpacing the swiftest Indians. Under his leadership, Boonesborough once again beat off its attackers.

Boone also fought against the British in the Revolutionary War and was made a major. But after the war, he lost his land because of a weakness in the title. He moved back to Virginia, only to lose his land a second time in another title dispute. Angry and bitter, the famous pioneer moved into the Louisiana Territory and became a subject of Spain. But the United States later took over Louisiana. And so Daniel Boone, who had done so much to speed American settlement of the West, died an American citizen.

tion of the territory reached 5,000 adult males, the territory could elect its own legislature. When any part of the territory had at least 60,000 people, that part of the territory could apply to Congress for permission to become a state. The law also declared that there were to be not less than three and not more than five states made out of the region.

The two laws passed by the Congress for the western lands marked a great advance in American democracy. 1. By putting aside money for education, the Land Ordinance set an example for the states. Many of our great state universities today are supported in part by money obtained from the sale of public lands. 2. The Northwest Ordinance guaranteed freedom of religion and other rights to the people of the Northwest. It also forbade slavery there. 3. Most important of all, the Northwest Ordinance provided that the Northwest Territory should eventually be made into states. These new states would be equal in every way to the thirteen original ones. This provision has been followed for almost all the other lands acquired by the United States. As a result, our country now consists of fifty equal states working together, instead of thirteen states ruling over an unfriendly empire.

EFFECTS OF THE NORTHWEST ORDINANCE

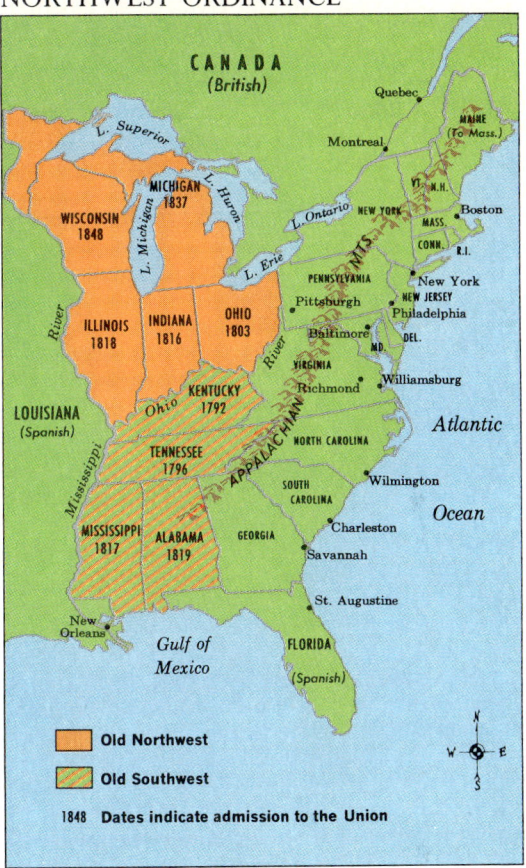

REVIEWING THE SECTION

A. Knowing New Terms

PART 1. In your notebook write the new terms in this section that best complete these statements.

1. A time of great danger is known as a _____.
2. In the period from 1783 to 1789, many people doubted that the United States could continue to exist. Those years have been called the _____ _____.
3. Our country's first constitution, in effect at that time, was called the _____ _____ _____.

105

4. The lands west of the Appalachian Mountains and north of the Ohio River were called the _____ Territory.
5. The law establishing governments for this territory was called the _____ _____.

PART 2. Copy each term and the meaning it has in the text. Underline the clues.

(In **A**) central government   (In **B**) confederation   (In **D**) ordinance
         treaties   amending
         ratified   unanimous vote

B. Knowing Important Facts

Here is a list of the powers of the central and state governments under the Articles of Confederation. In your notebook write "Central" if the power belonged to the central government. Write "States" if it belonged to the states. Write "Both" if it belonged to both the central government and the states.

1. To wage war
2. To maintain armed forces
3. To make treaties with foreign nations
4. To deal with Indian tribes
5. To admit territories as states
6. To establish a postal system for the United States
7. To sell the western lands
8. To return runaway slaves
9. To appoint and dismiss members of the Congress
10. To collect taxes
11. To control trade
12. To coin money
13. To enforce its laws
14. To govern the western lands
15. To return escaped criminals

Conclusion. Which was stronger under the Articles of Confederation, the central government or the states? Use the facts above to support your answer.

IMPROVING YOUR SKILLS

A. Reading the Time Line

Study the time line on page 100. Then answer the following questions:

1. Give the dates for the beginning and end of the Revolutionary War.
2. Give the dates of the Critical Period.
3. Which lasted longer, the Revolution or the Critical Period?
4. How old was the United States when the Articles of Confederation were adopted?

5. How long was the United States governed under the Articles?
6. How old was the United States when the present Constitution went into effect?
7. How long has the United States been governed under the Constitution?

B. Mastering the Map

Use the names and dates on the map on page 105 to complete these sentences.

1. When Americans referred to "the West" in 1787, they probably meant the part of the United States between the _____ Mountains and the _____ River.
2. This region was divided into two parts by the Ohio River. One part was the _____ Territory and the other was the _____ Territory.
3. The five states later admitted into the Union from the Northwest Territory were _____, _____, _____, _____, and _____.
4. The four states created from the Southwest Territory were _____, _____, _____, and _____.
5. Of the nine states, the first to be admitted to the Union was _____. It was admitted in the year _____.
6. The last of these states to be admitted was _____. It was admitted in the year _____.
7. The dates when the new states were admitted show that the _____ Territory was settled faster than the _____ Territory.
8. Because of poor roads, it was easier to ship goods by water than by land. From Pittsburgh, for example, farm products could be shipped down the _____ and _____ rivers.
9. The Mississippi and other rivers in the Southwest Territory passed through territory held by the country of _____.
10. Spain controlled a very important port near the mouth of the Mississippi River. This port was _____ _____.

C. Finding the Main Idea

A paragraph usually consists of a single idea, together with explanations and examples of that idea. Good readers learn to find the main idea and to keep their attention on it. Doing this helps them to remember what they have read. When they recall the main idea of a paragraph, the explanations and examples usually come to mind with it.

It is a rule of good writing to begin a paragraph with a sentence containing the main idea. You should therefore pay special attention to the first sentence in each paragraph.

It would, however, be difficult for the writer and dull for the reader if every paragraph began in this way. Most writers vary their approach. Sometimes the first sentence refers to the previous paragraph, and the main idea is contained in the second sentence. Sometimes the main idea is expressed in a later sentence —sometimes even in the last sentence, where it serves as a summary of the paragraph. And sometimes, as we shall see later, the main idea is not directly expressed at all.

In any case, there is a simple way to recognize the main idea of a paragraph. It is what all, or almost all, of the sentences in the paragraph are about. To see how this works out in practice, let us examine each paragraph in this section, beginning with the first paragraph in **A** on page 102.

The first paragraph in **A** tells us an important fact that many Americans do not know—that the United States has had two different governments and two different constitutions. This is the main idea, and it is found in the third sentence. The rest of the paragraph tells us that the Continental Congress was our first government, the Articles of Confederation our first constitution.

The second paragraph describes the government set up by the Articles of Confederation. The main idea is found in the first sentence, "The Articles kept the Continental Congress with only a few changes." The rest of the paragraph tells us the powers of the Continental Congress under the Articles of Confederation.

1. Go through the rest of the section. For each paragraph, write "Yes" in your notebook if the first sentence contains the main idea, "No" if it does not.
2. If you write "No," then identify the main-idea sentence.

What Were the Problems of the New Government?

A. The Basic Problem. How much power should the central government have, and how much power should be left to the states? This question has come up several times in our nation's history. Each time it has been difficult to find a good answer. We have already seen in the preceding section why a weak central government was set up under the Articles of Confederation. This government would not interfere with the states or threaten the people's liberties. But would it be strong enough to solve the problems of a new nation?

Some historians think that the Congress of the Confederation might have succeeded under normal conditions. But the Revolution, like most wars, was followed by a time of troubles. The Congress soon proved too weak to deal with these troubles.

B. Economic Troubles. 1. AN EMPTY TREASURY. The new government's biggest problem was that it was poor. During the Revolutionary War, the United States had borrowed large sums from France, Spain, and the Netherlands. These nations refused to make any more loans after the fighting ended. In 1782 the Congress asked the states for more than ten million dollars. They gave less than one and a half million. The government found itself without money to support the army and navy or to pay its workers. When the soldiers of the Continental Army were discharged from the service, they were paid in promissory notes—that is, in promises to pay sometime in the future!

2. ECONOMIC DEPRESSION. A second economic trouble was the depression, or period of hard times, that followed the war. During the Revolution, many Americans had found work making arms or other goods once imported from Great Britain. They were thrown out of work when the war ended.

To make matters worse, Americans lost their special rights under the British Trade Acts when they won their independence. Planters, farmers, and fur traders suffered because the British no longer bought all the goods they produced. Shipbuilders no longer received help from the British government. Shippers were allowed to carry to British ports only products of the state from which they had sailed. The rich American trade with the British West Indies was almost completely cut off.

If the central government had controlled foreign trade, it might have threatened to put high tariffs (customs duties) on British goods coming into the United States. This threat might have forced the British to change their policy. Under the Articles of Confederation, however, foreign trade was controlled by the states.

3. THE MONEY PROBLEM. Still another cause of depression was trouble with money. Gold and silver coins were very scarce in the early United States. Both the Congress and the state governments therefore printed their own currency (paper money). But people usually accept paper money at its full value only if it is backed by precious metals or by a government they have confidence in. The continental currency met neither of these conditions. It fell rapidly in value. Soon a hundred dollars in continental currency could not even buy a barrel of flour or a pair of shoes. Before the Revolution ended, the Congress stopped printing this currency because it cost more to print than the goods it could buy were worth. "Not worth a continental" became a popular saying for something of little value.

Most state currencies also fell in value. This confused situation was bad for business. Merchants found it hard to deal in thirteen different kinds of paper money, especially since the values of each kept changing.

Quarrels over the value of money arose between creditors (the wealthy people who lent money) and debtors (the poor people who borrowed it). In Rhode Island and North Carolina, the debtors gained control of the legislature. They passed laws forcing creditors to accept payment in currency. In these states, debtors chased their creditors in order to pay them with cheap paper! In other states, where the currency kept its value, debtors were often unable to pay back their creditors. They lost their farms or businesses, and many were thrown into jail (see page 31).

In Massachusetts this situation led to a small revolt known as Shays's Rebellion. Trouble started when former Revolutionary War soldiers began losing their farms because they could not pay their debts or taxes. The state legislature refused to help them. It did not even allow them to pay their taxes with the notes Congress had given them as payment for their war service. A band of veterans led by Captain Daniel Shays decided to take action. They drove out the judges who were ordering debtors to give their farms to creditors. They

Quarrel between a Massachusetts government supporter and one of Shays's followers. What was the basic reason for Shays's Rebellion?

also tried to seize a government building containing arms. Massachusetts asked the central government for help. But the Congress was, of course, unable to provide any troops. The state legislature then called up the militia. It quickly crushed the revolt.

C. Conflicts Among the States. Still other conflicts arose among the states. Most states tried to help their own farmers and business people by collecting tariffs on goods brought in from other states. (The tariffs raised the prices of these imported goods so that people would not buy them.) New York, for example, put tariffs on eggs from New Jersey and firewood from Connecticut. New Jersey and Connecticut struck back by putting tariffs on New York's goods. Such "tariff wars" cut trade between the states and stirred up much bad feeling.

Quarrels also broke out over state boundaries before the central government took over the western lands. New York, New Hampshire, and Massachusetts all claimed the territory that is now Vermont. The people in the disputed territory, however, wanted to form an independent state. A group of them actually asked Great Britain for help in case of war! Connecticut and Pennsylvania quarreled over a small piece of territory that both claimed (see map, page 86). When settlers from Connecticut entered the territory, Pennsylvania sent its militia to attack them. The troops burned down the settlers' homes and drove them into the wilderness. Europeans who read about these quarrels made fun of the "*Dis-United States of America.*"

D. Unfriendly Foreign Countries. Other countries took advantage of America's weakness. British policies, as we have seen, hurt American exports, shipping, and shipbuilding. Furthermore, the British government refused to sign a trade treaty with the United States. It would not even send a minister to represent Britain in this country. A high British official joked that his government did not know whether to send one minister to the Congress or thirteen to the states. Another compared the United States to a monster with thirteen fists and no head.

In the Treaty of Paris, the British had promised to give the United States all the land between the Appalachian Mountains and the Mississippi River. They refused, however, to give up their trading posts in the Northwest. British traders continued to carry on a million-dollar-a-year fur trade with the Indians. Since they usually paid the Indians with guns, the number of Indian raids on western settlements increased. The settlers appealed to Congress for help. But Congress could not, of course, afford to keep troops in the West.

An early stagecoach. Because of rough roads, a stagecoach traveled less than a hundred miles a day. How did the difficulty of traveling make it hard for the thirteen states to work together?

The United States hoped for better treatment from its former war partners, France, Spain, and the Netherlands. But Spain had dreams of taking America's Southwest Territory (see map, page 105). Spanish officials encouraged Indian raids on American settlements. They also stopped western farmers from exporting their goods by closing the port of New Orleans at the mouth of the Mississippi. They even bribed important Americans to set up a separate country in the Southwest under Spanish protection. Many western settlers were willing to accept Spanish help because the Congress could do so little for them.

France and the Netherlands refused the United States any special trading privileges. They also asked the Congress to pay back the money it had borrowed during the Revolutionary War. America's weakness became even plainer when North African pirates began seizing American ships at will. They held the passengers and crews for ransom or sold them into slavery. Without a navy, the Congress could not protect American shipping.

E. Calling of the Constitutional Convention. The weak government established by the Articles of Confederation might possibly have succeeded in time. It might have obtained money by selling the western lands. The states might have learned to work together, both with one another and with the central government. Certainly American shippers would have found new markets. They were already beginning to pick up furs on the Pacific coast to carry to distant China in exchange for tea and silks. In 1786 economic conditions even showed an improvement.

However, important Americans—chiefly merchants, creditors, and other business people—had already lost faith in the new government. They were upset by the nation's economic troubles, by the quarreling among the states, and by the unfriendliness of foreign nations. They were especially alarmed by Shays's Rebellion. Suppose other revolts broke out in states weaker than Massachusetts! The Congress, they knew, did not have the power either to improve conditions or to crush revolts.

A movement to strengthen the central government arose. One of its leaders was George Washington. At first this movement tried to amend the Articles of Confederation. Its attempts failed because amendments required a unanimous vote, and one state or another always vetoed them. Finally, in 1787, most of the states agreed to send delegates to a convention (meeting) to rewrite the Articles. The convention met in Philadelphia in the summer of 1787. Out of this historic meeting, called the Constitutional Convention, came our present Constitution.

REVIEWING THE SECTION

A. Knowing New Terms

In your notebook write the new terms in this section that best complete these statements.
1. A period of hard times, when business is bad and many people are out of work, is known as a _____.
2. Paper money is also known as _____.
3. People who lend money are called _____. People who borrow it are _____.
4. The attempt by debtors in Massachusetts to seize control of the courts is known as _____ _____.
5. Taxes on imports are known as _____.
6. The meeting of state delegates that drew up our present constitution was named the _____ _____.

B. Understanding the Facts

For each problem in the first column, write the *letter* of the weakness in the second column that made the problem difficult to solve. (The same letter may be used more than once.) Write the correct answers in your notebook.

Problems of the United States in the Critical Period	Weaknesses of the Central Government
1. Treasury of the central government empty, continental currency worthless	a. Could not collect taxes
2. Thirteen different state currencies with many different values	b. Could not support an army and navy
3. Shays's Rebellion	c. Could not regulate trade among the states
4. Tariff wars among the states	d. Could not control American trade with foreign lands
5. Quarrels among the states over territory	e. Could not regulate the value of money in the United States
6. Sharp drop in trade with Great Britain	f. Lacked courts to settle conflicts and a head of government to enforce their decisions
7. British refusal to send a minister to the United States or leave America's Northwest Territory	g. Failed to win the respect of foreign governments
8. Indian attacks in the West	
9. Port of New Orleans closed by Spain to American shipping	
10. Attacks on American ships by pirates	

IMPROVING YOUR SKILLS

Finding the Main Idea

Each group below consists of three statements taken from a single paragraph or group of paragraphs. Write in your notebook the *letter* of the statement in each group that contains the main idea. (You will probably have to go back to the text to find some of the answers. Note that the order the sentences have in the section has been changed for this exercise. Why do you think this was done?)

(In **A**)
1. a. "How much power should the central government have?" has proved a difficult question to answer. b. Under the Articles of Confederation, the central government was not strong enough to threaten the people's liberties. c. The Congress of the Confederation proved too weak to deal with the postwar problems of the United States.

(In **B**1)
2. a. Foreign nations were not willing to lend the United States any more money. b. The new government's biggest problem was an empty treasury. c. The states gave Congress only a small part of the money it asked for.

(In **B**2)
3. a. American trade with Great Britain dropped sharply. b. People who had made arms during the war lost their jobs. c. The Revolution was followed by an economic depression.

(In **B**3, pars. 1 and 2)
4. a. Each state printed its own currency. b. Trouble with currency values was another cause of the depression. c. The values of the different state currencies kept changing.

(In **B**3, par. 3)
5. a. Creditors and debtors quarreled over the value of money. b. In some states, debtors could pay off their creditors in worthless paper. c. In other states, where money kept its value, debtors could not pay back their creditors.

(In **C**)
6. a. Disputes between states were another problem. b. Several boundary disputes broke out among the states. c. Some states engaged in tariff wars with their neighbors.

(In **D**)
7. a. Great Britain refused to sign a trade treaty with the United States.

b. Foreign countries took advantage of America's weakness. c. Spain closed the port of New Orleans to American trade.

(In **E,** par. 1)
8. a. American shippers might have found new markets. b. Congress might have raised money by selling land in the West. c. The weak central government might have succeeded in time.

(In **E,** par. 2)
9. a. Many Americans had already lost faith in the Congress of the Confederation. b. Businessmen suffered because of the country's economic troubles. c. Creditors were frightened by Shays's Rebellion.

(In **E,** par. 3)
10. a. Attempts to amend the Articles of Confederation always failed. b. A convention was held in Philadelphia in 1787 to rewrite the Articles of Confederation. c. A movement to strengthen the central government arose.

MAKING HISTORY LIVE

1. Explain each of these statements.
   a. George Washington called the Confederation a "rope of sand." b. Europeans made fun of the *"Dis*-United States of America." c. One British official compared the United States to a "monster with thirteen fists and no head."
2. a. Pretend that you are a European in the 1780s. Join a group of other Europeans to discuss the question, "Will the United States succeed or fail?" b. Pretend that you are an American in 1787. Join a group of other Americans to discuss the question, "Should the Articles of Confederation be rewritten?" Write up your discussions.
3. Read a description of Shays's Rebellion in an encyclopedia or history book. Then tell the class whether you think the Rebellion was justified and why. Write it up.
4. Imagine you could go back in time and interview some typical Americans of the Critical Period, such as a small farmer, a large plantation owner, a wealthy banker, a settler on the western frontier, a small local merchant, or a shipowner or shipbuilder. Ask these citizens the question, "Should our central government be strengthened?"
5. Draw a cartoon showing:
   a. the steps by which a territory became a state under the Northwest Ordinance; b. the weaknesses of the central government under the Articles of Confederation; or c. the troubles of the United States in the Critical Period.

Chapter 7

MAKING THE CONSTITUTION

THE Constitution of the United States is now nearly two centuries old. A few state constitutions are older, but they have been changed a great deal over the years. The United States Constitution, on the other hand, has remained basically unchanged. So it may be considered the oldest written constitution in the world.

The Constitution established a strong central government for the United States. Under it our nation has prospered and grown great. Yet none of the people's liberties have been taken away. They have even actually increased. With good reason, one English leader called our Constitution "the most wonderful work ever struck off at a given time by the brain and purpose of man."

Who were the people who drew up this great document? How did they manage to do so well? What special features make our Constitution outstanding? In this chapter you will find answers to these three questions.

What Is the Federal System of Government?

A. The Constitutional Convention. In the summer of 1787, some fifty-five men met in Philadelphia. They were delegates from twelve of the thirteen states. They had been sent to Philadelphia to rewrite the Articles of Confederation. Only Rhode Island refused to send a delegation to the convention. That state was controlled by farmers, craft workers, and debtors. They were afraid that a strong central government run by the upper class would take away their power. Samuel Adams, Patrick Henry, and a few other leaders of the Revolution did not wish to serve as delegates because they, too, feared a strong central government.

The Founding Fathers (those who founded our present system of government) were a group of wealthy, educated men. Two-thirds were lawyers; the rest were mostly large landowners and merchants. Almost all had been active in the Revolution, in their state governments, and in Congress. Thus they brought the great advantage of practical experience to the writing of the Constitution. A number of them had also studied the English system of government and the form of democracy of the ancient Greeks.

George Washington, the most famous delegate, was quickly elected to the post of President of the Convention. Another leading delegate was Benjamin Franklin. At eighty-one, he was the oldest member of the Constitutional Convention. Still another very important delegate was James Madison, the new nation's outstanding expert on government. The convention was closed to the public in order to keep the delegates from being interrupted or influenced by outsiders. Madison, however, kept a careful record of the meetings that was later published. It is our main source of information about the Constitutional Convention.

B. The Federal System of Government. How to strengthen the central government was the most important question before the Constitutional Convention. Only a few delegates wanted the states to keep control of the central government. Some favored a strong central government that would control the states. The majority looked for a way to make the central government stronger without making the states weaker. This may seem impossible. Yet it was actually accomplished when the Founding Fathers invented the federal system of government.

Under this system, the central government came to be known as the federal government. It was given the powers it needed to deal with matters that concerned the people of *all* the states. The state governments were left the control of affairs within the states. Both governments could deal directly with the people. Every American thus became the citizen of *two* governments, the federal government and the government of his state.

1. THE DELEGATED POWERS. Article I, Section 8 of our Constitution (see page 712) lists some twenty powers of the federal government. These are known as the delegated powers because they were delegated (turned over) to the federal government by the states in the

The Constitutional Convention. Do you recognize any of the delegates?

Constitution. Most of these powers—such as the power to wage war, to raise an army and navy, and to coin money—had been granted earlier to Congress by the Articles of Confederation. But the Constitution also gave the new federal government additional powers. Two of these powers were especially important. Congress could now collect taxes directly from the people. So it no longer had to ask the states for money. It could also regulate interstate commerce—that is, trade among the states—and commerce with foreign nations. The power of regulating commerce with foreign nations meant that the federal government could place tariffs on goods imported from foreign countries. But neither the federal government nor the states were allowed to collect duties on goods going from one state to another. The Constitution further strengthened the new federal government by creating the office of President to enforce acts of Congress and a system of federal courts to try violations of federal law.

2. THE RESERVED POWERS. Article X of the Constitution states: "The powers not delegated to the United States [the federal government] by the Constitution, nor prohibited by it to the States, are reserved to the States respectively, or to the people. In other words, the states were left all the

DIVISION OF POWERS

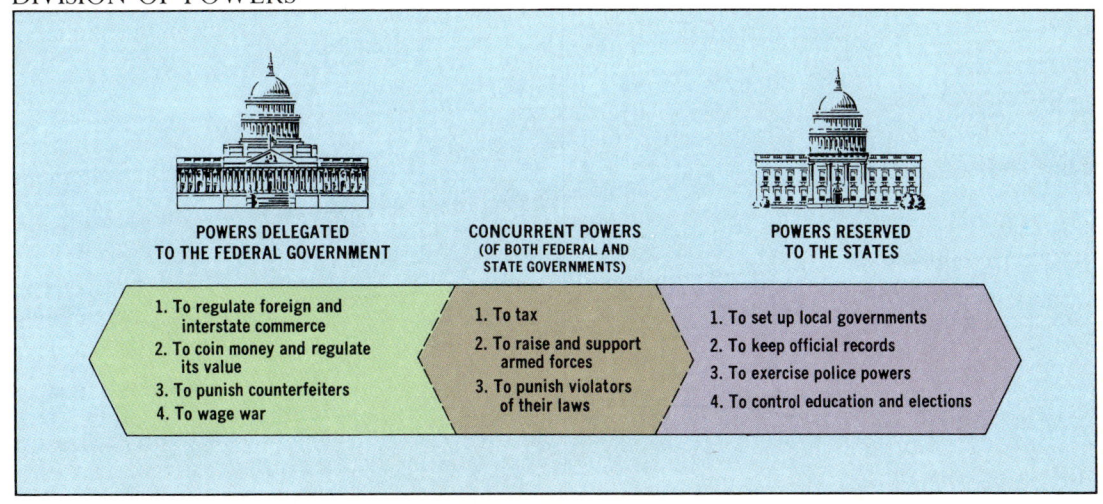

POWERS DELEGATED TO THE FEDERAL GOVERNMENT
1. To regulate foreign and interstate commerce
2. To coin money and regulate its value
3. To punish counterfeiters
4. To wage war

CONCURRENT POWERS (OF BOTH FEDERAL AND STATE GOVERNMENTS)
1. To tax
2. To raise and support armed forces
3. To punish violators of their laws

POWERS RESERVED TO THE STATES
1. To set up local governments
2. To keep official records
3. To exercise police powers
4. To control education and elections

GEORGE WASHINGTON: THE FATHER OF HIS COUNTRY

Most Americans know what George Washington looked like. His portraits and statues show that he was tall and strong, serious and dignified. But of course he was not so serious all the time. In his private life, Washington was relaxed and friendly, a good companion. He liked to entertain, and usually had a dozen or more guests staying at his home. He also liked dancing, riding, and fox hunting. Jefferson said that Washington was the "finest horseman" and "most graceful dancer" he knew. Above all, he liked to be with his family and to manage his large plantation. He watched over his land very carefully and tried new crops and methods. As a result, Mount Vernon was one of the most successful plantations in the country.

Washington had a strong sense of duty. He did what he thought right, regardless of the cost. His strong character helped the United States win its freedom from British rule. It also helped our nation again and again after the Revolution. Once, early in the Critical Period, some officers asked Washington to save the United States by becoming its king. He not only refused, but also spoke so strongly against the idea that it was never brought up again. Nevertheless, he was deeply dissatisfied with the weak Articles of Confederation. When Virginia and Maryland quarreled over use of the Potomac River, he asked officials of both states to meet in his home. This meeting led to the calling of the Constitutional Convention.

Washington did not want to serve in the Convention, and he certainly did not want to be its president. Because he had left school at an early age, he did not feel qualified to work with better educated men in political affairs. Yet he agreed to serve. This decision was very important. The American people had great confidence in Washington. His refusal would probably have ruined the Convention; his acceptance almost guaranteed that it would succeed. But his work did not end there. When the Constitution was finished, Washington's strong support made it possible to win the approval of the states. This done, he put off retiring to Mount Vernon until he had served two terms as the first President of the United States under the Constitution. We shall see later that he was as good a President as he was a farmer and general.

All in all, Washington played three important roles in establishing our nation. As general, he helped it to win its independence. As president of the Constitutional Convention, he helped to create a strong new government. As President of the United States, he got that government off to a good start. He certainly earned the title his fellow Americans gave him. He was truly the "Father of His Country."

powers they had before, *except* those the Constitution gave to the central government. These are known as the reserved powers because they were reserved (kept) by the states.

So many powers were kept by the states that only the most important ones will be mentioned. Each state has the power to set up local governments for its counties, cities, towns, and villages. Through these local governments, the state and its officials deal with citizens of the state for the whole of their lives. The state keeps records of birth, marriage, divorce, and death, and takes care of all legal matters regarding them. The state also holds the "police power." Under this power it protects the "health, safety, and welfare" of its citizens. The police and fire, health, sanitation and sewage, water supply and welfare departments of each state have all been created from this "police power." Control of education and elections are two other important powers reserved to the states.

3. THE CONCURRENT POWERS. A few powers are known as the concurrent powers because they are exercised by *both* the federal and state governments. Both have the power to tax. The federal government raises and maintains armed forces, but each state also has its own militia. (These state militias are known as the National Guard because they can be used by the President to keep order anywhere in the nation.) Both state and federal governments have their own separate systems of courts and prisons. Federal courts, however, try only people who break federal laws—draft laws, for example, or federal income tax laws. Most criminals and other lawbreakers are still tried under state laws by state courts.

C. Federal Supremacy. The Founding Fathers knew that there would be conflicts between the states and the federal government. To reduce the chances for disputes, they added two other important provisions to the Constitution. First, they denied to the states certain powers that they had given to the federal government. Article I, Section 10 (see page 714) forbids states to enter into treaties or coin money. It also forbids them to tax imports or exports, or to keep troops or warships in times of peace, without the consent of Congress. The states had held these powers under the Articles of Confederation. The resulting quarrels had weakened the United States during the Critical Period.

Secondly, the Founding Fathers added the so-called supremacy clause to the Constitution. "This Constitution, and the laws of the United States which shall be made in pursuance thereof, shall be the supreme law of the land." This clause has helped the federal government to win in disputes with the states.

D. The Federal System in Practice. The question of federal supremacy is still a live one. Over the years, the states have often charged the federal government with increasing its powers at their expense. They have accused it of violating "states' rights"—that is, of taking over powers reserved to the states. In 1965, for example, Congress passed a law to protect the right of blacks to vote. Several southern states insisted that this law violated states' rights. Only the states, they said, had the power to control elections.

Despite such conflicts, the federal system of government has been very successful. All the states work together through the federal government on matters that concern the whole nation, such as defense and foreign relations. At the same time, each state has its own government to deal with the special, local problems of its people. The states are also free to try out new ideas in government. New Jersey, for example, first allowed women to vote in 1790! If a reform proves worthwhile, it is usually adopted (taken over) by other states and the federal government. The federal system in the United States has been so successful that many other large countries, such as Canada, Brazil, and the Soviet Union, have adopted it.

REVIEWING THE SECTION

A. Knowing New Terms

In your notebook write the new terms in this section that best complete these statements.

1. The men who drew up our Constitution and set up our present system of government are often called the _____ _____.
2. Our type of government, in which power is divided between the central government and the states, is known as the _____ system.
3. The powers given to the federal government by the Constitution are known as the _____ powers.
4. The federal government was given the power to control trade among the states. This trade is called _____ _____.
5. The powers left to the states are called the _____ powers.
6. The powers held by both the federal government and the states are called the _____ powers.
7. The power of the states to protect the "health, safety, and welfare" of their people is known as the _____ power.
8. Because the state militia can be called up by the President to meet emergencies anywhere in the nation, it is known as the _____ _____.
9. In a dispute between the federal government and a state, the federal government usually wins because of the _____ clause.
10. Those who think the federal government is taking too much power usually complain that it is violating _____ _____.

B. Knowing Important People

For each important person in the first column, write the *letter* of the best description in the second column.

Important People
1. Samuel Adams
2. Benjamin Franklin
3. Patrick Henry
4. James Madison
5. George Washington

Descriptions
a. Expert on government who kept a record of the Constitutional Convention
b. Famous orator who made the opening speech at the Convention
c. Oldest member of the Convention
d. President of the Convention
e. New England revolutionary leader who opposed the Convention
f. Virginian revolutionary who refused to attend the Convention

C. Understanding the Facts

PART 1. Write "Federal" for each statement if it comes under a power delegated to the federal government by the Constitution. Write "States" if it comes under a power reserved to the states. Write "Both" if it is a concurrent power of both the federal government and the states. Write answers in your notebook.

1. Most Americans pay taxes on the income they earn each year.
2. Bonds are sold by the federal, state, and local governments.
3. The number of immigrants to the United States is limited by law.
4. It has been proposed that all high schools in the United States drop athletics to allow more time for study.
5. A general election for the office of mayor is held in September.
6. Large trucks and buses often have several license plates, including a small white one with the letters ICC (for Interstate Commerce Commission).
7. Modern pirates have sometimes seized control of an airplane while it was in flight.
8. A person may be arrested and imprisoned for counterfeiting money.
9. A resident of New York flew to Nevada for a quick divorce.
10. When a person returns from abroad, his baggage is searched by customs officials.

PART 2. For each problem in the first column write in your notebook the *letter* of the power in the second column that the new federal government could use to deal with the problem. (The same letter may be used more than once.)

Problems Under the Articles of Confederation

1. Empty treasury
2. Sharp decline in trade with Great Britain
3. Thirteen different currencies with many different values
4. Shays's Rebellion
5. Tariff wars among the states
6. British refusal to send a minister to the United States
7. British fur-trading posts in America's Northwest Territory
8. Indian attacks in the West
9. Port of New Orleans closed by Spain to American shipping
10. Attacks on American shipping by pirates

Powers of the New Federal Government

a. Control of foreign trade and power to make treaties with foreign nations
b. Control of interstate commerce
c. Power to coin money and regulate its value
d. Power to tax
e. Power to maintain an army and navy and to call up the National Guard

IMPROVING YOUR SKILLS

Finding the Main Idea

In your notebook write the *letter* of the sentence in each group that contains the main idea.

(In **A**)
1. a. All the states except Rhode Island sent delegates to the Constitutional Convention. b. The Constitutional Convention, composed of some fifty-five delegates, met in Philadelphia in 1787. c. Most delegates to the Constitutional Convention were wealthy and educated men.

(In **B**)
2. a. The Constitutional Convention found a way to make the central government stronger without making the states weaker. b. The state governments kept control of affairs within their borders. c. Under the federal system, the federal government could deal with matters that concerned the people of *all* the states.

(In **C**)
3. a. The Constitution makes federal laws supreme over state laws. b. The Constitution decreases the chances for disputes between the federal government and the states. c. The states have been denied important powers under the Constitution.

(In **D**)
4. a. The states often adopt new reforms before the federal government does. b. A number of foreign nations have adopted the federal system. c. The federal system of government has proved successful.

Why Is Our Constitution "a Bundle of Compromises"?

A. The Need for Compromise. Like any other group of people, the Founding Fathers had many different opinions. Almost all of them agreed that the central government should be strengthened. They also agreed that it would be easier to draw up a new constitution than to rewrite the old Articles of Confederation. But how much stronger should the new government be? How much power should be given to the common people? Should the large states—that is, those with a large population—have more power than the states with a small population? Would it be possible to please the different sections of the country even though they had different interests? The delegates had to settle these and other difficult questions in drawing up the Constitution.

When people have opposing views on an important matter, it rarely happens that one side gives in completely to the other. Usually each side gives in a little, and then, if necessary, a little more. The final result is a compromise. This is an agreement which combines some of the ideas of both sides, but which gives neither side all that it wanted.

So it was with the Constitutional Convention. It took the Founding Fathers four months to work out agreements on the questions facing them. The final result, our Constitution, has been called "a bundle of compromises." Like most compromises, it did not completely satisfy anyone. On the other hand, very few of the delegates were completely dissatisfied. Most of them felt that the Constitution they had written was the best possible under the circumstances. There were features in it to please almost every group of Americans. They hoped therefore that it would be adopted by the people when it was presented to them.

B. The Great Compromise. Under the Articles of Confederation, each state had one vote in Congress. How were the states to be represented in the new Congress? Was each state to have one vote? Or were those with the most people to have the most votes? Because control of the new government depended on the answer, the delegates from large and small states quarreled fiercely. The delegates from New Jersey, which had a small population, proposed that the system of equal representation under the Articles should be continued. Virginia, speaking for the large states, opposed the New Jersey Plan. It proposed instead that the number of representatives from each state should depend on its population. A New Jersey delegate angrily replied that the small states would be "swallowed up" if the Virginia Plan were adopted.

The dispute between the large and small states lasted for almost the entire four months of the Constitutional Convention. At times it threatened to break up the Convention. Finally Connecticut proposed a compromise that both sides were able to accept. The Great Compromise, as it is known, cleverly combined the main features of both the New Jersey and Virginia Plans. The new Congress would have two houses, the Senate and the House of Representatives. In the Senate, large and small states would be equal. Each would have two senators. In the House, on the other hand, representation would be based on population.

The Constitution also provided for a census (a count of the nation's population) every ten years. Representation in the House would be based on this census. The first House of Representatives in 1790 had sixty-five members, one for each 30,000 people. Since then the population of the United States has multiplied many times and is still growing. Congress has therefore fixed the total number of representatives at 435. Today, on the basis of the 1980 census, there is 1 representative for every 521,000 Americans. California—the state with the most people in 1983—has 45 representatives. Representation changes after each ten-year census. Representatives have always been elected by direct popular vote. (This is in contrast to senators. Senators, until 1913, were elected officially by state legislators.) No state may have fewer than 1 representative. Alaska, for example, has only about 402,000 people, but it is still entitled to one member in the House of Representatives.

C. Compromises Between the North and South. Another set of disputes proved almost as hard to solve as the question of representation. These arose between delegates from the northern and southern states. One dispute concerned slavery. The main question was, Should slaves be included in the census? By 1787 black slavery was disappearing in the North, but it was still increasing in the South. The southern states wanted their slaves counted in the census so that they would have more representatives. The northern states argued that slaves should not be counted because they were not citizens and had no political rights.

Another question in this dispute was, How long should slavery be allowed? Many northern delegates were opposed to slavery. They wanted to stop the cruel slave trade, which was still bringing thousands of unfortunate Africans to the southern states each year. Many southern delegates wanted the slave trade continued.

A third dispute between North and South arose over the control of foreign commerce. In the northern states, many people made a living through trade with foreign countries. They wanted the federal government to control this trade so that it could make favorable trade treaties. By threatening to place heavy tariffs on British goods, for example, Congress might force Great Britain to allow more American trade. The southern states, on the other hand, did not want the federal government to control foreign trade. Most of their income came from exports of tobacco, rice, and other raw materials. If Congress placed a tax on exports, these products would cost more in foreign countries and sales would fall. In return for their exports, southerners bought manufactured goods in Great Britain and other European countries. If Congress taxed imports, the European goods that Southerners bought would cost more.

METHODS OF ELECTION IN THE CONSTITUTION

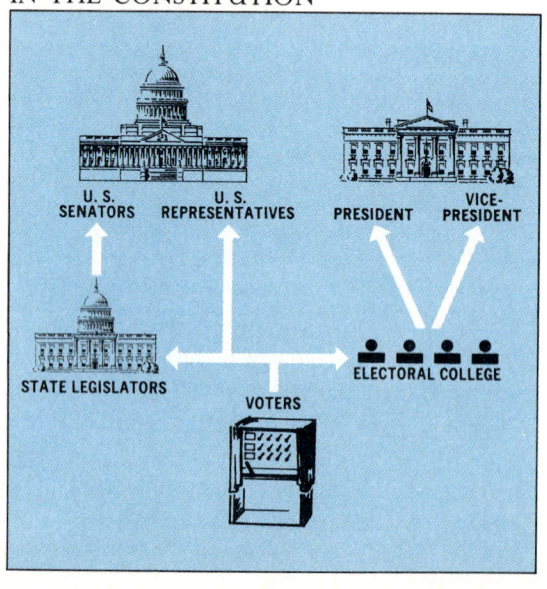

Ratification of the Constitution. How many states had already ratified when this cartoon was printed in a Boston newspaper? Why did the cartoonist expect Virginia and New York to ratify?

The Ninth PILLAR erected!
"The Ratification of the Conventions of nine States, shall be sufficient for the establishment of this Constitution, between the States so ratifying the same." *Art.* vii.
INCIPIENT MAGNI PROCEDERE MENSES.

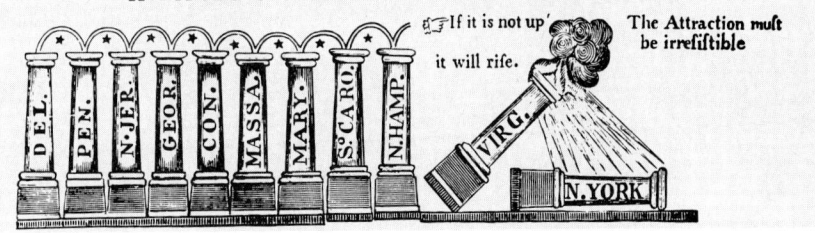

If it is not up it will rise. The Attraction must be irresistible

DEL. PEN. N.JER. GEOR. CON. MASSA. MARY. S.CARO. N.HAMP. VIRG. N.YORK

In the final compromise, the three differences were worked out together. 1. Three-fifths of the slaves in a state were to be counted for representation. This agreement is known as the "three-fifths compromise." 2. The slave trade was to be allowed, but only for twenty years—that is, only until 1808. 3. Congress would have the power to tax imports, but not exports.

D. Methods of Election. Still another question was, "How much power should the common people have?" Many wealthy, educated Americans were afraid that poor and illiterate people might take control of the new government. So they favored indirect elections and high qualifications for voting. In an indirect election, the voters would elect leading citizens, who would then elect the government officials. In this way, the common people would not be voting for the officials themselves.

Leaders of the common people, on the other hand, wanted direct elections in which *every* free man would have the right to vote and to run for office. They believed that a rich men's government would not care much about the people's needs or their liberties. Such a government might even establish a monarchy and a privileged class.

Once again the solution was a compromise. Each state was allowed, as before, to set the qualifications for voting. In addition, three different methods were adopted for electing federal officials. Representatives were to be elected directly by the voters. Senators were to be chosen by the state legislatures. The heads of the new government, the President and Vice-President, were to be chosen indirectly through an electoral college. This unusual method of election is described on pages 145-146.

E. Ratifying the Constitution. Before going home, the Founding Fathers made one other very important decision. They were afraid that some of the states would not ratify the Constitution. Their legislatures might well prefer the old Articles of Confederation under which they had more power. Therefore the Founding Fathers decided that the Constitution should be approved by the people instead of by the state legislatures. They arranged for the people to elect delegates to a special ratifying convention in each state. The Constitution was to go into effect as soon as it won a majority vote in nine of the thirteen conventions.

The American people quickly split into two opposing groups. Those who favored the Constitution and a strong federal government called themselves Federalists. They were led by wealthy landowners, bankers, merchants, and other business people. These people wanted a strong government to protect their property and trade. Against them were the Anti-Federalists, mainly small farmers, shopkeepers, and craft workers. To them, liberty was more important

A float in New York City's parade to celebrate the ratification of the Constitution. This float honored Alexander Hamilton, who led the fight for ratification in New York state. When did the Constitution go into effect?

than property. The Anti-Federalists also included many debtors, who wanted the states to keep printing cheap paper money (see page 109). The Anti-Federalists probably outnumbered the Federalists; but many of them were not able to vote because they owned little or no property.

In most states the elections were so hard fought that it looked as if the Constitution might not be ratified. Several small states led the way in voting for ratification. Being weak, they needed the help of a strong federal government. They were also satisfied because they were equal with the large states in the Senate under the Great Compromise. The Federalists also managed to win an easy victory in Pennsylvania. The outcome now depended on the vote in three large states—Virginia, Massachusetts, and New York. In all three states the vote was very close, but the Federalists won. The Constitution went into effect when the first elections for Congress and the President were held late in 1788. Rhode Island, which had not sent delegates to the Constitutional Convention, finally ratified the Constitution in May, 1790. By that time, the United States had already made a good start under its strong new federal government.

REVIEWING THE SECTION

A. Knowing New Terms

In your notebook write the new terms in this section that best complete these statements.
1. The agreement between the large states and the small states about representation in Congress is known as the _____ _____.
2. Congress consists of two houses, the _____ and the _____ _____.
3. The federal government counts our country's population every ten years. This count is called the _____.
4. The heads of the new federal government were called the _____ and the _____.
5. Those who favored the Constitution and a strong federal government called themselves the _____. Their opponents were the _____.

B. Understanding the Facts

Write the *letter* of the correct choice.
1. The Constitution was called "a bundle of compromises" because it: a. contained agreements between delegates with different ideas   b. had something to please almost every group of Americans.   c. did not completely please any of the delegates   d. was opposed by only a few of the delegates.
2. The total number of senators today is: a. 26   b. 50   c. 96   d. 100.
3. The total number of representatives today is: a. 65   b. 265   c. 435   d. 535.
4. The state with the largest number of representatives is: a. California   b. New Jersey   c. New York   d. Virginia
5. The smallest number of members of Congress (senators and representatives) that any state may have is a. 1   b. 2   c. 3   d. 5
6. The northern states objected to counting slaves for representation because they: a. had few slaves   b. disliked the cruel slave trade   c. wanted to abolish slavery   d. felt unfriendly toward the South.
7. The southern states were opposed to federal control of foreign trade because they: a. had little foreign trade   b. had large exports and imports   c. wanted high tariffs   d. felt unfriendly toward the North.
8. The Constitution originally stated that the United States senators from each state were to be chosen by: a. direct popular election by all adult white males   b. direct popular election by all property owners   c. vote of the state legislatures   d. vote by constitutional conventions.
9. Many wealthy Americans supported the Constitution because it: a. created a federal government strong enough to protect their interests   b. did not take any power away from the states   c. gave the wealthy more votes than the common people   d. made it easy to establish a monarchy and a privileged class.
10. Many of the common people opposed the Constitution because they: a. feared that a strong federal government might take away their rights   b. disliked anything the rich wanted   c. were not allowed to vote for federal officials   d. might be imprisoned by the federal government as debtors.

C. Summing Up the Chapter

To show the main compromises of the Constitution, complete the following sentences. Write the answers in your notebook.

1. *The Federal System of Government*
    Some delegates to the Constitutional Convention wanted a _____ central government with control over the states.
    Other delegates wanted a _____ central government and _____ state governments.

127

The final compromise gave the central government certain important powers. These are the _____ powers. The states were left with all other powers. These are known as the _____ powers.

2. *The Great Compromise*

The _____ states wanted equal representation in Congress.

The _____ states wanted representation based on population.

The Great Compromise provided that each state should have _____ members in the Senate; but the number of representatives it was to have would depend on its _____.

3. *The North-South Compromises*

The North wanted: a. to leave out _____ in determining a state's representation   b. to end the _____ _____   c. to have federal control of _____ commerce.

The South wanted: a. to _____ slaves for representation   b. to continue the _____ _____   c. to forbid federal taxes on both _____ and _____.

The compromises were: a. to include _____ of the slaves for representation   b. to end the slave trade after _____ years   c. to allow federal taxes on _____, but not on _____.

4. *Methods of Election*

Wealthy people wanted _____ qualifications for voting and _____ elections.

The common people wanted _____ elections in which every _____ could vote.

The Constitution allowed the qualifications for voting to be set by the _____. The methods of elections were to be: a. _____ election of representatives   b. selection of senators by the _____ _____   c. _____ election of the President and Vice-President.

IMPROVING YOUR SKILLS

A. Finding the Main Idea

The headings in this section are:

A. The Need for Compromise   **D. Methods of Election**
B. The Great Compromise   **E. Ratifying the Constitution**
C. Compromises Between North and South

Each of the following statements contains an explanation or fact about one of these headings. Write the *letter* of the heading under which it belongs.

1. The Constitution was to go into effect as soon as it won a majority in nine of the thirteen ratifying conventions.
2. Leaders of the common people were afraid that the wealthy might control the new government.
3. The main question was, Should slaves be counted in determining the number of representatives a state would have?
4. Many wealthy, educated Americans were afraid that poor and illiterate people might take control of the new government.
5. The most difficult dispute to settle was that between the states with a large population and those with a small population.
6. Merchants wanted the federal government to control foreign commerce so that it could win better treatment from European nations.
7. Our Congress has two houses, the Senate and the House of Representatives.
8. The outcome depended on the vote in three large states.
9. Plantation owners were opposed to taxes on imports and exports.
10. When two groups have opposing views on an important matter, both usually have to give in a little in order to reach an agreement.

B. Understanding the Picture

Compare the picture on page 108 with that on page 123. Both pictures show delegates of the states talking over problems that concern their states.

1. Why are they quarreling in the first picture?
2. Why are they shown as friends in the second picture?

MAKING HISTORY LIVE

1. Make a list of the activities of the federal government in your neighborhood or community.
2. Write an account of your activities on a typical day. How does the federal government influence them? How do your state and local governments influence them?
3. Clip newspaper accounts of at least five current events that show the power of the federal government. Be prepared to explain in class which of the delegated powers it is using in each case. Make notes.
4. Write a paragraph starting with these words: "If the Constitution had *not* been ratified, . . ."
5. Draw a chart or cartoon to illustrate *one* of the compromises in the Constitution. Help in making a classroom display of the best illustrations.

Chapter 8

THE LEGISLATIVE BRANCH

THE CONSTITUTION of the United States is not a very long document. It has only about 7,000 words. It can be printed on seven full pages of this book. Yet it contains the framework of our great government, so important to every American. See pages 708-731.

The Constitution opens with the Preamble or introduction. This is a stirring statement of American ideals. Like the second paragraph of the Declaration of Independence, it should be understood by freedom-loving people everywhere.

We, the people of the United States, in order to form a more perfect union, establish justice, insure domestic tranquility, provide for the common defence, promote the general welfare, and secure the blessings of liberty for ourselves and our posterity, do ordain and establish this Constitution for the United States of America.

The opening phrase, "We, the people of the United States," tells us that the Founding Fathers were acting as representatives of the American people. The rest of the Preamble lists the six purposes these men hoped to achieve by forming a new government:

1. ". . . to form a more perfect union"—that is, a better government—than the weak one under the Articles of Confederation.

2. To "establish justice" through a system of federal courts.

3. To "insure domestic tranquility"—that is, keep peace within the country—by preventing quarrels among the states and revolts like Shays' Rebellion.

4. To "provide for the common defence" by organizing an army and navy.

5. To "promote the general welfare" by improving the people's living and working conditions.

6. To "secure the blessings of liberty" by protecting the rights of all Americans.

Has the Constitution actually helped the American people to achieve these six great purposes? To answer this question, let us study this great document in detail.

How Is the Lawmaking Branch Organized?

A. The Three Branches of the Federal Government. The Founding Fathers decided to follow an example set by several of the states. They divided the government into three separate parts: the legislative branch (for making the laws), the executive branch (for enforcing them), and the judicial branch (for trying disputes arising from them). Article I of the Constitution (see pages 708-715) deals with the legislative branch.

B. The House of Representatives. As we have seen, the Great Compromise created a Congress of two houses, the Senate and the House of Representatives. Of these two bodies, the first described in the Constitution is the House. The Constitution states that the number of representatives from each state will depend upon its population. Each representative is to be elected by the people for a term of two years. The Constitution also states that representatives must meet three qualifications: They must be at least 25 years old, they must be citizens of the United States for at least 7 years, and they must live in the same state where they are elected. Although not written in the Constitution, it is now the custom for representatives to live in the district that elects them. The reason for this is clear. Representatives should be known by the people of the district. They should be able to tell their representatives what they want the government to do.

The House of Representatives elects its own officers. Most important is the Speaker, who serves as the presiding officer or chairperson of the House. The Speaker has great power in the House. Which members may speak when a law is debated is a decision of the Speaker. Officers and heads of committees are chosen with the

131

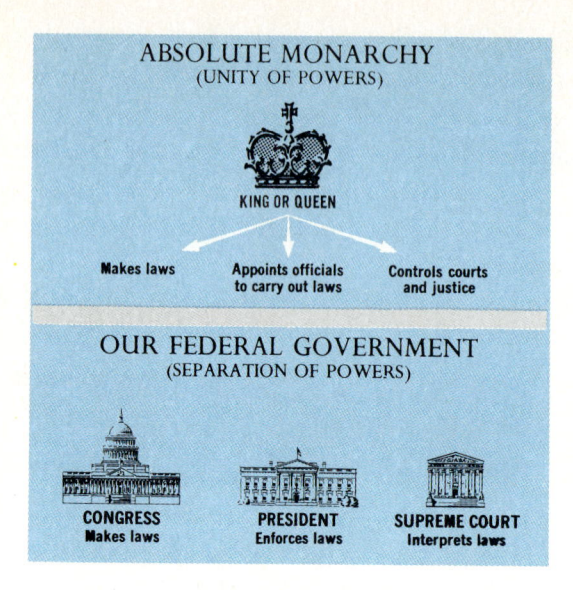

advice of the Speaker. (These will be discussed in the next section.) Because of the importance of the position, the Speaker is always a leading member of the political party with the most members in the House.

C. The Senate. The Senate is made up of two senators from each state. Their term of office is six years. For more than a century, senators were chosen by the state legislatures. But in 1913 the Constitution was amended to allow the people to elect senators directly, just as they elected representatives.

The House of Representatives has to be entirely reorganized every two years after each election. The Senate, on the other hand, is a continuous body. It can continue its work without interruption because only about one-third of the senators run for office every two years. The other two-thirds still have two or four years of their six-year terms to serve.

The qualifications for senator are higher than those for representative. Senators must be at least 30 years old and citizens for at least 9 years. Like representatives, they must live in the state that elects them.

The Senate elects all its officers except one. Its presiding officer under the Constitution is the Vice-President of the United States. The Vice-President is the chairperson when the Senate discusses a bill (a proposal for a new law). The Vice-President, unlike the Speaker of the House, may vote only in case of a tie vote. The Senate elects one of its members to be the leader when the Vice-President is absent. This member is called the president pro tempore (temporary presiding officer).

D. Rules of Congress. Congress meets at least once a year. January third has been the opening date of regular sessions since the adoption of the Twentieth Amendment to the Constitution in 1933. Congress may adjourn (end a session) whenever both houses agree on a date. In recent years Congress has usually remained in session for most of the year.

Congress keeps a journal, or daily record, of its proceedings. This is called the *Congressional Record*. It may be bought from the United States Government Printing Office in Washington, D.C. The *Congressional Record* gives the American people an idea of what Congress is doing.

Each house of Congress is "the judge of the elections, returns, and qualifications of its own members." This means that it may refuse to seat a new member if it finds that the member is not qualified or was elected unfairly. This power has rarely been used. Congress does not want to mix in disputes in different parts of the United States over the qualifications or elections of its members. It is also unwilling to keep out anyone the people have elected, even though they may make a poor choice.

E. Rights and Responsibilities of Members of Congress. Members of Congress are paid by the federal government—not by the states, as they were under the Articles of Confederation. Except for a few offenses listed in the Constitution, they are protected from arrest while Congress is in session. They may not be questioned elsewhere (in court, for example) about anything they have said in Congress. These rules are intended to protect members of Congress from pressure from the President or other government officials.

Unfortunately, members of Congress have sometimes used these protections to make unfair statements or to misbehave in other ways. The Constitution gives each house of Congress the power to punish its members. It may publicly censure (criticize) them or even expel a member by a two-thirds vote. These powers, like the power to refuse to seat newly elected members of Congress, have been used only a few times in our history.

No members of Congress may hold any other position under the federal government while serving in Congress. A person who was once a member of Congress is forbidden to take any federal position that was created, or for which a higher salary was provided, while that person was in Congress. These rules keep Congress from creating highly paid government positions into which its members can step after losing an election.

F. Differences Between the Two Houses. 1. Rules of Debate. There are several important differences between the two houses of Congress, besides the differences in qualifications and terms of office. One such difference is in rules for debating bills. The House of Representatives has a very large membership. In order to get bills passed without too much delay, it limits debate. Only a few members are permitted to speak for or against each bill, and they are allowed to talk for only a certain length of time. But in the Senate, which has fewer members, debate is unlimited. Any senator can speak on any bill for as long as he or she wants.

The right of unlimited debate in the Senate has made possible a practice called the filibuster. A few senators can "talk a bill to death." They can take turns talking about the bill, or anything related to it, until its supporters agree to drop it. In 1960, for example, some southern senators filibustered for nine days to prevent the passing of a civil rights bill. A filibuster can be shut off only by a three-fifths vote of the Senate. This vote is hard to obtain because the Senate is proud of its custom of unlimited debate. Moreover, many senators feel that they may want to use the filibuster themselves someday to kill a bill they strongly oppose.

2. Impeachment Proceedings. Under the

The House of Representatives (shown on the left) and the Senate in the early nineteenth century. Why were both houses of Congress much smaller then than they are today? Why was this an advantage?

Senate impeachment trial of President Andrew Johnson in 1868. The Senate failed by one vote to obtain the two-thirds majority necessary to remove him from office.

Constitution, each house of Congress also plays a different part in impeachment proceedings. These are the steps by which high government officials may be removed from office. First, officials must be impeached (accused of wrongdoing) by a majority vote of the House of Representatives. Then they must be tried by the Senate, which needs a two-thirds vote to remove them. To date, there have been only a dozen impeachments by the House. Only four (all cases involving federal judges) have resulted in removal from office by the Senate.

One President of the United States was impeached, but he did not lose his position. The vote to remove him in the Senate fell one short of the two-thirds required. The Founding Fathers made removal difficult in order to protect officials who took unpopular actions.

3. OTHER DIFFERENCES. Each house of Congress also plays a different part in the making of revenue bills (those dealing with money matters). Such bills must start in the House of Representatives. Only after the House has approved a revenue bill does it go to the Senate. There it may, however, be completely changed. The power of the House to start the bill is not, therefore, very important.

The Senate, on the other hand, has two important powers that the House does not have. 1. Every treaty the President makes with foreign nations must be ratified by two-thirds of the Senate. 2. All the President's appointments need a majority vote of the Senate for approval. A custom known as "senatorial courtesy" gives the Senate even greater power over appointments than the Constitution provided. Before appointing an official to serve in a certain state, the President is expected to ask the advice of senators from that state of the same political party. If those senators are not consulted, they may not approve the person chosen by the President. Thus many officials the President appoints are actually picked by the members of the Senate. Its special powers, longer terms, and higher qualifications for membership make the Senate more important than the House of Representatives.

REVIEWING THE SECTION

A. Knowing New Terms

For each new term in the first column, write in your notebook the *letter* of the best description in the second column.

Terms	Descriptions
1. Adjournment	a. Bringing charges against an official in the House of Representatives
2. *Congressional Record*	
3. Filibuster	b. Custom by which the President consults the senators of a state before appointing officials there
4. Impeachment	
5. Preamble	
6. President pro tempore	c. Ending a session of Congress
7. Revenue bill	d. The tactic of killing a bill in the Senate by talking a long time
8. Senatorial courtesy	
9. Speaker	e. Introduction to the Constitution
10. Vice-President	f. Presiding officer of the House of Representatives
	g. Regular presiding officer of the Senate
	h. Temporary presiding officer of the Senate
	i. Proposed law dealing with money matters
	j. Removal of officials from office by the Senate
	k. Publication that tells what has been happening in Congress

B. *Knowing Important Facts*

Copy this chart in your notebook and fill in the missing information.

	House of Representatives	Senate
1. Number of members	1.	1.
2. Term of office	2.	2.
3. Qualifications	3. a. b. c.	3. a. b. c.
4. Presiding officers	4.	4.
5. Rules of debate	5.	5.
6. Part in impeachment proceedings	6.	6.
7. Other special powers	7.	7. a. b.

Conclusion. Why is the Senate more important than the House of Representatives?

C. Finding the Reasons

One, two, or even all three answers to each question may be correct. Write the letters of *all* the correct answers in your notebook.

1. Why is the Preamble to the Constitution important?
   a. It lists the rights every American has. b. It lists the reasons for doing away with the Articles of Confederation. c. It lists the goals that the Founding Fathers hoped to achieve through the Constitution.
2. Why has it become the custom of representatives to live in the district that elects them?
   a. The voters can know them better. b. The voters can talk over problems with them. c. Representatives can learn what voters want.
3. Why is the Senate called a continuous body?
   a. Only two-thirds of its members are elected every two years; the rest of its membership is unchanged. b. It does not have to be reorganized after each election. c. It still follows the rules it adopted when it first met almost two centuries ago.
4. Why does Congress rarely refuse to admit a newly elected member?
   a. Members of Congress are usually qualified and fairly elected. b. Congress does not like to deprive the people of the representative they have chosen. c. Congress does not wish to get involved in disputes over elections or qualifications of its members.
5. Why do many senators refuse to shut off a filibuster, even against a bill they like?
   a. They usually need more time to study the bill. b. They are proud of the custom of unlimited debate. c. They want to show that the Senate is better than the House of Representatives.
6. Why does the Constitution give members of Congress certain special protections?
   a. As high government officials, they are entitled to more rights than ordinary Americans. b. They can be trusted not to take advantage of their privileges. c. They need to be free to say what they think without fear of punishment.
7. Why is it difficult for Congress to remove high government officials?
   a. Both houses of Congress must vote before an official is removed. b. A two-thirds vote of the House is required for impeachment. c. A two-thirds vote of the Senate is required for removal.

How Does a Bill Become a Law?

A. Lawmaking and the Constitution. Lawmaking is one of the most important jobs of government. For laws are the rules by which a government regulates the activities of its people. By telling them what they may or may not do, the government makes it possible for large numbers of people to live together in peace. Laws also deal with other important matters, such as the taxes people pay and the services they receive in return for taxes. These services include keeping order, helping people in need, and protecting the nation from its enemies.

In an absolute monarchy or dictatorship, laws are made by one person. This is probably the fastest and simplest way to make them. In a modern democracy, on the other hand, lawmaking is neither fast nor simple. The people elect hundreds of representatives. These people come from different parts of the country. They belong to different political parties and represent others with all sorts of interests. How do these representatives agree on what laws to make for our nation?

To find out how laws are made in the United States, we can start by reading the Constitution. But we will find that only one small section (Section 7 of Article I, on page 711) actually deals with the subject. This may seem strange until we recall that the Founding Fathers had had long experience with legislatures before they drafted the Constitution. So they did not have to spell out the lawmaking procedure in detail. Instead, they only outlined the procedure and let each house make its own rules for carrying it out. These rules have changed many times over the years. In this section you will learn how our laws are made today.

B. Introducing a Bill. The first step is for a member of Congress to introduce a bill. As we have seen, revenue bills must be introduced in the House of Representatives. All other bills may start in either house. When a member of Congress gets an idea for a bill, experts help to put it into exact legal language. To introduce it, the member merely drops a copy into a box near the desk of the presiding officer.

Several thousand bills are introduced at each session of Congress. But only a small number of them, perhaps one out of eight, finally pass. These have usually been changed a great deal by the time they become laws. To see why this happens, let us see what is done to a bill after it is introduced.

C. The Committee System. It would be impossible for the whole Congress to study, discuss, and vote on the thousands of bills introduced at each session. Instead, each bill is sent to a congressional committee. The name of the committee tells what sort of bills it handles. The names of some committees are the Agriculture, Judiciary, Human Resources, Rules, Ways and Means, and Foreign Relations committees.

The members of the committee study every bill that comes to them. If they consider a bill unsatisfactory or unimportant, they put it aside. Most bills "die in committee" in this way. If a bill seems worthwhile, however, the committee holds public hearings. Interested people come

The Senate Watergate hearings. Why do legislative committees hold hearings? What happens to a bill after a committee has recommended that it be considered?

to the hearings to speak for or against the bill. The committee may change the bill to meet the objections people have made. Then it may recommend that the bill be considered by the full house.

D. Organization of Congressional Committees. Since committees play a very important part in lawmaking, we should know how they are organized. The leaders of each house of Congress decide how many members each committee needs to do its work. Each of the two major political parties is assigned a certain number of these members, according to the number of seats it holds in the house. In 1978, for example, the Democrats had about two-thirds of the seats in the House of Representatives. Thus they were entitled to have ten members on a fifteen-member House committee.

Committee members are picked by the leaders of the two parties. Those with good records will usually be placed on important committees. A less outstanding member of Congress will be assigned to a less important one. That member, however, may ask for an appointment to a more important committee when a place opens up for a new member.

Usually members of Congress will serve on the same committee for as long as they keep their seats in the house. After many years, a member may become the chairperson of the committee. The chairperson is a member of the party that holds a majority of seats in the house. Choices are usually made on the basis of seniority. This means that the member of the majority party who has served longest on the committee is chosen. Many committee chairpersons have been Democrats from the South, reelected year after year, because the Democratic Party has been very strong in the South since the Civil War. (For details, see page 345.)

Committee chairpersons are powerful members of Congress. They make many decisions on which the life of a bill may depend. **They decide, for example, whether the committee should consider the bill. They also decide when**

A congressional committee questioning a witness. Congress may investigate any problem facing our nation to get information on which to base new laws. Why is this a very important power?

HOW A BILL BECOMES A LAW

| 1. Introduced (by a member of either house) | 2. Sent to committee—public hearings, study and changes, vote | 3. Brought before entire house—debate, changes, vote | 4. Sent to other house | 5. To committee—public hearings, study and changes, vote |
| 6. Brought before entire house—debate, changes, vote | 7. Sent to conference committee—(if bills from two houses differ) | 8. Sent back to both houses for vote | 9. Sent to President for signature or veto | 10. Sent back to Congress if vetoed—two-thirds vote needed to overrride veto |

public hearings should be held. They can rush through bills they favor. If they dislike a bill, they can hold it until late in the session when it has little chance of being passed. Most important of all is the chairperson of the Rules Committee of the House of Representatives. The Rules Committee decides when a bill will be discussed on the floor of the House. The Rules chairperson may "bottle up," that is, hold back, an unwanted bill for weeks, months, or even an entire session.

E. Voting on the Bill. Getting through the committee is the most difficult step in a bill's progress, but it is still only the beginning. The bill must next be debated and voted on by the full house. The chairperson of the committee, as a leading expert on the bill, opens and closes the debate. The committee's approval of the bill is enough, in most cases, to get it passed after a brief debate. But some bills deal with controversial issues—that is, with questions on which people have strong opposing opinions. The debate on such bills is often long and heated. In the Senate, a filibuster may be held to kill the bill. As a rule, important changes are made in a controversial bill to win over some of its opponents. Despite these changes, it may fail to get a majority when the vote is finally taken.

Members of Congress vote on most bills by calling out "Yea" or "Nay," or by standing to be counted. On important bills, however, a roll call is held. The names of all the members are called, and their votes are put on record. This means that the American people can know, by reading the *Congressional Record* or a good newspaper, how their representatives voted on important bills.

F. The Conference Committee. A bill that has passed one house of Congress still has to go through the same procedure in the other house. It has to be introduced, studied by the proper committee, recommended, debated on the floor, and passed by a majority vote. By that time, the bills passed by the two houses are usually quite different. The leaders of Congress therefore appoint a conference committee to work out the differences. This committee is made up of members from each house. It usually writes a compromise bill. But it may make changes of its own or even come up with an entirely new bill! The bill then goes back to both houses. There it is usually approved without change.

President Lyndon B. Johnson signing the Civil Rights Act of 1964. The President usually uses several pens to sign an important bill and gives them to supporters of the bill as souvenirs. Here President Johnson is giving a pen to a noted civil rights leader, Martin Luther King, Jr.

Any change means that it has to go back to the conference committee again.

G. The President's Part in Lawmaking. At last the bill goes to the President. At this point, there are three choices of action. 1. Usually, the President signs the bill and it becomes law. 2. In fewer cases, the President vetoes (kills) the bill. The bill must then be sent back to Congress with a message telling the reasons for the President's veto. Congress has the power to override a veto. This means that the bill becomes a law if it is passed again—this time by a two-thirds vote of both houses. 3. Suppose the President dislikes a bill but does not wish to anger Congress by vetoing it. In that case, the President takes no action for ten working days. If Congress is still in session at the end of that time, the bill becomes law without the President's signature. But if Congress has adjourned during the ten-day period, the bill is dead. This is called the "pocket veto" because the President has, so to speak, put the bill into a pocket and left it there to die.

The pocket veto is used much more often than the ordinary veto. The reason is that Congress usually rushes through several hundred bills during the last few days of the session. Many of these bills do not have strong support. Some may even have been introduced by members of Congress just to please the people at home. Congress can act in this way because it knows that the pile of last-minute bills will be examined by the President and the President's assistants. It knows that only the worthwhile bills will be signed. The rest will die by pocket veto.

H. Role of the Supreme Court. Even when a bill finally becomes a law, its troubles may not be over. Anyone who is harmed by the law can bring an action against the government in a federal court. Or people can refuse to obey the law, and so force the government to take action against them. Such cases, if they raise a question about the exact meaning of the Constitution, usually end up in the United States Supreme Court. If the Supreme Court declares the law unconstitutional—that is, contrary to the meaning of the Constitution—it is dead.

I. The Final Result. Now you have seen how carefully laws are made under our system of government. A bill is studied by a committee of members of Congress who know its subject; the public is given a chance to voice its opinion; and the bill is debated and voted on by the full house. This entire procedure is followed a second time in the other house of Congress. Then the bill goes to the President. It is studied again before the President decides whether to sign or veto it. Finally, the law may be tested in the courts. This is, on the whole, a slow process. But it guarantees that our laws will be helpful to a majority of the American people.

REVIEWING THE SECTION

A. Knowing New Terms

In your notebook write the new terms in this section that best complete these statements.
1. The rules by which a government regulates the activities of its people are called _____.
2. Any member of Congress may start the making of a law by _____ a bill.
3. The bill is sent to a group in the Congress called a _____.
4. The chairperson of each committee is the member of the majority party who has the longest service, or _____, on the committee.
5. When an important bill is voted on in either house, the vote is usually recorded by means of a _____ _____.
6. Differences between bills passed by the two houses of Congress on the same subject are settled by a special committee called the _____ committee.
7. After being passed by both houses of Congress, a bill goes to the President. The President usually signs or _____ (kills) it.
8. If the President leaves the bill untouched for ten working days and Congress adjourns, the bill dies. This is called the _____.
9. A bill vetoed by the President may still become a law if Congress, by a two-thirds vote of both houses, _____ the veto.
10. After a bill has become a law, the Supreme Court may still kill it by declaring it to be _____.

B. Understanding the Facts

Give the correct order of the following steps in the lawmaking procedure.
1. Sending the bill to a conference committee
2. Debating the bill
3. Declaring a law unconstitutional
4. Holding public hearings
5. Introducing a bill
6. Overriding the President's veto
7. Recommending the bill
8. Assigning the bill to the proper committee
9. Signing or vetoing the bill
10. Voting on the bill

IMPROVING YOUR SKILLS

A. Making an Outline

You have already learned how to remember what a paragraph is about by

141

finding the main idea. (For explanation, see page 107.) Even more useful is finding the main ideas of an entire section or chapter. This can be done by making an outline, a skill you will find helpful in other subjects besides history.

Outlining a textbook is usually easy. Most textbooks use heavy print to show the main ideas of a section or a chapter. By looking over these headings before you start to read, you can learn in a general way what a section or chapter is about.

To get a clear picture, let us practice outlining this section, "How Does a Bill Become a Law?" In this textbook, each heading in heavy print is usually followed by two or three paragraphs. Each of these paragraphs tells something different about the heading. To see how this works, let us find the main ideas of the three paragraphs under the first main heading, **Lawmaking and the Constitution** (see page 137). The first paragraph gives the reasons why lawmaking is important. The second paragraph explains why lawmaking is more complicated in a democracy than in an absolute monarchy or dictatorship. The third paragraph tells how our Constitution deals with lawmaking.

Let us now put this information in outline form.

A. Lawmaking and the Constitution

(Since you cannot use heavy print, underline each main heading in your notebook.)

1. Lawmaking is important because laws keep order by regulating the activities of the people.
2. Lawmaking is more complicated in a democracy than in an absolute monarchy or dictatorship.
3. The Constitution only outlines the procedure for making laws. Each house of Congress makes its own rules.

Outline the rest of this section by copying the main headings and filling in the main ideas of each paragraph.

B. Introducing a Bill

1.
2.

C. The Committee System

1.
2.

D. Organization of Congressional Committees

1.
2.
3.
4.

E. **Voting on the Bill**
  1.
  2.

F. **The Conference Committee**

G. **The President's Part in Lawmaking**
  1.
  2.

H. **Role of the Supreme Court**

I. **The Final Result**

Now look over your outline. You have before you on a page or two the main ideas of the entire section. You should go over this outline to prepare for classwork and tests. Be sure to recall the facts that belong with each main idea. If you cannot recall important facts, look them up again in the text. You will find that this procedure becomes easier with practice. Once you have mastered it, you will find it very helpful in your studies.

B. Understanding the Picture

Compare the picture on page 131 with that on page 137.

1. In the first picture, the congressman is shown leaving his district to go to the federal capital. What are the people of his district giving him?
2. How can you tell that the second picture shows present-day members of Congress?

MAKING HISTORY LIVE

1. Make a list of all the services our federal, state, and local governments provide for you and your family.
2. Keep track of an important bill now before Congress. Report to the class when it has either passed or died. What is the bill about?
3. Write letters to your members of Congress for or against an important bill now before Congress. Bring the letters to class first.
4. Write up a discussion of one of these controversial questions:
   a. Should chairpersons be chosen by members of each committee and not by seniority? b. Should we do away with one house of Congress to speed up lawmaking? c. Should the powers of the conference committee be reduced? d. Should the President be given thirty days to consider bills?

Chapter 9

THE EXECUTIVE AND JUDICIAL BRANCHES

WHEN Patrick Henry read the new Constitution, he was greatly troubled. He believed that it gave too much power to the federal government and especially to the President. Someday, he warned, the President would try to become a monarch. Since Henry's day, the powers of the federal government and the President have grown tremendously to keep up with our nation's growth. People often complain that our government and its head have become too powerful. Some fear, like Patrick Henry, that the President may become a dictator.

President Truman had a different view. He said that the presidency had become too big a job for one person. He called it "a man-killer, five or six full-time jobs, all different, all difficult." Has the presidency really become so big a job that no one person can fill it properly? Has the President become so powerful that our liberties are in danger? How do the Constitution and the federal courts protect our liberties? You will find the answers to these questions in this chapter, based on Articles II and III of the Constitution (see pages 715-719).

How Powerful Is the President?

A. Electing the President and Vice-President. The executive department of our federal government enforces the laws Congress passes. At its head are the President and Vice-President. The Constitution says that they must be citizens by birth, at least thirty-five years old, and residents of the United States for at least fourteen years. They are elected for four-year terms by a group of people known as the electoral college. The Founding Fathers adopted this system of indirect election because they did not trust the common people to pick the best leaders.

1. THE EARLY ELECTORAL COLLEGE. The Constitution provided that each state should have the same number of electors as its membership in Congress. Thus if a state had ten representatives and two senators, it was entitled to have twelve electors. The electors would be chosen in any way the state legislature decided. They would meet in their state capitals a few weeks after Election Day and cast their votes for two persons—the Americans who were their first and second choices for President. Their ballots would be sent to Congress to be counted. The person who received the largest number of votes and also had a majority of votes would become President. The person who received the next largest number would become Vice-President.

If there was a tie vote, or no candidate received a majority of the electoral college vote, Congress would decide the election. The House of Representatives would choose the President from among the leading candidates. The Senate would choose the Vice-President. Congress has actually chosen the heads of our government under this provision only twice in our history.

2. THE MODERN ELECTORAL COLLEGE. The Founding Fathers expected the electors to be outstanding Americans. Only such people, they felt, could be trusted to pick the President and the Vice-President. But their plan was soon changed by the rise of political parties. Each party nominates (chooses) two candidates, one for each post. Since 1832 this choice has been made by the nominating convention, a meeting of political leaders from all parts of the country. They usually choose as their candidate for President the one they think will win the most votes for their party. They usually choose a candidate for Vice-President who will "balance the ticket"—that is, appeal to voters who might not like the candidate for President. The nominating convention also draws up the party platform. This is a list of the ideas the party stands for and the actions it will take if its candidates win the election.

The political parties also choose the electors for each state. Many of the electors are unknown to the public. But voters do not have to know who they are. They simply vote for the political party whose candidates for President and Vice-President they prefer. The party that gets a majority of the popular vote in a state wins all the electoral votes of that state. The electors, in turn, are expected to cast their ballots for the party's candidates. That is why the results of a presidential election are known a few hours after the voting ends on Election Day, even though the electors do not actually vote until several weeks later.

145

The electoral college has been criticized for being complicated and undemocratic. It has elected a dozen men who did not get a majority of the popular vote. In fact, three of them received fewer votes than their rivals. They won because they carried enough states with a large number of electoral votes to get a majority in the electoral college (see map, bottom of page). States with a large electoral vote, like New York or California, have therefore become very important. Candidates from such states have a much better chance of being nominated than have persons from states with small populations. They can gain an advantage by carrying their own states with their larger number of electoral votes. Proposals have been made for changing the Constitution to do away with the electoral college. To date, however, none of these proposals has gained much support.

B. The President's Successors. If the President dies, resigns, or is disabled (unable to perform the duties), the Vice-President becomes President. The Constitution did not, however, take care of two problems. 1. It failed to explain what would happen if the Vice-President became President, died, or resigned. 2. More important, it did not explain how to tell when the President was disabled. Two Presidents, Garfield and Wilson, were unable to carry out their duties for months. In both cases, however, the Vice-President was unable to take over.

The question of presidential disability came to a head after President Eisenhower's three serious illnesses. It was finally settled by the Twenty-Fifth Amendment, adopted in 1967. If the President tells Congress of a disability, the Vice-President takes over as the Acting President. When the President has recovered, Congress is informed, and the President goes back to work. If the President is disabled but cannot or will not tell Congress, a different procedure is followed. Either the Vice-President and a majority of the cabinet, or some other body named by Congress, can say that the President is disabled. If they believe that the President is not ready to return to work, they can inform Congress of this. Congress can then decide, by a two-thirds vote of both houses, whether the President is still disabled and cannot go back to work. The Twenty-Fifth Amendment also provides that the President shall nominate a new Vice-President whenever the position falls vacant. Congress must approve his choice by a majority vote of both houses.

C. The President's Powers Under the Constitution. Under the Constitution, the President of the United States has been given many powers. Many other powers have developed over the years. In order to study these powers more easily, we shall group them under six headings.

1. EXECUTIVE POWERS. The President is the chief executive of the United States. This means that the President is responsible for enforcing the thousands of laws passed by Congress. There is assistance from the federal civil service, which consists of about three million workers. The most important assistants are the heads of the thirteen major executive depart-

THE CLOSE ELECTION OF 1976

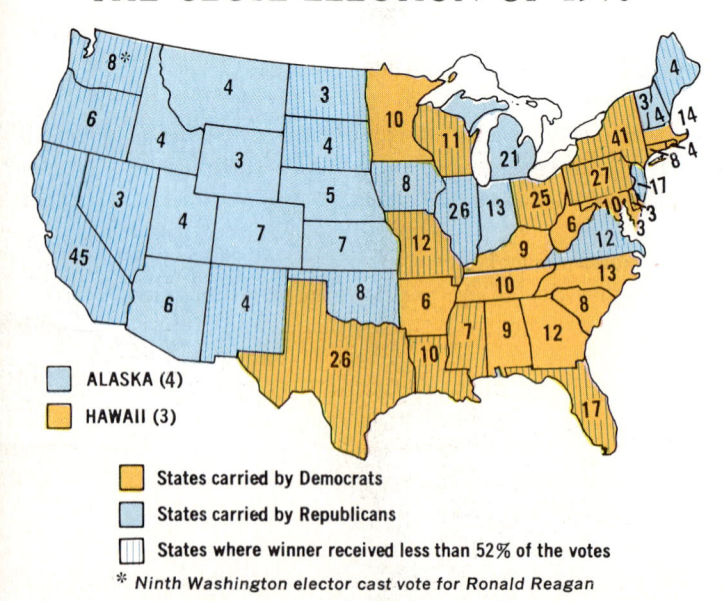

- States carried by Democrats
- States carried by Republicans
- States where winner received less than 52% of the votes

* Ninth Washington elector cast vote for Ronald Reagan

Numbers indicate electoral votes

ments. (These are shown in the chart.) The President appoints, with the Senate's consent, thousands of the highest officials in government. (See page 134.)

The department heads must report to the President on the work of their departments. The President may ask the heads to resign if their work is held to be unsatisfactory. Following a custom established by George Washington, the President meets with the department heads regularly to talk over the nation's problems. When the department heads meet in a group to advise the President, they are known as the President's cabinet.

2. LEGISLATIVE POWERS. The President has much to do with the making of laws. The President sends messages to Congress asking for laws the nation supposedly needs. The President may call Congress back for a special session if it adjourns without passing the laws asked for. As we have seen, the President can also veto bills passed by Congress.

3. JUDICIAL POWERS. The President appoints all federal judges, including the justices of the Supreme Court. Each appointment must, of course, be approved by the Senate. The President also has the power to pardon people who have broken federal laws, or to reprieve them (put off their punishment for a time).

4. MILITARY POWERS. The President is commander in chief of the armed forces, including the National Guard when he calls it into action. This is a tremendous power. Only Congress can declare war, but the President may move the armed forces in such a way that war results. This has happened in the Mexican, Korean, and Vietnamese wars. The President may also use troops within the nation. Both President Eisenhower and President Kennedy called out the National Guard to protect black students entering schools in which only white students had been allowed.

The President has the final say in all military matters. A President may even dismiss generals if it is necessary. During the Civil War, President Lincoln dismissed several generals for being either too careful or too reckless. During the Korean War, President Truman removed General MacArthur for criticizing the President's policies and for taking actions the President opposed.

5. CONTROL OF FOREIGN POLICY. The Constitution gives the President almost complete power over our foreign policy (our relations with the governments of other nations). Among

President Reagan delivering a message to both houses of Congress.

these duties are naming ambassadors and other ministers to represent our nation abroad. Also included are making treaties with the consent of two-thirds of the Senate and receiving ministers from foreign nations. The President may refuse to receive ministers of foreign countries if their governments are not considered to be legal governments.

6. Duties As Chief of State. In receiving foreign officials, the President acts as our chief of state. This means that he or she is the formal head of our government, much like the king or queen of a monarchy. As the chief of state, the President has to take part in many official ceremonies. The President must also attend other affairs, such as greeting important visitors, dinners of many kinds, college graduations, ball games, and charity drives.

D. Powers Outside of the Constitution. We have just seen that the Constitution gives the President many important powers. But other powers have been obtained in ways the Founding Fathers did not foresee. Political parties are one reason why these powers have grown. The first political parties in the United States were formed during the administration of George Washington. Soon afterward, the President was recognized as the head of his party. As a result,

President Reagan with Indira Gandhi, prime minister of India. Which two of the President's powers does this picture illustrate?

there are frequent meetings with political leaders from many parts of the nation. There are speeches in local election campaigns. These are heavy burdens, but they also increase the President's power. For example, the President can influence lawmaking by meeting with the party leaders in Congress.

The President's influence can be increased through federal appointments. Members of Congress who support the presidential program can be rewarded by having their followers named to federal posts. Those who oppose the President can be punished by having their requests for appointments refused.

Finally, the President's power and influence have grown greater and greater as newspapers, television, and other means of communication have developed. A President who speaks well on television can win strong popular support from the voters. The people in turn can bring pressure on Congress by writing or speaking to their member of Congress in behalf of the laws the President wants.

E. Lightening the President's Load. Is the presidency too big a job for any person? Judging by the long list of presidential powers, it would certainly seem so. Recent Presidents, however, have found two ways to lighten their burdens. The first is to place some of them on the shoulders of the Vice-President. The Constitution gives the Vice-President only one job—to serve as the presiding officer of the Senate. Nowadays, it is the custom for the Vice-President to perform ceremonial duties and to visit foreign lands as the President's personal representative. The second way of lightening the President's work load has been to provide a staff of assistants for this office.

Nevertheless, the President still has to make thousands of important decisions. There is a popular saying that most people can "pass the buck" when they want to avoid responsibility. President Truman kept a sign on his desk saying, "The buck stops here."

REVIEWING THE SECTION

A. Knowing New Terms

PART 1. In your notebook write the new terms in this section that best complete these statements.

1. The branch of our federal government that enforces the laws passed by Congress is called the _____ branch.
2. At the head of this branch is our chief executive, the _____.
3. If the chief executive dies, the _____ becomes the President.
4. The President and Vice-President are elected by a group of people known as the _____ _____.
5. Candidates for the presidency and vice-presidency are nominated by meetings of political leaders, called _____ _____.
6. The President is assisted by the heads of the executive departments. When they meet with the President to discuss government problems, they are known as the _____.
7. The department heads direct a huge force of government workers called the federal _____ _____.
8. The Constitution makes the President responsible for conducting our relations with foreign countries—that is, our _____ _____.

PART 2. Explain the following terms *in your own words*.

(In **A2**) "balancing the ticket"
(In **B**)   Twenty-Fifth Amendment
(In **C6**) chief of state

B. Understanding the Facts

PART 1. In your notebook complete this chart comparing the qualifications for President, senator, and representative (see pages 131, 132, and 145).

	President	Senator	Representative
1. Citizenship			
2. Age			
3. Residence			

PART 2. Complete the following chart comparing the powers of our President with those of an absolute monarch or dictator.

Powers of Absolute Monarch or Dictator	Powers of the President
1. Appoints all important officials	1.
2. Acts as the only lawmaker	2.
3. Appoints judges; can imprison or pardon people at will	3.
4. Commands armed forces	4.
5. Has complete control over foreign policy	5.
6. Presides at official ceremonies	6.
7. Heads the political party, if there is one	7.
8. Controls newspapers, television, and other mass media	8.

IMPROVING YOUR SKILLS

A. Mastering the Map

Examine the map on page 146. It shows the voting in the presidential election of 1976. That was a very close election. Out of a total of almost 80,000,000 votes, the Democrat Jimmy Carter received only a million and a half more votes than the Republican Gerald R. Ford. The electoral vote was 297 for Carter, 241 for Ford. To see why this happened and how easily the Republicans might have won, answer these questions:

1. How many states did the Democrats carry by a close margin (less than 52 percent of the popular vote)?
2. How many electoral votes did these states have together?
3. The Republicans had to take only 29 electoral votes from the Democrats to win the election. How many of the close states did they need to carry in order to win?

B. Making an Outline

Reread the instructions for making an outline on pages 141-143. Now let us carry your skill in outlining a step further. What should you do when the headings in the text have subheadings, as they do in this section? The answer is to use small letters (*a, b,* etc.) whenever there is more than one paragraph under a subheading. Your outline will look like this:

A. Electing the President and Vice-President
  1. THE EARLY ELECTORAL COLLEGE
    a. The electors cast two ballots. The man with the most votes became

President; the person with the next largest number became Vice-President. b. If there was a tie vote or no candidate won a majority, the House of Representatives chose the President.
2. THE MODERN ELECTORAL COLLEGE
a. The electoral college system has been changed by political parties, which nominate the candidates for President and Vice-President.
b. The political parties choose groups of electors in each state. The people cast a single vote for their party's group.
c. The electoral college system has been criticized as complicated and undemocratic.

Now complete in your notebook the outline of the rest of this section. Remember to use small letters whenever you have a subheading followed by more than one paragraph.

B. The President's Successors

1.
2.

C. The President's Powers Under the Constitution

1. EXECUTIVE POWERS
   a.
   b.
2. LEGISLATIVE POWERS
3. JUDICIAL POWERS
4. MILITARY POWERS
   a.
   b.
5. CONTROL OF FOREIGN POLICY
6. DUTIES AS CHIEF OF STATE

D. Powers Outside of the Constitution

1.
2.
3.

E. Lightening the President's Load

1.
2.

How Do the Judicial, Executive, and Legislative Branches Work Together?

A. Importance of the Courts. Courts and their judges play a very important part in our lives. They decide the guilt or innocence of anyone accused of breaking the law. They set the penalty if a person is guilty. In disputes, they decide which side is right and which wrong. If the law is not clear or the opposing sides disagree on its meaning, the courts interpret the law—that is, they explain exactly what it means in this particular case.

In every case, we expect the courts to carry out the democratic ideal of justice. This means that their decisions must be fair and in accordance with the law. The courts must also be strong enough to protect the poor and weak from the rich and powerful. Thanks to the protection the courts give us, we can carry on our daily activities and feel safe.

B. The Judicial Branch. 1. THE POSITION OF FEDERAL JUDGES. The Founding Fathers realized how important courts and justice are. Under the Articles of Confederation, the central government had no courts of its own. This weakness was corrected by Article III of the Constitution. Sections 1 and 2 (see pages 718-719) set up the third branch of our federal government, the judicial branch. It consists of the Supreme Court and a number of lower courts established by Congress.

The judges of all the federal courts are appointed by the President with the Senate's approval. They hold office "during good behavior." This means, in effect, that they can be removed only by impeachment. Moreover, their salaries may not be reduced while they hold office. Thus federal judges are protected by the Constitution from attacks by other government officials or the general public. They can feel free to give just decisions, even when such decisions may be unpopular.

2. TYPES OF FEDERAL CASES. The federal courts handle two types of cases: a. Violations of the Constitution, federal laws, or treaties between the United States and a foreign nation go to federal courts. So do cases involving American ships while they are at sea. Federal courts can also now try cases involving airplanes in flight. b. Cases involving the federal government, two or more states, a foreign government, or the representatives of a foreign government also go to federal courts. Under the Articles of Confederation, such cases might have been tried in the courts of two or more states. Each might have given a different decision. The Constitution changed this situation. Any case whose influence goes beyond the border of a single state is a federal case. The decision of the federal court is binding throughout the United States.

3. ROLE OF THE SUPREME COURT. Cases involving state or foreign governments go directly to the Supreme Court. Other cases are heard by the federal court in the district where the dispute started. In most cases, the decision of the district court is final. Suppose, however, that you are one of the parties in a case and you believe that the court's decision is wrong.

You may ask the United States Court of Appeals for a rehearing. There are only eleven appeals courts in the entire country today. They grant an appeal only if there is good reason. Suppose that the Court of Appeals accepts your case but supports the decision of the district court. You may then appeal to the Supreme Court in Washington, D.C. The Supreme Court, as its name indicates, is the highest court in the land. Its decision is final.

The Supreme Court hears only a small number of appeals each year. These are usually very important cases. They usually involve a conflict between the Constitution and a federal law or a conflict between federal and state laws. If a majority of the Supreme Court decides that a federal law violates the Constitution, then the law is unconstitutional. It becomes "null and void and of no effect, as if it had never been passed." A state law is also killed if it violates the Constitution or a federal law. (See the "supremacy clause" on page 721.)

The Constitution did not actually give the Supreme Court the power to declare laws unconstitutional. But the Court pointed out in an early decision (*Marbury* v. *Madison,* 1803) that someone had to have the last word in interpreting the Constitution. It was reasonable that this should be the highest federal court, the Supreme Court. Since that time, the Supreme Court has played an important role in our government. Its decisions have gradually increased the power of the federal government, especially by "stretching" the elastic and interstate commerce clauses of the Constitution (see page 160). In recent years, the Supreme Court has been a leading protector of the people's liberties and the rights of minority groups.

C. The System of Checks and Balances. Now that we have studied all three branches of our federal government, let us see how they work together. The Founding Fathers were afraid

The United States Supreme Court. Why is there no time limit to the terms of office of members of the Supreme Court? How can the Supreme Court check the power of Congress?

that the federal government, and particularly the President, might become too powerful. To prevent this, they divided the government's powers among the three branches. They also carefully balanced the powers of the different branches so that each would act as a check on the other two. This system of "checks and balances" is another outstanding feature of our Constitution.

1. CHECKS ON THE EXECUTIVE. The President is subject to the most checks. The President's appointments must be approved by the Senate. Treaties must be ratified by a two-thirds vote of that body. Congress can refuse to pass laws the President wants. It can cut the money needed to run executive departments. It can investigate the conduct of the President's staff. In extreme cases, Congress can impeach, try, and remove from office executive officials, including even the President.

The Supreme Court can also check the President. In 1952, for example, President Truman took over the steel mills to prevent a strike. He defended his action as a war measure. The steel was needed, he said, to make weapons for our armed forces in Korea.

The Supreme Court, however, declared the takeover unconstitutional. The President promptly returned the mills to their owners.

2. CHECKS ON THE LEGISLATURE. We already know about two important checks on Congress. The President can veto bills passed by Congress, and the Supreme Court can declare laws unconstitutional. In addition, the President can influence Congress through control of jobs, position as party leader, and speeches to the people. If Congress refuses to pass certain laws the President wants at a regular session, Congress can be called back for a special session. The President can also publicly criticize members of Congress and may even actively campaign against them when they run for office.

3. CHECKS ON THE FEDERAL COURTS. The judicial branch is subject to fewer checks than the executive and legislative branches. Congress can, however, increase or decrease the number of justices on the Supreme Court. It can also create or do away with lower courts.

It can reduce the funds of the judicial department and impeach judges. When a law has been declared unconstitutional, Congress can pass a new law on the same question. It can even propose an amendment to the Constitution (see page 720).

Presidents can check the federal courts by refusing to enforce decisions they do not like. They can also appoint judges who will support their views. President Franklin D. Roosevelt used these checks against the Supreme Court in the 1930s. At his request Congress had passed a large number of laws to help our country through a severe economic depression. The Supreme Court declared some of these laws unconstitutional. The President broadcast an appeal to the public over the radio. Then he asked Congress to let him appoint six additional judges to the Supreme Court. He expected that the six new judges, together with the minority of the Court that already supported his views, would give him the majority he needed. Congress refused to increase the number of justices.

CHECKS AND BALANCES

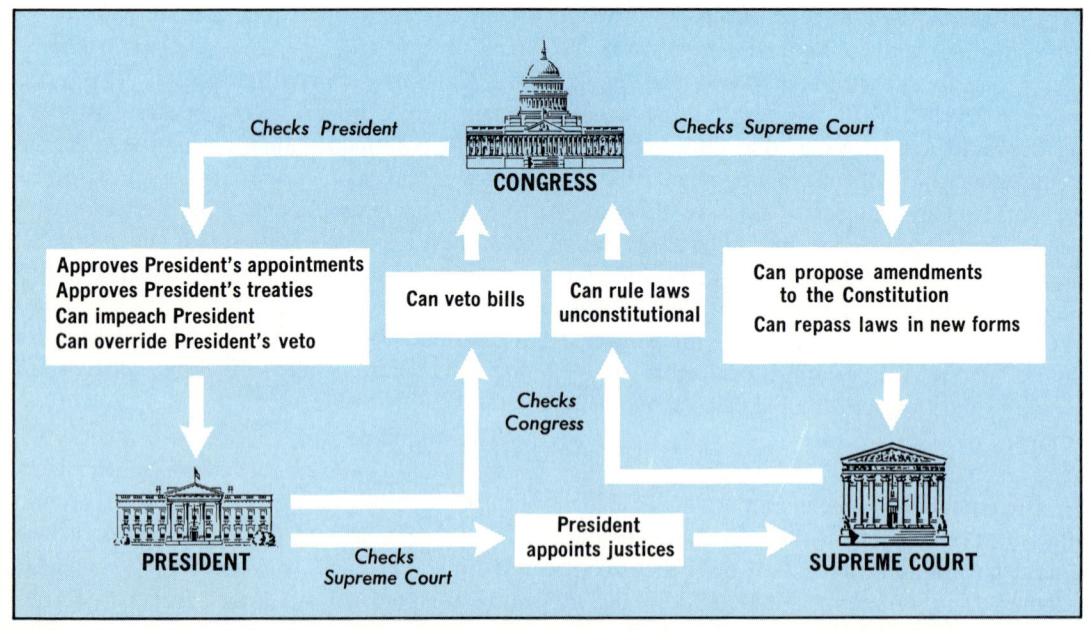

CONGRESS — Checks President / Checks Supreme Court

- Approves President's appointments
- Approves President's treaties
- Can impeach President
- Can override President's veto

Can veto bills | Can rule laws unconstitutional

- Can propose amendments to the Constitution
- Can repass laws in new forms

Checks Congress

PRESIDENT — Checks Supreme Court — President appoints justices — **SUPREME COURT**

But it did repass in different forms most of the laws the Supreme Court had declared unconstitutional. A majority of the justices now found these laws to be constitutional.

D. Opinions of Checks and Balances. The separation of powers, with its checks and balances, has been criticized for slowing down the work of our government. Sometimes it even appears to halt work altogether. This has usually happened when the President has belonged to one political party and one or both houses of Congress have been controlled by the other party.

Supporters of the system of checks and balances point out that it protects our liberties. It prevents the President or a group of members of Congress from gaining too much power. It also helps to insure that our federal government will not take hasty actions that may later prove unwise. Slow and careful action is especially necessary on controversial issues. Thanks to checks and balances, both sides have time to work out a compromise in Congress. The public also has time to get used to the changes the compromise will bring about.

In war or other emergencies, however, the government has to act quickly. At such times, the President usually takes over all the powers needed, becoming, in effect, dictator for a time. Congress, the federal courts, and the people usually permit this to happen. They feel certain that the President will not be able to make the dictatorship a lasting one, thanks to our system of checks and balances.

REVIEWING THE SECTION

A. Knowing New Terms

In your notebook write the new terms in this section that best complete these statements.

1. Laws are made by the _____ branch of our federal government; they are enforced by the _____ branch; they are interpreted by the _____ branch.
2. Federal judges hold office "during good behavior." This means that they can be removed only by _____ proceedings.
3. Most cases involving federal laws are first heard in a federal _____ court. This court's decision may be appealed by either party to the United States _____ _____. This court's decision may in turn be appealed to the _____ _____, whose decision is final.
4. If a federal or state law violates the Constitution, a federal court can declare the law _____.
5. To prevent dictatorship, the Founding Fathers set up the system of _____ _____ _____ among the three branches of the federal government.

B. Understanding the Facts

PART 1. Tell whether each of these cases would be tried in a federal or state court. Be prepared to give the reasons for your answers in class.

1. A bank robber killed a person during a robbery. He fled to another state, where he killed a trooper who tried to arrest him.
2. The citizens of a certain state sued to keep a newly elected congressman from taking his seat. Their reason was that he did not really live in their state.
3. A dispute arose between New York and New Jersey over the ownership of a small island in New York Harbor.
4. A man was arrested for telephoning an airline to say that he had hidden a bomb on one of its planes.
5. The German government sued for the return of property the American government had taken from its citizens during World War II.
6. A black man sued a local restaurant for refusing to serve him. His reason was that the Civil Rights Act passed by Congress in 1964 made discrimination in public places unlawful.
7. The owner of a yacht was charged with murder because two of the passengers disappeared while on a cruise in the Atlantic.
8. A Wisconsin hunter was arrested for shooting geese protected by a treaty between the United States and Canada.
9. A woman sued because she fell down broken stairs in Yellowstone National Park.
10. A mail-order firm was accused of cheating its customers by selling them a machine guaranteed to cure many kinds of illness by "electronic rays."

PART 2. Tell whether each of the following checks applies to the legislative, executive, or judicial branch of the federal government. (Some of the checks apply to two of these branches.)

1. Congress has the power to impeach federal officials.
2. Congress proposes amendments to the Constitution.
3. No money can be spent by federal officials unless it has been voted by Congress.
4. The Senate approves appointments and ratifies treaties.
5. The President appoints federal judges.
6. The President has the veto power.
7. The President can arouse public opinion against opponents.
8. The federal courts decide whether a law or other federal action is allowed by the Constitution.

C. Summing Up the Chapter

Write "Yes" in your notebook if you think each case following is allowed by the Constitution. Write "No" if you think it is unconstitutional. Be prepared to give the reasons for your answers in class.

1. Can a woman be elected President of the United States?
2. Under the Twenty-Fifth Amendment, can the Vice-President take power when he decides that the President is disabled?
3. Can a disabled President decide when to go back to work without outside approval?
4. If the President calls Congress back in special session to pass a certain law, can it adjourn without taking any action?
5. Can the President prevent the execution of a person sentenced to death by a federal court by granting him or her one reprieve after another?
6. Can Congress force the President to receive the minister of a country the President does not wish to recognize?
7. Can Congress require the President to appoint officials on merit—that is, on the basis of examinations that determine the people best qualified for jobs?
8. Can Congress reduce the number of Supreme Court justices to one or raise it to a hundred?
9. If Congress were afraid that the President was trying to seize power, could it refuse to vote funds for the armed forces?
10. Investigating committees from Congress have sometimes asked to see records kept by the executive department. Can the President refuse to show them these records?

MAKING HISTORY LIVE

1. Watch the newspapers carefully for a week. Make a list of the President's activities during that time. Then tell whether you think the President is overworked or not.
2. Clip a few newspaper articles that tell about conflicts between the different departments of the federal government. Do you think such conflicts are good or bad for our country? Why?
3. Make notes for a discussion of one of the following topics:
   a. The President of the United States has become too powerful. b. The nominating convention is a good show, but a poor way to pick the President. c. "Balancing the ticket" is a poor way to choose our Vice-President. d. A Representative represents a district, a Senator represents a state, but only the President represents the entire nation. e. The Constitution should be amended to give the Vice-President more powers. f. The Supreme Court should not have the final say on our laws. g. Our system of checks and balances should be changed.
4. Help make a classroom display of diagrams, cartoons, posters, and other illustrative materials about our executive and judicial departments.

Chapter 10

OUR CHANGING GOVERNMENT

THE United States has changed a great deal since 1789, the year our federal government was established under the Constitution. At that time our nation had only about four million people. Most of them earned their living by farming. There were only a few industries and these were carried on mainly in small shops and homes. Compared with the great European powers, the United States was a weak and undeveloped nation. Today our country has about 230 million people. It is the world's most advanced industrial nation and its leading power.

The Founding Fathers could not possibly foresee how much the United States would change. They did not know there would be great cities or inventions like the airplane and television. Yet their Constitution has guided our nation successfully through all these changes. That is why it is sometimes called "a living constitution." In this chapter we shall see:

1. How our government has changed to meet new conditions.

2. How our liberties have been preserved even though our government has become so powerful.

How Has Our Federal Government Changed Through the Years?

A. Amending the Constitution. The Founding Fathers knew that our government might have to correct mistakes in the Constitution and make other changes to meet new situations. This meant that the Constitution would have to be amended (changed) from time to time. Article V (see page 720) describes the ways in which amendments can be made. It divides the amending process into two parts, proposal and ratification. It gives two different ways of doing each part.

1. PROPOSING AN AMENDMENT. In the first way, amendments may be proposed by Congress by a two-thirds vote of both houses. In the second way, Congress may call a nationwide convention to propose amendments, if the legislatures of two-thirds of the states ask Congress to do so. This second method resembles the way the Constitution itself was written. It was probably meant to be used only if many changes were necessary. In 1967, for the first time in our history, there was a movement to call such a convention. However, it fell two states short of the two-thirds required by the Constitution. To date, every amendment has been proposed by Congress.

2. RATIFYING A PROPOSED AMENDMENT. When an amendment has been proposed, copies are sent to all the state governments. The amendment is adopted when it has been ratified by the legislatures of three-fourths of the states. This is the first method and it accounts for the ratification of all amendments but one. The second method calls for special conventions to be elected in every state. The amendment goes into effect when it has been ratified by three-fourths of these conventions. Only the Twenty-first Amendment has been ratified in this way.

3. A DIFFICULT PROCEDURE. Because a large majority vote is needed at each step, amending the Constitution is difficult. There have been only twenty-six amendments to date. The first ten amendments, known as the Bill of Rights, were adopted soon after the Constitution itself. Amendments Eleven and Twelve were needed to correct weaknesses in the document. Not counting these amendments, the Constitution has been changed only about four-

THE AMENDMENT PROCESS

AMENDMENT PROPOSED

By two-thirds vote of both houses of Congress *or* By national convention at request of two-thirds of states

AMENDMENT RATIFIED

By three-fourths of state legislatures *or* By three-fourths vote of special state conventions

The United States Customs Service at work. Where do you think this train might be coming from?

teen times in about 190 years. This makes an average of about once every fourteen years.

B. Reasons for the Growth of Federal Power. In spite of the difficulty of amending the Constitution, the federal government has greatly increased its powers through the years. Several reasons account for this. First, our country has grown rapidly, and the government has had to increase its powers in order to keep up. A second reason is the development of modern industry. Congress has had to pass many laws to regulate business, labor, and agriculture. Wars and depressions are a third reason. To deal with a severe depression in the 1930s, Congress passed a number of laws to help the people. For the first time in our history, for example, the federal government created jobs for the unemployed. During the First and Second World Wars, the President became almost a dictator. He raised and directed huge armed forces. He also decided what goods should be produced both for our fighting men and women and for the people at home.

C. Stretching the Constitution. This great increase in government powers has come about mostly without amending the Constitution. By "stretching" the meaning of provisions in the Constitution, our government has been able to make fuller use of the powers it was given. All three branches of the government have worked together to bring this about.

1. THE "ELASTIC CLAUSE." The easiest provision of the Constitution to stretch is the so-called elastic clause. The list of delegated powers (see pages 712-714) ends with the statement that Congress can "make all laws which shall be necessary and proper for carrying into execution [carrying out] the foregoing powers . . ." This clause proved important almost as soon as the new government was organized. The Constitution says nothing about a government bank. Yet the first Congress created the Bank of the United States as a "necessary and proper" means for collecting taxes. Since then, Congress has used the elastic clause many times to justify new laws for our nation. The Supreme Court has generally found such laws constitutional.

2. THE INTERSTATE COMMERCE CLAUSE. Another provision of the Constitution that has been greatly stretched is the interstate commerce clause. The word "commerce" ordinarily applies only to goods. But the word in the Constitution has been held to apply to people as well. Congress therefore has the power to regulate the movement of both people and goods from one state to another. It also controls the immigration of foreigners into the United States and the travel of Americans abroad.

In our nation's early days, when roads were bad, commerce was carried on mainly by water. Look closely at the major rivers of the United States (see map, pages 732-733). You will find that each river, or at least one of its branches, crosses a state border. In 1825 the Supreme Court ruled that Congress has power over every navigable American waterway. (These are waterways that boats can sail on.) Federal permission may therefore be needed to build a dam or bridge even on a small stream. The theory is that the dam or bridge may in some way interfere with interstate commerce.

Railroads were invented in the first half of the nineteenth century. They soon began to carry large amounts of goods overland from state to state. In 1887 Congress created a special federal agency, the Interstate Commerce Commission, to regulate all railroads crossing a state border. Later the commission's powers were broadened to include interstate trucks, buses, and pipelines.

A great deal of commerce now travels by air. Congress has therefore set up the Federal Aviation Agency to make sure that air travel is safe. Messages sent by wire or air are likewise considered a form of interstate commerce. The Federal Communications Commission was established to watch over the telegraph, telephone, radio, and television industries.

In a very important decision, the Supreme Court ruled that an industry is engaged in interstate commerce if its products are shipped across state lines. This ruling brought manufacturing, mining, and farming under Congress' power to regulate interstate commerce. For example, the Fair Labor Standards Act of 1938 set a minimum (lowest) wage for all workers in interstate commerce. This law may cover even the workers in your local dry-cleaning establishment if it does business in more than one state!

D. The "Unwritten Constitution." The federal government has also increased its powers in a third way—through the growth of practices not mentioned in the Constitution. Many of these practices have become firmly established through long use. They are so important that they are often called the "unwritten constitution."

Political parties are an outstanding example of the unwritten constitution. Though not foreseen by the Founding Fathers, they have become an important part of our government machinery. They name candidates for most elective offices in the federal, state, and local governments. As we have seen, they have changed the way the electoral college works and the relationship between the President and Congress. Other important customs are senatorial courtesy, the role of the President's cabinet in our government, and the requirement that representatives live in the district that elects them.

E. The Final Result. How much have the powers of the federal government grown? You can see how much just by looking at what has happened in the executive branch. George Washington was the head of four executive departments that had fewer than a hundred workers. He commanded a very small army and navy. Today the President must watch over thirteen executive departments, dozens of other federal agencies, and huge military bases throughout the world. As chief executive and commander in chief, the President is responsible for about three million workers in the federal civil service and another two million Americans in the armed forces. Some recent Presidents have been deeply concerned with wiping out discrimination and poverty. This makes the welfare of every American the President's concern.

Air traffic control tower at the Dallas-Fort Worth airport. What federal government agency is supposed to make sure air travel is safe? Which clause in the Constitution gives the government the power to deal with air travel?

REVIEWING THE SECTION

A. Knowing New Terms

In your notebook write the new terms in this section that best complete these statements.

1. Changes in the Constitution are known as _____.
2. A change in the Constitution must first be _____ by a two-thirds vote of Congress. Then it must be _____ by three-fourths of the states.
3. The federal government has grown more powerful by stretching parts of the Constitution, especially the _____ clause and the _____ _____ clause.
4. Our government has also changed because of new practices and customs. These are often called the _____ _____.
5. Two examples of such practices and customs are _____ _____ and _____ _____.

B. Understanding the Facts

Write "True" in your notebook if the statement is correct. If the statement contains an error, rewrite it so that it is correct.

1. Every amendment to the Constitution has been proposed by a two-thirds vote of Congress.
2. Every amendment has been ratified by three-fourths of the state legislatures.
3. The President has the power to veto proposed amendments.
4. The Constitution has been amended very few times because it is almost perfect.
5. A farming nation needs a stronger government than an industrial nation.
6. The American people now expect the government to help them through economic depressions.
7. Congress alone decides whether a law is "necessary and proper" under the elastic clause.
8. As a result of Supreme Court decisions, the interstate commerce clause has been stretched to include most types of business.
9. An amendment has to be proposed and ratified to change the "unwritten constitution."
10. The powers of Congress and the Supreme Court have decreased as the powers of the President have increased.

IMPROVING YOUR SKILLS

A. Making an Outline

Outline either **A** or **C** of this section in your notebook. (For a review of outlining, see pages 141-142, 150.)

B. Finding the Main Idea

For each statement below, write in your notebook the *letter* of the heading under which it belongs.

Headings:
- **A. Amending the Constitution**
- **B. Reasons for the Growth of Federal Power**
- **C. Stretching the Constitution**
- **D. The Unwritten Constitution**
- **E. The Final Result**

1. An amendment is adopted when it has been ratified by the legislatures of three-fourths of the states.
2. The Constitution has been changed, on the average, only about once in fourteen years.
3. The development of modern industry has made it necessary for Congress to pass laws on unfair business practices and labor disputes.
4. Political parties have become an important part of our government machinery.
5. Every amendment to date has been proposed by Congress.
6. The easiest provision of the Constitution to stretch is the elastic clause.
7. The first Congress created the Bank of the United States as a "necessary and proper" means for collecting taxes.
8. Today the President watches over thirteen executive departments, a large number of federal agencies, and huge military bases all over the world.
9. The Fair Labor Standards Act of 1938 set a minimum wage for all workers in interstate commerce.
10. The government had to grow as the nation grew in size and population.
11. In the 1930s the federal government gave help to the unemployed for the first time in our history.
12. Important customs we have studied are senatorial courtesy, the role of the President's cabinet, and the requirement that representatives live in the districts that elect them.
13. During the First and Second World Wars, the President became almost a dictator.
14. Federal permission may be needed to build a dam even on a small stream.

How Does the Constitution Protect Our Liberties?

A. Order With Liberty. The troubles Americans had under the Articles of Confederation showed them that a weak government could not hold the nation together. That is why the Founding Fathers created a much stronger government under the Constitution. But they were worried that this strong new federal government might be a threat to the liberties the people had fought so hard to win. "Could a nation enjoy both liberty and order?" they wondered. This question had to be solved to make the new government a success. The Founding Fathers found the answer in the system of checks and balances (see page 153), in a few special provisions of the Constitution, and in the Bill of Rights.

B. Safeguards in the Constitution. The Constitution contains several provisions designed to safeguard (protect) the people's rights. Two of these, derived from the old "rights of Englishmen," are especially important. Section 9 of Article I (see page 714) guarantees every American the right of *habeas corpus*. This means that persons cannot be arrested and held in jail without good reason. They must be told the charges against them. Arrangements must be made quickly for a hearing of the case or a trial. Otherwise, a lawyer can apply to a nearby court for a writ of habeas corpus. This is an order, signed by a judge, either to arrange for an early hearing or to set the prisoner free at once.

Section 10 of Article I forbids the states to impair contracts—that is, to interfere with agreements made by private companies or individuals. This provision is especially important for business people. They can carry on their dealings without having to worry that the government will suddenly upset them.

C. The Bill of Rights. When the Constitution was being ratified, the Anti-Federalists protested that it did not contain enough provisions to protect the people's liberties. The Federalists met this objection by promising to add more safeguards as soon as the Constitution went into effect. This promise was kept. The first Congress drew up ten amendments, modeled on the old "rights of Englishmen" and on provisions in some of the new state constitutions. These amendments are known as the Bill of Rights. They were quickly ratified by three-fourths of the states and added to the Constitution.

1. OUR FIVE BASIC LIBERTIES. The First Amendment is the most important of all. It guarantees the American people five basic liberties—freedom of religion, freedom of speech, freedom of the press, the right of assembly, and the right of petition. Freedom of religion means that people are free to worship as they please. In addition, the government is forbidden to support any church or to set up a religious test for any government post. According to the Supreme Court, the Constitution has "erected a wall" to separate church and state—to prevent the government from mixing in religious questions.

The freedoms of speech and press guarantee all Americans the right to say, write, and publish whatever they please. The Supreme Court has ruled, however, that freedom has its limits. A person has the right to express opinions even though most Americans may dislike them. But

IMPORTANT PROVISIONS OF THE BILL OF RIGHTS

FREEDOM OF SPEECH

FREEDOM OF RELIGION

FREEDOM OF THE PRESS

RIGHT TO ASSEMBLE

RIGHT TO TRIAL BY JURY

FREEDOM FROM UNREASONABLE SEARCH

people do not have the right, as one justice said, to shout "Fire!" in a crowded theater. In other words, the Constitution does not give people the right to harm other people by what they say or write. People guilty of making false charges can be sued by those hurt. In extreme cases, they can be charged with the crime of libel (see page 55).

The right of assembly means that people can come together for any lawful purpose, including criticism of the government. The right of petition allows Americans to complain to government officials and to ask for reforms without fear of punishment. These rights, too, are limited if the public's safety and welfare are in danger. Americans may hold meetings, parades, and demonstrations for many causes. But they may not interfere with traffic, block sidewalks and building entrances, or otherwise harm their fellow citizens.

2. SOME OTHER SAFEGUARDS. The next three amendments deal with other matters. Americans have the right to bear arms. The government may not station troops in their homes in peacetime without their permission. They are protected against "unreasonable searches and seizures." That is, government officials may not enter homes or places of business without a search warrant. To obtain a warrant, they must prove to a judge that a crime or wrong has taken place. The warrant must describe the place to be searched, the articles to be seized, and the people to be arrested. The courts have held that these safeguards do not apply in case of "hot pursuit." Police officers may, for example, enter a home without a warrant, if they are pursuing a thief.

3. THE RIGHTS OF ACCUSED PERSONS. Amendments Five through Eight all deal with the rights of a person accused of a crime or otherwise in trouble with the law. This part of the Bill of Rights is based on the old English

165

Demonstrators against the war in Vietnam trying to enter the Pentagon, where our Defense Department is located. Are such demonstrations allowed by the First Amendment? Was the government right in using force to keep the demonstrators from entering the Pentagon?

principle that a person is innocent until proved guilty "beyond a reasonable doubt." They also reflect the American feeling that the people need to be protected from unjust government officials.

Before a person can be tried for a crime, he or she must be indicted (accused) by a grand jury. The grand jury meets behind closed doors. It decides whether there is enough evidence to hold the accused for trial. If not, he or she is released. This spares the person the trouble and disgrace of a public trial.

Trying a person twice for the same offense (double jeopardy) is forbidden. This means that the government cannot bother a person with new arrests and trials once she or he has been acquitted. On the other hand, a person who has been found guilty is free to appeal for a new trial if she or he wishes.

People cannot be forced to be witnesses against themselves. In recent years, a number of people—including racketeers, Communists, and members of illegal organizations—have "taken the Fifth." Relying on the Fifth Amendment, they have refused to answer questions on the ground that they might incriminate themselves (involve themselves in criminal charges).

A person may not be "deprived of life, liberty, or property, without due process of law" —that is, without a fair trial or hearing. This clause has often been quoted by the Supreme Court in insisting on fairer treatment for people under arrest. The Court has said, for example, that a person must be told his or her rights by the police soon after being arrested. Confessions obtained through force are not admitted as evidence. Questioning a person for hours, without food or rest, has been forbidden as a kind of torture to force a confession.

When the government needs property for public use, it must pay a fair price for it. In case of disagreement with the owner, the price is usually fixed by a judge after a public hearing.

Under the Sixth Amendment, accused persons have the right to a "speedy and public trial, by an impartial [fair] jury" in the district where the crime was committed. They must be told the charges against them. They have the right to confront (to see and question) the witnesses against them. They can call up witnesses in their defense, and they can have a lawyer. If they cannot pay for a lawyer, the government must provide one.

The Eighth Amendment forbids excessive (very high) bail, excessive fines, and cruel and unusual punishments. Bail is money that an accused person leaves on deposit in order to get out of jail before the trial takes place. The amount of bail fixed by the court depends on the kind of crime that has been committed. Bail may be a few hundred dollars for a minor offense or thousands of dollars for a major crime. Cruel and unusual punishments—such as whipping, cutting off parts of the body, and execution by torture—were common in eighteenth-century Europe. The Bill of Rights outlawed them in the United States.

4. AMENDMENTS NINE AND TEN. The last two amendments of the Bill of Rights take care of any matters that might have been overlooked in Amendments One through Eight. Amendment Nine states that the people have other rights besides those listed above. Amendment Ten provides that powers not delegated to the federal government by the Constitution are reserved to the states and people.

D. Importance of the Bill of Rights. The liberties guaranteed by the Bill of Rights have been important to the growth of the United States. By guaranteeing freedom of religion, the Founding Fathers made it possible for people of many different faiths to live and work together in peace. Freedom of speech and the press has several advantages. Because people are free to express their ideas, the American people have an opportunity to choose those ideas they consider best. If an idea works badly, they are free to criticize it and to suggest other ideas. Their criticisms also make the government more efficient. Government officials know that they can be replaced if they do a poor job or fail to carry out the people's wishes.

Much of the Bill of Rights deals with justice for the individual. This emphasis on justice has proved very important. People are grateful to a government that treats them fairly. They are happy knowing that they will be able to enjoy what they have worked for because the government cannot arrest them without good cause or seize their property without payment. As a result, they work harder and the entire nation progresses faster.

The Bill of Rights does not, however, enforce itself. Congress and officials of the executive branch have sometimes violated the rights of individuals. They have usually been restrained by the courts, which have won a reputation as the main defenders of our liberties. But the courts, in turn, need the support of the American people. Supreme Court Justice William O. Douglas has said:

"In a democracy all government rests on the consent of the governed. If 'We the People' do not believe in the Bill of Rights, the courts will not be able effectively to enforce it. Federal judges stand out against the popular opinion of the moment to preserve the enduring principles of the Constitution. But they are able to do so only because the majority of people in the United States, however much they may disagree with a particular decision, agree with the basic principles of the written Constitution, including the power which we give our courts to interpret and enforce it."

Court room scene. Which amendment provides for trial by jury? Why is this right such an important part of the Bill of Rights? Why is it important for the accused to have the right to question witnesses against them?

REVIEWING THE SECTION

A. Knowing New Terms

In your notebook write the new terms in this section that best complete these statements.

1. To keep a person from being held in jail without good reason, the Constitution guarantees the right of _____ _____.
2. Our liberties are also safeguarded by the first ten amendments to the Constitution. They are known as the _____ _____ _____.
3. The First Amendment guarantees the American people freedom of _____, _____, and _____.
4. They also have the right of _____ (to meet for peaceful purposes) and the right of _____ (to ask the government for reforms).
5. Under the Fourth Amendment, an American's home or place of business cannot be searched without a special permit, called a _____.
6. Under the Fifth Amendment, accused persons must be _____ by a grand jury before they can be tried.
7. The Bill of Rights forbids trying persons more than once for the same offense—that is, they may not be placed in _____ _____.
8. Persons cannot be forced to be witnesses against themselves. When they refuse to answer questions that may incriminate them, they are said to be "_____ _____ _____."
9. A person may not be deprived of life, liberty, or property without "_____ _____ of law."
10. Under the Eighth Amendment, the judge cannot keep a person in jail before the trial by setting an excessive amount of _____.

B. Understanding the Facts

PART 1. To compare our rights with practices in a dictatorship, complete this chart in your notebook.

Practices in a Dictatorship	Democratic Rights
1. People held in jail for years without a trial	1.
2. Trial by judges appointed by the dictator	2.
3. Dictator opposes the church or controls it	3.

Practices in a Dictatorship	Democratic Rights
4. Government controls newspapers, TV, radio; criticism considered a serious crime	4.
5. Officials can enter homes whenever they wish	5.
6. Accused persons are forced to confess crimes	6.
7. People jailed and deprived of property without a trial	7.
8. Secret trials	8.
9. Little chance for an accused person to prepare a defense	9.
10. Years of hard labor for even minor crimes	10.

PART 2. Citizens in a democracy have many rights. In return, they are expected to be good citizens and to cooperate with the government. To see how this works out, write in your notebook the way a good citizen should behave in return for each right listed below.

Our Rights	Our Responsibilities
1. Trial by jury	1. (Sample answer) To serve when called for jury duty
2. Freedom of religion	2.
3. Freedom of speech and the press	3.
4. No unreasonable searches and seizures	4.
5. No self-incrimination	5.
6. Many rights of an accused person	6.

Conclusion. What other responsibilities of a good citizen can you mention?

PART 3. In school, many pupils refuse to tell on fellow pupils who are guilty of wrongdoing. Explain why you do or do not consider this an example of responsible citizenship. Give examples.

MAKING HISTORY LIVE

Write in your notebook what your decision would have been if you were the judge in each of the following actual cases. Give the clause in the Constitution on which you would have based your decision.

1. An atheist (a person who does not believe in God) was making a speech in a public park attacking all organized religions. Two police officers arrived and arrested the speaker for disorderly conduct. Was the speaker guilty?
2. A civil rights group marched down the main street of a city, even though the police commissioner had refused them a permit for the parade. They were arrested and charged with disorderly conduct. Were they guilty?
3. An extremist civil rights group wanted the Board of Education of a large city to place more black children in schools in white neighborhoods. Its members blocked the doorways of the Board's building, interrupted the Board's meetings, and encouraged pupils to stay out of school. Was such behavior legal?
4. A leading newspaper criticized officials of a state for the way they had treated civil rights demonstrators. The state charged the newspaper with libel. A state court found the newspaper guilty and ordered it to pay a half-million dollars in damages. Did the Supreme Court uphold the award?
5. Opponents of a government plan to build a new atomic power plant on public land staged a "sit-in" on the land. They refused to move when police asked them to. The police were carrying out a court order to remove the demonstrators from the building site. Could the protesters be arrested?
6. Prisoners are still flogged (whipped) in some states. In one case they appealed to the federal district court for protection from "cruel and unusual punishment." Did they win?
7. A woman charged with burglary was found guilty and sentenced to five years in prison. She appealed on the ground that she had been denied the constitutional right to have a lawyer. The state replied that it provided a lawyer only in cases involving the death penalty. Was the state upheld?
8. After a series of fires, the police arrested a man with a previous record as a firebug. They held him in jail for some time on the ground that they were protecting the public. The man appealed for his release. Did he win?
9. A police officer entered a private home without a search warrant. Unable to find what he was looking for, he questioned the woman living there. The woman refused to answer. So the officer arrested her for resisting an officer. Was the arrest legal?
10. A poor man arrested for robbery remained in jail for months because he could not afford to post the bail of several thousand dollars. His lawyer argued that such a large amount was excessive for her client. Did the lawyer win?

SUMMING UP THE UNIT

Did the Constitution Achieve Its Purposes?

A. The Critical Period. For a few years after the Revolutionary War, the United States struggled along under a weak central government, the Congress of the Confederation. These years have been called the Critical Period in American history. It looked as though the new nation might break up into thirteen quarreling states.

B. Drafting the Constitution. In 1787 a group of leading Americans met in Philadelphia and wrote the Constitution of the United States. This great document set up a much stronger central government than that under the Articles. It was called the federal government. The Constitution delegated (gave) to the federal government some twenty powers, including the power to collect taxes and to regulate foreign and interstate commerce. The post of executive and a system of federal courts were created to enforce the decisions made by Congress.

C. The Separation of Powers. To prevent the rise of a monarch or dictator, the Founding Fathers divided the powers of the federal government among three parts or branches. The legislative branch makes the laws; the executive branch enforces the laws; the judicial branch interprets them. The Constitution has carefully balanced the powers of the three branches so that each serves as a check on the other two.

D. The Legislative Branch. Congress is the legislative branch of the federal government. It makes the laws by a majority vote of both houses. The President has the power to veto a bill, but Congress can override that veto by a two-thirds vote of both houses. The Supreme Court is said to have the last word because it can declare laws unconstitutional.

E. The Executive Branch. The President is our chief executive or head of the executive branch. The President watches over thirteen executive departments, appoints government officials, commands the armed forces, conducts our rela-

Independence Hall in Philadelphia. This building played an important part in our early history. It housed meetings of both the Continental Congress during the Revolution and the convention that drew up the Constitution a few years later. It has been restored as part of a national historic park.

171

tions with foreign nations, and is a party leader. But these powers are checked. The Senate must approve treaties and appointments. Congress controls government spending. The Supreme Court can declare some actions illegal or unconstitutional.

F. The Judicial Branch. The judicial branch consists of a "ladder" of federal courts with the Supreme Court at the top. The federal courts deal with violations of the Constitution or federal laws. The federal courts also deal with cases involving the federal government, two or more states, or foreign nations. They have won a reputation as defenders of the people's liberties.

G. Growth of the Constitution. As our country has expanded, the Constitution has grown to keep up with its needs. Congress, the President, and the federal courts have all "stretched" the Constitution to meet new conditions. The elastic clause and the interstate commerce clause, in particular, have been interpreted more and more loosely through the years. The Constitution has also grown through new customs (the unwritten constitution) and through amendments.

H. The Bill of Rights. The most important amendments were adopted soon after the Constitution went into effect. They are the first ten amendments, known as the Bill of Rights. These guarantee the American people the five basic freedoms and many other precious rights. Some of these rights are especially important to persons accused of wrongdoing. The Bill of Rights has been followed by sixteen other amendments. In later units, we shall learn how these amendments have helped to make our government more democratic and efficient.

I. Conclusion. More than 190 years have passed since 1789, the year our Constitution went into effect. During that time, the Constitution has succeeded in carrying out the six purposes set forth in its Preamble. It has formed a far more perfect union than that under the Articles of Confederation. It has given the American people justice, peace at home, protection from foreign enemies, a high level of prosperity, and the "blessings of liberty." We shall now see how the Constitution has helped to achieve all these goals. Unit Three tells the early part of the story, how the new federal government dealt with the problems left by the Revolutionary War and the Critical Period.

REVIEWING THE UNIT

A. Knowing New Terms

For each term in the first column, write in your notebook the *letter* of the best explanation in the second column.

Terms	Explanations
1. census	a. Court order to release a person who is being held without a hearing
2. committee	
3. elastic clause	
4. filibuster	b. Argument that the federal government has too much power
5. impeachment	
6. habeas corpus	c. Refusal to answer questions on the ground that they may incriminate you
7. bail	
8. pocket veto	
9. "taking the Fifth"	d. Constitutional provision allowing Congress to make all "necessary and proper" laws
10. states' rights	
	e. Count of the American people, used to decide the number of representatives each state can have
	f. Court order releasing persons from prison
	g. Method used by a Senate minority to kill a bill it opposes
	h. First step in the removal of high officials by Congress
	i. Group of members of Congress, who study a bill after it is introduced
	j. Money put up by an accused person to obtain release from jail while awaiting trial
	k. Permission for government officials to search a private home or business
	l. Simple way for the President to kill a number of bills at the same time

B. Understanding the Facts

Choose the item in each group that does *not* belong with the others.

1. *Northwest Ordinance:* admission of territories as states, aid for education, dealings with Spain, prohibition of slavery
2. *Founding Fathers:* Benjamin Franklin, Abraham Lincoln, James Madison, George Washington
3. *Constitutional Convention:* Bill of Rights, federal system of government, Great Compromise, three-fifths compromise

4. *Great Compromise:* Congress, electoral college, House of Representatives, Senate
5. *North-South compromise:* Senators elected by state legislatures, slave trade allowed for twenty years, tax on exports forbidden, three-fifths of slaves counted for representation
6. *Separation of powers:* introducing laws, making laws, enforcing laws, interpreting laws
7. *Presiding officers in Congress:* President of the United States, president pro tempore, Speaker, Vice-President of the United States
8. *Making laws:* committee system, public hearings, roll call, Supreme Court decisions
9. *Powers of Congress:* to coin money, to control foreign commerce, to conduct foreign policy, to raise an army and navy
10. *Constitutional powers of the President:* chief executive, chief of foreign policy, commander in chief of the armed forces, party chief
11. *President's influence on lawmaking:* calling a special session of Congress, impeachment, making appointments, "State of the Union" message
12. *Amending the Constitution:* proposal by Congress, proposal by the President, ratification by state conventions, ratification by state legislatures
13. *Growth of the Constitution:* amendments, elastic clause, interstate commerce clause, supremacy clause
14. *Types of voting in the Constitution:* simple majority, two-thirds, three-fourths, unanimous
15. *Parts of the Constitution:* Articles I-IV, Bill of Rights, Declaration of Independence, Preamble

MAKING HISTORY LIVE

1. Tell about an experience that you or someone you know had, in which the rights guaranteed by the Bill of Rights proved important.
2. Make notes for a class debate on one of the following questions:
a. Should the federal government establish the same requirements for voting throughout the United States? b. Should sixteen-year-olds be allowed to vote? c. Should the leaders of congressional committees be selected by the members of the committees and not by seniority? d. Should the electoral college be abolished and the President be elected directly by the people? e. Should the Constitution be amended to reduce the President's powers? f. Should the voters have the last word, through a nationwide vote, whenever the Supreme Court declares a law unconstitutional?

3. Serve as one of four speakers in a panel discussion. The first speaker should represent Congress, the second the President, the third the Supreme Court, and the fourth the people of the United States. Tell the class what your powers are. Then let the class question you on the ways in which your powers are limited. At the end of the discussion, the class should decide by vote which one of the four is the most powerful of all. Prepare by making notes on each of the four positions.
4. If you have visited Washington, D.C., tell about the government activities and other interesting things you saw. If you have not made such a visit, go to the library and write a report on them.

RECOMMENDED READING

A. Historical Books

ACHESON, P. C. *Our Federal Government: How It Works*. rev. ed. New York: Dodd, Mead, 1979.

BOGGS, J. *American Revolution: Pages from a Negro Worker's Notebook*. New York: Monthly Review Press, 1963.

BRECKENRIDGE, A. C. *Electing the President*. Lanham, Md.: Univ. Press of America, 1982.

CHIDSEY, D. B. *Mr. Hamilton and Mr. Jefferson*. Nashville: Nelson, 1975.

COOKE, D. E. *America's Great Document—the Constitution*. Maplewood, N.J.: Hammond, 1970.

DUPUY, R. E., and DUPUY, T. N. *An Outline History of the American Revolution*. New York: Harper & Row, 1975.

JEFFERSON, T. *Democracy*. Ed. S. K. Padover. Reprint of 1939 ed. Westport, Conn.: Greenwood Press, n.d.

LAWSON, D. *The Changing Face of the Constitution*. New York: Franklin Watts, 1979.

LIEBERMAN, J. K. *Free Speech, Free Press, and the Law*. New York: Lothrop, Lee & Shepard, 1980.

NORTON, M. B., ed. *Liberty's Daughters: The Revolutionary Experience of American Women, 1750–1800*. Boston: Little, Brown, 1980.

RADDING, C. *The Modern Presidency*. New York: Franklin Watts, 1979.

B. Biographies

FARRAND, M. *Fathers of the Constitution*. Chronicles of America, vol. 13. New York: U.S. Pubs.

FLEXNER, J. T. *Washington: The Indispensable Man*. Boston: Little, Brown, 1974.

KENNEDY, J. F. *Profiles in Courage*. New York: Harper & Row, 1961. Stories of brave Senators, written by one of our former Presidents, when he was a young Senator.

MEANS, M. *The Woman in the White House*. New York: Random House, 1963. The stories of twelve outstanding "First Ladies."

WHITNEY, D. C. *American Presidents: Biographies of the Chief Executives from Washington Through Carter*. Garden City, N.Y.: Doubleday, 1979.

WILLIAMS, S. R. *Demeter's Daughters*. New York: Atheneum, 1976.

C. Historical Fiction

BEERS, L. *The Crystal Cornerstone*. New York: Harper & Row, 1953.

FAST, H. *April Morning*. New York: Bantam, 1962. A boy at the battle of Lexington.

UNDER MY WINGS EVERY THING

Above, New Orleans in 1803; below, New Orleans in 1852.

Unit Three

OUR NATION BECOMES STRONG

A visitor to New York City in 1840 reported: "All is hurry and bustle; the very carts, instead of being drawn by horses at a walking pace, are often met at a gallop. [The people] seem to enjoy this bustle, and add to it by their own pace."

Why did Americans so early gain a reputation as a fast-moving, hard-working people? For one thing, in the United States hard work was rewarded with success. For another, there was much work to be done. Americans had half a continent to settle. Their labors quickly changed the wilderness to fertile farmlands and busy cities.

A large part of this great task was accomplished in the half-century or so after the Constitution went into effect. The population of the United States multiplied almost six times in two generations. From 4,000,000 in 1790 it grew to 23,000,000 in 1850. In the same period the nation's area more than tripled. The number of states rose from thirteen to thirty-one, and the number of cities increased from just a half-dozen to more than eight thousand! In 1850 America's farms and plantations produced more than a billion dollars' worth of food and raw materials. Its industries turned out almost as much in manufactured goods.

In this unit we shall see why the United States developed so rapidly. We shall learn the following:

1. *How the early Presidents established a strong government.*
2. *How the United States fought Great Britain a second time and grew stronger as a result.*
3. *How economic progress changed each section of the United States.*
4. *How American democracy continued to advance.*
5. *How the United States expanded westward to the Pacific.*
6. *How American culture progressed.*

UNIT 3: 1789-1849

1789	Hamilton's financial program
1793	Washington's Proclamation of Neutrality
1794	Jay's Treaty / Whiskey Rebellion
1789-1800	Undeclared war with France
1803	Purchase of Louisiana
1812-1814	War with Great Britain
1823	Monroe Doctrine
1825	Erie Canal
1832	South Carolina threatens to leave the Union / Jackson's war on the Bank of the United States
1837	Panic of 1837
1846-1848	Mexican War
1848	Gold discovered in California

Chapter 11

BEGINNING THE NEW GOVERNMENT

IN 1789, when the new federal government began its work, the situation of the United States was still critical. Many Americans questioned whether the new government would be strong enough to handle the nation's problems. Others feared that it would be too strong or that the President would want to become a monarch.

Almost every American, however, had complete confidence in one man—"The Father of His Country," George Washington. By unanimous vote of the electoral college, he became the first President of the United States. Washington had been a great general, but he had had little experience in government. "Would he also be a great political leader?" people wondered. Would he be able to build an effective government on the foundation the Constitution provided? Would he be able to solve the nation's economic problems, unite the quarreling states, and win the respect of foreign nations?

How Did the New Government Handle Its Problems at Home?

A. The First Cabinet. As the first President, Washington had a very heavy responsibility. "I walk on untrodden ground," he said. "There is scarcely any part of my conduct which may not hereafter be drawn into precedent." In other words, almost any of his actions might become an example for later governments to follow. One important precedent was Washington's creation of a cabinet made up of the heads of the executive departments (see page 147).

The first cabinet consisted of four very able men. Washington appointed Thomas Jefferson, author of the Declaration of Independence, as his secretary of state. Jefferson had many years of political experience. He had served as a member of the Continental Congress, as governor of Virginia, and as minister to France. The secretary of the treasury, Alexander Hamilton, was a brilliant young lawyer who had served as Washington's aide in the Revolutionary War. At the Constitutional Convention, Hamilton had fought for a very strong central government. The secretary of war, Henry Knox, had been one of Washington's best generals during the Revolution. Attorney General Edmund Randolph was, like Jefferson, a former governor of Virginia. He later took Jefferson's place as secretary of state.

B. Hamilton's Financial Program. As secretary of the treasury, Hamilton held the most important cabinet position during Washington's first term. The Congress of the Confederation had left the nation with an empty treasury and heavy debts. Because it could not pay these debts, it had lost the confidence of foreign nations and American business people.

Hamilton placed before Congress a three-part program to solve the nation's financial (money) problems. His goals were to pay back the nation's debts, to balance its income and spending, and to restore the people's confidence in the government. He especially wanted to win the support of wealthy business people. They would strengthen the new government, he believed, and lead the United States to prosperity.

1. PAYING THE DEBTS. The nation had three kinds of debts, all dating back to the Revolutionary War. The first kind was the foreign debt. The central government owed about $12,000,000 to France, the Netherlands, and Spain. Congress quickly agreed that this money should be paid back in full.

The second kind was the domestic debt—that is, money owed to American citizens. This consisted largely of promissory notes issued by the central government to veterans of the Revolutionary War (see page 109). With interest, the domestic debt amounted to about $45,000,000. Hamilton's plan called for repaying this amount in full.

This part of his program met with strong opposition in Congress. Most of the original holders of the notes, needing money, had sold them to wealthy business people. They had usually received only a small part of the face value—as little as ten cents on the dollar! Even while Congress was discussing Hamil-

180

ton's proposal, business people were buying up large numbers of notes from holders who did not know what was happening. If Congress agreed to pay the full amount, these rich people would make a great profit at the taxpayers' expense. Some members of Congress suggested that only original holders of the notes should be paid in full. Hamilton insisted, however, that all note holders had to be paid if the people were to have confidence in the new government. Hamilton's proposal was finally accepted by Congress.

The third kind of debt was owed by the states. Like the central government, the states had borrowed to meet the heavy expenses of the Revolutionary War. Some states had paid all or most of their debts; others had paid little or nothing. Hamilton proposed that the federal government should take over all unpaid state debts. These amounted to well over $20,000,000. He argued that all Americans should help to pay these debts because the money had been spent to win the independence of the entire country. He also wanted to show that the federal government was stronger than the states.

Members of Congress from states that owed large sums supported Hamilton. The rest objected to paying the debts of other states. The bill for paying these debts was defeated in the House of Representatives by two votes. But Hamilton did not give up. Virginia's representatives, who had voted against the bill, wanted the new capital of the federal government built in the South. Hamilton made a deal with them. If they voted for his plan, he would help them obtain the votes they needed to locate the new capital in Virginia. They agreed, and the bill to pay the state debts was passed by Congress. Hamilton kept his part of the bargain. The city of Washington, named in honor of the President, was built on a piece of land that Virginia gave to the federal government. This tiny federal territory was named the District of Columbia (see map, page 214).

2. RAISING THE NECESSARY FUNDS. The debts taken over by the federal government amounted to about $75,000,000. Since the new government did not have such a large sum, Hamilton printed government bonds, which he offered in exchange for the old notes. People made the exchange because they believed that the new government would be able to pay off the bonds when they fell due. Until then, it would pay them interest each year.

To pay the interest, the treasury needed several million dollars a year. It needed several million dollars more to pay the salaries of government workers and to carry on the activities the Constitution had delegated to the federal government. Hamilton wanted to pay the government's expenses mainly by placing a small tariff on goods imported from abroad. He also wanted Congress to pass some federal excise taxes—that is, taxes on goods made or sold within the United States. The main excise tax was on the manufacture of large amounts of whiskey.

Congress voted all the taxes Hamilton asked for. The Whiskey Tax, however, aroused strong opposition, chiefly in the newly settled lands west of the Appalachian Mountains. The

Washington's first inauguration. A statue of Washington marks the spot on Wall Street in New York City where he took the oath of office. The federal government moved to Philadelphia a year later.

Cause of the Whiskey Rebellion: Whiskey took up only one-sixth as much space as the grain from which it was made.

western farmers could not send their grain to market because distances were long and roads were bad. So they made the grain into whiskey, which was much easier to ship. They insisted that the Whiskey Tax was unfair because they were the only group of ordinary Americans that had to pay it. In western Pennsylvania groups of farmers rose in protest. They sent a strongly worded message to Congress, refused to pay the tax, and attacked the tax collectors. These were the very same methods that had once been used against the British.

Hamilton seized this opportunity to show how strong the new federal government was. He persuaded Washington to call up fifteen thousand militiamen. He accompanied the troops, under the command of Henry Lee, across the mountains to crush the "Whiskey Rebellion." The farmers fled as the force approached. Nevertheless, he managed to capture a few of the leaders. Two were tried and found guilty of treason, but were pardoned by President Washington. The speed with which the Whiskey Rebellion was put down pleased merchants. They remembered Shays's Rebellion (see page 109) and were glad that the new government meant to keep order.

3. Establishing the Bank of the United States. The third part of Hamilton's program also met with strong opposition. He proposed that Congress should charter a special bank. It was to be known as the Bank of the United States. Despite its name, this bank was to be owned and controlled by private individuals. It would have three functions. First, it would handle the government's financial affairs. It would hold the money collected by the government in taxes, pay the government's bills, and lend the government money. Second, it would open branches all over the country to serve business people. Third, it would give the nation a sound currency. People would accept the bank's notes as money because they were backed by the government's funds.

Congress passed the bank bill. When it reached the President, he asked members of his cabinet for their opinions. Jefferson objected to the bank on the ground that its wealthy owners would have too much power. He also thought that it was unconstitutional because the right to charter a bank had not been mentioned among the powers delegated to Congress. Hamilton argued, however, that the bank was constitutional under the elastic clause (see page 160). Washington agreed with Hamilton and signed the bank bill.

C. Results of Hamilton's Financial Program. The Bank of the United States issued ten mil-

Bank of the United States in Philadelphia. This fine building shows how important the bank was. Why did Jefferson oppose the bank?

lion dollars' worth of stock (shares sold to the public). The entire amount was sold in a few hours, mostly to rich business people. The success of the stock sale showed that the country was prosperous and that merchants had confidence in the new government. Hamilton had clearly succeeded in achieving his main goals. He had taken care of the nation's debts, he had put the new government's finances in order, and he had won the support of the wealthy business class.

REVIEWING THE SECTION

A. Knowing New Terms

In your notebook write the new terms in this section that best complete these statements.
1. By creating a cabinet of the heads of the executive departments, Washington set an example, or _____, still followed today.
2. The new federal government agreed to pay back both the money owed to European nations, or the _____ debt, and the money owed to American citizens, or the _____ debt.
3. To meet the government's financial needs, Congress used two kinds of taxes: _____ on goods imported into the United States and _____ taxes on goods made and sold within the United States.
4. The government's funds were handled by a new bank, called the _____ _____ _____ _____ _____. This bank was controlled by the wealthy business people who bought most of the shares of its _____.

B. Understanding the Facts

Complete this chart by listing the part of Hamilton's financial program that achieved each of his goals.

Hamilton's Goals	His Financial Policies
1. To pay the nation's debts 2. To put the nation's finances in order 3. To win the support of wealthy business people	1. 2. 3.

C. Finding the Reasons

One, two, or even all three answers to each question may be correct. Write the letters of *all* the correct answers in your notebook.

1. Why was Washington unanimously elected the first President under the Constitution?
   a. He had played the leading part in winning the Revolutionary War. b. He had had a great deal of political experience as a member of the Continental Congress. c. The American people trusted him.
2. Why was Washington's responsibility greater than that of later Presidents?
   a. He had no other Presidents to follow as his models. b. His actions set many precedents for future chief executives. c. He had to live up to his reputation as "The Father of His Country."
3. Why did many in Congress object to paying the domestic debt in full?
   a. The Continental Congress had given away its notes to many people who did not deserve the money. b. Many original holders of the notes had sold them to rich business people at low prices. c. The people who had bought the notes would make a fortune if the government paid them in full.
4. Why did Hamilton want the federal government to pay the state debts?
   a. He expected that the states would help to pay the federal debt. b. He had bought many notes himself and expected to make a large profit on them. c. He wanted to show that the federal government was strong.
5. Why did the farmers of western Pennsylvania oppose the Whiskey Tax?
   a. They bought and drank a good deal of whiskey. b. It was a tax on the small amounts of whiskey they made for their own use. c. It was a tax on the large amounts of whiskey they made for sale.
6. Why did Hamilton create the Bank of the United States?
   a. It would handle the government's funds. b. It would give the nation a sound currency. c. It would help win the support of wealthy business people for the new federal government.
7. Why did Jefferson object to the Bank of the United States?
   a. He believed that the federal government did not have power under the Constitution to charter the bank. b. He objected to giving power to the wealthy people who owned most of the bank's stock. c. He was jealous because President Washington liked Hamilton's ideas better than his.

IMPROVING YOUR SKILLS

A. Reading the Time Line

Look at the time line on page 178. Then answer the following questions:
1. What are the dates for the beginning and end of this unit?
2. How many years does this unit cover?
3. How many years have passed since the end of the unit?

4. How much of our history as an independent nation will you be studying in this unit?
5. Name three wars that took place during the period shown here.
6. Did the War of 1812 occur before or after the Monroe Doctrine was issued?
7. During which decade did the United States suffer an economic depression? What was the depression called?

B. Interpreting the Graph

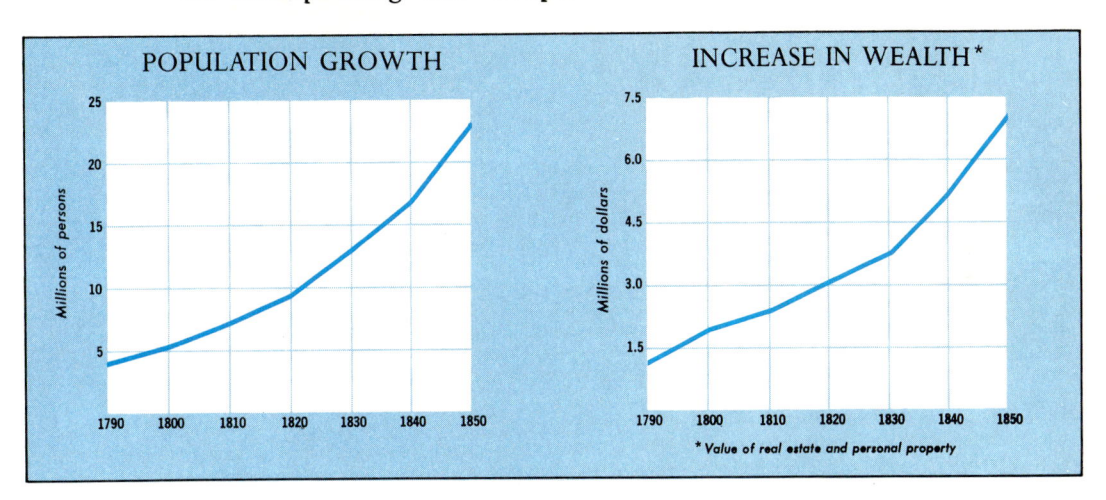

After studying these graphs, answer the following questions.

GRAPH 1. Population Growth
1. During which decades (ten-year periods) did the population of the United States increase?
2. During which decade did the population increase the least?
3. During which decade did the population increase the most?
4. How many times as large was the population in 1850 as in 1790?

GRAPH 2. Increase in Wealth
1. During which decades did the wealth of the United States increase?
2. During which decade did the wealth increase the least?
3. During which decade did it increase the most?
4. How many times as large was the wealth of the United States in 1850 as in 1790?

Conclusion. Which of the following phrases best describes the way the population and wealth of the United States increased between 1790 and 1850? a. Slow but steady b. Slow and uncertain c. Fast and steady d. Fast but uncertain.

How Did President Washington Deal With Foreign Nations?

A. The French Revolution and Its Effects. George Washington considered himself a planter and military man, not a politician. He had not wanted to become President of the United States. As his term of office neared its end, he spoke with pleasure of returning to his estate at Mount Vernon. But Jefferson and Hamilton persuaded him to run for office a second time. They insisted that the nation still needed him because it now faced a crisis in its foreign policy.

The new crisis arose as a result of the French Revolution. In 1789, the same year that our federal government began, the French people revolted against their absolute monarchy. The French Revolution was not very violent at first. Its leaders left the king on the throne, but limited his powers. They also made some other long-needed reforms and issued an important document, the Declaration of the Rights of Man. This expressed the same democratic ideals as our Declaration of Independence and Bill of Rights.

After a short while, however, events in France took a different turn. The leaders of the Revolution were not able to solve the nation's problems. To hold the people's support, they declared war on the monarchs of Europe! France was soon invaded by several enemy armies. Then the government fell into the hands of a group of radicals (people who wish to make great changes). They declared France a republic, arrested the king and queen, and began the Reign of Terror. They executed thousands of people, many from the upper and middle class. After about a year of bloodshed, the radicals were overthrown and the Reign of Terror ended. But the wars between France and the other European powers continued, with hardly a break, for another twenty years.

B. Washington's Proclamation of Neutrality. The war in Europe created a difficult problem for the United States. The new French government asked our government for military aid. There were some strong reasons for agreeing to help. France had been our ally in the Revolutionary War. It was still our ally under the treaty signed at that time (see page 80). The European monarchies it was fighting included Great Britain, which we still considered our enemy. Finally, the French people were struggling for liberty and democracy, just as we had done.

Most Americans wanted the United States to help France. When a new French minister visited the United States, he was greeted by cheering crowds wherever he went. In the President's cabinet, Jefferson favored aid to France short of getting into the war.

Hamilton, on the other hand, again expressed the business people's point of view. He argued that American aid to France would anger Great Britain. Since the British were the main buyers of American products and their fleet ruled the seas, they could easily ruin American trade. They might even declare war on the United States. Our nation, Hamilton argued, was still young and weak. It needed a long period of peace to build up its wealth and strength.

Once again President Washington sided with Hamilton. In 1793 he issued a statement of America's foreign policy known as the Proclamation of Neutrality. The President told the American people and the world that the United States intended to remain neutral—that is, it would help neither side in the European war. Washington's proclamation aroused violent public protest in the United States. According to Vice-President Adams, "Ten thousand people in Philadelphia [then the federal capital] day after day threatened to drag Washington out of his house, and effect a revolution in the Government, or compel it to declare war in favor of the French Revolution and against England."

C. Jay's Treaty With Great Britain. President Washington soon took a second unpopular step. He sent a special minister, Chief Justice John Jay, to settle our differences with Great Britain. The British fleet had seized almost two hundred American ships that were attempting to trade with the French West Indies. The crews had been thrown into prison or forced to serve in the British navy. (For details, see page 207.)

A second cause of trouble between Great Britain and the United States had developed over the Northwest Territory. The British had agreed in the Treaty of Paris to give this region to the United States. Yet they continued to hold forts and fur-trading posts there. British traders gave the Indians guns and whiskey for their furs. Once armed and aroused by "firewater," the Indians often attacked American settlers who had settled on Indian land.

John Jay succeeded in settling some of these differences. The British agreed to leave the Northwest Territory and to pay for the ships they had seized. In return, the United States agreed to pay back debts owed by Americans to British merchants since the Revolutionary War. The British refused, however, to discuss their treatment of American sailors. They also continued to restrict American trade with the West Indies.

Jay's Treaty was bitterly attacked by the American public. The Supreme Court Justice was labeled "Sir John Jay, the traitor." His effigy (image) was hanged from lampposts all over the country. Nevertheless, Washington persuaded the Senate to ratify his treaty because it was the best the United States could obtain at the time. The President also raised an army to fight the Indians in the Northwest Territory. The American force, led by General "Mad Anthony" Wayne, a Revolutionary

Burning Jay's effigy. In the eighteenth century people showed their dislike of an important person by burning a straw figure. How do people show their dislike today?

Mount Vernon in Virginia. George Washington inherited the estate from his half brother and made additions to the mansion. Why is it important to preserve such historic sites?

War hero, won a decisive victory over the hostile Indian tribes.

D. The Treaty With Spain. The President now turned to the problems of settlers in the Southwest. Spain, seeking to control the territory, had closed the Mississippi River and the port of New Orleans to American trade (see map, page 201). It was also encouraging Indian tribes in Florida to attack American settlers across the border.

Washington sent another special minister to Spain to deal with both problems. Strangely enough, the Spaniards welcomed him. Because of Jay's Treaty, they were afraid that the Americans and British had reached a secret agreement to attack Florida and Louisiana. They readily agreed to sign a treaty granting Americans free use of the Mississippi River. This included the right to transfer goods from riverboats to ocean-going vessels at New Orleans without paying tariff duties. The treaty also established the boundary between Florida and the United States. This was set much farther south than the Spanish had earlier claimed it should be.

E. Washington's Retirement. By this time Washington was worn out by the strains of the presidency. He was also angered by bitter attacks on his policies and his character. He refused to run for a third term of office. His decision set another precedent, that a President should serve only two terms.

When Washington took office in 1789, many people doubted whether the new federal government of the United States would succeed. When Washington left the presidency eight years later, the nation was secure and prosperous. Government bonds were selling at a price far above their face value. American trade, thanks in part to the war in Europe, was growing rapidly. The United States had managed to remain neutral in the war and to gain the respect of the European powers. As a result of its treaties with Great Britain and Spain and its victory over the Indians, the western lands were being rapidly settled. "The Father of His Country" had good reason to feel satisfied when he retired at last to his beloved Mount Vernon.

REVIEWING THE SECTION

A. Knowing New Terms

Write the meanings of these important terms in your notebook *in your own words.*

(In **A**) radicals
      Reign of Terror

(In **B**) Proclamation of Neutrality
      neutral

(In **C**) effigy

B. Understanding the Facts

PART 1. Write "True" in your notebook if the statement is correct. If the statement contains an error, rewrite it so that it is correct.

1. President Washington refused to run for a second term.
2. There was much more fighting among the French during the French Revolution than among Americans during the American Revolution.
3. The wars started in Europe by the French Revolution lasted much longer than the Revolutionary War in America.
4. Most Americans, including business people, wanted the American government to help France.
5. Hamilton argued that Great Britain was much more important to the United States than France was.
6. President Washington took Hamilton's advice to side with Great Britain in the war.
7. Jay's Treaty failed to settle any of the important differences between Great Britain and the United States.
8. After Jay's Treaty, American settlers in the Northwest Territory were not troubled by Indian attacks for years.
9. Because of Jay's Treaty, Spain was more willing to sign a treaty with the United States.
10. The treaty with Spain was more favorable to the United States than the treaty with Great Britain.

PART 2. Here is a list of the most important actions taken during President Washington's two terms in office. Write "Good" in your notebook if you think an action was good for the United States. Write "Bad" if you think an action hurt our country. Write "Mixed" if you think an action had both good and bad effects. Be prepared to defend your answers in class.

1. Starting the President's cabinet
2. Paying all debts—foreign, domestic, and state
3. Using tariffs to raise the money the government needed
4. Collecting excise taxes on whiskey and other American products
5. Crushing the Whiskey Rebellion
6. Founding the Bank of the United States
7. Refusing to help France—proclaiming the neutrality of the United States
8. Signing a treaty with Great Britain
9. Signing a treaty with Spain
10. Setting the precedent that a President shall not serve more than two terms

Conclusion. Was George Washington a great President?

IMPROVING YOUR SKILLS

Making an Outline

You have learned to make an outline by following the headings, subheadings, and paragraphs in the text (see pages 141 and 150). Sometimes it is necessary to go a step further because a single paragraph may contain several important facts, causes, or results. This section contains six such paragraphs. Their headings are given below. Outline at least two of them. First copy the heading into your notebook. Then fill in the important facts.

HOW DID PRESIDENT WASHINGTON DEAL WITH FOREIGN NATIONS?

B. Washington's Proclamation of Neutrality
   1. Arguments for American Aid to France
      a.
      b.
      c.
   2. Arguments Against American Aid to France
      a.
      b.
      c.

C. Jay's Treaty With Great Britain
   3. Terms of Jay's Treaty
      a.
      b.

D. The Treaty With Spain
   2. Terms of the Treaty With Spain
      a.
      b.
      c.

E. Washington's Retirement
   1. Reasons Why Washington Refused a Third Term
      a.
      b.
   2. Washington's Achievements
      a.
      b.
      c.
      d.
      e.

How Did Political Parties Arise?

A. The Reason for Political Parties. In President Washington's Farewell Address to the American people, he warned against two dangers. One was involvement in Europe's wars. The other was "the baneful [harmful] effects of the spirit of party." The second part of his warning referred to the two new political parties that had just been formed. Washington thought that political parties were a great evil because they divided the American people into rival groups, each violent in its attacks on the other. Such behavior, Washington believed, would keep the American government from acting in the best interests of the nation.

In spite of the warnings of Washington and other Founding Fathers, political parties soon became important. There is a basic reason why political parties spring up in democracies. People tend to join with other people who have ideas like their own. By forming groups, they can win greater support. When they are strong enough, the government will usually adopt their ideas. That is why the American people divided into two groups, the Patriots and the Loyalists, during the Revolutionary War. That is why they became Federalists and Anti-Federalists when the Constitution was being ratified (see page 125). It was only natural that they should divide a third time over Hamilton's financial program, which affected most Americans in one way or another.

B. The Federalist Party. Like the supporters of the Constitution a few years earlier, Hamilton and his followers called themselves Federalists. The name showed that they supported a strong federal government. They also believed that the government should be controlled by a small ruling class of "the rich, the wellborn, and the able." The Federalists naturally attracted the support of bankers, shippers, merchants, and other wealthy business people. They were also backed by most of the clergy, teachers, and other educated people, who helped them to win over many ordinary voters. They were especially strong in the Northeast, where most of the country's trade and industry was centered. Because of their business interests, they favored friendly relations with Great Britain. The French Revolution, with its radical ideas and bloodshed, frightened them.

C. The Democratic-Republican Party. Thomas Jefferson led the people who opposed Hamilton and his program. Feeling that Washington had been won over by the Federalists, Jefferson left the cabinet in 1793. He was then free to organize an opposition party. He called it the Democratic-Republican party to show that it favored a republic run by the common people.

The Democratic-Republican party was supported by small farmers, shopkeepers, and craftworkers, especially in the South and West. They probably outnumbered the Federalists, but many of them did not own enough property to vote or were not interested in politics. To arouse and organize them, Jefferson started political clubs and newspapers all over the country.

The Democratic-Republicans attacked Ham-

ALEXANDER HAMILTON: ARISTOCRATIC COMMONER

Alexander Hamilton was a remarkable man. Born of poor parents on a small island in the British West Indies, he became through his own efforts one of the most important men in the United States. Even as a boy, Hamilton was outstanding. At the age of fourteen, he was running his uncle's store and writing articles for the local newspaper. One article about a hurricane attracted the attention of some wealthy people. They raised money to send young Alexander to college on the American mainland.

In 1774, at the age of seventeen, Hamilton won nation-wide fame by writing pamphlets urging the colonists to rebel against British rule. When the Revolution began, he enlisted. He soon won praise for his bravery and skill as an officer. General Washington, who recognized his gifts, made him an aide. Hamilton, the general said, could do more work than ten other aides put together.

After the war, Hamilton became a leading lawyer in New York City. But government was his main interest. In 1782 he proposed that the Congress of the Confederation should have the power to raise taxes. When this proposal failed, he worked for a convention to create a strong new central government. Chosen a delegate to the Constitutional Convention, he offered a plan for a very strong central government. This plan too was defeated. Hamilton nevertheless joined with Madison and Jay in writing a series of articles defending the new Constitution. These articles, known as the *Federalist Papers,* convinced many Americans that the Constitution should be ratified. Soon afterward Hamilton became the first secretary of the treasury of the new government. He did so much to make it a success that he has often been called our greatest secretary of the treasury.

After leaving the government in 1795, Hamilton remained active as a leader of the Federalist party in New York. There he clashed often with Aaron Burr, a leader of the Republicans. In 1800 Hamilton kept Burr from becoming President instead of Jefferson. In 1804 he kept his rival from being elected governor of New York. Angered, Burr challenged Hamilton to a duel. Hamilton, who was against dueling, accepted the challenge because he did not want people to think him a coward. But he did not fire at his opponent. Burr, on the other hand, took careful aim and fatally wounded the man he hated.

Hamilton was only forty-seven years old when he died. He had performed great services for our nation. Yet his influence was already declining. For he believed, in spite of his own humble background, in government by an upper class or aristocracy. "All countries," he had written, "divide themselves into the few and the many. The first are the rich and wellborn; the other the mass of the people, turbulent [stormy] and changing. They seldom judge or determine right. Give therefore to the first class a distinct, permanent share in the Government." Our nation's future, as we know, did not lie with the aristocracy Hamilton wanted. It lay with those who, like Thomas Jefferson, believed in democracy.

THOMAS JEFFERSON: ARISTOCRAT FOR DEMOCRACY

Thomas Jefferson was a member of the upper class by birth. His father was a plantation owner; his mother belonged to one of Virginia's leading families. He was educated in one of the best colonial colleges and moved in the best society. Yet Jefferson was a champion of democracy. The common people, he wrote, "may safely be trusted to hear everything true and false, and to form a correct judgment." He also had other ideas ahead of his time. He believed in equality, religious toleration, freedom of speech and the press, free education for the poor, and freedom for slaves. He also believed that the people have the right to rebel against unjust rulers. "A little rebellion now and then," he wrote, "is a good thing; the tree of liberty must be refreshed from time to time with the blood of patriots and tyrants."

Jefferson worked hard to put his ideas into practice. Before the Revolution, he was a member of Virginia's Committee of Correspondence. When the war began, he served in the Continental Congress and wrote the Declaration of Independence. Then he became governor of Virginia and helped to write its new state constitution. Next he went as minister to France, where he helped to spread American ideals of democracy. After his return to the United States, he served as our secretary of state, founded the Democratic-Republican party, and became our third President.

Politics was only one of Jefferson's interests. From an early age, he studied and wrote for hours every day. He knew a half-dozen different languages and could discuss almost any field of knowledge. Yet he liked horseback riding, dancing, and music. Like Washington, he was an excellent farmer and experimented with new crops and methods on his plantation. He was also an architect. He designed his own home at Monticello, the University of Virginia, and several other famous buildings. Jefferson was an inventor too. Visitors to Monticello can still see his seven-day clock, revolving desk, and other interesting home improvements. Far more important, however, was the plow he invented. It came into wide use because it dug more deeply into the ground than the other plows of the time.

After he left the presidency, Jefferson continued to work hard. He wrote on many subjects and kept in touch with hundreds of people at home and abroad. Historians have collected more than fifty volumes of his writings—and over fifty thousand letters besides!

Jefferson died on July 4, 1826, the fiftieth anniversary of the Declaration of Independence. The words on his tombstone, which he had written himself, tell us what he considered his greatest achievements. They read: "Here lies Thomas Jefferson, Author of the American Declaration of Independence, of the Statute [law] of Virginia for Religious Freedom, and Father of the University of Virginia."

ilton's policies. They were especially angered by the Whiskey Tax, the crushing of the Whiskey Rebellion, and the Bank of the United States. They were against a strong federal government because they feared that it would side with the wealthy against the common people. In foreign affairs, they supported the French and their revolution. Unlike the Federalists, they thought of the British as enemies, not customers.

The Democratic-Republicans soon dropped the first part of their long name and called themselves just Republicans. This early Republican party should not be confused, however, with the modern Republican party, which was born more than a half-century later. (For details, see page 310.) It is the modern Democratic party, as we shall see later, that traces its beginnings to Thomas Jefferson and his followers.

D. The Election of 1796. The two parties used strong language in their attacks on each other. The Federalists called the Republicans the "ignorant mob" or the "stupid populace" and their leaders "dangerous radicals" or "wild men." The Republicans called the Federalists "aristocrats," "monarchists," "tyrants," and "enemies of liberty." Even President Washington was not safe from such attacks. They were an important reason why he would not accept a third term.

Washington's decision to retire forced the Federalists to find another candidate for the presidency. They could not nominate their leader, Alexander Hamilton, because too many people disliked him. So they chose Vice-President John Adams instead. Adams was noted for his honesty and courage. He had also played an important role in the Revolutionary War. Since he came from Massachusetts, the Federalists "balanced the ticket" by nominating a southerner for Vice-President.

The Republicans nominated Thomas Jefferson for President. Since he was a Virginian, they chose a New Yorker for Vice-President. The election was a close one. Adams received the largest number of electoral votes and became President. Jefferson, with the second largest number of votes, was elected Vice-President.

E. War With France. President Adams had to deal at once with a new crisis in foreign affairs. The French, angered by Washington's policy of neutrality and Jay's Treaty, began seizing American ships bound for British ports. Adams sent delegates to France to work out a peaceful settlement. They were met by three French officials, who demanded a bribe of a quarter of a million dollars and a large loan for their government! They also said that France would attack American ports if their demands were not met.

In reporting to President Adams, the American delegates referred to the three Frenchmen

This drawing shows how Burr killed Hamilton. Why was dueling a foolish custom?

as "Mr. X," "Mr. Y," and "Mr. Z." So the incident was called the XYZ Affair. The insulting behavior of the French made Americans angry. With the support of both parties in Congress, Adams organized a navy. He also gave the captains of American merchant ships permission to attack French shipping. Though war was not declared, the United States and France were soon fighting at sea.

During the next few months, Americans seized 85 French ships. But the Americans lost only one of their own. The American people were happy about these victories. But they felt less so as the war continued and Congress found it necessary to pass new tax laws. One was a stamp tax on documents, like the tax Americans had protested against so strongly thirty years earlier. Meanwhile, in France, a military hero named Napoleon Bonaparte overthrew the revolutionary government. When the new French dictator offered the United States a peaceful settlement, President Adams quickly accepted. The undeclared naval war came to an end in 1800, nearly two years after it had begun.

F. The Alien and Sedition Acts. Many Federalists were angry with Adams for ending the war. They had already taken advantage of the anti-French feeling aroused by the war to strengthen their party. They had put through Congress several laws known as the Alien and Sedition Acts. These laws were supposed to protect the United States from the spread of radical French ideas. They were actually used, however, to attack the Republican party.

One of the laws required aliens (foreigners) to wait 14 years, instead of 5 years as before, to become citizens. Large numbers of the French and other Europeans had migrated to the United States in the 1790s to escape the troubles in Europe. Many had become supporters of the Republican party. This law kept them from becoming citizens and voters.

A second law required all aliens to register with the federal government. If aliens were suspected of actions dangerous to the government, the President could deport them (send them back) to Europe without a hearing.

A third law, the Sedition Act, forbade American citizens to commit acts that were dangerous to the government. It was a crime, for example, to make or publish "false, scandalous, and malicious" statements about the government, Congress, or the President. The maximum (highest) penalty was a $5,000 fine and five years in prison.

Within the next few months, twenty-five Republican newspaper editors and printers were arrested. Ten of them were sentenced to prison. Their arrests convinced many Americans that the Federalists were trying to take away liberties the First Amendment to the Bill of Rights had guaranteed. They thought of the jailed Republicans as heroes fighting for the cause of freedom. One Republican editor was elected to Congress while in jail. He was greeted with a big parade on his release.

G. The Election of 1800. Since many Americans now disliked the Federalist policies, Adams lost to Jefferson in the election of 1800. Still, Americans could see that, during their twelve years in power, the Federalists had done much that was good. They had established a strong government, opened the West to settlement, and avoided a major war. Yet they never again gained control of the federal government. Their party, with its old-fashioned ideas of government by the "rich and wellborn," finally died out after the War of 1812 (see page 218).

Meanwhile the United States faced a new problem. Would the Republicans, who favored a federal government of limited powers, be able to govern well? Or would the nation return to the weakness and confusion of the Critical Period?

REVIEWING THE SECTION

A. Knowing Important People

For each important person in the first column, write in your notebook the *letter* of the correct description in the second column.

Important People	Descriptions
1. John Adams	a. Federal judge who tried Republican editors under the Sedition Act
2. Alexander Hamilton	b. Federal judge called a traitor because of his treaty with Great Britain
3. John Jay	c. Federalist President who was not reelected
4. Thomas Jefferson	d. Leader who warned against political parties
5. George Washington	e. First secretary of state
	f. First secretary of the treasury

B. Knowing Important Facts

Complete this chart comparing the two early political parties.

	Federalist Party	Democratic-Republican Party
1. Name of leader	1.	1.
2. Main supporters	2.	2.
3. Where popular	3.	3.
4. Main ideas	4. a. b. c. d.	4. a. b. c. d.

C. Finding the Reasons

In your notebook write the letters of *all* the correct answers to each question.

1. Why was President Washington against political parties?
   a. They divided the American people into opposing groups. b. They gave the common people a much stronger voice in the government. c. They had helped the British during the Revolutionary War.
2. Why did the Federalists win the elections of 1792 and 1796?
   a. Nearly all Americans believed in their main ideas. b. Many Americans who liked Washington thought he sided with the Federalists.

  c. Many Republicans could not vote because they did not own property.
3. Why did President Adams allow American merchant ships to attack French shipping?
  a. He was anxious to win the support of New England shipowners. b. He wanted to show the French that they could not insult the United States. c. He wanted to end the French seizures of American ships.
4. Why were many Americans against the Alien Acts?
  a. These laws violated the democratic ideal of justice because aliens could be punished without a trial. b. Aliens were not permitted to become American citizens if they had voted for Republicans. c. A number of Republican leaders were deported to Europe.
5. Why did many Americans object to the Sedition Act?
  a. It provided that American citizens could be imprisoned without a trial if they criticized the government. b. It violated the constitutional guarantee of freedom of the press. c. It was used by the Federalists against the Republicans.
6. Why did the Federalist party grow weaker after 1800?
  a. It no longer had the support of George Washington. b. Many Americans thought it was not democratic. c. Large numbers of the common people suddenly gained the right to vote.

D. Summing Up the Chapter

In your notebook give the correct order of the three events in each group.

Group A	Group B
1. Adoption of Hamilton's financial program	1. Jay's Treaty with Great Britain
2. Creation of the President's cabinet	2. Washington's Proclamation of Neutrality
3. Crushing of the Whiskey Rebellion	3. Treaty between the United States and Spain

Group C
1. Alien and Sedition Acts
2. Undeclared war with France
3. XYZ Affair

IMPROVING YOUR SKILLS

Understanding the Picture

Study the picture on page 191. Then answer the following questions.
1. Why are the two speakers shown wearing different kinds of clothing?

2. Which political party does the man on the left represent? Why do you think so?
3. Which party does the man on the right represent? How can you tell?
4. What would be a good title for this picture?

MAKING HISTORY LIVE

1. Read and write up descriptions of: a. Washington's trip to New York City for his first inauguration; b. the inaugural ceremonies; or c. New York City at that time.
2. Use pictures or sketches to show how American clothing changed in the 1790s under the influence of the French Revolution.
3. At Washington's funeral, a speaker said that he was "first in war, first in peace, and first in the hearts of his countrymen." Prove that Washington was or was not outstanding in these three ways.
4. If you had been a voter in 1800, would you have voted for John Adams or Thomas Jefferson? Explain why.
5. a. Why did the Federalists call themselves the party of "the rich, the wellborn, and the able"? b. Why did the Republicans call them "aristocrats, monarchists, and enemies of liberty"? c. Why did the Federalists call the Republicans "the ignorant mob"? d. Which descriptions, if any, were justified? Explain.
6. a. Why was the Sedition Act called a "gag bill"? b. During World War II, aliens were required to register with the government. The courts held that they could be deported without a hearing if suspected of plotting against our government. Congress also made it a crime to "teach or advocate" the overthrow of the government by force. Compare these actions with the Alien and Sedition Acts 150 years earlier. c. Why are actions of this sort often taken during a war?
7. Take part in a class debate on the question: Should political parties be abolished? Prepare by writing the views of both sides in the debate.

Chapter 12

THE FIRST REPUBLICAN PRESIDENTS

THE ELECTION of Thomas Jefferson has been called "the revolution of 1800." For the new President expected to bring about a revolution (a great change) in the government of the United States that would make it more democratic. In his First Inaugural Address (the speech he made when he was sworn in as President), Jefferson told the people what he planned to do: He would protect freedom of speech and the press, even for his opponents, the Federalists. He would put the needs of the common people before those of the wealthy upper class. Finally, he would limit the powers of the federal government. He said, "Let the general [federal] government be reduced to foreign concerns only, to a very simple organization and a very inexpensive one—a few plain duties to be performed by a few servants."

Could President Jefferson keep his promises? Could he really make the federal government both less powerful and more democratic? If he did, would he also be able to govern the country effectively?

Did Jefferson Really Change the American Government?

A. Jefferson's Democratic Ways. The new President lost little time in putting his democratic ideas into practice. Washington and Adams had dressed like European nobles—with powdered hair, fancy jackets, and velvet knee breeches. Jefferson wore such plain clothing that one visitor said he looked like "a tall, large-boned farmer." Instead of traveling in a splendid coach, he rode a horse or walked. In fact, he walked to his own inauguration! Washington and Adams had held a formal dinner every week, to which only important people were invited. These people were seated in order of their importance. Jefferson held "open house" several days a week. He welcomed all sorts of visitors, and his guests could sit anywhere they wished.

B. Other Republican Changes. For two years Jefferson's policies as chief executive followed his principles. The President pardoned the men who had been jailed for violating the Sedition Act. That law and the Alien Acts were allowed to die out. Congress changed the waiting period for citizenship from 14 years back to 5 years again.

For a time President Jefferson also kept his promise to reduce the cost of the federal government. He made the largest cuts in the army and navy. The nation's new warships, built for the undeclared war against France, were taken out of service. In their place the government built a "mosquito fleet" of small gunboats to patrol the American coastline. The Whiskey Tax, which had brought in a million dollars a year, was repealed (ended). Nevertheless, the government was able to pay off its debts, which had increased under the Federalists.

C. The Louisiana Purchase. Jefferson's belief that the federal government should be less powerful and more thrifty was suddenly challenged by events in 1803. The new French dictator, Napoleon Bonaparte, had persuaded the king of Spain to give Louisiana back to France. The warlike French dictator was a dangerous neighbor for the United States. Soon his officials forced Americans using the port of New Orleans to pay tariff duties. This meant ruin for thousands of western farmers. They could not afford to pay duties and had no other way to ship out their goods.

Jefferson clearly saw the danger in this situation. He said, "There is on the globe one single spot the possessor of which is our natural enemy. It is New Orleans, through which the produce of three-eighths of our territory must pass to market." He promptly sent delegates to France with an offer to buy New Orleans. If Napoleon refused to sell, they were to go to Great Britain to ask for military help against France.

The Americans arrived in France at just the right moment. Bonaparte's fortunes had suddenly turned for the worse. He had sent a large army to the little island of Santo Domingo in the West Indies. There the army was supposed to crush a revolt of black slaves, then sail on to Louisiana. But Bonaparte's plan failed. Almost the entire force was wiped out in Santo Domingo by enemy attacks and

LOUISIANA PURCHASE

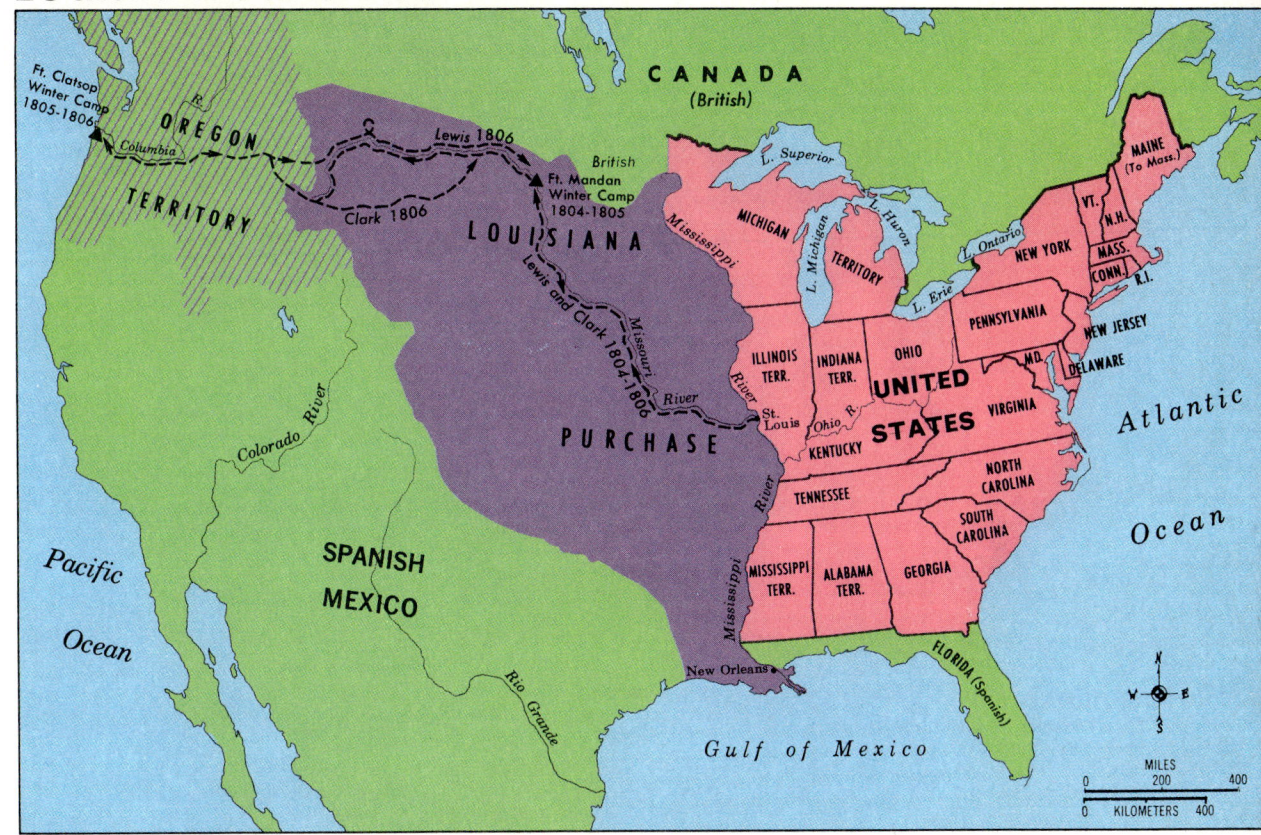

yellow fever. Moreover, a war was brewing against him in Europe, and he needed money to prepare for it. So when the Americans came, he was ready to offer them a great bargain, the entire Louisiana Territory for only $15,-000,000.

The Americans accepted the offer. But Jefferson was not sure that he could approve it. "Did the Constitution," he wondered, "give the executive the power to buy territory?" Because he was unsure, he thought for a time of asking for a constitutional amendment. But he also knew that Bonaparte might withdraw the offer if he delayed. He finally decided that he would get Louisiana while he could by using the President's power to make treaties. So he approved the purchase of Louisiana in the form of a treaty with France and asked Congress to provide the money. The Federalists now tried to block his action on the ground that he was trying to "stretch" the Constitution! Interestingly enough, such about-faces have happened several times in our history. The party in power has usually interpreted the Constitution loosely—that is, stretched it to do what it thought necessary. The party out of power has usually objected.

D. Importance of the Louisiana Territory. The Louisiana Purchase has been called "the greatest real-estate bargain in history." For only fifteen dollars a square mile, the United States obtained almost a million square miles of territory in the rich Mississippi River Basin (see map above). This territory almost doubled the nation's size. It also gave the

Toussaint L'Ouverture. He led the people of Haiti in their struggle for freedom against the French. Haiti became the second nation in the Western Hemisphere to win independence.

United States complete control of the Mississippi River. Furthermore, it opened the way for future expansion westward to the Pacific Ocean.

President Jefferson chose two Virginians, Meriwether Lewis and William Clark, to explore the new territory. The Lewis and Clark expedition set sail up the Missouri River from St. Louis in the spring of 1804. They spent the winter in what is now North Dakota. When spring came, they crossed the Rocky Mountains. Then they sailed down the Columbia River to the Pacific. In order to see more of the country, they returned by a somewhat different route. They came back to St. Louis in 1806, after covering eight thousand miles in two years with the loss of only one man. Lewis and Clark were the first Americans to cross this continent. Their reports of the wonders they had seen and the dangers they had overcome thrilled the American people. Their expedition also strengthened the American claim to the Oregon Territory (see map, page 201).

E. War With Tripoli. As in the Louisiana Purchase, Jefferson "stretched" his powers to deal with another problem. The rulers of the Barbary States in North Africa were pirates. They collected a tribute (forced payment) from many nations. If a country refused to pay the tribute, the Barbary rulers declared war on that country. Then they claimed the right to seize any of its ships passing off their shores. They usually sold the ships and cargoes and held the passengers and crews for ransom. If ransom was not paid, they sold the unfortunate captives into slavery.

The Federalists had paid tribute to the Barbary States. Jefferson refused to do so. The ruler of the state of Tripoli declared war on the United States and began to seize Ameri-

Sacajawea, a Shoshone Indian, acting as a guide for the Lewis and Clark expedition. How did the expedition benefit the United States?

can ships. The President, acting as commander-in-chief, sent warships and marines to punish him. After some daring attacks by the Americans, the ruler of Tripoli agreed to respect American shipping. Jefferson had won; but he had, in effect, waged war without a declaration by Congress.

F. Internal Improvements. Jefferson also "stretched" his powers to deal with another problem. The farmers in the rapidly growing settlements of the West needed roads, canals, and bridges to ship their goods to market. In the East, such internal improvements (projects to improve transportation inside the nation) were built by private companies. They made a profit by collecting tolls from the people who used their projects. But they would not build improvements in the West because there were still too few people in the West to make the projects profitable. So the western settlers asked the federal government to lend them the money to build the roads or to do the job itself. Jefferson now had to decide whether the Constitution gave the federal government the power to spend money for internal improvements.

The President sympathized with the small farmers, especially those in the West. He finally decided that federal aid was constitutional if the improvement crossed from one state to another. If it did, it fell under Congress's power to regulate interstate commerce. At Jefferson's request, Congress voted money for a highway from Maryland across the Appalachians to the western part of Virginia. The National Road, as it was named, was about 80 feet wide and paved with crushed stone. It was used by large numbers of Americans going to the West and by western farmers trading with the East.

REVIEWING THE SECTION

A. Knowing New Terms

Write the meaning of the following terms in your notebook *in your own words*.

(In the Introduction) Inaugural Address
(In **C**) loose interpretation of the Constitution
(In **E**) tribute
(In **F**) internal improvements
toll roads

B. Understanding the Facts

In your notebook write the *letter* of the correct choice.

1. When Jefferson took office, he promised:
a. greater freedom of speech and the press   b. more consideration for the needs of the common people   c. a weaker federal government   d. all of these.

203

2. As President, Jefferson actually:
    a. allowed complete freedom of speech and the press   b. refused to stretch the powers of the federal government   c. spent very little government money   d. did all these things he had promised.
3. The Louisiana Purchase has been called "the greatest real-estate bargain in history" because it:
    a. was very large   b. contained rich natural resources   c. included the important port of New Orleans   d. had all these advantages.
4. The Lewis and Clark expedition was important because it:
    a. explored much of the Louisiana Territory   b. aroused the American people's interest in the new territory   c. gave the United States a stronger claim to the Oregon Territory   d. did all these things.
5. President Jefferson supported the National Road under the government's power to:
    a. make treaties   b. regulate interstate commerce   c. promote the general welfare   d. carry on all these activities.

IMPROVING YOUR SKILLS

A. Mastering the Map

Study the map on page 201. Then complete the following sentences in your notebook.

1. The boundaries of the Louisiana Territory were the British colony of _____ on the north, the _____ River on the east, and the _____ ___ _____ on the south.
2. Between the Louisiana Territory and the Pacific Ocean were the _____ Territory and lands owned by _____.
3. The city of New Orleans is located near the mouth of the _____ River.
4. Lewis and Clark made most of their journey along the _____ and _____ rivers.

B. Finding the Main Idea

Here are three topics. Under them are ten facts. Under which heading does each of the facts belong?

Headings:

A. Changes Made in Federalist Policies by the Republicans
B. The Louisiana Purchase and Its Importance
C. The Question of Internal Improvements

Facts:
1. The Alien and Sedition Acts were allowed to die.
2. The federal government paid off a large part of its debt.
3. Slaves seized control of Santo Domingo and defeated Napoleon's army.
4. The federal government built a road across the Appalachian Mountains.
5. Large warships were replaced by a "mosquito fleet" of small gunboats.
6. Americans had to pay tariffs for using the port of New Orleans.
7. Private companies could not afford to build roads, bridges, and canals in the West.
8. The United States expanded westward toward the Pacific Ocean.
9. President Jefferson made a treaty with Napoleon that the Federalists called unconstitutional.
10. The Whiskey Tax was repealed.

C. Answering Essay Questions

In making outlines, you have seen how this book organizes and presents information. You can easily learn to do this yourself. The first step in answering an essay question is to list important facts or reasons. (For a review of this first step, turn to page 190.) Suppose you are asked to answer the question, Why did President Jefferson purchase Louisiana? By looking over the headings in this section, you find that **C** is the one that deals with the purchase of Louisiana. After rereading **C,** you list the important facts on scrap paper as follows:

C. The Louisiana Purchase
1. Bonaparte took Louisiana from Spain. His officials collected tariffs on American goods passing through New Orleans. This meant ruin for the settlers of the American West.
2. President Jefferson tried to buy New Orleans from France.
3. Needing money, Bonaparte offered him the entire Louisiana Territory for only $15,000,000.
4. Jefferson decided to accept the offer because the price was so low.

The next step is to write your answer. An answer in essay form should begin with a topic sentence that lets the reader know what the answer is about. You will find that it usually helps to use the words of the question in writing your topic sentence. In this case, you might write, "There were some good reasons why President Jefferson decided to buy Louisiana."

You follow up with several sentences that give, in your own words, the facts listed in your outline. It is usually a good idea to use a separate sentence for each fact. To finish off smoothly, you might have a closing sentence that again repeats the words of the question.

Now write your answer in your notebook according to these instructions. Be sure to write complete sentences in good English.

Why Did the United States Declare War on Great Britain?

A. Renewal of the War in Europe. In 1800 Thomas Jefferson won the presidency by a close vote. Four years later he defeated his Federalist opponent by the one-sided electoral vote of 176 to 14. It was clear that the work he had done in his first four years in office had won him the support of the American people. But when Jefferson left the presidency in 1809, the American people had again changed in their feeling toward him. Like Washington, he was criticized so much during his second term of office that he was happy to retire to private life. Like Washington, too, Jefferson became unpopular mainly because of troubles with foreign nations.

The European war that Napoleon had been preparing for broke out in 1805. For several years the French ruler won victory after victory. He defeated every one of his enemies except Great Britain. The powerful British fleet kept him from crossing the English Channel to invade the British Isles.

Napoleon then decided to fight the British with other weapons. He ordered the nations of Europe to stop buying British goods. The British government replied by ordering all ships bound for Europe to stop at British ports. British officials were to seize all war materials on board and collect duties on the remaining cargo. Napoleon replied by ordering his officials and those of his allies to seize any ship that had stopped at a British port. American shippers were caught in the middle of this struggle between the two giants. If they obeyed Britain, France would seize their ships. If they obeyed France, their ships would be seized by Britain.

B. Impressment of American Sailors. The British gave American shippers more reason to complain than the French. Since their fleet controlled the seas, they captured more American ships than the French did. In addition, they "impressed" many American sailors—that is, they forced Americans to serve as sailors on British warships.

The reason for impressment was that the British had great trouble in getting and keeping sailors. The food in the British navy was bad. the pay was low, and the discipline was very harsh. It is hardly surprising that sailors deserted whenever they could. Many of them fled to the United States and became American citizens. Some became sailors on American ships, which offered much higher pay and better conditions.

So the British adopted the impressment policy. They stopped American ships, examined the crews, and took off deserters. They paid no attention to American citizenship papers. When Americans protested, the British answered, "Once an Englishman, always an Englishman." In other words, it did not matter that some of the English had become citizens of other countries. Under British law, they were still British subjects. Worse still, British officers needed sailors so desperately that they made many so-called mistakes. Of the ten thousand Americans they impressed, probably only about one thousand had ever been British citizens.

The impressment of American sailors had begun in Washington's day. Jay's failure to stop it was one reason why his treaty had been bitterly attacked (see page 187). Now, during Jefferson's second term, the problem became much worse because American trade with Europe was much larger. The warring nations needed American goods and were willing to pay very high prices for them. Even though one ship out of three was seized, American shippers made large profits. They built hundreds of new ships. To attract the new seamen they needed, they paid high wages and gave bonuses (extra money) for successful voyages. Thousands of young Americans risked the danger of impressment to make quick fortunes. The rest of the country also prospered from the boom in shipbuilding, shipping, and foreign trade. Despite these benefits, however, anger over the seizure of American ships and the impressment of American sailors continued to grow.

C. The Chesapeake Affair. In 1807 a crisis developed in the relations between the United States and Great Britain. An American warship, the *Chesapeake*, was leaving the port of Norfolk in Virginia when it was met by a British man o' war, the *Leopard*. The British commander ordered the American vessel to stop. When it refused, the British opened fire, killing three Americans and wounding eighteen. The British then boarded the *Chesapeake* and impressed four men—a British deserter, a native-born white American, a black American, and an Indian. The *Chesapeake* Affair aroused the American people. President Jefferson sent a strong protest to the British government. The British agreed to pay damages, but once again they refused to talk about the whole question of impressment.

D. The Embargo Act. President Jefferson now decided to strike back at both Great Britain and France with an economic weapon, the embargo. At his request, Congress forbade American ships to set sail for any foreign ports. Since Europe needed American foods and other goods, Jefferson expected Great Britain and France to change their policies.

Unfortunately, the Embargo Act hurt the United States more than it did the two giants. It caused a severe economic depression in this country. About 150,000 men—sailors, shipbuilders, longshoremen, and other workers in port cities—were thrown out of work. In New York City, one observer reported, "The streets near the waterside were almost deserted, the grass had begun to grow upon the wharfs." American tobacco, grain, and other exports piled up in the warehouses. Prices fell sharply as a result. American merchants and farmers began to smuggle goods into Canada, from where they could be shipped to Great Britain. Unemployed sailors crossed into Canada to find jobs on British ships. In New England, which was very hard hit, the Federalists threatened to impeach the President and to

Impressing sailors from the *Chesapeake*. How does the artist attempt to arouse your feelings against the British?

British buying scalps from Indians. Why were cartoons like this a cause of the War of 1812?

secede (withdraw) from the Union.

Jefferson had to admit that he had made a mistake. Congress repealed the Embargo Act fifteen months after passing it. In its place, a bill was passed that forbade trade only with British and French ports. This made it possible for Americans to trade with Great Britain and France through other European nations. American shipping and commerce now recovered, but seizures and impressment continued. As Jefferson left the presidency, he wondered what the new President, his friend James Madison, would do about the situation.

E. Increased Anti-British Feeling. At President Madison's suggestion, Congress again changed the law. This time, Americans were allowed to trade with Great Britain and France for one year. If during that time one of them agreed to stop seizing American ships, the United States would stop trading with the other. In this way Madison hoped to set the British and French competing with each other for American trade. But his plan, like Jefferson's embargo, had unexpected results. The British refused the American terms. The crafty Napoleon, who agreed to them, never intended to keep them. After Madison ordered trading with the British stopped, Napoleon told his officials to continue seizing American ships!

The American people did not know of Napoleon's trick. Their anger was directed solely at the British government for refusing Madison's offer. They became even angrier at the British when a new Indian war broke out in the Northwest Territory. Once again, British fur traders were accused of arming the Indians to attack the settlers. Many Americans also believed that the British were paying the Indians for American scalps, as a newspaper drawing of the time showed.

F. The Declaration of War. The strongest anti-British feelings were expressed by a group of young members of Congress, mostly from the Southwest. These people were so eager for war with Great Britain that they became known as the "War Hawks." The War Hawks wanted to seize Canada, with its rich fur trade, as soon as war broke out. The Canadian people, they thought, would be happy to join the United States. In fact, one of them boasted that his state's militia would be able to conquer Canada by itself. Since Spain was at that time an ally of Great Britain, some of them also hoped to seize Florida.

The War Hawks persuaded President Madison to ask Congress for a declaration of war against Great Britain. Meanwhile British merchants, suffering from the American boycott, convinced their government to stop seizing American ships. While the ship carrying the good news from Great Britain was crossing the Atlantic Ocean, Congress voted the declaration of war.

G. Causes of the War of 1812. In his message to Congress, President Madison listed four reasons for going to war: 1. the impressment of American sailors; 2. violations of American waters by British warships; 3. seizures of American ships; 4. encouragement of Indian attacks. Most historians agree that the President was wrong about the fourth charge. The Indians attacked because American settlers were taking away their lands. The first three charges were justified. But strangely enough the northeastern states, which were most affected by British actions, voted against the declaration of war.

Historians suggest that two additional factors, rooted in the American past, were responsible for the War of 1812. One was dislike of the British because of the Revolutionary War. This feeling was strengthened by event after event, from the *Chesapeake* Affair to the Indian war. Many Americans felt that if the British were ever to respect our nation they would have to be taught a lesson. The second factor was a desire for territory. The Louisiana Purchase had actually increased the American appetite for land. Some of the War Hawks spoke confidently of seizing not only Canada and Florida but also the rest of North America.

REVIEWING THE SECTION

A. Knowing New Terms

In your notebook write the new terms in this section that best complete these statements.
1. The British angered the American people by seizing or _____ American sailors to serve on their ships.
2. The law forbidding Americans to ship their goods abroad was called the _____ Act.
3. If this law was not repealed, the New England states threatened to withdraw, or _____, from the Union.
4. Members of Congress who wanted the United States to declare war on Great Britain were known as _____ _____.

B. Understanding the Facts

Write "True" in your notebook if the statement is correct. If the statement contains an error, rewrite it so that it is correct.
1. President Jefferson was very unpopular during his first administration, but became popular during his second term in office.
2. The American people disliked Jefferson's domestic policy.
3. The British government ordered all ships bound for America to stop at British ports to be searched and to pay taxes.

4. Napoleon ordered the seizure of any ship that stopped at a British port.
5. Poor food, low pay, and bad treatment caused thousands of British sailors to desert.
6. Under the Embargo Act, Americans were forbidden to buy goods abroad.
7. Many New Englanders showed their dislike of the Embargo Act by smuggling goods into Florida.
8. In case of war, the War Hawks expected the Canadian people to fight against the United States.

C. Summing Up the Chapter

Arrange the following events in the correct order.

1. Declaration of war on Great Britain
2. *Chesapeake* Affair
3. Embargo Act
4. Indian war in the Northwest Territory
5. Lewis and Clark expedition
6. Louisiana Purchase
7. Renewal of war in Europe

IMPROVING YOUR SKILLS

Answering Essay Questions

You learned on page 205 how to answer a simple essay question. A similar approach can be used for more complicated questions. In one type of question, you have to evaluate (weigh) the facts on both sides and then reach a conclusion.

Suppose you are asked, "Was Thomas Jefferson a great President?" To answer this question, you must first go through the entire chapter to get the facts. On scrap paper make a list in two separate columns of the good and bad things he did. They might be called his "successes" and "failures," or his "achievements" and "mistakes."

President Jefferson's Successes	President Jefferson's Failures
1.	1.
2.	2.
3.	3.
4.	4.
5.	5.
6.	6.

It will take three paragraphs to write up these facts properly. The first paragraph should deal with Jefferson's successes. Your topic sentence might be, "Thomas Jefferson did a great deal for the United States when he was President." The second paragraph should deal with his failures. (What would be a good topic sentence?) In the third paragraph, you will want to state your conclusion. The opening words might be, "On the whole, I think that Jefferson was (or was not) a great President because . . ."

MAKING HISTORY LIVE

1. a. Report on Jefferson's achievements in one of the following roles: (1) as member of the Continental Congress; (2) as governor of Virginia; (3) as ambassador to France; (4) as secretary of state; (5) as founder and leader of the Democratic-Republican party; (6) as President of the United States; (7) as ex-President; (8) as scientist, inventor, and architect; (9) as a leader in the development of liberty and democracy. b. Why was Jefferson a very remarkable man?
2. Imagine that you are an American sailor who was impressed by the British and who managed to escape and return to the United States. Write a letter to your family telling about your experiences.
3. a. An *embargo* and a *boycott* are opposites. Explain the difference between them. b. Why are they both considered *economic* weapons? c. How did Jefferson's experience with the embargo show that an economic weapon can be a "two-edged sword"?
4. Join in a staging of the Senate debate on President Madison's war message. Take a role of a War Hawk or a New England senator opposed to war with England. Make notes for each side of the debate. Be prepared to defend your point of view.
5. Many English people were surprised when their "American cousins" declared war on Britain while it was engaged in a life-and-death struggle with Napoleon. Take part in a discussion between some typical English people in 1812 on the question, Was the American declaration of war justified? Write up the main points on both sides of the question.

Chapter 13

THE WAR OF 1812

"WE HAVE licked the British twice, and we can lick them again." This was a popular saying of Americans in the nineteenth century. We know that the United States defeated Great Britain once in the Revolutionary War. But did our nation really beat its powerful enemy a second time in the War of 1812? Did it gain enough important benefits from the war to make up for the cost in lives and wealth? Or was the War of 1812 a mistake that Americans were too proud to admit? To answer these questions, let us examine the war and its results as fairly as we can.

The bombardment of Fort McHenry. Francis Scott Key described the "bombs bursting in air" in "The Star-Spangled Banner."

Who Won the War of 1812?

A. Strength of the Opposing Sides. When the War of 1812 began, the War Hawks were sure that the United States would be able to seize Canada without much trouble—perhaps Florida too. Most Americans were also confident that our nation would win a quick and easy victory. They reasoned that the United States was much bigger and stronger than it had been during the Revolution. They believed that the Canadian people would be happy to join a democratic country like ours. Even if the Canadians decided to fight, they numbered only a half million. They could be no match for seven million Americans. Great Britain could send them little help because it was still fighting a long and difficult war against Napoleon. The British government was also having money troubles, and the British people wanted peace.

There were, however, several important factors that confident Americans overlooked. First, the American armed forces had been seriously weakened by the Republicans' policy of cutting costs. The army had only seven thousand men, and many of its commanders were aged veterans of the Revolutionary War. The navy had only sixteen warships and some almost useless small gunboats. Second, the Canadians were fighting in defense of their homeland. As a result, they had a higher morale (fighting spirit) than the American invaders. In addition, the Americans had to march and carry supplies for long distances over very poor roads. In short, they were now up against the very same difficulties that had caused the British to lose the Revolutionary War. Third, the United States was a divided nation. The people of the Northeast, especially New England and New York, were bitter about "Mr. Madison's War." The harmful effects of this attitude and of America's military weakness soon became clear.

B. The Fighting Along the Canadian Border. President Madison called on the states to raise 100,000 militiamen for a triple invasion of Canada. One force was to advance from eastern New York along Lake Champlain. A second was to march from western New York across the Niagara River. A third was to move from Detroit at the western end of Lake Erie (see map, page 214). This ambitious plan was a complete failure. The first two forces, composed mainly of militia from the Northeast, refused to advance onto foreign soil. The commander of the Detroit force succeeded in leading two thousand men through the woods into Canada. But when he heard that a strong British and Indian force was approaching, he quickly retreated. He surrendered Detroit and his army without a fight. Since the Indians had earlier captured Fort Dearborn (now Chicago), the entire Northwest Territory was open to British invasion.

The next year, 1813, brought a change for the better. An American naval commander, Commodore Oliver H. Perry, built a small fleet at the eastern end of Lake Erie. Then he boldly sailed across the lake and attacked and defeated a larger British fleet near Detroit. "We have met the enemy and they are ours," he proudly reported. Perry's words and deeds

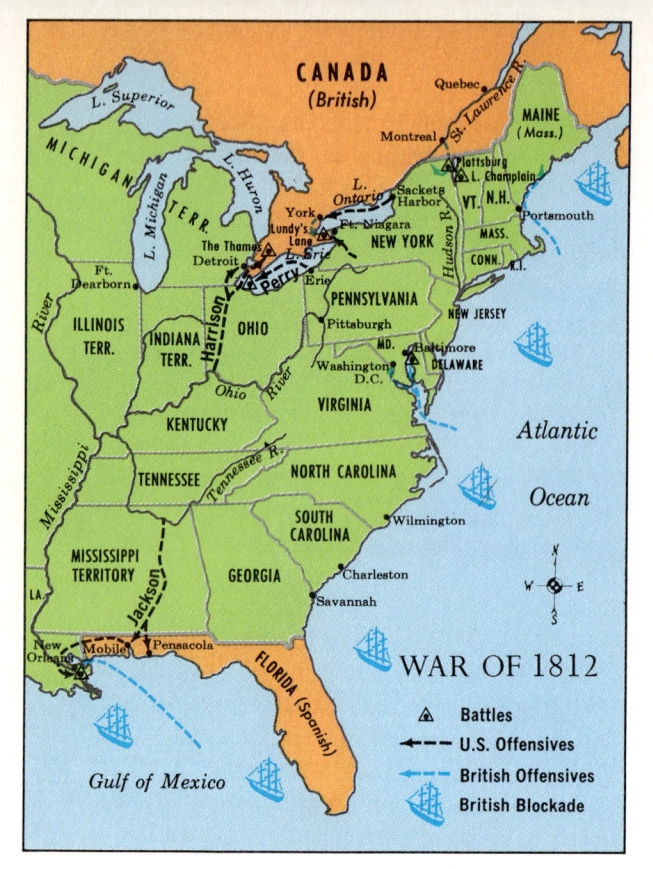

WAR OF 1812
- ▲ Battles
- ←--- U.S. Offensives
- ←--- British Offensives
- ⛵ British Blockade

cheered the American public. His victory also forced the British to withdraw from Detroit because supplies could no longer be shipped to them across Lake Erie.

The governor of Indiana Territory, William Henry Harrison, quickly followed up Perry's victory. He defeated a British and Indian force at the Thames River in Canada (see map above). Harrison did not, however, dare to advance much farther into enemy territory. Two other American attempts to invade Canada from eastern and western New York ended in failure.

C. The War at Sea. In the fighting at sea, the situation was reversed. There the Americans got off to a good start. Though outnumbered fifteen to one, American warships managed to win a few victories by fighting their enemies one at a time. In addition, the American government allowed some five hundred merchant ships to attack British shipping. The Americans succeeded in capturing almost fourteen hundred British ships worth about $40,000,000.

D. A Dark Year. In 1814, the third year of the war, the tide turned again. Great Britain and its allies finally managed to crush Napoleon. The British were now free to put more effort into their war against the United States. Their mighty fleet soon captured the American warships or drove them from the seas. It also blockaded the United States, cutting off almost all imports and exports.

The British even established a base on American soil in Maine. From this base, they carried out a series of damaging raids along the American coast. One British force invaded Washington, D.C. It set fire to the Capitol, the White House, and other public buildings in revenge for an earlier American raid on the capital of Canada. Only a heavy thunderstorm saved the entire city from the spreading flames. The same British force next attacked the port of Baltimore. This time, however, it was stopped by a strong defense. An American lawyer, Francis Scott Key, watched the battle all night. Proud of the American victory, he wrote the poem that became our national anthem, "The Star-Spangled Banner."

President Madison, who had been forced by

Perry's victory on Lake Erie. The victorious American commander is approaching the British flagship to take it over.

Battle of New Orleans in 1815. Word that the peace treaty had already been signed did not reach the two sides in time to stop the fighting. Why might such a thing be less likely to happen today?

the British to flee from the White House, faced other serious setbacks during 1814. The government's income from tariffs dropped sharply because the British blockade cut off foreign trade. Attempts to borrow money were not very successful. Most of the wealthy bankers and merchants of the Northeast refused to buy government bonds. In New England, the leaders of the Federalist Party called a meeting to condemn the war. They demanded a number of changes in the Constitution to weaken the federal government's powers. They threatened that New England would secede from the Union if their demands were not met.

E. The Final Battle. In January 1815, a strong British force advanced on the important Mississippi River port of New Orleans. The government called on a Tennessee lawyer, Andrew Jackson, to defend the city. Jackson had earlier become famous by defeating the Creek Indians and driving them into Florida.

General Jackson quickly gathered a mixed force of regular army troops, state militia, western sharpshooters, and even pirates. After the British forces landed, he guessed the route they would take to march on New Orleans. Across this route he built a high wall of earth, strengthened with cotton bales and sugar barrels. Jackson stationed his troops behind the wall. When the British charged, they were met by a deadly hail of American fire. They were forced to retreat after suffering more than two thousand casualties. The Americans lost only seventy-one men.

F. The Peace Terms. The Battle of New Orleans was like a tonic for the discouraged American President and his people. It did not, however, affect the outcome of the war. The peace treaty had already been signed a week earlier. The ship bearing the good news was nearing the American shore when the battle was fought.

At the peace conference, the British acted at first like victors. They demanded a large slice of American territory. The Americans insisted that they had not lost the war and so would not yield any territory at all. The deadlock ended when a quarrel broke out among the European countries that had defeated Napoleon. It began to look as though Great Britain would soon be fighting some of its former allies. The British decided to accept the American terms before a new war started.

The peace treaty provided only for a return of prewar conditions. No boundary lines were changed. The main causes of the war, the seizing of American ships and impressment of American sailors, were not even mentioned. These were no longer important issues since Napoleon's defeat. As one of the American delegates put it, "We have brought back nothing but peace."

REVIEWING THE SECTION

A. Knowing Important People

For each important person in the first column, write in your notebook the *letter* of the statement in the second column that tells what he did in the War of 1812.

Important People
1. William Henry Harrison
2. Andrew Jackson
3. Francis Scott Key
4. James Madison
5. Oliver H. Perry

Descriptions
a. Had to flee from his home
b. Suffered severe military defeat
c. Won naval victory on Lake Erie
d. Won great victory at New Orleans
e. Won victory on Canadian soil
f. Wrote about successful American defense

B. Finding the Reasons

In your notebook write the letters of *all* the correct answers to each question.

1. Why did most Americans believe that the United States would easily conquer Canada and win the War of 1812?
   a. The United States had defeated Great Britain once before. b. The United States had almost fifteen times as many people as Canada. c. Great Britain was engaged in a long and costly war with Napoleon.
2. Why was it a mistake for Americans to feel so confident of victory?
   a. Great Britain had a much larger army and navy than the United States. b. It could be expected to send much help to Canada. c. Its commanders were more experienced than American commanders.
3. Why was it difficult for the United States to conquer Canada?
   a. Canada was very large. b. The roads into Canada were few and poor. c. The Canadians fought hard to defend their land.
4. Why was 1814 the worst year of the war for the United States?
   a. The British blockaded our shores. b. British forces attacked the American coast. c. The American government was short of money.
5. Why was the Battle of New Orleans important?
   a. It made the American people feel proud. b. It opened the Mississippi River so that American farmers could trade with Europe. c. It forced the British to give the United States better peace terms.
6. Why did the American government accept the peace terms?
   a. It was glad to end a war that was going badly. b. It gained a great deal of new territory. c. It won the right to trade with Europe in wartime.

IMPROVING YOUR SKILLS

A. Mastering the Map

Study the map on page 214. Then complete the following statements.
1. Most of the battles in the War of 1812 took place on American soil—in the states of _____ _____, _____, and _____, in _____ Territory, and in the city of _____.
2. Additional battles took place in two foreign possessions: _____, owned by _____, and _____, owned by _____.
3. The easiest invasion route from the United States to Canada was across lakes _____ and _____.
4. Because the British controlled the seas, they were able to attack the American coast at widely separated points in the states of _____, _____, and _____.

B. Answering Essay Questions

You have already learned how to answer two types of essay questions. (For a review of the two types, turn to pages 205 and 210.) A third type of essay question is the comparison. Like the evaluation, the comparison should be answered in three paragraphs. The first and second paragraphs should describe the two sides you are comparing. The third paragraph should contain your conclusion.

QUESTION: Which side was stronger at the start of the War of 1812, the United States or Great Britain?

Step 1. Read **A** carefully. Then list on a separate sheet of paper each side's important strong points or advantages.

American Strong Points	*British Strong Points*
1.	1.
2.	2.
3.	3.
4.	4.
5.	5.

Step 2. In your first paragraph, put down the strong points of the United States. Be sure to have a topic sentence and to use at least one sentence for each fact you have listed.

Step 3. Your second paragraph should deal with British strong points. Write at least one sentence for each fact on your list.

Step 4. In your concluding paragraph, tell which side you consider stronger and why.

What Were the After-Effects of the War of 1812?

A. Direct Effects of the War. The War of 1812 was by modern standards a very small conflict. Fewer than two thousand Americans died in battle. Yet this "little war" had a number of important effects both on our country and on foreign nations.

Almost every part of our country gained some benefit from the war. In the Northeast, merchants built hundreds of factories to make goods that Americans had once bought from Great Britain. In the Northwest and Southwest, settlement was speeded because the Indian tribes had been defeated.

B. The Growth of Nationalism. Another important effect of the war was the growth of nationalism—that is, a feeling of loyalty to the nation. Most Americans had been used to thinking of themselves as citizens of their state rather than the United States (see page 103). But their working and fighting together against a common enemy during the war gave them a feeling of unity and national pride.

They began to speak of themselves as Americans, citizens of the United States. They felt proud of the American triumph at New Orleans and the victories won by American warships on the Great Lakes and the Atlantic.

The new spirit of nationalism was strikingly shown at a patriotic dinner in 1816. A naval hero, Stephen Decatur, proposed this toast: "Our country! May she always be in the right; but our country, right or wrong." Decatur's toast soon became an American motto. More important, two generals of the war, Andrew Jackson and William Henry Harrison, were elected to the presidency in later years.

C. The "Era of Good Feeling." American nationalism also showed itself in another way. The Federalist party fell into disgrace because it had not supported the nation's efforts to win the war. In the election of 1816 the Republican candidate for President, James Monroe, defeated his Federalist opponent by a very large margin. President Monroe toured New England the next year. He was greeted everywhere by cheering crowds. The United States, as one Boston newspaper noted, had entered an "Era of Good Feeling."

The spirit of nationalism was shown even more clearly in the election of 1820. This time the Federalist party did not even name a candidate. President Monroe received every electoral vote cast except one! Soon afterward the Federalist party passed out of existence. The Republicans were left as the only political party.

D. New Republican Policies. Strange to say, the basic ideas of the Federalist Party were now adopted by the Republicans. Their war experience had taught them the need for a strong government. Clearly, the United States had suffered because it had been unprepared when the war began. So the Republicans now spent large sums on building a strong army and navy. They also changed their views on other important issues. So marked was the change

The death of Tecumseh. The Shawnee Indian chief believed that no Indian tribe could sell Indian land since it belonged to all Indians. He was killed at the Battle of the Thames, but not by General Harrison as this picture shows and many people believed.

that one observer was prompted to say, "The Republicans out-federalized the Federalists."

Before the war, the Republicans had opposed high tariffs. They had argued that only a few business people benefited from them. Most other Americans did not benefit because tariffs raised the prices they had to pay for imported goods. When the war ended, however, British manufacturers "dumped" their products in the United States at very low prices. They hoped in this way to ruin the business of the new factories built in this country during the war. American manufacturers asked the government for help. Congress promptly raised tariff duties to protect America's "infant industries" from the competition of cheaper British goods. The protective tariff was to remain a Republican policy for many years.

Jefferson, Madison, and Monroe had all opposed the Bank of the United States. When the bank's charter had expired in 1811, Madison had allowed it to die. But when the war began a year later, the government found it very difficult to collect taxes and to borrow money. Worse still, the states had chartered a large number of banks, each of which printed its own notes. If a bank was well run and backed up its notes with gold and silver, the notes kept their value. Most banknotes, however, soon fell in value. Some became completely worthless. The fact that people used the "cheap" or worthless paper money to pay their taxes added to the government's financial troubles. Business people also suffered because they found it confusing to handle so many different kinds of money. With the President's approval, Congress chartered a second Bank of the United States in 1816. Its banknotes once again gave the nation a sound currency.

Thomas Jefferson had broken with Republican principles by asking Congress for funds to build the National Road (see page 242). Congress now voted more money for this project. In time the National Road was extended almost as far west as the Mississippi River.

E. Work of the Supreme Court. The powers of the federal government were also greatly increased during this period by the Supreme Court. Its Chief Justice, John Marshall, was a loyal Federalist who had always favored a strong federal government. Taking advantage of the new spirit of nationalism, he led the court in a series of decisions that increased federal power. In these decisions, the Supreme

JOHN MARSHALL: CHIEF JUSTICE OF THE SUPREME COURT

Jefferson's victory in the election of 1800 was a severe blow to the Federalists. They lost not only the presidency but also both houses of Congress to the Republicans. Only the federal courts were still under their control. To strengthen their hold, the Federalists rushed through a law adding sixteen new judges to the federal district courts. These new judges became known as the "midnight judges." Adams, it seems, stayed up late the night before he left the presidency to sign their appointments. As you might expect, he chose sixteen strong Federalists. For the post of chief justice of the Supreme Court, his seventeenth appointment, Adams chose another strong Federalist. His choice was John Marshall of Virginia.

Marshall, the son of pioneers, grew up in the mountains of western Virginia. Though well educated, he liked the outdoor life better than studying. At the age of twenty-one, he joined his father in enlisting to fight in the Revolution. He soon rose from lieutenant to captain and won praise for his courage under fire. After the war he became a successful lawyer and a member of the Virginia assembly. He took a leading role in supporting the Constitution when it came up for ratification. He especially praised the new system of federal courts.

Marshall's Federalist ideas, legal skill, and strong character made him an ideal choice for chief justice. His appointment turned out to be the most important action Adams took as President. Marshall remained chief justice for thirty-four years. Because of his keen mind, he easily persuaded the other justices to follow his lead. He wrote more than five hundred decisions, many of which greatly strengthened our federal government.

One of Marshall's first cases dealt with the "midnight judges." Jefferson had refused to give his approval to one of the appointments. Marshall upheld the President's action. But he cleverly used the case to prove that the Supreme Court had a great power not mentioned in the Constitution, the power to declare laws unconstitutional. In later cases Marshall used the "elastic" and interstate commerce clauses of the Constitution to "stretch" the powers of Congress (see page 160). He also ruled a number of state laws and state court decisions unconstitutional. Thus he clearly established the supremacy of the federal government over the states.

Because Marshall's decisions were so important and well reasoned, many experts consider him the greatest Supreme Court justice in our nation's history. Others may disagree with this opinion. But even they must admit that John Marshall did more than any other American—except George Washington and Alexander Hamilton—to make the new federal government strong and successful.

Court overruled state courts or declared state laws unconstitutional.

Two cases were especially important. In the first case, the Court upheld the Second Bank of the United States as a "necessary and proper" use of federal power. It also struck down a tax placed on the bank by the state of Maryland. Its reason was that states might use such taxes to destroy the bank or other agencies of the federal government. In the second case, the Supreme Court killed a charter granted by New York State to a steamboat line on the Hudson River. It ruled that all navigable waterways came under the federal government's power to regulate interstate commerce (see page 117).

F. A Strong Foreign Policy. The War of 1812 also affected American foreign policy. It has been called our "second war for independence" because it taught Great Britain and other foreign nations to respect our country. The British government now wanted to establish friendly relations with the United States. In 1816 the two nations finally signed a trade treaty. In the next year, they agreed to destroy all fortifications and remove all warships from the Great Lakes. In the year after that, they set the forty-ninth parallel as the boundary between the United States and Canada west of the Great Lakes (see map, page 271). Both countries promised not to build forts or keep troops near their common border. That promise has been kept to this day; the border between the United States and Canada is still the longest unfortified frontier in the world.

Spain likewise showed a new respect for the United States. Florida had for many years been a hiding place for Indians, smugglers, pirates, and runaway slaves who wanted to escape American law. The Seminole Indians, in particular, used Florida as a base from which to raid the neighboring states. In 1818 President Monroe sent Andrew Jackson to punish the Indians. The famous war hero pursued the Seminoles into Florida, captured several Spanish forts, and court-martialed and executed two British citizens who had been arming the Indians.

General Jackson's actions clearly violated international law (the set of rules governing the conduct of nations). But Great Britain did not protest. Instead, it admitted that the two Englishmen had been wrong. Spain did make a strong protest, however. President Monroe replied that it should either keep order in Florida or turn the colony over to the United States. Fearing that he meant to seize Florida, the Spanish government gave the territory to our country in 1819 for about $5,000,000.

G. The Monroe Doctrine. Spain's action showed its weakness as well as America's

Simón Bolívar was called the Liberator. He is the most famous of the brave people who led the Spanish colonies in their wars of independence from Spain.

strength. The king of Spain was a cruel absolute monarch. He used extreme methods to stamp out the ideas of liberty and equality that had been spread by the American and French revolutions. His cruelty drove his subjects to rebel, both in Spain itself and in its American colonies. Other European rulers were troubled by these rebellions. They sent troops to crush the revolt in Spain and spoke of sending armies to America.

The United States became alarmed. It feared that the European powers might seize some of Spain's holdings as a reward for their efforts. This country did not want such powerful neighbors. It was especially concerned about France and Russia. There were reports that these great powers intended to divide Mexico between them. Fortunately, the United States had the support of Great Britain. British merchants, who had built up a rich trade with the former Spanish colonies, wanted them to remain independent.

In 1823 President Monroe made a statement that has become known as the Monroe Doctrine. In it he warned the European powers not to interfere in the affairs of the Western Hemisphere or establish new colonies there. The powers dropped their plans to invade America. They did so mainly because Great Britain, with its powerful fleet, backed the United States. The Monroe Doctrine was nevertheless very important. It has remained basic to our foreign policy since 1823. In later years the United States became strong enough to protect the Western Hemisphere without British help.

H. The Situation in 1824. It would be a mistake to think of the United States as already a great power in 1824. On the other hand, it was no longer a weak country that could be tossed about by events in Europe. For the next 70 years, most of the American people were to pay little attention to foreign affairs. They were too busy developing the rich resources of the large territories they had gained. In so doing, they met with a number of difficult problems. Differences on how to handle these problems soon brought an end to the "Era of Good Feeling" that had followed the War of 1812.

President Monroe with his cabinet. Monroe is explaining the warning he is about to give the European powers (the Monroe Doctrine). What other country supported the warning?

REVIEWING THE SECTION

A. Knowing New Terms

PART 1. In your notebook write the new terms in this section that best complete these statements.

1. A feeling of extreme loyalty to one's nation is known as _____.
2. The short period after the War of 1812, when all sections of the United States supported the President, has been named the "era of _____ _____."
3. A high tariff, intended to protect American manufacturers by keeping out foreign products, is called a _____ tariff.
4. The rules which nations are supposed to follow in their dealings with one another are called _____ law.
5. President Monroe's warning to the European powers not to interfere in the Western Hemisphere or to establish colonies there is known as the _____ _____.

PART 2. Explain these terms *in your own words.*

(In **D**) dumping
infant industries
cheap money

(In **F**) "second war for independence"
unfortified frontier

B. Knowing Important People

For each description below, write the *letter* of the important person it applies to. You may use two letters for one description if it applies to more than one person. You may also use the same letter again if a person is described more than once.

Important People:

A. Stephen Decatur
B. William Henry Harrison
C. Andrew Jackson
D. John Marshall
E. James Monroe

Descriptions:

1. Author of warning to the European powers
2. Purchaser of Florida
3. Leading Federalist in the government during the 1820s
4. Military hero of the War of 1812, later elected President of the United States
5. Naval hero of the War of 1812
6. Noted Indian fighter, whose actions persuaded Spain to sell Florida

7. President elected by almost unanimous vote of the electoral college
8. Chief executive during the "Era of Good Feeling"
9. Military man who proposed a toast that became a national motto
10. Republican President who followed Federalist policies

C. Understanding the Facts

Here is a list of the principles of the early Republican party. Write "Same" if the principle was still being followed by the Republicans in the 1820s. If it was not, write "Different." Then tell what the party did that differed from its principles.

1. Against a strong federal government
2. Against a large army and navy
3. Against friendship with Great Britain
4. Against the Bank of the United States
5. Against government aid to business
6. For low tariffs
7. For small western farmers
8. For thrift in government
9. For freedom of speech and the press

Conclusion. Explain the statement, "The Republicans out-federalized the Federalists."

IMPROVING YOUR SKILLS

Finding the Main Idea

Here are eight topics. Under them are ten facts. Under which heading does each of the facts belong?

Headings:

A. Direct Effects of the War
B. The Growth of Nationalism
C. The "Era of Good Feeling"
D. New Republican Policies
E. Work of the Supreme Court
F. A Strong Foreign Policy
G. The Monroe Doctrine
H. The Situation in 1824

Facts:

1. Americans spoke with pride of their nation's victories in the war.
2. British merchants had built up a large trade with the new nations in the Western Hemisphere.
3. The European powers wanted to help Spain reconquer its colonies in America.

4. Great Britain signed treaties with the United States to fix the border between the United States and Canada and to settle other differences.
5. The Republicans maintained a strong army and navy, adopted a protective tariff, and established the Second Bank of the United States.
6. Maryland's tax on a branch of the Bank of the United States was declared unconstitutional.
7. People began to think of themselves as Americans rather than as citizens of a certain state.
8. President Monroe was greeted by cheering crowds in New England.
9. Spain sold Florida to the United States.
10. The war speeded the development of American industry.

MAKING HISTORY LIVE

1. Practice the skills you learned in previous lessons by answering these essay questions:
   a. (Evaluation question) Who do you think won the War of 1812, the United States or Great Britain? Prove your answer. b. (Comparison question) Who did more to strengthen the federal government, the Federalists or the Republicans?
2. a. Why did the Federalists call the War of 1812 "Mr. Madison's War"? b. How did the American people show their dislike of the Federalists' attitude after the war was over?
3. a. Explain the significance of the motto: "Our country! May she always be in the right; but our country, right or wrong." b. Tell why you agree or disagree with it.
4. History is full of "ifs" (events which might have happened very differently if the circumstances had been slightly different). If, for example, the transatlantic cable or telephone had existed before 1812, how might our history have been different?
5. Report on the early life and military career of Andrew Jackson, the daring exploits of Stephen Decatur in two wars, or the naval victories of Oliver H. Perry.
6. Report on the Hartford Convention, held by the Federalists to protest against the War of 1812. Tell why the convention met, what changes in the federal government it proposed, and how it helped kill the Federalist party.
7. Contribute to a bulletin-board display of famous American slogans. Use pictures or drawings to show the conditions that prompted each slogan.
8. Make drawings or models of the uniforms, military equipment, or warships used in the War of 1812.
9. Go over the words of "The Star-Spangled Banner." Tell how they describe conditions during the siege of Baltimore and the War of 1812.

Chapter 14

THE RISE OF SECTIONALISM

In 1824 the United States had only one political party, the Republicans. Yet the presidential election in that year was hotly fought by four rival candidates. They were (1) Andrew Jackson of Tennessee, famous Indian fighter and hero of the Battle of New Orleans; (2) John Quincy Adams of Massachusetts, President Monroe's secretary of state and the son of our second President; (3) William H. Crawford of Georgia, Monroe's secretary of the treasury; and (4) Henry Clay of Kentucky, Speaker of the House of Representatives and a leader of the War Hawks. The vote in the electoral college was 99 for Jackson, 84 for Adams, 41 for Crawford, and 37 for Clay. No candidate had a majority. The election therefore went to the House of Representatives. Since it had to choose the President from among the three men with the most votes, Clay was out of the running. He threw his support to Adams, who became President.

The election of 1824 was also unusual in another way. Of the four candidates, only the military hero, Andrew Jackson, received electoral votes in all parts of the nation. The other three candidates were supported mostly by voters in their own section of the country. Adams was strong in the Northeast, Crawford in the South, and Clay in the West. Thus the election highlighted an important development in American politics. This was sectionalism, a feeling of loyalty to a section of the United States rather than to the nation as a whole.

In this chapter we shall find the answers to three questions:

1. How did sectionalism arise in the United States?
2. How was each section different from the others?
3. What policies did each section want the federal government to follow?

RISE OF SECTIONS OF THE UNITED STATES

Legend:
- Fishing
- Shipping
- Textiles
- Iron mills
- Tobacco
- Lumber
- Sugar
- Cotton
- Wheat
- Corn
- Pork
- Beef
- Rice

How Did Industry and Commerce Grow in the Northeast?

A. Growth of Fishing, Shipping, and Trade. The Northeast consisted of both the New England states and the middle states (see map, page 227). Most of the people in this region still made a living by farming during the first half of the nineteenth century. But the other occupations which had been important before the Revolution—shipping, shipbuilding, fishing, and trade—continued to grow. Ships from New England's ports roamed the seven seas to hunt down the world's largest animal, the whale. The slender Yankee clippers, the fastest sailing ships ever built, traveled halfway around the globe to obtain silk, tea, and other valuable products from China.

B. Large-Scale Manufacturing. The Northeast also led the way in developing large industries. The first power-driven machines and the first factories to house them had been built in Great Britain during the eighteenth century. That country produced cloth, iron goods, and other machine-made products at very low prices. It sold them in so many other countries that it became known as the workshop of the world. Anxious to hold its lead, the British government did not allow other countries to obtain the new machines or the plans for making them.

A bright young man named Samuel Slater outsmarted his government. After memorizing the plans of some of the new machines, Slater came to the United States. He built the first American textile mill (factory for making cloth) in Rhode Island in 1790. Only a few other factories were built in the United States before the War of 1812. But afterwards textiles quickly became New England's main industry. Other factories were built to make shoes, paper, clocks, and other products once bought from the British.

New England had important advantages as a center for manufacturing. Since the region is mountainous, it has many swift-flowing rivers and waterfalls. These provided power for driving the machines. Raw materials were available or could be brought in easily by sea. There were plenty of skilled workers, for young people were eager to leave their rocky farms and

Slater's textile mill in Pawtucket, Rhode Island. Why were early factories often built near waterfalls?

228

immigrants continued to pour in from Europe. Business people had the capital (money) needed to build factories and buy machines.

Industry also developed in Pennsylvania, mainly because of its rich deposits of iron ore and coal. These provided raw materials for a large iron industry. Foundries were built to make the iron into machines, farm tools, and other important products. Coal also became important as fuel for the steam engine, which was coming into wide use for driving machines, boats, and locomotives.

C. Improvements in Transportation. 1. THE STEAMBOAT. The first successful steamboat was built by an American, Robert Fulton, in 1807. He tested it on the Hudson River and then organized a company to navigate there. The steamboat was a great success because it could travel upstream against the current. Within a short time, a hundred steamboats were carrying passengers and cargo between New York and Albany. An even larger number traveled the Mississippi and Ohio rivers. They brought the western farmers into closer contact with the outside world.

2. THE STEAM LOCOMOTIVE. The steam locomotive was perfected by a British subject, George Stephenson, in 1825. It could pull heavy loads over smooth iron rails at high speed. The United States, with its great distances, soon had more railroads than Great Britain. Most American rivers flow from north to south. Railroads provided a means of carrying people and goods from east to west. By 1860 a half-dozen railroads had been built across the Appalachian Mountains, linking the Atlantic coast with the Mississippi Valley.

3. THE CANALS. The use of steamboats and railroads spread slowly because they were expensive to build and used up great amounts of coal. The most important improvement in transportation between 1820 and 1850 was the canal. So many canals were built during this period that it has been called the golden age

GROWTH OF MANUFACTURING

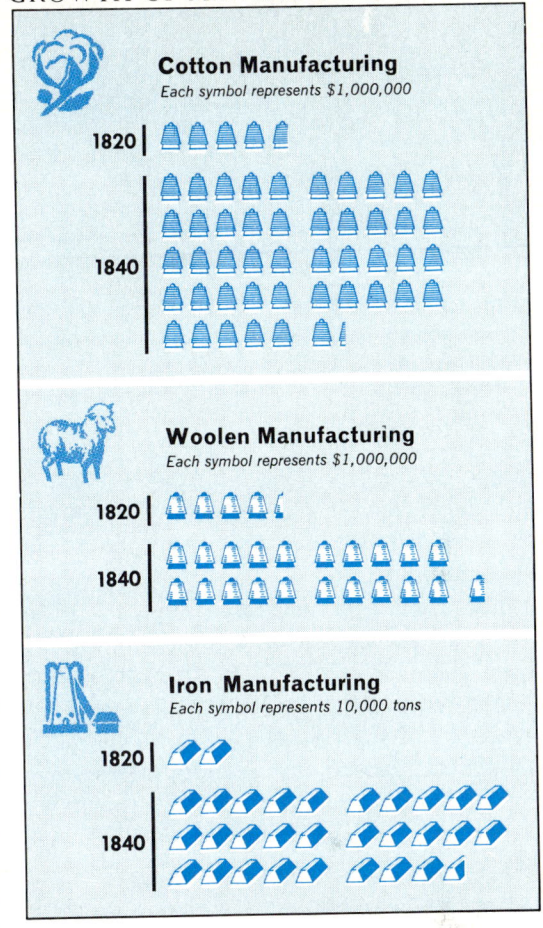

Cotton Manufacturing
Each symbol represents $1,000,000

Woolen Manufacturing
Each symbol represents $1,000,000

Iron Manufacturing
Each symbol represents 10,000 tons

of canal building. Canals were dug either to get around waterfalls or to connect rivers. They made it possible to ship goods long distances by water at low cost.

The most successful example of canal building was the Erie Canal. The "big ditch," completed in 1825, was over 350 miles long. It connected the Hudson River with the eastern end of Lake Erie (see map, page 227). This made it possible to ship grain and other farm produce from the Great Lakes region to New York City much faster than before. More important, the shipping cost was cut from a hundred dollars a ton to less than ten dollars. From New York City, the produce could be

229

Race between the Tom Thumb locomotive and a horse-drawn car. Why were such races held? Which would you expect to win?

sent to other ports along the Atlantic coast or to Europe. Manufactured goods for the people of the Northwest Territory could return by the same route.

The building of the Erie Canal had other important results. Factories sprang up in New York and neighboring New Jersey to manufacture products for the West. New York City, the center of this booming trade and industry, became the largest city in the United States. Population also increased rapidly along the Hudson River, the Erie Canal, and the Great Lakes.

D. Conditions of the Industrial Workers. In time, the growth of trade and industry made the Northeast the richest and most populous section of the United States. However, it also created serious problems, especially for workers in industry. Working conditions in the new factories were very poor. Hours of work were long—usually from sunrise to sunset, six days a week. Wages were only a few dollars a week for men. Women and children worked the same long hours, but were paid much lower wages.

You may wonder why people took such jobs. For many immigrants, these jobs were the quickest way to save money to buy farms. For native Americans, they offered other important advantages. Life on the farms was usually quite lonely. Farmers earned little cash, hardly enough to buy necessities. Factory jobs, on the other hand, provided cash, companionship, and a gayer life in a town or city.

E. Political Policies of the Northeast. The owners of the new factories, steamship lines, and railroads—unlike their workers—were usually wealthy men. Many also had large interests in commerce and banking, or worked closely with people who did. Often these rich business people disagreed among themselves on a certain question. But they almost always agreed on what they wanted the federal government to do for them. They wanted: 1. high tariffs to protect American industries from foreign competition; 2. a sound currency, like that provided by the Second Bank of the United States; 3. unrestricted immigration, because it gave them a large supply of workers willing to accept low wages. They were only partly successful, however, in getting the government to give them what they wanted. For the leaders of the other sections were demanding different policies suited to their own interests.

REVIEWING THE SECTION

A. Knowing New Terms

In your notebook write the new terms in this section that best complete these statements.

1. A feeling of loyalty to one's nation is called nationalism. A feeling of loyalty to a part or section of the nation is called _____.
2. The three sections of the United States after 1820 were the _____, the _____, and the _____.
3. Great Britain sold its machine-made goods in so many different places that it became known as the _____ of the world.
4. The first large factories in the United States were the clothmaking, or _____, mills.
5. Three important improvements in transportation in the first half of the nineteenth century were the _____, the _____, and the _____.
6. Especially successful was the _____ Canal, which helped make _____ _____ the most populous city in the United States.

B. Knowing Important People

For each important person in the first column, write the *letter* of the best description in the second column.

Important People
1. John Quincy Adams
2. Henry Clay
3. Robert Fulton
4. Samuel Slater
5. George Stephenson

Descriptions
a. Builder of America's first textile machines
b. Inventor of the canal
c. Inventor of the first useful steamboat
d. Inventor of the steam locomotive
e. Son of a President who became President himself
f. Congressman who first became famous as a War Hawk

C. Finding the Reasons

In your notebook write the letters of *all* the correct answers to each question.
1. Why did John Quincy Adams win the election of 1824?
    a. He won a majority of the votes in the electoral college. b. He won electoral votes in every section of the United States. c. Thanks to the support of Henry Clay, he was elected President by the House of Representatives.
2. Why did New England become the main manufacturing center of the United States?
    a. It had swift-flowing rivers and good seaports. b. It had a large supply of labor. c. It had many wealthy business people.
3. Why did Pennsylvania become a manufacturing center?
    a. Its ports and shipping were superior to New England's. b. It had a larger supply of skilled labor than New England. c. It had much more coal and iron ore than New England.

4. Why did steamboats quickly become popular in the United States?
a. Since roads were poor, Americans preferred to ship their goods by water. b. The United States had many navigable rivers. c. The current usually carried boats downstream, but power was needed to make the return trip.
5. Why were most American railroads built from east to west?
a. There were few mountains to cross. b. Few rivers ran in that direction. c. There was no other way for settlers in the West to send their goods to market.
6. Why did New York become the most populous city in the United States after the Erie Canal was built?
a. It was the port through which the farmers of the Great Lakes region sent their produce to market. b. It was the port through which European manufactured goods were sent to the Northwest. c. It became a manufacturing center for goods for the western farmers.
7. Why did many native Americans and immigrants take jobs in the new factories?
a. Wages of factory workers were high. b. Working hours were shorter in the factories than on the farms. c. Life in the city was usually more interesting than life on the farm.
8. Why did members of Congress from the Northeast want high tariffs, sound money, and unrestricted immigration?
a. High tariffs protected the Northeast's manufacturers from foreign competition. b. Sound money made it easier for workers to save up to buy farms. c. Immigrants were usually willing to work for low wages.

IMPROVING YOUR SKILLS

A. Mastering the Map

Study the map on page 227. Then answer the following questions.
1. List the names of the states and territories in each section of the United States in 1830.
    a. Northeast
    b. South
    c. West
2. Which was the largest section in area? The smallest section?
3. Which section had the most states and territories? The least?
4. What were the main products of each section?
    a. Northeast
    b. South
    c. West

B. *Interpreting the Graph*

Study the graph on page 229. Then complete these statements in your notebook.
1. Cotton manufacturing was about _____ times as large in 1840 as in 1820.
2. Woolen manufacturing was about _____ times as large in 1840 as in 1820.
3. About _____ times as much iron was made in 1840 as in 1820.
4. The value of the cotton goods made in 1840 was more than _____ times as large as the value of the woolen goods made the same year.

How Did the Plantation System Develop in the South?

A. A Beautiful Picture. You have probably seen motion pictures of southern plantations before the Civil War. They usually show a large mansion surrounded by broad lawns and tall trees. The owner and his family lead a life of luxury. They have many black slaves to serve them. They wear fine clothes and amuse themselves with fox hunting, fancy balls, and other costly entertainments.

This picture is true as far as it goes; but it shows only a very small part of life in the South at that time. There were fewer than ten thousand large plantations, and most of them were less prosperous than the films lead us to believe. To find out why this was so, we must look beneath the bright surface to see how the plantation system actually worked.

B. The Spread of Cotton Growing. Tobacco continued to be the main cash crop (crop sold for money) in Maryland, Virginia, and North Carolina during the first half of the nineteenth century. Rice was still the main crop in the wet lowlands of South Carolina. Sugar growing early became the main occupation in Louisiana. Elsewhere in the South, however, cotton quickly became the main crop after the invention of the cotton gin by Eli Whitney in 1793.

Before Whitney's invention, only small amounts of a special kind of cotton were grown. It did not pay to grow ordinary cotton because it took a slave an entire day to pick the seeds out of a single pound. With the early cotton gin, however, a slave could remove the seeds from fifty pounds a day. With a larger gin and water power, a slave could clean a thousand pounds a day! It now became profitable to grow cotton wherever the summer sea-

A planter's mansion. How did the system of slavery enable wealthy plantation owners to afford to live in homes like this one?

son was long enough. Production shot up from 100,000 bales in 1800 to over 2,000,000 bales in 1850. Cotton became not only the main crop of the South but also the main export of the United States. "Cotton is King" became a southern boast.

C. Disadvantages of the Cotton Plantation System. It is dangerous to depend on a single cash crop. The price paid for cotton changed a great deal from year to year. When bad weather reduced the crop, the shortage of cotton forced the price up. Nevertheless, many planters lost money because they had only a small amount of cotton to sell. Surprisingly, they might be even worse off when the crop was very large. At those times, the oversupply of cotton forced the price down. Only the most careful planters could make a profit when the crop was poor or when the price was low. Those who failed to plan carefully, or lived too richly, sank into debt. Many ended by losing their plantations.

There was a second reason why many planters went bankrupt: cotton, like tobacco, wore out the soil. Very few planters went to the trouble and expense of using fertilizers, changing crops, or leaving land idle to regain its strength. Instead, they continued to grow cotton on every foot of available land until the soil was worn out. Then they tried to borrow money to buy new plantations in the Southwest.

Because of the need for fresh soil, the "Cotton Kingdom" spread rapidly westward. As the new plantations were opened, the supply of cotton increased rapidly and the price fell. Planters who stayed in the southeastern states found it even more difficult to manage than before. They often made a smaller profit by growing the cotton than the northern merchants did who shipped and sold it.

D. Treatment of the Slaves. The largest single expense in running a plantation was the cost of the field hands, the slaves who worked in the fields. To show a profit, the planter had to obtain the most work from these slaves at the lowest possible cost. A careful planter planned the work so that the slaves were kept busy almost all the time. They usually went out into the fields before dawn and continued to toil until dark. Since slaves were not paid, they had little reason to work hard. For this reason, men, women, and children were put together in large groups or gangs and directed by an overseer. To make them work hard, the overseer carried a whip and used it often. In addition, many plantations required each field hand

PRODUCTION OF RAW COTTON

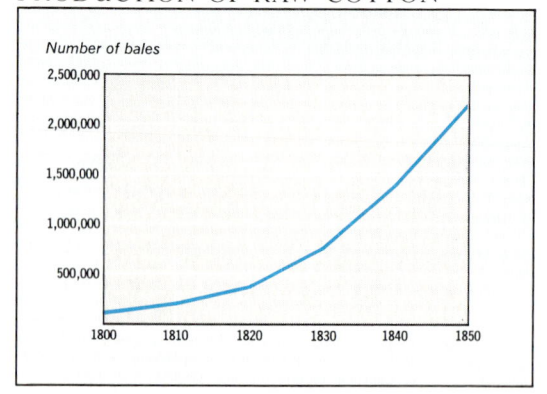

234

to do a certain amount of work every day. Those who fell behind were whipped.

After a long day's work, the slaves returned to their homes. These were usually small huts with dirt floors and a few crude furnishings. There they prepared a simple supper of the food provided by the planter—usually some corn meal and a piece of salted fish or meat. To improve their diet, slaves generally tended a small garden plot after their day's work. They also tried to find time for a little hunting or fishing. Their clothing consisted of a few cheap garments their masters supplied. The total cost of keeping a slave was less than fifty dollars a year.

Slaves who worked in the mansion as house servants were usually better treated than the field hands. So were skilled workers, who made most of the tools, furniture, clothing, and other articles the plantation used. A master often allowed skilled slaves to work for other people, provided that he, the master, received a share of their wages.

E. "The Other South." Though the plantation system was the oustanding feature of southern life, most southern whites were not plantation owners. The South also had several hundred thousand "family farms" like those in the Northeast and the West. Their owners raised some cotton or tobacco as a cash crop. Since these crops were produced mostly by cheap slave labor, the prices paid for them were low. Southern small farmers therefore had small cash incomes. Most earned so little that they became known as the "poor whites."

There were also thousands of merchants and craftworkers in the southern towns and cities. Few became rich, because their market was limited—that is, they had few good customers. The plantations made almost everything they needed, and imported the rest from Great Britain. Most of the small farmers were too poor to buy much.

The cotton gin invented by Eli Whitney.

F. Southern Society. Class lines were sharply drawn in southern society. At the bottom were the slaves and some free blacks. Above them were the poor whites, the other small farmers, and the townspeople. At the top were the planters. A planter's social position depended on the size of the plantation and the number of slaves owned. A few thousand families, the owners of the largest plantations, made up the "planter aristocracy," or ruling class. Because of their wealth and education, the planters controlled the southern governments. They even chose the representatives from their districts. The majority of white southerners usually followed the lead of this small planter aristocracy without question.

G. Policies of the Planters The southern planters were completely opposed to the demands the Northeast made on the federal government. They were against protective tariffs because most of their trade was with Great Britain and other European countries. High tariffs raised the prices of the goods they

235

SLAVEOWNING IN THE SOUTH IN 1850

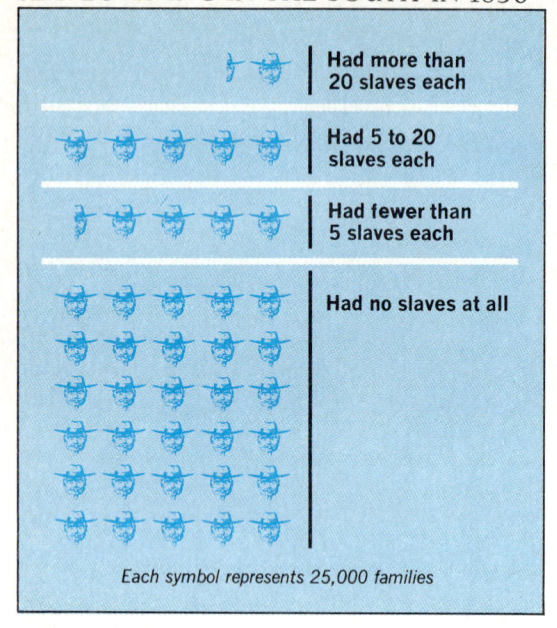

🧑	Had more than 20 slaves each
🧑 🧑 🧑 🧑 🧑	Had 5 to 20 slaves each
🧑 🧑 🧑 🧑 🧑	Had fewer than 5 slaves each
🧑 🧑 🧑 🧑 🧑 🧑 🧑 🧑 🧑 🧑 🧑 🧑 🧑 🧑 🧑 🧑 🧑 🧑 🧑 🧑	Had no slaves at all

Each symbol represents 25,000 families

imported from Europe. Yet they would not switch to American products for fear that the Europeans would buy less American cotton.

Southerners also differed from the Northeast on the Bank of the United States. The bank maintained a sound currency and was strict in making loans. But southerners often had to borrow to buy land and slaves. So they preferred "cheap money" and easy credit.

They likewise disliked a large immigration because it helped the other sections but did little for them. Few immigrants came to the South, where they would have to compete with slave labor. They settled in the Northeast instead, or pushed on to the West. As a result, the other sections were growing faster than the South.

Southerners opposed a strong federal government because they feared the Northeast would win control of it. They became the leading supporters of states' rights (see page 119).

Finally, southerners had one demand of their own. They were always looking for fresh land for cotton growing. For this reason, they wanted the United States to acquire new territories with a warm climate. First they asked for Florida, then for Texas and California, and finally even for Cuba and Central America. These demands became still another cause for disagreement between the Northeast and the South.

REVIEWING THE SECTION

A. Knowing New Terms

For each group listed below, write in your notebook whether it belonged to the upper class of southern society at this period, to the middle class, or to the lower class.

1. Small farmers
2. Field hands
3. House servants
4. Merchants and craftworkers
5. Plantation owners
6. Free blacks

B. Understanding the Facts

To compare the policies northern business people and southern planters favored, complete the second column of the following chart in your notebook.

Policies Favored by Northern Business People	Policies Favored by Southern Planters
1. High protective tariffs	1.
2. Sound money	2.
3. Sound loans	3.
4. Continuation of the Second Bank of the United States	4.
5. Large immigration	5.
6. A strong federal government	6.
7. End of westward expansion	7.

Conclusion. Why were the two sections rivals for control of the federal government?

C. Finding the Reasons

In your notebook write the letters of *all* the correct answers to each question.
1. Why is the usual picture of the luxurious life on southern plantations during the early nineteenth century misleading?
   a. Few southern people owned plantations. b. Many planters did not own large mansions or lead a life of luxury. c. Many planters lived well for a time, but then became poor.
2. Why did cotton become the main southern crop in the early nineteenth century?
   a. Better varieties of cotton were introduced. b. The cost of cleaning the raw cotton was greatly reduced. c. Cotton dresses became very fashionable.
3. Why did many planters lose money?
   a. The price of cotton fell because too much was grown. b. Cotton wore out their lands. c. Keeping slaves was very expensive.
4. Why did slaves usually work in gangs?
   a. They were used to working this way in Africa. b. They worked better together. c. They could be watched more easily by the overseer.
5. Why did the large planters control the South?
   a. They were usually wealthy and educated. b. The middle class was small and weak. c. Most small farmers were poor and uneducated.

IMPROVING YOUR SKILLS

A. Telling Facts From Opinions

In answering essay questions, you have learned to reach a conclusion after listing and examining the facts. Many people do not take the trouble to do this.

Instead, they draw conclusions before they have enough facts or state their own opinions as if they were facts. To think clearly and reach correct conclusions, you should learn to tell the difference between facts and opinions.

The main difference is that facts can be proved, but opinions cannot. Are you, for example, taller than the pupil who sits next to you? This is a question of fact because it can be settled simply by measuring the two of you. Are young people today taller than their parents? This is more difficult to prove. But it is still a question of fact because it is possible to find a definite answer by gathering the necessary information. Are Americans taller than Africans? This question is difficult to answer because we would have to get the figures from African countries on their peoples' heights. Yet even this is a question of fact because it can be settled by taking the necessary measurements.

On the other hand, how would you answer the question, Who is a kinder person, you or the pupil in the next seat? You could, of course, find evidence to prove that you are a kind person, and your neighbor could do likewise. Each of you could also gather facts to prove that the other is not a kind person. But could you arrive at a final answer which everyone, including the other pupil, would have to accept as fact? Obviously not. There is no way to measure "kindness" accurately, and people have very different ideas of what makes a person kind. Any question that involves people's values and judgment is a question of opinion. It cannot be answered with certainty because people have different standards and values on which they base their opinions.

Now practice finding the difference between facts and opinions. Write "Fact" for each statement below that can be proved by getting the necessary information. Write "Opinion" if you think the answer depends on a person's values and judgment. Write the correct answers in your notebook.

> EXAMPLES. 1. "Most southern plantation owners in the early nineteenth century lived in large mansions." The answer is "Fact" because it is possible to prove or disprove this statement by looking up nineteenth-century records.
>
> 2. "Most southern plantation owners led happy lives." This is a question of opinion because even well-informed people would disagree on the answer. What is happiness and how is it measured? Different people would certainly give different answers to this question. It would be impossible to decide what percentage of the plantation owners were happy, or how much of the time they felt that way.

Reread the explanation above to make sure that you understand it. Then write "Fact" or "Opinion" for each of the following statements.

1. Cotton was the main crop in the South in 1850.
2. The cotton gin made cotton growing profitable.
3. Cotton growing was more important to the progress of the United States than industry.

4. Cotton growers suffered whether the crop was very good or bad.
5. It would have been better for the planters to take care of their soil than to keep moving westward.
6. It was necessary to whip the slaves to make them work hard.
7. Southern slaves led better lives than northern factory workers.
8. The small farmers and merchants of the South would have been better off if slavery had been abolished.
9. The policies of the planter aristocracy benefited the large planters rather than the small farmers.
10. Southerners had good reasons for opposing the policies favored by the northern business people.

For extra practice, apply this test to other sources of information. Read an account of slavery by a northerner or southerner of the early nineteenth century. Examine it to see how much of it is fact, how much opinion.

In the daily newspaper, news items are supposed to contain facts. Editorials and special columns usually give the opinions of the writers. Find an editorial and a news item on the same topic. Compare them to see whether they follow this general rule.

B. Interpreting the Graph

Study the graphs on pages 234 and 236. Then write "True" in your notebook for each statement if it is correct according to the graphs. If it is wrong, write the correct answer.

GRAPH 1. Production of Raw Cotton

1. The production of raw cotton increased steadily from 1800 to 1850.
2. Only about 100,000 bales of cotton were produced in 1800.
3. More than 500,000 bales were produced in 1820.
4. More than 1,500,000 bales were produced in 1840.
5. More than 2,000,000 bales were produced in 1850.
6. The total production of raw cotton in 1850 was more than twenty times as large as in 1800.

GRAPH 2. Slaveowning in the South in 1850

1. The smallest group of slaveowners were those owning more than twenty slaves per family.
2. The largest group of slaveowners were those owning less than five slaves per family.
3. The total number of slaveowning families was less than 250,000.
4. The number of southern families without slaves was more than double the number that owned slaves.

Why Did Settlers Move to the "Old West"?

A. Stages of Settlement. The frontier people or pioneers—with their buckskin suits, raccoon caps, and long rifles—are figures known to every American. We think of them as brave and able people, equally at home in the forests, prairies, or mountains. They really deserve our thanks as well as our admiration. They opened the way for the conquest of the great American wilderness from the Appalachian Mountains to the Pacific Ocean.

The frontier people lived by hunting, fur trapping, and trading with the Indians. When they returned East to sell their furs, they brought back glowing accounts of the new lands they had explored. They told of fertile valleys and magnificent forests filled with wild game, birds, and fish. Their stories made listeners long to go west. Some frontier folk also served as guides. They led migrants to the West and helped them settle there. Without such leadership and help, the settlement of the West would have been even more difficult than it actually was.

Following the frontier folk were backwoods people. They found land, settled for a while, and moved on. These were hardy people, prepared for a rough life in the backwoods. They usually built a small cabin near a brook or a spring. Often they did not bother to cut down trees in order to clear the land. Instead, they only killed the trees around the cabin by cutting out the bark in a ring around the trunk. Corn and vegetables were planted between the trees. Families kept a cow or two and some pigs. The pigs ran wild to find their own food. The women and girls took care of the cabin, made all the clothes for the family, and helped in the garden besides. Always there was a rifle handy, for hunting and protection. Like the frontier people, these early settlers were always eager to explore new lands. It has been said that when they saw the smoke from a neighbor's chimney, they felt crowded, and moved westward again.

Third came the permanent settlers. These were the people who changed the wilderness into farmland. They cut down trees and built fences around their lands. They built comfortable homes for themselves and roomy barns for their animals. The family members were partners in the work of the frontier. Men hunted, did the work in the fields, and defended their lands. Women performed household work, made butter, cheese, soap and candles, and took care of the cows and poultry. Where settlements had favorable locations, at a crossroads or the meeting place of two rivers, villages sprang up. Some later became large cities. Thanks to the efforts of the pioneers and later settlers our vast country was settled within a century.

B. Defining the "West." The frontier (the line of new settlements) was always moving westward. It is therefore hard to say exactly where the "West" was located at any particular time. After the Revolutionary War, settlers began to cross the Appalachian Mountains in large numbers. Fifty years later, they were beginning to cross the Mississippi River. In the period we are now studying, the West was still mainly the region between the Appalachians and the Mississippi (see map, page 227).

This region is still sometimes called the Old West. However, the "cotton belt" states of Alabama, Mississippi, and Louisiana were usually considered part of the South rather than the West. They had the same economic interests as the southern states and usually voted with them in Congress. Kentucky and Tennessee, on the other hand, were generally considered western, rather than southern, states.

C. A Picture of Westward Migration. The settlement of the West proceeded with amazing speed. As one Illinois settler put it, "No poor man in the eastern states who has feet and legs and can use them has any excuse for remaining where he is, a day or even an hour." Many Americans left their worn-out farms in the East every year to find fresh lands in the West. Townspeople from the East and immigrants from Europe swelled the flood of settlers.

Every spring the roads and rivers leading westward were crowded with this traffic. Most families loaded their household furnishings in wagons and took along their cattle and sheep. Single people usually rode on horseback, their belongings tied to their saddles. The poor went on foot. They pushed their few possessions in a handcart or wheelbarrow or carried them in packs on their backs. When they reached a river, the migrants crowded aboard flatboats or barges. A fully loaded riverboat was certainly a striking sight; but traveling on one was not a very comfortable experience.

The entire journey usually took a month or two if all went well. But the way was filled with difficulties and dangers: bad weather, illness and accidents, robbers, and Indian attacks. Several families generally traveled together for safety. Because of the strain, the migrants often quarreled with one another. But some became lifelong friends. Many young men and women who met on the journey were married before it ended.

D. Routes to the West. Poor roads presented still another serious difficulty. Most American roads at that time were no more than dirt trails full of ruts and holes. In wet weather they oozed mud. When the weather was dry, they sent up clouds of choking dust. The most important exception was the National Road, begun in Jefferson's day. This road was wide, paved with crushed stone, and carefully graded to eliminate steep rises or dips. It was also free of tolls. This was important because most of the migrants had little cash. The National Road soon became one of the main routes for westward migration.

Another major route to the West, the Wilderness Road, ran from northern Virginia across the Appalachians into Kentucky (see map, page 242). Water transportation, however, was much better than overland transportation. Once the migrants reached the Ohio River or some other branch of the Mississippi, they boarded a riverboat. The current carried them slowly down river to their destination.

E. Acquiring Land. When they arrived, the migrants had to get land. Under the Land Act

Fairview Inn on the National Road. Why did Americans already have a traffic problem over a hundred years ago?

241

ROUTES TO THE OLD WEST IN 1840

of 1785, the government had offered public lands in 640-acre sections at a dollar an acre. Very few Americans, however, could afford to pay out $640 at one time. So land companies formed by rich eastern business people bought the sections instead. Then they sold them to settlers in small plots at a much higher price per acre. Complaints led Congress in 1800 to offer half-sections for sale at two dollars an acre, with four years to pay. This still proved too expensive for most people. In 1820 eighty-acre plots were made available at $1.25 an acre. A family could obtain a farm from the government for one hundred dollars and take several years to pay.

Even so, many people became "squatters" —that is, settlers on unused land. In 1841, the government gave each squatter 160 acres of land. They had to agree to pay for it over a period of a year. Finally, in the Homestead Act of 1862, the government gave people 160 acres of land free of charge, provided they settled on it for five years. This "cheap land" policy of the federal government was one of the reasons why the West was settled so fast.

F. Influence of the West. By 1850 nearly one-half the people of the United States were living west of the Appalachian Mountains. The entire territory east of the Mississippi had already been made into states. Four states west of the river, Texas, Iowa, Missouri, and Arkansas, had also been admitted to the Union.

From these new western states, great amounts of wheat and corn, pork and beef, lumber and cotton traveled southward by the Mississippi or eastward by the Erie Canal. There was more than enough to supply the needs of the South and Northeast. The surplus not needed in the United States was exported to Europe. In return, the West bought large amounts of manufactured goods from the Northeast and Europe.

The development of the West also led to the strengthening of democracy. There were few wealthy people of the frontier. There, a person's ability to handle difficult situations counted for more than family background. Westerners felt that people should be allowed to vote and

GROWTH OF POPULATION IN THE OLD WEST

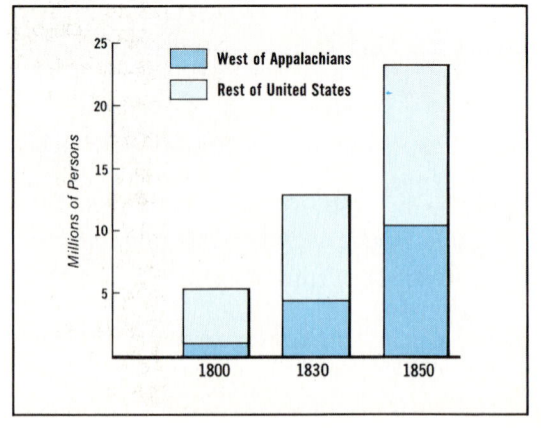

and hold office even if they did not own property. New western states were therefore the first to do away with property qualifications (see page 53). Also, women played an important part in taming the frontier. They enjoyed respect and rights they did not have in the older parts of the country.

G. The Western Program. The West, like the other two sections of the United States, had its own special needs. Westerners wanted a strong federal government to supply them with cheap land. They wanted internal improvements and protection from the Indians. They were also interested in expanding farther westward to the Pacific Ocean.

The Northeast and South competed for the support of the westerners in Congress. At first, representatives from the Northeast were opposed to cheap land and federal aid for internal improvements. So many people were moving westward, they complained, that entire towns were being left empty. But their attitude changed when they discovered that the West was buying more and more northeastern factory products. So they supported the western demands, and the westerners in turn supported their demands for protective tariffs and free immigration. On one issue, however, the West and Northeast could not agree. Most westerners were in debt for land and farm equipment. For this reason, they opposed the Bank of the United States, which stood for sound money and hard-to-get credit.

Both the West and South agreed that they wanted cheap land, easy credit, and more territory. But these sections disagreed on three points. The West favored a strong federal government; the South favored states' rights. The West wanted federal aid for internal improvements; the South did not, because it had many rivers down which cotton could be shipped to the coast. Most important, the South wanted territorial expansion in order to get more land for cotton growing. But this meant the spread

Cyrus McCormick giving a demonstration of his invention, the reaper. McCormick's invention was important in settling the West because it enabled a farmer to harvest a large crop without hiring extra workers.

of slavery. On this issue, as we shall see, the West sided with the Northeast.

H. Revival of the Two-Party System. Disagreements among the three sections and their political leaders made the administration of John Quincy Adams a difficult one. Adams began by appointing Clay as his secretary of state. Jackson's supporters said that the appointment was Clay's reward for helping Adams to become President. They charged that this "corrupt [dishonest] bargain" had robbed their leader of the presidency. For the next four years, the Jackson men in Congress carried on a merciless fight against the Adams-Clay group.

Since Jackson and Clay were both westerners, their feud split the West. Clay sided with John Quincy Adams and the Northeast. The Jackson men therefore turned to the South for support. They reached an agreement with John C. Calhoun of South Carolina. Calhoun was to be the candidate for Vice-President on

243

Jackson's ticket when the "hero of New Orleans" ran again in 1828.

The Jackson-Calhoun group took the old name of Democratic-Republicans (see page 191). The change showed that they favored the common people over the rich business people of the Northeast. A few years later, they became known as the Democrats. This group, founded by Andrew Jackson's followers on principles laid down earlier by Thomas Jefferson, was the beginning of the modern Democratic party. The annual Jefferson-Jackson Day dinner is a very important political event for Democrats to this day.

The Adams-Clay group called themselves the National-Republicans to show that they favored a strong national (federal) government. They soon became known as the Whig party. In the 1850s a part of the Whig party helped to found the modern Republican party. Thus the feud between Jackson and Clay, together with the spirit of sectionalism, led to the revival of the two-party system in American politics.

REVIEWING THE SECTION

A. Knowing New Terms

PART 1. In your notebook write the new terms in this section that best complete these statements.

1. The buckskin suit, raccoon cap, and long rifle were symbols of the _____ _____.
2. People who changed the wilderness into farmland and stayed on the land were _____ settlers.
3. The place where settlements ended and the wilderness began was known as the _____.
4. People who settled on land that did not belong to them were known as _____.
5. The federal government sold land to settlers at lower and lower prices. It finally gave them 160 acres free of charge under the _____ Act.
6. In the 1830s the Republican party split into two new parties—the Democratic-Republicans, or _____, and the National-Republicans, or _____.

PART 2. Explain each term *in your own words.*

(In **B**) cotton belt states (In **H**) corrupt bargain
(In **E**) cheap land policy

B. Knowing Important People

For each important person in the first column, write the *letter* of the best description in the second column.

Important People	*Descriptions*
1. John Quincy Adams	a. Head of the Democratic party
2. John C. Calhoun	b. Last important leader of the Federalists
3. Henry Clay	c. Political leader of the Northeast
4. Andrew Jackson	d. Political leader of the South
5. Eli Whitney	e. Westerner who helped form the Whig party
	f. Yankee who invented the cotton gin

C. Understanding the Facts

In your notebook write the *letter* of the correct choice.

1. The frontier people:
   a. explored the West   b. advertised its advantages   c. guided settlers there   d. did all these things.
2. The backwoods people usually:
   a. cleared some land for farming   b. built comfortable houses and barns   c. established villages   d. did all these things.
3. Permanent communities were established in the West mainly by the:
   a. frontier people   b. backwoods people   c. later settlers   d. federal government.
4. People migrating to the West included large numbers of:
   a. farmers from the East   b. townspeople from the East   c. immigrants from Europe   d. all these groups.
5. Water routes were better than roads for traveling West because they:
   a. required less effort   b. were faster   c. were safer   d. had all these advantages.
6. The West led the way in:
   a. ending property qualifications for voting and officeholding   b. granting women the same rights as men   c. reducing the differences between social classes   d. all these ways.
7. Between 1820 and 1850, the Northeast drew closer to the West because:
   a. it wanted western support against the South in Congress   b. trade between the two sections increased greatly   c. more western settlers came from the Northeast than the South   d. it was influenced by all these factors.
8. The Jackson-Calhoun group represented:
   a. the Northeast and South   b. the Northeast and West   c. the South and West   d. all three sections.

D. Summing Up the Chapter

Copy the following chart in your notebook. To compare what the different sections wanted, write either "For" or "Against" in each box.

	Northeast	South	West
1. High tariffs			
2. Bank of the United States			
3. Large immigration			
4. Strong federal government			
5. Expansion of slave territory			

Conclusion. Which section did the West agree with more, the Northeast or South?

IMPROVING YOUR SKILLS

A. Telling Facts From Opinions

Write "Fact" for each statement that can be proved by getting the necessary information. Write "Opinion" if you think the answer depends on values and judgment. (For a review, see pages 237-238.)

1. The pioneers who opened the West are usually praised in our films, TV programs, and books.
2. Every American should feel gratitude as well as admiration for the work of the pioneers.
3. The backwoods people were a hardy people accustomed to a rough and simple life.
4. Alabama, Mississippi, and Louisiana had the same economic interests as the older southern states and usually voted with them in Congress.
5. Since the western lands were very fertile, no poor person should have remained in the Northeast or South.
6. Many migrants used the National Road because it charged no tolls.
7. The cheap land policy of the federal government was an important reason why the West was settled so fast.
8. The West played a more important part in the growth of American democracy than the Northeast or South.

B. Mastering the Map

After examining the map on page 242, complete the following sentences:
1. Two roads connecting states east of the Appalachian Mountains with the West were the _____ _____ and the _____ _____.
2. The West and South were connected by one very long road, the _____ _____.
3. The section of the United States where the most roads, canals, and railroads were built was the _____.

4. The two sections connected by the new means of transportation were the _____ and the _____.

C. Interpreting the Graph

Study the graph on page 242. Then complete these sentences in your notebook.
1. The total population of the United States in 1800 was a little over __ million.
2. In 1830 the total population was about __ million.
3. In 1850 the population of the United States was about __ million.
4. The population of the United States increased almost __ times from 1800 to 1850.
5. The population of the West in 1800 was about __ million.
6. In 1850 the West had over __ million people.
7. The population of the West increased more than __ times from 1800 to 1850.
8. The population of the West increased __ times as fast as the population of the entire country.

MAKING HISTORY LIVE

1. Pretend you are an immigrant coming to the United States in the 1830s. In which section would you settle—the Northeast, South, or West? Explain the reasons for your choice.
2. Explain each statement and tell why you agree or disagree with it:
   a. "Cotton is King."   b. "The curse of slavery was fastened on the South by a Yankee inventor."
3. After reading actual accounts of the time, imagine that you traveled westward in the 1830s.
   a. Tell what you took with you on the trip. b. Write a letter to a friend in the East about your experiences.
4. Report on the achievements of an important American associated with the developments described in this chapter. Examples are:
   a. Political leaders like Andrew Jackson, John Quincy Adams, Henry Clay, and John C. Calhoun; b. Economic leaders like Samuel Slater, Eli Whitney, and Robert Fulton; c. Pioneers like Davy Crockett and James Bowie.
5. a. Make a model of a train, steamboat, canal boat, or flatboat of the early nineteenth century. b. Sing or play folk songs of the period.
6. Join one of three groups representing the different sections of the United States during the first half of the nineteenth century. Help prepare a display to show life in your section.

Chapter 15

PRESIDENT JACKSON AND DEMOCRACY

In the election of 1828, Andrew Jackson defeated John Quincy Adams by an electoral vote of 178 to 83, or by more than two to one. "The hero of New Orleans" was a new kind of President. The first chief executive from a poor family, he had become wealthy through his own efforts. He was also the first President from the West and often showed it in his rough and ready ways. He had, for example, fought and won five pistol duels. Though he had never received military training, his military record was outstanding. He filled his men with confidence, made decisions quickly, and carried them out successfully.

In politics, Jackson was a great admirer of Thomas Jefferson and his democratic ideas. Like Jefferson, he dressed simply and walked to his own inauguration. Jackson also shared Jefferson's belief that the President should help the common people. "Equal rights for all, special privileges for none," was one of his slogans.

The people almost worshiped Jackson. On Inaugural Day, Washington was crowded with about ten thousand visitors—"countrymen, farmers, gentlemen, mounted and dismounted, boys, women, children, black and white," wrote an eyewitness. After the ceremony, the crowd rushed into the White House. They damaged the furnishings and almost crushed the new President. One observer called the scene "the reign of King Mob." It was a fitting start for the administration of "the People's President," as Jackson liked to be called.

Jackson served two terms as President. His successor, whom he picked, served one term. This twelve-year period saw so many changes that it

President-elect Jackson on his way to Washington. How does this picture show that Jackson was "the People's President"?

has been called the "Age of Jackson" and the "Era of Jacksonian Democracy." In this chapter you will find answers to three questions:
1. Was Jackson a great President?
2. Did he really promote the interests of the common people?
3. Why has his period been called an era of democracy?

Was Jackson Really "the People's President"?

A. The "Spoils System." One of President Jackson's first moves was to dismiss hundreds of officials who had worked for the government a long time. They were mostly educated members of the upper class from the Northeast. In their places, the President put his own supporters, many of them poor and uneducated westerners. Jackson called this policy "rotation [change] of office." He defended it on the ground that government officials paid less attention to the people when they remained in office too long. It was therefore in the interests of democracy to replace them with "new blood" every few years. Jackson also pointed out that a newly elected President needed officials whom he could trust to carry out his policies. He admitted that many of his

249

"The Trail of Tears." Why did the Cherokees give their westward migration this sad name?

men lacked education and experience. But he did not consider these serious handicaps. "The duties of all public offices are so plain and simple," he said, "that men of intelligence may readily qualify for them."

This policy of rotation had already begun long before Jackson's election. It came under bitter attack in later years. By then it had become the custom for newly elected heads of government—governors and mayors, as well as Presidents—to fill government positions with their supporters. Many of the new officials were dishonest or unskilled. Others were not even needed. This policy became known as the "spoils system." *Spoils* is an old word meaning "prizes taken in battle." Like conquerors of old, the winners of an election felt that they should take all they could from the losers.

B. Removal of the Indians. Jackson's second important move was to resettle all the Indian tribes who lived east of the Mississippi River. Even though federal treaties guaranteed the Indians their lands, settlers were determined to take them away. Georgia, for example, sought to expel the powerful Cherokee Indians. The Indians brought their case to the Supreme Court. The Court, still headed by Chief Justice Marshall, declared Georgia's action unconstitutional. But the President refused to protect the Indians. He is reported to have said, "John Marshall has made his decision. Now let him enforce it."

Jackson believed that the Indians would have to make way for white settlers sooner or later. So he thought the government should move them out before trouble started. During the next few years, he persuaded or forced almost a hundred tribes, including the Cherokees, to move to the western side of the Mississippi. They suffered greatly as a result.

C. South Carolina and Nullification. 1. THE THEORY BEHIND NULLIFICATION. Jackson's spoils system and the removal of the Indians were both popular policies. His third move, however, did not please his supporters in the South. In 1828 Congress raised tariff rates to a new high to protect the industries of the Northeast. Vice-President Calhoun led a strong attack on the tariff law. He based his attack on the theory of states' rights (see page 119), which he carried to a new extreme.

According to Calhoun, the Constitution was an agreement among the states. Therefore the states, rather than the Supreme Court, should have the power to decide what the Constitution means. If a state thought that a federal law violated the Constitution, it should be able to nullify (kill) the law. The protective tariff, Calhoun said, should be nullified because it helped one section of the country at the expense of the others.

Daniel Webster, a noted senator from Massachusetts, made a stirring reply to Calhoun's arguments. Webster said that the federal union had been created by the people, not by the states. If every state was free to disobey federal laws, the United States would return to the unhappy conditions existing under the Articles of Confederation. This would mean disagreements among the states, civil wars, and finally the breakup of the Union.

Calhoun expected Jackson, who was known as a "states' rights man," to back up his southern supporters. At the next Jefferson Day dinner, the President was called on to offer the first toast. To Calhoun's surprise, Jackson said firmly, "The federal union—it *must* be preserved." The Vice-President, knowing that he could not support Jackson's position, resigned. South Carolina then elected Calhoun to the Senate. There he led the states' rights movement for the next twenty years.

2. The Threat of Civil War. Congress reduced tariff rates in 1832. But South Carolina was still not satisfied. Its governor called a special convention, which voted to nullify the new tariff act. The convention declared that South Carolina would leave the Union if the federal government tried to collect customs duties within its borders. The governor also called for volunteers to fight against any "federal invasion."

Jackson quickly met this challenge. "The laws of the United States must be executed," he warned the people of South Carolina. He asked Congress to give him the right to use the army and navy, if necessary, to enforce federal laws there. Privately, he told some members that he planned to send 50,000 troops into South Carolina. "If one drop of blood be shed there in defiance of the laws of the United States," he said, "I will hang the first man of them I can get my hands on to the first tree I can find."

The threat of civil war soon ended, however, because Henry Clay worked out a compromise settlement. Congress passed a new tariff law, which provided for a gradual lowering of rates to the level of 1816. President Jackson accepted the settlement, but he did not like it. He had wanted to end the battle over nullification by forcing South Carolina to back down. He saw that the state was encouraged by its success. He predicted that it would use the threat to secede from the Union again in the years ahead.

D. Jackson's War Against the Bank. President Jackson also met another challenge to the federal government's power—this time by the business interests of the Northeast. The Second Bank of the United States had opened branches throughout the nation. It had become one of the richest and most powerful banks in the world. Its banknotes gave the United States a sound currency. It also kept close watch over other banks to make sure they did

Webster's reply to the South. In a stirring speech, the New England Senator attacked the theory of nullification as a threat to our federal union. He finished his speech with the famous words: "Liberty and union, now and forever, one and inseparable."

not lend money without good security.

Nevertheless, President Jackson was against the bank. He said it was an undemocratic "money power." It gave a few hundred men, the owners of its stock, power over the entire nation. It was especially unfair to the South and West. The people of these sections had borrowed large sums from the bank. Every year they had to pay millions of dollars in interest to the rich easterners who owned it.

The bank's charter, issued in 1816, was good until 1836. But Henry Clay introduced a bill to renew the charter in 1832. Clay expected to run against Jackson in the presidential election that year. He thought that Jackson would be afraid to veto the bank bill, or that he would lose many votes if he did.

Congress quickly passed the new charter; Jackson just as quickly vetoed the bill. His veto message contained such a strong attack on the bank that Congress did not dare to override his veto. To save the bank, its owners spent large sums to help Clay win the election. But the electoral vote was 219 for Jackson, only 49 for Clay. The American people clearly supported Jackson's attack on the bank, as well as his other policies.

Jackson was angry because the bank had supported his opponent. "The Bank is trying to kill me," he said, "but I will kill it." He withdrew the federal government's funds and deposited them in state banks. This action killed the Bank of the United States even before its charter ran out.

E. The Panic of 1837. Jackson's victory over the bank had a harmful aftereffect. It helped to bring on a severe "panic" (economic depression), which began in 1837 and lasted six years. The main causes of the panic were easy credit and land speculation (see page 31). After Jackson killed the Bank of the United States, the state banks began printing notes and making loans as they pleased. Many banks, especially in the West, became known as "wildcat banks." They printed large amounts of "wildcat currency" (banknotes without backing) and lent the money to almost anyone who asked for it. Many people used wildcat currency to buy government lands, which they sold a few months later at a higher price. Land prices skyrocketed. In the little town of Chicago, a single lot cost as much as $7,000.

The United States Treasury soon found itself holding large amounts of almost worthless paper money. In 1836 President Jackson ordered that only gold and silver should be accepted as payment for land. Since these metals were very scarce, people were no longer able to buy land. Those who had borrowed money and bought land in the hope of making a quick profit could not repay their loans. The

Which of Jackson's actions does this cartoon criticize?

BORN TO COMMAND.

KING ANDREW THE FIRST.

ANDREW JACKSON: OUR FIRST PRESIDENT FROM THE WEST

Even on the Carolina frontier, where he was born and grew up, Andrew Jackson was considered a "wild one." According to a friend, he would rather fight than study, and never gave up a fight, even against much larger boys. Andrew was only thirteen years old when the British invaded the Carolinas during the Revolutionary War. In one unfortunate incident, a British officer ordered Andrew to shine his boots. When the boy refused, the officer struck him with his sword. Jackson bore the scar—and a deep hatred of the British—for the rest of his life.

Andrew's father died shortly before he was born. His mother died during the Revolution. Soon afterward a distant relative left the youth a small fortune. He quickly spent it, mostly on horse racing and gambling. After studying law for a short time, he moved to the frontier in Tennessee. He became a circuit (traveling) judge in the "back country." It was a hard job to bring law and order to the tough frontier people. But Jackson did so well that he was elected to Congress when Tennessee became a state. Then he served on the state supreme court. At the same time he ran a store, speculated in land and cotton, managed race horses, and became a major in the state militia. He was often deep in debt. But in time he made a fortune and bought a fine plantation.

Though a judge, Jackson was ready to fight anyone who insulted him or his beloved wife, Rachel. In one duel he was shot near the heart, yet carefully took aim and killed his enemy. He was seriously wounded a second time in a vicious hand-to-hand fight. The two bullets were never removed and often caused Jackson a great deal of pain. He also suffered for many years from tuberculosis and other diseases. But Jackson never let illness slow him down. His soldiers called him "Old Hickory" because he was as tough as a hickory tree.

Jackson was recovering from his second wound when the War of 1812 began. The War Department called on him to fight the Creek Indians. Allies of the British, the Creeks were attacking frontier settlements. Jackson quickly raised an army, marched against the Indians, and crushed them. Then he marched to New Orleans and defeated the British there. Two years later he defeated the Seminole Indians in Florida. These victories made Jackson a great national hero. Though he wanted to retire to his plantation, his friends insisted on nominating him for the presidency.

Jackson was old and not well when he became President. Yet he was one of our strongest and most active Presidents. What is more, he remained active in politics for years after leaving the presidency. His last important act was to help our country acquire a large and rich western territory, Texas, in 1845. This was a fitting end for the life of our first pioneer President, a true westerner.

wildcat banks, unable to collect the money they had lent, failed. Banks and businesses that had dealings with the wildcat banks also suffered heavy losses. Many went bankrupt. Thousands of people were thrown out of work. The Panic of 1837 was the worst depression the United States had suffered up to that time.

F. A "Strong President." President Jackson retired just before the depression began. In his eight years in office, he had shown how powerful a "strong President" could be. He had carried out his policies against determined opponents, he had vetoed more bills than all the Presidents before him combined, and he had defied the Supreme Court. The precedent he set was to be followed by Abraham Lincoln and other strong Presidents in the years to come.

Jackson's Vice-President, Martin Van Buren of New York, followed him as President. Van Buren supported Jackson's ideas. But he lost the election of 1840 because he was blamed for the panic, which started soon after he took office. The Whigs, whose ideas were much like those of the old Federalists, next took control of the government. The "Era of Jacksonian Democracy" seemed to have ended. We shall see, however, that many of its ideas lived on, some even to this day.

REVIEWING THE SECTION

A. Knowing New Terms

For each new term in the first column, write in your notebook the *letter* of the best description in the second column.

New Terms
1. Panic
2. Nullification
3. Secession
4. Spoils system
5. Wildcat currency

Descriptions
a. Practice of replacing old officials with the supporters of a newly elected executive
b. Democratic system for choosing candidates for President and Vice-President
c. Paper money with very little backing
d. Period of business failures and unemployment
e. Right of a state to kill any law it considers unconstitutional
f. Right of state to withdraw from the Union

B. Understanding the Facts

To see how the different sections were affected by President Jackson's policies, complete the chart on the next page. Go down one column at a time. Write "For" in a box if that section had reason to like the President's policy. Write "Against" if it had reason to oppose the policy. If a certain policy had no important effects on the section, leave the box blank. Write in your notebook.

Jackson's Policies	Northeast	South	West
1. Rotation in office (spoils system)			
2. Removal of the Indians			
3. Opposition to nullification and secession			
4. War on the Bank of the United States			

Conclusions. 1. Which section did President Jackson's policies most favor?
2. Which of his policies were clearly intended to help the common people?
3. Was Jackson really "the People's President"?

C. Finding the Reasons

In your notebook write the letters of *all* the correct answers to each question.

1. Why was Jackson called "the People's President"?
   a. He came from a poor family and grew up in the West. b. His military victories made him a popular hero. c. He believed in the democratic ideas of Thomas Jefferson.
2. Why did President Jackson think rotation in office was democratic?
   a. New officials were more likely to do what the people wanted. b. A newly elected President's supporters would carry out his policies loyally. c. Uneducated officials would understand the needs of the common people.
3. Why did the President remove the Indian tribes living east of the Mississippi?
   a. He wanted the Indians to have richer lands. b. He had to win the support of southern and western voters. c. He believed that the Indians could not hold out against the settlers who wanted their lands.
4. Why did Jackson want to deal harshly with South Carolina after it adopted the policy of nullification and secession?
   a. He did not believe in states' rights. b. He favored high tariffs. c. He considered South Carolina's action a danger to the existence of the United States.
5. Why did President Jackson fight the Bank of the United States?
   a. He thought it was undemocratic for a small group of business people to have so much power. b. He considered it unfair that the bankers of the Northeast took large amounts of interest from the West and South. c. The bank interfered in politics and supported his opponents.
6. Why was the death of the Bank of the United States followed by the Panic of 1837?

a. Some state governments chartered banks that did not have enough gold and silver to back their operations. b. Many kinds of paper money with many different values came into circulation. c. Cheap money and easy credit were used for speculation, especially in land.
7. Why was Jackson known as a strong President?
a. He fought duels and won battles. b. He carried out his policies in spite of strong opposition. c. He insisted that he had the right as President to disagree with Congress and the Supreme Court.

IMPROVING YOUR SKILLS

Looking at Both Sides

How can we tell whether a source of information is reliable? You already know one test—whether its statements are supported by facts and so are not just opinions. Another test is whether the source presents both sides of controversial questions fairly. (Controversial questions are those for which there is no single correct answer.) Let us apply this test to sources on President Jackson. Since he was a controversial President, many books and articles have been written for and against him and his policies. A good project is to select one of his policies, to find several sources agreeing or disagreeing with it, and to compare their arguments. The last step is to decide which source you consider the most reliable because it presents both sides fairly.

Now use this section of the text to practice finding evidence on both sides. Choose *one* of President Jackson's policies in **A** through **D**. Then summarize *in your own words* the arguments that are given for and against it in the text. Use the two-column form shown here. (If the class forms four groups, it can cover all four policies.)

POLICY 1. Rotation in Office (the Spoils System)

Pro (arguments for the policy)	Con (arguments against it)
a. b. c.	a. b.

POLICY 2. Removal of the Indians

Pro	Con
a. b.	a. b. c.

POLICY 3. Opposition to Nullification and Secession

Pro	Con
a. b.	a. b.

POLICY 4. Killing the Bank of the United States

Pro	Con
a. b. c.	a. b. c. d.

Conclusion. Does this text try to present both sides fairly?

Why Were the 1830s Called an "Era of Democracy"?

A. The Spirit of Reform. The 1830s were a period of great democratic progress in the United States. Up to that time, the country had been concerned mainly with political questions—that is, with improvements in government. Now, however, new reform movements were springing up to deal with the social and economic problems of workers, women, and other groups. The reformers (people who wanted to make improvements) believed that everyone had the right to a full and satisfying life. That ideal has not been forgotten. In this century, it inspired the labor movement and the fight for civil rights and women's rights.

B. Political Reforms. The new spirit of reform showed itself in President Jackson's policies. It also influenced many states to end property qualifications for voting and officeholding. It was most noticeable in a new democratic method for choosing the candidates for President and Vice-President. This was the nominating convention.

Before 1830 members of each party in Congress had made the nominations. Sometimes state legislatures had also named candidates. Neither method allowed for the views of people all over the nation. The nominating convention was first tried in the election of 1832. In that year leaders of each political party in all parts of the United States came together. They chose the candidates and drew up the party platforms. This method worked so well that it has been used in every presidential election since Jackson's day.

C. Helping the City Workers. 1. PRESIDENT JACKSON'S ATTITUDE. The new spirit could also be seen in President Jackson's attitude toward the working class. Jefferson had been interested mainly in helping the small farmers. Jackson promised to help all the "humble members of society—its farmers, mechanics, and laborers." His attitude showed that the "mechanics and laborers"—that is, the city workers—had become an important group. Their numbers were growing rapidly as commerce and industry expanded. They were also voting in greater numbers as property qualifications were ended. Under President Jackson, the Democrats succeeded in winning their support. The Democratic party has usually had their support ever since.

2. THE TEN-HOUR DAY. Up to that time, workers had been used to a twelve- to fifteen-hour day. During the Jackson era, however, they demanded a ten-hour day. This would last from 6 A.M. to 6 P.M., with an hour off for breakfast and a second hour off for lunch. President Jackson ordered the ten-hour day for all workers in government shipyards. President Van Buren extended the order to all workers on government projects. During the 1840s two states ordered a ten-hour day for children under twelve. Two other states extended the ten-hour day to all workers. Many other states followed suit in later years.

3. THE TRADE UNION MOVEMENT. The Jackson era also saw a rapid growth of workers' organizations, the trade unions. The workers joined together in unions to be stronger when they bargained with their employers. If an employer refused to meet their demands, they could strike—that is, they could walk off the job altogether. Skilled workers formed the earliest American unions. They usually won their strikes because the employer could not find other skilled workers to replace them.

The trade unions called many strikes in the early 1830s. But they soon ran into two problems. First, the courts outlawed both strikes and unions under an old rule making it a crime to interfere with commerce. Then the Panic of 1837 caused thousands of workers to be laid off. The unions were unable to collect dues or call successful strikes. Most of them passed out of existence.

Despite this setback, unionism made some gains. In 1840 a Massachusetts court ruled that a strike might be legal if the workers behaved properly. Two years later the Supreme Court held that unions were legal, provided they used "fair, honorable, and lawful means." Almost a hundred years passed, however, before unions finally gained full protection under our laws. It took even longer to end child labor.

D. The Women's Rights Movement. Women form half the world's population. Yet rarely in history have they enjoyed the same rights as men. Though better treated in the United States than in Europe, they still had a low position in the early nineteenth century. Very few girls received an education. The only occupations open to them were teaching, factory work, and work in homes—all very poorly paid. The average woman was married off by her parents at an early age. She spent the rest of her life keeping house and raising a family. This was hard work at a time when almost everything had to be made or done by hand.

In spite of all the work they did, women were considered the "weaker sex." A woman possessed few legal rights. She could not own property. Any valuables she had and any wages she earned went to her husband. Her children were also her husband's legal responsibility. He kept them in case of divorce and could name their guardian in case of his death. If he left property, his widow had to

Three famous women reformers. Amelia Bloomer (left) fought for women's rights. Lucretia Mott (center) was a leader of the movement to end slavery. Dorothea Dix (right) helped the insane and other unfortunates.

find a man to take care of it for her.

The movement for women's rights began when a bold Scotswoman, Frances ("Fanny") Wright, dared to speak on the subject all over the United States. A few courageous American women followed her example. They called themselves feminists, from the Latin word *femina,* meaning "woman." The feminists organized a strong reform movement in 1848. They issued a clever revision of the Declaration of Independence that said, "All men *and women* are created equal." It listed the many grievances (complaints) women had against men and the rights they wanted. As one of the feminist slogans put it, "Men their rights, and nothing more; women their rights, and nothing less."

Most men opposed the feminist movement. They accused its leaders of wanting to "wear the pants" in the family and of seeking to destroy the American home. Hoodlums often pelted the women with eggs and vegetables, or sometimes even struck them. But the feminists bravely continued to fight for women's rights. Gradually they began to make headway.

In the 1830s the first coeducational college and the first college for women were opened. A few years later the first woman minister and the first woman doctor graduated. The achievements of these women showed that women are not inferior to men in intelligence. The feminist cause was also helped by the growing number of women workers in the new factories. Once women earned money for themselves, it was hard to "keep them in their place." By 1850 seven states had granted women the right to hold property in their own names. In 1869 the territory of Wyoming gave them the right to vote.

Yet the women's struggle for their rights was to prove as long and hard as that of the workers. Not until 1920 did the Nineteenth Amendment guarantee all American women the right to vote. Discrimination in employment because of a person's sex was not forbidden until 1964.

E. Public Education. Another large part of the population, the children, benefited from the public school movement. This reform had the support of both the trade unions and the feminists. Workers wanted to end child labor

259

A country school. Note the crude furniture and the different ages of the pupils. Do you think it was hard to teach under such conditions? Why?

because children worked for very low wages and took jobs away from adults. They also wanted their children to be educated so that they could have a better chance for advancement. The feminists wanted schools open to girls as well as boys. Many other far-sighted Americans also supported the public school movement. They knew that education would make the American people more skillful workers, wiser voters, and better citizens.

The United States had been a pioneer in public education in the colonial period (see page 56). Yet its educational system was in poor condition in the early part of the nineteenth century. Most of the southern and western states had no public schools at all. In the other states, most schools were simply small one-room cabins with little equipment and few books. They were open for only three or four months a year and taught only the three Rs (reading, 'riting, and 'rithmetic). Teachers were very poorly paid, and many were poorly educated. Yet even these crude public schools charged high fees. Only a few charity students could go to school free. Nevertheless, the public education movement met with strong opposition—especially from private schools and well-to-do taxpayers. The well-to-do sent their children to private schools. They did not want to pay for a second school system.

In Massachusetts, Horace Mann gave up a very successful career as a lawyer to work for reforms in education. Mann made hundreds of speeches and wrote dozens of articles to expose the bad conditions in the schools. He also toured Europe to learn what improvements could be made.

Under Mann's guidance, Massachusetts once again became the leader in public education. In 1839 it started the first school for training teachers. It also opened the first public high schools, as well as many new elementary schools. In 1852 it passed the first compulsory education law. This law required children be-

Horace Mann addressing the Massachusetts legislature.

tween the ages of 8 and 14 to attend school for at least twelve weeks a year. In 1855 Massachusetts ordered public schools open to all children, regardless of race or religion. One by one the other states followed its lead. In less than a century, our small and crude public school system became the largest and most costly in the world.

F. Treatment of Unfortunates. The fourth large group to attract the reformers' attention were the unfortunates—criminals, debtors, the feeble-minded, the insane, the blind, and the deaf. Prisons in the early nineteenth century were terrible places. They were little more than large rooms, often unbearably hot in summer and terribly cold in winter. There, all types of offenders, regardless of age or background, were thrown together. Because of bad food and unsanitary conditions, many died of "prison fever" or other diseases.

Many prisoners were debtors. Every year about 75,000 people were jailed for owing money. The prisons in one city in 1830 had twenty-four prisoners with debts ranging from six to ninety cents!

The feeble-minded and insane were often thrown into the same prisons as criminals—or given even worse treatment. "Confined in cages, closets, cellars, stalls, pens; chained, naked, beaten with rods, and lashed into obedience"—these words describing their mistreatment were written to the Massachusetts legislature by a young teacher, Dorothea Dix. Shocked by what she had seen, Miss Dix devoted her life to bringing these evils to public attention.

Once again, it took time and effort to bring about reforms. Imprisonment for debt was the first of these evils to be ended. In time, separate prisons were built for different types of offenders and prisoners were given individual cells. In general, conditions were made more healthful. Special institutions (asylums, homes, and shelters) were established for the feeble-

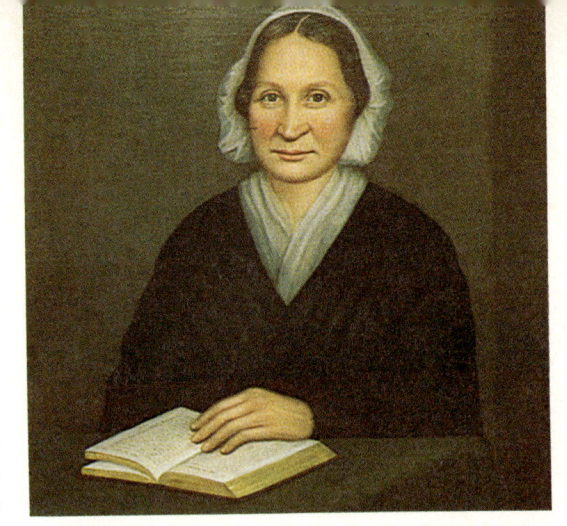

Mary Lyon, the founder of Mount Holyoke in Massachusetts. This school for women opened in 1837 and became a women's college in 1893.

minded and insane. Schools were founded for blind and deaf children, who had been treated like the feeble-minded. Yet the struggle to help these unfortunate people is still far from over. Even today, much more could be done to help them lead more normal lives and become more useful citizens.

G. Other Social Reforms. Two other reform movements were also born in the 1830s. The temperance movement taught the evils of alcoholic liquors. To stop people from drinking them, temperance leaders asked people to sign a pledge. They also asked state governments to forbid the manufacture and sale of liquors. In 1846 Maine became the first state to adopt prohibition—that is, to outlaw alcoholic liquors completely. Other states followed its example. The federal government also adopted prohibition for the brief period from 1920 to 1933.

Perhaps the most important reformers of all were the abolitionists. Their goal was to abolish (end) black slavery in the United States. In the next unit we shall learn more about the important part the abolitionists played in bringing on the Civil War and ending slavery.

REVIEWING THE SECTION

A. Knowing New Terms

In your notebook write the new terms in this section that best complete these statements.

1. People who want to make political, economic, or social improvements are known as _____.
2. In the 1830s many states gave the poor political rights by ending the _____ _____ for voting and officeholding. Another political reform of the time was a new way to choose candidates for President and Vice-President, the _____ _____.
3. To improve their conditions, city workers formed organizations called _____ _____. Their most powerful weapon against employers was the _____.
4. Getting equal rights for women was the goal of the _____ movement.
5. To make sure that all children would be educated, the states established _____ schools and passed _____ _____ laws.
6. Laws prohibiting the manufacture and sale of alcoholic liquors were demanded by the _____ movement.
7. People who wanted to end slavery were called _____.

B. Knowing Important People

For each person in the first column, write the *letter* of the best description in the second column.

Important People
1. Martin Van Buren
2. Dorothea Dix
3. Horace Mann
4. Daniel Webster
5. Frances Wright

Descriptions
a. Founder of the women's rights movement in the United States
b. Leader of the movement to help unfortunates
c. Leader of the public education movement
d. Leader of the states' rights movement
e. Leader of the Democratic party
f. Leading opponent of the states' rights movement

C. Understanding the Facts

PART 1. Tell whether each of the following items is a political, economic, or social reform.

1. Abolitionist movement

2. End of property qualifications for voting and officeholding
3. Presidential nominating convention
4. Public education movement
5. Ten-hour day
6. Trade unions
7. Helping the unfortunate
8. Women's rights movement

PART 2. In your notebook write the *letter* of the correct choice.
1. The most democratic way to choose candidates for President and Vice-President is by vote of:
   a. the electoral college   b. members of each party in Congress   c. state legislatures   d. nominating conventions.
2. In the 1830s the trade union movement was helped by:
   a. the support of Presidents Jackson and Van Buren   b. decisions of the courts   c. great prosperity   d. all these factors.
3. Women were called the "weaker sex" in the early nineteenth century because they:
   a. were less intelligent than men   b. were not allowed to work hard   c. had fewer legal rights than men   d. suffered from all these disadvantages.
4. Most men opposed the women's rights movement because it wanted to:
   a. make women more important than men   b. destroy the American family   c. give women rights that men wanted only for themselves   d. achieve all these purposes.
5. In the second half of the nineteenth century, women advanced toward equality by:
   a. forming organizations to fight for their legal rights   b. getting an education and entering the professions   c. going to work in factories and stores   d. carrying on all these activities.
6. The public education movement was strongly supported by:
   a. political and religious leaders   b. feminists and trade unions   c. wealthy merchants and planters   d. all these groups.
7. Massachusetts became the leader in public education by:
   a. founding a special school to train teachers   b. opening public high schools   c. requiring children to attend school twelve weeks a year   d. making all these advances.
8. Among the unfortunates badly treated in the early nineteenth century were:
   a. debtors and criminals   b. the feeble-minded and insane   c. the blind and deaf   d. all these groups.

IMPROVING YOUR SKILLS

Understanding the Picture

Study the picture on page 257. Then answer the questions below.

1. How can you tell that the people in the crowd represent factory workers?
2. Who does the man facing the crowd represent?
3. What requests might these nineteenth-century workers be making?

MAKING HISTORY LIVE

1. Report on the life and work of any nineteenth-century reformer mentioned in this chapter.
2. Investigate a reform movement active in your community today. Find out:
   a. when the movement began; b. what it has done so far; c. what it would like to accomplish in the future.
3. a. Prepare to be a speaker from a reform movement to address your class. Discuss whether the class should help this movement. b. In your library, find out about an institution for unfortunates. Then discuss what is being done for them and whether it is enough.
4. Suppose you were an American in the 1830s. Which reform movement would you have liked most to support? Why?
5. Prepare to debate the policies of the Jackson administration. Present arguments for and against each of Jackson's policies. Then discuss whether Jackson was a great President.
6. Compare the achievements of Andrew Jackson with those of Thomas Jefferson. Which President did more for democracy?
7. a. Draw a poster for one of the reform movements mentioned in this section. b. Draw a cartoon that shows what you think about the "Era of Jacksonian Democracy."

Chapter 16

A PERIOD OF EXPANSION AND PROGRESS

Few nations in history have grown faster than the United States. Our country advanced three thousand miles, from the Atlantic to the Pacific, in the short space of sixty-five years. This territorial growth was accomplished in three giant steps and a few smaller ones.

The first giant step was the peace treaty of 1783, which gave our new nation the territory from the Atlantic to the Mississippi. The second giant step was the purchase of Louisiana Territory from France twenty years later. This brought the United States as far west as the Rocky Mountains. Another step was the purchase of Florida from Spain in 1819. Thus our nation took possession of almost two-thirds of its present mainland holdings in less than forty years.

The remaining one-third consisted of large, important territories owned by Mexico and Great Britain. American settlers—searching for adventure, a quick fortune, or cheap land—were soon pressing forward into these territories. They talked of our nation's "manifest destiny," a popular slogan at that time. The word *manifest* means "clearly shown" or "plain to see." Destiny means "fate"—that is, something sure to happen. So when Americans used the term "manifest destiny" they meant that it was clearly the fate of the United States to expand westward to the Pacific Ocean.

In this chapter we shall see how the United States fulfilled its manifest destiny. In a third giant step, it took more than a million square miles of territory stretching from the western border of Louisiana to the Pacific. How did it get all this territory? What other advances did our nation make in this period? You will find the answers to both questions in this chapter.

How Did the United States Expand to the Pacific?

A. The "Lone Star Republic." 1. THE SETTLING OF TEXAS. Texas became a target for American expansion soon after Florida was purchased. It was a good target. For Texas was a large territory, larger than such European countries as France and Spain. It had fertile soil and a warm climate. It belonged to Mexico, a weak country that had just gained its independence from Spain. It was thinly populated because few Mexicans had settled there.

In early 1821 a rich American named Moses Austin persuaded the Spanish authorities to let him establish a settlement in Texas. More than 20,000 Americans poured into the region during the next dozen years. Among them were hundreds of slave owners, who established cotton and sugar plantations.

2. THE TEXAN WAR FOR INDEPENDENCE. The Mexican government grew alarmed by the flood of American settlers. In 1830 it ordered a halt to American immigration into Texas and the end of slavery there. The settlers ignored these orders because the Mexican government was too weak to enforce them. (Mexico had fifty-seven different heads of government during the first fifty years of its independence from Spain.) Four years later, however, the new head of the Mexican government, General Santa Anna, decided to enforce the orders. He also issued a new constitution, which ended the Texans' right to govern themselves. They replied by seceding from Mexico. Santa Anna led an army into Texas to crush the rebellion. He trapped a little band of less than two hundred Texans in a fortified mission called the Alamo. After a gallant thirteen-day defense, the brave defenders were completely wiped out.

"Remember the Alamo!" became the Texans' battle cry. Under the able leadership of Sam Houston, the Texans retreated until help arrived. Then they caught Santa Anna by surprise, defeated his army, and captured him. He was released after agreeing to the independence of Texas. The Mexican Congress refused, however, to accept the agreement because it had been obtained by force.

3. THE QUESTION OF ANNEXATION. Texas became an independent country in 1836. It was known as the "Lone Star Republic" because its flag carried a single star. The new republic soon asked for admission to the United States. But many Americans opposed the annexation (takeover) of Texas. Some were afraid that it would mean war with Mexico. Others, especially in the Northeast, were sure that Texas would become slave territory. They did not want to strengthen the South and slavery by taking over a territory from which four or five slave states might be made.

President Jackson, nearing the end of his second term, left the question of annexing Texas to his successor. President Van Buren, who was strongly opposed to slavery, refused to act. So Texas remained an independent nation for a while.

B. American Settlements in the Far West. Meanwhile other Americans had built up trade with the territory of New Mexico by way of the Santa Fe Trail (see map, page 379). Several hundred American settlers had also reached far-off California. They were attracted by an American sea captain's report that it was "the richest, most beautiful, the healthiest country in the world." Both New Mexico and California were legally part of Mexico, but the weak Mexican government had little control over them.

To the north of California was the Oregon country, which reached all the way to Alaska. Both British and American citizens had established trading posts there to get otter and beaver furs from the Indians. In 1818 Britain and the United States agreed to a joint occupation of Oregon. Later, missionaries led by Jason Lee, Marcus and Narcissa Whitman, and Father Pierre De Smet went to Oregon to convert the Indians to Christianity. Word of Oregon's fertile soil and pleasant climate was sent back East. In the early 1840s, many Americans traveled there in covered wagons over the long and rugged Oregon Trail (see map, page 379).

C. The Election of 1844. William Henry Harrison, who was elected President in 1840, died after a few months in office. His successor, Vice-President John Tyler, was a southerner who wanted to annex Texas. But when he placed the annexation treaty before the Senate, it was voted down by northern senators.

In the election of 1844 Henry Clay ran for the presidency for the third time. He was the candidate of the Whig party. Clay was opposed to annexing Texas. Andrew Jackson had the Democrats nominate his friend, James K. Polk of Tennessee, who strongly favored annexation. To please the North, the Democrats announced that they would also take over the entire Oregon country. They hinted that they would fight Great Britain if it did not agree.

Clay pointed out that the United States would probably have to fight both Mexico and Great Britain if the Democrats tried to carry out their promises. Nevertheless, Polk won the election. President Tyler hailed Polk's victory as proof that the American people favored the annexation of Texas. He again laid the matter before Congress, and this time it was approved. Texas became a part of the United States in 1845.

D. The Outbreak of War. When Polk became President, he tried at first to settle the two border problems peacefully. He offered Mexico $50 million if it would accept the loss of Texas and give up New Mexico and California. But the Mexican government refused his offer. The new President was more successful with the British. The United States and Great Britain reached an agreement to divide Oregon at the forty-ninth parallel (see map, page 271).

President Polk then sent an army into Texas. The exact boundary line between Texas and Mexico had never been fixed. It was not clear to whom one small region north of the Rio Grande belonged. Polk ordered Zachary Taylor, the American commander, to advance

Capture of the Alamo. In this reconstruction of the battle, the Texans are shown clearly outnumbered and surrounded.

into the disputed region. A Mexican force crossed the river to drive out the Americans, and a brief battle resulted. As soon as Polk heard the news, he called on Congress to act. He told Congress, "Mexico has passed the boundary of the United States, has invaded our territory, and shed American blood upon American soil." Congress declared war on Mexico at once. Most Americans, believing in manifest destiny, supported the Mexican War. Opposition came mainly from New England. There the conflict was called a war of conquest, planned to gain more slave territory for the South.

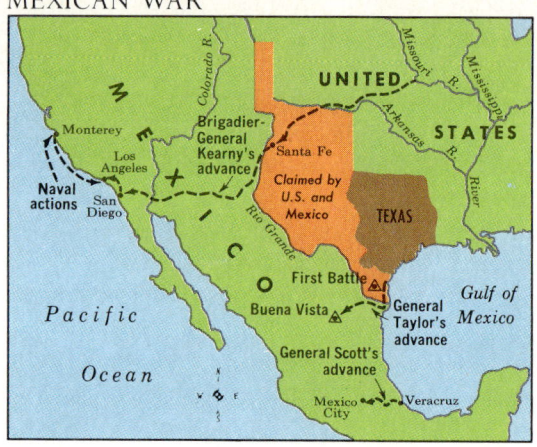

E. The Mexican War (1846-1848). President Polk quickly ordered an attack on Mexico by three American armies. Each army was small and had to travel a great distance, often through deserts and up steep mountains. But the Mexicans were so poorly led that their resistance proved weak.

The first army under General Taylor advanced across the Rio Grande and defeated the Mexicans in two hard-fought battles. The second army marched from Kansas to New Mexico, which it took with hardly a fight. Then it marched on California. Meanwhile a noted explorer, Captain John C. Frémont, led a successful revolt of the American settlers in California. A small American naval force also landed there. Together, the three groups took possession of California. The third American army landed at the port of Veracruz on Mexico's east coast. Advancing inland, it captured the capital, Mexico City (see map above). The Mexican government then agreed to end the fighting and discuss peace terms.

F. The Triumph of Manifest Destiny. The Mexican government, defeated on every front, had to accept peace terms. It recognized the annexation of Texas and ceded (gave up) New Mexico and California to the United States. In return, the American government paid Mexico $15,000,000. It also agreed to pay several million dollars that the Mexican government owed to American citizens.

The Mexican Cession (the territories ceded by Mexico) proved another good bargain for the United States. California was especially

Three Mexican War heroes who later ran for the presidency:

John C. Frémont   Winfield Scott    Zachary Taylor

valuable. Two weeks before the peace treaty was signed, gold was discovered there. A great gold rush followed. Within two years, California had 80,000 settlers and was applying for admission as a state.

In 1853 the United States paid $10 million to Mexico for a strip of land it needed for a southern railroad. The Gadsden Purchase (named after the man who arranged it) brought the mainland United States to its present-day boundaries. The promise of manifest destiny had been fulfilled.

Gold mining in California. Why did so few of these people become wealthy?

REVIEWING THE SECTION

A. Knowing New Terms

In your notebook write the new terms in this section that best complete these sentences.
1. The slogan of the Americans who wanted the United States to reach the Pacific was "_____ _____."
2. The motto of the Texans in their war for independence was "_____ _____ _____."
3. During the ten years Texas remained an independent nation, it was known as the _____ _____ _____.
4. The two main routes to the Far West in the 1840s were the _____ _____ Trail in the Southwest and the _____ Trail in the Northwest.
5. California was quickly settled and admitted to the Union as a result of the _____ _____.

B. Knowing Important People

For each important person in the first column, write the *letter* of the best description in the second column.

Important People
1. Moses Austin
2. Zachary Taylor
3. Sam Houston
4. James K. Polk
5. John Tyler

Descriptions
a. Leader of first American settlers in Texas
b. Leader of the Texans' war for independence
c. Presidential candidate who opposed annexation of Texas
d. President who annexed Texas
e. President who acquired Oregon and the Mexican Cession
f. Victorious Mexican War general

C. Understanding the Facts

Complete this chart by showing the steps in the territorial expansion of the United States.

Territory	Date	How Acquired	From Whom
Original United States	1783	Treaty of peace after the Revolutionary War	Great Britain
Louisiana Territory			
Florida			
Texas			
Oregon Territory			
Mexican Cession			
Gadsden Purchase			

Conclusion. Most countries have enlarged their territories by conquest. Americans often claim that our country has not. Judging by the facts above, are they right? Explain your opinion.

D. Finding the Reasons

In your notebook write the letters of *all* the correct answers to each question.

1. Why did many Americans want this country to expand westward to the Pacific?
   a. They believed in the idea of manifest destiny. b. They wanted fresh land for farming and cotton growing. c. They were attracted by stories about Oregon and California.
2. Why did thousands of Americans settle in Texas in the 1820s?
   a. In Texas, they were free to rule themselves as they pleased. b. The Mexican government was more democratic than the American. c. The warm climate made Texas suitable for cotton growing.
3. Why did the Texans revolt against Mexican rule?
   a. The Mexican government insisted that they obey its laws and abolish slavery. b. It wanted to take away their rights of self-government. c. It ordered them to return to the United States.
4. Why did the United States wait ten years before annexing Texas?
   a. Many members of Congress were afraid of war with Mexico. b. Northern members of Congress did not want to add slave territory to the United States. c. Presidents Jackson, Van Buren, Harrison, and Tyler were all opposed to annexation.
5. Why did the United States win the Mexican War?
   a. The American troops were experienced fighters. b. The Mexican government was weak and inefficient. c. Mexican military leaders were not very able.

IMPROVING YOUR SKILLS

A. Mastering the Map

Study the map below. Then complete the following statements in your notebook.

1. The largest territory ever acquired by the United States was the _____ _____.
2. The smallest territory acquired by the United States before 1860 was the _____ _____.
3. The last three territories acquired before the Civil War were the _____ _____, the _____ _____, and the _____ _____.
4. The United States made its greatest gains in the 1840's when it acquired _____, _____ _____, and the _____ _____.

EXPANSION OF THE UNITED STATES

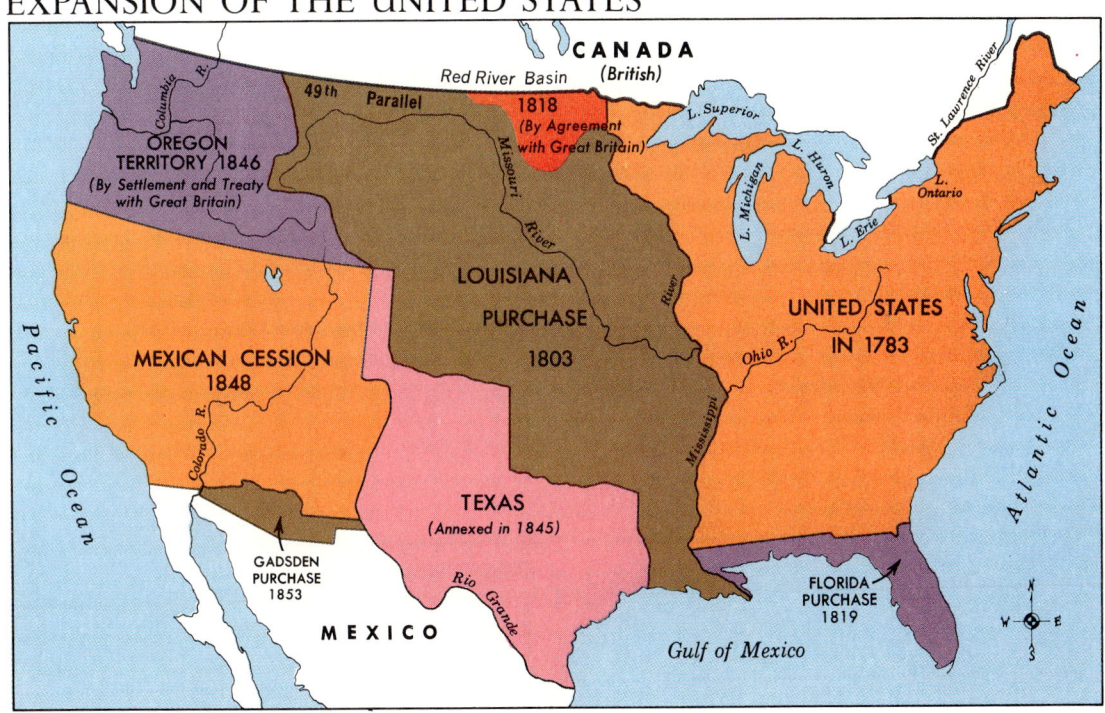

B. Looking at Both Sides

Read the two quotations, one from Mexican sources, the other from American sources, on the next page. Then write in your notebook the answers to the questions that follow.

1. The Mexican Account

The United States desired to extend its territory to the Rio Grande. Its people invaded Mexican territory, claimed so-called rights, and made demands that could not be satisfied.

The Texan revolt would not have happened if the colonists had depended only on their own scant resources; but they were strengthened by the support of the United States, which supplied them with arms and even soldiers, who called themselves "deserters from the American army."

2. The American Account

The people of the United States watched the heroic struggle of the Texans with interest. To many it seemed a contest of free people against dictatorship.

Our government tried to remain neutral during the Texas revolution. Since Texas had maintained its independence for nine years, and since it wished to come into the Union, we had a right to annex it.

1. Which quotation do you consider more reliable? Why? (*Hint:* Compare the number of facts, rather than opinions, in each.)
2. a. Imagine that you are a Mexican high school student. Write a letter to an American student, explaining why you think the United States was to blame for the war between the two countries. b. As an American, write an answer to this letter. c. Which side do you think was actually more to blame? Why?

How Did the United States Progress Within Its Borders?

A. Advances in American Culture. In 1820 a noted English minister wrote:

"In the four quarters of the globe, who reads an American book? Or goes to an American play? Or looks at an American picture or statue? What does the world yet owe to American physicians and surgeons? What new substances have their chemists discovered?"

This feeling that Americans were a people without culture was justified. Most of them worked so hard that they had little time for culture. Americans who had leisure and a good education believed that Europe was far ahead of the United States. So they were content to look to Europe for literature, science, and art.

Yet this state of affairs was already beginning to change even as the Englishman was writing his criticism. A spirit of nationalism had already led Americans to make important reforms and to acquire additional territory. Pride in their nation also inspired them to produce original works in almost every field of culture.

B. Progress in Literature. More than a dozen great American writers, whose works are still widely read today, appeared before 1850. Those listed below wrote books that young people as well as adults find interesting. How many have you read or heard about?

1. Washington Irving told charming stories about the early history of New York. Best known are the legends of the headless horseman of Sleepy Hollow and of Rip Van Winkle, who took a twenty-year "nap."

2. James Fenimore Cooper won fame by writing the first adventure novels about Indians and frontier people. His hero, Natty Bumppo, surpassed even the Indians in woodcraft and cunning.

3. Herman Melville wrote stories of life at sea. His most famous novel describes the hunt for a great white whale, Moby Dick.

4. Edgar Allan Poe created a new type of short story, full of mystery and horror. He also wrote poems notable for their musical language and rhythms.

5. New England produced three famous poets—Henry Wadsworth Longfellow, John Greenleaf Whittier, and William Cullen Bryant. All three wrote beautiful nature poems and stressed the value of good character, political democracy, and social reforms.

During the same period, Margaret Fuller edited *The Dial*. This journal published the writings of Ralph Waldo Emerson and Henry David Thoreau. Fuller later became the first woman on the staff of a leading New York newspaper. She also wrote an important book on women's rights.

The number of Americans reading printed matter also increased at this time. One reason

This painting by John James Audubon is of a blue crane or heron.

for this increase was that the new literature about America interested Americans. A second reason was that the public schools were teaching more people to read. A third reason was that printing had become less costly, thanks to some new inventions.

As a result, the sales of books and of a number of new popular magazines grew rapidly. In 1833 appeared the first newspaper the average family could afford to buy. It was the *New York Sun*. By taking in a large amount of advertising, the *Sun's* publisher could sell his paper for only a penny a copy. Sarah Josepha Hale was the editor of *Godey's Lady's Book*, one of the most popular magazines of the time.

American culture also gained from the lecture system, which became popular at this time. Famous writers and scientists traveled around the country speaking to large audiences on many subjects. They helped to stimulate interest in learning.

C. Science and Invention. The United States also produced some great scientists during the first half of the nineteenth century. John James Audubon won world-wide fame for the beautiful pictures and accurate descriptions in his book *The Birds of America*. Asa Gray was an expert on plants, Louis Agassiz on animals and the earth. Joseph Henry performed important experiments in electromagnetism, which made possible the invention of the telegraph, telephone, and electric motor. Matthew F. Maury became known as the "pathfinder of the oceans." Maury produced accurate charts of the winds, ocean currents, and ocean bottom. His charts made ocean voyages safer and faster in many parts of the world.

Americans soon won a reputation for their ability as inventors. The outstanding example was Eli Whitney. Besides inventing the cotton gin, Whitney developed the idea of mass production. This made possible the manufacture of articles in large quantities at low prices.

In the 1830s two American inventions opened the Great Plains west of the Mississippi River to farming. John Deere's steel plow cut through the tough layer of grass that covered the Great Plains. Cyrus McCormick's reaper made it possible to harvest crops without using large numbers of workers. The reaper was especially important in the West because labor was very scarce there.

In the 1840s Samuel Morse invented the telegraph, a device for sending messages through wires at almost the speed of light. Elias Howe invented the sewing machine, which made possible the modern garment and shoemaking industries. Charles Goodyear discovered how to vulcanize (toughen) rubber. Several American doctors successfully used anesthetics to make operations painless by putting the patient to sleep.

D. The Arts. The arts, too, showed Americans' pride in their nation. In 1800 American painters usually turned out portraits of wealthy people in a stiff imitation of European models. Then a group of artists decided to paint America's beautiful scenery instead. They were called the "Hudson River School" because the valley of the Hudson was one of their favorite subjects for painting. One American painter, George C. Bingham, started a new fashion in art by showing how ordinary people lived, especially on the western frontier where he had grown up.

In music, Stephen Foster led the way by composing the first popular American folk songs, notably "Old Folks at Home" and "My Old Kentucky Home." Another new type of American music was the black spiritual. The typical spiritual was a song about the sufferings of blacks under slavery. "Swing Low, Sweet Chariot" and "When Israel Was in Egypt Land" are well-known examples.

E. Improved Living Standards. At the beginning of the nineteenth century, American customs and manners were very crude in most places. Europeans who visited America at that time described the people as rough tobacco chewers and hard drinkers. American inns for travelers, they also reported, were unpleasant places. The food, usually poorly prepared and greasy, was put on the table in one large dish. Diners had to grab their share fast or else go hungry. The average inn had only a few bedrooms. Strangers often had to sleep together, three or four to a single bed.

By 1850 American manners had greatly improved in the older, settled parts of the country. America had many satisfactory inns with good food and comfortable furniture. American homes had also become more pleasant and attractive. The iron stove and bright gaslight were replacing the smoky open fireplace and dull whale-oil lamp.

The greatest changes took place in the cities. In 1800 sidewalks, paved streets, and street lights were rare. Water was drawn from wells, and garbage was thrown into the street for dogs and pigs to eat. There was no regular police force. Firefighters were unpaid volunteers with little equipment. No wonder city dwellers were often troubled by disease epidemics, crime, and fires. On a windy day, a fire might burn down an entire neighborhood before it could be brought under control.

By 1850 many American cities enjoyed

sanitary water supply and sewage systems and paved streets lit by gas lamps. Uniformed police and fire departments were being organized. A few cities could even boast of a new means of transportation, the horse-drawn omnibus—the ancestor of our modern motor bus.

F. Immigration and Its Effects. Immigration, which played an important part in America's rapid progress, increased greatly in the 1830s and 1840s. Europe suffered from a number of revolutions and crop failures during this period. Most of the revolutions failed, and many people with advanced ideas had to flee for their lives. This was especially true in Germany, where absolute monarchy was still strong. The worst crop failures occurred in Ireland. There several million people faced starvation during the "potato famines" of 1845 and 1846.

Large numbers of Germans, Irish, and other Europeans were attracted to the United States by its cheap land, economic prosperity, and democratic government. But they met with an unexpected problem, a growing feeling among Americans of dislike for foreigners. Most of the Irish were very poor. Since they could not afford to buy farms, they settled in the cities. There they performed the most difficult and unpleasant types of work for very low wages. Native American workers resented the Irish for keeping wages down and for taking away jobs. The newcomers were also disliked because they were generally uneducated, had very low living standards, and were Catholic.

Immigrants on their way to New York City. Why did these people migrate to the United States?

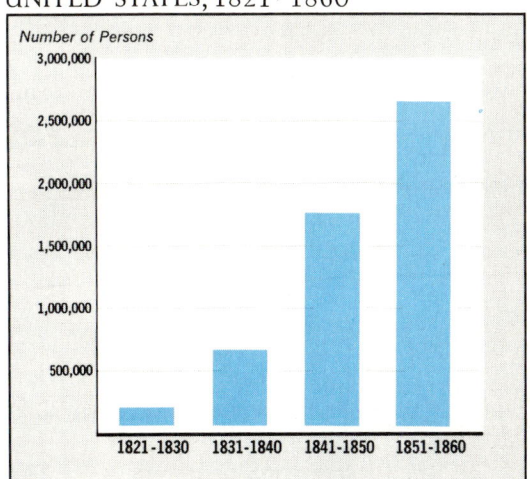

The German immigrants, unlike the Irish, were mostly Protestants with some training or skill. Many became prosperous farmers, opened businesses, or went into the professions. They took an active part in politics and in social reform movements. Lovers of music, they formed choruses, bands, and orchestras. Yet they too were resented by many Americans. They were accused of "putting on airs"—that is, of acting superior to their native-born neighbors.

In the early 1850s, antiforeign feeling led to the formation of a third political party, the American party. It soon became known as the Know-Nothing party because its members, when questioned about their views, were supposed to answer, "I know nothing." The Know-Nothings wanted to reduce immigration and raise the waiting period for citizenship to

IMMIGRATION INTO THE
UNITED STATES, 1821-1860

275

twenty-one years. The party soon died out. It was important mainly because it showed that the old dislike for foreigners, which had inspired the Alien Act over 50 years earlier, was still alive. Yet the United States certainly could not have made its remarkable progress without the labor, wealth, and new ideas that immigrants supplied.

REVIEWING THE SECTION

A. Knowing Important People

In your notebook identify each important American listed below as an author, a poet, a scientist, an inventor, a painter, an editor, or a composer.

1. Louis Agassiz
2. John James Audubon
3. George C. Bingham
4. Margaret Fuller
5. James Fenimore Cooper
6. John Deere
7. Stephen Foster
8. Charles Goodyear
9. Sarah Josepha Hale
10. Joseph Henry
11. Elias Howe
12. Washington Irving
13. Henry Wadsworth Longfellow
14. Matthew F. Maury
15. Cyrus McCormick
16. Herman Melville
17. Samuel Morse
18. Edgar Allan Poe
19. Eli Whitney
20. John Greenleaf Whittier

B. Finding the Reasons

In your notebook write the letters of *all* the correct answers to each question.

1. Why did a clearly American culture develop slowly in our nation's early years?
   a. Most Americans had to work very hard. b. Most educated Americans looked to Europe for literature, science, and art. c. The spirit of nationalism hurt the development of culture.
2. Why did Americans read much more in the generation after 1820?
   a. Books and newspapers cost less. b. More books were written about the United States by American writers. c. More public schools were built.
3. Why were farm machines first developed in the United States?
   a. Americans were very good farmers. b. Many American farms were large. c. There was a shortage of farm workers, especially in the West.
4. Why was living in a city less safe in the early nineteenth century than it is today?
   a. There were no regular police, fire, or sanitation departments. b. The

drinking water often carried disease germs. c. Bandit gangs frequently made raids on the cities.
5. Why did many Europeans come to the United States in the 1830s and 1840s?
a. They hoped to earn a better living and to give their children a better opportunity. b. They wanted to escape political persecution. c. They wanted to escape religious persecution.
6. Why did many Americans dislike Irish immigrants?
a. Most of them settled in the cities. b. They were mostly uneducated and worked for low wages. c. They were Roman Catholics.
7. Why did many Americans dislike German immigrants?
a. Most of them settled on farms or started businesses. b. Many were educated and cultured. c. They usually worked hard and became successful.
8. Why were immigrants important for the development of the United States?
a. They brought many new ideas. b. They helped to settle the West. c. They provided skilled workers for industry.

IMPROVING YOUR SKILLS

Interpreting the Graph

Study the graph on page 275. Then complete the following statements in your notebook.

1. The smallest number of immigrants to the United States entered during the decade (ten-year period) from _____ to _____.
2. The number of immigrants during that period was about _____.
3. The largest number of immigrants entered during the decade from _____ to _____.
4. During that decade, about _____ people entered the United States.
5. The total number of immigrants from 1821 to 1860 was about _____.

MAKING HISTORY LIVE

1. Skim through a story by one of the authors mentioned in this section, then tell what it is about and why you liked or disliked it.
2. Report on the life and work of one of the following cultural leaders: Ralph Waldo Emerson, Herman Melville, Elizabeth Palmer Peabody.

3. Visit your local historical society or museum. Write a report about some of the interesting things you learned there about your community. If your community is old enough, take special note of conditions before 1850.
4. Draw sketches, make models, or bring in pictures to illustrate conditions in American cities before 1850. b. Play, sing, or recite the words to music of that period. Copy the words in your notebook.
5. Discuss these questions:
   a. Were Americans justified in considering Irish immigrants "lower-class"? b. Were they justified in resenting German immigrants for "putting on airs"? c. Were the Know-Nothings really good Americans?

SUMMING UP THE UNIT

How Did the United States Become a Strong Nation?

A. Domestic Developments Under the Early Presidents. This unit has covered the sixty-year period from 1789 to 1850. At the beginning of the period, many people doubted that the United States would succeed. It had less than a million square miles of territory—and that mostly wilderness. It had a weak government, unsound finances, and a low standing among the nations of Europe.

What a great change took place after the Constitution went into effect! Under our first President, George Washington, the nation prospered and its finances improved. At this time the first political parties were born. The Federalists, helped by Washington's great popularity, managed to elect John Adams as his successor. But their attempt to crush the Democratic-Republicans by means of the Alien and Sedition Acts backfired. Thomas Jefferson, friend of the common people, won the election of 1800.

President Jefferson tried at first to put through a "revolution" in the federal government. He limited the government's powers, cut its expenses, and ended unpopular laws. But events soon forced Jefferson to change his views. He doubled the nation's size by buying the Louisiana Territory. He also fought the Barbary pirates and started the National Road.

B. Foreign Policy. In foreign affairs, the main problems of the young nation arose from wars in Europe. President Washington proclaimed a policy of neutrality that his successors followed. Except for a short undeclared naval war with France under President Adams, the United States managed to stay out of Europe's wars for twenty years. In 1809 President Jefferson put an embargo on trade with Europe. He hoped to keep America neutral and to stop British and French attacks on American shipping. But he soon had to end the embargo because it brought about an economic depression in the United States.

As the British continued to seize American ships and impress American sailors, the anger of the American people grew. An Indian war in the Northwest further aroused feeling against Great Britain. The War Hawks, eager to seize Canada, finally brought Congress to declare war on Britain in 1812.

C. Progress After the War of 1812. The War of 1812 was a small one, but it had important effects. In politics, the American people became much more nationalistic. The Federalist party, which had opposed the war, died out. The Republicans now took over the Federalist idea of a strong federal government. They passed high protective tariffs, chartered the Second Bank of the United States, and encouraged westward migration.

The war also helped develop the American economy. In the 1820s the Northeast became the main industrial section of the nation. Cotton growing on plantations and small farms spread across the South. Migrants from the East and Europe settled the West. Differences among these sections ended the "Era of Good Feeling" that had existed under President Monroe. The Republican party split and two new parties, the Democrats and the Whigs, were formed.

In the 1830s the first Democratic Presidents, Jackson and Van Buren, held office. Their administrations saw important democratic advances in political, economic, and social life. In the 1840s the nation completed its expansion to the Pacific by acquiring more than a million square miles of territory—the Mexican Cession and Oregon Territory.

In 1850 the United States was already one of the largest nations in the world in area. Its fast-growing population, farm production, industry, and commerce made it one of the most important nations as well. The European powers now treated it with respect. It was recognized as a leader in democracy. It was also rapidly developing a culture of its own. Its people, looking back at the great progress they had made since 1789, had good reason to feel proud that they were Americans.

REVIEWING THE UNIT

A. Knowing Where Things Happened

On an outline map of the United States, do the following:

1. Mark all large bodies of water with light-blue crayon or pencil shading.
2. Label:
    a. the Atlantic and Pacific oceans, Gulf of Mexico, Great Lakes; b. the Appalachian and Rocky mountains; c. the Mississippi, Ohio, Missouri, St. Lawrence, and Columbia rivers and the Rio Grande.
3. Show the westward expansion of the United States by labeling each of the following regions. Also mark its boundaries and write the date when it was acquired.
    a. the United States in 1783 b. the Louisiana Territory c. Florida d. Texas e. the Oregon Territory f. the Mexican Cession g. the Gadsden Purchase.

B. Knowing When Things Happened

For each event listed below, write in your notebook the *letter* on the time line showing the period in which it happened.

1. Alien and Sedition Acts
2. Annexation of Texas
3. California gold rush
4. Constitutional Convention
5. Critical Period
6. Era of Good Feeling
7. Era of Jacksonian Democracy
8. First Bank of the United States
9. First political parties
10. Mexican War
11. Monroe Doctrine
12. Purchase of Florida
13. Purchase of Louisiana
14. Rise of sectionalism
15. South Carolina's nullification
16. Whiskey Rebellion

A	B	C	D
1783 — 1789	1789 — 1812	1812 — 1828	1828 — 1850

C. Knowing Important People

"Who Am I?" is an interesting game that also serves as a good review. Divide the class into two teams of equal size. Have pupils on each team bring in five questions on five different slips of paper. Collect all the slips. Players on each team take turns drawing a question and answering it. Players are counted out of the game when they miss. When one team has lost all its players, the other team wins.

The following exercise shows the type of questions used in this game. For each famous person in the first column, write in your notebook the *letter* of the best description in the second column.

PART 1.

Presidents

1. John Adams
2. John Quincy Adams
3. Andrew Jackson
4. Thomas Jefferson
5. James Madison
6. James Monroe
7. James K. Polk
8. John Tyler
9. Martin Van Buren

Descriptions

a. Because of sectional rivalries, my administration was called the "era of bad feeling."
b. I annexed the Lone Star Republic.
c. I doubled the size of the United States.
d. I fought an undeclared war rather than pay bribes to a foreign government.
e. I fought our "second war of independence."

Presidents	Descriptions
10. George Washington	f. I fulfilled the "manifest destiny" of the United States.
	g. I set more precedents than any other President.
	h. I warned the European powers to stay out of the Western Hemisphere.
	i. I was elected for three terms.
	j. I was known as a strong President.
	k. I was unfairly blamed for a severe panic.

PART 2.

Famous Americans	Descriptions
1. John C. Calhoun	a. As chief justice, I strengthened the Supreme Court and the federal government.
2. Henry Clay	b. As our first secretary of the treasury, I put our country's finances into good shape.
3. Alexander Hamilton	
4. Sam Houston	
5. Dorothea Dix	c. I defended the federal Union from the attacks of states' rights congressmen.
6. Meriwether Lewis	
7. John Marshall	d. I explored the Louisiana Territory.
8. Horace Mann	e. I won fame with my naval victory in the War of 1812.
9. Daniel Webster	
10. Sara Josepha Hale	
	f. I fought for more and better public schools.
	g. I edited a popular women's magazine.
	h. I led South Carolina's fight against high tariffs and a strong federal Union.
	i. I led the Texans' war for independence.
	j. I formed a political party to oppose President Jackson's policies.
	k. I worked to improve the living conditions of the insane.

D. Knowing Important Terms

Choose the item in each group that does *not* belong with the others. Be prepared to explain in class why it does not belong.

1. *Political parties:*
   a. Democrats   b. Federalists   c. Feminists   d. Whigs
2. *Causes of the War of 1812:*
   a. Impressment of sailors   b. Indian attacks   c. Monroe Doctrine   d. War Hawks

3. *Social classes in the South:*
   a. Immigrants   b. Planter aristocrats   c. Poor whites   d. Slaves
4. *Groups that settled the West:*
   a. Backwoods people   b. Frontier people   c. Pioneers   d. Mechanics
5. *Problems of the Jackson administration:*
   a. Nullification and secession   b. Panic of 1837   c. Protective tariff   d. States' rights
6. *Causes of the Panic of 1837:*
   a. Bank of the United States   b. Cheap money   c. Easy credit   d. Land speculation
7. *Reform movements of the Jackson Era:*
   a. Prison reform   b. Public education   c. Temperance movement   d. Whiskey Rebellion

RECOMMENDED READING

A. *Historical Books*

ANDRIST, R. K. *Andrew Jackson, Soldier and Statesman.* New York: Harper and Row, 1963.

ASIMOV, I. *Our Federal Union.* Boston: Houghton Mifflin, 1975. The United States from 1816 to 1865.

BRISTOW, G. *Golden Dreams.* New York: Lippincott & Crowell, 1980. An anecdotal history of the Gold Rush.

BUGG, J. L., JR., and STEWART, P. C. *Jacksonian Democracy.* 2d ed. New York: Holt, Rinehart & Winston, 1976.

CORWIN, E. S. *John Marshall and the Constitution.* Chronicles of America, vol. 16. New York: U.S. Pubs.

CUMMINS, D. D., and WHITE, W. G. *The Federal Period.* New York: Glencoe/Macmillan, 1973.

DODD, W. E. *The Cotton Kingdom.* Chronicles of America, vol. 27. New York: U.S. Pubs.

FARR, N. *Americans Move Westward 1800–1850.* rev. ed. Eds. D. Calhoun, and L. Bloch. West Haven, Conn.: Pendulum Press, 1976.

———, and DOSTERT, D. *The United States Emerges: 1783–1800.* rev. ed. Ed. L. W. Bloch. West Haven, Conn.: Pendulum Press, 1976.

FAIRFAX, D. D. *Texas and the War with Mexico.* New York: American Heritage, 1961.

FULLER, C. *Pioneer Paths.* Broken Bow, Nebr.: Purcells, 1974.

GATTEY, N. *The Bloomer Girls.* New York: Coward, McCann, 1967.

GUTMAN, H. G. *The Black Family in Slavery and Freedom, 1750–1925.* New York: Random House, 1976.

HAWKE, D. F. *Those Tremendous Mountains: The Story of the Lewis & Clark Expedition.* New York: Norton, 1980.

HULBERT, A. B. *The Paths of Inland Commerce.* Chronicles of America, vol. 21. New York: U.S. Pubs.

LANGDEN, W. C. *Everyday Things in American Life.* Vol. 2, *How Americans Lived from 1776–1876.* New York: Scribner, 1941.

LAWSON, D. *The United States in the Mexican War.* New York: Abelard-Schuman, 1976. From the Alamo to Mexico City's fall.

Lyon, J. D. *Clipper Ships and Captains.* New York: Harper & Row, 1963.
McCready, A. L. *Railroads in the Days of Steam.* New York: Harper & Row, 1960.
Nabokov, P., ed. *Native American Testimony.* New York: Crowell, 1978. Indian/white relations from early times.
Paine, R. D. *The Fight for a Free Sea.* Chronicles of America, vol. 17. New York: U.S. Pubs. War of 1812.
Poatgieter, H. *Indian Legacy.* New York: Messner, 1981. Influences on sports, foods, language, etc.
Slossen, E. E. *The American Spirit in Education.* Chronicles of America, vol. 33. New York: U.S. Pubs.
Stinchcombe, W. *The XYZ Affair.* Westport, Conn.: Greenwood Press, 1980.
Tunis, E. *The Young United States 1783–1830.* New York: Harper & Row, 1976.
Wayne, B. *The Founding Fathers.* Westport, Conn.: Garrard, 1975.

B. Biographies

Baker, R. *Angel of Mercy: The Story of Dorothea Lynde Dix.* New York: Messner, 1955.
Bloomer, D. C. *Life and Writings of Amelia Bloomer.* New York: Schocken, 1975.
Commager, H. S. *Crusades for Freedom.* Garden City, N.Y.: Doubleday, 1962.
Davis, B. *Old Hickory: A Life of Andrew Jackson.* New York: Dial, 1977.
DeGering, E. *Wilderness Wife: The Story of Rebecca Bryan Boone.* New York: McKay, 1967.
Dillon, R. *We Have Met the Enemy: The Life of Commodore Oliver Hazard Perry.* New York: McGraw-Hill, 1978.
Flexner, E. *Century of Struggle.* Cambridge, Mass.: Belknap/Harvard Univ. Press, 1975. The women's suffrage movement.
Flynn, J. *Jim Bowie: A Texas Legend.* Burnet, Tex.: Eakin Publications, 1980.
Guiko, M. *The Black Hawk War.* New York: Crowell/Harper & Row, 1970.
Jensen, M. *Phyllis Wheatley: Negro Slave.* New York: Lion, 1982.
Moore, V. *The Madisons: A Biography.* New York: McGraw-Hill, 1979.
Reck, F. M. *The Romance of American Transportation.* New York: Crowell/Harper & Row, 1962.
Sterling, D. *Speak Out in Thunder Tones.* Garden City, N.Y.: Doubleday, 1973. Letters and writings of black Northerners, 1787–1865.
Stevens, W. O. *Famous American Statesmen.* New York: Dodd, Mead, 1953. Madison, Monroe, Jackson, Clay, Calhoun, and Webster.
Vail, P. *The Great American Rascal.* New York: Hawthorn/Dutton, 1973. The stormy life of Aaron Burr.
Wayne, B., ed. *Four Women of Courage.* Westport, Conn.: Garrard, 1975.
Wibberly, L. *The Gales of Spring: Thomas Jefferson, The Years 1789–1801.* New York: Farrar, Straus & Giroux, 1965.

C. Historical Fiction

Allen, T. D. *Doctor in Buckskin.* New York: Harper & Row, 1951. Marcus Whitman in Oregon.
Collier, J. L., and Collier, C. *Jump Ship to Freedom.* New York: Delacorte Press, 1981. Daniel escapes a dishonest master.
Dohan, M. H. *Mr. Roosevelt's Steamboat.* New York: Dodd, Mead, 1981.
Hough, E. *The Covered Wagon.* New York: Pocket Books, n.d. Crossing the continent to California.
Tharp, L. H. *Until Victory: Horace Mann and Mary Peabody.* Boston: Little, Brown, 1953.
Yolen, J. *The Gift of Sarah Barker.* New York: Viking Press, 1981.

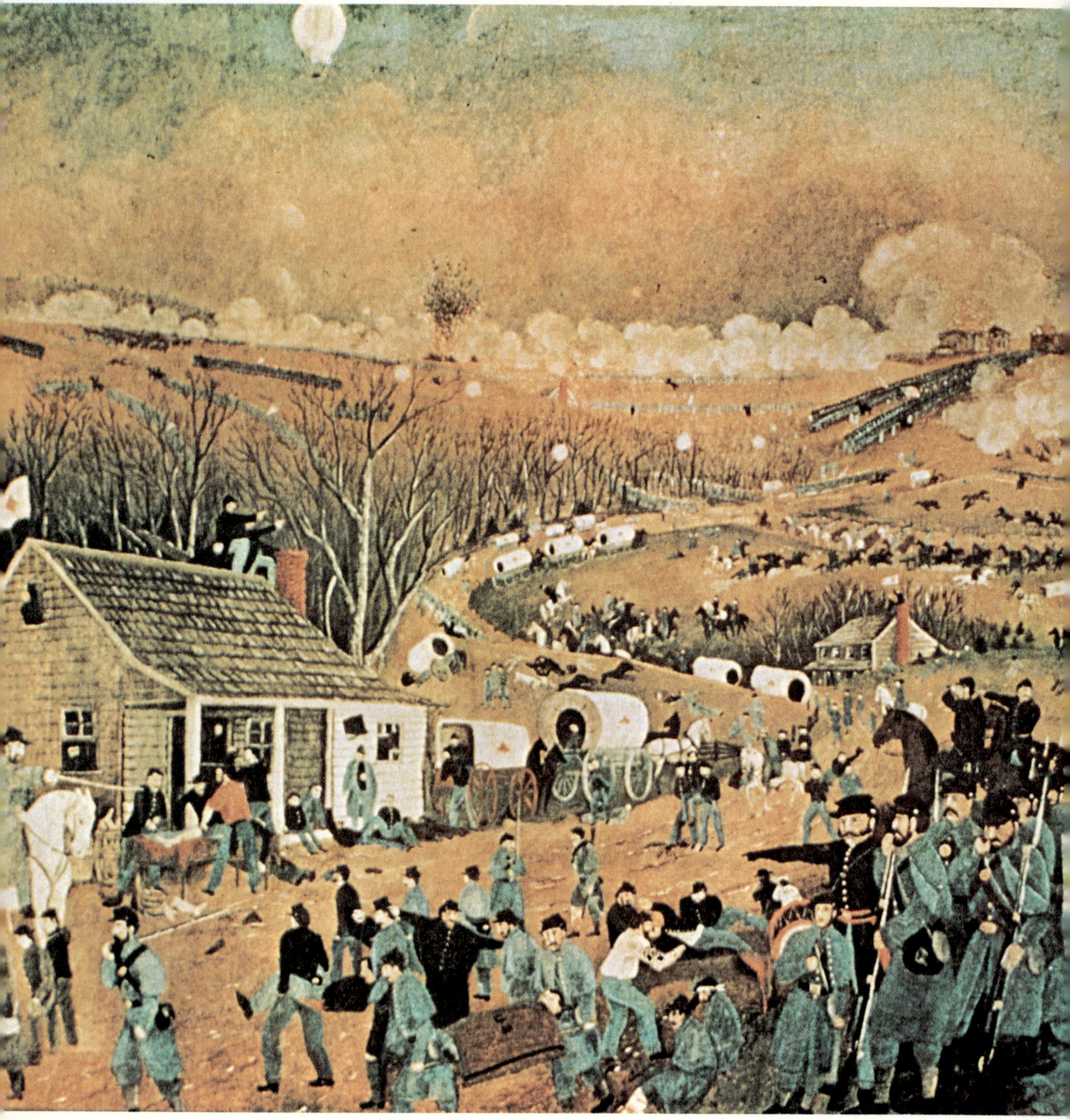

Unit Four

THE CIVIL WAR

In most families, brothers and sisters may tease one another, wrestle a bit, or even quarrel now and then. But people are shocked when they see brothers and sisters in a real fight. "How can children of the same parents, living under the same roof, fight one another?" they wonder. For this reason, a civil war—that is, a war between rival groups within a nation—is considered especially terrible. The citizens of a nation speak the same language, have the same background, and feel the same loyalty to their country. When they go to war against one another, it is like members of the same family fighting each other.

Like family fights, civil wars usually have deep-rooted causes. Since both sides feel very strongly, the war is often a long and cruel one. This was certainly true of the Civil War, or the War Between the States, as it is also called. For four terrible years, from 1861 to 1865, the Civil War tore the United States apart. It was one of the most bitterly fought and costly conflicts of the nineteenth century.

More Americans were killed in the Civil War than in any other war the United States has ever been in. Do you think that people in 1861 realized how long and cruel the war was going to be?

In studying the American Civil War, you will find answers to the following questions:

1. *What were the reasons for bad feeling between the North and the South?*
2. *What events led our nation into the Civil War?*
3. *How did the North win the war?*
4. *How did the North and South deal with the problems arising from the war?*
5. *Why do we hear people say, "We are still fighting the Civil War today"?*

UNIT 4: 1849-1877

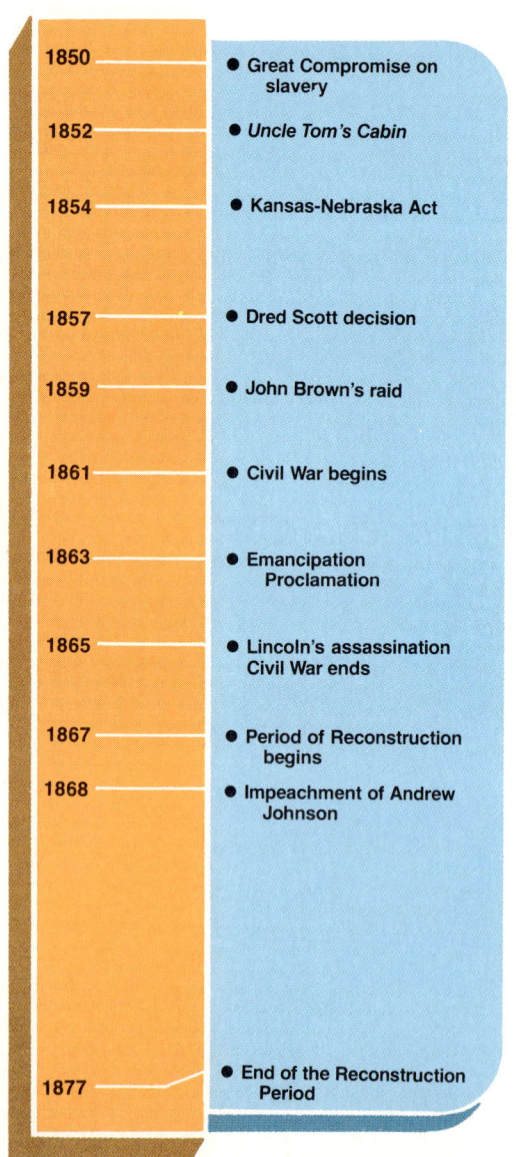

1850	Great Compromise on slavery
1852	*Uncle Tom's Cabin*
1854	Kansas-Nebraska Act
1857	Dred Scott decision
1859	John Brown's raid
1861	Civil War begins
1863	Emancipation Proclamation
1865	Lincoln's assassination / Civil War ends
1867	Period of Reconstruction begins
1868	Impeachment of Andrew Johnson
1877	End of the Reconstruction Period

Chapter 17

THE PROBLEM OF SLAVERY

SLAVERY in the United States no longer exists. It is hard to believe that human beings were once considered private property, just like furniture or cattle. It may be even harder to believe that slavery could exist when it was so costly to the South. Slaves had to be supported whether they could work or not, and they had little to gain by working hard. As we have seen, slavery kept the South from progressing as fast as the Northeast and West. Why then was this system introduced in the thirteen colonies? Why did it die out in the northern states but become firmly established in the South? How did it become a cause of conflict between the North and the South? We shall find out how and why in this chapter.

Slaves working on a plantation in South Carolina. The number of slaves increased from over half a million in 1776 to about 4 million in 1861.

How Did Slavery Become Established in America?

A. Slavery in Ancient Times. History tells us that slavery began thousands of years ago and that it has existed in every known civilization. In ancient times, people usually became slaves because of wars or crop failures. Conquering armies made slaves of the prisoners they took in battle or in raids on cities. When crops failed, farmers who fell into debt often had to sell their families and themselves. Anyone, even a monarch, might become a slave if things went wrong. For these reasons, slavery was not considered a disgrace, but rather a misfortune that might overtake even the best of people.

Most ancient peoples had a small number of slaves whom they treated fairly well. People who had been made slaves through debt were usually given their freedom after a few years. Educated slaves were put to work as teachers or as managers of their masters' businesses. Slaves with special skills were allowed to hire themselves out and to keep part of their wages. When slaves had saved enough money, they could buy their freedom. A few ancient peoples, like the Egyptians and the Romans, had many slaves and treated them cruelly. Even among such peoples, however, the law recognized that slaves were human beings and offered them some protection. They were usually given a few days of rest each month. They were not supposed to be punished without cause.

B. The Decline of Slavery in Europe. Slavery reached its peak in the Roman Empire about two thousand years ago. The Romans owned slaves from every part of the known world. Though they often mistreated their slaves, they did not consider one group inferior to another because of race, skin color, or place of birth.

Slavery began to decline as Christianity spread through the Roman Empire. The new religion taught that all human beings are equal in the sight of God. Christian masters were expected to treat their slaves with kindness and consideration. Since marriage was sacred, they were not supposed to break up slave families. They were also encouraged to emancipate (free) their slaves as an act of charity.

Slavery was further weakened by the fall of the Roman Empire and the rise of a new way of life (feudalism) in western Europe. Though there were still slaves in Europe during the Middle Ages, most people were serfs. They had to obey their masters, work for them, and give them a large share of all they produced. But serfs were much better off than slaves. They could not be sold away from their land and their family. They could keep what was left of their produce after they paid their dues to their lords.

As conditions in Europe improved, the serfs and slaves gradually obtained their freedom. In the seventeenth century, when the English colonies in America were founded, both serfdom and slavery were disappearing in western Europe. Slavery had already come to an end in England. Strangely enough, this evil practice got a fresh start in the New World just when it was ending in the Old World.

C. Slavery in Latin America. Portuguese explorers began to bring blacks from Africa to Europe during the fifteenth century. Most of

288

Two inside views of a slave ship. Note how carefully slave traders arranged their "goods" to pack in the largest number. Why did so many die on the way from Africa to America?

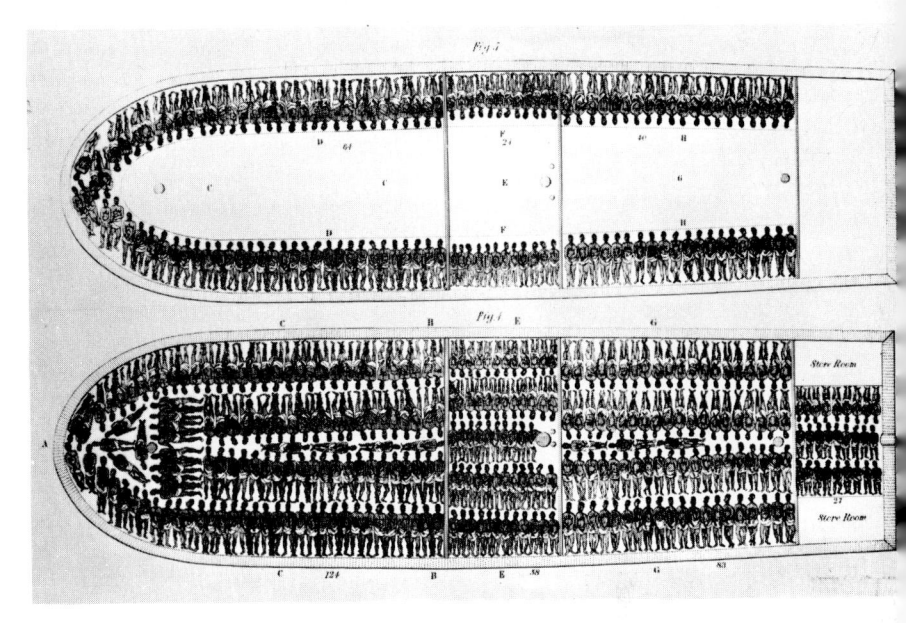

the blacks were kept as slaves. But some were set free, and these were treated as equals by the white Portuguese. Blacks received much the same treatment in Spain as in Portugal. Some free blacks accompanied the early Spanish and Portuguese explorers of the New World and took part in its settlement.

A great deal of labor was needed to develop the resources of the American continents. This need was met by a rapid growth in the slave trade. Between 1550 and 1850, almost 15 million human beings were carried off from Africa to the Americas by slave traders. For a long time almost all of the slaves went to the Spanish and Portuguese colonies. There they were often treated harshly. But royal laws gave them some protection, and the Catholic Church insisted that they should be granted their natural rights as human beings. Many gained their freedom. Free blacks were treated as equals in the colonies, as in the mother countries. There was a good deal of intermarriage (marriage between the races). Today many Latin Americans have black ancestry, and Latin American culture shows a strong African influence.

D. Slavery in the Thirteen Colonies. 1. Its Beginning. The first Africans in the thirteen English colonies were brought to Virginia by a Dutch trader in 1619. For the rest of the seventeenth century, only a few thousand blacks were imported. They were sold in almost every colony. Since slavery was unknown to the colonists, the first blacks were treated like white indentured servants. They were set free after a few years' service and were helped to start a new life on their own.

The change from indentured servants to slaves took place gradually. One colony after another deprived blacks of their rights. Instead of being freed after a few years, they were required to serve their masters for a lifetime. Then the law ordered that their children, too, should continue to serve the same master. Slaves were also denied the right to own property or to bring complaints against their masters. Thus they had less protection in the thirteen colonies than in Latin America or in many ancient lands.

2. Reasons for the Growth of Slavery. Why were blacks made into slaves and treated so harshly? The first and most im-

A slave auction in Virginia. What evils of slavery does this picture show?

portant reason was the need for labor. The Indians were few in number. Many had been wiped out by diseases brought to the New World by Europeans. White indentured servants could be kept for only a few years, and many ran off before their term was up. Blacks, on the other hand, could be brought in from Africa by the thousands. Most of them were used to doing farm work in their homelands. Because of their color, they could easily be found if they tried to run away. Once their children were also declared to be slaves, the labor supply increased with each new generation.

A second reason why blacks were made into slaves was that their appearance, languages, and customs were strange to the English settlers. Even though many blacks came from civilized lands, the colonists looked upon them as savages. The belief spread that they could perform only simple tasks and could not possibly manage for themselves. Blacks who showed outstanding ability were thought to be exceptions. This false notion that blacks were an inferior race made it easy for the colonists to accept slavery as fair.

Once slavery was accepted, it came to play a very important part in the economic life of the thirteen colonies. In fact, the slave trade was one of the main reasons for New England's prosperity in the eighteenth century (see map, page 62). By 1775 there were over half a million slaves in the colonies, or more than one-sixth of the population. Few were found in the northern colonies. Most people in these colonies owned small farms or shops and depended on their families to help them. Even on large farms, it did not pay to keep slaves. They had to be fed in the wintertime, when there was little for them to do. In the South, on the other hand, black slaves could be kept busy most of the year. Moreover, the work on a plantation could be broken up into simple tasks, which slaves could do without the expense of long-term training. It was in the South, where conditions were most suitable, that black slavery took root and grew.

A cotton plantation in Mississippi.

REVIEWING THE SECTION

A. Knowing New Terms

Explain these new terms in your notebook *in your own words*.

(In the unit introduction) civil war
    the Civil War
(In the chapter introduction) slave

(In **B**) emancipating a slave
    serf

B. Understanding the Facts

PART 1. In your notebook write the *letter* of the correct choice.

1. In ancient times, slaves were usually:
   a. given a chance to gain their freedom   b. given the same rights as free people   c. taken from the educated upper class   d. treated like animals.
2. Among the ancient Romans:
   a. most slaves were treated with kindness   b. the number of slaves was very large   c. only blacks could be slaves   d. slaves had no protection under the law.
3. The Christian religion helped the slaves by teaching that:
   a. families should be kept together   b. all people deserved consideration because they were equal in the sight of God   c. freeing slaves was an act of charity   d. all these things were true.
4. Serfs in Europe during the Middle Ages were better off than slaves because they could not be:
   a. beaten by their lords   b. forced to work for their lords without pay   c. sold to another lord in a different place   d. mistreated in any of these ways.
5. Slavery in Latin America was different from slavery in the thirteen colonies in that:
   a. fewer slaves were imported   b. they came from a more civilized part of Africa   c. they were usually treated well   d. many were given their freedom.
6. Indentured servants were different from slaves because they:
   a. could refuse to obey orders without fear of punishment   b. gained their freedom after a certain number of years   c. had to be white people   d. were paid for their work.
7. Blacks were made into slaves in the thirteen colonies because they:
   a. were uncivilized when they arrived from Africa   b. were needed to work the plantations   c. could not learn to do skilled work   d. were inferior in ability to whites.

8. Slavery grew in the South, but died out in the North, because:
   a. there were many more plantations in the South than in the North
   b. unskilled workers were more useful on plantations than on small farms   c. farm work went on for most of the year in the South, but not in the North   d. the South offered slaveowners all these advantages.

PART 2. In your notebook complete this chart on slavery in different places and times.

	In Ancient Times	In Latin America	In the Thirteen Colonies
Where slaves came from To which race they belonged Usual type of work How they were treated How they were protected Their chance of emancipation			

Conclusions. 1. Where were slaves given the least protection and the fewest rights? 2. Why did this happen?

IMPROVING YOUR SKILLS

A. Reading the Time Line

Look at the time line on page 286. Then answer these questions in your notebook.

1. In what year did the Civil War begin?
2. In what year was an attempt made to settle the dispute between the North and the South?
3. List three events that led to the Civil War.
4. What President was assassinated at the end of the Civil War?
5. The attempt to "reconstruct" the South began when the Civil War ended. How many years did the Reconstruction Period last?
6. How many years does this unit cover?

B. Choosing Reliable Sources

Let us suppose that some of your friends have quarreled. When you try to find out what happened, you are told several different stories. How do you know what or whom to believe?

Those who actually saw the quarrel are, of course, more reliable witnesses than those who only heard about it. But even eyewitnesses often disagree, and so you have to decide which ones you can trust. "Is the witness taking sides in the quarrel?" "Is the person neutral?" "Is the witness truthful and accurate?" These are questions you have to ask yourself. Once you have decided who the reliable witnesses are, you listen carefully to all they have to say. When you get through, you may still not be sure about some small details. But usually you find that the reliable witnesses have agreed on enough important facts to give you a fairly clear picture of what really happened.

Historians have a much more difficult task. They have to discover the truth about events that occurred in distant places long ago. Since they cannot question witnesses, they have to study their accounts very carefully. Like you, they prefer eyewitness, or firsthand, accounts to secondhand or thirdhand ones. They find out as much as they can about each source of information to determine how reliable it is. Finally, they must test to determine whether the source gives facts rather than opinions, and whether it presents both sides fairly (see pages 237 and 256). Only when historians find at least two reliable sources that agree do they consider their accounts likely to be proven or factual.

Ordinary people are not trained like historians and do not have time to do research. How then can they find out the truth about important questions? For one thing, they should read only reliable sources. For another, they should use at least two sources with different viewpoints. To see how this works out, do *one* of the following exercises.

1. Read accounts of slavery in the American South or in other countries. Test each account to determine how reliable it is. You should compare several accounts to see which are the most reliable and what facts on slavery they agree on.
2. Choose a controversial topic in the news today. Look it up in two or more newspapers or news magazines. a. List the points of agreement and disagreement. b. Tell which source you consider the most reliable and why.
3. Compare an editorial or special column in your favorite newspaper with a news item on the same topic. a. Why should the news item be more reliable? b. What evidence can you find to prove that it is?

After going over each of these exercises, you will see how hard it is to get the facts in history. But you will also see why it is important to get them—and from the most reliable sources you can find.

Why Did the North and South Clash Over Slavery?

A. The Rise of Antislavery Feelings. It was impossible for a liberty-loving people like the Americans to allow slavery without question. Opposition to slavery soon arose. It grew steadily stronger, until it finally became a cause of the Civil War.

The earliest known white protest against slavery was made by a group of Quakers sometime before the end of the seventeenth century. They felt that slaveholding violated the Christian belief in the brotherhood of man. They even threatened to expel slaveholders from their church. The first antislavery society was formed by the Quakers in 1775.

The Declaration of Independence appeared a year later. It clearly stated that *all* men are created equal and have a right to "life, liberty, and the pursuit of happiness." Thomas Jefferson saw that slavery violated these ideals. So he condemned slavery in the Declaration of Independence and blamed the king of England for bringing it to the colonies. But these ideas were cut out in the final writing. Other members of the Continental Congress felt that it might cause trouble with the South.

B. Black Achievements. In the Revolutionary War about five thousand blacks, both freemen and slaves, served in the American armed forces. A number of them won special honors for their courage in battle. Some slaves who fought were emancipated by their masters as a reward.

In the years after the Revolution, blacks appeared among the leaders of American culture. Benjamin Banneker was well known as an astronomer and mathematician. His work was highly praised by Jefferson, and he was employed to help plan the new capital of Washington, D.C. Phillis Wheatley became known for her poems on patriotic subjects. Gustavus Vassa wrote an autobiography that can still be read with interest today. It tells how he was kidnapped by slave traders as a child in Africa, how he was treated as a slave, and how he managed to win his freedom. Other blacks showed great skill as craftworkers, mechanics, and business people. Such achievements were made despite slavery and new laws that often prevented thousands of free blacks from voting or attending schools.

C. Steps Toward Freedom. As we have seen, most northern states abolished slavery during the Revolution or soon afterward. The Congress of the Confederation forbade slavery in the Northwest Territory in 1787. One of the compromises in the Constitution fixed the year 1808 as the date for ending the slave trade. It actually stopped a few years before.

Even in southern states like Maryland and Virginia, there were proposals to free the slaves gradually. It was suggested, for example, that masters should free their slaves in their wills or grant slave children their liberty when they became old enough to support themselves. It was also proposed that the government pay slaveowners the value of any slaves they emancipated.

Southerners also took up the problem of what to do with the blacks after they were freed. The most popular proposal was that they should be "returned" to Africa. The colony of Liberia ("Land of the Free") was established on the west coast of Africa in 1822 as a home for former slaves. Several thousand were settled there. But the newcomers were not prepared for the kind of life they had to lead in Liberia. Many died of disease. Others tried to return to their real homeland, the United States. As one black leader made clear, "This is our home, and this is our country. Beneath its soil lie the bones of our fathers; for it, some of them fought, bled, and died. Here we were born, and here we will die."

D. The Strengthening of Slavery. Strangely enough, the movement to end slavery was reversed by a northerner, Eli Whitney. His gin strengthened slavery by making cotton growing very profitable. Slave labor seemed perfectly suited for this occupation. Only a few simple operations were needed, which groups of slaves could easily perform under the watchful eye of an overseer. There was work to be done all year round; so the master did not have to feed idle slaves.

As cotton growing spread, so did slavery. Even the older southern states, where the soil was exhausted, benefited. Planters in these states raised not only farm crops but also slaves, whom they sold to slaveholders in the "Cotton Kingdom." The importing of slaves from Africa, though illegal, began again. The total number of slaves rose from 600,000 in 1775 to over 4,000,000 in 1860. Yet the demand for slaves was so great that the price of a field hand rose from less than $500 to more than $1,500 during this period.

The treatment of slaves varied from plantation to plantation. But many slaves suffered from extreme cruelty, whippings, and torture. So as the number of slaves increased, the fears of slave revolts grew. Then, in 1791, the slaves on the West Indian island of Haiti staged a successful revolution. In the battles, hundreds of white and black people were killed. During the next half-century, there were many slave revolts and acts of individual resistance. The most violent was the Nat Turner revolt in Virginia in 1831. Turner and his followers killed over 50 white men, women, and children before the revolt was crushed. The black leaders of the revolt were hanged.

Fear of slave revolts led the southern states to pass very harsh laws, known as the "slave codes" or "black codes." Blacks—free people as well as slaves—were forbidden to hold meetings of any sort without a white person present. They were not allowed to go out at night without a pass. Teaching slaves to read and write was made a crime. The emancipation of slaves was discouraged for fear that free blacks might more easily organize revolts.

BLACKS IN THE UNITED STATES

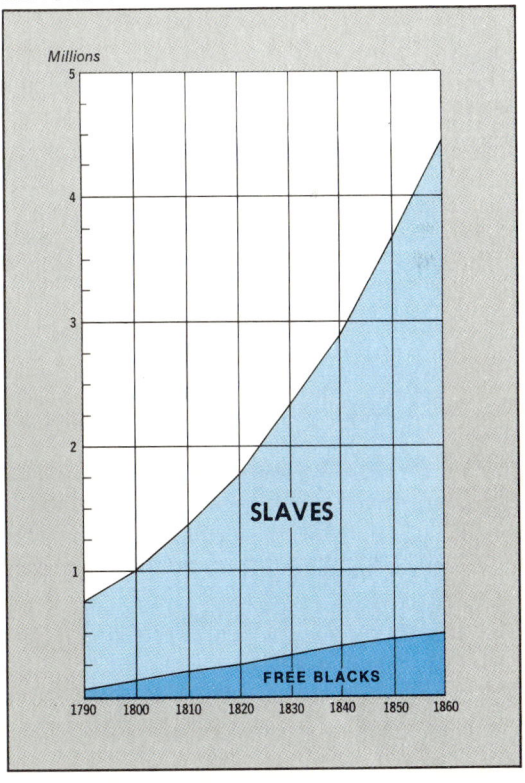

295

Three black abolitionists. From left to right: Frederick Douglass, Sojourner Truth, Harriet Tubman.

E. The Abolitionist Movement. At the very time when slavery was being strengthened in the South, the social reform movement was spreading in the North and abroad (see page 257). One of the main goals of the reformers was the abolition of slavery. A number of countries in Europe and Latin America abolished slavery during the first half of the nineteenth century. Especially important was the example set by Great Britain. The British government outlawed the slave trade in 1807. It ordered slavery ended throughout its vast empire in 1833.

Abolitionist societies sprang up in the United States. Most of them favored a moderate policy, such as gradual emancipation of the slaves with government payments to the slaveowners. Others took the extreme position that slavery must be abolished at once without payment.

The extreme abolitionists, because of their fiery words and actions, attracted the most attention. One of their leaders, William Lloyd Garrison, started a newspaper called *The Liberator* in Boston in 1831. In his first issue, Garrison boldly announced: "On this subject [slavery], I do not wish to think, or speak, or write with moderation. No! No! Tell a man whose house is on fire to give a moderate alarm, but urge me not to use moderation in a cause like the present. I will not excuse—I will not retreat a single inch—and I will be heard." The extreme abolitionists included blacks like Frederick Douglass and Sojourner Truth. They aroused their listeners with eyewitness accounts of the mistreatment slaves suffered at the hands of their masters.

The extreme abolitionists argued that slavery had to be ended at once because it was a crime against humanity. Slaves, they pointed out, were treated more like animals than human beings. They were branded with their master's mark, whipped often, with or without cause, and horribly beaten if they tried to resist or escape. In the slave markets, they were examined just like horses or cattle. Children were often sold away from their parents and wives from their husbands.

The abolitionists used lectures, newspapers (such as Douglass's *North Star*), and books to

THOMPSON, THE ABOLITIONIST.

That infamous foreign scoundrel THOMPSON, will hold forth *this afternoon*, at the Liberator Office, No. 48, Washington Street. The present is a fair opportunity for the friends of the Union to *snake Thompson out!* It will be a contest between the Abolitionists and the friends of the Union. A purse of **$100** has been raised by a number of patriotic citizens to reward the individual who shall first lay violent hands on Thompson, so that he may be brought to the tar kettle before dark. Friends of the Union, be vigilant!

Boston, Wednesday, 12 o'clock.

Poster attacking a British abolitionist. Printed in Boston in 1835, this poster calls on people to tar and feather the abolitionist. Why were many people in this city, the "cradle of our liberty," against the abolitionists?

spread their ideas throughout the northern states. They flooded the southern mails with pamphlets. They also sent hundreds of petitions against slavery to Congress and the state legislatures. Not content with words alone, they formed a secret organization, known as the "Underground Railroad," to help slaves escape to the North and Canada. The Underground Railroad consisted of places, called "stations," where runaway slaves hid until a "conductor" could lead them safely to the next station. The most famous conductor was an escaped slave, Harriet Tubman. She led more than three hundred fugitives to safety. The Underground Railroad helped about 75,000 slaves to escape in the years before the Civil War.

F. Objections to Extremism in the North. Most people in the North opposed the extreme abolitionists. Among them were northern business people and workers who depended on trade with the South. Many other northerners felt that the extremists' attacks, by angering the South, made a peaceful end of slavery impossible. The abolitionists' meetings were often broken up by hecklers. Their meeting houses were set afire and their printing presses smashed. Garrison was almost hanged by a mob in Boston in 1835 Another abolitionist leader, Elijah Lovejoy, was attacked and killed by a mob in Illinois two years later. Frederick Douglass had to flee to England to escape being arrested and returned to slavery. But the abolitionists did not stop their attacks on the slave system. Slowly they won public support throughout the North. Some years before the Civil War, they boasted of having formed more than two thousand antislavery societies, with some 200,000 members.

G. The Southern Reaction. Southerners, of

The Underground Railroad. This dramatic painting shows a white farm family helping some slaves to escape.

course, objected much more strongly than northerners to the attacks of the extreme abolitionists. They accused the abolitionists of twisting the facts and spreading outright lies. In defending their position, southerners did an about-face. At one time they had defended slavery as a necessary evil. That is, while they had admitted that slavery was bad, they had insisted that the prosperity of the Cotton Kingdom and the United States depended on it. Now they began to defend slavery as good.

The following statement is typical of the southern arguments for slavery. "In all social systems, there must be a class to do the mean duties, to perform the drudgery of life. The difference between us [the North and the South] is that our slaves are hired for life and well compensated [paid]; there is no starvation, no begging, no want of employment among our people. Yours are hired by the day, not cared for, and scantily compensated. Why sir, you meet more beggars in one day, in any single street of New York City, than you would meet in a lifetime in the whole South. Our slaves are black, of another inferior race. Your slaves are white, of your own race. You are brothers in one blood."

The southern defenders of slavery, like the extreme abolitionists, took strong action. They burned abolitionist writings sent through the mails. In Congress, they put through a rule that abolitionist petitions should be put away without being read. Though this "gag rule" was a clear violation of the Bill of Rights, it remained in effect for eight years. Southern "slave-catchers" traveled through the northern states hunting for runaway slaves. They kidnaped suspects, including free blacks, and carried them off to the South. Some northern states passed laws to stop this practice. The abolitionists once again favored direct action. They formed armed bands to attack the "slave-catchers" and free their victims.

H. Bad Feeling Between North and South. As the moderates had foreseen, bad feeling between the North and South grew rapidly. This made it more and more difficult to solve the problem of slavery peacefully. It is important to remember, however, that there already were other causes for disagreement between the two sections. Northerners made a living from industry, commerce, and small-scale farming. The southern economy depended on cotton and other cash crops, raised mainly on large plantations. In Congress, northern representatives had favored high protective tariffs and the Bank of the United States. The South had opposed the bank and had tried to nullify the protective tariff. The effect of the slavery issue was to deepen these earlier differences, and finally to bring them to a head.

REVIEWING THE SECTION

A. Knowing New Terms

In your notebook write the new terms in this section that best complete these statements.

1. Americans sent emancipated blacks to the colony of _____ in Africa.
2. Laws regulating the behavior of blacks in the southern states were called the "_____ _____" or "_____ _____."

3. People who wanted to end slavery were known as _____.
4. Those who wanted to end slavery gradually and pay the slaveowners were called the _____ _____. Those who wanted to end slavery immediately without paying the slaveowners were known as the _____ _____.
5. Slaves were helped to escape to the North by a network of hiding places called the "_____ _____."

B. Knowing Important People

For each important person in the first column, write in your notebook the *letter* of the best description in the second column.

Important People
1. Benjamin Banneker
2. Frederick Douglass
3. William Lloyd Garrison
4. Elijah Lovejoy
5. Harriet Tubman
6. Nat Turner
7. Gustavus Vassa
8. Phillis Wheatley

Descriptions
a. Conductor on the Underground Railroad
b. Founder of Liberia
c. Leader of a slave revolt
d. Murdered abolitionist leader
e. Black leader of the extreme abolitionists
f. Early black poet
g. Noted black scientist
h. Black author of an interesting autobiography
i. Publisher of the abolitionist newspaper *The Liberator*

C. Finding the Reasons

In your notebook write the letters of *all* the correct answers to each question.

1. Why did some Americans want to end slavery in the late eighteenth century?
   a. It went against Christian teaching and American ideals. b. Black slaves wanted to be free of their masters' cruel treatment. c. Importing slaves was no longer a profitable business.
2. Why did many Americans think that slavery would end in the late eighteenth century?
   a. It was outlawed by the northern states and forbidden in the Northwest Territory. b. The Constitution outlawed the importing of slaves after 1808. c. Several southern states ordered the gradual emancipation of slaves.
3. Why did the movement to end slavery die out in the South during the early nineteenth century?
   a. The cotton gin made cotton growing very profitable. b. Blacks who had been freed were unable to take care of themselves. c. The

attempt to settle freed blacks in Liberia failed.
4. Why did many northerners dislike the black codes?
a. These laws applied to free blacks as well as slaves. b. They made it almost impossible for blacks to improve themselves. c. They made it much harder for southerners to free their slaves.
5. Why did the abolitionist movement spread rapidly in the 1830s and 1840s?
a. This was a period of democratic reforms. b. Great Britain freed all the slaves in its vast empire. c. The extreme abolitionists gained many supporters in both the North and the South.
6. Why did many northerners object to the extreme abolitionists?
a. They were afraid that the South might reduce its trade with the North. b. They wanted to preserve slavery in order to hold down wages in the North. c. They thought that the methods used by the extremists would prevent a peaceful settlement of the slavery question.
7. Why did southerners defend slavery much more strongly in the 1840s than they did a half-century earlier?
a. They were angered by the attacks of the extreme abolitionists. b. They wanted to help the factory workers in the North. c. They wanted to stop the slaves from escaping to the North.
8. What were the reasons for bad feeling between the North and the South in the 1840s?
a. The two sections had developed different economic systems. b. They both wanted to control the federal government. c. They held opposite views on slavery.

IMPROVING YOUR SKILLS

A. Interpreting the Graph

Study the graph on page 295. Then write "True" in your notebook for each statement if it is correct according to the graph. If it is wrong, write the correct answer.
1. The total number of blacks in the United States increased steadily from 1790 to 1860.
2. The number of free blacks and the number of slaves both increased steadily during this period.
3. The number of free blacks increased more rapidly than the number of slaves.
4. The number of blacks in the United States grew from 1,000,000 in 1790 to about 4,500,000 in 1860.
5. There were almost 1,000,000 free blacks in the United States in 1860.

6. There were about 4,000,000 slaves in the United States in 1860.

B. Looking at Both Sides

Read the quotation in **G** carefully. Then do the following:

1. Make a list of the arguments you agree with.
2. Make a list of the arguments you disagree with. (Be prepared to explain why in each case.)
3. On the whole, do you think southerners were right to defend slavery? Tell why or why not.

MAKING HISTORY LIVE

1. a. In what ways was slavery bad for the slaveowners and other southerners? b. Explain the following statement, made by a famous writer in this period: "If you put a chain around the neck of a slave, the other end fastens itself around your own neck."
2. Report on the life and work of a leading abolitionist or black cultural leader of the first half of the nineteenth century.
3. Read eyewitness accounts of how slaves lived and how they were treated. Compare these accounts, discuss why they are different, and decide which are reliable.
4. Imagine that you are either a northerner or a southerner in the 1830s. Write a letter to a relative in the other section explaining how you and your friends feel about slavery.
5. Prepare for a debate on the question: Did the extreme abolitionists do more harm than good? Write the views for both sides.
6. Draw a cartoon or poster either to attack or to defend slavery.
7. Help prepare a class display of pictures, drawings, and songs about slavery in the United States.

Chapter 18

THE ROAD TO CIVIL WAR

WOULD SLAVERY have ended peacefully in the United States if the Civil War had not broken out? Some historians think so. They point out that slaves were becoming more and more expensive to buy and keep. At the same time, the soil in the Cotton Kingdom was being worn out and crops were getting smaller. Long before the Civil War, planters in the older southern states found it hard to get along. Their economic troubles were the main reason why they complained about high tariffs and the Bank of the United States. In time the entire South might have been forced to find a better system of farming than plantations worked by slave labor.

Slavery also hindered the progress of the South in another way. Immigrants preferred to settle in the Northeast and West, where they did not have to compete with cheap slave labor. As a result, the population of these two sections increased much faster than that of the South. Moreover, the two sections drew closer together as railroads were built connecting them. The Northeast bought the West's farm products and the West bought its manufactured goods from the Northeast.

Together, the free states in the Northeast and the West held a majority of the seats in the House of Representatives in 1850. Southerners were determined to keep these free states from gaining control of Congress. They insisted that the Senate had to remain evenly divided between the slave states, or South, and the free states, or North. But this could happen only if new territories in the West were opened to slavery. These territories would provide both fresh soil for cotton growing and new slave states for keeping the balance in the Senate. If slavery were not allowed in the territories, the North was certain to control both houses of Congress. Southerners were afraid that they would be at the mercy of the abolitionists if this happened.

Actually, most northerners were not abolitionists. But they disliked slavery and did not want to see it spread. Thus the contest between North and South centered on a single issue: Should slavery be allowed in the western territories? In this chapter we shall see how Congress tried to settle this issue, why it failed, and how its failure led to the Civil War.

How Did Congress Deal With the Western Territories?

A. The Early Laws. 1. THE "OLD WEST." The issue of free or slave territory had first come up before the Constitution was adopted. The Northwest Ordinance of 1787 had forbidden slavery in the Northwest Territory. Five free states were eventually formed from this territory. In the region south of the Ohio River, slavery was allowed. There, four slave states were formed. The later admission of Florida as a slave state kept the balance between free and slave states.

2. THE MISSOURI COMPROMISE. The issue arose again in 1819. In that year Missouri applied for admission to the Union as a state to be formed from the Louisiana Territory. There were at the time twenty-two states in the Union, eleven free and eleven slave. Missouri was slave territory. A northerner in Congress proposed that it should be admitted only if it promised to free its slaves. Southerners in Congress angrily replied that the North had no right to require this. The debate became so bitter that the aged Thomas Jefferson wrote: "This momentous question, like a firebell in the night, awakened and filled me with terror. I considered it at once as the [death] knell of the Union."

Henry Clay managed, however, to end the dispute. He worked out a compromise that Congress adopted in 1820. Missouri was admitted as a slave state. Maine, which had long wanted to break away from Massachusetts, was admitted as a free state. Thus the balance was kept in the Senate. To prevent disputes like this one in the future, the rest of the Louisiana Territory was divided into two parts. The northern part was to be free territory, the southern part slave territory (see map, page 309).

B. The Election of 1848. The question of slavery was so explosive that both political parties avoided it for the next twenty-five years. But it came up again as a result of the Mexican War. A northern congressman pro-

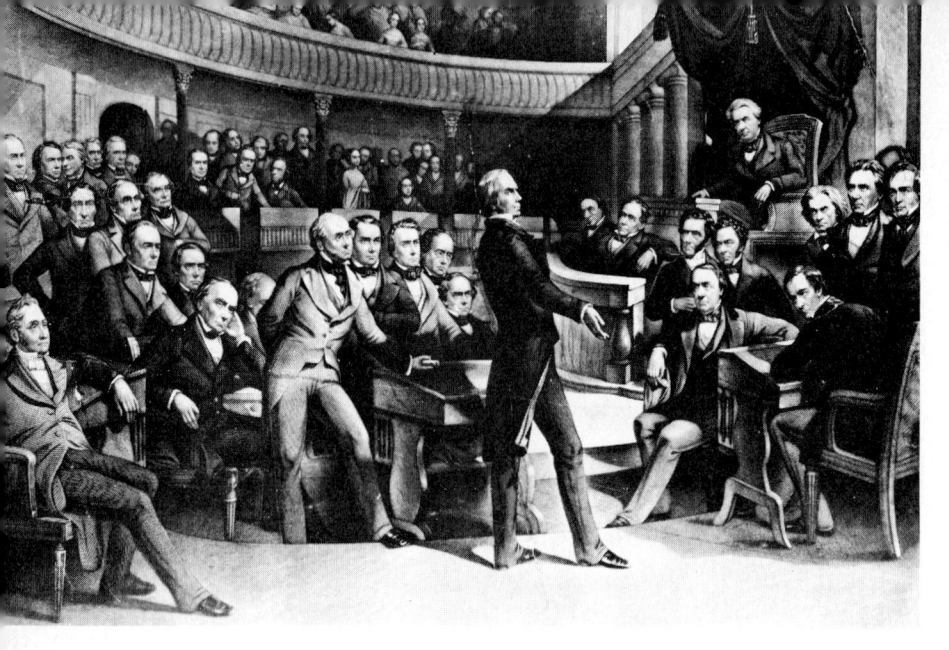

Henry Clay addressing the Senate in 1850. The "Great Compromiser" is making a proposal to settle the dispute over slavery in the territories.

posed that slavery should be forbidden in any territory taken from Mexico. His proposal passed the House of Representatives, but was defeated in the Senate. This incident proved to southerners that they could not afford to let the North gain control of the Senate.

In the election of 1848, both parties tried to avoid the issue of slavery in the Mexican Cession. The Whigs' main strength was in the North. To win votes in the South, they chose a southern slaveowner as their candidate for President. He was the Mexican War hero General Zachary Taylor. The Democrats, who were strong in the South, nominated a northerner, the governor of Michigan. People who opposed slavery were so disgusted by the tactics of both parties that they formed a third political group, the Free Soil party.

The Free Soilers proposed to "keep the soil free" in the new territories. That is, they proposed to forbid slavery so that ordinary farmers and laborers could settle there. They did not plan to abolish slavery in the southern states or territories where it already existed. However, many moderate abolitionists supported the Free Soilers as the best of the three parties. The Free Soil candidate, former President Martin Van Buren, took enough votes away from the Democrats to give the Whigs the victory. General Taylor became President. He died after a year in office and was succeeded by Vice-President Millard Fillmore of New York.

C. The Compromise of 1850. Despite the politicians' efforts, the problem of slavery in the new territories could not be put aside. When California applied for admission as a free state in 1849, southerners objected. California, they said, would give the North a majority in the Senate. This dispute was even more bitter than the one in 1820. For months northerners in Congress attacked slavery while southerners threatened to secede from the Union.

Henry Clay, now 73 years old and in poor health, worked out the final compromise of his long career. California was to be admitted as a free state. In return, the South would get something it had wanted for many years. This was a strong federal law for the return of runaway slaves. The rest of the Mexican Cession was to be divided into two parts—New Mexico Territory in the south, Utah Territory in the north (see map, page 309). In each territory, the question of slavery was to be decided in a new way, by the vote of the settlers.

Members of Congress liked the idea of letting the settlers decide. This compromise relieved them of a difficult decision. Actually, they knew, nature would make the decision. If a territory proved suitable for the plantation system, many slaveowners would move in and vote to make it slave territory. If not, it would become free soil. Thus both New Mexico and Utah territories were likely to become free states because they were too dry for cotton growing.

D. Effects of the Compromise of 1850. Every part of Clay's compromise was passed by Congress. The votes in both houses were very close. Many congressmen supported parts they disagreed with just to settle the dangerous issue of slavery in the territories. They thought the issue would never rise again.

Nevertheless, the slavery question continued to trouble the nation, mainly because of the new Fugitive Slave Law. Under this law, slaveowners or their agents could arrest any black suspected of being a runaway slave. They could call on local officials and bystanders for help. Those who refused to help could be fined or imprisoned. Accused black people were to be brought to a federal commissioner for a hearing. They could not speak or have witnesses on their behalf. The commissioner's fee was doubled if he decided to return the suspects to the South instead of releasing them.

The Fugitive Slave Law encouraged "slave-catchers" to increase their activities in the North. But it seemed so unfair to northerners that ten states passed laws to keep it from going into effect within their borders. These laws forbade state officials to help in arresting or holding a runaway slave. Suspects could be released under habeas corpus (see page 164). They were to be given a jury trial, instead of a hearing before a federal commissioner. Nevertheless, northerners often took the law into their own hands. Northern mobs freed a number of suspects by attacking the men who were arresting them. Sometimes they freed the suspects by storming the jails where they were being held. These developments caused southerners to complain bitterly. They had let the North gain control of Congress, but now it was going back on its part of the bargain of 1850.

E. A Temporary Truce. The early 1850s were a period of great economic prosperity. Gold flowed from California and business

What weakness of the Compromise of 1850 does this poster show?

CAUTION!!
COLORED PEOPLE
OF BOSTON, ONE & ALL,
You are hereby respectfully CAUTIONED and advised, to avoid conversing with the
Watchmen and Police Officers of Boston,
For since the recent ORDER OF THE MAYOR & ALDERMEN, they are empowered to act as
KIDNAPPERS
AND
Slave Catchers,
And they have already been actually employed in KIDNAPPING, CATCHING, AND KEEPING SLAVES. Therefore, if you value your LIBERTY, and the *Welfare of the Fugitives* among you, *Shun* them in every possible manner, as so many HOUNDS on the track of the most unfortunate of your race.
Keep a Sharp Look Out for KIDNAPPERS, and have TOP EYE open.
APRIL 24, 1851.

Harriet Beecher Stowe. President Lincoln called her "the little woman who wrote the book that made this great war."

Both parties nominated Mexican War heroes rather than political leaders. Both supported the Compromise of 1850 and appealed for friendship between the sections. The Democratic candidate, Franklin Pierce of New Hampshire, won the presidency. The Free Soil party received only half as many votes as it had four years earlier. This showed that the American people, like Congress, considered the issue of slavery in the territories settled.

F. An Important Book. At this time, however, a new novel about slavery was published. It was called *Uncle Tom's Cabin*. Its author, Harriet Beecher Stowe, was a New England woman who sympathized with the extreme abolitionists. She made the villain of her book a cruel overseer named Simon Legree, and her hero a religious old slave named Uncle Tom. The overseer eventually beats old Uncle Tom to death. Another character was the slave girl Eliza. To prevent being separated from her little child, Eliza runs away. She barely escapes the bloodhounds of her pursuers by crossing the ice-filled Ohio River.

Uncle Tom's Cabin was a very popular book and later an equally popular play. It was important because it kept the question of slavery before the American people. Northerners shuddered at what they believed to be a true picture of the slave system. Southerners resented what they thought a very unfair description by a northern woman who knew very little about the South.

boomed. Many factories, railroads, telegraph lines, and highways were built. Immigration continued on a large scale. Some southerners complained because the North was growing faster than the South. But most Americans seemed to be losing interest in the slavery question.

In the election of 1852, both the Whigs and the Democrats again tried to calm the public.

REVIEWING THE SECTION

A. Understanding the Facts

To see which side gained more from the compromises of 1820 and 1850, copy the two charts on the next page in your notebook. Fill in the blank spaces and answer the questions.

CHART 1. *The Compromise of 1820*

Gains of the North	Gains of the South
a. _____ was admitted as a free state.	a. _____ was admitted as a slave state.
b. The _____ part of the Louisiana Territory was to be free soil.	b. The _____ part of the Louisiana Territory was opened to slavery.

Conclusion. Examine the map on page 309. Which side gained more in this compromise?

CHART 2. *The Compromise of 1850*

Gains of the North	Gains of the South
a. _____ was admitted as a free state.	a. A strong _____ _____ Law was passed.
b. The rest of the Mexican Cession was divided into two parts, _____ _____ Territory and _____ Territory. Slavery in these territories was to be decided by the votes of the _____ .	

Conclusion. Examine the map on page 309. Which side gained more in this compromise?

B. Finding the Reasons

In your notebook write the letters of *all* the correct answers to each question.

1. Why do some historians think that slavery would have died out in time?
   a. The price of slaves was high in 1850 and was still going up. b. The soil in the cotton growing states was rapidly being worn out. c. The United States had no more new lands suitable for plantations.
2. Why did southerners want additional territories opened to slavery?
   a. They needed fresh soil for growing cotton. b. They had a surplus of slaves for whom they had to find work. c. They needed new slave states to keep the North from gaining control of Congress.
3. Why did the Compromise of 1820 settle the question of slavery in the territories for thirty years?
   a. It gave the North and South an equal number of states. b. It decided which parts of the Louisiana Territory would be free and which would be open to slavery. c. The United States did not acquire any more new territories until the 1840s.
4. Why did Congress let the settlers decide the future of the new territories by their votes in the Compromise of 1850?

a. By adopting this method, Congress no longer had to make the difficult decisions itself. b. Letting the people of the territories decide their future themselves was a democratic policy. c. In effect, nature would make the decision because the climate of a territory would decide whether it was suitable for slavery or not.
5. Why did northerners strongly oppose the Fugitive Slave Law?
a. They thought the South had gained an unfair advantage in the Compromise of 1850. b. Northerners were required to help capture blacks suspected of being runaway slaves. c. The suspects were denied their rights as Americans.
6. What reasons for complaint did southerners have in the 1850s?
a. The Underground Railroad was helping thousands of slaves to run away. b. Northern states were violating the Compromise of 1850 by refusing to enforce the Fugitive Slave Law. c. The North held a majority in both houses of Congress.
7. Why was *Uncle Tom's Cabin* a very important book?
a. It gave the American people a clear and accurate picture of slavery.
b. It aroused northerners with its vivid account of the evils of slavery.
c. It angered southerners because it gave an unfair picture of their way of life.

IMPROVING YOUR SKILLS

A. Choosing Reliable Sources

Reread the discussion of reliable sources on pages 292–293. Then write in your notebook the *letter* of the *most reliable source* for the information required in each item below. (Be prepared to defend your choice in class.)

1. How slaves were treated in ancient Egypt:
a. Paintings in the tombs of Egyptian rulers and nobles   b. The account of a famous Greek historian who visited Egypt in ancient times   c. The story of Moses and the Hebrews in the Old Testament   d. The diary of a modern visitor who questioned Egyptians about their past.
2. How slaves were treated in Latin America:
a. Reports to the monarchs of Spain by the governors of their colonies   b. Petitions to the monarch by missionaries asking for laws to protect the slaves   c. Letters to the monarch by plantation owners explaining why such laws were not needed   d. Records of an investigation by a special court to decide whether the laws were really necessary.
3. How slaves were treated in the South:
a. Descriptions of southern life by southerners   b. *Uncle Tom's Cabin* and other accounts by abolitionists   c. Stories told by runaway slaves   d. Accounts of Europeans who traveled through the South.

4. Why the Compromise of 1850 was adopted:
   a. The *Congressional Record* (see page 132)   b. Articles in southern newspapers at the time   c. Articles in northern newspapers at the time   d. A biography of Henry Clay

B. Mastering the Map

Look at the map below. Then do the following:

1. List in two columns in your notebook the free and slave states in 1850.

   Free States   *Slave States*

   a. States on the Atlantic Coastal Plain
   b. States formed from the "Old West"
   c. States west of the Mississippi River

2. List in three columns the free territories, the slave territories, and those whose future had not yet been decided.

   Free Territories   *Slave Territories*   *Undecided*

   Conclusion. Judging by the map, which side was stronger in 1850, the North or the South?

FREEDOM AND SLAVERY IN THE UNITED STATES IN 1850

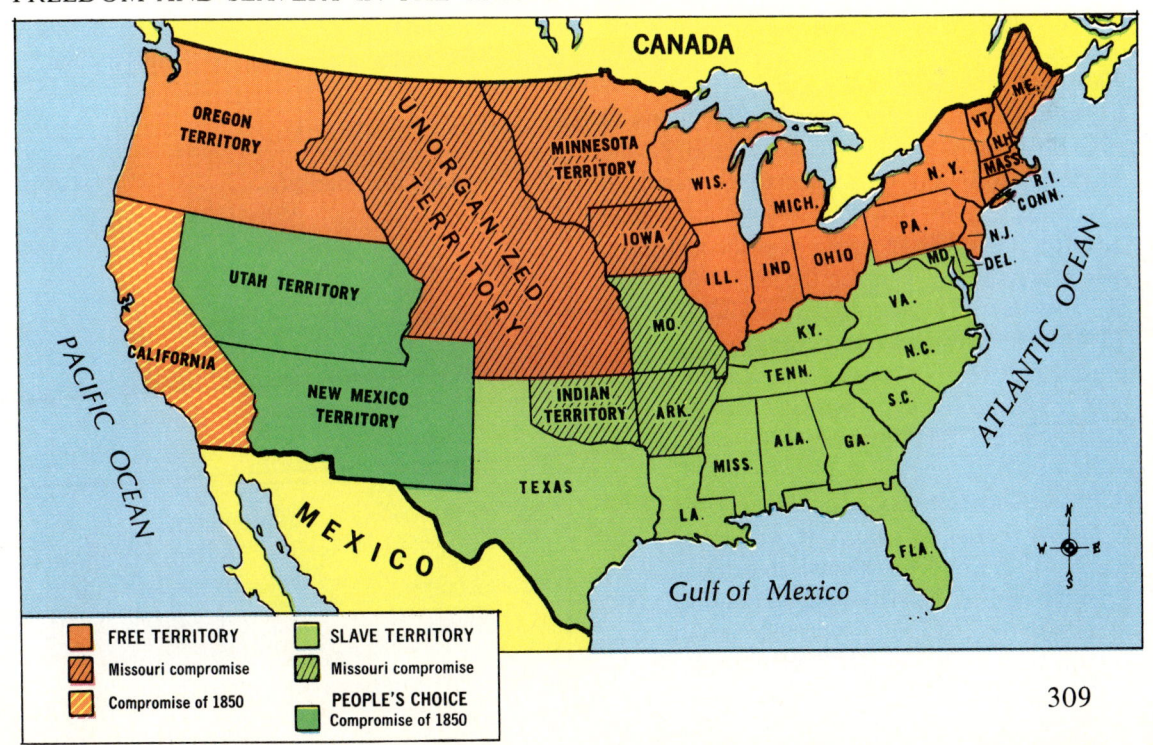

Why Did the North and South Go to War?

A. The Kansas-Nebraska Act (1854). Could the Civil War have been avoided? It is, of course, impossible to tell. We do know, however, that for a few years after the Compromise of 1850 bad feelings lessened between the North and South. Then a senator from Illinois, Stephen A. Douglas, made a serious mistake. He reopened the issue of slavery in the territories. His action touched off a series of events that led our nation step by step into the Civil War.

Senator Douglas was interested in plans to build a railroad from Chicago to the Pacific coast. To promote the railroad, he had to attract settlers to that part of the Louisiana Territory the railroad would pass through. The region was free soil under the Missouri Compromise. However, Douglas introduced a bill dividing it into two parts, Kansas and Nebraska (see map on this page). Whether each part would be free or slave was to be decided by the votes of the settlers.

B. "Bleeding Kansas." The Kansas-Nebraska bill soon passed Congress. It was attacked in the North because it opened free territory to slavery. To keep Kansas free, abolitionists and other antislavery groups formed a society to settle northerners there. Southerners quickly formed a group to settle slaveholders in the same region. Soon after the rival groups began to arrive, fighting broke out between them.

On one occasion, southerners attacked the town of Lawrence, the main antislavery settlement in Kansas, and killed two men. However, word spread that five had been killed. "An eye for an eye," said an extreme abolitionist named John Brown. He and his followers entered a southern settlement at night, called out five men, and killed them. The fighting in "Bleeding Kansas" went on year after year. It stirred up hatred in both the North and the South.

C. Birth of the Republican Party. The bad feeling became so intense that it split the Whig party. Southern Whigs joined the Democratic party. Northern Whigs united with the Free Soilers to form a new party, the Republican party. The Republicans took over the Free Soil platform. They did not attack slavery in the southern states, but they did pledge themselves to stop its spread in the territories.

In the election of 1856, the Democrats nominated James Buchanan of Pennsylvania.

KANSAS-NEBRASKA ACT

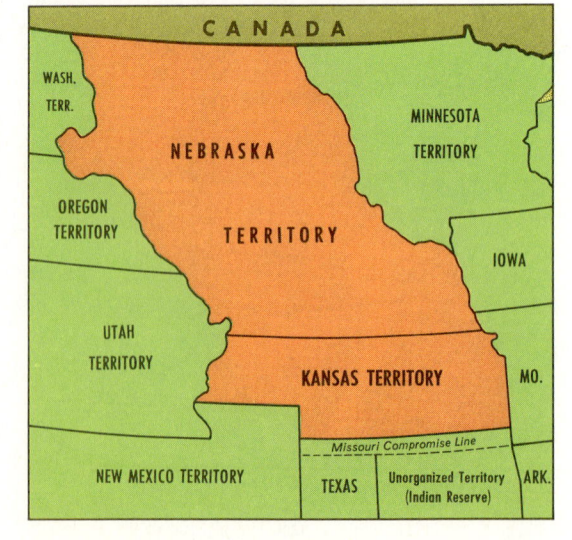

310

The Battle of Hickory Point was part of the fighting in "Bleeding Kansas."

Buchanan had served for several years as ambassador to Great Britain. So he had not become involved in the quarrels over slavery in the territories. Buchanan won the election. But the Republicans did very well for a new party. Their candidate, the Mexican War hero John C. Frémont, carried eleven northern states.

D. The Dred Scott Decision (1857). A few days after President Buchanan took office, the Supreme Court handed down a very important decision. A slave named Dred Scott had been taken by his master from a slave state, Missouri, into the free part of the Louisiana Territory and then back to Missouri. Dred Scott claimed that he had become a free man once he had entered territory where slavery was forbidden. The Supreme Court decided against him. As a slave, the Court ruled, he was not a citizen and so did not have the right to sue. More important, the Court held that Congress did not have the power to prohibit slavery in the territories. It pointed out that slaves were property. Since the Fifth Amendment forbade the federal government to take away a person's property without due process of law, the Missouri Compromise was unconstitutional.

The Supreme Court hoped by this decision to settle the question of slavery in the territories once and for all. Instead, the Dred Scott decision made the quarrel even more bitter than before. It angered the North because it threw open all federal territories to slavery. It also threatened to wreck the new Republican party, whose main goal was to keep slavery out of the territories. Fortunately for the Republicans, a little-known backwoods lawyer named Abraham Lincoln found an answer to the Dred Scott decision.

E. The Lincoln-Douglas Debates (1858). In 1858 Senator Douglas was the Democratic candidate for reelection to the Senate from Illinois. Lincoln was his Republican opponent. The two men agreed to hold a series of debates on the great issues facing the nation. The Lincoln-Douglas debates interested the whole country because Douglas was a well-known senator and a likely candidate for the presidency in 1860. Most Americans, however, had never heard of Lincoln. As yet he had an unimportant record in politics. He had only served several terms in the state legislature and a single term in the House of Representatives. Yet those who knew Lincoln thought highly of his character and ability. He was skillful in getting to the heart of a problem. He knew how to use an interesting story or a simple illustration to make even a complicated question clear to his listeners.

During the debates, Lincoln used all his skill to put his rival in a difficult position. Douglas and the Democratic party had accepted the

Dred Scott decision, which forbade Congress to regulate slavery in the territories. Yet Douglas had also introduced the Kansas-Nebraska Act, which gave the settlers in a territory the power to forbid slavery. How could Congress, Lincoln wanted to know, give the settlers a power it did not have itself?

Douglas had to admit that the settlers did not have the legal power under the Dred Scott decision to prohibit slavery. But in practice, he insisted, they could make it impossible for slavery to continue by refusing to protect the rights of slaveowners. Wherever a majority of the settlers opposed slavery, Douglas stated, it would surely die.

Though Douglas won the election to the Senate, his answer cost him dearly. By admitting that the settlers could keep slavery out of a territory, he angered the South. The Democratic party soon split into Douglas supporters, mainly in the North, and anti-Douglas men, mainly in the South. Lincoln, on the other hand, was hailed by the Republicans. If slavery could be kept out of the territories, the Dred Scott decision was no longer important. By splitting the Democrats, moreover, Lincoln had greatly strengthened the position of the Republican party.

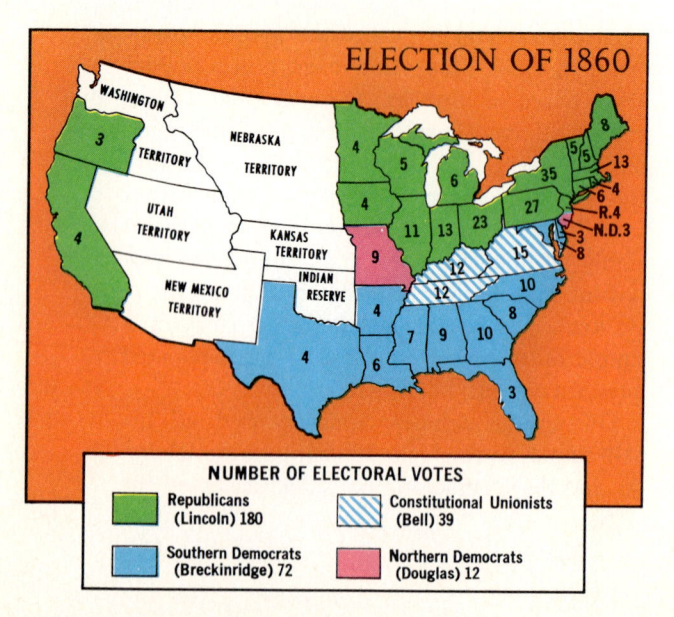

F. John Brown's Raid (1859). The extreme abolitionist John Brown was responsible for the next step toward war. Leading a small band of armed men, Brown seized the federal arsenal (storehouse for weapons) at Harpers Ferry, Virginia. He probably meant to arm the slaves in that area for a revolt against their masters. But his plan failed. The slaves were unwilling to take up arms. Federal troops quickly surrounded the arsenal and killed or captured his entire band. John Brown and the other survivors were quickly tried, found guilty, and hanged.

In the North, John Brown was hailed as a martyr who had sacrificed his life to free the slaves. "John Brown's body lies a-mould'ring in the grave, but his soul goes marching on," sang the northern army in the Civil War. Southerners, on the other hand, were angered and horrified by his action. They lived in fear of slave uprisings. What sort of people, they wondered, would arm slaves to massacre helpless men, women, and children?

G. The Election of 1860. In the summer of 1860 northern Democrats nominated Senator Douglas for the presidency. Southern Democrats nominated Vice-President Breckinridge of Kentucky. The Republicans chose Abraham Lincoln. A fourth candidate was named by a small group that hoped to preserve the Union by ignoring the question of slavery altogether.

With the Democrats split, the Republicans were confident of victory. Lincoln, a westerner born in a log cabin, could be expected to win the votes of small farmers and workingmen in the West and Northeast. The Republican platform was also sure to appeal to these two sections. It promised westerners free land, a railroad to the Pacific coast, and other internal improvements. To the business people of the Northeast, it promised a protective tariff and a sound banking system. In an effort to reassure the South, the Republicans once again said that they did not wish to abolish slavery.

ELECTION OF 1860

NUMBER OF ELECTORAL VOTES
- Republicans (Lincoln) 180
- Constitutional Unionists (Bell) 39
- Southern Democrats (Breckinridge) 72
- Northern Democrats (Douglas) 12

They wanted only to stop its spread in the territories.

The Republican appeal was very successful. Though Lincoln won only 40 percent of the popular vote, he carried almost every state in the Northeast and West. This gave him a large majority in the electoral college and the presidency.

H. Formation of the Confederacy. Events now moved rapidly toward a climax. Southern extremists had sworn that they would not stay in the Union if the Republicans won the election. South Carolina was the first state to secede. Soon after, ten other southern states joined South Carolina in founding a new nation, the Confederate States of America (see map, page 320). The constitution of the Confederacy was much like that of the United States. But, as you might expect, it protected slavery, forbade a protective tariff, and guaranteed states' rights.

President Buchanan declared that the secession of the southern states was illegal. Yet he insisted that the federal government had no power to prevent it! By the time Lincoln was inaugurated, the Confederacy was well established. In his inaugural address, Lincoln pleaded with the South for peace. But at the same time he reminded southerners that he had a sacred duty to save the Union:

"In your hands, my dissatisfied fellow countrymen, and not in mine, is the momentous issue of civil war. The government will not assail you. You can have no conflict without yourself being the aggressors [attackers]. You have no oath registered in heaven to destroy the government, while I shall have the most solemn one to 'preserve, protect, and defend' it."

I. The Opening Shots (1861). Almost at once, the new President was faced with a critical decision. The Confederate government had taken over almost all the federal property within its borders, including military bases.

The firing on Fort Sumter. Confederate soldiers bombarded the fort for 34 hours and forced its surrender. What made the incident so important, even though no one was killed?

Only four bases still remained in federal hands. From one of these bases—Fort Sumter, in the harbor of Charleston, South Carolina—came a call for help. Lincoln had to decide whether or not to send reinforcements. He chose to follow a middle path—to send food and supplies, but not soldiers and arms. To avoid a clash, he let the governor of South Carolina know of his plan. But the Confederate government ordered the fort taken at once. The Confederate attack on Fort Sumter in April, 1861, started the Civil War.

J. Basic Causes of the Civil War. Why did section turn against section and plunge the nation into civil war? Slavery was clearly a basic cause of the war. It was mainly over slavery that the North and South had quarreled during the ten-year period before the war began. Most northerners considered slavery a great evil. Abolitionists wanted to end it at once. Moderates wanted to stop its spread in the territories and hoped that it would gradually die out in the southern states. Southerners, on the other hand, defended slavery as necessary to their way of life and good for their slaves. They refused to give it up. As one southern leader put it: "Rather than yield our dearest rights and privileges, we should see the Union scattered to the winds."

It is important to remember, however, that rivalry among the sections had begun many years earlier. This sectional rivalry was a second basic cause of the war. In 1830 South Carolina had threatened to secede over the tariff. In 1860 the Republicans had promised to pass a high protective tariff and other measures the South had long opposed. Their victory turned over control of the federal government to an alliance of the Northeast and West. It left the South too weak to defend its interests.

Southern leaders now decided that they had more to gain by establishing a separate nation than by staying in the Union. They expected the Confederacy to profit from lower tariffs and increased trade with Great Britain. Some even dreamed of building a mighty slaveholding empire by taking territories in the Caribbean, Mexico, and Central America. Many northerners, on the other hand, felt that secession could not be allowed because it would mean the end of the United States as a great democratic nation. The third basic cause of the Civil War, in President Lincoln's words, was that "one side would *make* war rather than let the nation survive, and the other would *accept* war rather than let it perish."

REVIEWING THE SECTION

A. Knowing New Terms

Explain each term in your notebook *in your own words*.

(In **B**) "Bleeding Kansas"
"An eye for an eye"

B. Knowing Important People

For each important person in the first column, write the *letter* of the best description in the second column.

Important People
1. Abraham Lincoln
2. Dred Scott
3. Harriet Beecher Stowe
4. John Brown
5. Stephen A. Douglas

Descriptions
a. Author who attacked slavery
b. Democratic leader responsible for the Kansas-Nebraska Act
c. Extreme abolitionist who used violent methods
d. First Republican President
e. President at the time the southern states seceded
f. Slave involved in an important Supreme Court decision on slavery in the territories

C. Understanding the Facts

In your notebook write the *letter* of the correct choice.

1. Senator Douglas introduced the Kansas-Nebraska bill in order to:
   a. encourage the building of a railroad to the Pacific coast   b. open additional territory to slavery   c. win the support of the abolitionists   d. accomplish all these purposes.

2. The Kansas-Nebraska Act was a mistake because it:
   a. angered even northerners with moderate views on slavery   b. reopened a successful settlement of the question of slavery in the territories   c. resulted in fighting between northerners and southerners   d. had all these bad results.

3. The new Republican party consisted mainly of:
   a. Free Soilers and northern Democrats   b. Free Soilers and northern Whigs   c. northern Democrats and southern Whigs   d. southern Democrats and northern Whigs.

4. The Supreme Court ruled against Dred Scott on the ground that:
   a. Congress could not deprive slaveowners of their property without due process of law   b. the Missouri Compromise was unconstitutional   c. a slave did not have rights as an American citizen   d. all these arguments made his suit illegal.

5. As a result of the Dred Scott decision:
   a. the question of slavery in the territories was finally settled   b. the Republican party was in a difficult position   c. slavery spread to the northern states   d. all these developments took place.

6. Through his debates with Senator Douglas, Abraham Lincoln managed to:
   a. show up a weakness in the Dred Scott decision   b. cost Senator Douglas the support of many southern Democrats   c. make himself well known to the Republican party   d. accomplish all these things.

7. The southern states seceded from the Union because President Lincoln had:
   a. promised to abolish slavery in the southern states   b. threatened to use force against any state that seceded   c. won the support of the Northeast and the West   d. done all these things.

8. The immediate cause of the Civil War was:
   a. the firing on Fort Sumter   b. the dispute between the North and South over slavery   c. the economic rivalry between the Northeast and South   d. President Lincoln's desire to preserve the Union.

D. Summing Up the Chapter

Arrange the three events in each group in chronological order.

1. a. Compromise of 1850
   b. Kansas-Nebraska Act
   c. Missouri Compromise
2. a. Formation of Free Soil party
   b. Formation of Republican party
   c. Split of Democratic party
3. a. Dred Scott decision
   b. John Brown's raid
   c. Lincoln-Douglas debates
4. a. Firing on Fort Sumter
   b. Formation of the Confederacy
   c. Lincoln's victory in the presidential election

MAKING HISTORY LIVE

1. a. Why did Henry Clay become known as the "Great Compromiser"? b. Why was the Compromise of 1850 a great achievement? c. Why did it fail?
2. a. Explain President Lincoln's statement: "One side would *make* war rather than let the nation survive, and the other would *accept* war rather than let it perish." b. Tell why you agree or disagree with it.
3. On the basis of outside reading, write a report on *one* important person or exciting incident described in this chapter.
4. As an "inquiring reporter," interview "typical Americans" in the spring of 1861 on the question: Whom do you blame for the Civil War? (The interviews should include both northerners and southerners with moderate or extreme views.) Write them up.
5. Complete and write on *one* of these topics:
   a. "The Civil War might have been avoided if Senator Douglas had not . . ." b. "The Civil War might have been prevented if President Buchanan had . . ." c. "The Civil War might have been prevented if President Lincoln had . . ." d. "The Civil War could not have been prevented because . . ."
6. a. Draw a campaign poster for either the northern Democrats, the southern Democrats, or the Republicans in the presidential election of 1860. b. Draw a cartoon to show how events led the United States step by step into the Civil War.

Chapter 19

THE CIVIL WAR AND ITS RESULTS

Three months after the attack on Fort Sumter, a northern army advanced from Washington toward the Confederate capital of Richmond, only a hundred miles away. It was an unusual army. The soldiers, wearing the colorful uniforms of different state militias, walked along at a leisurely pace. Now and then some of them broke ranks to take a drink, pick flowers, or rest in the shade of the trees. With the army was a crowd of people in carriages and on horseback. Dressed in their Sunday best and carrying picnic baskets, they had come along to watch the "show."

Thirty miles west of Washington, near a stream called Bull Run, the Union and Confederate forces met in battle. The fighting raged for hours, taking a heavy toll of lives on both sides. At first the Union troops advanced. But then fresh Confederate forces arrived and the Union commander called a retreat. Suddenly panic swept through the crowd of onlookers. It quickly spread to the inexperienced Union troops. Soldiers joined with civilians in a wild dash back to Washington. Fortunately for the Union, the Confederate forces were also disorganized. Many southern soldiers stopped to pick up enemy guns and equipment. Some, thinking the war was over, went home. If they had pressed on, they might easily have captured the capital of the United States.

The Battle of Bull Run was important because it woke the American people from their dreams. Before the battle there had been talk in the North of a ninety-day war. "One big victory will finish it!" northerners had been saying. The South had been talking about the "cowardly Yankees" who would not fight at all or who would give up after their first defeat. Both sides discovered too late that they had been wrong. The Civil War was to last four years and cost more than a million casualties. In this chapter you will find the answers to these questions:

1. Why was the conflict so long and costly?
2. Why did the North win?
3. How did the war change the United States?

How Did the North Win the Civil War?

A. Strength of the Confederacy. At the start of the war, as the Battle of Bull Run showed, southerners were better fighters than northerners. They were more used to life outdoors, and they knew better how to handle guns and horses. The South also had more able officers than the North. Without a doubt its most able officer was General Robert E. Lee of Virginia. It has been said that the North might have won the war in a few months if Lee had stayed with the United States Army, as Lincoln had asked him to do. But Lee felt loyal to Virginia and joined the Confederacy instead. Time and again Lee's military skill helped the Confederate armies to defeat much larger Union forces.

The Confederacy had one other important advantage over the North—it was waging a defensive war. Its troops had very high morale because they were fighting for their homes. They also knew the land they fought for better than northerners did, and they had shorter supply lines. Most important, they had only to hold out until the North grew tired of fighting. The Union forces, on the other hand, had to invade the South and smash the Confederate armies to win.

B. Greater Strength of the North. Nevertheless, the North was stronger than the South in some important ways. With twice as many states as the South, it had more than double the South's population, industries, railroads, capital, and food production. The Union government was well organized and experienced. Moreover, it still controlled most of the prewar army and almost the entire navy.

Blacks also helped to make the North stronger. Though they made up more than a third of the population of the eleven Confederate states, they did not fight for the South. Southerners, unwilling to trust blacks with guns, used them as laborers in their armies. The Union forces, on the other hand, accepted blacks—both freemen from the North and runaway slaves from the South—as soldiers. Before the war's end, almost 200,000 of them were in northern uniform. Black regiments fought bravely in a number of important battles.

The Confederacy also lacked industries to

Company E of the 4th U.S. Colored Infantry. Black troops played an important part in some of the hardest fought battles of the Civil War.

supply its armed forces. It did not have enough railroads to move its troops quickly from one battlefront to another. Its government, being new, was not experienced enough to conduct the war effectively. It was also hindered by quarrels growing out of the strong southern belief in states' rights. When it began to draft men for the armed forces, for example, several governors objected. South Carolina even threatened to secede from the Confederacy.

In spite of these weaknesses, the South won most of the battles in the early part of the war. As the fighting continued, however, the North's greater resources and manpower counted more and more heavily. At the end of the war, the Union had a million men under arms and two million more in reserve. The South had less than a quarter of a million—and these were short of food, clothing, and equipment.

C. President Lincoln's Problems. President Lincoln also played an important part in winning the war. At the start, there was great danger that the four slave states bordering on the North would join the Confederacy (see map, page 320). If they did, the North and South would be more nearly equal in strength. The President acted swiftly. He sent troops into Maryland and Kentucky to arrest the leaders of a movement to secede from the Union. He also gave strong support to the governments of Missouri and Delaware, which favored the Union cause. To reassure the slaveowners in all four states, Lincoln said over and over again that the North was fighting to save the Union, not to end slavery.

Northerners who opposed the war were another great danger to the Union. A large group called the Copperheads (a copperhead is a poisonous snake) attacked the President and the war. They tried to discourage young men from entering the armed forces. Some of them

SOUTH vs. NORTH IN 1860

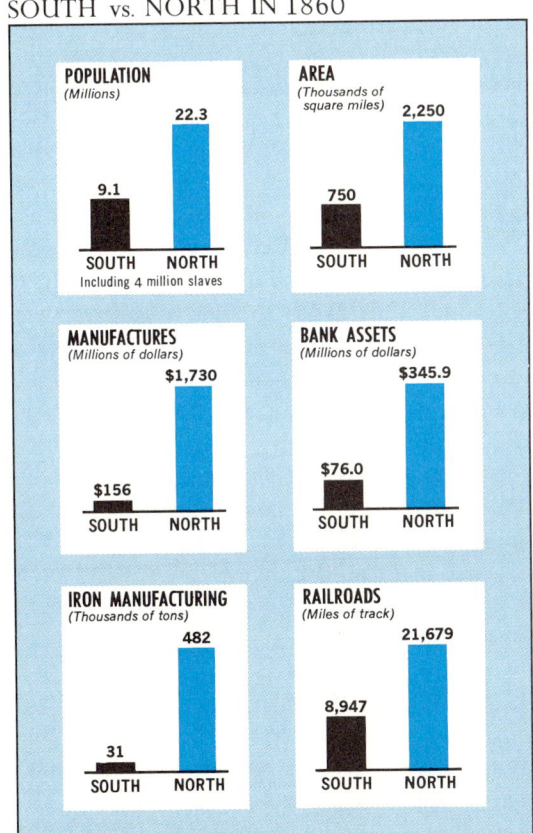

POPULATION (Millions)
- SOUTH: 9.1 (Including 4 million slaves)
- NORTH: 22.3

AREA (Thousands of square miles)
- SOUTH: 750
- NORTH: 2,250

MANUFACTURES (Millions of dollars)
- SOUTH: $156
- NORTH: $1,730

BANK ASSETS (Millions of dollars)
- SOUTH: $76.0
- NORTH: $345.9

IRON MANUFACTURING (Thousands of tons)
- SOUTH: 31
- NORTH: 482

RAILROADS (Miles of track)
- SOUTH: 8,947
- NORTH: 21,679

OPPOSING SIDES IN THE CIVIL WAR

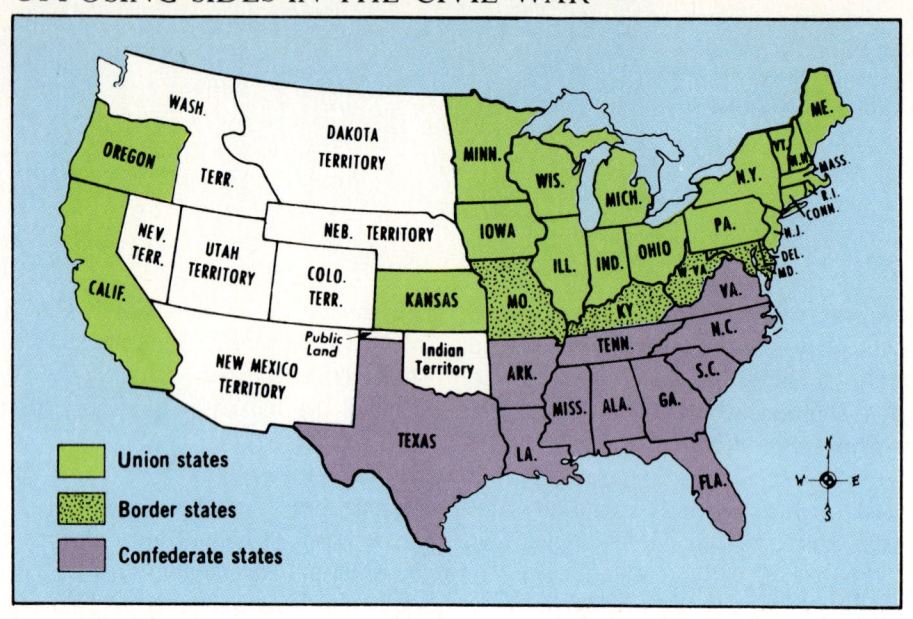

even spied for the South. They gained strength as the North lost battle after battle. In 1863, when the government began to draft men for the army, they played a part in starting riots in a few northern cities. Once again President Lincoln acted quickly. He sent troops to the cities to crush the draft riots. In some places he called for martial law (military rule) and suspended the right of habeas corpus (see page 164). Thousands of persons believed to be Copperheads were arrested and held in prison without a trial.

For a time the Union also faced the danger that the British and French governments would openly support the South. President Lincoln worked hard to win over the British. Early in the war, a northern warship stopped a British vessel and removed two Confederate officials. Lincoln quickly apologized to the British government and released the men. To gain the support of the democratic middle class and workers of Great Britain, he repeatedly said that the North was fighting to save American democracy. He won their full support later in 1862 when he freed the slaves. Soon afterward the North finally won some major victories. The British government then adopted a policy of strict neutrality. Eventually the ruler of France followed the British lead.

Finding able generals was another problem for the President. Time and again he changed commanders in order to find a general who had the will to fight and win. His actions were bitterly criticized on the ground that he was not a military man and should not interfere in military matters. The attacks on Lincoln increased as the Union armies suffered defeat after defeat. Indeed they became so violent that he expected for a time not to be reelected in 1864. But, like George Washington in the Revolutionary War, he carried on until the final victory.

D. The War in the East. The Civil War was fought on three fronts—in the East, in the West, and on the sea. In the East, the chief goal of the Union forces was to capture the Confederate capital of Richmond. After the

ABRAHAM LINCOLN: A SUCCESSFUL FAILURE

Abraham Lincoln was the son of a poor laborer on the western frontier. He was born on February 12, 1809 in a rude log cabin in Kentucky and grew up in the backwoods of Indiana. His mother died when he was a little child. He received little schooling and had to go to work at an early age. Young Abe settled in a frontier town in Illinois. There he worked at various jobs, such as field hand, ferryman, rail splitter, and surveyor. Twice he went into business with a partner. Both times the store failed and he was left to pay the debts. He was almost forty years old by the time they were paid.

Lincoln also had bad luck in his personal life. He was a tall and homely man, with long arms and legs and large hands and feet. It was hard to find a girl who wanted to marry him. When he did find her, she died suddenly. For months he was so sad that friends feared he would kill himself. Later he became engaged to an attractive but hot-tempered young lady. He broke off the engagement, went through another spell of sadness, and then married her. She was a difficult wife. The couple had four sons, each of whom he loved deeply—but two of them died very young.

Meanwhile Lincoln had become a successful lawyer. His main interest, however, was politics. He served for many years as a member of the state legislature, but his efforts to win a higher position failed. He was elected to the House of Representatives in 1846, but served only one term. When he ran for the Senate in 1858, he lost again.

It may seem strange that a man with such a poor record in politics was nominated for the presidency in 1860. But Lincoln was a rare person. He was unusual in character as well as in appearance. People who got to know him found that he was very wise, honest, and kind. His suffering seemed to have taught him to understand and sympathize with others. Lincoln's personal qualities won him many friends. They stood by him loyally through the long years of failure and disappointment.

This wise and kindly man proved to be a great President. For he did not bear grudges against people who hurt him. Though he hated slavery, he did not hate slaveowners. He often said that if he had been brought up as they had, he would have behaved in the same way. Even after four terrible years of war, Lincoln did not hate white southerners. He hoped by treating them kindly to heal the wounds of war and win fair treatment for the newly freed blacks. Our nation's history might have been very different if he had lived to carry out his plans.

defeat at Bull Run, Lincoln appointed George B. McClellan to command the main northern force, the Army of the Potomac. An excellent organizer, General McClellan soon built up a powerful army. But he was too cautious to make good use of it. He refused to advance overland on Richmond because the way was blocked by rivers, swamps, and woods. He chose instead to carry his troops by boat to a peninsula that provided an easier approach to the Confederate capital (see map below). At first the Peninsular Campaign was successful. In spite of strong opposition, McClellan advanced slowly inland. But when the Union forces were only a few miles from Richmond, Lee counterattacked and drove them back. Though McClellan had much larger forces than Lee, he called for more troops. He would not renew the attack until he got them. Lincoln, disappointed by McClellan's failure to act, removed him and called off the offensive.

The President then appointed a general who promised to fight. Advancing boldly overland toward Richmond, this general was thoroughly beaten by Lee's forces in the Second Battle of Bull Run. Lee now took the offensive. He advanced into Maryland, hoping to win over that slave state and to gain British support for the South through a great victory. McClellan, reappointed by the President, defeated the Confederates at Antietam Creek. But Lincoln again removed him because he failed to go after the retreating Confederates.

During the next year, Lincoln appointed two more generals in the East. Each advanced on Richmond only to suffer a severe defeat. In the summer of 1863, Lee made a supreme effort to win the war for the Confederacy. He marched northward into Pennsylvania, hoping to force the North's surrender by capturing some important cities. His advance was stopped by the Union army at the little town of Gettysburg (see map below). After three days of heavy fighting, in which the Confederates suffered almost 30,000 dead and wounded, Lee was forced to retreat. Though few knew it at the time, the Battle of Gettysburg was the turning point of the war.

E. The War in the West. General Lee had to gamble on ending the war quickly because the Union armies were winning in the West. There General Ulysses S. Grant had captured two Confederate forts and was advancing southward along the Mississippi River. Admiral David Farragut had led a strong naval force into the mouth of the Mississippi. He had captured New Orleans after a hard fight and was advancing upstream to meet Grant. Separating the two northern commanders was the city of Vicksburg, standing like a fort on cliffs high above the river. It took Grant a half-dozen hard-fought battles and a long siege to force Vicksburg's surrender. The city fell on July 4, 1863, the day after Lee's defeat at Gettysburg. Grant then gained control

A scene from the Battle of Gettysburg.

Lincoln's Gettysburg Address (1863)

Four score and seven years ago our fathers brought forth on this continent a new nation, conceived in liberty, and dedicated to the proposition that all men are created equal.

Now we are engaged in a great civil war, testing whether that nation, or any nation so conceived and so dedicated, can long endure. We are met on a great battlefield of that war. We have come to dedicate a portion of that field as a final resting place for those who here gave their lives that that nation might live. It is altogether fitting and proper that we should do this.

But, in a larger sense, we cannot dedicate—we cannot consecrate—we cannot hallow—this ground. The brave men, living and dead, who struggled here, have consecrated it far above our poor power to add or detract. The world will little note nor long remember what we say here, but it can never forget what they did here. It is for us, the living, rather, to be dedicated here to the unfinished work which they who fought here have thus far so nobly advanced. It is rather for us to be here dedicated to the great task remaining before us—that from these honored dead we take increased devotion to that cause for which they gave the last full measure of devotion—that we here highly resolve that these dead shall not have died in vain—that this nation, under God, shall have a new birth of freedom—and that government of the people, by the people, for the people, shall not perish from the earth.

Lee, on the right, surrenders to Grant. After the war, Lee became president of Washington College (now Washington and Lee University).

of the Mississippi, cutting the Confederacy in two (see map, page 322).

Grant next headed eastward through Tennessee, planning to split the Confederacy a second time. At last President Lincoln had found a general who won battles. Early in 1864 he appointed Grant to command all the Union armies.

F. The War at Sea. The North did best of all in the war at sea. The navy blockaded the South so effectively that cotton exports fell from almost $200,000,000 a year to only $4,000,000. As a result, the South could not pay for the war. It was also unable to import from Great Britain the military equipment and other supplies it desperately needed.

The Confederates tried to break the northern blockade. They armed a warship named the *Merrimac* with iron plate and a ram and sent it to attack the blockading fleet. The *Merrimac* easily destroyed two wooden warships off the coast of Virginia. But the Union government was already prepared to meet this threat to the blockade. It had built a strange-looking iron-plated vessel of its own called the *Monitor*. The two ironclads soon met in a furious battle. Neither ship could seriously damage the other. So the northern blockade continued.

Though the Battle of the *Monitor* and *Merrimac* did not change the war, it was one of the most important naval battles in history. It marked the end of wooden warships and the beginning of modern steel navies.

G. The Final Triumph. In the spring of 1864, General William T. Sherman carried out Grant's bold plan to split the Confederacy east of the Mississippi. Beating back Confederate attacks, he marched eastward across the states of Tennessee and Georgia to the port of Savannah. Then he advanced slowly northward along the Atlantic coast, through South Carolina and into North Carolina (see map, page 322). Sherman spread his forces across a belt sixty miles wide. He ordered them to destroy everything of value that lay in their path—especially railroads, factories, crops, livestock, and barns. The damage done by Sherman's "march to the sea" was so great that even to this day southerners recall it with bitterness. But it undoubtedly helped to end the war quickly. Sherman's victories also helped Lincoln to defeat the Democratic candidate, General McClellan, in the election of 1864.

Meanwhile Grant was fighting his way overland toward Richmond. In an almost continuous series of battles, known as the Wilderness Campaign, he lost more than a thousand men a day. But he continued his sledge-hammer blows without a pause until he reached Petersburg, through which supplies for Richmond passed. He took the city after a long siege. Then he quickly captured Richmond and surrounded Lee's forces. Early in April of 1865, Lee surrendered to Grant at Appomattox Court House in Virginia. Soon afterward, the remaining Confederate forces surrendered to Sherman. At last, a full four years after the firing on Fort Sumter, the Civil War was over.

REVIEWING THE SECTION

A. Knowing New Terms

PART 1. In your notebook write the best meaning for each of the words in italics.

1. *at a leisurely pace:*
   a. foolishly   b. directly   c. quickly   d. slowly
2. *panic:*
   a. cowardice   b. great danger   c. strong attack   d. wild fear
3. *disorganized:*
   a. disorderly   b. discontented   c. dismayed   d. dismissed
4. *defensive:*
   a. attacking   b. resisting attack   c. powerful   d. weak
5. *martial law:*
   a. federal law   b. state law   c. local law   d. military law

PART 2. Explain each term in your notebook *in your own words.*

(In the chapter introduction) ninety-day war   (In C) Copperheads
"cowardly Yankees"

B. Knowing Important People

For each important person in the first column, write the *letter* of the best description in the second column.

Important People
1. David Farragut
2. Ulysses S. Grant
3. Robert E. Lee
4. George B. McClellan
5. William T. Sherman

Descriptions
a. Able but very cautious northern military commander
b. Commander in chief of the northern armies and fleets
c. Leading Confederate commander
d. Most successful northern naval commander
e. Northern commander who destroyed everything of value in his advance through the South
f. Northern military commander who won decisive victories in both the West and East

C. Understanding the Facts

PART 1. To compare the strength of the two sides at the start of the Civil War, do the following exercise in your notebook. Write "North" if the Union

325

was stronger in a certain way; write "South" if the Confederacy was stronger. (Be prepared to explain your answers in class.)

1. Skilled soldiers
2. Able officers
3. High morale
4. Knowledge of the land
5. Manpower
6. Industries, railroads, capital
7. Food production
8. Strong, experienced government
9. Strong navy
10. Support of blacks

Conclusions. 1. Why did the South win at first? 2. Why did the North win in the end?

PART 2. In your notebook write "North" if the battle was won by the Union forces, "South" if it was won by the Confederates, and "Draw" if neither side won.

1. First Battle of Bull Run
2. Peninsular Campaign
3. Second Battle of Bull Run
4. Battle of Antietam Creek
5. Battle of the *Monitor* and *Merrimac*
6. Capture of New Orleans
7. Battle of Gettysburg
8. Battle of Vicksburg
9. Wilderness Campaign
10. "march to the sea"

Conclusion. How does this study show that the Union forces grew stronger as the war went on?

IMPROVING YOUR SKILLS

A. Mastering the Map

Study the map on page 322. Then complete the following sentences in your notebook.

1. In the East, most of the fighting in the Civil War took place in the state of _____. This state contained the Confederate capital, _____, and bordered on the Union capital, _____, ____.
2. In the West, the Union forces cut the Confederacy in two by winning control of the _____ River. General Grant started his western campaign in the state of _____. He advanced southward through the states of _____, _____, _____, and _____. He finally joined forces with Admiral Farragut in the state of _____.
3. General Sherman again cut the Confederacy in two when he marched across the state of _____ to the port of _____. Next he advanced northward through the state of _____ _____ into the state of _____ _____.

B. Interpreting the Graph

Answer these questions based on the graph on page 319.

1. In which ways was the North more than ten times as strong as the South?
2. In which way was the North almost five times as strong as the South?
3. In which ways was the North more than twice as strong as the South?
4. If we leave out slaves, the North's population was how many times as large as that of the South?

How Did the Civil War Change the United States?

A. Costs of the War. The Civil War has been called the first modern war. It was fought by large armies of citizen soldiers and involved large numbers of civilians. As a result, casualties were very heavy. Besides the large number killed in battle, several hundred thousand men died in hospitals and prisons. Altogether, more than a half million young Americans perished as a result of the war — a much larger number than in any other war our nation has fought, including even World War II.

The Civil War was also very costly from an economic standpoint. It cost the North and South together about five billion dollars. Both sides used more of the nation's wealth to pay for the war than the United States did for World War II. The North was left with a heavy war debt that took many years to pay. The Confederate government could not pay its debts at all. People who held Confederate bonds or currency lost the full value. Slaveowners lost another two billion dollars when their slaves were freed. In addition, Sherman's march to the sea and the many battles fought on southern soil resulted in heavy damage to property in many parts of the South.

What did the United States obtain for the

AMERICAN CASUALTIES IN WARS

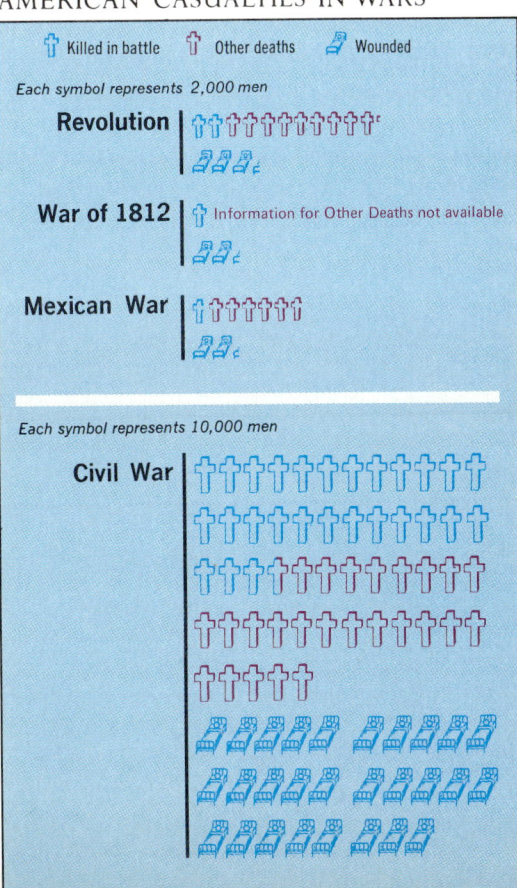

huge price it paid in lives and wealth? The Civil War helped to bring about a number of far-reaching changes that made the United States a much stronger nation. But the war also created problems so serious that they still concern us greatly today.

B. Political Effects of the War. 1. PRESERVING THE UNION. By winning the Civil War, the North succeeded in saving the Union. Its success settled a question that the Constitution had not answered—whether a state could legally secede. Since the defeat of the Confederacy, no state has tried to leave the Union.

2. ABOLISHING SLAVERY. The war also settled a second question, slavery. In his Emancipation Proclamation, President Lincoln declared that all slaves in rebel territory were to be considered free on January 1, 1863. Because it applied only to areas still under Confederate control, the Proclamation did not free a single slave at first. But the slaves gained their freedom as the northern armies advanced into Confederate territory. By the end of the war, most of them had been emancipated.

A few months later, the Thirteenth Amendment was ratified by the states and went into effect. This amendment forbade slavery anywhere in the United States. At long last our nation joined most other civilized countries in outlawing one of the greatest evils the world has ever known.

3. STRENGTHENING THE PRESIDENCY. In the Emancipation Proclamation, Lincoln had stretched the President's powers. To fight the war, he stretched his constitutional powers in still other ways. To raise an army quickly at the start of the war, he spent money that Congress had not yet voted. As the war continued, he ordered martial law and suspended the right of habeas corpus in some places to deal with spies, Copperheads, and draft rioters. As a result, thousands of Americans were arrested and held without a trial or were tried by military courts. Hundreds of newspapers were shut down for attacking the government and its policies. Private letters were opened by federal officials who censored (cut out) any information that might help the South.

President Lincoln admitted that his actions violated the Constitution. But he held that he was acting to meet an emergency that placed the nation in danger. Lincoln set an important precedent. Other Presidents since his time have also exercised great power in emergencies. This was especially true of Presidents Wilson and Roosevelt during the first and second world wars.

4. PURCHASING ALASKA. One of the most important results of the Civil War came about

Sherman's march to the sea. His troops burned Atlanta and spread destruction through Georgia and South Carolina. Why are the Union soldiers tearing up the railroad tracks?

almost by accident. The czar (king) of Russia was angry with Great Britain and France because they had defeated his country in a war a few years earlier. Since they favored the South, he announced his friendship for the North. He even sent fleets to visit San Francisco and New York as proof of his friendship. When the war ended, the czar asked the United States to buy Alaska from him. Secretary of State Seward persuaded the President and Congress to accept the offer. For $7,200,000, the United States acquired over a half-million square miles of territory.

At the time, many Americans made fun of the purchase. They called Alaska "Seward's Folly" or "Seward's Icebox" because they thought it too cold for any use. But it has paid for itself many times over in gold, furs, salmon, and recently oil. The 800-mile oil pipe line, from the Arctic Ocean to ice-free waters off southern Alaska, was completed in 1977. Alaska's location is also important. It is near the Soviet Union and on the main air route between most of the United States and the Far East.

C. Economic Results of the War. 1. THE "NEW SOUTH." The Civil War also had some important economic results. The South, as we have seen, suffered heavily because of war damage, the failure of the Confederate government to pay its debts, and the freeing of the slaves. Without slave labor, the plantation system could no longer continue. Many plantations were broken up and sold as small farms. Others were saved by a new system of labor known as sharecropping. Under this system, the landowners rented plots of land to poor whites and blacks, who paid them a share of the crop as rent.

The sharecropping system created two serious problems. First, sharecroppers did not have either the skills or the money to take care of the soil. Already exhausted by plantation farming, it became less and less productive

Sharecroppers ploughing the soil for rice. Why did most of what they earned go to pay for land use, tools, seeds, and fertilizer?

as the years passed. Secondly, sharecroppers were usually at the mercy of their landlords. Landlords could dispossess sharecroppers—that is, throw them off the farm—at any time. Sharecroppers, on the other hand, might not be free to leave if they wished. To get started, a sharecropper needed tools, seeds, and other supplies. The landlord usually provided these items—but as a loan, not as a gift. Landlords added interest at a very high rate to the cost of the items until all of the loan was repaid. Many sharecroppers were unable to pay their debt. In fact, they usually had to borrow again each spring to plant a new crop. As long as they owed money, they were not allowed to leave the farm. Thus they were bound to the land, almost like serfs in Europe during the Middle Ages.

In spite of these weaknesses, sharecropping was certainly better than the old plantation system. Sharecroppers, unlike slaves, could not be sold. Families could not be separated. They could not be made to work without pay. Sharecroppers had a chance to earn money by raising larger crops. The cruel overseer with his whip was no longer considered necessary and disappeared from the South.

The Civil War had one other important economic effect. It awakened southern leaders to the fact that their section had fallen behind the North. So they began to modernize the South by building industries, railroads, and public schools. They built new textile mills in the Cotton Belt and founded a new iron and steel industry in Birmingham, Alabama. They also developed the coal and timber resources of the Appalachian Mountain region. Slowly but steadily, a new South arose from the ruins of the Civil War. By 1900 southern cotton production was more than twice that of 1860, and industrial production was more than four times the prewar level.

2. ECONOMIC PROGRESS IN THE NORTH. In the northern states, the war did little damage. Indeed, it actually helped economic progress. The needs of the armed forces created a very large demand for manufactured goods and foods. Prices and profits rose. Business people used the profits to expand and modernize their factories. Farmers used them to buy farm machinery.

The government encouraged progress by carrying out the promises of the Republican platform of 1860. To speed the settlement of the West, it gave settlers free land and helped build a railroad to the Pacific coast. To aid business, the government raised tariffs to new high levels and created the national banking system.

It was easy to start a national bank. Five or more persons had only to buy federal bonds worth $30,000 or more and apply to the federal government for a charter. A national bank could print its own bank notes with the bonds as backing. It could use the notes to make loans to business people. It therefore collected double interest—both on the loans and on the government bonds that backed them.

The national banking system helped the government win the support of bankers. More important, it helped the government sell bonds to pay for the war, and it gave the nation a sound currency. The system remained unchanged for fifty years. In fact, there are still many national banks in existence today.

D. Social Effects of the War. The most important social change brought about by the Civil War was the emancipation of the slaves. (It will be discussed in the next chapter.) Another important change was an improvement in the position of women in American society. With men busy fighting, women had a chance to show their abilities. Many managed plantations or farms; others gave help to the armed forces. Since the South had few factories, southern women made clothing and bandages for the Confederate army. In the North, women raised money for the Sanitary Commission. This was an organization established to improve conditions in military hospitals, camps, and prisons. Many women worked as nurses, an occupation thought suitable only for men before the war. One woman, Clara Barton, rose to fame through her work with the Sanitary Commission. When the American Red Cross was established after the Civil War, she became its first president. Achievements like hers helped women in their long struggle for equal rights with men.

E. Two Unsolved Problems. One bad effect of any war is the hatred it stirs up between the opposing sides. This hatred usually continues after the war. The winning side usually wants to punish and weaken the losing side by making it pay dearly for the war. The loser, in turn, wants revenge for its defeat and punishment. Would the North, like most winners, deal harshly with the South? Or would it wisely see that kind treatment would be better if northerners and southerners were to live together as fellow Americans? What would be done about the four million blacks freed from slavery? The way the North dealt with these two problems was sure to have important effects on the development of the United States for many years to come.

REVIEWING THE SECTION

A. Knowing New Terms

In your notebook write the new terms in this section that best complete each statement.

1. President Lincoln's order to free the slaves in Confederate territory was called the _____ _____.
2. Slavery was outlawed everywhere in the United States by the _____ Amendment.
3. The plantation system in the South was replaced by a new system of farming called _____.
4. Banks chartered by the federal government during the Civil War were called _____ _____.
5. After winning fame for her work with the Sanitary Commission, Clara Barton became the first president of the American _____ _____.

B. Knowing Important Facts

Complete this chart in your notebook by filling in the missing facts.

COSTS AND RESULTS OF THE CIVIL WAR

Costs	Results

1.
 2.
 3.
 4. Problems left by the war
    a.
    b.
	1.
	 2.
	 3.
	 4.
	 5.
	 6.
	 7.

Conclusions. 1. Which do you consider the most important result of the Civil War? Why? 2. On the whole, were the results of the war worth its costs? Explain.

C. Understanding the Facts

Write "True" in your notebook if the statement is correct. If the statement contains an error, rewrite it so that it is correct.

1. The Civil War is considered a modern war because both sides used large armies composed mainly of professional soldiers.

2. If its cost is measured against what the nation could afford, then the Civil War is the most expensive war the United States has ever fought.
3. Since the Civil War, no state has tried to secede because the Constitution was amended to forbid secession.
4. The Emancipation Proclamation did not free a single slave during the Civil War.
5. President Lincoln violated the people's right of freedom of speech and the press, as well as other rights guaranteed by the Constitution.
6. Alaska was nicknamed "Seward's Folly" because many Americans thought it foolish to buy a territory in the frozen Arctic.
7. Southern sharecroppers after the Civil War were treated much like slaves before the war.
8. The notes issued by the national banks served as an important part of our nation's currency for more than fifty years.
9. The Civil War gave American women a chance to prove that they could do work once thought suitable only for men.
10. The sudden freeing of several million black slaves created serious problems for both the South and the North.

D. Finding the Reasons

In your notebook write the letters of *all* the correct answers to each question.

1. Why did President Lincoln stretch the powers of the President under the Constitution?
   a. He wanted to show that he was a strong President. b. He wanted to set an example for future Presidents to follow. c. He acted to keep the Copperheads and other opponents of the war from interfering with the war effort.
2. Why has Alaska proved valuable to the United States?
   a. It has important natural resources. b. It is located on an important air route between the United States and the Far East. c. It is very near our main rival, the Soviet Union.
3. Why were sharecroppers more like serfs than slaves?
   a. They could not be bought and sold. b. They could not leave or be put off the land they worked. c. After giving the landlord part of their crop, they could keep the rest.
4. Why did southern leaders decide to build industries in the South after the Civil War?
   a. With the plantation system ruined, wealthy southerners had to find another way to invest their capital. b. They discovered that industry had made the North stronger than the South. c. They planned to build up their strength for a war of revenge.

5. How did the Civil War encourage the rapid growth of industry and agriculture in the North?
   a. The army's needs created a great demand for food and manufactured goods. b. Business people and farmers made large profits that they put back into their factories and farms to increase production. c. New laws of the federal government helped business people and western farmers.

IMPROVING YOUR SKILLS

Interpreting the Graph

Study the graph on page 327. Then answer these questions in your notebook.

1. In which war was the total number of American casualties (killed and wounded) the smallest?
2. About how many Americans were killed in the first three wars combined? About how many were wounded?
3. About how many Americans were killed in the Civil War? How many were wounded?
4. Is it correct to say that the casualties of the Civil War were more than twenty times as large as those of the three previous wars combined?

MAKING HISTORY LIVE

1. Find out if any members of your family were affected by the Civil War. If so, tell the class how they were affected.
2. If you have visited a Civil War battlefield, tell your classmates what you saw. Show them any pictures or other souvenirs you obtained there.
3. After visiting a local museum, report on:
   a. the part your community played in the Civil War; or b. how the war affected its development.
4. Write a report on an eyewitness account that tells what fighting was like during the Civil War. Try the library for assistance.
5. Write part of the imaginary diary of a young soldier in the Civil War.
6. Prepare for a debate on the question, Were the results of the Civil War worth its costs? Write the views of both sides.
7. Imagine you are a nurse in a military hospital in the Civil War. Write a letter to your family at home telling them what your work is like.
8. Play Civil War songs. Go over the words carefully to see what they tell you about the war. Bring the words of one you like to class.

Chapter 20

THE RECONSTRUCTION OF THE SOUTH

To *reconstruct* means to rebuild. The South certainly needed rebuilding in 1865. Large areas had been ruined, the Confederate government had collapsed, and Confederate money was worthless. The railroads had broken down and trade had come to a standstill. In many places, people were starving, and ordinary goods like cloth, shoes, and needles and thread could not be obtained.

To make matters worse, the labor supply needed for rebuilding was sharply reduced. A large number of young white men had been killed or crippled. The slaves had been freed. Many of the freedmen and freedwomen, as they were called, chose to remain with their former masters. But many other freedpeople left to start a new life elsewhere or to find loved ones from whom they had been separated.

The wanderings of the freedpeople caused still another problem. They traveled in bands about the countryside, gathered in towns and cities, or attached themselves to the northern armies. Thousands died of hunger and disease.

The northern army and government took some steps to help freedpeople. Private charities from the North also helped the freedpeople by sending them supplies and by starting schools. But not much more was done to help the South recover socially and economically. The federal government's plans for reconstruction dealt for the most part with political problems created by the Civil War.

In this chapter we shall find answers to the following questions:

1. How did the President propose to set up new governments in the southern states and readmit them to the Union?

2. Why did Congress kill the President's plan and put a plan of its own into effect?

3. Why did southerners call the congressional plan "the crime of Reconstruction"?

What Were the Opposing Plans for Reconstruction?

A. President Lincoln's Viewpoint. In his Second Inaugural Address, President Lincoln expressed the hope that North and South might begin the work of reconstruction in a spirit of friendly cooperation. He said:

"With malice [ill will] toward none, with charity for all, let us strive on to finish the work we are in; to bind up the nation's wounds, to care for him who shall have borne the battle, and for his widow and his orphan; to do all which may achieve a just and lasting peace."

The President spoke out strongly against those who favored malice and revenge. He told his cabinet that he did not want to see the South and its leaders punished. He hoped that "there would be no persecution, no bloody work. Enough lives have been sacrificed. We must extinguish [end] our resentment if we expect harmony and union." Lincoln even spoke of asking Congress for $400,000,000 to pay southerners for the loss of their slaves.

B. The Lincoln-Johnson Plan. The President's plan for Reconstruction showed his desire to win over the South. As he saw it, the southern states had never had the right to secede and thus were still legally members of the Union. So he set up machinery that would restore them to their former position quickly and easily. Under his plan, only 10 percent of the men who had voted in the election of 1860 and had taken an oath of allegiance to the United States were needed to form a new state government. The new government would be recognized as soon as it ratified the Thirteenth Amendment abolishing slavery.

Lincoln had no clear plan for dealing with the freedpeople. He hoped that the southern whites would work out a wise policy of their own. He expected that they would grant the vote to educated blacks and black war veterans.

Unfortunately, Lincoln did not live to see his "10% Plan" put into effect. A few days after General Lee's surrender, the President went to the theater for an evening of relaxation. As he sat in his box watching the play, an insane actor named John Wilkes Booth crept up behind him and fired a bullet into his brain. The assassination of President Lincoln

The assassination of President Lincoln by John Wilkes Booth in Ford's Theater. What effect did Lincoln's death have upon the South?

was part of a plot to help the Confederacy by killing some important Union leaders. The plot failed. Its only effect was to deprive the South of a powerful friend.

Lincoln's successor, Vice-President Andrew Johnson, had been chosen to "balance the ticket" (see page 145). Johnson was a Democrat and a slaveowner. Like most southerners, he considered blacks an inferior race. But the Republicans trusted him because he had remained loyal to the Union and was known to dislike the wealthy planter aristocrats.

Johnson continued Lincoln's plan with only a few small changes. By the end of 1865, ten of the former Confederate states had met the easy conditions set by Lincoln and Johnson. The last state, Texas, was getting ready to do so.

C. Developments in the South. Another important federal action was the creation of the Freedmen's Bureau. This bureau was established to help freedpeople—men, women, and children. It gave them food and medical care, started schools for them, and found them work. In general, the Bureau encouraged freedpeople to continue as farmers. It settled several thousand on deserted plantations. It helped others to obtain fair terms for work they did as laborers or sharecroppers for white landowners.

As the new southern state governments took over, however, conditions changed. In the new governments were many officers of the old Confederate government—including the vice-president of the Confederacy, 4 generals, 6 cabinet members, and 58 members of Congress. Some of them made bold speeches in which they openly defied the North. One congressman expressed the anger of many northerners when he said, "Who do they think won the war anyway?"

The new southern governments soon began to undermine the work of the Freedmen's Bureau. They passed a number of laws "to keep the Negro in his place." These laws, like the earlier laws for slaves (see page 295), were known as the "black codes." The new black codes gave the freedpeople only a few rights. They were allowed to own property and could bring court actions or serve as witnesses in cases involving other blacks. But they were not allowed to vote or hold office, serve on juries, carry arms, or testify in cases involving whites. These new laws also made it a crime for a black to show disrespect, by either word or gesture, to a white person. Blacks were forbidden to do skilled work unless they had a special license. They had to agree to work for the same employers for years and to permit their children to work as apprentices without pay.

Blacks who did not obey these laws could be arrested as vagrants (persons who have no home or work). If they were arrested, they were ordered to pay a heavy fine. If they could not pay it, they were hired out until they worked it off. Often, "vagrants" were put to work for their old masters. It seemed to many northerners that the South had created a new form of slavery to replace the old one.

D. Northern Opposition to the Lincoln-Johnson Plan. From the start, a small group of congressmen had objected to the Lincoln-Johnson Plan of Reconstruction. They thought it too easy on the South. These congressmen called themselves Radical Republicans because they wanted to make radical (extreme) changes in the South. The Radicals demanded that blacks be given full rights as American citizens immediately. One of their leaders, Representative Thaddeus Stevens of Pennsylvania, wanted to destroy the southern aristocracy by taking away its plantations. Stevens wanted to divide these plantations into forty-acre farms for black families. He wanted the rest of the land to be sold to help pay for the war.

The Radicals won wide support in Congress for three reasons. First, Congress as a whole felt that the President had grown too powerful during the war. So it tried to regain power by taking over the reconstruction of the South. Second, the Republicans were afraid they would lose control of the government to the Democrats. There were still a number of northern Democrats in Congress. The new congressmen from the South were almost certain to be Democrats. President Johnson was a Democrat. If the Democrats obtained a majority in Congress, they would be able to repeal the entire Republican program. The Republicans were determined to see that this did not happen. "The party that saved the nation must rule it" became their slogan. Third and most important of all, the actions of the new southern governments aroused great anger, both in Congress and among the general public. The Radicals received a large vote in the elections of 1866. They controlled Congress for the next six years.

E. Congressional Reconstruction. Congress killed the Lincoln-Johnson Plan by refusing to seat the congressmen the southern states had elected. Then it put through an entirely new plan of its own.

1. THE FOURTEENTH AMENDMENT. To guar-

Outside and inside views of a school for freedpeople in Vicksburg, Mississippi. Why had most slaveowners not allowed their slaves to get an education? How did these schools benefit blacks?

antee the freedmen equal rights, Congress proposed the Fourteenth Amendment to the Constitution. The amendment begins with these words, "All persons born or naturalized [granted citizenship] in the United States, and subject to the jurisdiction thereof, are citizens of the United States and of the State wherein they reside." Up to this time, Americans had been citizens of just their states. By making them citizens of the United States, the amendment put the freedmen under the protection of the federal government.

The Fourteenth Amendment also forbade any state to "deprive any person of life, liberty, or property, without due process of law" and to "deny any person within its jurisdiction the equal protection of the laws." If a state kept citizens from voting, its representation in Congress was to be reduced. People who had been active in the Confederacy could not hold federal or state office. Finally, the southern states were forbidden to pay any Confederate debts. (This was an added punishment for the wealthy southerners who had bought Confederate bonds.)

2. THE FIFTEENTH AMENDMENT. As a further guarantee of the freedmen's right to vote, Congress proposed the Fifteenth Amendment. This forbids a state to keep a citizen of the United States from voting "on account of race, color, or previous condition of servitude [slavery]."

3. THE RECONSTRUCTION ACT OF 1867. Of the eleven southern states, only Tennessee ratified the Fourteenth Amendment. The other ten states refused. Congress then passed the Reconstruction Act of 1867. The existing Lincoln-Johnson governments were declared illegal. The ten southern states were placed

Two leaders of congressional reconstruction. On the left is Representative Thaddeus Stevens of Pennsylvania; on the right, Senator Charles Sumner of Massachusetts. Why did they want the defeated states to be treated like "conquered provinces"?

MILITARY RULE

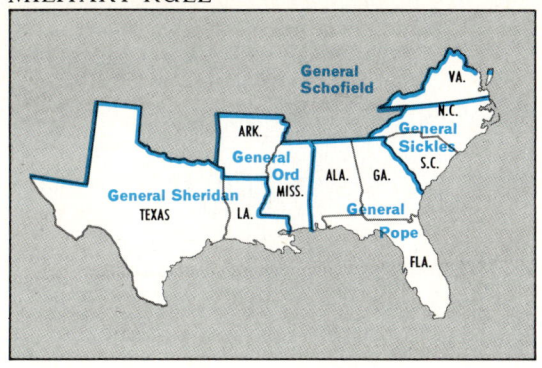

under military rule—that is, northern generals and troops were sent to govern them.

According to Congress, the southern states had lost their rights when they had seceded. They had to apply to Congress to return to the Union, just as a new territory had to do. To be readmitted, they were required to meet a number of conditions. They had to draft new constitutions that Congress approved; guarantee freedmen the right to vote and hold office; deny these rights to all people who had been active in the Confederacy; and ratify the Fourteenth and Fifteenth Amendments. This Congressional plan for reconstruction was much harsher than President Lincoln's proposals. It remained to be seen whether it would work any better.

REVIEWING THE SECTION

A. Knowing New Terms

In your notebook write the new terms in this section that best complete each statement.

1. The way the federal government dealt with the South after the Civil War has been called "_____."
2. The first plan for the South was worked out by two Presidents. It is known as the _____-_____ or _____ Plan.
3. To help the newly freed blacks, Congress created the _____ Bureau.
4. To control the freed blacks, the new governments of the southern states passed laws known as the "_____ _____."
5. The actions of the southern whites angered the North and gave control of Congress to the extreme or _____ Republicans.
6. Blacks were granted equal rights as citizens of the United States by the _____ Amendment.
7. Blacks were guaranteed the right to vote by the _____ Amendment.

B. Knowing Important Facts

PART 1. Compare the reconstruction plans of the President and Congress by completing the following chart in your notebook.

	Presidential Plan	Congressional Plan
1. Admission of southern states to the Union	1.	1.
2. Treatment of former Confederates	2.	2.
3. Treatment of blacks	3.	3.

PART 2. To test your knowledge of the three "Civil War amendments," write "13," if a statement is a provision of the Thirteenth Amendment, "14," if it is a provision of the Fourteenth Amendment, and "15," if it is a provision of the Fifteenth Amendment.

1. Former Confederates were forbidden to vote or hold office.
2. Slavery was forbidden in the United States.
3. The states were forbidden to deny citizens the right to vote because of their "race, color, or previous condition of servitude."
4. The states were forbidden to deny citizens of the United States any of their rights.
5. The southern states were forbidden to pay Confederate debts.
6. All Americans were made citizens of the United States.
7. The representation of southern states in Congress might be reduced under certain conditions.

Conclusion. Which of the three do you consider the most important amendment? Why?

C. Understanding the Facts

In your notebook write the *letter* of the correct choice.

1. The economic problems of the South in 1865 included:
   a. widespread war damage   b. lack of good money and transportation   c. shortages of food and manufactured goods   d. all these problems.
2. The federal government's plans for the reconstruction of the South dealt with:
   a. economic problems   b. political problems   c. social problems   d. all three kinds of problems.
3. President Lincoln favored:
   a. kindly treatment of the South   b. paying slaveholders for the property they had lost   c. admitting the southern states to the Union on easy terms   d. all these things.
4. Lincoln's "10% Plan":
   a. allowed 10 percent of the white voters in a southern state to set up a new government if they had taken an oath of allegiance to the United States   b. freed 10 percent of the slaves   c. admitted 10

percent of the southern states to the Union   d. paid 10 percent of the cost of rebuilding the South's war damage.
5. The assassination of President Lincoln:
a. helped the South by making a southerner President   b. helped the South to get better treatment from Congress   c. hurt the South by depriving it of Lincoln's support   d. had little effect on the reconstruction of the South.
6. The Freedmen's Bureau helped the blacks by giving them:
a. food and medicine   b. education   c. jobs   d. all three kinds of aid.
7. The laws passed by the 10% governments in the South:
a. brought back slavery   b. did nothing to help the freedpeople   c. gave the freedpeople a few rights, but kept them under strict control   d. gave blacks equal rights with whites.
8. Many northerners objected to the Lincoln-Johnson Plan on the ground that it:
a. left the former Confederate leaders in power   b. did not give blacks a chance to better their lot   c. threatened to give the Democrats control of the federal government   d. had all these faults.
9. The Fourteenth Amendment:
a. freed the slaves   b. made the freedpeople citizens of the United States   c. guaranteed freedpeople the right to vote   d. did all these things.
10. By the Reconstruction Act of 1867, Congress:
a. took over control of Reconstruction   b. killed the 10% Plan   c. made it harder for the southern states to return to the Union   d. did all these things.

IMPROVING YOUR SKILLS

Mastering the Map

Study the map on page 339. Then answer the following questions:

1. List the southern states in each of the five military districts set up by the Reconstruction Act of 1867.

   a.
   b.
   c.
   d.
   e.

2. Compare this map with the one on page 320. Which former Confederate state was *not* placed under military rule?

341

How Did Congress' Plan for Reconstruction Work?

A. The Impeachment of President Johnson. If Lincoln had lived, could he have kept Congress from taking over the reconstruction of the South? We shall, of course, never know the answer to this question. We do know that his successor, Andrew Johnson, failed to do so. Johnson was, like Lincoln, a poor boy from the old West who had risen through his own efforts. He was intelligent, vigorous, and courageous. But he did not have Lincoln's understanding of people nor his skill in dealing with them.

Johnson soon angered Congress by criticizing its actions and pardoning a large number of Confederate leaders. In the election of 1866, he openly supported the Democrats. As we have seen, the Radical Republicans won control of Congress in that election. They put through the Reconstruction Act and other bills dealing with the South. Johnson vetoed these bills, but Congress repassed them over his veto. The President then set out on a nationwide speaking tour to win the support of the American people. Republican speakers followed him. They interrupted his speeches to contradict what he said. Johnson often lost his temper and argued with the hecklers. Such undignified behavior by the President shocked the American people. It cost Johnson the support he had hoped to gain.

The Radicals then struck back at Johnson with two laws that sharply cut his powers. One law forbade him to remove important officials without the Senate's consent. The other law deprived him of control of the army. Johnson defied Congress by removing the secretary of war, who had been working closely with the Radicals. Congress replied by starting impeachment proceedings against the President.

Clearly, President Johnson should not have been impeached. He was not guilty of any of the offenses that the Constitution gives as grounds for impeachment. In fact, the Supreme Court later ruled that it was Congress that had acted illegally. It had deprived the President of powers that were rightfully his under the Constitution. But at the time feeling against Johnson was so strong that the House of Representatives quickly voted his impeachment. His trial before the Senate was obviously unfair. Yet, when the vote to remove him was finally taken, it fell only one short of the two-thirds required by the Constitution. Thus our system of separation of powers was saved by a single vote. For if Johnson had been removed, a precedent would have been set for Congress to impeach any President who dared to challenge its policies.

Ticket of admission to the impeachment trial of President Johnson.

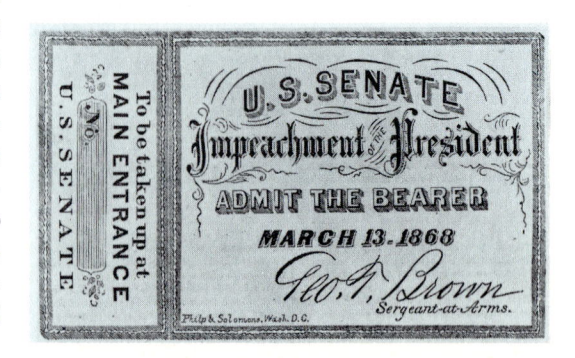

B. The "Carpetbagger" Governments. Meanwhile new governments had been set up in the southern states under the Reconstruction Act. Blacks were now allowed to vote, but thousands of whites were disqualified or refused to vote. As a result, the Republicans won every election. Many blacks, generally men of education and culture, were elected to the state governments. Sixteen of them were even elected to Congress—fourteen to the House, two to the Senate.

Nevertheless, the new state governments were run by white men, both northerners and southerners. Most southerners looked down on white men who worked with blacks. They called the southerners in the new state governments "scalawags" (scoundrels). The northerners were called "carpetbaggers." This was a very insulting term. It meant that these men, when they had come South, had carried all their belongings in a cheap bag made of a piece of carpet. Many carpetbaggers and scalawags were indeed poor men who were interested mainly in making a quick fortune for themselves. Many others, however, were honestly interested in helping the freedpeople.

C. Policies of the Carpetbagger Governments. The carpetbagger governments passed the most progressive laws the South had ever seen. They abolished the black codes and allowed all men the right to vote and hold office. Recognizing that education was the blacks' greatest need, the new governments started the first public school systems in the South. They also spent large sums to repair war damage, to feed the unemployed, and to improve roads and railroads. Under them, debtors' prison was finally abolished in the South and women were given the right to own property. They greatly increased taxes on the wealthy, which had been very low before the war. They also saw to it that the Fourteenth and Fifteenth Amendments were ratified and became part of the Constitution.

The first black senator and representatives were wealthy, well-educated men.

Unfortunately, the Reconstruction governments earned a reputation for waste and dishonesty. Probably they were no more dishonest than the northern governments of the time or the southern governments of the late 1870s. The Reconstruction governments spent large sums on fancy public buildings and on fine clothing and other luxuries for themselves. Millions of dollars voted for public works disappeared, while officials suddenly became wealthy. The war-damaged South was poor to begin with. Taxes now rose higher and higher and so did government borrowing. By 1874 the southern states had run up debts of $100 million. Their credit was so poor that they had to accept a 75 percent discount on loans. In other words, to get one million dollars they had to agree to pay back four million.

D. A Reign of Terror. The southern whites did not stand idly by while these developments were taking place. Their leaders formed secret organizations to regain power by driving out the carpetbaggers and scalawags. Best known was the Ku Klux Klan. Its members covered themselves and their horses with white robes, both to disguise themselves and to frighten the blacks. The Klan and other new organizations soon turned to violence. They whipped, tarred and feathered, and even lynched (killed) people they disliked. Their main targets were black leaders and whites who helped the blacks. They also set fire to many black homes, schools, and churches.

This reign of terror lasted several years. To deal with it, Congress passed a law in 1871 outlawing groups like the Ku Klux Klan. Under this law, federal officials, aided by troops, arrested several thousand people. Military rule was used to restore law and order in districts where the worst violence was occurring. These efforts checked outbreaks for a time. But then congressional Reconstruction suddenly ended.

E. The End of Reconstruction. To understand why Reconstruction ended in the South, we must go back to the election of 1868. It was won by the North's outstanding military hero, General Ulysses S. Grant. Grant, who knew little about politics, proved to be a weak President. When it became known that his officials were stealing money from the federal government, he lost the support of many Americans. Despite this, Grant ran again in 1872 and was reelected.

A number of important Republican leaders decided that the time had now come to end Reconstruction. People in the North, they believed, had become tired of the troubles in the South. By failing to enforce the Reconstruction Act, these leaders hoped to regain support for the Republican party in the North and even to win over a large number of southerners. They persuaded President Grant to come around to their way of thinking. On their advice, he pardoned most of the former Confederate leaders and began to withdraw federal troops from the South. Even before the soldiers left, southern whites began to take control in one state after another.

Reconstruction was dealt the final blow in the election of 1876. The result of this election remained in doubt for weeks. The carpetbagger governments in three southern states had sent in one set of election returns, the southern white governments another. Congress had to decide which would be counted. The Democratic and Republican leaders of Congress finally settled the matter in a secret deal. The Republican candidate, Rutherford B. Hayes of Ohio, was given all the disputed votes and became President. In return, he withdrew the remaining federal troops from the South. Reconstruction came to an end early in 1877.

F. The Aftereffects of Reconstruction. 1. BAD FEELING BETWEEN NORTH AND SOUTH. Historians have called the Reconstruction Period the "Tragic Era" of American history. Presi-

Two members of the Ku Klux Klan. They used terror, whippings, and lynchings against blacks and also against carpetbaggers and scalawags.

dent Lincoln had hoped that the North and South would cooperate to solve the problems left by the Civil War. But they never did. Instead, extremists on both sides made the situation worse than it already was. In the end, the southerners won the battle over Reconstruction. They regained control of their own states. But this second clash between the two sections made them worse enemies. Years later, many southerners still spoke of the "crime of Reconstruction."

2. THE "SOLID SOUTH." Once the southern whites regained power, they made sure they would not lose it again. They found several different ways to keep blacks from voting. They required voters to meet property qualifications, to pass a literacy test, and to make a cash payment known as the poll tax. Since most blacks were poor and uneducated, they could not meet these new requirements. Voting officials could also use the literacy test to disqualify educated blacks by asking them very difficult questions. Another new provision was the "grandfather clause." This said that a person could vote only if his grandfather had been qualified to vote. Very few, if any, southern blacks could meet this requirement.

The poll tax and property qualifications also kept many poor whites from voting in the South. This made it easier for a small group of political leaders to take and keep control of the state and local governments. These leaders were all Democrats. Few southern whites supported the Republicans, whom they blamed for the "crime of Reconstruction." In every presidential election for the next half-century, the South gave all of its electoral votes to the Democratic candidates. It also elected Democrats to Congress and to the state governments. The "Solid South," as it came to be called, had, in effect, a one-party system. Only since World War II have the Republicans been able to make gains there.

3. REPUBLICAN STRENGTH IN THE NORTH. The same kind of development took place in the North. For years Republican leaders reminded their hearers that the Democrats were the party of the South. They blamed their opponents for the Civil War, the assassination of President Lincoln, and the mistreatment of the freedmen. Since the North continued to grow much faster than the South, the Republicans were able to keep control of the federal government for a long time. Between 1860 and 1932, only two Democrats were elected President.

4. THE RACE PROBLEM. The most troublesome aftereffect of the Civil War was the race problem. Most southern whites would not treat blacks as equals. Lincoln hoped that whites would deal fairly with the freedpeople. The fight over Reconstruction destroyed this hope. Many southern whites were determined to keep blacks as second-class citizens—and they succeeded. Blacks could neither vote nor enjoy the rights all Americans were supposed to have. They were prevented from taking any but the lowest and worst-paid jobs. By the 1890s, blacks were segregated (separated) from whites in schools, parks, trains, hotels, restaurants, theaters, and many other places. In every case, facilities for blacks were far inferior to those for whites.

Without the right to vote, blacks had few legal ways to change the system. Lacking money and education, they found it very difficult to improve their economic and political position. Black churches and community organizations worked hard to better conditions. But many blacks moved to northern cities. Almost everywhere, the race problem prevented blacks from obtaining equality.

In later sections, we shall see what steps the nation has taken to deal with the race problem. We shall see to what extent black Americans have achieved the equal rights to which they are entitled by the Fourteenth and Fifteenth Amendments. In some areas, progress has been slow. Segregation by law no longer exists in this nation. But equal rights and opportunities have not yet been achieved in all areas of American life.

REVIEWING THE SECTION

A. Knowing New Terms

In your notebook write the new terms in this section that best complete each statement.

1. Northerners who held government posts in the South during the Reconstruction Period were nicknamed "_____."
2. A secret organization formed by southern whites to regain control of the state governments was named the _____ _____ _____.
3. Because the southern states almost always elected Democrats to office in the period from the Civil War to after World War II, those states were called the "_____ _____."
4. In order to vote, the people in most southern states had to pay a special tax known as the _____ tax.
5. To keep the blacks "in their place," southern whites established a system of separate facilities for the two races. This system is called _____.

B. Knowing Important People

For each important person in the first column, find the *letter* of the best description in the second column. Write them together in your notebook.

Important People	*Descriptions*
1. Ulysses S. Grant	a. Leader of the Radical Republicans
2. Rutherford B. Hayes	b. President during most of the Reconstruction Period
3. Andrew Johnson	c. President who ended Reconstruction
4. Thaddeus Stevens	d. President who was impeached
	e. Secretary of war who sided with the Radicals against the President

C. Finding the Reasons

In your notebook write the letters of *all* the correct answers to each question.

1. Why did the Radical Republicans impeach President Johnson?
a. He had committed offenses that the Constitution gave as grounds for impeachment. b. He had violated the rights of Congress under the Constitution. c. He was strongly opposed to congressional Reconstruction.
2. Why did most southern whites hate the carpetbagger governments?
a. These governments were controlled mainly by northerners. b. They

allowed blacks to vote and to hold office. c. They spent large sums of money but failed to make any reforms.
3. Why were the Ku Klux Klan and other terrorist organizations successful?
a. They had the support of many southern whites. b. Federal troops in the South secretly sided with them. c. The federal government gave up the attempt to crush them after a short time.
4. Why was General Grant a weak President?
a. He knew little about politics. b. Many of his officials were dishonest. c. He did not have the support of Congress.
5. Why has the Reconstruction Period been called the "Tragic Era"?
a. Southerners, feeling that they had been mistreated, hated the North. b. Northerners were angry because the South refused to obey the laws Congress had passed. c. Blacks suffered because the southern whites took strong measures to keep them down from 1866 until 1877.
6. How did the policy of segregation adopted by the southern whites affect the blacks?
a. It provided them with inferior facilities. b. It improved most blacks' economic position. c. It denied them equality of opportunity.

MAKING HISTORY LIVE

1. Explain why you agree or disagree with the following statements:
a. The South lost the Civil War but won the peace. b. The southern whites were justified in "keeping the Negro in his place." c. From the Civil War until the late 1940s, the South had, in effect, a one-party system. d. Reconstruction was a crime committed by the North against the South. e. The southern whites should have blamed themselves, not the North, for the troubles of Reconstruction. f. Many southern whites benefited from laws passed by the carpetbagger governments.
2. Discuss what you learned by reading about one of these topics:
a. An early black educational institution in the South, such as Hampton or Tuskegee Institute. Take special note of the difficulties it had during its early years. b. The life and achievements of Booker T. Washington, Ira B. Wells Barnett, George Washington Carver, or W. E. B. Du Bois. c. Reconstruction in one southern state. Show how trouble developed there between the northerners and the southern whites.
3. Prepare for a debate on the question of which is better, the presidential policy of Reconstruction or the congressional policy. Write the views of both sides of the debate. Try to work out a compromise that might have been more effective than either.
4. Complete and write on one of these topics:
a. If the South had accepted the congressional plan of Reconstruc-

tion . . ." b. "If Congress had seized the plantations of the Confederate leaders and had given the freedmen farms of their own. . . ."

SUMMING UP THE UNIT

What Were the Results of "a Generation of Conflict"?

A. The Reasons for Conflict. The Constitution, it has been pointed out, had one serious weakness. It did not say whether a state might legally secede from the United States. The southern states insisted that they had this right. They thought of seceding because the Northeast and West were growing much more rapidly than their own section and were drawing close together. Both northern sections opposed slavery. Southerners felt that their way of life depended on it.

B. The Steps to War. A clash was prevented in 1850, when a compromise settled the issue of slavery in the territories. During the next ten years, however, bad feeling grew between the sections and drove them further apart. Americans in both the North and South were angered by the fighting in Kansas, the Dred Scott decision, John Brown's raid, and other events involving slavery. In 1860 Abraham Lincoln became the first Republican President. Since his support came entirely from the Northeast and the West, southerners believed that these two sections had gained complete control of the federal government. Eleven southern states soon seceded from the Union. Lincoln refused to recognize their secession. When the Confederates attacked Fort Sumter, the Civil War began.

C. The Civil War and Its Results. This bloody conflict between fellow Americans raged for four years before the North finally won. The Civil War was very costly. It left a million Americans dead or injured. War damage and military costs totaled in the billions of dollars. The war's most important results were the saving of the Union and the freeing of the slaves.

D. The Period of Reconstruction. After the war ended, a new conflict between North and South arose over what to do with the freed blacks. Southerners were determined to see that they remained poor and humble workers. But northern extremists, the Radical Republicans, demanded that blacks be given equal rights as American citizens. The Radicals used troops and martial law to force their plan of Reconstruction on the South. White southerners resisted. They won after a decade of struggle. Federal troops were withdrawn from the South, southern whites took control once more, and blacks were reduced to second-class citizenship.

E. Continued Economic Progress. The conflict between North and South lasted from 1850 to 1877—an entire generation. But even during this troubled period the United States continued to grow. Immigrants from Europe were far greater in number than the casualties of the war. Settlement of the West was speeded up. Northern industry expanded rapidly to meet the needs of war. The South, rid of the burden of slavery, developed more quickly after the Civil War than it had before. In fact, the period after the Civil War saw such rapid progress that it has become known as the period of the "Economic Revolution."

REVIEWING THE UNIT

A. Knowing Where Things Happened

On an outline map of the United States, do the following:
1. Use light blue crayon or pencil shading to mark all large bodies of water.
2. Label:
   a. the Atlantic and Pacific oceans, Gulf of Mexico, Great Lakes; b. the Appalachian and Rocky mountains; c. the Mississippi, Ohio, Missouri, St. Lawrence, and Columbia rivers and the Rio Grande; d. the Old Northwest Territory, Louisiana Territory, Texas, Oregon Territory, and Mexican Cession.
3. Use two different colors to show the regions that were free and those that were open to slavery before the Civil War.
4. Write in the names of the eleven Confederate states and mark them with hatching (diagonal lines).

B. Knowing When Things Happened

Arrange the events in each group in the correct order.
1. a. Compromise of 1850
   b. Missouri Compromise
   c. Northwest Ordinance
2. a. Compromise of 1850
   b. Kansas-Nebraska Act
   c. Mexican War
3. a. Dred Scott decision
   b. John Brown's raid
   c. Strong Fugitive Slave Law
4. a. Firing on Fort Sumter
   b. Formation of the Confederacy
   c. Lincoln's first election
5. a. Battles of Gettysburg and Vicksburg
   b. First and Second Battles of Bull Run
   c. Wilderness Campaign
6. a. Congressional Reconstruction
   b. Election of President Hayes
   c. Presidential Reconstruction

C. Knowing Important People

Choose the person in each group who does *not* belong with the others.
1. *Black cultural leaders:*
   a. Benjamin Banneker   b. Nat Turner   c. Gustavus Vassa   d. Phillis Wheatley
2. *Leaders of the extreme abolitionists:*
   a. Frederick Douglass   b. William Lloyd Garrison   c. Sojourner Truth   d. Harriet Beecher Stowe
3. *Political leaders before the Civil War:*
   a. John C. Calhoun   b. Henry Clay   c. Stephen A. Douglas   d. Dred Scott

4. *Northern commanders in the Civil War:*
   a. David Farragut   b. Ulysses S. Grant   c. Robert E. Lee   d. George B. McClellan
5. *Important figures in Reconstruction:*
   a. Stephen A. Douglas   b. Rutherford B. Hayes   c. Andrew Johnson   d. Thaddeus Stevens

D. Knowing Important Terms

Choose the term in each group that does *not* belong with the others.
1. *Associated with slavery:*
   a. black codes   b. emancipation   c. Liberia   d. serfdom
2. *Opposed to slavery:*
   a. abolitionists   b. Copperheads   c. Free Soilers   d. Underground Railroad
3. *Developments that led to the Civil War:*
   a. "Bleeding Kansas"   b. Dred Scott decision   c. John Brown's raid   d. Missouri Compromise
4. *Formation of the Republican party:*
   a. Democratic party   b. Free Soil party   c. Kansas-Nebraska Act   d. Whig party
5. *Helpful to blacks:*
   a. Thirteenth Amendment   b. Fourteenth Amendment   c. Fifteenth Amendment   d. Sixteenth Amendment
6. *Harmful to freedpeople:*
   a. carpetbaggers   b. Ku Klux Klan   c. poll tax   d. segregation
7. *Presidential Reconstruction:*
   a. Thirteenth Amendment   b. Freedmen's Bureau   c. "grandfather clause"   d. 10% Plan
8. *Congressional Reconstruction:*
   a. martial law   b. carpetbagger governments   c. impeachment of President Johnson   d. black codes

RECOMMENDED READING

A. *Historical Books*

   American Heritage:
     The Battle of Gettysburg.
     Ironclads of the Civil War.
   Bishop, J. *The Day Lincoln Was Shot* (Harper, 1955).

GILDNER, G. *Letters from Vicksburg*. Greensboro, N.C.: Unicorn Press, 1976.
GOLDSTON, R. *The Coming of the Civil War*. New York: Macmillan, 1972.
HALEY, A. *Roots*. Garden City, N.Y.: Doubleday, 1976.
JACKSON, F. *The Black Man in America, 1861–1877*. New York: Franklin Watts, 1972.
LAWSON, D. *The United States in the Indian Wars*. New York: Abelard-Schuman, 1975.
Lincoln's Own Yarns and Stories. Grand Rapids, Mich.: Bengal Press, 1980.
MCPHERSON, J. M. *The Abolitionist Legacy, From Reconstruction to the N.A.A.C.P*. Princeton, N.J.: Princeton Univ. Press, 1976.
———. *Ordeal by Fire: the Civil War and Reconstruction*. New York: Alfred A. Knopf, 1982.
MELTZER, M., ed. *In Their Own Words*. New York: Crowell, 1965. A history of the American Negro, 1865–1916.
MITCHELL, J. B., LT. COL. *Decisive Battles of the Civil War*. New York: Putnam, 1955. From First Manassas to Petersburg.
TRELEASE, A. W. *Reconstruction, The Great Experience*. New York: Harper & Row, 1971.
WILEY, B. I. *Confederate Women*. Westport, Conn.: Greenwood Press, 1975.
———. *The Life of Billy Yank*. Baton Rouge, La.: Louisiana State Univ. Press, 1978.
———. *The Life of Johnny Reb*. Baton Rouge, La.: Louisiana State Univ. Press, 1978.

B. Biographies

GRAHAM, L. *John Brown*. New York: Crowell, 1980. Who led the raid on Harper's Ferry.
GRANT, M. G. *Clara Barton*. Mankato, Minn.: Creative Education, 1974.
———. *Robert E. Lee*. Mankato, Minn.: Creative Education, 1974.
JAY, D., and CRAINE, E., eds. *Living Black in White America*. New York: William Morrow, 1971. Twenty-two autobiographical selections.
JOHANNSEN, R. W. *Stephen A. Douglas*. New York: Oxford Univ. Press, 1973.
MCFEELY, W. S. *Grant: A Biography*. New York: Norton, 1981.
MELTZER, I. S. *Frederick Douglass, Great Abolitionist*. Ed. N. Thomas. North Bergen, N.J.: Book-Lab, 1972.
OATES, S. B. *The Fires of Jubilee*. New York: Harper & Row, 1975. Nat Turner's rebellion.
ORTIZ, V. *Sojourner Truth*. New York: Harper & Row, 1974.
SANDBURG, C. *Abraham Lincoln: The Prairie Years & the War Years*. New York: Harcourt Brace Jovanovich, 1974.
WRIGHT, R. *Black Boy*. New York: Harper & Row, 1945.

C. Historical Fiction

ALLEN, M. *Johnny Reb*. New York: McKay, 1952. About the fighting in Virginia.
BUTLER, O. E. *Kindred*. Garden City, N.Y.: Doubleday, 1979. A black woman's time-travel to save her family.
CRANE, S. *The Red Badge of Courage*. New York: Macmillan, 1962. A great novel about a young soldier who learned courage in battle.
HEIDISH, M. *A Woman Called Moses*. Boston: Houghton Mifflin, 1976. A novel about Harriet Tubman.
L'AMOUR, L. *Bendigo Shafter*. New York: Dutton, 1979. Founding a town in Indian territory.
MITCHELL, M. *Gone With the Wind*. New York: Macmillan, 1961. The longest and best-known novel about the Civil War.
SMUCKER, B. *Runaway to Freedom: A Story of the Underground Railway*. New York: Harper & Row, 1978.
STOWE, H. B. *Uncle Tom's Cabin*. Various editions. The book that helped start the war.

THE CONVERTERS

Casting ingots.

Unit Five

THE ECONOMIC REVOLUTION

The entire history of the United States is a story of rapid growth. But no period in American history shows a larger and more rapid growth than the fifty years after the Civil War. Between 1865 and 1916, the output of American factories increased almost ten times. This was the highest rate of increase the world had ever seen. By 1900 the United States had surpassed Germany and Great Britain as the world's leading industrial nation. It has held this position ever since.

Transportation, farming, and other types of business also expanded and changed a good deal during this period. Historians call this great and rapid change in the American economy after the Civil War the Economic Revolution.

The Economic Revolution brought our nation the benefits of great wealth and power. But the progress was made at a high cost. Rapid change brought suffering to millions of farmers and workers and used up our resources at a tremendous rate. For a time it even seriously threatened our democracy.

Making steel by the Bessemer process, one of the key inventions of the Economic Revolution.

In this unit we shall learn the following:

1. *How new inventions changed American industry, transportation, and agriculture.*
2. *How these changes affected industrial workers, farmers, and other Americans.*
3. *What problems the nation faced because of its rapid progress.*
4. *What was done to solve these problems.*

UNIT 5: 1865-1916

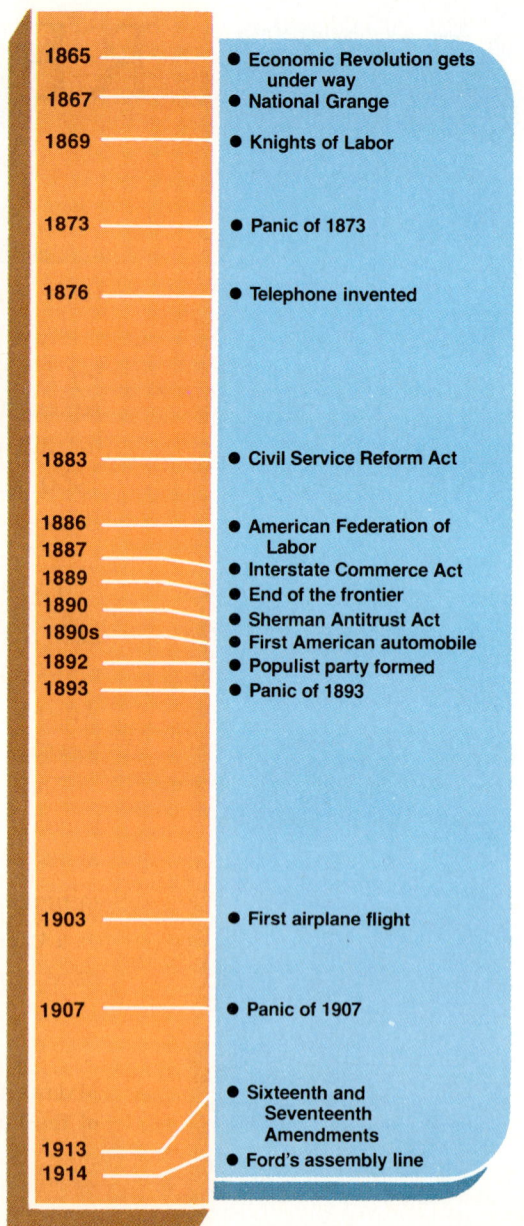

1865	Economic Revolution gets under way
1867	National Grange
1869	Knights of Labor
1873	Panic of 1873
1876	Telephone invented
1883	Civil Service Reform Act
1886	American Federation of Labor
1887	Interstate Commerce Act
1889	End of the frontier
1890	Sherman Antitrust Act
1890s	First American automobile
1892	Populist party formed
1893	Panic of 1893
1903	First airplane flight
1907	Panic of 1907
1913	Sixteenth and Seventeenth Amendments
1914	Ford's assembly line

354

Chapter 21

THE REVOLUTION IN INDUSTRY

WHY DID the United States become the world's leading industrial nation after the Civil War? First of all, our nation had important advantages even before the war. It was very rich in coal, iron ore, petroleum, and other natural resources. It was also rich in human resources. Thanks to a high birth rate and large-scale immigration, it had a large and growing population. This included many educated people, experienced business people, and skilled workers. But even unskilled workers were valuable. They ran the new machines, built the railroads, mined the coal and iron ore, and helped to settle the West.

Secondly, the Civil War stimulated our nation's economic progress in several ways. 1. Industry and agriculture expanded to meet the needs of the armed forces. After the war, the fast-growing population continued to provide a good market—that is, enough people to buy the growing output of American factories and farms. 2. Business people and farmers made large profits during the war. They used these profits to buy new factories, land, and machinery. 3. The government helped business people and farmers. It raised tariffs to keep out foreign goods, provided money to build railroads, and gave away western lands to settlers.

Finally, the American spirit encouraged progress. Americans had long believed that they could better themselves through hard work. This belief was especially strong in the period after the Civil War. Manufacturers, farmers, and workers of the time were filled with confidence in the future. They looked forward to rich rewards for their efforts as the nation's economy continued to expand faster and faster. In this chapter we shall see whether their hopes came true.

How Did the United States Become a Great Industrial Nation?

A. Expansion of Existing Industries. 1. Development of the Railroads. The railroads played a very important part in our nation's economic growth. Their total mileage doubled during the ten years after the Civil War and doubled again in the 1880s. By 1916 American railroads had a quarter of a million miles of track, 40 percent of the world's total.

Most of the new railroads were located in the Northeast. But many were also built in the South and West. A half-dozen lines ran all the way across the West to the Pacific coast. This "web of steel" tied the different sections of our large country closer together and increased trade between them.

The half-century after the Civil War also saw many improvements in railroad service. Most early railroads were "short lines," only 50 to 150 miles long. The trains of one railroad could not be used on another because the railroads had different gauges (different widths between the rails). To go from New York to Chicago, a traveler had to change trains at least five or six times. By 1900, however, most railroads had been combined into large systems.

They used the same gauge so that trains could move from one railroad system to another. As a result, passengers could enjoy "through service" for long distances.

Inventions helped to make travel by rail faster and safer. Steel rails soon replaced iron rails because they were twenty times as strong. They made it possible to use more powerful locomotives, which could pull larger loads at higher speeds. With air brakes, trains could be stopped quickly. Automatic signals greatly reduced the danger of trains crashing into one another. Thanks to such improvements, the "iron horse" became our nation's most important means of transportation. It carried most American travelers until the 1920s, when the automobile and airplane began to cut into its passenger traffic. It still transports most of our nation's freight to this day.

2. Other Important Industries. The iron and steel industry expanded greatly to meet the needs of the railroads. It also provided the materials for bridges, skyscrapers, and many kinds of machines. Iron and steel have been called, with good reason, the "backbone of modern industry."

The railroads also helped to change other industries. Before the Civil War, clothing and shoes were made in small shops for people living close by. During the war, however, factories sprang up to make them for the armed forces. These factories began to ship their products all over the country by rail once the war was over. By using the new sewing machines, they were able to undersell the local shops making clothing and shoes by hand.

Meat packing became a large industry when the refrigerator car came into use. To ship live animals to market was expensive. The refrigerator car made it cheaper to slaughter all the livestock in one place and ship the meat to market. Flour milling and canning, mining and lumbering, were other fast-growing industries. The department store, chain store, and mail-order house began to take the place of the old general store. They sold large quantities of manufactured goods to people all over the nation at low prices.

B. The Rise of New Industries. 1. INDUSTRIES BASED ON PETROLEUM. Science and invention also made possible a number of new industries. Some of these were based on a dark, thick liquid called petroleum or "rock oil." Petroleum became important when a scientist showed that it could be refined to obtain kerosene, lubricating oil, paraffin (wax), and other valuable products. The problem then was to find the petroleum underground and bring it to the surface. The modern petroleum industry was born when the first successful oil well was drilled in Pennsylvania in 1859. Soon "forests" of oil derricks could be seen in many parts of the nation.

At first kerosene, which took the place of whale oil in lamps, was the most valuable petroleum product. But then gasoline was discovered. It became even more important than kerosene because it contains a great deal of energy and burns without leaving an ash. It made possible the development of a small but powerful new type of engine. In the 1890s gasoline engines were used to drive the first successful automobiles. Ten years later the Wright brothers used an engine of this type to drive the first airplane. Thus the gasoline engine made possible two of our leading industries, automobile manufacturing and aviation.

2. ELECTRICITY AND ITS MANY USES. Electricity was a second important new form of energy. It was first used to improve communication. In 1844 Samuel Morse invented the telegraph, which sends messages by means of electrical "dots and dashes." The telephone, invented by Alexander Graham Bell in 1876, sends the human voice through wires by changing the sound into electricity. Thomas A. Edison invented the first useful electric light. He also built the world's first central powerhouse in New York City in 1882. People marveled when

A steel mill. By 1914, the United States had become the leading steel-producing nation in the world.

he turned on hundreds of street lights at one time simply by closing a switch!

Edison also helped to develop the electric motor, the phonograph, and the motion-picture projector. Clean and quiet electric motors soon began to replace the noisy, smoky steam engine in transportation and other industries. They now drive vacuum cleaners, dishwashers, refrigerators, and other appliances that make life easier for those doing household tasks.

Edwin L. Drake (wearing the high hat) drilled the first successful oil well, which was located in Pennsylvania.

THOMAS ALVA EDISON: THE "WIZARD OF MENLO PARK"

"Genius is 2 percent inspiration and 98 percent perspiration." The man who said this, Thomas Edison, showed by his own life that it was true. Edison was born in Ohio in 1847. Even as a child, he was interested in finding out how things worked. Twice he started fires by experimenting with chemicals, once in his father's barn and once in the baggage car of a railroad for which he worked. The second fire cost him his job. The conductor also gave young Tom a blow on the ear that may have started his ear troubles. For Edison became deaf at an early age and suffered all his life from terrible earaches. But he never let pain interfere with his work.

In the nineteenth century, railroads used the telegraph to communicate from station to station. Young Edison soon became an expert telegraph operator and started experiments to improve the device. Busy at his experiments, he neglected his appearance, and even his work. This made it hard for him to hold a job. He became a "tramp" operator, wandering from place to place in search of a job.

When Edison was twenty-two years old, however, his luck suddenly turned. He sold one of his inventions for $40,000, a very large sum in those days. He used the money to set up a laboratory and to hire assistants. All his life he kept putting the profits from his inventions back into his work. In later years his laboratory at Menlo Park, New Jersey, employed hundreds of scientists and technicians. It became world famous. His basic idea—that scientists can get more done by working in teams in a well-equipped laboratory—has since been taken over by large companies everywhere.

Edison himself worked harder than any of his workers. "Life is too important to waste in excessive snoring," he once said. He rarely slept more than four hours a night. Often he did not go to bed at all, but only napped in a chair. He never became discouraged if an idea did not seem to work. Ten thousand experiments failed, for example, before he finally made a successful storage battery.

Before his death at eighty-four, Edison obtained over 1,000 patents from the government on his inventions. Most of them—like the electric light, phonograph, and motion picture—used electricity to make life easier and better for the American people. "Inspiration" had a great deal to do with Edison's success. For he had a keen mind, a remarkable memory, and a powerful imagination. But "perspiration," his willingness to work hard for many long hours a day, year after year, was even more important. It enabled him to carry out most of the projects he started and to become known all over the world as the "wizard of Menlo Park."

Early Ford assembly line. In spite of hundreds of improvements, today's assembly line is still based on Henry Ford's ideas.

C. Mass Production. Still another great change took place in the way goods were manufactured. The new way was called "mass" production because it produced large amounts of goods. Credit for perfecting mass production is usually given to Henry Ford. He used this new method to assemble automobiles in the early 1900s. Ford placed his workers along both sides of a power-driven belt that ran from one end of his assembly plant to the other. At the beginning of this assembly line, workers placed one auto frame after another on the belt. As the belt carried the frames down the line, each worker quickly added or fastened a single part in place. By the time the frame reached the end of the line, it had become a finished automobile, ready to be driven away.

Mass production turned out a large number of goods and also made better products at lower cost. Each worker had a single simple job, which was done over and over. Workers soon learned to do their job simply, quickly, and accurately. Even very complicated articles could now be made easily just by breaking down their manufacture into many small jobs.

The cost of labor was reduced because the workers were able to get much more done in the same time. Moreover, machines were used to replace human labor wherever possible. In Ford's plant, parts were made by machine, brought to the workers by the power-driven belt, and fastened into place with power-driven tools. Thanks to these methods, an entire automobile could be put together in less than an hour and a half. Ford was able to sell his Model T, or "flivver," for as little as $300!

D. Results of Industrial Progress. Thanks to the Economic Revolution, the American standard of living rose after the Civil War. Many Americans could now buy articles that only the wealthy could afford before. Since workers did less by hand, it became possible to shorten their hours. In time, it became unnecessary to hire children.

These benefits did not happen at once, however. In fact, the boom in industry seemed for a time to add to our country's problems. America had "shot up" too fast. Like many a teenager, it was suffering from "growing pains."

REVIEWING THE SECTION

A. Finding Word Meanings

PART 1. In your notebook copy each term and the meaning it is given in the text. Underline the word clues (see pages 34-35).

   (In the unit introduction) Economic Revolution
   (In the chapter introduction) a good market
   (In **C**) mass production

PART 2. There are no clues for the following terms. You must get the meaning from the context (see pages 43-44). Write each term in your notebook and give its meaning *in your own words*.

   (In **A1**) "web of steel"   (In **C**)   assembly line
              through service

PART 3. Explain these statements *in your own words*.

   (In **A2**) Iron and steel are the backbone of modern industry.
   (In **D**)   The United States was suffering from "growing pains."

B. Knowing Important People

For each person in the first column, write in your notebook the *letter* of the best description in the second column.

Important People	*Descriptions*
1. Alexander Graham Bell	a. Developed modern mass production
2. Thomas A. Edison	b. Flew the first successful airplane
3. Henry Ford	c. Invented the first practical electric light
4. Samuel Morse	d. Invented the air brake
5. Wright brothers	e. Invented the telegraph
	f. Invented the telephone

IMPROVING YOUR SKILLS

A. Making an Outline

Copy the following outline into your notebook and fill in all the missing parts.

HOW DID THE UNITED STATES BECOME A GREAT INDUSTRIAL NATION?

A. Expansion of Existing Industries
  1. Development of the Railroads
     a.
     b.
     c.
     d.
  2. Other Important Industries
     a.
     b.
     c.

B. The Rise of New Industries
  1. Industries Based on Petroleum
     a.
     b.
  2. Electricity and Its Many Uses
     a.
     b.

C. Mass Production
  1.
  2.

D. Results of Industrial Progress
  1.
  2.

B. Reading the Time Line

Study the time line on page 354. Then complete the following statements.

1. In this unit we shall study the Economic Revolution that took place in the United States between the years _____ and _____.
2. The frontier was officially closed in _____.
3. The Economic Revolution helped cause three great panics, or depressions, in the years _____, _____, and _____.
4. Three important inventions of this period were the _____, _____, and _____.
5. Three important organizations formed during this period were the _____ _____ for farmers and the _____ _____ _____ and _____ _____ _____ _____ for industrial workers.
6. Three important laws passed at this time were the _____ _____ Act, the _____ _____ Act, and the _____ _____ Act.

7. The _____ and _____ Amendments were passed in 1913.
8. A political party begun during the 1890s was _____.

C. Interpreting the Graph

Study the graphs below. Then write in your notebook the *letter* of the correct answer to each question.

VALUE OF AMERICAN MANUFACTURES, 1859-1919

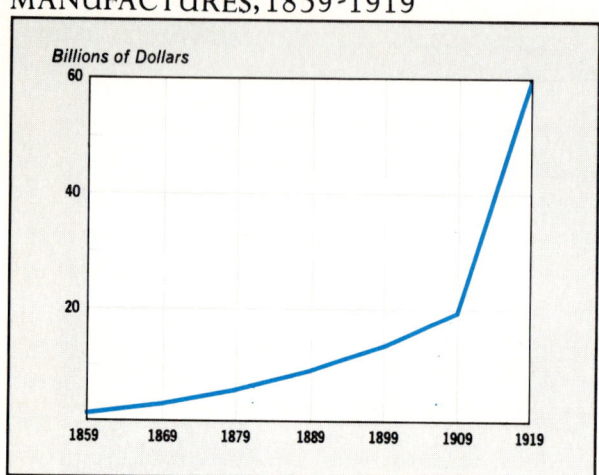

RAILROAD MILEAGE IN THE UNITED STATES, 1860-1920

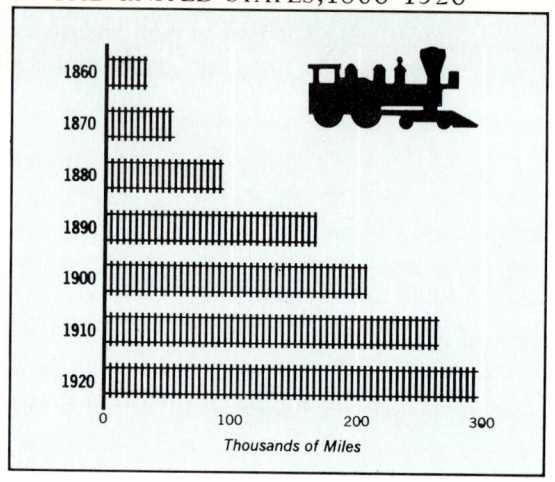

GRAPH 1. Value of American Manufactures, 1859-1919
  1. During which decade (ten-year period) did the value of American manufactures increase the least? a. 1859-1869 b. 1869-1879 c. 1879-1889 d. 1889-1899.
  2. During which decade did the value of manufactures increase the most? a. 1879-1889 b. 1889-1899 c. 1899-1909 d. 1909-1919.
  3. How large was the increase in value between 1909 and 1919? About: a. ten billion dollars b. twenty billion dollars c. thirty billion dollars d. forty billion dollars.
  4. How many times as large was American industrial production in 1919 as in 1859? About: a. ten times b. twenty times c. forty times d. a hundred times.

GRAPH 2. Railroad Mileage in the United States, 1860-1920
  1. During which decade was the greatest mileage of new railroads built? a. 1870-1880 b. 1880-1890 c. 1890-1900 d. 1900-1910.
  2. How many times as large was the railroad mileage in 1920 as in 1860? About: a. five times b. ten times c. fifteen times d. twenty times.

What Problems Did Big Business Create?

A. A True Success Story. Andrew Carnegie was thirteen years old when he arrived in the United States from Scotland and found a job in a cotton mill. He earned only $1.20 a week for six days' work, twelve hours a day. After studying the Morse Code in his spare time, young Andrew became a telegraph operator for a large railroad. His speed and accuracy, together with his friendly personality and willingness to work hard, won him rapid promotion. At the age of twenty-two, Andrew was put in charge of an entire branch of the railroad.

Though he helped support his family, young Carnegie managed to save a large part of his salary. He invested his savings in a company that manufactured sleeping cars. By persuading the directors of his railroad to buy the cars, he made a small fortune. Not long after, Carnegie noticed that the railroads were replacing wooden bridges with iron ones. He bought a mill to manufacture iron bridges and again made a large profit. When the railroads began to use steel rails, Carnegie went to England to study the new Bessemer method for making steel quickly and cheaply (see picture, page 352). He introduced it in this country and became a leading steelmaker.

Carnegie soon found other ways to cut the cost of making steel. He hired expert managers and scientists, often at very high salaries, to make improvements in his plants. But he paid his ordinary workers very low wages. As a result, he was able to undersell other steel manufacturers. He bought out many of them or put them out of business. He also bought coal and iron mines, ore ships, a railroad, and mills to make all sorts of iron and steel products. By bringing every step in iron and steelmaking under his control, Carnegie was able to bring costs down still further. It became his boast that he could sell steel for only one cent a pound and still show a profit!

When Carnegie retired in 1901, he sold his share of his company for $250,000,000. He spent the rest of his life giving away his money to worthy causes, especially for the improvement of American education.

In this section we shall see why many other business people were able, like Carnegie, to make fortunes during the Economic Revolution. We shall also see how their activities helped our nation and what problems they created.

Four men who helped build our nation's industrial greatness:

Andrew Carnegie, manufacturer of iron and steel.

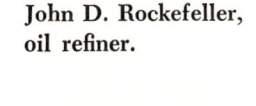

John D. Rockefeller, oil refiner.

J. Pierpont Morgan, banker.

Henry Ford, automobile maker.

B. Waste of Natural Resources. During the Economic Revolution, alert business people could make fortunes in one of three ways—by developing our nation's natural resources, by building big businesses, or by serving as bankers for big business. People who owned or developed mines, oil wells, and forests found a profitable market in the fast-growing industries. But in their haste to make money, they used the nation's resources recklessly. Lumberers destroyed entire forests without replanting new trees. Mineowners dug out only the richest ore, then abandoned the mines. Owners of oil wells allowed surplus oil to spill out on the ground. They burned up great amounts of natural gas because they had no use for it. Because of such waste, our nation now suffers from shortages of some resources and has had to take steps to conserve (save) or import them.

C. The Powers of Big Business. The second wealthy group were the "captains of industry," people who built up large businesses. As Carnegie's story shows, an able person could make a fortune by working hard, saving money, and investing it in a fast-growing industry. However, such a person had to be willing to put most of the profits back into the business. By building it up into a big business, the owner gained important advantages over competitors.

The Economic Revolution was a period of "cut-throat competition." Business people were ready to use any methods, even dishonest ones, to "cut the throats" of rival firms. The bigger the business, the better its chances of winning in this sort of competition. A big company could buy larger and more efficient machines than its smaller competitors could. It could hire scientists and other experts to find new products and improve methods of production. It could force the firms it bought from to give it low prices and other special privileges. Most important of all, a big business could afford to lose money on its products in one neighborhood because it made money in others. Once it had put the local firms out of business, it could raise its prices as high as it wished.

D. Monopolies or "Trusts." As a result of cut-throat competition, many small firms were driven out of business. In one industry after another, a few large firms became the leaders. Such firms often got together to form a monopoly—that is, an organization with complete control of an industry.

1. TWO TYPES OF MONOPOLY. The simplest form of monopoly was the merger. Several large firms merged (combined) to form a single giant company. This new company was usually so strong that it could easily force smaller firms to join. If they refused, it could put them out of business.

As a rule, however, "captains of industry" did not want to give up their power by merging their companies. So they looked for ways to rid themselves of competition without losing their independence. One way was to form a special type of company called a trust. A trust decided which territory each member company should control and what prices it should charge. The most famous example was the Standard Oil Trust. It was formed in 1882 by a wealthy oil refiner from Ohio, John D. Rockefeller. The Standard Oil Trust was so successful that trusts were organized in many other industries. Eight years later Congress declared trusts to be illegal. To this day, however, people still use the word *trust* to mean "monopoly."

2. THE "MONEY TRUST." Bankers played a very important part in forming mergers, trusts, and other large combinations. They helped, for example, by lending a company money to buy out its competitors or by selling the stock of a merged firm to the public. The first billion-dollar company, U.S. Steel, was organized by J. P. Morgan and Company, a Wall Street, New York City, banking firm. The same firm reorganized most of the nation's railroads by merging a number of small lines to form a few large ones. The banks charged very high fees

for their services. By 1900 they had become so wealthy and powerful that they were known as the "Money Trust."

3. OBJECTIONS TO MONOPOLY. There were three main reasons why the American people objected to monopolies. First, monopolies charged very high prices because they did not have to worry about competition. Second, they were so powerful that they easily crushed unions and forced their workers to accept low wages. Third, they gained great political influence by giving large sums to election campaigns and by bribing officials. Many local and state governments, and even members of Congress, fell under the influence of the trusts.

4. THE SHERMAN ANTITRUST ACT. Complaints by small-business people, farmers, and workers led Congress to pass the Sherman Antitrust Act of 1890. The Sherman Act declared that "combinations or conspiracies [secret agreements] in restraint of trade" were illegal. Heavy penalties were provided for breaking the law.

The federal government began to enforce the Sherman Act by bringing suit against the "Sugar Trust." But the Supreme Court dismissed the case. It ruled that the manufacture of sugar was not a form of trade. Because of this narrow decision, the government did not try to enforce the Sherman Act for the next ten years. Nevertheless, some Americans approved. They felt that business was doing a great deal for the country and should be let alone.

E. Extremes of Wealth and Poverty. There probably were fewer than four hundred millionaires in the United States in 1860. In 1900 there were more than four thousand and they owned one-fifth of the nation's wealth! Some of them, like Andrew Carnegie, gave large sums for education and charity. John D. Rockefeller gave more than $300,000,000 to a foundation for improving health and living standards in the United States and other countries.

Most millionaires, however, used their wealth selfishly. They stuffed themselves with expensive foods and bought luxuries such as furs and jewels. They built huge mansions, which they

"Next!" Why does the cartoonist show Standard Oil as an octopus holding the Capitol in Washington, state legislatures, and important industries in its grasp? Who does he think may be the next victim?

The Breakers in Newport, Rhode Island, was the summer "cottage" of the Vanderbilts. Cornelius Vanderbilt was able to build it with some of the wealth gained by owning railroads.

filled with fancy furniture and works of art. They competed with one another in giving huge banquets and balls to attract public attention. The guests of one millionaire rode their horses into the dining room of a luxurious hotel and ate their dinners on horseback. The horses were fed, too—on flowers and champagne. On other occasions, all the guests received cigarettes wrapped in hundred-dollar bills and oysters containing real pearls.

Because of these displays, the first part of the Economic Revolution, from about 1865 to 1900, has been called the "Gilded Age." The surface of the period was bright, as if it had been painted in gold or gilt. Underneath the bright surface, however, were dark and dismal conditions. America still had a large middle class. But the Economic Revolution had created a much larger lower class of factory workers, miners, and small farmers. Members of the lower class did not share in the nation's growing wealth. Millions of them were very poor. Many even faced starvation. In the next few sections we shall consider the problems of these people, the victims of economic progress.

REVIEWING THE SECTION

A. Knowing New Terms

In your notebook write the new terms in this section that best complete these statements.

1. The people who built and ran big businesses were called "_____ _____."
2. To destroy rival firms, businesses often engaged in "_____ competition."
3. By gaining complete control of an industry, business people created a _____.
4. When two or more companies combined to form a single large company, their combination was called a _____.
5. A special company, formed to end competition in a certain industry, was named a _____.

6. A few large banking firms had so much power that they became known as the "_____ _____."
7. The first federal law to prevent monopoly was the _____ _____ Act.
8. Because of the manner in which many rich people lived, the last part of the nineteenth century has been called the "_____ _____."

B. Finding the Reasons

Write the letters of *all* the correct answers to each question.
1. Why was Andrew Carnegie so successful?
   a. He had great ability. b. He became involved in two fast-growing industries, railroads and steelmaking. c. He spent large sums to attract public attention.
2. Why did the United States have to import lumber, iron ore, and other natural resources in the twentieth century?
   a. American industry grew so large that it needed more resources. b. Large amounts of these resources had been wasted by greedy business people in the nineteenth century. c. Patriotic businessmen imported these materials to conserve our nation's resources.
3. Why was a big business often able to destroy its smaller competitors?
   a. It could afford better machines and managers. b. It could gain special favors from the firms it dealt with. c. It could afford to sell at a loss in order to drive rivals out of business.
4. Why did Congress pass the Sherman Antitrust Act?
   a. Small-business people, farmers, and unions all objected to monopolies. b. These groups bribed members of Congress to pass the law. c. Congress found that monopolies were preventing the growth of American industry.
5. Why was the Sherman Act useless for many years?
   a. The law was long and hard to understand. b. The government made only a weak attempt to enforce it. c. The Supreme Court interpreted the law very narrowly.
6. Why did many Americans defend big business and monopoly?
   a. Big business was playing an important part in the nation's economic growth. b. It helped make our government more democratic. c. Some "captains of industry" gave large sums to charity.

IMPROVING YOUR SKILLS

A. Telling Facts From Opinions

Write "Fact" for each statement that can be proved by getting the necessary information. Write "Opinion" if you think the answer depends on values and judgment. (For a review, see pages 237-238.)

1. Andrew Carnegie was the most able business person of his time.
2. Carnegie was one of the richest people in history, but Rockefeller was even richer.
3. Carnegie and Rockefeller were both leaders of fast-growing industries.
4. Business people who wasted our country's natural resources were unpatriotic.
5. Our imports of raw materials would be lower today if business people had been more careful with them during the Economic Revolution.
6. The trust was a better form of monopoly than the merger.
7. Congress purposely wrote the Sherman Antitrust Act so that it would be hard to enforce.
8. American society was less democratic in 1900 than in 1850.
9. American business people spent much more on personal luxuries during the Gilded Age than they gave to charities.
10. American millionaires should not have lived so richly when many other Americans were so poor.

B. Looking at Both Sides

PART 1. List in your notebook all the services that big business performed for American society during the Economic Revolution. Also list the problems it created. (See explanation on page 256.)

Services

1.
2.
3.
4.
5.

Problems

1.
2.
3.
4.
5.

Conclusion. Should the government have tried to prevent the rise of big business? Give reasons why or why not.

PART 2. A millionaire businessman explained his methods in these words: "First you hit your enemies in the pocketbook, hit them hard. Then you either buy them out or take them in with you."
1. Explain what he meant by "hit your enemies in the pocketbook."
2. Why did he consider this the right way to behave?
3. What objections might be raised to such behavior today?

What Problems Did the Workers Face?

A. Bad Working Conditions. Imagine a cellar full of noisy, steaming machines. Workers are busy tending the machines or racing up and down the narrow aisles carrying bundles from one machine to another. They have to work fast. For they are paid by piecework—that is, for each article they make. The wages of the men are very low. Women and children make even less, usually only two to three dollars a week. Adults work at top speed twelve hours a day, six days a week. They barely make enough to support their families. Because of poverty and poor working conditions, many of the workers suffer from tuberculosis or some other disease.

Such factories, crowded and poorly ventilated, were known as "sweatshops." They were especially common in the garment industry during the Gilded Age. In other important industries—such as steelmaking, coal mining, and meat packing—accidents were a greater danger than disease. Accidents were considered the workers' fault unless they could prove that the employer was responsible. Such proof was usually impossible to get. So most injured workers could not collect damages and most employers did not bother with safety devices.

The greatest danger of all was unemployment. Thousands of skilled workers were displaced yearly by machines that could be run by unskilled workers. Every few years many thousands more lost their jobs because of panics (depressions) far worse than those of the early nineteenth century. Since there were no government organizations to help the unemployed, many of them suffered from hunger, cold, and disease.

B. Bad Living Conditions. As American industry expanded, cities grew larger. Many now boasted such modern improvements as streets with pavements and lights, trolley cars and "els" (elevated railroads), water supply and sewage systems, and police and fire departments. The rich and well-to-do built many fine homes.

Nevertheless, the living conditions of most city workers probably worsened during the Gilded Age. Most of them lived in slums—that is, run-down neighborhoods full of old wooden shacks and tall tenement houses. A tenement

Women and children were hired to cut string beans in this New York City sweatshop. How have working conditions changed since then? Why?

house was designed to squeeze a large number of people into a small space. It had five or six floors, each divided into several apartments. The rooms were very small. Most opened into tiny courtyards which let in very little light or air. There was usually only one washroom with a single cold water faucet on each floor. Yet rents were so high that two families often had to share a single apartment. Even the dark, damp basements were occupied.

C. Large-Scale Immigration. Why was the average American worker probably worse off during the Gilded Age than a half-century earlier? The main reason was a surplus of labor. For the first time since the founding of the thirteen colonies, America had more workers than it needed. This oversupply was greatest in the cities. Each year many young men and women left the farms and came to the cities for work. An even larger number of immigrants came pouring in from Europe. Most of them settled in the cities of the Northeast. So the labor surplus was worst there.

The "new immigrants," as they were called, differed in several ways from the "old immigrants" who had first settled our country. The "old immigrants" came mostly from the advanced countries of northern and western Europe. Almost all were Protestants. A great number spoke or understood English. Many were farmers or skilled workers. Most "new immigrants," on the other hand, came from the less advanced countries of southern and eastern Europe—from Italy, Poland, Russia, and the Balkan Peninsula. The majority were Catholics and Jews. They were for the most part too poor to buy farms. Lacking the special skills American industry needed, they could not get the better-paid jobs.

The newcomers had to be content with low-paid, unskilled work in factories or mines. Some, unable to find work, turned to crime. The poverty, high crime rate, and strange customs of the newcomers revived the old feeling against immigrants (see page 275). Soon the public demanded laws to cut down immigration. Labor unions supported these demands in order to reduce the oversupply of workers.

The first immigration laws were passed in 1882. One law forbade Chinese, thousands of whom had settled on the West Coast, to enter the United States. A second law barred the insane, the feeble-minded, exconvicts, and persons not able to support themselves. Not until the 1920s, however, did Congress limit immigration from Europe (see page 505).

Altogether, more than 20,000,000 immigrants entered the United States during the period of the Economic Revolution. They created some difficult problems for our nation. They themselves suffered a great deal before they became used to American ways. But they also played a very important part in our nation's progress. Their labor helped to build the railroads, work the mines, and run the factories that made the United States the world's leading industrial power. They also added many new

Four immigrants who enriched our nation with their talent:

Carl Schurz, political leader, from Germany.

Joseph Pulitzer, newspaper publisher, from Hungary.

Michael Pupin, scientist and inventor, from Serbia.

Sergei Rachmaninoff, composer and pianist, from Russia.

Immigrants passing through the streets of New York. Notice the faces of the bystanders. Why do you think they are sneering at the newcomers?

skills, customs, and ideas to the rich mixture of our American culture.

D. Opposition to Unions. Still another problem of factory workers in the Gilded Age was the lack of unions to fight for better treatment. Existing unions consisted almost entirely of skilled workers. These could bargain successfully with the employer because he could not replace them if they went on strike. Factory workers, on the other hand, were mostly unskilled. If they struck, the employer could easily hire immigrants or blacks from the South to take their places.

The growth of big business made it still harder for workers to organize successful unions. If they called a strike in one plant, the company could shut down the plant and lock out the workers. The lockout was a powerful new weapon of the employers. Since most workers had no savings, they usually had to return to work on the employer's terms after a few weeks.

The government and public were also hostile to unions. Government officials were usually quick to send police or troops to help employers in labor disputes. The courts gave employers a second powerful weapon against their workers, the injunction. This was a court order that forbade workers to hurt the employer's business. Workers who disobeyed an injunction suffered heavy penalties for "contempt of court."

E. A Period of Violence. The workers deeply resented the bad conditions and harsh treatment. As a result, a number of violent labor disputes occurred during the Gilded Age. Most violent and costly was the Great Railroad Strike of 1877. Trouble began as a result of a severe depression in 1873. During the next four years thousands of railroad workers lost their jobs. The rest were paid lower and lower wages. When one large railroad announced still another wage cut, the workers struck. They were soon joined by railroad workers in other parts of the country. Three large railroad unions, formed only a few years earlier, came to their aid. So did thousands of the unemployed. Angry mobs began to steal and damage railroad property. Two states called out the militia to restore order. But fighting broke out between the rioters and the militia, and the federal government had

Strikers and strikebreakers battling at the Carnegie steel plant in Homestead, Pennsylvania, in 1892.

to send regular army troops to assist the states. The strike finally ended when the railroad companies agreed to give their workers better conditions. The Great Railroad Strike cost more than a hundred lives, millions of dollars in property damage, and many millions more in lost wages and business.

In most other cases, government help made it possible for businessmen to break strikes. In 1892, for example, the workers in one of Carnegie's steel plants struck because of bad conditions and wage cuts. The company hired a force of private police to break the strike. A small war broke out between the strikers and the strikebreakers. The governor called out the state militia, which defeated the strikers. They had to return to work on the company's terms. Their defeat destroyed their union.

In 1894 a second great railroad strike crippled the nation. Federal courts jailed the union leaders for disobeying an injunction, and the President sent troops to escort the trains. Once service was restored, the strike collapsed.

F. A Few Successes. Nevertheless, the picture was not completely dark for American labor. Workers in a few skilled trades managed to form large national unions. These could bargain on equal terms with big business. Several attempts were also made to organize unskilled workers. Most successful was the Knights of Labor. It was started by Uriah Stephens, a Philadelphia tailor, in 1869. The Knights of Labor was to be "one big union" for all American workers, skilled or unskilled. It planned to help the workers by putting pressure on the government rather than by calling strikes. Its chief goal was to get Congress to order an eight-hour day for all workers.

The Knights of Labor allowed women as members. Women suffered in a special way in the industrial age. Prejudice and lack of opportunity for the same education as men kept women from hope of advancement in jobs. Whether single or married with children, women workers received less pay than men who were doing the same work. Many had to work twelve hours a day and run a household besides. In most cases, male workers objected to women in unions.

The Knights of Labor grew rapidly. But it ran into trouble because it could not control its 700,000 members. They called strike after strike—and lost most of them. One demonstration in Chicago ended in a bloody riot. This incident and its other failures caused a loss in membership. The organization died out by the end of the nineteenth century.

An immigrant cigar maker, Samuel Gompers, formed the American Federation of Labor in 1886. Gompers did not organize workers directly like the Knights. In the A.F. of L., workers joined existing unions in a federation like that of the states and the federal government. Also, only unions of skilled workers were admitted. This made the American Federation of Labor a strong organization. Since skilled workers received high wages, they could pay high dues. Because they were hard to replace, their strikes were often successful. Furthermore, Gompers did not seek political and social reforms. He urged the A.F. of L.'s member unions to work for better hours, wages, and working conditions in their trade.

These policies were successful. A.F. of L. members made important gains and improved working conditions. By 1900 the organization had more than one and a half million members. It has grown a great deal since. In fact, it is still our country's leading labor organization.

The American Federation of Labor and other strong unions gradually forced employers to consider the needs of their workers. At the same time, as we shall see, public opinion was turning against big business. An important part in this change was played by farmers, who, like the factory workers, were suffering because of the nation's rapid growth.

UNION MEMBERSHIP
IN THE UNITED STATES, 1870-1920

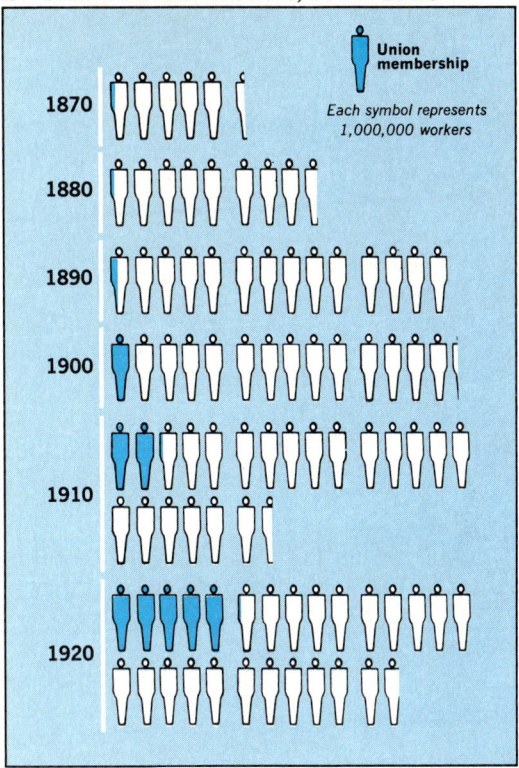

Each symbol represents 1,000,000 workers

REVIEWING THE SECTION

A. Knowing New Terms

In your notebook write the terms in this section that best complete these statements.

1. When workers are paid according to the number of items they turn out, they are said to be doing _____ work.
2. A factory that was unhealthy because of crowding and poor ventilation was called a _____.
3. People who came to the United States from southern and eastern Europe during the late nineteenth century were often called the "_____ _____."
4. In labor disputes, employers often shut down the factory until the workers accepted their terms. This was called a _____.

373

5. The workers who suffered from prejudice and low pay, and who were often expected to run a household besides, were _____ workers.

B. Knowing Important People

For each important person in the first column, write the *letter* of the best description in the second column.

Important People
1. Andrew Carnegie
2. Samuel Gompers
3. J. P. Morgan
4. John D. Rockefeller
5. Uriah Stephens

Descriptions
a. Leading Wall Street banker
b. Leader of the Great Railroad Strike of 1877
c. Leader of the oil industry
d. Leader of the steel industry
e. Leader of a successful nation-wide labor organization
f. Leader of a nation-wide labor organization that failed

IMPROVING YOUR SKILLS

A. Interpreting the Graph

Study the graph on page 373. Then answer these questions in your notebook.
1. During which ten-year period did the number of union members drop?
2. During which period did union membership show the smallest increase?
3. During which periods did the number of union members more than double?
4. How many workers were there in the United States in 1920? How many were union members? What percentage of the workers were union members?

B. Answering Essay Questions

Write a paragraph or two to answer each part of the following essay questions. Note that your answer to part a and b of each question should contain the facts and your answer to part c should contain your conclusion about the facts.

1. a. Compare the "new immigrants" with the "old immigrants." b. Compare the "new immigrants" with the Irish immigrants of the 1840s. Check an encyclopedia or other reference work for information on this part. c. Should the United States have passed laws to keep out the "new immigrants"? Give reasons for your opinion.
2. a. List the achievements of big business in the Gilded Age. b. List the problems it created. c. On the whole, was big business good or bad for our nation's development? Give reasons for your opinion.

ELIZABETH BLACKWELL AND BELVA LOCKWOOD: TWO WHO OPENED DOORS

The notion that only men were capable of healing the sick was destroyed by an English immigrant to the United States, Elizabeth Blackwell. Turned down by eight medical schools that she tried to enter, Elizabeth was finally accepted at Geneva Medical College in New York in 1847. After her graduation she went to Paris and then to London. However, there her diploma was not recognized. In France she lost the sight in her left eye as the result of a disease she contracted. That blow ended her dream of becoming a surgeon.

Returning to New York in 1853, she was again not allowed to practice her profession. She was abused, threatened, and ridiculed. But Blackwell opened her own dispensary in the slums. Shortly, hundreds of the poor sought her out as a caring, understanding doctor and friend. Four years later, she opened the New York Infirmary for Poor Women and Children. A training school for nurses was soon added. All the staff were women. Ten years later, a Women's Medical College was opened—the first of its kind in America.

Elizabeth Blackwell spent her latter years in London. For 32 years, until she retired in 1907, she was a professor at the London School of Medicine. Dr. Blackwell, the first woman doctor of medicine in modern times, was largely responsible for the fact that there were 7,000 women doctors in the United States by 1900.

Belva Lockwood was a young school teacher in a small town in New York State when she decided to become a lawyer. She faced the same kinds of rejection as Dr. Blackwell. She was turned down by several law schools on the grounds that her presence would disturb the study of male students. When she graduated from the National Law School in Washington, her diploma was withheld for several months. President Ulysses S. Grant, honorary president of the school, finally got it for her.

Because she was a woman, she was later denied the right to try a case before a federal court. As a result of her pressure, in 1879, Congress did pass a bill allowing women to practice before the Supreme Court. Lockwood was interested in the rights of the Cherokee Indians. In 1900 she sponsored a congressional bill which forbade reducing the size of their territories. She argued the case against the United States in which the Cherokees won a judgment of five million dollars.

Twice, Belva Lockwood was nominated for the presidency by the National Equal Rights party. On several occasions she represented the State Department at international conferences. She was an eloquent orator. With great fervor, Lockwood demanded suffrage for women in the western states that had been admitted to the Union shortly after the turn of the century.

Belva Lockwood did not only fight for the equal treatment of women, she also won her battles. She was the first woman to argue cases before the United States Supreme Court—a giant step in gaining respect for women in the law.

Elizabeth Blackwell

Belva Lockwood

Chapter 22

THE AGRICULTURAL REVOLUTION

W<small>E ALL KNOW</small> from motion pictures and TV what the "Wild West" was like. A typical western town had a few dozen wooden houses, including an inn, a general store, two or more saloons, a sheriff's office, and a jail. All through the week, the town seemed to be asleep. On Saturday night, however, people rode in from the surrounding countryside for a little fun. Tying up their horses in front of a saloon, they went in to drink, dance, and gamble until they had spent all their money. Many people carried guns because a gunfight, robbery, or murder might happen anytime. Sometimes bandits terrorized the town or even took control of it. Eventually, however, a tough sheriff or federal marshal helped honest citizens to establish law and order.

Such was the "Wild West." Its daring heroes have captured the imagination of millions of people, not only in the United States but also in foreign lands. Yet it existed for only a short time and only in a single region of the United States. The region was the territory between the Mississippi River and the Pacific coast; the time was the forty-year period after the Civil War. What happened in the West during that period was part of a great agricultural revolution that took place at the same time as the revolution in industry in the East.

This chapter will tell you:
1. How the West was settled.
2. What other changes took place in American agriculture.
3. What problems arose because of these changes.
4. What was done to solve the problems.

How Was the Wild West Tamed?

A. The "Great American Desert." California and Oregon in the Far West were settled before the Civil War. But most of the land between the Mississippi and these territories remained unsettled for years. It was made up of two quite different regions—one very mountainous, the other grassy and flat (see map, page 2). The flatland is known as the Great Plains.

The Great Plains, strange to say, were the last part of the Far West to be settled. There were several reasons for the delay. First, the climate was harsh. Extremes of heat and cold, tornadoes and blizzards, and light, uncertain rainfall made farming difficult. Second, trees, on which settlers depended for fuel and home building, were few in number. Third, the land was covered with tough grass, very hard to plough under. Fourth, the Indians of the Great Plains sometimes attacked those settlers who tried to cross or take over their hunting grounds. This was because many of these Indians depended upon the bison (buffalo) for their food, clothing, and shelter. Great herds of bison grazed on the vast stretches of grassland. To maintain their way of life, the Indians had to protect their hunting grounds. The Indians and the harsh climate made this area so forbidding that travelers called it the "Great American Desert."

B. The "Mining Frontier." The mountain region was opened to settlement in 1859. As the California gold rush ended, prospectors began to explore the mountains nearby. They made two rich "strikes" in land that is now Nevada and Colorado. In the next twenty years the Nevada find, the famous Comstock Lode, produced more than $300,000,000 worth of silver and gold. At the same time prospectors were making strikes elsewhere in the mountain country. In 1890, when the veins of silver and gold were finally giving out, the new electrical industry created a demand for copper, lead, and zinc. Then new mines were opened to obtain these minerals.

A mining "boom" usually lasted for only a few years, until the best veins were used up. Then the mines were either abandoned or taken over by large companies, which could make a profit by working them with modern machinery. Most mining centers eventually became deserted "ghost towns." By that time, however, the mountain states had been admitted to the Union and many permanent communities had been started by ranchers and farmers.

C. The "Cattle Kingdom." Cattle ranchers followed the prospectors to the Far West. The cattle-raising industry began in Texas. When Americans, both black and white, first settled there, the Mexicans taught them their methods of handling cattle. Americans also adopted Mexican-style outfits and some of their customs.

For many years, Texans killed cattle mainly for their hides because they could not ship the meat to market. After the Civil War, however, the fast-growing cities of the East provided a good market for beef, and the railroads provided the means for shipping it. Cattle raising quickly became a big business. Every spring Texas cowboys set out on the "long drive." They drove huge herds of cattle hundreds of miles northward to the Great Plains. There the cattle were fattened by grazing on the unsettled lands and then sold at the nearest railroad.

The vast "Cattle Kingdom" on the Great Plains lasted less than twenty-five years. It was destroyed by a combination of factors. The number of cattle grew so large that the region began to suffer from overgrazing. At the same time, the area suitable for grazing became smaller as sheep herders and farmers moved in. Sheep bit off the grass so close that there was nothing left for the cattle. Farmers put up barbed-wire fences to keep the cattle off their lands. The cattle herders fought the newcomers bitterly, but they had to give in when the federal government sent marshals to stop the violence. In the year 1886 came the final blow. First there was a long drought (dry spell). The cattle were too thin to sell and too weak to drive back south. Then came a terribly cold winter, with blizzards that covered the grass with ice. Most of the cattle that had lived through the drought died of hunger and cold.

The cattle herders then retreated from the open range to parts of the Great Plains too dry for farming. There they started ranches on which they bred fine cattle instead of wild longhorns and raised hay and alfalfa to feed them. The cattle industry continued; but the romantic days of the "Wild West" ended when the cowboy became just a ranch hand.

D. Arrival of the Farmers. 1. THE HOMESTEAD ACT. The Federal government was anxious to have the West settled by farmers. In 1862, during the Civil War, Congress passed the Homestead Act. This act gave a homestead, or family farm, of 160 acres free (except for a small registration fee) to anyone willing to settle on the land and work it for five years. Settlement of the Great Plains by farmers began while the war was still being fought. It increased after the war was over. Among those who came were many former soldiers, especially unhappy southerners who wanted to start a new life in the West

2. THE TRANSCONTINENTAL RAILROADS. The government knew that the farmers would have to ship their goods to market. So it gave two companies the right to build the first transcontinental railroad—that is, the first railroad that could carry goods from the East all the way to the Pacific coast. The Union Pacific was to lay tracks westward from Omaha, Nebraska, where an earlier railroad ended. The Central Pacific was to build eastward from California (see map next page). The government promised each company ten square miles of land and a large sum of money for each mile of track it laid. The result was a fierce competition between the two companies to see which could build faster.

Each company hired thousands of laborers—mostly Irish for the Union Pacific, Chinese for the Central Pacific. To house the workers, they built "towns on wheels," which moved along as the tracks were laid. Huge amounts of rails

Left, cattle roundup; center and right, portrait photographs from the era of the "Cattle Kingdom." Why did the "Cattle Kingdom" last less than 25 years?

ROUTES TO THE FAR WEST

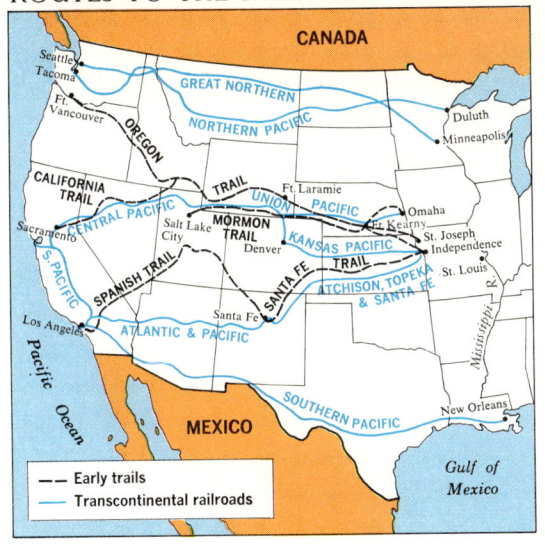

and other supplies were shipped in over great distances. To deal with the great bison herds and Plains Indians, the Union Pacific hired a large force of riflemen. Union Pacific workers were able to lay as many as six miles of track a day. The Central Pacific advanced more slowly because it had to dig tunnels through towering mountains and throw bridges over deep canyons. On May 10, 1869, four years after work began, the "wedding of the rails" finally took place. The last spike connecting the two lines was driven near Ogden, Utah. An American could now travel by rail from the Atlantic to the Pacific.

The first transcontinental railroad was quickly followed by four others. To earn profits, the railroads needed large numbers of customers. So they put on advertising campaigns in the East and in Europe, offering land to settlers at very low prices. By 1900 they had brought about 5,000,000 people into the Far West.

E. Hardships of the Early Farmers. The early farmers on the Great Plains had a very difficult time. Their main problems were the harsh climate and the lack of wood and water. To overcome these handicaps, they had to master new ways of farming and living. They dug up sod (grass-covered earth) in long strips, cut it into "bricks," and used it to build their houses. A sod house gave shelter from the heat and cold; but it dripped dust in dry weather and leaked on rainy days. For fuel, the settlers used almost anything that would burn, including "buffalo chips" (manure) and cornstalks. They also learned methods of "dry farming"—that is, how to raise crops with little water.

Settlers on the Great Plains faced two other serious difficulties. Every few years huge swarms of grasshoppers appeared. They were so thick they often stopped trains. They ate

A train on its way to the Pacific. What two companies were responsible for building the first transcontinental railroad?

A sod home on the Great Plains. Why were the settlers willing to live in such an uncomfortable house?

up the crops and anything else they could possibly chew. Droughts were even worse. For lack of water, crops and cattle died, and the topsoil blew away in great "dust storms." Thousands of early settlers left in despair—but others soon arrived to take their places.

F. Reasons for Success. The hard work of the early settlers on the Great Plains was finally rewarded with success. But they probably could not have succeeded without the help of American industry. Factories produced strong steel ploughs that cut through the tough grass to the fertile soil beneath. Other new farm machines prepared the soil, planted the seeds, and harvested the crops. These machines made it possible to farm large areas of level land with few workers. Well-digging machines found underground water, and pumps powered by windmills raised it to the surface. The railroads carried out the crops and brought back materials for building houses and coal for heating them.

As we have seen, the federal government helped settle the West by giving away farms under the Homestead Act and by encouraging railroad building. It also protected the settlers against the Indians. In a series of wars, federal troops defeated the Plains tribes and drove them into reservations (land set aside for their use). In addition, the federal government gave the states large grants of land to support agricultural colleges and research centers. Government scientists developed new kinds of grain that could withstand droughts and extremes of heat and cold. They also developed new kinds of livestock and better methods of farming on the Great Plains. The sons of farmers learned about these new improvements in the agricultural colleges.

Thanks to the settlers, the government, and science and industry, the "Great American Desert" was completely changed by the year 1900. It became the main source of American wheat and one of the richest farming regions in the world.

G. The "Passing of the Frontier." On the morning of April 22, 1889, thousands of people on horseback or in wagons lined up along the borders of Oklahoma Territory. Exactly at noon, bugles blared and the greatest land rush in history was on. By nightfall 50,000 people had staked claims to free government land. Less than twenty years later, Oklahoma became a state. Soon afterward, in 1912, Arizona and New Mexico became the last of the forty-eight mainland states to be admitted to the Union.

The opening of Oklahoma Territory marked an important development in American history, the "passing of the frontier." Less than three hundred years after the first English settlement at Jamestown, our country no longer had any large areas of unoccupied land.

The passing of the frontier had two far-reaching effects. One was a movement to conserve (save) our nation's natural resources. Americans had long acted as though these resources were unlimited. Planters in the South had raised the same crop year after year until the soil was exhausted. Then they moved on. In the Appalachian Highlands, farmers had cut down the forests that kept the precious topsoil from washing away. On the Great Plains, farmers had plowed up the grasses that held the topsoil down. Miners had used up a large part of the nation's minerals. Hunters had destroyed much of our wildlife. With the passing of the frontier, Americans began to see that such waste should not be allowed to continue.

The second effect of the frontier's passing was an increasing demand for economic and social reforms. Since poor and unemployed people in the East could no longer dream of going West, they became more insistent that the government help them. Western farmers also demanded reforms. These farmers had conquered the forces of nature. But now, as we shall see in the next section, they found themselves facing some difficult problems created by society.

REVIEWING THE SECTION

A. Knowing New Terms

In your notebook write the new terms in this section that best complete these statements.

1. Because of the widespread violence and lawlessness, the Far West became known in its early days as the "_____ _____."
2. The region between the Mississippi River and the Rocky Mountains is called the _____ _____.
3. For a long time this region was thought to be unfit for settlement. It was nicknamed the "_____ _____ _____."
4. The part of the Rocky Mountain region that miners opened to settlement became known as the "_____ _____."
5. The parts of Texas and the Great Plains used to graze longhorn cattle were known as the "_____ _____."
6. An American could have a family farm just by working a piece of land for five years and paying a small registration fee under the _____ Act.
7. The railroads connecting earlier railroads with the Pacific coast were known as the _____ railroads.
8. Methods of raising crops with less water in regions with light, uncertain rainfall are called _____ _____.
9. The settling of the last large area of good farmland, Oklahoma Territory, marked an important step in American history. It marked the "_____ _____ _____ _____."

381

B. Understanding the Facts

PART 1. Write the events in each group in the correct order.

A
1. The "Cattle Kingdom"
2. Farming on the Great Plains
3. The "Mining Frontier"

B
1. Completion of the first transcontinental railroad
2. Passage of the Homestead Act
3. The "passing of the frontier"

C
1. Establishment of cattle ranches
2. Killing cattle for hides
3. The "long drive"

D
1. Development of copper mines
2. Discovery of gold in California
3. Discovery of silver and gold in Nevada

PART 2. Tell how each of these obstacles to the settlement of the Far West was overcome. Use your notebook.

Obstacles to Settlement	How Overcome
1. Rugged Rocky Mountain region	1.
2. Light and uncertain rainfall on the Great Plains	2.
3. Lack of wood for houses and fuel	3.
4. Tough grass	4.
5. Bison herds	5.
6. Invasion of Indian lands	6.
7. Conflict of cattle herders with sheep herders and homesteaders	7.
8. End of open range for cattle	8.
9. Long distance to eastern markets	9.
10. Shortage of workers	10.

PART 3. In your notebook list the ways each of the following helped settle the Far West.

1. The federal government
   a.
   b.
   c.
2. The transcontinental railroads
   a.
   b.
   c.
3. Scientists and inventors
   a.
   b.

Conclusion. Which of the three do you think played the most important part in the settlement of the Far West? Give reasons to support your opinion.

IMPROVING YOUR SKILLS

A. Mastering the Map

Study the map on page 379. Then complete the following sentences.
1. The northernmost of the early routes to the Pacific coast was the _____ Trail.
2. The southernmost route was the _____ _____ Trail.
3. The transcontinental railroad that followed almost the same route as earlier trails was made up of the _____ _____ and the _____ _____.
4. The two transcontinental railroads built to the north of the old trails were the _____ _____ and the _____ _____.
5. The transcontinental railroad built far to the south of the old trails was the _____ _____. This railroad began in the city of _____ _____ and ended in the city of _____ _____.

B. Telling Facts From Opinions

In the following exercise, tell which statement in each group is the hardest to prove. If one of the statements is an opinion, then it is, of course, the hardest to prove. But if all three statements are facts, you will have to decide which one would be the hardest to check. In either case, be prepared to explain your answer in class.
1. a. Indians fought the new settlers to protect their hunting grounds. b. Railroads brought many benefits to the Indians. c. The true Indian heroes are those who fought to preserve their people's land.
2. a. Mining is a very important industry because it supplies the raw materials industry needs. b. Mining is a very destructive industry, because it uses up natural resources and often damages the countryside. c. The damage mining does is greater than the benefits it brings.
3. a. To prevent soil damage, the dry parts of the Great Plains should not have been opened to farming. b. Sheep herding should also have been discouraged because sheep, by biting off the grass close to the roots, expose the soil. c. The government should have allowed the cattle ranchers to keep out the farmers and sheep herders by force.
4. a. Much of the land the government gave away under the Homestead Act was taken over by land speculators. b. The federal government gave the transcontinental railroads more help than they needed. c. The West would have been settled just as quickly if the government had not helped at all.
5. a. The early settlers of the Great Plains suffered a great deal from illness. b. Only the toughest settlers were able to survive the many hardships. c. Those who managed to stay for five years usually became successful farmers.

Why Were the Farmers Dissatisfied?

A. The Revolution in Agriculture. Farming in the United States, like industry, went through a revolution between 1865 and 1900. As the Far West was settled, the amount of farmland almost doubled. Thanks to improved methods of farming, crops were almost four times as large. Yet fewer farmers were needed to raise these crops, mainly because of farm machines. It had once taken a farmer an hour to raise a bushel of wheat. With machines and improved methods, the same work took only ten minutes. By 1900 only 40 percent of the American people worked on farms, as compared with 80 percent in 1865. Yet they raised enough food, cotton, and other produce to supply all the people of the United States. They even shipped a large surplus to Europe.

B. The Farmer's Complaints. 1. Low Prices. Strangely enough, the great increase in production was the main reason for the farmers' problems. The farmers of the Midwest (the northern part of the Mississippi River Valley) were raising huge amounts of wheat and corn for sale as cash crops. As a result, they faced the same problem that had once troubled cotton and tobacco growers in the South. The price they received for their products depended on the world market. In the 1880s and 1890s, farm production grew rapidly in a number of countries besides the United States. This led to overproduction and a sharp drop in prices. As prices fell, farmers planted more in order to keep up their incomes. But the more they produced, the lower prices fell.

2. High Costs. While the incomes of farmers were going down, their costs were going up. In the days of the small family farm, most American farming families had raised their own food. They made almost everything else they needed. Big commercial farmers, on the other hand, had to buy machinery, other farm equipment, and fertilizer. They also bought machine-made clothing and household supplies instead of making them. Because of high tariffs and monopolies, the prices of these items were going up at the very same time farm prices were falling.

3. Complaints Against the Railroads. Most farmers did not know that their real problem was overproduction. But even if they did, they could not do anything about it. In their discontent, they began to blame the businesses they dealt with—especially the railroads that shipped their grain, the elevators and other warehouses that stored it, and the banks that lent them money. In many places, they said, it "cost a bushel of wheat to ship a bushel of wheat." In other words, much of their total income went for shipping and storage costs.

The farmers also accused the railroads of dealing unfairly with them. A railroad often charged more for a "short haul" of a few hundred miles in a farm area than for a "long haul" between big cities like New York and Chicago. Most railroads, farmers knew, also secretly gave rebates (reductions in rates) to monopolies and other big businesses. To make up for what they lost on rebates, the railroads raised rates for farmers and other small customers.

4. Complaints Against the Banks. High interest rates were still another serious problem

A Grange meeting. One of the signs reads: "Let us organize and educate, for knowledge is power."

for most farmers. Farmers who needed money to buy machinery and other costly equipment usually gave the bank a mortgage on their property as security for a loan. This meant that the bank could take their farms if they failed to pay the interest each year or to repay the loans when they fell due. Interest rates on farm mortgages were high in the West and even higher in the South. During periods of falling prices or crop failures, the banks took over many farms. In 1900 fully one-third of all the farms in the United States were being worked by people who did not own the land. A midwestern farm editor wrote bitterly:

"There are three crops raised in Nebraska. One is a crop of corn, one a crop of freight rates, and one a crop of interest. One is produced by the farmers who by sweat and toil farm the land. The other two are produced by men who sit in their offices and behind their bank counters, and farm the farmers."

C. Attempts to Improve the Situation. 1. The Granger Movement. The farmers tried to deal with their problem in several different ways. They hit on the first almost by accident. In the Midwest, where farms were large and far apart, farmers and their wives were often lonely. A government official, Oliver H. Kelley, encouraged them to establish meeting places in the towns. These were called *granges* (on old word meaning "farmhouses"). Farmers used the granges at first mainly for dances, lectures, and other social activities. The idea caught on rapidly, especially in the Midwest. Within a few years the Granger movement had more than a million members.

Once farmers got together, they talked politics. Soon the granges were supporting candidates who promised to help the farmers. In the 1870s Granger candidates won a majority in the legislatures of several midwestern states. They passed laws regulating the rates charged by railroads, grain elevators, and other farm warehouses. But the companies complained to the courts that the "Granger laws" were depriving them of their property without due process of law. The courts usually decided in favor of

385

the companies. Finally, in 1886, the Supreme Court ruled that state government could regulate only businesses conducted entirely within the state. This meant that most railroads, because they were engaged in interstate commerce, could be regulated only by the federal government.

After this defeat, the Granges turned to Congress for help. The result was the Interstate Commerce Act of 1887. This law created a special government agency, the Interstate Commerce Commission. Its job was to make sure the railroads charged "reasonable and just" rates. The ICC could also order a railroad to stop giving rebates and charging more for short hauls than for long ones. When the new government agency tried to enforce its orders, however, the courts almost always ruled against it.

Weakened by these defeats, many granges shut down. Others remained open, but only as social centers. Yet the Granger movement had not failed completely. It had taught the farmers to work together for political ends. Moreover, the Granger laws and Interstate Commerce Act had set an important precedent. Both the federal and state governments have since passed many laws to regulate private business.

2. THE "CHEAP MONEY" MOVEMENT. A second approach to the farm problem was the "cheap money" movement. This movement was based on the fact that the value of money changes. When there is an oversupply of money, it becomes "cheaper"—that is, its value falls. People can tell this is happening when prices go up and they can buy less for a dollar. In other words, when money is cheap, prices are high.

The first cheap money movement, the Greenback party, started soon after the Civil War. Before the war, paper money was backed by gold and had a yellow back. To meet its war expenses, the government printed large amounts of money with no backing. This currency had a green back so that people would know that it was different. The "greenbacks" dropped in value during the war. The Greenback party wanted the government to keep printing large amounts of this "cheap money." Its demand was supported by both farmers and debtors. Farmers hoped that farm prices would rise as the value of money fell. Debtors, many of whom were farmers, knew that it would be easier to pay their debts with cheap money. Opposing them were creditors and other wealthy business people who would lose if the value of money fell. Congress sided with this group. In 1875 it ordered that all American currency should be backed by gold.

At about this time, the new western mines began to turn out great amounts of silver and the price of that precious metal fell. When the mineowners asked the government to buy up the surplus silver, many farmers supported them. They wanted the government to issue more silver coins and large amounts of currency backed by silver. This too, they believed, would cheapen money and force prices up. Congress gave in to the demands of the farmers and mineowners. It passed silver purchase acts in 1878 and 1890. But the President in office each time was opposed to cheap money. He bought as little silver as he could under the law and printed only a limited amount of silver-backed currency. Money did not fall in value and the prices of farm products did not rise.

3. THE FARMERS' ALLIANCES. The strongest farm protest movement, the Farmers' Alliances, started in the late 1880s. Two alliances were formed in the South, which was hard hit by a drop in the price of cotton. Some 3,000,000 white farmers joined one alliance; 700,000 black farmers joined the other. Two other strong alliances, with more than a half-million members, were formed in the Midwest and Far West. The alliances tried to unite, but differences on the question of admitting blacks kept them apart.

The Farmers' Alliances, like the Granges before them, began as a social movement. But soon they were educating their members in better methods of farming and supporting can-

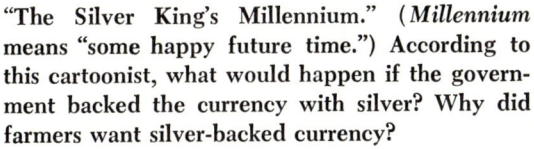

"The Silver King's Millennium." (*Millennium* means "some happy future time.") According to this cartoonist, what would happen if the government backed the currency with silver? Why did farmers want silver-backed currency?

According to this cartoonist, what effect would a "gold standard" (backing money with gold only) have on farmers and workers? With which of the two cartoons do you agree? Who benefited most from a gold-backed currency?

didates for public office. They won control of several state governments. They also elected several dozen members of Congress, who helped pass the second Silver Purchase Act and the Sherman Antitrust Act. In the election of 1892, the Farmers' Alliances joined forces with other reform groups. The result was a new political party, the Populist ("People's") party.

To help the farmers, the Populist Party called for cheap money, government loans at only 2 percent interest a year, and government ownership of the railroads. It also tried to win over the city workers by asking for shorter hours and limits to immigration. In the election of 1892, the Populist candidate for President received more than a million votes.

The Populists were a threat to the two old parties, the Republicans and the Democrats. Experts at the time foresaw three possibilities. The first was that the Populists might win over enough farmers and workers to become a major party. They could then use the power of the government to make reforms. The second possibility was that one of the old parties might borrow Populist ideas. In that case, too, reforms would be made. The third possibility was that the reform movement might fail completely. If that happened, the experts were afraid, the unhappy workers and farmers might turn to violence, or even to revolution.

REVIEWING THE SECTION

A. Knowing New Terms

In your notebook write the new terms in this section that best complete these statements.
1. The great improvements in American farming after 1865 are known as the _____ Revolution.
2. The main reason why the prices of farm products fell after the Civil War was _____.
3. The first important farmers' organization that fought for political reforms was the _____ movement.
4. The new federal agency to regulate the railroads was named the ICC or _____ _____ _____.
5. Farmers wanted the government to raise prices by issuing either currency backed by silver or currency without any backing, known as "_____."
6. In the 1880s farmers formed several new organizations known as the _____ _____. These helped organize the new _____ party.

B. Understanding the Facts

Complete this chart in your notebook.

Farm Problems	Actions Before 1892	Populist Platform
1. Low prices	1.	1.
2. High costs	2.	2.
3. Complaints against railroads	3.	3.
4. Complaints against banks	4.	4.

C. Finding the Reasons

In your notebook write the letters of *all* the correct answers to each question.
1. Why did the United States become the greatest farming nation in the world?
    a. It had large areas of fertile land with abundant rainfall. b. American farmers used modern machinery and methods. c. The government told farmers which crops they had to plant.
2. Why did the prices of wheat and other farm products fall in the 1880s?
    a. The amount grown was greater than the demand. b. The railroads, grain elevators, and bankers charged high rates. c. There was too much money in circulation.

3. Why did attempts to regulate railroad rates fail?
a. The Supreme Court ruled that the states could not regulate interstate railroads. b. Congress refused to pass a law dealing with this problem. c. The ICC lost most of the cases it brought against the railroads.
4. Why did farmers back the Greenback party and the silver purchase movement?
a. They wanted to reduce the federal government's spending and taxes. b. They wanted to help the manufacturers of paper money and the owners of silver mines. c. They thought these measures would raise the prices of farm products.
5. Why did the founders of the Populist party choose this name?
a. They were appealing to all the American people. b. They wanted to attract ordinary people, like farmers and city workers. c. They represented the farmers, who formed a majority of the American people.

IMPROVING YOUR SKILLS

Interpreting the Graph

UNITED STATES AGRICULTURE, 1860-1920

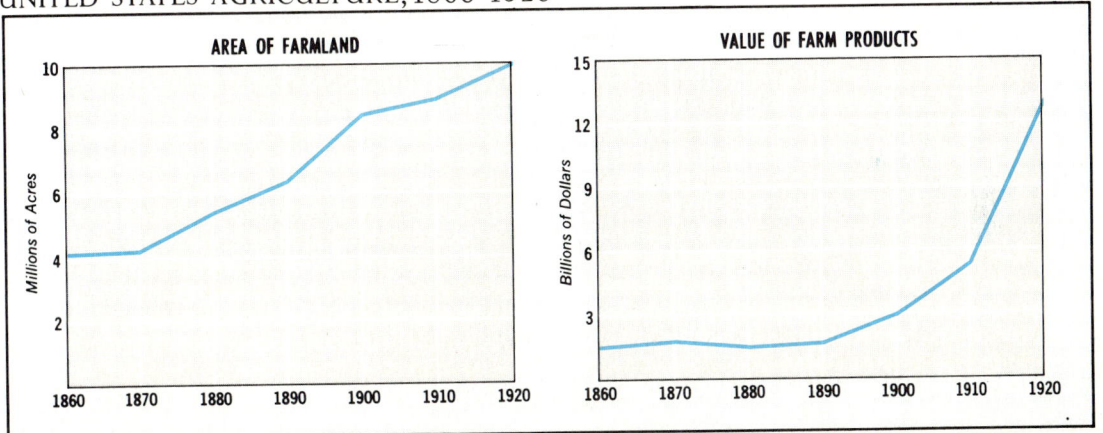

Study the graphs above. Write "True" if a statement is correct according to the graphs. If it is wrong, write "False" and give the correct answer. If the graphs do not give the answer, write "Not answered." Use your notebook.

1. The smallest increase in the area used for farming took place from 1860 to 1870.
2. The greatest increase in farm acreage occurred between 1870 and 1880.
3. The decade from 1870 to 1880 was the only time that the total value of farm products fell.

4. The greatest increase in the value of farm products occurred between 1890 and 1900.
5. The increased value of farm products was the result of both higher prices and larger production per acre.

MAKING HISTORY LIVE

1. a. Explain the quotation at the end of **B4**. b. Tell why you agree or disagree with it.
2. Explain the statement: "Farming was once a way of life; but the Agricultural Revolution made it into a business."
3. Read eyewitness accounts of life on the mining, cattle, or farming frontiers after the Civil War. Write a report on what you have learned.
4. Imagine that you are the son or daughter of an early settler on the Great Plains. Write a letter or sections of a diary to describe the hardships you are suffering.
5. One account of life on the Great Plains in the 1870s and 1880s contained this description: "Farm wives are not much better off than slaves. It is a weary, monotonous round of cooking and washing and mending, and as a result the insane asylum is one-third filled with wives of farmers." a. Why was life on the Great Plains often harder for the women than for the men in farm families? b. How does this help to explain why the Granger movement grew so fast?
6. Find old songs about the problems of the workers and farmers described in this chapter and the last one. Sing or read them and copy one.
7. a. Draw a poster such as the railroads might have used to attract settlers to the West. b. Draw a poster such as a settler might have made to criticize the railroad after losing his or her farm.

Chapter 23

POLITICS AND CULTURE IN THE GILDED AGE

In 1871 investigators checked the records of a courthouse being built in New York City. The courthouse was supposed to cost a quarter of a million dollars, but it had already cost eight million dollars and was still far from finished. The plasterers alone, the investigators found, had received three million dollars. Another firm had been paid a million dollars for repairs, even though the building had not yet been used! The investigation led to the arrest and imprisonment of William M. Tweed, the "boss" (head) of the Democratic party in New York City. Further investigation showed that Boss Tweed and his followers had stolen between 50 and 200 million dollars from New York City's taxpayers in ten years.

Such great corruption (dishonesty) did not exist in New York City alone during the generation after the Civil War. It was also found in many other cities, in state governments, and in the federal government. The worst cases of corruption in the federal government occurred during the two terms when Ulysses S. Grant was President (1869-1877). A military man, Grant knew little about politics. Though honest, he unwisely accepted gifts from business people and appointed relatives and friends to high government posts. His brother-in-law used the government's power to raise the price of gold so that a few of his friends might make a large profit. His personal secretary sold government tax stamps to whiskey makers for only a small part of their value and kept the money. The secretary of war helped himself to funds intended for the Indians on government reservations. Some members of Congress and other federal officials took bribes from one of the companies that built the first transcontinental railroad.

Why was there so much corruption in government during the Gilded Age? What else was wrong with our democracy at that time? Why did the government do so little to help the common people? And how was it able, after a time, to begin working again for democratic ideals? You will find answers to all four questions in this chapter.

What Was Wrong With Our Government in the Gilded Age?

A. Reasons for Corruption. An important reason for the corruption in government during the Gilded Age was "machine politics." Many city governments, and even some state governments, were controlled by "bosses" like Tweed. A boss's power depended on his "political machine," an organization made up of his party's leaders in the local districts. The job of the leaders was to "get out the vote"—that is, to get as many people as possible to the polls on Election Day to vote for their party's candidates. The leaders gave favors and bribes to people who regularly supported their party. They also "stuffed the ballot boxes" with fake votes or bribed the officials who counted the ballots. As a result, the candidates the boss picked almost always won. Once these men were in office, the boss could get them to do what he wanted because they owed their election to him. The boss could also count on the loyalty of his district leaders. Under the "spoils system" (see page 250), he could reward them for their service with appointments to well-paid government posts.

A second reason for the political corruption of the Gilded Age was the nation's sudden wealth. Many politicians forgot about honesty in their greed for easy money. Like the business people of the period, they believed that wealth meant success, even wealth obtained dishonestly. So businesses could easily get special favors from machine politicians either with bribes or with large gifts to the party's campaign fund.

B. Other Weaknesses of the Major Parties. Still another reason for corruption was the failure of the two-party system. Normally the two major parties try to win elections by giving the people what they want. In the generation after the Civil War, however, both parties could easily win elections without working for reforms. The Republicans still had the support of eastern business people and western farmers, whom they had won over during the Civil War. They could also count on most other northerners to vote for them because they were the party of Abraham Lincoln, who had saved the Union and freed the slaves. The Democrats, once Reconstruction ended, could count on the Solid South. They also had the support of political machines in the big eastern cities, which had been for the Democrats ever since the days of Jefferson and Jackson.

"A group of vultures waiting for the storm to blow over." This cartoon was one of a series by Thomas Nast that destroyed the Tweed Ring. They stirred up the people of New York City and led to Tweed's arrest.

Neither party wished to tackle the problems caused by the Economic Revolution. In their campaigns, they nominated war heroes or other popular candidates and avoided important issues. Since there was little real difference between Republicans and Democrats, many Americans lost interest in politics. And as long as the voters did not seem to care, politicians felt free to do favors for business people in return for bribes or gifts to their party.

Still another reason why the two-party system failed to work was the even balance between Republicans and Democrats in the federal government. The Republicans usually won the presidency and a majority in the Senate. The Democrats usually gained control of the House of Representatives. At such times, the system of checks and balances (see page 153) resulted in a deadlock. Neither party could hope to do very much even if it wanted to.

C. Civil Service Reform. The situation improved only when large numbers of Americans became angry enough to demand reforms. This happened in the case of the federal civil service. The struggle to reform it began in 1877, when Rutherford B. Hayes of Ohio became President. Hayes wanted to staff the government with able officials. He refused to appoint many people suggested by the bosses. He forbade federal workers to take an active part in politics. Most important, he asked Congress to set up a merit system, under which government workers would be chosen on the basis of examinations. However, the machine politicians refused to carry out Hayes's orders. What is more, they refused to nominate him for a second term.

At the Republican nominating convention in 1880, there was a sharp division between the machine politicians and the reformers. After a long struggle, an honest Republican leader, James A. Garfield of Ohio, was nominated for President. A machine politician, Chester A. Arthur of New York, was chosen for Vice-President. Once again, the Republicans won the election. But Garfield was shot by a disappointed job seeker a few months later. Arthur, the choice of the bosses, became President.

To everyone's surprise, the new President joined the cause of reform. With the support of the public, which had been aroused by Garfield's assassination, he got Congress to pass the Civil Service Reform Act in 1883. This law created the Civil Service Commission to give examinations for government positions. Arthur himself ordered that 15,000 jobs, almost one-eighth of the total number, should be filled only by people who had passed the examinations. Later Presidents kept raising the number. Eighty-five percent of all federal positions come under the merit system today.

D. A "Watchdog" President. In 1884 the Republicans nominated a popular congressman for President even though he had been involved in a corrupt deal. The Democrats nominated the governor of New York, Grover Cleveland, who was well known for his honesty. Cleveland won by a very close vote. He became the first Democratic President since the Civil War.

Cleveland doubled the number of federal workers under the merit system. He also made himself a "watchdog" of public money. He carefully studied every spending bill and vetoed those he did not think worthwhile. For example, he vetoed many bills giving pensions to Civil War veterans or providing money to build unnecessary post offices. Cleveland also recovered for the government some 80,000,000 acres of public land that the railroads and other big businesses were holding illegally.

E. The Tariff Issue. President Cleveland now found himself facing a very unusual problem, a large surplus in the treasury. He decided that the best way to end the surplus was to cut tariffs, which were the federal government's main tax at the time. The Republicans opposed him. They argued that high tariffs were needed to protect America's "infant industries" and the high wages of American workers. Cleveland replied that American industries were now strong enough to meet foreign competition without government support. He also showed that protected industries did not pay their workers higher wages than other industries. He concluded that high tariffs resulted mainly in high prices for the public and high profits for business people.

CIVIL SERVICE EMPLOYEES
IN THE UNITED STATES, 1891-1941

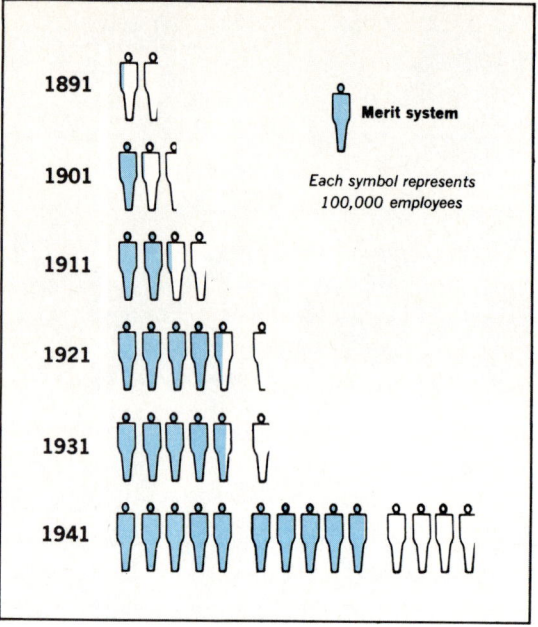

Each symbol represents 100,000 employees

Tariffs became the main issue in the election of 1888. Business people gave large sums to elect the Republican candidate, Benjamin Harrison of Indiana, grandson of a former President. Cleveland won a majority of the popular vote, but Harrison won a majority in the electoral college and became President.

Harrison was a weak President who let Congress do what it pleased. It soon raised tariff rates even higher than they had been before. As a result, the prices of many products rose. The surplus in the treasury did not increase, however, because Congress voted to spend more than a billion dollars in a single year. The money went mainly for a new steel navy and many public works. The "billion-dollar Congress," as it came to be called, left the treasury with a debt instead of a surplus.

It is hardly surprising that Cleveland was reelected in 1892. But his second administration was a great disappointment to his supporters. A severe depression began soon after he was inaugurated and lasted the four years he was in office. To improve conditions, Cleveland asked Congress to cut tariff rates. It agreed to only a few small reductions. The President refused to take any further action to help the suffering farmers and workers. It was the people's duty to support the government, he said, not the government's duty to support the people. Cleveland also turned down pleas for cheap money. He insisted instead on backing the currency with gold and had the silver purchase act repealed. Finally, he used federal troops to break the railroad strike of 1894 (see page 372). Many reformers who had supported Cleveland in 1892 now turned against him.

F. The Election of 1896. With the Democrats divided, the Republicans were sure they could win in 1896. Their convention quickly nominated Senator William McKinley of Ohio, a strong supporter of big business, sound money, and high tariffs. The Democratic party, on the other hand, made an unusual choice. A young congressman from Nebraska, William Jennings Bryan, made a speech that held the convention spellbound. Bryan demanded reforms to help the common people—the farmers, wage earners, and small business people. His main proposal was that silver, as well as gold, should be used to back the American dollar. In effect, he called on the Democratic party to adopt the Populist platform (see page 387). This dramatic speech won Bryan the Democratic nomination.

The campaign that followed was one of the most exciting in American history. Bryan traveled widely, telling cheering crowds everywhere how the government would help them if he won. To discredit Bryan, the Republicans charged that he was a dangerous radical who wanted to destroy the American way of life. They promised that a victory for McKinley, on the other hand, would mean the return of prosperity and

McKinley's "front porch campaign." Why do you suppose McKinley did not travel around the country speaking to crowds as Bryan did?

a "full dinner pail" for the worker. Just before Election Day, many business people warned their workers that they would close their plants if Bryan won. Bankers warned farmers that their loans would not be renewed. Such threats were probably unnecessary. McKinley received the votes of many Democrats who were afraid of cheap money and other Populist proposals. He won an easy victory over Bryan.

G. The McKinley Administration (1897-1901). Prosperity returned to the nation soon after McKinley took office. The Republicans claimed all the credit. Republican policies like the protective tariff, they said, had helped business and business had helped the country to recover. This was a good reason, the Republicans felt, to raise tariffs again. The new Congress soon did so. Cheap money supporters, on the other hand, insisted that the nation owed its recovery to a decline in the value of money. New gold mines, they pointed out, had just been opened in Africa. More gold had resulted in more money in circulation, and this in turn had caused prices to rise. Farm experts disagreed with both the Republicans and the cheap money supporters. The chief reason for America's recovery, they said, was a drop in European farm production. This had helped American farm prices to rise. Whatever the reason, prosperity had returned, and McKinley benefited. When he ran again against Bryan in 1900, he won another easy victory. For a few months, it looked as though the cause of reform was dead. However, it was soon to win some surprising victories.

REVIEWING THE SECTION

A. Knowing New Terms

PART 1. In your notebook write the new terms in this section that best complete these statements.

1. The head of a political party in a city or state during the Gilded Age was called the "_____."
2. His organization, made up of his party's leaders in the local districts, was called his "_____ _____."
3. Faithful supporters of a political party expected to be appointed to well-paid government jobs under the "_____ system."
4. The practice of appointing government officials on the basis of examinations is called the _____ system.
5. Examinations for government jobs are given by a special government agency, the _____ _____ Commission.

PART 2. Explain the following expressions in your notebook *in your own words*.

    (In **A**) "Getting out the vote"
                "Stuffing the ballot boxes"
    (In **D**) A "watchdog" President
    (In **E**) The "billion-dollar Congress"
    (In **F**) A "full dinner pail"

B. Knowing Important People

For each important person in the first column, write the *letter* of the best description in the second column.

Important People
1. Chester A. Arthur
2. William Jennings Bryan
3. Grover Cleveland
4. James A. Garfield
5. Ulysses S. Grant
6. Benjamin Harrison
7. Rutherford B. Hayes
8. William McKinley
9. William M. Tweed

Descriptions
a. Great general who was a poor President
b. Machine politician who became a reforming President
c. Only President to be elected, defeated, and then reelected
d. Only President who was the grandson of a former President
e. Outstanding example of the corrupt politician
f. President during a period of prosperity after a severe depression
g. President who started the movement for civil service reform
h. President who favored reforms to help the farmers and workers
i. President whose death led to civil service reform
j. Unsuccessful presidential candidate, who favored cheap money backed by silver

C. Understanding the Facts

First, copy the chart in your notebook. Then compare the Republican and Democratic parties in the Gilded Age. Put a check in the correct column to show which party supported each of the following proposals.

	Republicans	Democrats
1. Civil service reform		
2. Less government spending		
3. Lower tariffs		
4. Cheap money, backed by silver		
5. Reforms to please the farmers and workers		

Conclusion. Which party would you have supported? Why?

IMPROVING YOUR SKILLS

A. Telling Facts From Opinions

In your notebook write the *letter* of the statement in each group that is hardest to prove. Be prepared to explain your choice in class. (For a review, see page 383.)

1. a. There was a great deal of corruption in the Democratic party during the Gilded Age. b. There was also much corruption in the Republican party at that time. c. Corruption was greater among the Democrats than among the Republicans.
2. a. Both major parties usually nominated honest men for President during the Gilded Age. b. The machine bosses often nominated dishonest men whom they could easily control. c. If the American people had controlled the nominations, they would have chosen only honest men.
3. a. Hayes was an honest but weak President. b. If Garfield had not been shot, civil service reform would not have been passed by Congress. c. Despite his earlier record as a machine politician, Arthur was an honest President.
4. a. Reformers had good reason to support Cleveland in 1892. b. They had good reason to be disappointed in him by 1896. c. Cleveland could have prevented a split in the Democratic party by taking up the cause of reform.
5. a. The Republicans had good arguments for protective tariffs in 1820. b. President Cleveland had good arguments against protective tariffs in 1890. c. Congress usually voted for high tariffs just to please business people.

B. Interpreting the Graph

Study the graph on page 394. Then write "True" in your notebook if the statement is correct according to the graph. If it is wrong, rewrite it so that it is correct.

1. The largest increase in the number of government workers under the merit system occurred between 1931 and 1941.
2. The smallest increase in the number of workers under the merit system occurred between 1891 and 1901.
3. The number of workers under the merit system increased about three times between 1891 and 1901.
4. The number of federal workers not under the merit system was smallest in the year 1911.
5. The number of federal workers not under the merit system was highest in 1941.

What Did Reformers Accomplish?

A. The Humanitarian Movement. People who are deeply interested in helping their fellow human beings are called humanitarians. The humanitarian spirit has a long history in our country. On the frontier, for example, people often got together to help a needy neighbor. Sometimes they even cleared a plot of land and built a house for a new settler. The same spirit of friendly cooperation inspired the reformers of the Jackson era in the 1830s. During the Civil War, the Sanitary Commission helped wounded soldiers. After the war many northerners helped the freed blacks in the South. The humanitarian spirit became even stronger in the late nineteenth and early twentieth centuries. As our country's problems increased, earlier reform groups grew larger and new ones came into being.

The humanitarians of the Gilded Age were especially interested in helping the poor and needy in the large industrial cities. Some started charities to provide needy people with food, clothing, and fuel. During the depressions of the 1870s and 1890s, however, these private charities found that they could not do the job alone. So they started a movement to make local governments help the needy. In the next generation they succeeded in getting government help for the poor in most large cities. Such help is known as "relief" or "welfare."

Another important humanitarian group helped the poor to help themselves. These humanitarians started centers, known as settlement houses, in the slum districts of big cities. The most famous was Hull House, opened by Jane Addams in 1889 to serve the people of a Chicago slum neighborhood. Hull House had a nursery where working mothers could leave young children. It also had club rooms and a gymnasium for older children, an employment agency for the jobless, and classes in English for the foreign-born. Jane Addams also worked for reforms to help all the poor people in Chicago. Her drives to clean up the tenement houses and to improve the courts and jails were especially successful. They inspired humanitarians in many other parts of the United States.

The humanitarians won strong support from the churches. The Roman Catholic Church had

A social worker visits an immigrant couple in their kitchen. How did Americans try to improve living conditions of the poor?

long ago created special orders of monks and nuns to help the needy. These orders now found much to do in the eastern cities where the new immigrants, many of them Catholic, had settled. Protestant churches also supported missions to help the poor. One was the Salvation Army, which helped even the poorest members of society, the down-and-out.

B. Other Reform Movements. The temperance movement became very active again during the Gilded Age. Alcoholism (drunkenness) was especially serious in the slums. Many workers spent so much on drink that their families starved. In the 1870s the Women's Christian Temperance Union, Anti-Saloon League, and Prohibition party were formed. These groups tried to deal with the problem in two ways. They taught people about the evils of drink. They also fought for laws to limit the manufacture and sale of alcoholic beverages. Their efforts finally resulted in the adoption of the Eighteenth Amendment at the end of World War I in 1919. This amendment outlawed the manufacture or sale of "intoxicating liquors"

Jane Addams with children in Hull House. She was also a leader in the women's suffrage movement. Addams won the Nobel Peace Prize in 1931 for her work for international peace.

anywhere in the United States. Though it was later repealed, many states and local districts still have prohibition laws today.

Leaders of another reform group, the women's rights movement, organized the National Association for Woman Suffrage in 1869. They won the support of many political reformers, who expected women to fight for honest government once they got the vote. By 1900 women were allowed to vote in four western states. The Nineteenth Amendment, ratified at the end of World War I, finally gave the right to vote to all American women.

C. Growth of Education. Another force for progress in the second half of the nineteenth century was the rapid growth of education. In this period the first kindergartens were established for preschool children. The number of elementary schools was increased, the school year was made longer, and the age for compulsory school attendance was raised to fourteen in most states. As a result, the number of Americans who could not read or write dropped sharply. Many public high schools were also built at this time, mainly in the cities. These new schools provided commercial and vocational courses for students who did not plan to go to college. The number of colleges and the subjects they offered also increased greatly.

The South had only a few public schools until the Reconstruction Period. Many schools were built at that time. They were open to both white and black children. After Reconstruction ended, however, the public schools were usually open only to white children. Private humanitarian groups then started new schools for blacks. These schools usually followed the principles set forth by the leading black educator of the period, Booker T. Washington. These schools prepared most students to be skilled workers, farmers, and owners of small businesses. Some schools educated teachers and other professionals.

D. Realists and Muckrakers. Once again, as in the time of President Jackson, improvements in education affected American literature. The United States in the Gilded Age could boast of more than a dozen outstanding writers. Still widely read today is the humorous writer Mark Twain. One of his books, *The Gilded Age,* gave this period in American history its name. In this book Mark Twain made fun of the dishonest business methods and selfish spending of the newly-rich. Far better known, however, are his novels about life along the Mississippi as seen through the eyes of two adventurous boys, Tom Sawyer and Huckleberry Finn.

Many writers of this period were realists. Their books described the way most Americans really lived. Two examples are *The Red Badge of Courage* by Stephen Crane and *Little Women* by Louisa May Alcott. Crane described the experiences of a young soldier fighting in the Civil War. Alcott wrote about the teenage adventures of four sisters. She based her book largely on her own life. Other realists wrote about the sufferings of the poor in the city slums and the hardships of farmers on the Great Plains.

Newspapers and magazines became very important during the Gilded Age, thanks to improved printing methods and lower prices. One newspaper, *The World,* won a very large number of readers by exposing evils in New York City and then leading "crusades" to change them. Several popular magazines soon followed *The World*'s example. They hired skilled writers to uncover conditions needing reform. Such writers were called "muckrakers" because they raked up the filth or muck of corruption. The most famous muckraker was Lincoln Steffens. In a series of articles called *The Shame of the Cities*, he exposed corruption and injustice in city government. A second muckraker, Ida Tarbell, exposed corruption in big business by showing how Rockefeller had built the Standard Oil Trust. A third, John Spargo, described the evils of child labor in articles justly named *The Bitter Cry of the Children.* Both the muckrakers and the realists aroused the American people to the need for reforms.

E. The Rise of Radicalism. One of the most popular books of the Gilded Age was Edward Bellamy's *Looking Backward.* The hero of the book awakens from a long sleep in the year 2000. He finds a world filled with marvels, such as air travel, television, and electric heating. The people are all healthy and happy. Bellamy wanted to show his readers that Americans could enjoy wonderful lives if they changed the nation's economic system. He argued that poverty, suffering, and crime existed because the capitalists (owners of businesses) took advantage of their workers. He believed that these evils would disappear under socialism, an economic system under which the government would own all business.

At the time Bellamy wrote, socialist parties were growing in many European countries. This was largely because European capitalists and government officials were doing very little to tackle the problems modern industry had

A march for women's suffrage in front of the White House in 1917. Why did women take part in fund drives, speeches, hunger strikes, and jailings to win the right to vote?

created. Many poor European workers joined socialist parties or other radical movements that promised to help them. In the United States, however, the socialist movement grew very slowly. A Socialist party was finally formed in 1904. It reached its peak eight years later, when its candidate for President received about a million votes.

F. Signs of Progress. Why did socialism gain so few followers in the United States? The main reason was that most Americans believed in the future. They felt sure that the nation would continue to progress and that existing evils would be corrected under the capitalist system. By 1900 many signs of progress could already be seen. Private charity and public education were helping the poor. The revolution in agriculture was making food cheaper and more plentiful. Industry was turning out more and more goods at lower prices. Thanks to machinery, people did not have to work so hard or so many hours each day.

Many Americans devoted their new-found leisure to culture. Art galleries, concert halls, opera houses, orchestras, and music societies multiplied. A number of talented American composers appeared. The best known, Edward MacDowell, wrote music that suggested the mood and spirit of America. His *Woodland Sketches* and *Indian Suite* are good examples.

Many other Americans found recreation in sports. At this time professional baseball became the nation's leading "spectator sport," the game millions of people watched every year. Bicycle riding was probably the most popular active sport. An entire family would often "go for a spin" on a Sunday afternoon. Many a young couple pedaled along together "on a bicycle built for two."

In 1900 life was becoming easier for many Americans as the economy prospered under the McKinley administration. Nevertheless, the demands for reform did not stop. In fact, the next sixteen years were to prove an even greater period of progress than the Jackson Era.

REVIEWING THE SECTION

A. Knowing New Terms

For each term in the first column, write in your notebook the *letter* of the best description in the second column.

Terms
1. Capitalists
2. Humanitarians
3. Muckrakers
4. Realists
5. Socialists

Descriptions
a. People who wanted to help the poor and unfortunate
b. Owners of private businesses
c. Radical reformers who believed that all business should be owned by the government
d. Reformers who opposed the manufacture and sale of intoxicating liquors
e. Writers who described the way ordinary people actually live
f. Writers who exposed corruption in government and industry

B. Knowing Important People

In your notebook write the *letter* of the best description in the second column for each important person in the first column.

Important People

1. Edward Bellamy
2. Ida Tarbell
3. Lincoln Steffens
4. Mark Twain
5. Booker T. Washington

Descriptions

a. Author noted for humorous accounts of life along the Mississippi
b. Author who described the experiences of an ordinary soldier in the Civil War
c. Author who believed Americans would lead better lives under socialism
d. Writer who told of corruption in big business
e. Leading black educator of the time
f. Muckraker who wrote about corruption in big cities

C. Understanding the Facts

In your notebook write the *letter* of the correct choice.

1. During the late nineteenth century, the humanitarians were most successful in:
a. changing the American economic system   b. ending poverty   c. finding jobs for the unemployed   d. providing the needy with food, clothing, and fuel.
2. Settlement houses were started in the slum districts of industrial cities because:
a. buildings were cheaper in the slums   b. farmers and other people in the rural areas did not need help   c. the slums contained many immigrants and other people who needed help   d. most slum dwellers and humanitarians were Catholics.
3. The Eighteenth Amendment made it a crime to:
a. make or sell intoxicating liquors   b. drink alcoholic beverages   c. offer an alcoholic drink to a friend   d. do any of these things.
4. During the second half of the nineteenth century, public education:
a. was born in the United States   b. grew very rapidly   c. was made available to every young American   d. was better than it is today.
5. The muckrakers were important because they:
a. aroused the American people to the need for reforms   b. organized a new political party to fight for reforms   c. supported reform candidates for Congress and the state legislatures   d. helped to sell more newspapers and magazines.
6. Socialism grew strong in Europe, but not in the United States, because:
a. less was being done to help European workers than Americans

  b. Europeans have always made reforms faster than Americans   c. Europeans were better educated than Americans   d. most European countries had weaker governments than the United States.
7. Which statement about actions of reformers in the late nineteenth century is not accurate?
  a. Fighting alcoholism was a goal of reformers.   b. Churches did not become involved in helping the poor.   c. Women were leaders in many reform movements.   d. Europe was the source of many reform ideas.

D. Summing Up the Chapter

In your notebook write "Yes" if each condition is still common today; write "No" if it is no longer a problem.

1. Bribing voters and "stuffing the ballot box"
2. The spoils system
3. Little discussion of important issues by the two major parties
4. High tariffs
5. Large-scale spending by the federal government
6. Terrible slums
7. Widespread alcoholism
8. Inferior position of women
9. Inferior schools for blacks in the South
10. Growth of unemployment

IMPROVING YOUR SKILLS

A. Looking at Both Sides

The following statement is taken from the Populist platform of 1892. Read it carefully. Then follow the instructions below it.

"We meet in the midst of a nation on the edge of ruin. Corruption dominates the ballot-box, the state legislatures, Congress, and even the courts. The newspapers are bribed and public opinion is silenced. Homes are covered with mortgages, labor is impoverished [very poor], and the land is concentrated in the hands of capitalists. Workmen are denied the right to organize unions in self-protection, immigrants beat down their wages, and private armies [strikebreakers] are hired to shoot them down. The fruits of the toil of millions are boldly stolen to build up colossal fortunes for a few."

1. Make a list *in your own words* of the evils this passage mentions.
2. How can you tell that this is a one-sided statement?

3. Pretend you are a Democratic or Republican politician of the time. How would you answer these charges?

B. Understanding the Sketch

Study the picture at the top of page 399. Then answer the questions below.

1. Name the reform movements in the picture.
2. What did these movements try to do?

MAKING HISTORY LIVE

1. a. Explain the statement: "The two great parties were like two bottles. Each bore a label telling the kind of liquor it contained, but each was empty." b. How does this statement explain why a number of third parties arose during the Gilded Age?
2. a. Why did both Republicans and Democrats fail to deal with important issues during the late nineteenth century? b. Who are better citizens: the independent voters who vote for the candidates and principles they think best, or the people who always vote the straight party ticket? Why?
3. Many black leaders today condemn the segregated vocational education that Booker T. Washington called for.
a. Was Washington right or wrong in calling for such education in his day? Explain your opinion. b. Do you think blacks should accept such education today? Explain.
4. a. Report on one case of corruption that happened during Grant's term of office. b. Tell what should have been done to prevent it.
5. Write a report on the life and work of a leading reformer or muckraker of the Gilded Age.
6. a. Draw a poster either for or against socialism in the late nineteenth century. b. Draw a cartoon to show what the humanitarians accomplished at that time.

Chapter 24

THE PROGRESSIVE ERA

"SHOULD THE GOVERNMENT pass laws to regulate business?" This question was raised by many people who were troubled by the evils of the Gilded Age. For many years business people, government officials, and a large part of the public said "No." They argued that free enterprise, which left businesses free to do as they chose, had made the United States rich and powerful. Government regulation, they warned, would hurt business and slow the nation's progress. This belief in free enterprise was an important reason why the government did little to help the workers and farmers in the Gilded Age.

The Socialists thought differently. They wanted the government to take over all businesses, farms, and natural resources. Only in this way, Socialists believed, could business be run for the benefit of the common people.

A group of reformers known as the Progressives wanted the United States to take a middle path. The Progressives believed that the nation would progress faster under capitalism than under socialism. But they also felt that the government should "police" business to protect the public.

The Progressives won wide support. Humanitarians, ministers and teachers, and many workers and farmers joined them. In this chapter, first we shall see what reforms local and state governments made as a result of the Progressive movement. Then we shall see how two Presidents—the Republican Theodore Roosevelt and the Democrat Woodrow Wilson—fought for reforms in the federal government. So successful were the Progressives that the fifteen-year period after the Gilded Age, from 1901 to 1916, has become known as the Progressive Era.

What Reforms Were Made in Local and State Governments?

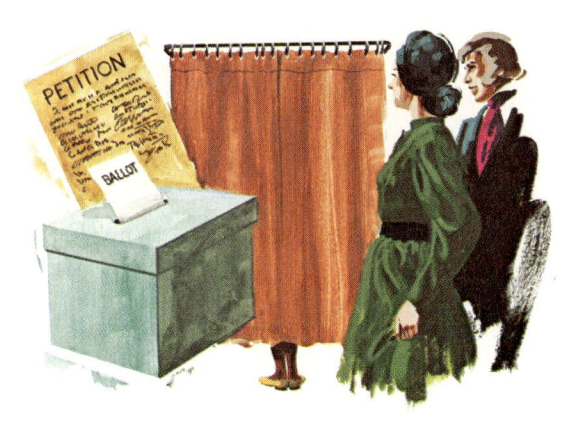

A. Improving Our Democracy. "The cure for the evils of democracy is more democracy," said the Progressives. They proposed that the American people should be given a greater voice in running their governments—federal, state, and local. This, they believed, would arouse the people's interest in politics. An aroused public would put a stop to corruption and bring about needed reforms. To make governments more democratic, the Progressives called for the adoption of a number of new democratic ideas. These had been tried successfully in some of the western states and in some foreign countries.

1. THE SECRET BALLOT. Before 1900 most states had open voting. Voters marked their ballots in an open place in front of other people. This led to a number of abuses. Corrupt politicians could "steal" an election by bribing people to vote for their candidates. They could "stuff the ballot boxes" by hiring hundreds of people to vote in one polling place after another. They could also bribe the officials who counted the ballots.

The Progressives won several reforms to make voting more honest. Most important was the secret ballot. This provided that voters mark their ballot in a closed booth and drop it into a locked box. Since no one could tell how they voted, they were free to choose the candidates they wanted. Politicians were discouraged from bribing voters because they could no longer be sure how the people they had bribed were voting. For many years now, voting machines have been widely used. They make it almost impossible for dishonest politicians to steal elections.

2. THE PRIMARY ELECTION. The Progressives found that it was not enough to make elections more honest. Machine politicians still kept control by nominating (naming) all the candidates for their party. The Progressives therefore asked that candidates should be nominated by the voters in a special election. This was named the primary ("first") election because it was held several weeks before Election Day.

Under the primary system, any citizen has the right to become a candidate for office. A person only has to get the signatures of a certain number of voters on a nominating petition. That person's name is then placed on the primary ballot. On the primary day, the party members decide by their votes the party's candidates who will be in the regular election.

3. THE INITIATIVE AND REFERENDUM. The Progessives also knew that legislatures often refused to consider laws that many people wanted, or passed laws that many people did not want. So they called for two reforms that would give the people more control over lawmaking. These were the initiative and the referendum. The initiative allows the voters to initiate (start) laws they want by getting a certain number of signatures on a special petition. When these signatures have been obtained, the legislature must either pass the law or put it to the voters in a referendum.

A referendum is a "Yes" or "No" vote on a single question. Amendments to the constitution, proposals to spend large sums, and other important measures passed by the legislature are decided by referendum in many states today. That is, they go into effect only if a majority of the voters supports them. Thus the referendum keeps legislatures from taking actions the people do not approve.

4. THE RECALL. Another problem of democracy is that officials may not keep their promises to the voters. Or they may prove lacking in honesty or ability. This is most serious in the case of judges because they usually have very long terms of office. The recall was the Progressives' answer to this problem. It gives the people the power to remove unwanted officials before their term in office ends. After a

At right: A modern voting machine. How has its use protected the secrecy of the ballot? Why is the secret ballot so important? Below: A voter studies the ballot in New Hampshire's primary election, in which the state's candidates for President and Vice-President are nominated. The American people watch the results of this election closely because it is the first presidential primary in the nation.

certain percentage of the voters has signed a recall petition, the official's name is placed on the ballot. Voters then decide whether or not the official remains in office.

5. OTHER REFORMS. Progressives also fought for ways to limit the political influence of big business. Employers often controlled their workers' votes by threatening to discharge them if they did not vote as they were told. The secret ballot ended this practice. In addition, laws were passed to limit the amount any person or company could give to an election campaign and the amount a candidate could spend.

The Progressives suggested several reforms to end the corruption the muckrakers had found in city government. Most important was the city manager government. The voters elect a trained manager, rather than a political leader, to run their city. Such city managers are given great power. They are watched closely by voters. If they fail to do a good job, they can usually be removed by the voters. Today, many American cities are governed by city managers.

The Progressives also called for two other reforms to make democracy stronger. These were votes for women and the direct election of senators (see page 418). Check your own local and state governments to see which of the Progressives' reforms described in this section have been adopted. Also check to see how well they have worked. In general, these reforms have made American government more democratic by giving more power to the voters. But they have not stopped political machines or corruption entirely. This shows that it is not enough to reform the machinery of government. It is also necessary for the people to elect good officials and to make sure that they govern honestly and well.

B. Reforms to Help the Workers. Besides making improvements in government, the Progressives got the states to pass laws to help the workers. Every state, for example, passed a workers' compensation law. This law requires employers to buy a special insurance policy for their workers. The policy provides free medical care for any worker who is hurt on the job. It also pays workers a part of their wages (usually one-half to two-thirds) until they can return to work. If they are not able to work for a long time, it pays them a lump sum, the amount depending on how badly they were disabled. Finally, it pays workers who have developed a disease or illness caused by the job, like the lung disease of miners and stone workers. To keep costs down, state governments and insurance companies made employers adopt safety measures. As a result, the number of accidents and industrial diseases dropped sharply.

Working women and children clearly needed special protection. Some states passed laws forbidding them to work at night, in dangerous occupations, or more than a certain number of hours a week. (The earliest laws set the limit at ten hours a day for six days a week!) Many states also gave welfare help to widows with young children so that they could stay at home and care for their families. Tenement laws were still another important reform. These laws made builders design tenements so that each apartment had sunlight and fresh air, fire escapes, and a bathroom.

C. The Need for Federal Action. Several reform laws, chiefly those dealing with the labor of women and children, were declared unconstitutional by the Supreme Court. The Court ruled that some of the laws interfered with the workers' freedom of contract—that is, their right to take a job on any terms they wished. Others, the Court held, interfered with interstate commerce, which only the federal government could regulate. It soon became clear to the Progressives that local and state action was not enough. Luckily they were able, as we shall soon see, to win powerful support in Washington.

REVIEWING THE SECTION

A. Knowing New Terms

For each term in the first column, write in your notebook the *letter* of the best description in the second column.

Terms
1. Free enterprise
2. Progressive movement
3. Secret ballot
4. Primary election
5. Initiative
6. Referendum
7. Recall
8. Workers' compensation
9. Tenement laws
10. City manager government

Descriptions
a. Allowed the public to introduce bills
b. Protected voters from being influenced by corrupt politicians and employers
c. Fought for reforms to help the workers and other common people
d. Required builders to make better houses for city workers
e. Gave the public a way to dismiss bad officials
f. Let the public decide whether a law should be passed
g. Made it possible for the public to nominate candidates
h. Gave business people the opportunity to run their businesses as they pleased
i. Paid workers who were hurt or became ill because of their jobs
j. Prevented big business from making large contributions to political campaigns
k. Provided a better way to run local affairs

B. Finding the Reasons

In your notebook write the letters of *all* the correct answers to each question.

1. Why did many humanitarians, ministers, and teachers support the Progressive movement?
   a. They did not like free enterprise. b. They favored socialism for the United States. c. They wanted the government to deal with the problems of the Economic Revolution.
2. Why did Progressives want a more democratic government?
   a. They believed that democracy is a good form of government. b. They thought that people would be more interested in politics if they had a greater voice in government. c. They expected government officials to be more honest and efficient if the people watched them closely.

3. Why was the secret ballot important?
   a. People who bribed voters could not be sure how those bribed would vote. b. Employers could not find out how their workers had voted. c. Voters no longer had to vote for the candidates of a single party.
4. Why were the initiative and referendum important?
   a. These reforms gave the voters a voice in lawmaking. b. They kept the state legislatures from passing unpopular laws. c. The people could remove the officials from office if they did not do what the people wanted.
5. Why did the Progressives turn to the federal government?
   a. The state governments would not pass the laws they wanted. b. The federal courts had declared many state reforms unconstitutional. c. It was easier to influence the federal government than the state governments.

IMPROVING YOUR SKILLS

Getting Different Viewpoints

You have already learned to look at both sides of a controversial question. (For a review, see page 256.) You will find, however, that questions often have more than two sides. This is especially true when they affect a number of groups with different interests. Each group looks at the question differently, and each is usually sure that it is right. As citizens in a democracy, we should learn to examine and understand the different viewpoints. Then we can decide which should have our support.

Let us now examine the controversial questions of the Progressive Era to see how the American people felt about them. Let us divide the people into four groups: big business people, small business people, farmers, and workers. In the following exercise, each group's feeling about a question has been given. "For" means that most of the group took a favorable stand on the question. "Against" means that most of the group took an unfavorable stand. "Mixed" means that most had good reasons for feeling both favorable and unfavorable. "Not interested" means that it did not affect the group much. In each case, write in your notebook *why* the group probably felt as it did. (The first exercise has been done for you as a sample.)

1. **Free enterprise** (the freedom of business people to follow the policies they think best without government interference)
   a. Big business people: "For." They liked free enterprise because it had helped them become wealthy and powerful. It also left them free to deal with other business people, workers, and consumers in any way they wanted.
   b. Small business people: "Mixed." They wanted to be free to run their businesses as they pleased. But they also wanted the government to

protect them from monopolies and unfair practices of big business.
- c. Farmers: "Mixed." They wanted to run their farms as they pleased. But they also wanted the government to regulate railroads and banks and to break up monopolies.
- d. Workers: "Mixed." They knew that the country was growing fast under free enterprise. But they also wanted the government to help them get shorter hours, workers' compensation, and other reforms.

2. **Socialism** (government ownership of businesses and farms)

    a, b, c. Big business people, small business people, and farmers: "Against."

    d. Workers: "Mixed."

3. **Political reforms** (secret ballot, primary elections, initiative and referendum, recall)
    - a. Big business people: "Not interested."
    - b, c, d. Small business people, farmers, workers: "For."

4. **Economic reforms** (workers' compensation, laws to protect working women and children, tenement laws)

    a, b. Big business people and small business people: "Against."
    - c. Farmers: "Not interested."
    - d. Workers: "For."

MAKING HISTORY LIVE

1. a. Explain *in your own words* each of these Progressive reforms—the secret ballot, primary elections, initiative and referendum, recall, city manager. b. Which do you consider the most important reform? Why?
2. Study the election procedures for the student government in your school. a. Make a list of its strong and weak points. b. Suggest improvements based on the reforms of the Progressive movement.
3. Draw a poster for an election in the early 1900s either for a candidate supported by a political machine or for a candidate who wants the Progressives' support.
4. Study elections in your community. Besides reading your local newspapers, talk to local political leaders and visit polling places if you can. a. Report on at least one of the following questions: (1) How many of the eligible voters in your community actually vote? (2) Do most people vote a "straight party ticket" or do they vote for the candidates and platforms they like best? (3) How important are the local political clubs? How do they influence community affairs? (4) Are voting machines used? In what other ways does your community make sure elections are honest? (5) Which of the Progressive reforms described in this section has your community adopted? How have they worked? Suggest ways to improve politics in your community.

Why Was Theodore Roosevelt Considered a Progressive?

A. An Outstanding President. Theodore Roosevelt—Americans often called him "Teddy" or "TR"—was one of our most remarkable Presidents. "TR" was born into a wealthy and important family in New York City. As a boy, he was weak and sickly and spent most of his time reading. But in his teens he built up his body by exercising and taking part in sports. He became a member of his college boxing team, a lover of the outdoors, and even for a time a rancher in the "Wild West." Yet he kept up his reading. He also wrote many books on American history, ranching, and outdoor life.

After graduating from law school, TR entered politics as a Republican. He served as a member of the New York State legislature, a New York City police commissioner, a federal civil service commissioner, and an assistant secretary of the navy. In each post he did an outstanding job. But he angered machine politicians because he refused to take orders and fought corruption.

When the Spanish-American War began in 1898, TR formed a special regiment called the "Rough Riders." He became a national hero by leading them in a charge against a well-defended enemy position on San Juan Hill in Cuba. On his return, he was elected governor of New York. Once again he displeased the machine politicians, this time by trying to put through reforms. To get rid of him, the bosses had him nominated for the vice-presidency. In TR's day the post was considered a "political graveyard." The man who became the Vice-President had so little to do that people usually forgot him. TR was elected Vice-President in 1900 as McKinley's running mate. But the bosses' trick backfired. A year later McKinley was assassinated and Theodore Roosevelt became President of the United States.

B. Meaning of the "Square Deal." TR, as you might expect, was a strong President. Like Andrew Jackson and Abraham Lincoln, he was eager to lead Congress and willing to stretch the

Republican campaign poster for the election of 1900. What symbols did the artist use? Why? What does the slogan mean?

413

Constitution. He was also strongly influenced by the Progressive movement. His main purpose, he said, was to give a "square deal" (fair treatment) to every American. TR explained the "Square Deal" in these words:

"I mean not merely that I stand for fair play under the present rules of the game, but that I stand for having these rules changed so as to work for a more substantial equality of opportunity and reward."

C. Aid to Labor. Great discontent among the anthracite (hard coal) miners gave the new President a chance to prove that he meant what he said. The average miner worked ten hours a day at a hard and dangerous job. Yet he earned only about $300 a year. He was paid according to the weight of the coal he mined each day. Company officials, who did the weighing, often cheated him. Moreover, the company usually owned the town he lived in and charged him a high rent for a small, poorly built house. It also charged high prices for everything he bought at the company store.

Early in 1902 the miners' union called a strike for higher wages, shorter hours, and better treatment. The public was on the side of the strikers from the start. But the mineowners did not seem to care. They refused even to talk with the union leaders. The strike dragged on month after month. Hard coal became so scarce that its price rose from five to thirty dollars a ton. Millions of Americans found that they could no longer afford to buy coal to heat their homes.

With winter coming on, TR decided to step into the dispute. He called representatives of the mineowners and miners to the White House. He asked them to choose arbitrators (referees) to help them work out a settlement. The union agreed to the idea, but the mineowners refused. Instead they urged the President either to sue the union for violating the Sherman Antitrust Act or to break the strike with troops. TR not only refused their request; he also threatened to take over the mines unless they agreed to arbitration. The mineowners finally gave in. The workers won a 10 percent wage increase, a nine-hour working day, and the right to have fellow workers weigh their coal.

The hard-coal strike was important because it was the first labor dispute in which the federal government sided with the workers. At TR's request, Congress also passed two laws to help labor. One law gave workers' compensation to federal workers; the other established the Department of Labor. This meant that workers now had an important government official to look out for their interests.

D. Regulation of the Railroads. Under TR the government finally began to regulate the railroads. The President persuaded Congress to pass a law making the Interstate Commerce Commission stronger. This law had three important provisions: 1. It gave the ICC power to cut very high railroad rates. 2. It gave the commission control of oil pipelines, ferryboats, and warehouses owned by railroads. 3. It forbade rebates and free passes. (The railroads had been giving out thousands of free passes each year to lawmakers, newspeople, and others they wanted to influence.) The ICC acted quickly to carry out the new law. It forced the railroads to make large cuts in their rates.

E. The "Trust-Buster." When TR became President, the Sherman Antitrust Act was almost useless because of a Supreme Court decision (see page 365). Nevertheless, the new President ordered his attorney general to sue when the leading Wall Street banker, J. P. Morgan, combined three large railroads in the Northwest. To the surprise of big business, the government won its case by a five-to-four vote of the Supreme Court.

TR started more than forty other antitrust suits against powerful monopolies such as Standard Oil and the American Tobacco Company. The government won most of these cases. The Supreme Court usually ordered the monopoly broken up into several separate companies. Because of his reputation for breaking up trusts, TR became known as the "trust-buster."

F. Protecting the Consumer. Several muckrakers had written about the ways dishonest business people were cheating consumers (the people buying and using their products). One book, *The Jungle* by Upton Sinclair, gave a vivid picture of unsanitary conditions in the meat-packing industry. TR was so shocked by the book that he asked Congress for laws to protect comsumers. Congress passed two such laws. One law gave federal officials the right to inspect all meat shipped in interstate commerce. The other law set up a new government agency, the Food and Drug Administration. The FDA could seize foods and drugs shipped in interstate commerce if they were impure, unsafe, or wrongly labeled. A number of states followed the federal government's lead. They required the inspection of products made and sold within the state.

G. Conserving Our Natural Resources. Because he loved the outdoor life, TR soon took up the cause of conservation (the saving of natural resources). He set aside more than 150,000,000 acres of public land, chiefly forests, as national parks. He also stopped the sale of public lands to private companies at low prices. Instead he leased (rented) the lands for a certain number of years. This kept them under the control of the government. Ranchers were forbidden to graze more than a certain number of cattle on each acre. Lumberers had to plant new trees to replace those they cut down.

In many speeches and articles, TR educated the American people about the importance of conserving natural resources for future generations. Through his efforts, the National Conservation Commission was created to promote conservation. He also persuaded the governors of most of the states to set up state conservation departments.

The irrigation of desert lands, especially in the dry Southwest, was another of TRs many interests. He approved more than twenty large irrigation projects. Most of these projects called for the building of large dams. The dams not only stored water for irrigation but also prevented floods and produced electricity.

H. A Very Popular President. In 1904 TR scored a one-sided victory over his Democratic opponent and became President in his own right. He could certainly have been elected again in 1908. But he refused to run. Though TR had been elected President only once, he

A popular cartoon about Theodore Roosevelt. What does it tell you about his career? Why was he such a popular President?

"And in his time a man plays many parts."
Shakespeare.

Cowboy | Historian | Police Commissioner | Naval Secretary | Rough Rider | Governor of New York | Vice President | President | Peacemaker | Mighty Hunter all the time

insisted that he had already served two terms. So, following the example of Washington and Jefferson, he refused a third term. He made sure, however, that the Republicans nominated his close friend William H. Taft for the presidency. With TR's support, Taft easily defeated Bryan, who was once again the Democratic candidate. As soon as Taft took office, TR went off to Africa to start a new career—big-game hunting.

REVIEWING THE SECTION

A. Knowing New Terms

In your notebook write the terms in this section that best complete these statements.

1. Theodore Roosevelt called his program to give every American equal treatment the "_____ _____."
2. Because TR broke up trusts by bringing suit against them under the Sherman Antitrust Act, he became known as the "_____."
3. A person who buys and uses goods is called a _____.
4. The federal agency that protects consumers from unsafe foods and drugs is called the _____ _____ _____ _____.
5. To save our nation's natural resources, TR started a program of _____.

B. Understanding the Facts

Write the *letter* of the correct choice in your notebook.

1. TR was the only President who:
   a. held a number of important political posts   b. was a scholar and writer   c. was a sportsman and military hero   d. was outstanding in all these ways.
2. The vice-presidency was considered a "political graveyard" because:
   a. the Vice-President becomes President when the President dies   b. the Vice-President works so hard that his health is usually ruined   c. the Vice-President is usually forgotten by the public   d. candidates for Vice-President are usually unimportant people.
3. In the hard-coal strike, the mineowners angered President Roosevelt by:
   a. mistreating their workers.   b. refusing to recognize the union   c. turning down his suggestion to arbitrate the dispute   d. raising the price of hard coal.
4. Under TR, Congress gave the Interstate Commerce Commission the power to:
   a. order a railroad to reduce its rates if they were very high   b. regulate all oil pipe lines, ferries, and warehouses in the United States   c. forbid

rebates and free passes under certain conditions   d. do all these things.
5. The Food and Drug Administration protects consumers from:
    a. unsafe products   b. false advertising   c. unfair business practices   d. all these evils.
6. TR's conservation policy was intended to save our nation's:
    a. farmland   b. forests   c. mineral resources   d. natural resources of every kind.
7. TR was a very popular President because he:
    a. led a varied and interesting life   b. helped the common people   c. educated the American people about the nation's problems   d. did all these things.

IMPROVING YOUR SKILLS

Getting Different Viewpoints

For each of TR's policies below, write "For" in your notebook if you think most members of a group favored it; "Against" if you think they opposed it; "Mixed" if you think they had good reasons to be both for and against it; "Not interested" if you think it did not matter much to them. Be prepared to give the reasons for your answers.

1. **Proposing arbitration to settle the hard-coal strike**
    a, b. Big and small-business people
    c. Farmers
    d. Workers
2. **Improving railroad regulation**
    a. Big business people
    b, c. Small business people, farmers
    d. Workers
3. **Enforcing the Sherman Antitrust Act**
    a. Big business people
    b, c, d. Small business people, farmers, workers
4. **Protecting the consumer**
    a, b. Big and small business people
    c, d. Farmers and workers
5. **Conservation and irrigation**
    a, b. Big and small business people
    c. Farmers
    d. Workers

Conclusions. 1. To which groups did TR's policies appeal most? 2. To which did they appeal least? 3. Why did TR receive such a large vote in 1904?

Were Presidents Taft and Wilson Progressives?

A. Achievements of the Taft Administration. The Progressive movement continued under President Taft. The new President started twice as many antitrust suits as Roosevelt. He added greatly to the number of federal positions under the merit system. He set aside several million acres of mineral lands as a conservation measure.

Congress also passed a number of progressive measures during the Taft administration. It increased the Interstate Commerce Commission's power to regulate railroads. It also gave the Commission control over telephone and telegraph companies. Even more important, it passed the Sixteenth and Seventeenth Amendments to the Constitution and sent them to the states for ratification. The Sixteenth Amendment allowed the federal government to collect a graduated income tax. This meant that the larger a person's income was, the larger the share paid to the government. The Seventeenth Amendment provided for the direct election of senators. They were now to be elected directly by the voters, just as representatives were, instead of by the state legislatures. Progressives considered this a very important reform. Under the old system, the Senate had become "a rich men's club." Many of its members were rich men or had been chosen by rich men to represent their business interests. Once senators were elected by the people, it was expected they would represent the public rather than big business.

B. Progressive Opposition to Taft. In spite of this record, many Progressives opposed Taft. There were two main reasons why. One was his attitude toward the presidency. Taft was a friendly, easy-going, cautious person—very different from the forceful Roosevelt. Unlike TR, he did not believe in a strong presidency. He would, he said, use "only those powers expressly authorized by law." Since he did not give Congress strong leadership, he received no credit for the reforms it passed.

The second reason for the Progressives' opposition to Taft was their feeling that he was too friendly to eastern big business people. This feeling first arose during a fight over the tariff in 1909. When Congress met, Taft asked it to lower tariff rates. His reason was that many American industries no longer needed protection from foreign competition. Business people representing these industries replied by asking Congress for more protection. Since Taft did not fight hard for reductions, the business people won. The tariff bill passed by Congress raised far more tariff rates than it cut. Angry Progressives called on Taft to veto the bill. But he not only signed it; he also called it "the best tariff bill that the Republican party has ever passed."

After two other disagreements with Taft, the Progressives asked Roosevelt to come home and help them. TR returned to the United States in 1910. A few months later he made a speech strongly supporting the Progressives and attacking Taft. The two old friends became bitter enemies.

C. The Election of 1912. Republican party politics took an exciting turn in 1912. Both

Taft and TR announced that they would be candidates for the presidency. Taft's supporters controlled the party's nominating convention and quickly nominated him. TR's followers then left the Republican party. They formed the new Progressive party and nominated Roosevelt as their candidate for President.

With the Republicans split, the Democrats had an excellent chance to win the election. They nominated a strong candidate, Woodrow Wilson. Wilson was a former college professor, not a politician. He was an expert on government, a fine speaker, and a supporter of reform. As president of Princeton University, he had attracted public attention by forbidding special clubs for rich students. The political bosses in New Jersey had then nominated him for governor, expecting to control him because he was not experienced in politics. But Wilson had proved a strong governor. He had smashed the political machine and put through a number of progressive laws.

The platform on which Wilson ran in 1912 was almost as progressive as TR's. The Socialists nominated a labor leader named Eugene V. Debs and asked for even more reforms than the two major parties. On Election Day, Wilson received 42 percent of the popular vote, Roosevelt 28 percent, Taft 24 percent, and Debs 6 percent. Thus the three candidates running on reform platforms won more than 75 percent of the vote, or three times as many votes as Taft. Though Wilson did not receive a majority of the popular vote, he won a tremendous victory in the electoral college. Thanks to the Republican split, he carried thirty-nine of the forty-eight states.

A cartoon about Roosevelt's third-party movement in 1912. The Progressives were called the Bull Moose party because TR boasted that he felt strong, "like a bull moose." How does the cartoon make fun of TR and his new party? How did the new party affect the election of 1912?

Inauguration Day, 1913. Woodrow Wilson, on the left, is about to take over the presidency from William H. Taft. How did the administrations of the two Presidents differ? In what ways were their policies similar?

D. Wilson's "New Freedom." Wilson, like TR, believed in a strong presidency. In his inaugural address, he announced a program of reforms he expected Congress to pass. This program would give the American people a "new freedom," the freedom to lead better and richer lives, by reducing the powers of big business.

1. REDUCING THE TARIFF. Wilson went to work at once. He called a special session of Congress to lower tariff rates. Hundreds of business people came to Washington to block tariff reform. But Wilson, unlike Taft, aroused the public to support him. As a result, he won the first great reduction in the tariff since 1857. Congress lowered rates on more than a thousand items and placed another hundred on the free list.

2. THE FEDERAL RESERVE SYSTEM. The American banking system was the next subject for reform. In 1913 a Senate committee reported on the reasons for a panic a few years earlier. The committee's report showed that the panic had been caused by two major weaknesses in the old National Banking System (see page 330). First, each bank had to depend on itself. It could not get help in case of emergency. Second, eastern bankers controlled most of the nation's credit. As a result, people in the West and South found it harder to borrow money and had to pay much higher interest rates than easterners.

To correct these weaknesses, Congress passed a law setting up the Federal Reserve System. The law divided the United States into twelve districts. A special "bankers' bank," called the Federal Reserve Bank, was established in each district. Banks in the district could join the Federal Reserve Bank by buying a certain amount of its stock. In return, they could ask for its help in case of emergency. Any district that needed more credit could borrow from the Federal Reserve Bank of another district.

One question was hard to answer: Who would control the new banking system? The bankers wished to keep control, as in the past. But President Wilson thought that the new system should be under government control. The final decision was a compromise. Each Federal Reserve Bank was to be controlled by its member banks. The entire system, however, would be guided by the Federal Reserve Board. The members of this board would be appointed by the President.

3. NEW ANTITRUST LAWS. In 1911 the Supreme Court handed down a decision that weakened the Sherman Antitrust Act again. It held that a combination violated the law only if the government could clearly prove that it was harming the public. Since such proof was hard to get, the chances of the government's winning a case were small.

President Wilson therefore had Congress pass two new antitrust laws. One law, the Clayton Antitrust Act, listed a number of unfair business practices that were to be considered illegal. The second law set up the Federal Trade Commission. Its job was to watch for violations of the antitrust laws, to look into complaints of unfair practices, and to take action against offenders.

4. AID TO FARMERS AND WORKERS. President Wilson also acted to help the common people. At his request, Congress set up special government banks to lend money to farmers at low interest rates. It also provided funds for building roads in farm areas and for teaching farmers new methods. To help the workers, Congress provided funds for vocational schools and passed an eight-hour-day law for railroad workers. Two laws were passed to outlaw child labor, but these were declared unconstitutional by the Supreme Court.

Wilson's reforms, like those of TR, won him much popular support. His foreign policy, on the other hand, was far less successful. In the next unit we shall see how President Wilson tried, but failed, to keep our nation out of the First World War. We shall see how the American people, busy with the war, soon lost interest in the Progressive movement and in reform.

REVIEWING THE SECTION

A. Knowing New Terms

PART 1. For each term in the first column, write in your notebook the *letter* of the best description in the second column.

Terms

1. Clayton Antitrust Act
2. Federal Reserve System
3. Federal Trade Commission
4. Sixteenth Amendment
5. Seventeenth Amendment

Descriptions

a. Allowed the federal government to tax people with higher incomes more heavily than people with lower incomes
b. Enforced the Clayton Antitrust Act
c. Forbade certain unfair practices by business
d. Helped banks, especially in the West and South
e. Provided aid for the common people
f. Provided that senators should be elected directly by the voters

PART 2. Write the meaning of the following terms *in your own words*.

(In **A**)   "a rich men's club"   (In **D2**)   "bankers' banks"

B. Finding the Reasons

In your notebook write the letters of *all* the correct answers to each question.

1. Why could Taft claim to be a Progressive President?
a. He enforced the Sherman Antitrust Act. b. He strengthened the merit system and the conservation policy. c. He proposed the Sixteenth and Seventeenth Amendments.
2. Why did the Progressives turn against Taft?
a. He was not a strong President like Roosevelt. b. He asked Congress to pass the program eastern business people favored. c. He signed a bill that raised tariffs instead of reducing them.
3. Why did many Progressives vote for Woodrow Wilson in 1912?
a. He was an experienced politician. b. He had put through important reforms as governor of New Jersey. c. He promised to make progressive reforms if he was elected President.
4. Why did President Wilson call his program the "New Freedom"?
a. He promised to protect freedom of speech, the press and religion. b. He promised the common people freer and better lives. c. He believed business people should be free to run their affairs as they pleased.

5. Why was the new Federal Reserve System better than the old National Banking System?
   a. A member bank could get help from the Federal Reserve Bank in its district. b. The Federal Reserve Bank in one district could borrow from reserve banks in other districts. c. Officials chosen by the President watched over the Federal Reserve Banks.
6. Why did the Progressive movement come to an end in 1916?
   a. The problems resulting from the Economic Revolution had all been solved. b. The American people were tired of reforms. c. The American government and people were faced with new problems arising from the First World War.

C. Summing Up the Chapter

For each item below, write in your notebook the *letter* of the President to whom it applies.

A. Theodore Roosevelt   B. William H. Taft   C. Woodrow Wilson

1. Anthracite coal strike
2. Clayton Antitrust Act
3. Conservation of forest lands
4. Direct election of Senators
5. Federal Reserve Act
6. Federal Trade Commission
7. Food and Drug Act
8. Graduated income tax
9. New Freedom
10. Square Deal
11. Tariff increases
12. Tariff reductions
13. Formation of the Progressive party
14. Rough Riders
15. "Trust-buster"

Conclusion. Which of the three Presidents do you consider the most progressive? Explain why you think so.

IMPROVING YOUR SKILLS

A. Getting Different Viewpoints

For each of the following policies, write "For" in your notebook if you think most members of a group favored it; "Against" if you think they opposed it; "Mixed" if you think they had good reasons to be both for and against it; and "Not interested" if you think it did not matter much to them. Give the reasons for your answers.

1. **The graduated income tax**
   a. Big business people
   b. Small business people
   c, d. Farmers and workers
2. **Direct election of Senators**
   a. Big business people
   b, c, d. Small business people, farmers, and workers
3. **Lower tariffs**
   a, b. Big and small business people
   c. Farmers
   d. Workers
4. **The Federal Reserve System**
   a. Big business people
   b, c. Small business people and farmers
   d. Workers
5. **New antitrust laws**
   a. Big business people
   b, c, d. Small business people, farmers, and workers
6. **Aid to farmers and workers**
   a, b. Big and small business people
   c, d. Farmers and workers

THE UNITED STATES IN 1916

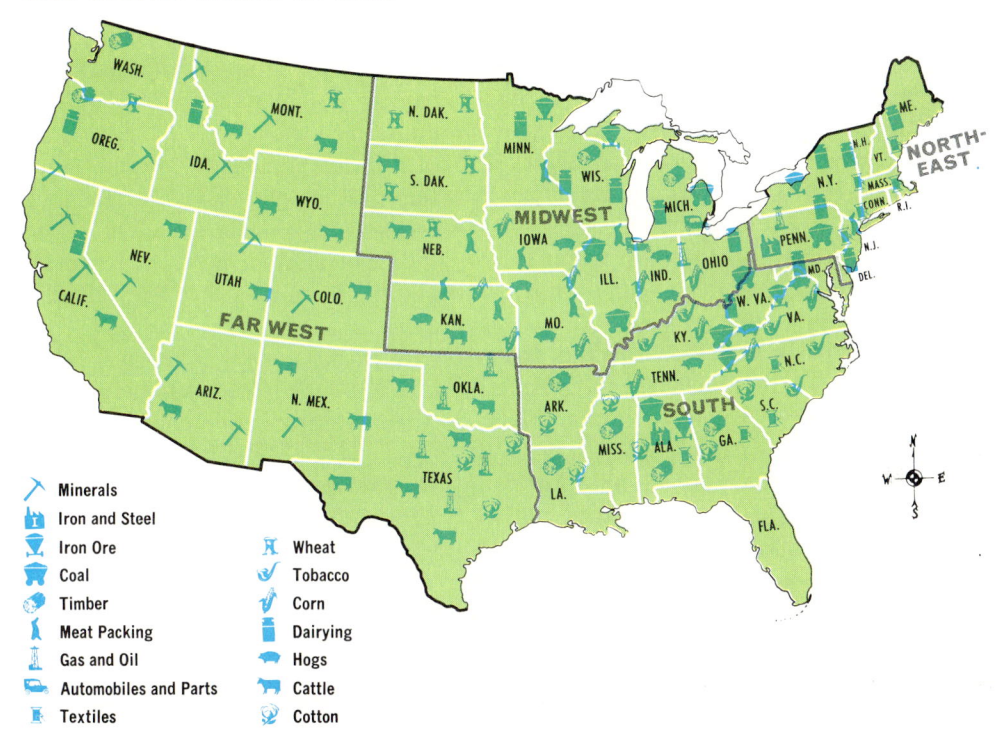

- Minerals
- Iron and Steel
- Iron Ore
- Coal
- Timber
- Meat Packing
- Gas and Oil
- Automobiles and Parts
- Textiles
- Wheat
- Tobacco
- Corn
- Dairying
- Hogs
- Cattle
- Cotton

B. Mastering the Map

Study the map above. Then answer these questions in your notebook.
1. What were the four geographic sections of the United States in 1916?
2. What were the main products of each section?
3. Which section had the largest area?
4. a. Which was the smallest section? b. Why was it important in spite of its small size?

SUMMING UP THE UNIT

How Did the United States Progress Between 1865 and 1916?

A. The Revolution in Industry. In the second half of the nineteenth century, American industry grew with amazing speed. The railroads and the iron and steel industry played an important part in this rapid growth. So did petroleum and electric power. They provided new sources of power to run machines and brought about amazing changes in transportation and communication. Still another important new development was mass production. It enabled industry to turn out great amounts of goods at lower prices. Thanks to their new industries, machines, and methods, Americans could enjoy more leisure and a higher standard of living than ever before.

B. Problems Arising from the Growth of Industry. Unfortunately, the rapid growth of American industry gave rise to some serious problems. One was the waste of our country's precious natural resources. Another was the power of big business people to take advantage of their workers, smaller business people, and consumers. Some big business people even built monopolies that controlled entire industries. Still another problem was the extremes of wealth and poverty in America. While a small number of Americans became millionaires, millions of other Americans remained poor.

The city workers probably benefited less from economic progress than any other group. A surplus of labor, caused by large-scale immigration, kept their wages low and their hours of work long. Working and living conditions, especially in the sweatshops and slums of big cities, were worse than they had ever been. So workers formed unions and called many strikes. But they won few victories before 1900. One of their victories was the establishment of a nation-wide labor organization, the American Federation of Labor.

C. The Revolution in Agriculture. A revolution in farming took place side by side with the revolution in industry. Miners, ranchers, and farmers settled the western half of our nation. Western farmers had to work especially hard. The land they settled had a harsh climate, light rainfall, and few trees. Thanks to improved farm machinery and methods, they finally turned the "Great American Desert" into one of the world's richest farming regions. But success brought with it other problems, namely overproduction and low prices. Western farmers also found themselves at the mercy of railroad companies, warehouses, and banks that overcharged them.

To change their situation, farmers formed the Granger movement, the Farmers' Alliances, and the Populist party. They asked for government regulation of the railroads, antitrust laws, and cheap money. They won some of their demands, but their situation improved only when overproduction ended.

D. The Politics of the Gilded Age. While the American economy was advancing, government was passing through a period of corruption and weakness. Congress voted only a few reforms between 1865 and 1900. These were the merit system, the Interstate Commerce Act, and the Sherman Antitrust Act. Reformers finally won control of the Democratic party in 1896. But the Republicans, who favored laws that helped big business, won the election.

E. The Humanitarian Movement. Until 1900 humanitarians and other reformers did more for progress than the government. Settlement-house workers like Jane Addams helped the poor in the large cities. The temperance movement fought to stamp out drinking among slum workers. The women's rights movement continued to press for votes for women. The muckrakers and other writers awakened the public to the need for reform in government and industry. The same period also saw rapid strides in public education. More and better schools resulted in a drop in illiteracy among Americans. Discontent among workers in this period also led to the founding of the Socialist party. Its goal was to end the capitalist system by taking ownership of property and resources from private hands and giving it to the government.

F. Achievements of the Progressive Era. When economic conditions improved after 1900, the influence of socialism decreased. People interested in reform turned instead to the new Progressive movement. Local, state, and federal governments, influenced by the Progressives, made a number of political and economic reforms during the next sixteen years.

The Progressives helped both city workers and farmers. Their basic idea, that the government was the servant of the people, was accepted by both major parties. The Progressives also succeeded in limiting the power of big business and political machines. Above all, they restored the people's faith in democracy. They proved that Americans could get the reforms they wanted if they were willing to organize and fight for them.

REVIEWING THE UNIT

A. Knowing New Terms

For each term in the first column, write in your notebook the *letter* of the item in the second column with which it belongs.

PART 1

1. Big business
2. Capitalism
3. Lockout
4. Monopoly
5. Panics
6. Socialism
7. Sweatshop

a. Antitrust laws
b. Free enterprise
c. Government ownership
d. Mass production
e. Piecework
f. Spoils system
g. Strike
h. Large-scale unemployment

PART 2

1. Agricultural Revolution
2. American Federation of Labor
3. "Bossism"
4. Civil service reform
5. Granger movement
6. Homestead Act
7. Knights of Labor
8. Populist party

a. "Aristocrats of labor"
b. Farmers' Alliances
c. Interstate Commerce Act
d. Merit system
e. New immigrants
f. "One big union"
g. Overproduction of wheat and corn
h. Passing of the frontier
i. Political machines

B. Knowing Important People

Choose the person who does *not* belong with the others in the group.

1. *Inventors:* Alexander Graham Bell, Thomas A. Edison, William M. Tweed, the Wright brothers
2. *Captains of industry:* Andrew Carnegie, Henry Ford, Uriah Stephens, John D. Rockefeller
3. *Presidents who favored civil service reform:* Chester A. Arthur, James A. Garfield, Ulysses S. Grant, Rutherford B. Hayes
4. *Muckrakers:* Lincoln Steffens, John Spargo, Ida Tarbell, Booker T. Washington
5. *Other famous American writers:* Edward Bellamy, Samuel Gompers, Louisa May Alcott, Mark Twain
6. *Presidents of the Progressive Era:* William Jennings Bryan, Theodore Roosevelt, William H. Taft, Woodrow Wilson

C. Knowing When Things Happened

Arrange the events in each group in the correct order.

A
1. Civil War
2. Gilded Age
3. Progressive Era

B
1. Invention of the electric light
2. Invention of the telegraph
3. Invention of the telephone

C
1. Ford's assembly line
2. Invention of the gasoline engine
3. First successful oil well

D
1. Formation of the A.F. of L.
2. Formation of the Knights of Labor
3. Great Railroad Strike

E
1. Completion of the first transcontinental railroad
2. Passage of the Homestead Act
3. Settling of Oklahoma Territory

F
1. Cattle Kingdom
2. Farming on the Great Plains
3. Mining Frontier

G
1. Formation of the Farmer's Alliances
2. Formation of the Granger movement
3. Organization of the Populist party

H
1. Civil Service Reform Act
2. Interstate Commerce Act
3. Sherman Antitrust Act

I	J
1. Administration of Theodore Roosevelt	1. Western states approve voting rights for women
2. Administration of William H. Taft	2. Most states begin to use the secret ballot system
3. Administration of Woodrow Wilson	3. Direct election of senators

D. Knowing Where Things Happened

Do the following on an outline map of the United States:

1. Use light blue or pencil shading to mark all large bodies of water.
2. Label: a. the Atlantic and Pacific oceans, Gulf of Mexico, Great Lakes; b. the Appalachian and Rocky mountains; c. the Mississippi, Ohio, Missouri, St. Lawrence, and Columbia rivers and the Rio Grande.
3. Use different colors to mark the four main regions—the Northeast, the South, the Midwest, and the Far West.
4. Use different kinds of pencil markings (▨   ▨   ▨   ▨) to show: a. regions with a great deal of industry; b. regions rich in mineral resources; c. regions important for food crops; d. main cotton- and tobacco-growing regions.
5. Make a key for your map.

MAKING HISTORY LIVE

1. Write a report on the life and achievements of one famous person mentioned in this unit. Be sure to describe the events or people that influenced the person you have selected. You may have to use the resources of your library for additional information.
2. a. Draw a cartoon showing how the Progressive movement helped the United States; or b. Draw a poster for one of the candidates in the presidential election of 1912.
3. Explain: a. Why socialism grew strong in many European countries; b. Why it did not become powerful in the United States.
4. Write a paragraph beginning with the words: "If there had been no Progressive movement, the United States might have . . ."
5. Write up notes for a debate or discussion on the question: Does the United States need a new Progressive movement today?
6. Contribute to a bulletin-board display on life in the United States during the period this unit covers.

RECOMMENDED READING

A. Historical Books

ADAMS, J. T., ed. *Album of American History, 1853–1893*. New York: Scribner, 1969.
AMERICAN HERITAGE. *Indians of the Plains*. New York: American Heritage, 1960.
ASIMOV, I. *The Golden Door: The United States from 1865–1918*. Boston: Houghton Mifflin, 1977.
BLUMENTHAL, S. *Coming to America: Immigrants from Eastern Europe*. New York: Delacorte Press, 1981.
BORNSTEIN, J. *Unions in Transition*. New York: Messner, 1981.
BUCK, S. J. *Agrarian Crusade: Farmers in Politics*. Chronicles of America, vol. 45. New York: U.S. Pubs.
CONRAT, M., and CONRAT, R. *The American Farm: A Photographic History*. Boston: Houghton Mifflin, 1977.
DEGLER, C. N. *The Age of the Economic Revolution: 1876–1900*. 2d ed. Glenview, Ill.: Scott, Foresman, 1977.
FARR, N., and DOSTERT, D. *The Industrial Era: 1865–1915*. Ed. L. W. Bloch. West Haven, Conn.: Pendulum Press, 1976.
GATEWOOD, W. B., Jr. *Black Americans and the White Man's Burden 1898–1903*. Champaign, Ill.: Univ. of Illinois Press, 1975.
GREENLEAF, B. K. *America Fever*. New York: Four Winds Press, 1970.
GURKO, M. *The Ladies of Seneca Falls*. New York: Macmillan, 1974.
HENDRICK, B. J. *The Age of Big Business*. Chronicles of America, vol. 39. New York: U.S. Pubs.
HOOBLER, D., and HOOBLER, T. *Photographing the Frontier*. New York: Putnam, 1980. Recording the settlement of the West.
HOWLAND, H. J. *Theodore Roosevelt and His Times*. Chronicles of America, vol. 47. New York: U.S. Pubs.
KATZ, W. L. *The Black West*. rev. ed. Garden City, N.Y.: Anchor Books/Doubleday, 1973.
LAVENDAR, D. S. *History of the Great West*. New York: American Heritage, 1965.
LEINWOLL, S. *From Spark to Satellite*. Ed. F. Shunaman. New York: Scribner, 1979.
MARZELL, E. S. *Great Inventions*. Minneapolis, Minn.: Lerner Pubns., 1973.
MILLER, D. C. *Ghost Towns of the Southwest: Arizona, New Mexico & Utah*. Boulder, Colo.: Pruett, 1980.
PARKMAN, F. *The Oregon Trail*. New York: Dodd, Mead, 1964. Life on the Great Plains and Rockies.
THOMPSON, H. *Age of Invention*. Chronicles of America, vol. 27. New York: U.S. Pubs.
WAITLEY, D. *The Roads We Traveled*. New York: Messner, 1979. The early days of the automobile.
WARE, N. *The Labor Movement in the United States 1860–1895*. Magnolia, Mass.: Peter Smith, n.d.

B. Biographies and Autobiographies

BALDWIN, M., and O'BRIEN, P. *Wanted!* New York: Messner, 1981.
BROWN, D. *The Westerners*. New York: Holt, Rinehart & Winston, 1974. From the Conquistadores to wagon trains and Indian fighters.
COMMAGER, H. S. *Crusaders for Freedom*. Garden City, N.Y.: Doubleday, 1962.
CURRIE, B. *Railroads and Cowboys in the American West*. Ed. M. Reeves. New York: Longman, 1974.

Davis, A. F. *American Heroine: The Life and Legend of Jane Addams.* New York: Oxford Univ. Press, 1975.

Earp, W. S. *Wyatt Earp: His Autobiography.* Ed. G. G. Boyer. Bisbee, Ariz.: Yoma V. Bissette, 1981.

Farr, N. C. *Thomas Edison—Alexander Graham Bell.* West Haven, Conn.: Pendulum Press, 1979.

Fielder, L., et. al. *Buffalo Bill & the Wild West.* Pittsburg: Univ. of Pittsburg Press, 1982.

Grant, M. G. *Elizabeth Blackwell.* Mankato, Minn.: Creative Education, 1974.

Horan, J. D. *The Authentic Wild West: The Outlaws.* Vol. 2. New York: Crown, 1977.

Kaplan, J. *Mark Twain and His World.* New York: Crown, 1983.

Kurland, G. *John D. Rockefeller: Nineteenth Century Industrialist and Oil Baron.* Ed. D. S. Rahmas. Outstanding Personality Series #35. Charlotteville, N.Y.: SamHar Press, 1972.

Lerner, G., ed. *Black Women in White America.* New York: Random House, 1972. A history in their own words.

McCullough, D. *Mornings on Horseback.* New York: Simon & Schuster, 1981. The young manhood of Teddy Roosevelt.

Meltzer, M. *Taking Root.* New York: Farrar, Straus & Giroux, 1976. Jewish immigrants in America.

Merriam, E., ed. *Growing Up Female in America.* Garden City, N.Y.: Doubleday, 1971. Ten lives, in ten different times.

Morrison, D. N. *Chief Sarah.* New York: Atheneum, 1980. Her fight for Indian rights.

Morrison, J., and Zabusky, C. F. *American Mosaic.* New York: Dutton, 1980. Personal stories of immigrants.

Swetnam, G. *Andrew Carnegie.* Boston: Twayne Publications, 1980.

Washington, B. T. *Up From Slavery.* Garden City, N.Y.: Doubleday, 1963.

Weisberger, B. P. *Captains of Industry.* New York: American Heritage, 1966.

Werstein, I. *Labor's Defiant Lady.* New York: Crowell, 1969. Mary Harris, who made the picket line her battlefield.

Wilson, D. *Bright Eyes: The Story of Susette La Flesche.* New York: McGraw-Hill, 1974. Omaha Indian fighting racism and the atrocities committed against her people.

C. Historical Fiction

Adams, S. H. *Pony Express.* New York: Random House, 1953.

Alcott, L. M. *Little Women.* Various editions.

Bellamy, E. *Looking Backward.* Various editions.

Brand, M. [F. S. Faust] *Best Western Stories.* New York: Dodd, Mead, 1981.

Cohen, D. *The Great Airship Mystery.* New York: Dodd, Mead, 1981. A UFO of the 1890's.

Curtis, E. S., and Bierhorst, J., eds. *The Girl Who Married a Ghost.* New York: Four Winds Press, 1978. Indian folk tales, illustrated with photographs.

Finney, J. *Time and Again.* New York: Simon & Schuster, 1970. A fantasy of New York City in 1882.

Forman, J. *People of the Dream.* New York: Farrar, Straus & Giroux, 1972.

Gipson, F. *Old Yeller.* New York: Harper & Row, 1964. A dog's-eye view of the Old West.

Murphy, C. G. *Buffalo Grass.* New York: Dial, 1966. Buffalo hunters on the Great Plains.

Snow, R. *The Burning.* Garden City, N.Y.: Doubleday, 1981. The destruction of a lumber town by fire.

Strete, C. *The Bleeding Man.* New York: Greenwillow, 1974. Science fiction stories based on American Indian legends.

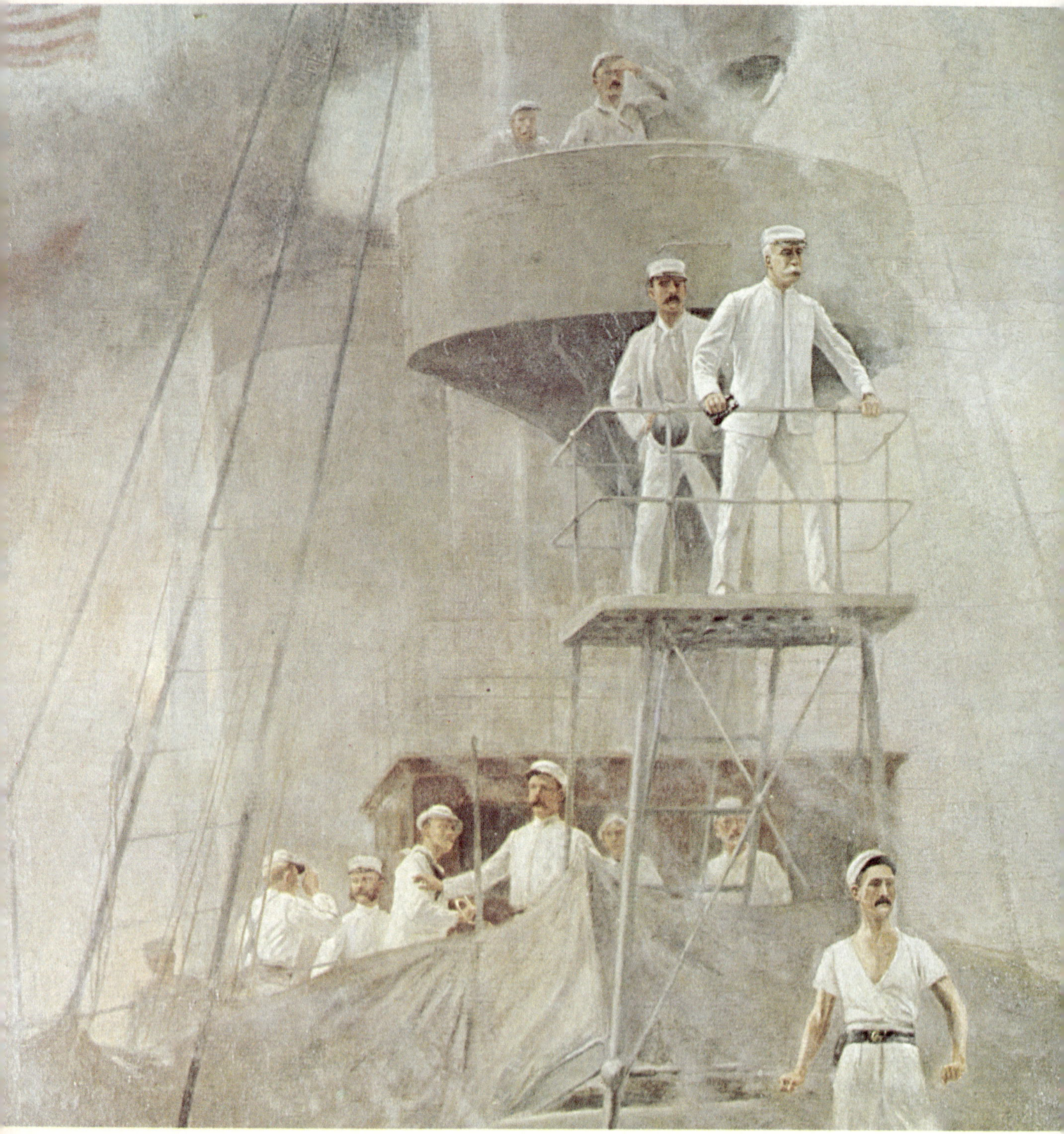

Unit Six

OUR NEW FOREIGN POLICY

When George Washington was President, the French government asked the United States for help in a war against Great Britain and other European countries. France had helped the United States to defeat Great Britain in the Revolutionary War only a few years earlier. Yet President Washington refused the French request. He declared that the United States would help neither side in the war. It would stay neutral. He also warned the American people to "steer clear" of Europe's troubles.

The policy begun by Washington later came to be known as isolationism. It got that name because our country isolated itself (kept itself apart) from foreign nations. Though it traded with them, it refused to sign any alliances. When wars and other disputes between nations arose, it stayed neutral.

Isolationism remained the basis of our country's foreign policy (its relations with other nations) for a long time. In the second half of the nineteenth century, however, this policy began to change.

Admiral Dewey's defeat of the Spanish fleet at Manila showed that the United States had become a world power. What are some of the problems and advantages of being a world power?

In this unit we shall see the following:
1. *Why American foreign policy changed*
2. *How the United States was drawn into the affairs of foreign nations—first in the Far East, then in Latin America, and finally in Europe*
3. *Why the American people were disappointed with the new policy and tried to return to isolationism after the First World War*

UNIT 6: 1789-1932

1793	• Washington's Proclamation of Neutrality
1807	• Jefferson's embargo
1812	• War with Great Britain
1823	• Monroe Doctrine
1841	• Opening of China by Great Britain
1853	• Opening of Japan by Commodore Perry
1867	• Purchase of Alaska
1889	• Pan-American Union
1898	• Spanish-American War Open Door policy in China
1903	• Panama Canal Treaty
1914	• Start of World War I
1917	• United States enters World War I
1919	• Paris Peace Conference League of Nations
1931-1932	• Japan's conquest of Manchuria

Chapter 25

AMERICA ACQUIRES AN EMPIRE

IN THE 1790s, when Washington started the policy of isolationism, the United States was a young and weak nation. It needed a long period of peace to develop a strong government and prosperous economy. At that time, moreover, it took several weeks to cross the Atlantic Ocean. This physical separation from Europe made it easier for the United States to stay out of European affairs. During the next hundred years, the American people worked hard to build their nation. They moved westward to the Pacific, turned a vast wilderness into farmland, and built many great industrial cities. Busy with affairs at home, they saw little reason to change the policy of isolationism their first President had begun.

By the end of the nineteenth century, however, the United States had become one of the largest and most powerful nations in the world. The Atlantic Ocean had "shrunk" as steamships cut the time required to cross it to a few days. Because of the Economic Revolution, American trade with other nations had grown by leaps and bounds. It reached a total of over two billion dollars in 1900.

As conditions changed, American foreign policy also changed. The United States became involved with other nations. There were three main reasons for this change in policy—to increase American trade, to help less developed lands, and to show that the United States was a great power. As Theodore Roosevelt put it:

In foreign affairs we must make up our minds that, whether we wish it or not, we are a great people and must play a great part in the world. It is not open to us to choose whether we will play that part or not. We have to play it. All we can decide is whether we shall play it well or ill.

In this chapter we shall see how the United States first took up the role of a world power.

How Did the United States Become Involved in the Far East?

A. The "Opening" of China. In the eighteenth century, China was the largest and most populous country in the world. Europeans were eager to obtain its silk, tea, and other valuable products. They were also eager to use its several hundred million people as a market for European goods. But the Chinese government did not trust the "Westerners" (people from lands to the west of China). So it limited their trade and did not allow them to enter the country.

During the nineteenth century, however, the Chinese government was weakened by revolts and other troubles. The European powers took advantage of its weakness. British merchants, for example, made large profits by selling opium, a harmful drug, to the Chinese people.

When Chinese officials tried in 1840 to stop this trade, Great Britain sent a fleet to protect its merchants. A war followed, which the British easily won. The defeated Chinese were forced to open some of their main ports to foreign trade. The result was a great increase in trade with China for American merchants, as well as for Europeans. The fast American clipper ships brought furs and other raw materials to China. They brought back valuable cargoes of fine Chinese goods.

B. The "Opening" of Japan. The islands of Japan lie only a short distance from the coast of China. Their large population made them, like China, a profitable market for Western businesses. The Japanese, however, were even more suspicious of Westerners than the Chinese were. To keep out the foreigners, they even killed sailors who happened to be shipwrecked on their shores.

In 1852 the President of the United States sent a naval force under Commodore Matthew C. Perry to Japan. Perry's orders were to make a treaty opening Japan to American traders and giving protection to American sailors. Perry decided not to use force. Instead, he impressed the Japanese by giving their rulers modern weapons and machines. He was surprisingly successful. The Japanese agreed to open their ports and to protect foreign sailors. Even more important, they began to "westernize" their country— that is, make it more like the countries of the West. Japan's progress was so rapid that it soon became a powerful nation. It even became a rival of the Europeans and Americans in China.

C. Our First Overseas Colonies. 1. THE HAWAIIAN ISLANDS. The trip from New England to the Far East, around the tip of Africa or South America, was a very long one. Ships needed places along the way where they could stop to make repairs and get fresh food and water. In the 1820s American sailors established a base at Honolulu in the Hawaiian Islands (see map on this page). This base also became a center for whaling in the South Pacific. So many Americans settled there that the town of Honolulu, a visitor said, looked like a New England seaport.

The descendants of the early American settlers started sugar plantations in Hawaii. They also built a large trade with the United States. Hawaiians, ruled by Queen Liliuokalani, were alarmed by the wealth and power of the "Americans" as they were still called. She tried to limit the activities of the "Americans." But they revolted and seized power. They asked the United States to annex (take over) the Hawaiian Islands. Congress did so in 1898. Hawaii was our first important possession outside the continent of North America.

2. OTHER POSSESSIONS IN THE PACIFIC. American sailors had also established bases on a number of other islands in the Pacific. One base was located in the Samoan Islands (see map right). The British and Germans, who had also set up bases there, were hostile to the Americans. On one occasion fighting almost broke out between American and German warships. In 1899, however, the three powers settled their differences by dividing the islands.

In the same year, the United States took the Philippine Islands and Guam from Spain (see page 442). A year later, our nation annexed Wake, an island in the Central Pacific. Together with Hawaii, Guam, Midway, and the Philippines, Wake Island provided American sailors with a "stepping stone" across the Pacific Ocean to China, Japan, and other parts of Asia (see map right).

Liliuokalani, the last ruling monarch of the Hawaiian Islands. Why was she forced to give up her royal power?

UNITED STATES
PACIFIC POSSESSIONS IN 1900

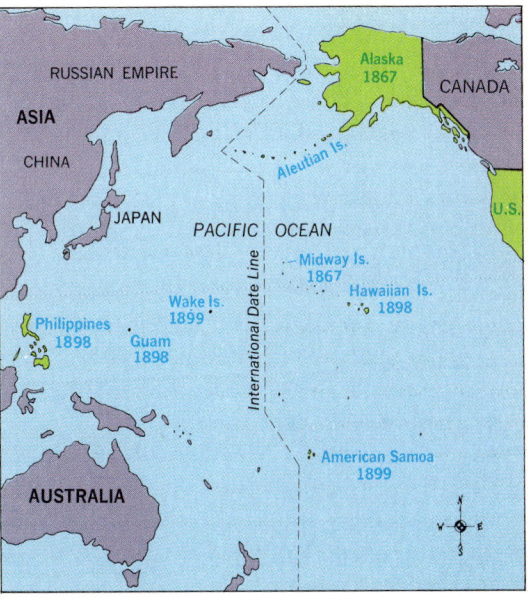

435

D. American Defense of China. 1. THE OPEN DOOR POLICY (1899). By this time, China was so weak that Japan and the great European powers were able to control large parts of its territory. Their activities threatened to cut off America's rich trade with China. Alarmed, President McKinley's secretary of state sent them a note stating that all nations should have an equal right to trade with China. His statement became known as the "Open Door" Policy because it tried to keep the door of China open to all foreign trade.

2. THE BOXER UPRISING (1900). The Chinese government also tried very hard to save itself. It encouraged secret societies, called the "Boxers," to drive out the "foreign devils." The Boxers murdered more than two hundred foreigners and destroyed much foreign property. But then the powers sent in troops equipped with modern weapons. They easily crushed the Boxer Uprising.

The United States now had even greater reason to be alarmed. It looked as if the other powers would use the Boxer Uprising as an excuse to take over more Chinese territory. Our government therefore insisted that China should only have to pay for the damage the Boxers had done. Great Britain, which also wanted to keep China open to trade, backed the American position. The powers agreed to collect damages of $300,000,000. The American share was about $25,000,000. This amount proved to be much larger than the real damages to American citizens and their property. So the United States returned most of the money to the Chinese government, which used it to send Chinese students to American colleges. Because of this generous action and the Open Door Policy, the United States gained the good will of many educated Chinese.

E. Troubled Relations with Japan. 1. THE RUSSO-JAPANESE WAR. American relations with Japan, on the other hand, started off well but gradually went bad. In 1904 Japan and Russia went to war over some Chinese territory which both countries wanted. Most Americans hoped that their "little friend" would not be "crushed by the Russian bear." To their surprise, Japan won a series of smashing victories, both on land and on the sea. But the war was very costly, and Japan was a poor nation. Its government secretly asked President Roosevelt to help arrange a peace settlement.

"Teddy" arranged for the Russians to meet with the Japanese in the United States. After a good deal of bargaining, the two powers agreed on peace terms. The Japanese received some territory, but they could not get the Russians to agree to pay their war costs. They put the blame for their failure on President Roosevelt. Demonstrations against America broke out in Japan.

2. DISCRIMINATION IN THE UNITED STATES AGAINST THE JAPANESE. At the same time, a second source of trouble was developing in the United States. About 75,000 Japanese had settled on the West Coast. Still more were coming each year. The Japanese worked hard and behaved well. But their growing number alarmed the people on the West Coast. States and towns began to pass laws discriminating against them. The state of California, for example, would not allow them to buy land. The city of San Francisco made Japanese school children, even though there were less than a hundred of them, attend a separate school. The Japanese government, angered by these insults to its citizens, made a strong protest to our government.

TR, as usual, acted quickly. He persuaded California and San Francisco to make changes in their laws. He also won an agreement from the Japanese government to stop emigration to the United States. These actions helped our relations with Japan for a short time. But discrimination against Japanese citizens on the West Coast and Japan's ambitions to take over large parts of China continued to make trouble for many years.

REVIEWING THE SECTION

A. Knowing New Terms

In your notebook write the new terms in this section that best complete these statements.

1. For more than a hundred years, the United States avoided alliances with other nations. This policy has been called _____.
2. A nation that helps neither side in a war is said to be _____.
3. A nation's way of dealing with other nations is called its _____ _____.
4. Since Europe is located to the west of Asia, the Chinese called Europeans _____.
5. The American government tried to keep other powers from shutting off its trade with China by announcing the _____ _____ Policy.
6. The Chinese tried to drive out foreigners in 1900 by means of the _____ _____.
7. The United States again became involved in Far Eastern affairs when President Roosevelt helped to end the _____ War.

B. Understanding the Facts

PART 1. In your notebook complete the following chart comparing the reasons for American foreign policy in 1790 and in 1900.

Reasons for Isolationism in 1790	Reasons for a Changed Foreign Policy in 1900
1. The United States was a young, weak nation.	1.
2. Crossing the Atlantic took several weeks.	2.
3. The American people were busy settling the West and developing their economy.	3.

PART 2. Historians give three main reasons why the United States, like the European powers, wanted overseas possessions: a. *economic* reasons—to help businesses; b. *nationalistic* reasons—to please patriotic citizens; c. *humanitarian* reasons—to help other peoples. Write in your notebook which reason lies behind each of the following statements.

1. Americans wanted to obtain silk, tea, and other valuable products from China.
2. China was considered a great market because of its huge population.

3. Japan was also considered valuable because of its large population.
4. The Japanese were killing American sailors shipwrecked on their shores.
5. The Hawaiian Islands became a base for American merchant and whaling ships.
6. People of American descent overthrew the government of Queen Liliuokalani and asked the United States to annex the Hawaiian Islands.
7. The Samoan Islands were a center for trade in the South Pacific.
8. The United States, Germany, and Great Britain were rivals for possession of the Samoan Islands.
9. Hawaii, the Philippines, Guam, Midway, and Wake were valuable as "stepping stones" for ships crossing the Pacific to the Far East.
10. American missionaries went to the newly acquired islands to teach the natives Christianity.
11. Our government asked that China be kept open to foreign trade.
12. The United States asked the powers not to take over Chinese territory as punishment for the Boxer Uprising.
13. President Roosevelt helped to end the Russo-Japanese War.
14. The United States did not want Japan to become too powerful in China.

Conclusion. Which was the most important reason for American actions in the late nineteenth century?

IMPROVING YOUR SKILLS

A. Reading the Time Line

Study the time line on page 432. Then answer the following questions.
1. When did the American policy of isolation begin?
2. When did the United States first become involved in the Far East?
3. When did the United States acquire most of its overseas possessions?
4. During which ten-year period did the United States follow an active foreign policy both in the Far East and in Latin America?
5. When did the United States become actively involved in European affairs?

B. Mastering the Map

Study the map on page 435. Then answer the following questions.
1. Which American possessions served as "stepping stones" across the Pacific Ocean to the Far East?
2. Which was the northernmost of our Pacific possessions?
3. Which was the southernmost of our Pacific possessions?

Was the Spanish-American War Justified?

A. An Easily Won War.

"One, two, three, and Cuba will be free,
There'll be a hot time in the old town tonight."

These lines from a popular song of the time show the light-hearted spirit of the American people when they entered the Spanish-American War in 1898. They were sure that the United States would quickly defeat Spain and free Cuba. They were right. The United States won a quick and easy victory. But this victory had some unexpected results. In this section you will learn both the causes and the results of the war with Spain.

B. Causes of the Spanish-American War.

1. THE CUBAN STRUGGLE FOR INDEPENDENCE. The causes of the Spanish-American War go back to the 1820s, the period when most of Spain's empire in the Americas won its freedom. Cuba, the largest and most valuable possession still under Spanish rule, also wanted to be free. The Cuban people had good reason to be dissatisfied with Spanish rule. Though their island was rich, they were poor. Most of the wealth they produced went to the Spaniards who owned the large plantations. Yet they had to pay heavy taxes to support corrupt Spanish officials and a large Spanish army.

The Cubans rebelled several times. One revolt lasted ten years (from 1868 to 1878), but it won only a few reforms. Another revolt broke out in 1895. High American tariffs on sugar and tobacco, Cuba's main cash crops, were partly to blame. When the prices of these products rose, Americans bought less. Many Cuban workers lost their jobs as a result. Others, though they were making only a bare living, had to take a cut in wages. In despair, thousands of them joined the struggle for independence. The rebels hid in the mountains and staged many guerrilla raids on Spanish troops and property.

2. REASONS FOR AMERICAN INVOLVEMENT. The United States could not shut its eyes to developments in Cuba. The island was on our doorstep, only ninety miles from Florida (see map, page 441). Americans had already invested some $50,000,000 there, mainly in plantations and sugar refineries. The yearly trade between the United States and Cuba was twice that amount.

The Cuban rebels tried very hard to draw the United States into the struggle. They made raids on American property. Thousands of them came to the United States and became American citizens, but continued the fight for freedom. They smuggled arms into Cuba and made raids along its coasts. If they were caught, they claimed the protection of the American government as American citizens. To put a stop to these troubles, Presidents Cleveland and McKinley both offered to help the Spanish government settle the war. But the proud Spaniards refused their help.

3. INFLUENCE OF THE "YELLOW PRESS." The American people sympathized with the Cubans from the start. American newspapers, especially a few sensational newspapers known as the "yellow press," played on these sympathies. They reported that the Spanish com-

mander had put the people of entire villages into special camps to keep them from helping the guerrillas. Without food, water, and medicines, thousands of them, including women and children, died. The yellow press described their sufferings in great detail. It also told exaggerated, or even untrue, stories about tortures Cubans suffered at the hands of Spanish soldiers. These stories aroused great hostility against the Spaniards in the United States.

4. TWO UNFORTUNATE INCIDENTS. American feeling reached a fever pitch early in 1898 because of two unfortunate incidents. One was the de Lôme letter; the other was the sinking of the *Maine*. Señor de Lôme was a high Spanish official in the United States. In a letter to a friend in Cuba, he called President McKinley, among other things, "weak, a bidder for the admiration of the crowd, a would-be politician." The de Lôme letter was stolen from the mails by a Cuban and printed on the front page of a leading yellow newspaper, the *New York Journal*. The Spanish government apologized at once and recalled de Lôme. But the American people were angered by the insult to their President.

Less than a week later the American battleship *Maine,* which had been sent to Cuba to protect American citizens, was sunk by an explosion. Two hundred and sixty American sailors died. The cause of the explosion remains unknown to this day. Nevertheless, the *Journal*'s headline read: "The warship *Maine* was split in two by an enemy's secret infernal machine!" Most Americans were sure that Spain was responsible for the sinking. "Remember the *Maine*" became an American battle cry.

Fearing war, the Spanish government finally agreed to accept American terms for ending the Cuban rebellion. President McKinley, together with many high officials and leading business people, did not want war. But the President gave in to the storm of public demands for action. He asked Congress to act against Spain, and it voted for war. Congress made it clear that the United States did not intend to annex Cuba. Once peace was won, it stated, the United States would "leave the government and control of the Island to the people."

C. The Opposing Sides. Once again, war found the United States poorly prepared. Soldiers were supplied with old rifles, canned meat almost impossible to eat, and woolen uniforms too warm for a war in the tropics. Many of the officers were either too old or not very able. Unsanitary conditions in army camps led to outbreaks of disease. These killed ten times as many Americans as the actual fighting. Nevertheless, our army easily crushed the poorly led and battle-weary Spanish forces.

Our navy did even better, mainly because it had a number of new steel ships (see page 394). Despite its lack of war experience, it

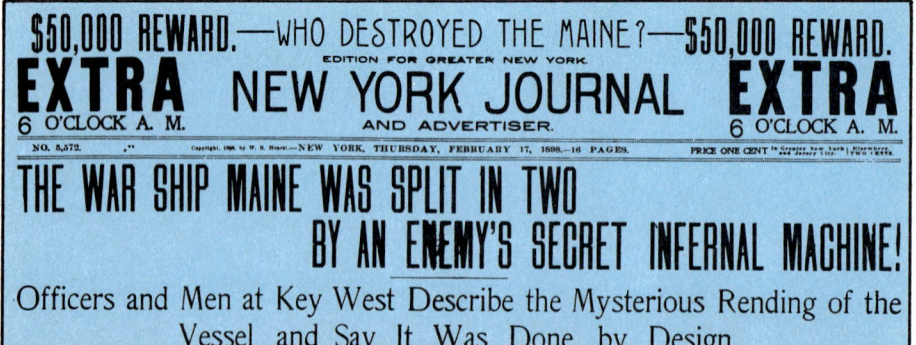

Lead article, *New York Journal,* February 17, 1898. Why was this front-page story misleading? How did articles like it help cause the Spanish-American War?

easily defeated the Spanish fleet, which still had many wooden vessels.

D. The Major Battles. The Spanish-American War had only a few major battles. Strangely enough, the first battle was fought halfway around the world from Cuba. Assistant Secretary of the Navy Roosevelt, expecting the war, had ordered the Pacific fleet to stand by for action. As soon as war was declared, Admiral George Dewey set sail for the Philippine Islands (see map, page 435). Boldly entering Manila Bay, he destroyed the entire Spanish fleet anchored there. Not a single American was killed in the battle, and only seven were wounded. A few weeks later American troops took the city of Manila, capital of the Philippines.

The next two battles were fought in Cuba. There the American army slowly fought its way toward the key port of Santiago. It was in this fighting that TR and his Rough Riders won fame by charging up San Juan Hill. Meanwhile, an American fleet had trapped Spain's Atlantic fleet in the harbor of Santiago. When the American army captured the heights overlooking the harbor, the Spanish admiral decided to risk death by fleeing rather than surrender. As his ships steamed one by one out of the narrow harbor, they were destroyed by the waiting American fleet. American casualties were only two men—one killed, the other wounded.

The final campaign was the American invasion of Puerto Rico, only a short distance from Cuba. Our troops were welcomed by the people and met with almost no military opposition. By this time, Spain was ready to surrender. An armistice (agreement to stop fighting) was signed only four months after the war began.

SPANISH-AMERICAN WAR

Spanish-American War in the Caribbean

Spanish-American War in the Pacific

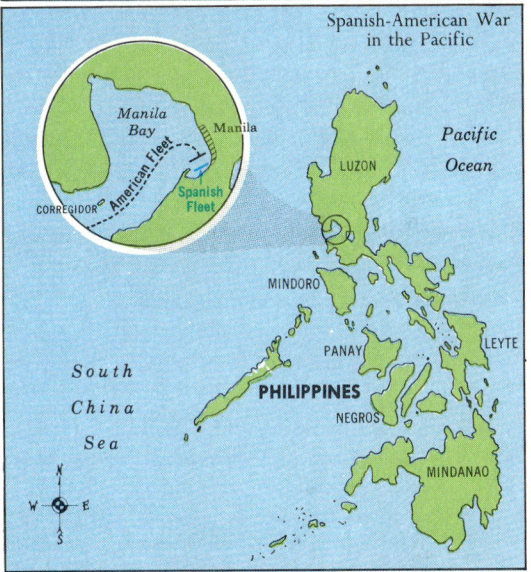

Teddy Roosevelt and his "Rough Riders" the day after the battle of San Juan Hill.

E. Results of the War. The Spanish-American War has been called "a little war with big results." Spain agreed to give Cuba its freedom. It also gave the United States Puerto Rico, Guam, and the Philippine Islands. (Our government agreed to pay $20,000,000 for the Philippines.) Thus the United States gained a sizable empire.

Another result of the Spanish-American War was that the United States now found itself responsible for Cuba. American military rule of the island lasted for over three years. During this time, the United States Army fed the Cuban people and built roads and public schools. Even more important, army medical teams set out to control diseases like yellow fever and typhoid that had killed off several thousand American soldiers. By using brave human volunteers, Major Walter Reed proved that yellow fever was carried by a certain type of mosquito. Colonel William C. Gorgas cleaned up the breeding grounds of the mosquito. He also eliminated the unsanitary conditions that had caused typhoid and other diseases. The health of the Cuban people greatly improved, and their numbers increased rapidly. Our government also helped the island's economy by reducing the tariff on Cuban sugar. Soon American businesses began to invest heavily in sugar plantations.

Before the army withdrew, the new Cuban government signed a special agreement with the United States. Cuba agreed not to make any treaty that would weaken its independence. It also agreed not to borrow more money from foreign nations than it could repay. Moreover, it gave the United States the right to start a naval base on Cuban territory. As the site for this base, the navy chose Guantanamo Bay, which it still holds today. Finally, Cuba gave the United States the right to step into Cuban affairs if it thought that either law and order or the island's independence was threatened. In short, Cuba became an American protectorate—that is, a country under the protection of the United States—rather than a completely independent nation.

The Spanish-American War also had several other important, though unexpected, results: 1. Thanks to the strength shown by our navy, the United States was now recognized as a great power. 2. Our nation became much more actively involved in foreign affairs than before. 3. As we shall soon see, our government faced some difficult problems in governing its new empire.

REVIEWING THE SECTION

A. Knowing New Terms

In your notebook write the meaning of each new term or *phrase* in your own words.

(In **B2**) on our doorstep
(In **B3**) yellow press
(In **B4**) de Lôme letter
　　　　　 sinking of the *Maine*
(In **E**) protectorate

B. Knowing Important People

For each important person in the first column, write the *letter* of the best description in the second column.

Important People
1. George Dewey
2. William C. Gorgas
3. William McKinley
4. Walter Reed
5. Theodore Roosevelt

Descriptions
a. Asked Congress to take strong action against Spain
b. Defeated the Spanish fleet in the Philippines
c. Discovered the cause of yellow fever
d. Greatly reduced yellow fever and typhoid in Cuba
e. Opened Japan to foreign trade
f. Ordered our Pacific fleet to be ready for action against the Spanish fleet in the Philippines

C. Finding the Reasons

In your notebook write the letters of *all* the correct answers to each question.

1. Why did the Cuban people revolt against Spanish rule?
   a. Wealthy Spaniards owned large plantations and paid their Cuban workers very low wages. b. Corrupt Spanish officials taxed the Cuban people heavily. c. High American tariffs caused unemployment and wage cuts in Cuba.
2. Why was it hard for the United States to stay out of Cuban affairs?
   a. Cuba is very near the United States. b. American businesses had large economic interests there. c. Cuban revolutionaries used tactics designed to involve the United States.
3. Why did the United States declare war on Spain in 1898?
   a. American businesses wanted war as an excuse to take over Cuba and the Philippines. b. The American people sympathized with the sufferings of the Cuban people under Spanish rule. c. The Spanish government refused to apologize for the de Lôme letter or accept American offers to help end the Cuban rebellion.
4. Why did the United States easily defeat Spain?
   a. The United States was well prepared for the war. b. Most American commanders were experienced and able. c. Spain had a very weak army and navy.
5. Why was the Spanish-American War important?
   a. The United States gained a good deal of territory. b. Europeans now saw that the United States had become a great nation. c. Colonial peoples all over the world looked to the United States to help them gain their freedom.

D. Understanding the Facts

Complete this chart by giving reasons for and against the American declaration of war on Spain.

Reasons for the Declaration of War	Reasons Against the Declaration of War

1. American interest in Cuba
   a.
   b.
2. American sympathy for the sufferings of the Cuban people
3. Influence of the yellow press
4. Two incidents
   a.
   b.
	1.
	
	2.
	
	3.
	4.

Conclusion. On the whole, do you think the United States was justified in declaring war on Spain or not? Explain why you reached that conclusion.

IMPROVING YOUR SKILLS

A. Mastering the Map

Study the map on page 441. Then complete the following statements.

1. The Americans who attacked Cuba captured the port of _____, at the _____ end of the island.
2. To the east of Cuba lies the island of Hispaniola, which contains two little countries, _____ and the _____ _____.
3. To the east of Hispaniola is another island that the United States took in the Spanish-American War, _____ _____.
4. Other islands in the West Indies were _____ possessions.
5. In the Philippines, Americans took the port of _____.

B. Telling Facts From Opinions

Write "Fact" for each statement that can be proved by getting the necessary information. Write "Opinion" if you think the answer depends on values and judgment. (For a review, see pages 237–238.)

1. The average American had little interest in Cuba before 1895.
2. The Cubans were justified in revolting against Spanish rule.
3. America was partly responsible for the Cuban revolution of 1895.

4. The interests of American businesses in Cuba were one of the basic causes of the Spanish-American War.
5. The United States might have stayed out of the war by refusing American citizenship to Cuban refugees.
6. The war could have been avoided if the yellow press had not stirred up the American people.
7. The de Lôme letter and the sinking of the *Maine* were the immediate causes of the Spanish-American War.
8. "Teddy" Roosevelt played an important part in our taking of the Philippines.
9. America had to make a protectorate of Cuba to protect American interests there.
10. The American occupation brought important benefits to the Cuban people.

How Has the United States Governed Its Possessions?

A. The Debate Over the Colonies. President McKinley had a hard decision to make in 1899. Should the United States keep the Philippines, return them to Spain, or give them their independence? As we know, he decided to keep the Philippines, as well as Puerto Rico and Guam. His decision became the main issue in the election of 1900.

"Don't haul down the flag"—that is, don't give up the new overseas possessions—was the chief Republican slogan in the election. The Republicans argued that there were good reasons for keeping the new colonies. They could serve the nation as military bases. They might also be valuable as sources of raw materials and markets for American industry. Their people, the Republicans said, would surely benefit from American rule.

The Democrats, led by William Jennings Bryan, tried to disprove each of these arguments. "The colonies will weaken the United States militarily," they said. "Being so far from our shores, they will be hard to defend. They will also be a heavy expense to the United States. A few businessmen will probably profit from trade and investments. But the government will spend much more to protect and develop the colonies than American business will make. Finally, their people are different from us. They are not ready to govern themselves. We shall have to rule over them, and in doing so we shall have to violate our democratic ideals. In spite of our sacrifices, the people of the colonies will dislike us because they will want their freedom."

As we know, the Republican candidates, McKinley and Roosevelt, won the election of 1900 by a wide margin. But they soon found

445

themselves facing some of the problems the Democrats had foreseen.

B. The Question of Self-Government. One problem arose at once: Were the people of the colonies entitled to the same democratic rights as Americans? If a person in the Philippines committed murder, for example, was he or she to be tried by a jury of fellow Filipinos? Several cases of this sort soon reached the Supreme Court. The Court ruled that the people of our new island possessions were *not* American citizens. Congress was therefore free to deal with them as it thought best, provided only that it respected their basic rights as human beings.

Congress gradually worked out a way of governing the possessions by stages or steps. The first step was rule by a governor appointed by the President of the United States. The people had only limited rights. They might be allowed to elect an assembly to advise the governor. But the governor was responsible for all decisions. Only the federal government—the President, Congress, or Supreme Court—could check the governor's actions. The people of the possession did not have any right to be represented in the federal government.

In the second step, Congress declared the possession a "territory," just like the old Northwest Territory (see page 103). This meant that the people became American citizens with full democratic rights. They could travel freely on American soil and sell their goods in the United States without paying tariffs. They could also elect their own legislature and a delegate to sit in the House of Representatives. The governor, however, was still appointed by the President. Acts of the territorial legislature could be vetoed by the governor, the President, and Congress.

The final step was for the territory to gain complete self-government. If it became a state, its citizens could elect their own governor, as well as their legislature. They had complete control of all domestic affairs, subject only to the limits set by the Constitution. They elected members to both houses of Congress and took part in presidential elections. In short, they had all the same rights as the older states.

In practice, Congress applied this step-by-step procedure in a very free way. That is, it dealt with each possession according to its needs and its readiness to govern itself. Thus the Hawaiian Islands became a territory as soon as they were annexed in 1898. Some possessions—mainly small places valuable as military bases—are still ruled by an American governor today. To see how this procedure has actually worked, let us examine the way Congress has dealt with our main possessions outside the American mainland, including Alaska.

C. Statehood for Alaska and Hawaii. Alaska was treated like a territory from the time it was purchased from Russia in 1867 (see page 328). For the next thirty years, however, few Americans settled there because of the cold climate. Gold strikes in 1896 and 1899 eventually brought thousands of prospectors to Alaska. Many of them stayed on. They built up the salmon fishing industry and the fur trade. In 1912 Alaska had enough people to elect a territorial legislature and a delegate to the House of Representatives.

Population increased again in the 1930s and 1940s. When many Americans lost their farms during the Great Depression of the 1930s, the federal government encouraged them to settle in southern Alaska. Here the climate was milder than most people thought. During World War II, the United States Army built airfields and bases in Alaska because of its nearness to Japan. Many veterans stayed on after the war as workers, farmers, or business people. In 1959, when Alaska finally had about 200,000 people, Congress admitted it to the Union as the forty-ninth state.

The Hawaiian Islands, because they were ruled by people of American descent, were

Mount McKinley in Alaska. The 1867 price for Alaska was about two cents an acre. Since then, Alaska has produced billions of dollars worth of gold, oil, fish, and timber. Why does Alaska's location make it important militarily?

made a territory from the start. Since Hawaiians could ship goods to the United States without paying tariffs, their sugar and pineapple plantations prospered. The pleasant, sunny climate and beautiful scenery also helped them to build a rich tourist trade. They had a third important source of income in the great American naval base at Pearl Harbor.

Despite Hawaii's prosperity, Congress delayed its admission as a state. The main reason was that so many Japanese and Filipinos had settled there. Congress felt that the newcomers needed time to become Americanized. Hawaii finally became the fiftieth state in 1959, only a few months after Alaska.

D. Independence for the Philippines. Of all the new possessions, the Philippines presented the most difficult problems. They were made up largely of mountainous and jungle-covered islands. Their people were a mixture of many groups speaking different languages and belonging to different religions. In the north, most of the Filipinos were Roman Catholics. Some of them spoke Spanish and had a Latin culture. In the south many were Moslems. In other places there were different cultures, or ways of life. Spain had done little to improve living conditions. Most of the people were poor and could not read or write.

For many years Filipinos had a strong independence movement. The Filipinos had revolted against Spanish rule in 1896. They had helped the American forces take Manila only because they expected to gain their independence. When it became clear that the United States meant to rule them, they again rose in revolt. It took a large American army three years to crush their revolt. This conflict cost more in lives and dollars than the Spanish-American War.

Even before the fighting ended, President McKinley sent a group of able officials, led by William H. Taft, to govern the islands. Taft first became famous for his success in the Philippines. Under his leadership, large estates were divided into small farms and sold to the peasants on easy terms. The American government spent large sums on public works, such as roads, schools, hospitals, and water supply and sewage systems. On Taft's recommendation, Congress gave Filipinos almost all the rights of American citizenship. It also did away with tariff duties on shipments of Philippine goods to the United States. As a result, American business people started plantations to grow coconuts, sugar, and other tropical products that the United States needed. The life of Filipino families showed a marked improvement. They could expect to live better and longer than they had under Spanish rule. Their children were given the opportunity of learning to read and write and had the chance to advance in life.

The United States also prepared the Filipinos for self-government. In 1907 they were allowed to elect one house of the legislature. Ten years later they were allowed to elect the members of both houses. In 1934 they were given the right to elect their own president. They were also promised complete independence in twelve years.

When the United States entered World War II, Filipinos fought bravely side by side with Americans against the Japanese. At the war's end, Congress gave the islands their independence and $600,000,000 to repair war damages. On the fourth of July, 1946, the Philippines became an independent nation. Later, it signed a military treaty and a special trade agreement with the United States. These agreements, together with the ties of friendship built through the years, keep the two nations closely linked to this day.

E. The Commonwealth of Puerto Rico. Puerto Rico is only a short distance from the United States. Its mountains, forests, and surrounding seas make a beautiful place. The language and customs were Spanish. Most of the island's one million people were poor and could not read or write. Puerto Ricans had a long history of struggle for independence. In 1897 they had forced Spain to give them the right to vote and have representatives in the Spanish Cortes (congress). Their system of government changed when the United States took over.

Congress gave Puerto Ricans the right to elect the lower house of the island's legislature. But Puerto Ricans had no right to vote in the U.S. Congress. They could export their goods to the United States without paying tariffs. American business people invested large sums in plantations to raise sugar, tobacco, and other tropical products. The federal government built roads, schools, sanitary facilities, and other public works.

In 1917 Congress gave Puerto Rico all the rights of territories like Alaska and Hawaii. Its people became American citizens. They could enter the United States freely. They could elect both houses of their legislature and send a nonvoting delegate to the House of Representatives. The President continued to appoint their governor.

Partly because of American public health measures, the population of Puerto Rico almost doubled in one generation. Thousands of people had neither land of their own nor jobs. In 1930 Puerto Rico was hit by the Great Depression that began in the United States. It spread to Puerto Rico because mainland Americans bought less of the island's products. The number of Puerto Ricans without jobs increased sharply. Many of them joined a movement for independence from the United States.

After World War II, the Puerto Ricans were given the chance to decide their own future. They voted to become neither a state nor an independent nation, but a "commonwealth." As a commonwealth, the island could govern itself and still be a part of the United States.

The Commonwealth of Puerto Rico came into being in 1952. It has its own constitution. Its people elect their own governor and members of the legislature, who have complete control over all domestic affairs. At the same time Puerto Ricans share a common citizenship, foreign policy, tariff duties, and money system with mainland Americans. Like a territory, Puerto

Carlos Romero Barceló was elected governor of Puerto Rico in 1976. He favors statehood rather than a commonwealth or independence for Puerto Rico.

Skilled factory worker checking stereo equipment. Puerto Rico gets its largest income from manufacturing. The United States is its main customer.

Rico can send a delegate to the House of Representatives, but its people cannot elect members of Congress or vote in presidential elections.

As a commonwealth, Puerto Rico has certain special advantages. Its people do not pay some federal taxes. Its government is also allowed to keep all that it collects in tariff duties and receives financial help from the United States besides. Since becoming a commonwealth, Puerto Rico has made remarkable economic progress. Its government has limited plantations to five hundred acres and has sold the surplus land to landless people. It has taught farmers to grow many kinds of crops besides sugar and tobacco. Most important, it has encouraged industry and attracted a large tourist trade. The average Puerto Rican now has the highest standard of living in Latin America. Nevertheless, the rate of unemployment is twice that in the United States. In the 1950s many workers came to the United States to look for jobs.

Several times the Puerto Rican people voted on their future. More than 60 percent of the voters wanted the island to remain a commonwealth. Nearly all the others voted for admission as a state of the United States. There are groups who favor Puerto Rican independence. But in recent elections, candidates favoring statehood or the commonwealth won easily.

F. Governing the Small Possessions. The remaining American possessions are too small to become either independent countries, states, or commonwealths. Most are ruled by an American governor who is usually helped by an assembly elected by the people. The people of these possessions have all or most of the rights of American citizens. Like the people of the Philippines and Puerto Rico, they have benefited from public works built by the Americans. On the whole, their people seem content to remain under American rule.

449

REVIEWING THE SECTION

A. Understanding the Facts

PART 1. In your notebook complete these charts to show how the Republican and Democratic arguments in the election of 1900 were proved or disproved by later events in two of our possessions, the Philippines and Puerto Rico.

Arguments of the Republicans	Actual Developments in the Philippines and Puerto Rico
1. Colonies can serve as bases. 2. They can supply raw materials and markets for American industry. 3. Their people will benefit from American rule.	1. 2. 3.

Arguments of the Democrats	Actual Developments in the Philippines and Puerto Rico
1. Colonies will weaken the United States militarily because they are far from our shores. 2. They will be a heavy expense to our government. 3. The people are not ready for democratic government, but will dislike being ruled by us.	1. 2. 3.

Conclusion. Judging by developments since 1900, which party was right? Explain your answer.

PART 2. Complete this chart to show the steps by which American possessions have advanced to statehood.

Step 1. Possession	Step 2. Territory	Step 3. State
1. The people have only basic rights as human beings. 2. The governor is appointed by the President of the United States. 3. Even if the people elect an assembly, it only advises the governor.	1. 2. 3.	1. 2. 3.

Step 1. Possession	Step 2. Territory	Step 3. State
4. The governor's actions can be checked only by the federal government.	4.	4.
5. A possession has no voice in the federal government.	5.	5.

Conclusion. In what ways is the political position of a state superior to that of a possession or territory?

B. Summing Up the Chapter

Arrange the three events in each group in the order they occurred.

A

1. American occupation of overseas territories
2. Beginning of large-scale American trade with the Far East
3. Beginning of the Economic Revolution in the United States

B

1. Establishment of American stopping-off place in Hawaii
2. Opening of China to western trade
3. Opening of Japan to western trade

C

1. Boxer Uprising
2. Open Door Policy
3. Russo-Japanese War

D

1. Establishment of American protectorate in Cuba
2. American annexation of the Philippines, Guam, and Puerto Rico
3. Beginning of the Spanish-American War

E

1. Commonwealth status for Puerto Rico
2. Independence for the Philippines
3. Statehood for Alaska and Hawaii

IMPROVING YOUR SKILLS

Telling Facts From Opinions

For each group of three statements, write in your notebook the *letter* of the one that would be the hardest to prove or disprove. Be prepared to explain your choice in class. (For a review, see page 383.)

1. a. The climate of Alaska will always be too cold for large-scale settlement. b. Alaska's location makes it an important military base. c. Alaska's natural resources make it valuable to the United States.
2. a. The prosperity of Hawaii depends on its trade with the United States. b. Hawaii could easily survive as an independent nation. c. The Hawaiian people are loyal to the United States, even though most of them have never visited the mainland.
3. a. The Philippines would be better off as a commonwealth than they are as an independent nation. b. A majority of the Filipinos prefer independence to American rule. c. The Filipinos benefited more from American rule than the people of any other possession.
4. a. The people of Puerto Rico probably preferred American rule to Spanish rule in 1898. b. The United States should have let Spain keep Puerto Rico. c. Puerto Rico has progressed more rapidly as a commonwealth than it did as a possession or territory.
5. a. A colony often adds to the ruling country's military strength. b. Colonies usually cost the ruling country more money than they bring in. c. Colonial peoples are usually better off when they become independent.

MAKING HISTORY LIVE

1. Discuss parts of articles printed in the yellow press about the Spanish-American War.
2. Write question and answers for interviews with "typical Americans" about the Spanish-American War:
a. Just after Congress declared war on Spain; b. A few months after the end of the war; c. A few years after the war.
3. On the basis of outside reading, write a report on what has been happening in recent years in Alaska, Hawaii, the Philippines, or Puerto Rico. (Books, magazines, and newspapers can be found in the library.)
4. Draw a travel poster to attract tourists to one of the island possessions.
5. Write both sides of a debate on one of these questions:
a. Should the United States have kept out of the Far East? b. Would the United States have been better off if it had not acquired overseas possessions? c. Would the people of the island possessions have been better off if the United States had given them their freedom at once?
6. Assume you are a Puerto Rican voter today. In a paragraph, tell why you would or would not favor independence for the island.

Chapter 26

OUR INVOLVEMENT IN LATIN AMERICA

SOUTH of the Rio Grande live more than 364,000,000 people whose ways are quite different from ours. We call them Latin Americans; they call us *Norteamericanos* (North Americans). We are all neighbors in the Western Hemisphere (the western half of the globe). Yet many of us know very little about one another.

What sort of people are our neighbors to the south? Why are they called *Latin* Americans? In what ways are they different from us? Why are we interested in them? Why have they been friendly at some times and unfriendly at other times? You will find the answers in this chapter.

LATIN AMERICA

How Did the United States Protect Latin America?

A. The Land of Latin America. Latin America is made up of Mexico and Central America, the islands of the Caribbean Sea, and the continent of South America (see map, page 454). It stretches about five thousand miles from the Rio Grande to Cape Horn at the southern tip of South America. Because of its vast size, Latin America contains a great variety of climates and land features. It has large areas of fertile farmland, broad grazing lands, valuable forests, and mountains rich in natural resources. On the other hand, large parts of Latin America are poor in natural resources. Other parts that are rich are hard to develop. Thick tropical jungles cover much of the vast Amazon River Valley, Central America, and the Caribbean islands. Deserts and other dry regions extend through Chile and elsewhere. The towering Andes and other mountain ranges run the full length of the west coast of the continent. They are the greatest handicap of all. They make many parts of Latin America hard to reach and too cold and rocky for farming.

B. The People of Latin America. The people of Latin America likewise show great variety. Many blacks live in the tropical regions, especially along the east coast. More temperate regions have a large white population of European origin. In hard-to-reach places, especially deep inside the continent and in the western

Left: a chemical plant in Brazil. Right: cattle ranching in Argentina.

La Paz, administrative center of Bolivia and the world's highest capital. Despite the mining of tin, silver, copper, oil, and other resources, a majority of Bolivians remain poor farmers.

regions, most of the people are Indians. In the five hundred years since the discovery of America, there has been a good deal of intermarriage among the three races.

C. Latin American Culture. Spain, as we know, took over most of Latin America. However, the largest country, Brazil, once belonged to Portugal. Both the Spanish and Portuguese languages come from Latin, the language of the old Roman Empire. The entire region is called Latin America because most of its people speak these two Latin languages.

Other features of Latin American culture are also Spanish and Portuguese in origin. Most Latin Americans dress and act much like the people of Spain and Portugal. They take *siestas* (afternoon rests or naps) and enjoy gay festivals called *fiestas*. Most of them belong to the Roman Catholic Church, the established church of Spain and Portugal. Their architecture, literature, art, music, and dancing likewise owe much to Spain and Portugal. But their culture also shows strong African and Indian influences, especially in the music and dancing of the common people. Some of their songs and dances have been very popular in the United States and Europe.

D. Economic and Political Problems. Only a few parts of Latin America still belong to European nations today. Some twenty of the region's republics won their independence from Spain and Portugal in the early nineteenth century (see page 222). Most of them drew up constitutions modeled on that of the United States. Yet very few of them have been able to establish strong and lasting democratic governments. Because of economic and political problems, dictators were able to take over in some countries.

The main economic problem was the unequal sharing of Latin America's wealth. A small but powerful upper class controlled most of the fertile land and other resources. The large majority of the people were very poor. As you might expect, the people often tried to revolt to improve conditions. The wealthy supported military dictators, who used force to keep the people down. Rival leaders won the people's support by promising to make reforms. If they succeeded in gaining power, however, they usually broke their promises.

Successful leaders of a revolution usually made themselves dictators. They and their followers lived in luxury at the people's expense. They sent money to foreign countries, where they could flee if their government were overthrown by another revolution. To pay for their waste and luxury, they taxed the people heavily and borrowed large sums from European bankers. The next dictators often refused to pay back these loans. Such refusals, as we shall see, led European powers to interfere in Latin American affairs a number of times.

E. Reasons for United States Involvement. The United States became involved in Latin America soon after its peoples won their independence. In 1823 it seemed to President Monroe that Russia and France might seize some of the new republics. Both European nations were too powerful and warlike to be good neighbors. So the President issued a strong statement on the matter. Monroe warned all the European powers not to interfere in the affairs of the Western Hemisphere or to establish new colonies there. His warning, known as the Monroe Doctrine, has become an important part of our Latin American policy.

During the nineteenth century, the United States became more and more interested in Latin America. At first the region was important mainly for its sugar, coffee, bananas, and other tropical products. When the United States grew into a great industrial nation, Latin America became much more important. American businesses were eager to obtain raw materials, sell manufactured goods, and make investments there. The United States Navy also wanted bases in the Caribbean area.

F. Enforcing the Monroe Doctrine. 1. THE MAXIMILIAN AFFAIR (1863). Our government again showed its interest in Latin America forty years after President Monroe announced his doctrine. While the United States was fighting the Civil War, Emperor Napoleon III of France tried to seize control of Mexico. The Mexican government could not repay loans from French bankers. Napoleon III used this failure as an excuse to send an army into Mexico. He set up a new government there under a European prince named Maximilian.

President Lincoln asked Napoleon to withdraw his troops. The French emperor refused. As soon as the Civil War ended, our government sent a strong army to the Rio Grande and repeated its request. This time Napoleon withdrew his army. Maximilian was put to death and Mexico regained its independence. The Maximilian Affair was important because it showed the European powers that the United States meant to enforce the Monroe Doctrine.

2. THE VENEZUELAN BOUNDARY DISPUTE (1895). Thirty years later, the United States felt strong enough to challenge even Great Britain. The boundary between British Guiana and Venezuela (see map, page 454) had never been fixed. When gold was discovered in the border region, both nations claimed the area. President Cleveland offered to help them fix the boundary, but the British refused his offer. Angered, he asked Congress to appoint arbitrators to settle the question and promised to enforce their decision. Cleveland's statement was almost a threat of war. The British decided that the good will of the United States was more important to them than the disputed area. They agreed to let arbitrators settle the boundary.

3. THE VENEZUELAN DEBT QUESTION (1903). A few years later Venezuela again became a source of trouble. Its dictator refused to pay back large sums that earlier governments had borrowed from European bankers. Great Britain, Germany, and Italy sent warships to blockade Venezuela. The Germans shelled two Venezuelan warships and a town. The American people were alarmed. They were afraid the European powers might try to take control of Venezuela. President Roosevelt asked the Europeans to call off the blockade and let arbitrators settle the debt question. They agreed to do so. Thus the United States succeeded, for the third time in forty years, in protecting Latin America from European powers.

G. The Pan-American Union. The United States also took the lead in bringing the independent nations of the Western Hemisphere together. In 1889 our government invited delegates of all the Latin American republics to meet in Washington, D.C. There they agreed to form a new international organization, the Pan-American Union. The purposes of the Pan-American Union were to promote friendship and trade among the member nations and to increase their knowledge of one another's culture. The member nations promised to meet often to talk over their problems. It is now part of the Organization of American States, whose headquarters are still in Washington.

REVIEWING THE SECTION

A. Knowing New Terms

In your notebook write the *letter* of the statement that best explains each italicized new term.

1. *Latin America* consists of: a. all of the countries in South America b. all of the countries south of the Rio Grande c. all of the Spanish-speaking nations in the Americas d. all of the countries in the Western Hemisphere except the United States.
2. The *Monroe Doctrine:* a. warned European nations not to interfere in the Western Hemisphere b. invited the Latin American nations to cooperate with the United States c. insisted on arbitration to settle all disputes in the Western Hemisphere d. asked the wealthy landowners of Latin America to divide their large estates among the common people.
3. The *Maximilian Affair* refers to: a. the Mexican fight for independence from Spain b. an attempt by the French to set up a government in Mexico c. a dispute over the boundary of Venezuela d. the refusal of the United States to let European powers use force to collect debts in Latin America.
4. The *Pan-American Union* was formed to promote: a. friendship between the United States and the Latin American nations b. a better understanding of one another's culture c. trade among the member nations d. all of these.

B. Understanding the Facts

Write the letter of the item that does *not* belong in each group.

1. *Geography of Latin America:* a. Large areas of fertile land b. Large areas of land unsuitable for settlement c. Overpopulation d. Rich natural resources.
2. *Obstacles to Latin America's development:* a. Cold climate b. Deserts c. Jungles d. Mountains.
3. *Major races of Latin America:* a. Indians b. Blacks c. Whites d. Asians.
4. *Features of Latin American culture:* a. Derived mainly from the cultures of Spain and Portugal b. Influenced by the Roman Catholic Church c. Influenced by African and Indian cultures d. Popular only in Latin America.
5. *Problems of Latin America:* a. Democratic governments that allow the people too much freedom b. Frequent revolutions c. Large, poor, and illiterate lower class d. Small, wealthy, selfish upper class.
6. *Reasons for United States interest in Latin America before 1900:* a. Fear that great European powers would establish colonies there b. Need for

minerals and tropical products   c. Need for territory   d. Desire for new markets and investments.

IMPROVING YOUR SKILLS

A. Mastering the Map

Study the map on page 454. Then complete the following statements.

1. Latin America is made up of three parts—Mexico and _____ America, the islands of the _____ Sea, and the continent of _____ _____.
2. Central America comprises a number of little republics. The northernmost is _____; the southernmost is _____.
3. The largest country in Latin America is _____.
4. The longest river in Latin America is the _____.
5. The equator crosses the South American countries of _____, _____, and _____.
6. The South American countries whose climate is temperate because they are far from the equator are _____, _____, and _____.
7. The most mountainous countries in South America are _____, _____, _____, and _____.

B. Getting Different Viewpoints

This exercise tells you how various groups felt about United States involvement in Latin America before 1900. Give reasons why each group probably felt the way it did.

1. **The American People**
   a. Big business people: For.
   b. Small business people: For.
   c. Farmers: Not interested.
   d. Workers: For.
2. **Latin Americans**
   a. Most of the common people: Not interested.
   b. Most educated people: For.
   c. Nationalists (very patriotic people): Against.
3. **Europeans**
   a. Banks and other businesses: Mixed.
   b. Nationalists: Against.

Why Did Latin Americans Object to Our New Policy?

A. Beginning of Latin American Suspicion. "Teddy" Roosevelt, William H. Taft, and Woodrow Wilson were three very able Presidents. Their intentions were good. They really wanted to promote the best interests of both the United States and Latin America. To do so, they took a very active part in Latin American affairs. But their actions alarmed the people they were trying to help. Latin Americans began to call the United States the "Bully of the North." In fact, much of their fear of the United States remains to this day.

Latin America's suspicion was first aroused by the Spanish-American War. The United States entered the war to free the Cuban people from misrule by Spain. After winning the war, however, our government made Cuba a protectorate and built a naval base on the island. It also took possession of the nearby island of Puerto Rico and built a second base there.

B. The Panama Canal Affair. 1. THE NEED FOR A CANAL. The main purpose of both bases was to protect a canal which the American government wanted to build to connect the Atlantic and Pacific oceans. Our nation first became interested in building such a canal during the California gold rush in 1849. The distance from the east coast to the west coast by sea around Cape Horn (the tip of South America) was over 14,000 miles. It was a very long and costly journey. To make the trip shorter and cheaper, thousands of Americans sailed to Panama. There they planned to go the fifty miles of jungle and mountain on foot and then board ships bound for the west coast (see map, page 454). Many who took this route, however, died of tropical diseases in Panama.

A French company started to build a canal across Panama in the 1880s. It failed largely because of yellow fever and other tropical diseases that felled many of its workers. Our government decided to finish the canal. President Roosevelt wanted it so that our navy would be able to move quickly from one ocean to the other. The Spanish-American War had shown the need for such a project. An American warship, the *Oregon,* had taken almost ten weeks to sail from the Pacific to the Atlantic. Eastern business people also wanted the canal because it would cut the cost of shipping goods to the West Coast and the Far East.

2. THE PANAMA REVOLUTION (1903). TR offered the French canal company $40,000,000 for its property and rights. He also offered Colombia, which owned Panama, a $10,000,000 cash payment and $250,000 a year for a strip of land on which to build the canal. Colombia's president accepted the offer, but the Colombian senate would not approve it. The senators hoped to get more money from the United States by waiting until the rights of the French company ran out a few months later. TR angrily condemned their action as "blackmail."

The owners of the French company knew that they would lose out if an agreement was not reached quickly. So a high official of the company helped start a revolution in Panama. American warships, which had recently arrived, also took part. They kept Colombian troops from landing to crush the revolt. Panama announced its independence at once, and the

United States quickly recognized the new government. The two nations soon signed a treaty with the same terms that Colombia had refused.

TR later admitted that he had supported the Panama revolution to speed the building of the canal. "I took the Canal Zone," he said, "and let Congress debate; and while the debate goes on, the canal does also." His bold action undoubtedly made it possible to build the canal a year or two sooner. But it earned the distrust of all Latin America. Years later, Congress voted Colombia $25,000,000.

3. BUILDING OF THE CANAL. Roosevelt gave the United States Army the responsibility for building the Panama Canal. It was a tremendous task. The army had to conquer yellow fever and the other diseases that had ruined the French company. This task was given to the Medical Corps under Colonel William C. Gorgas, the man who had wiped out tropical diseases in Cuba. Gorgas succeeded so well that the disease rate among canal workers was lower than it was among Americans on the mainland. Meanwhile the army's engineers under Colonel George W. Goethals had to blast a path for the canal through the mountains of Panama. They finally finished the project in 1913 at a total cost of almost a half-billion dollars.

The Panama Canal was well worth the cost. It served America's navy and merchant ships and the ships of many foreign nations too. In fact, it soon became so busy that talk about building a second canal began. To date, however, no definite plans for building such a canal have been drafted.

C. Roosevelt's Extension of the Monroe Doctrine. Meanwhile, TR had taken another bold step in our relations with Latin America. Troubled by the Venezuelan debt dispute, he decided to keep the European powers from interfering again in Latin American affairs. So he announced an extension (stretching) of the meaning of the Monroe Doctrine. The United States, he said, would exercise "an international police power" in the western hemisphere. It would step in whenever a Latin American government was unable to pay its debts to other nations or was "guilty of chronic [long-time] wrongdoing."

A few months later the Dominican Republic declared itself unable to pay its debts. TR sent in financial advisers and marines. Dismissing corrupt officials, the Americans were soon able to collect enough in tariff duties to start repaying the nation's debts. They were also able

Locks of the Panama Canal. The locks are like giant elevators. Water is pumped into them to raise a ship or pumped out to lower it. A series of locks is needed to carry ships over the high land of Panama.

to collect enough to make improvements within the country. A year later President Roosevelt sent troops to Cuba because the Cuban government had proved weak and corrupt. The Americans quickly improved conditions there.

President Taft carried Roosevelt's extension of the Monroe Doctrine a step further. He encouraged American bankers and business people to make large loans and investments in Latin America. By substituting American for European investment he hoped to reduce the need for our government to step in. But when Honduras, the Dominican Republic, and Nicaragua failed to repay American loans, Taft sent marines into all three little countries. American troops remained in Nicaragua, with only two short breaks, until 1933.

Woodrow Wilson did not approve of what Roosevelt and Taft had done. He told the Latin Americans that the United States would "never again seek one additional foot of territory by conquest." But Wilson also thought that the United States should teach Latin Americans how to run their governments democratically. To do this, he sent the marines into Haiti, Nicaragua, the Dominican Republic, and Cuba. He also extended American power by buying the Virgin Islands from Denmark to have another base protecting the Panama Canal. Most important, Wilson involved the United States deeply in Mexico's affairs.

D. Wilson's Actions in Mexico. 1. THE OCCUPATION OF VERACRUZ. In 1911 a military dictator who had ruled Mexico for thirty-five years was finally overthrown. An honest reformer then became president. Unfortunately, the reformer was murdered by one of his generals. Victoriano Huerta, the general, made himself president of Mexico. President Wilson refused to recognize the Huerta government. He also allowed rival Mexican leaders to obtain arms in the United States. When Huerta ordered arms in Germany, Wilson sent warships to the Mexican port of Veracruz to keep the arms from being unloaded. The Americans took the port after a fight that cost more than two hundred lives.

Latin Americans were shocked by the American occupation of Veracruz. Three leading countries (Argentina, Brazil, and Chile) offered to settle the dispute. Wilson accepted their offer. The outcome was that President Wilson withdrew American troops from Veracruz and Huerta resigned as president.

2. THE PURSUIT OF PANCHO VILLA. Another Mexican general, Pancho Villa, hoped to take Huerta's place as president. When he failed to get the position, he blamed the United States. In revenge, he killed a number of Americans in Mexico. Then he crossed the border into the United States and shot some more Americans. Since the Mexican government was unable to

"The Big Stick in the Caribbean Sea." In explaining his foreign policy, TR said, "Walk softly, and carry a big stick." What do you think TR meant? How does the cartoon interpret what he said?

deal with Villa, President Wilson sent an American military force to capture him. The small American army wandered through Mexico for months before it finally gave up the chase. By that time President Wilson was faced with far more serious problems, for the United States had become involved in the First World War.

E. Results of Our New Policy in Latin America. Between 1898 and 1918, the United States helped Cuba and Panama gain their independence. It acquired Puerto Rico and the Virgin Islands, built the Panama Canal, and acted forcefully in most of the nations bordering the Caribbean Sea. Its businesses also invested several billion dollars in this region. Latin Americans charged that the Caribbean had become "an American lake."

The Americans brought important benefits to the countries they protected. They took care of the sick and hungry, restored law and order, and established honest government. They built roads, schools, hospitals, water supply and sewage systems. They stamped out tropical diseases and developed natural resources.

Yet the people of Latin America disliked America's stepping into their affairs. They seemed to prefer their own governments, corrupt and weak though they might be, to honest and efficient administrations run by *norteamericanos*. They chiefly disliked the use of American troops to "police" them. Even in those countries where no troops were sent, the United States was accused of trying to gain control through its loans and investments.

Left: Pancho Villa. How did he show his dislike for America's actions in Mexico? Right: General John J. Pershing. He led an American force into Mexico. Why do you think he was unable to capture Villa?

In the 1920s our government began to change the policy that had created so much ill will. (For details of the Good Neighbor Policy, see pages 534-535). To this day, however, Latin Americans are still suspicious of the "Bully of the North." No matter what the circumstances, they object strongly to the use of American troops in any country of Latin America.

REVIEWING THE SECTION

A. Knowing New Terms

Explain each of these terms in your notebook *in your own words*.

(In **A**) "Bully of the North" (In **E**) "an American lake"
(In **C**) "an international police power"

B. Knowing Important People

For each person in the first column, write the *letter* of the best description in the second column.

Important People
1. George W. Goethals
2. William C. Gorgas
3. Victoriano Huerta
4. Theodore Roosevelt
5. William H. Taft
6. Pancho Villa
7. Woodrow Wilson

Descriptions
a. President who made the United States "an international policeman"
b. Builder of the Panama Canal
c. Doctor who cleaned up tropical diseases in the Panama Canal region
d. Mexican dictator whose actions angered the President of the United States
e. Mexican general who killed Americans on American soil
f. Mexican ruler who encouraged American investments
g. President who sent American troops into Mexico
h. President who encouraged American loans and investments in Latin America

C. Understanding the Facts

In your notebook write the *letter* of the correct choice.
1. Latin Americans came to distrust the United States because it:
a. protected them from European nations b. helped Cuba win its independence from Spain c. used force to restore order in a half-dozen nations around the Caribbean Sea d. did all these things.
2. The United States wanted a canal across Panama to:
a. move its warships more quickly from one ocean to another b. send goods from the east coast to the west coast more cheaply c. cut the cost of trading with the Far East d. do all these things.
3. President Roosevelt aroused the anger of Latin Americans by:
a. planning to build a canal through Panama b. making a treaty with the French canal company c. supporting Panama's revolution against Colombia d. admitting what he had done.
4. The Americans, unlike the French, were able to build the Panama Canal because they:
a. had modern canal-building machinery b. knew how to control tropical diseases c. used only American workers d. were better engineers than the French.
5. President Roosevelt sent marines into several Latin American nations to:
a. prevent European powers from interfering b. set up democratic governments c. show how strong the United States was d. teach the people a lesson.

6. Woodrow Wilson interfered in Mexico's affairs to:
   a. establish a more democratic government   b. keep out the French and Germans   c. protect American investments   d. show that the Democrats were as nationalistic as the Republicans.
7. Because of our nation's actions between 1898 and 1918, the nations around the Caribbean Sea:
   a. became democracies   b. developed modern industries   c. enjoyed a high standard of living   d. got more loans and investments from the United States.

D. Summing Up the Chapter

Complete this comparison in your notebook. (You will find the answers in both sections of this chapter.)

Actions That Latin Americans Liked	*Actions That Latin Americans Disliked*
1.	1.
2.	2.
3.	3.
4.	4.

Conclusion. If you were an educated Latin American in 1917, how would you have felt toward the United States? Tell why.

MAKING HISTORY LIVE

1. Prepare questions for interviews in which the "inquiring reporter" asks typical Latin Americans and *norteamericanos* in 1917 what they think of American policies in Latin America. Answer them.
2. After reading outside sources, explain whether you approve or disapprove of one of these American actions: a. TR's support of the Panama revolution; b. TR's extension of the Monroe Doctrine; c. Wilson's occupation of Veracruz; d. The attempt to capture Pancho Villa.
3. Discuss your points of view on the question: "Did the United States follow the right policy in Latin America between 1898 and 1918?"
4. Make a report on a recent important event in Latin America that involved the United States. Tell what the United States did, why it acted in this way, and how Latin Americans felt about its action.
5. Draw a cartoon to show how most Latin Americans felt about the United States either before 1900 or afterwards.
6. a. Play Latin American songs and copy the words of one song; or
   b. Use drawings, models, or dolls to show the clothing styles of the common people in different parts of Latin America.

Chapter 27

THE UNITED STATES AND WORLD WAR I

ON A pleasant day in June, 1914, an Austrian prince visited the capital of Bosnia, one of his country's possessions. He knew there was danger that Bosnians who were demanding independence from Austria might try to kill him. So he had a heavy police guard. But a Bosnian student broke through the guard and shot both him and his wife.

For years disputes among the great powers had kept Europe on the edge of war. The shooting of the Austrian prince plunged it into armed conflict. Austria-Hungary declared war on its neighbor Serbia, which it blamed for the murder. Russia, which had promised to help Serbia, declared war on Austria-Hungary. Germany, an ally of Austria-Hungary, declared war on both Russia and its ally France. Great Britain, which had a treaty with France and Russia, declared war on Germany. Within the next few months, other nations joined both sides and the fighting spread from Europe to Africa and Asia. The conflict, the largest in history up to that time, soon became known as the World War.

President Wilson, a former professor of government, had studied the way the United States became involved in a European war in 1812 (see pages 206-209). He was determined to avoid the mistakes made at that time by Presidents Jefferson and Madison. In spite of his efforts, however, the United States once again failed to keep out. How did the United States get involved in the First World War (World War I)? Once it entered the war, what did it do to help win the victory? You will find the answers to both questions in this chapter.

How Did the United States Become Involved in the War?

A. Wilson's Policy of Neutrality. In 1914 the United States was still following a policy of isolationism—that is, it avoided alliances with other nations. Most Americans were not interested in foreign affairs. They knew little about developments in Europe and were surprised when the war broke out. They expected the United States to stay out of the conflict. "Thank God for the Atlantic Ocean" was a popular saying.

President Wilson was confident that he could keep the United States out of the war. He issued a proclamation of neutrality soon after it started. He called on the American people to remain "neutral in fact as well as in name . . . impartial [favoring neither side] in thought as well as in action." The American people wanted to be neutral, but they were certainly not impartial in thought. Most of them sided with the Allies, led by Great Britain and France. The United States had been on good terms with Great Britain, its "parent country," for many years. France had once been America's ally. Both countries were, like the United States, democratic nations.

Germany and Austria-Hungary, the leading Central Powers, were not democracies. Yet they too had the sympathy of millions of Americans. These were mostly people of German and Austrian origin. Many Irish Americans, however, also sided with the Central Powers. They were angry with Great Britain because of the way it ruled Ireland. They believed that Ireland would win its independence if Britain lost the war.

B. The Influence of Propaganda. Both the Allies and the Central Powers tried to win the support of the American people. The British had one great advantage: They controlled the ocean cable lines by which news from Europe reached the United States. As you would expect, British news reports contained much propaganda (information favoring their side). They stressed the fact that the German government was undemocratic and that its emperor was warlike. They exaggerated, or even made up, stories about the cruelty of German soldiers. The Germans were not able to explain their nation's policies to the American public as well as the British did. In the long run, however, what each side did had far more effect on Americans than what its propaganda said.

C. British Violations of American Neutrality. The powerful British navy blockaded the Central Powers soon after the war started. In enforcing the blockade, the British often violated America's rights as a neutral nation. Under international law, warships had the right to stop and search neutral ships. If they found that a ship was carrying war materials to the enemy, they could either seize or sink it, provided that they saw to the safety of the passengers and crew. The British obeyed these rules in general. But they considered even food and raw materials like cotton "war materials." They seized American ships carrying such cargoes, even if they were bound for neutral nations.

President Wilson protested to the British

government against these violations of America's "freedom of the seas"—that is, its right as a neutral nation to carry on trade. But the President took no other action against Great Britain. There were two main reasons why. First, he himself sided with Great Britain because it was a democratic nation. Second, the United States was getting huge orders for arms, raw materials, and food from the Allies. In 1916 this trade amounted to more than three billion dollars. On the other hand, the United States had almost no trade with the Central Powers. They were not able to get American goods because the British fleet controlled the seas.

D. German Violations of American Rights.
1. SUBMARINE WARFARE. Germany, like Great Britain, violated America's "freedom of the seas"—but in a very different way. To break the British blockade, the Germans built a large fleet of submarines. The submarine, a new weapon in those days, was far less powerful and dangerous than it is now. If it rose to the surface to stop and search a ship, it could easily be sunk by ramming or shelling. For this reason, the Germans decided to torpedo enemy vessels without warning. This was a clear violation of international law. In defending their policy, the Germans said that their nation was fighting for its life. So it had the right to do anything it could to save itself. They pointed out that the British were also breaking international law. Finally, they accused the United States of not being really neutral because it was sending so much help to the Allies.

Early in 1915, a great British passenger liner named the *Lusitania* set sail from New York. As the *Lusitania* was approaching the British Isles, it was torpedoed by a German submarine. The liner sank very quickly. Some 1,200 people, including 128 Americans, were lost. The American people were horrified. Newspapers accused the Germans of "mass murder." Teddy Roosevelt demanded that President Wilson break off relations with Germany at once. But the secre-

A headline on the sinking of the *Lusitania*. Why was the American public aroused, even though the *Lusitania* was a British ship?

The New York Times.

EXTRA 5:30 A. M.

"All the News That's Fit to Print."

VOL. LXIV...NO. 20,923. NEW YORK, SATURDAY, MAY 8, 1915.—TWENTY-FOUR PAGES. ONE CENT

LUSITANIA SUNK BY A SUBMARINE, PROBABLY 1,260 DEAD; TWICE TORPEDOED OFF IRISH COAST; SINKS IN 15 MINUTES; CAPT. TURNER SAVED, FROHMAN AND VANDERBILT MISSING; WASHINGTON BELIEVES THAT A GRAVE CRISIS IS AT HAND

SHOCKS THE PRESIDENT
Washington Deeply Stirred by the Loss of American Lives.
BULLETINS AT WHITE HOUSE
Wilson Reads Them Closely, but Is Silent on the Nation's Course.
HINTS OF CONGRESS CALL
Loss of Lusitania Recalls Firm Tone of Our First Warning to Germany.
CAPITAL FULL OF RUMORS
Reports That Liner Was to be Sunk Were Heard Before Actual News Came.

SOME DEAD TAKEN ASHORE
Several Hundred Survivors at Queenstown and Kinsale.
STEWARD TELLS OF DISASTER
One Torpedo Crashes Into the Doomed Liner's Bow, Another Into the Engine Room.
SHIP LISTS OVER TO PORT.
Makes It Impossible to Lower Many Boats, So Hundreds Must Have Gone Down.
ATTACKED IN BROAD DAY
Passengers at Luncheon—Warning Had Been Given by Germans Before the Ship Left New York.

A German zeppelin. These large, gas-filled airships were used to bomb London and other Allied cities. How did this use of the zeppelin make Americans feel toward the Germans?

tary of state, William Jennings Bryan, disagreed. He thought that the United States should avoid trouble by forbidding Americans to travel on the ships of nations at war. President Wilson chose to take neither course. Instead, he sent Germany several strong protests and demanded payment for the damage its submarines had caused.

2. GERMAN SABOTAGE. Germany finally agreed not to torpedo merchant ships without warning. Nevertheless, it tried to stop the flow of American aid to the Allies in other ways. Its secret agents encouraged strikes in American war industries, blew up American plants making arms, and started fires on American ships carrying war materials. Such planned destruction of property is called "sabotage."

E. The Election of 1916. In the election of 1916, Wilson pointed with pride to his success in promoting prosperity and peace. "He kept us out of war" became a popular Democratic campaign slogan. But in fact Wilson was afraid that the United States might still be dragged into the war. He asked Congress to vote large sums for building up the army and navy. He also tried several times to bring both sides together for peace talks. But each time his efforts failed.

The presidential election of 1916 was one of the closest in our history. Wilson's success in keeping the United States neutral was an important reason for his victory. A few months later, however, the picture suddenly changed.

F. Renewal of Submarine Warfare. In two and a half years of fighting, the Central Powers had won many battles. Nevertheless, the war seemed no closer to an end. As it went on and on, the Central Powers began to fear that they would lose. For the Allies had a much larger population. They could also obtain supplies by sea from all parts of the world. So the Germans decided to gamble. They would try to cut the Allied supply lines by renewing their submarine warfare. They knew that this was a dangerous course, for it might bring the United States into the war. But they believed they had a good chance to win the war before American help could make a difference.

In January 1917, the German government declared the waters around Europe a war zone. Enemy vessels found in these waters would be sunk without warning. Neutral vessels entered them at their own risk. As a special favor, the United States would be allowed to send one ship a week to Great Britain. This ship would, of course, carry no war materials. It was to be clearly marked with red and white lines, set sail on Wednesday, and follow a certain path. The American people considered the offer an insult. Wilson replied by breaking off relations with Germany. But he still hoped to keep the United States out of war.

G. The Declaration of War. A few days later, the British secret service made public a note which the German Foreign Secretary, Arthur Zimmermann, had sent to the German minister in Mexico. If the United States entered the war against Germany, the note said, the minister was to talk Mexico into declaring war on the United States. He was to promise Mexico the return of Texas and all the territories it had lost in 1848. When the Zimmermann Note was published, the American people became even angrier with Germany than before.

During the next few weeks, five American merchant ships were sunk by German submarines. President Wilson finally called a special session of Congress. In a stirring speech, he asked Congress to declare war on Germany. The Germans, he pointed out, had destroyed American lives and property. By renewing submarine warfare, they were forcing the United States to enter the war. Finally, Germany was a warlike, undemocratic nation. Its victory would be a threat to democratic governments everywhere. America had to fight, the President concluded, because "the world must be made safe for democracy."

Congress quickly voted the declaration of war. President Wilson was, nevertheless, an unhappy man. He knew that the war would mean the end of his reform program (see page 420). He was afraid that it would also weaken American democracy. The actual effects of the war, as we shall see, were even more harmful than he predicted.

REVIEWING THE SECTION

A. Knowing New Terms

PART 1. In your notebook write the new terms in this section that best complete these statements.
1. The great war which began in Europe in 1914 is now called the _____ World War or World War __.
2. The warring nations led by Great Britain and France were known as the _____.
3. The opposing side, led by Germany and Austria-Hungary, was called the _____ _____.
4. One-sided information is called _____.
5. An incident that aroused the American people early in the war was the sinking by a German submarine of a British passenger liner, the _____.
6. The planned destruction of someone else's property is called _____.
7. The German plan to get Mexico into the war was revealed in the _____ Note.

PART 2. Explain each of these phrases *in your own words*.
(In **A**) "Thank God for the Atlantic Ocean."
(In **C**) freedom of the seas
(In **G**) "The world must be made safe for democracy."

B. Finding the Reasons

In your notebook write the letters of *all* the correct answers to each question.

1. Why did the Allies and Central Powers go to war in 1914?
a. Officials of one of the Allies shot the ruler of one of the Central Powers. b. The powers on both sides had been rivals for years. c. Many of the European powers were tied to one another by military alliances.
2. Why did President Wilson and most Americans want to stay neutral in 1914?
a. They had no personal interest in either the Allied countries or the Central Powers. b. There was little difference between the governments on both sides. c. The idea of isolationism was still strong in the United States.
3. Why did President Wilson send stronger protests to Germany than to Great Britain?
a. The British government was more democratic than the German government. b. The British seized American property, but the Germans destroyed both lives and property. c. American businesses and farmers made large profits trading with the Allies.
4. According to the German government, why was Germany justified in sinking American ships?
a. Germany was fighting for its life. b. The British were breaking international law. c. The United States was not really neutral.
5. Why did the Germans start submarine warfare again in 1917?
a. They were sure of winning the war in a few months. b. They thought that the United States would not dare to declare war on Germany. c. They decided to take a gamble in the hope of winning the war quickly.

IMPROVING YOUR SKILLS

Looking at Both Sides

Complete each of the following lists in your notebook.

PART 1. Compare the British and German violations of American rights as a neutral nation.

British Violations	German Violations
1.	1.
2.	2.

Conclusion. Which violations do you consider worse and why?

PART 2. Compare America's reasons for going to war in 1812 with its reasons for entering World War I.

Reasons for the War of 1812	*Reasons for America's Entry into World War I*

1. British violations of American rights
   a. Seizure of American ships
   b. Impressment of American seamen
	1. German violations of American rights
	   a.
	   b.

2. British arming of the Indians, who attacked Americans	2.
3. American desire for territory	3.

Conclusion. In which case do you think our government had better reasons for declaring war?

PART 3. Compare the way most Americans defended their government's actions with the way Germans defended theirs.

Arguments Defending America's Actions	*Arguments Defending Germany's Actions*
1. As a neutral nation, the United States had the right to trade freely with most other nations.	1.
2. German submarine warfare and sabotage violated international law.	2.
3. The Zimmermann Note showed that Germany was plotting against the United States.	3.
4. Germany was a warlike, undemocratic nation, a threat to democracy everywhere in the world.	4.

Conclusion. Which side do you think had the stronger arguments?

How Did the United States Help Win the War?

A. Weakness of the Allies. The year 1917, when the United States entered the war, was a critical one for the Allies. The French were so tired of fighting that many of their soldiers mutinied. In Russia a group of extreme socialists, called Communists, staged a successful revolt against the government. Once in power, they pulled Russia out of the war. In the meantime, Germany and Austria-Hungary won victories in Italy, in the Balkan Peninsula, and at sea. German submarines were sinking one-fourth of the ships carrying goods to or from the British Isles. With only seven or eight weeks' grain supply left, Great Britain faced the threat of starvation.

B. Stopping the Submarines. Fortunately, the United States Navy was ready for action. It quickly crossed the Atlantic to help the British fight the submarines. Moreover, American officers persuaded the British to have their merchant ships travel in groups under the protection of warships. These groups were called convoys. Though convoys moved slowly and were hard to keep together, they were less likely to be attacked by submarines than ships traveling alone.

At the same time, American shipyards began turning out dozens of small warships, known as "subchasers," to escort the convoys. A new listening device and improved depth charges (underwater explosives) made it easier to track and destroy submarines. A vast minefield was laid across the North Sea to trap them as they entered or left their bases in Germany. As a result of these measures, in 1918 the Allies were able to sink submarines faster than the Germans could build them.

C. Raising an Army. The American army, unlike the navy, was neither large nor well-prepared when the United States entered the war. It could send only one small force to France in 1917. Spread thinly among the Allied troops, these American soldiers could do little more than show that help was coming. But the important question was "How soon would it arrive?" According to experts, it would take at least two years to raise, train, equip, and send to France the large army that was needed. But the American commander, General John J. Pershing, warned, "The Allies are very weak and we must come to their relief in 1918. The year after may be too late."

The United States met the challenge. Congress quickly passed the Selective Service Act, or draft law. This required all men of fighting age, except for married men and men with dependents, to register with local draft boards. The government also quickly built thirty-two huge training camps and set up training centers in many colleges. In less than a year and a half, more than four million young men were taken into the armed forces. Half of them were sent to France, where almost 1,500,000 took part in the fighting.

D. Organizing the American Economy. President Wilson warned the American people, "It is not [just] an army that we must shape and train for war—it is a nation." Congress voted the President broad powers to organize the American economy for war. Wilson set up a half-dozen new agencies for the purpose and chose leading business executives to run them.

The most important new government agency was the War Industries Board. This board drew up plans for building new factories and for making over existing factories for war production. It also decided which industries would get scarce materials, to whom they would sell their products, and even how much they would charge. The head of the War Industries Board had so much power that he was called an "economic dictator."

The War Shipping Board had to find ships to send the army and its equipment overseas. It seized all enemy ships in American ports, bought or rented ships from neutral nations, and asked American shipyards to rush production. It also borrowed many ships from Great Britain. In 1918 American troops were being carried across the Atlantic at the rate of 10,000 a day, or 300,000 a month.

Two other boards controlled the railroads and trade. The Food Administration and the Fuel Administration watched over wheat and meat, sugar and fats, coal and oil. To increase the output of these important foods and fuels, the government offered producers much higher prices for them. It raised the price of wheat, for example, to more than two dollars a bushel. As a result, farmers greatly increased production. The American people were also asked to use less. There were "Meatless Mondays" and "Wheatless Wednesdays." Automobiles were not supposed to be driven on Sundays or holidays. On certain days Americans even had to do without heat. Because the winter of 1917-1918 was very cold and there was a flu epidemic, this seemed the greatest sacrifice of all. Still the American people cooperated willingly with the government to help win the war.

E. Increasing the Labor Supply. With millions of men in the armed forces and industry expanding, a shortage of labor soon developed. Women therefore took over many jobs once held by men. They worked in factories, as trolley car conductors, and taxi drivers. This wartime service helped the passage of the Nineteenth Amendment. Through it, women won the right to vote. Black people also benefited from the war. Many left the South to serve in the armed forces or work in northern industries.

The labor shortage grew worse in 1917 because rising prices caused an outbreak of strikes. The War Labor Board won a promise from the leading unions not to strike. In return, it asked employers to raise wages, establish a 48-hour week, and recognize the unions. Union membership doubled as a result, and the wages of organized labor rose faster than prices. But most workers were still unorganized, and they suffered greatly from rising prices.

F. Paying for the War. Organizing an entire nation on a scale never tried before proved very expensive. The American government spent more than thirty-two billion dollars in two and a half years, including loans of over ten billion dollars to the Allies. One-third of this huge sum was raised through taxes; the rest was borrowed. Taxes on personal incomes and business profits were greatly increased. Congress also taxed amusements, railroad tickets, telephone calls, phonograph records. chewing gum, and other luxuries.

The government borrowed more than twenty billion dollars, mainly by selling bonds directly to the people. These "Liberty Bonds" were available in amounts as low as fifty dollars. Even school children could buy them by filling books with war savings stamps, which sold for as little as ten cents each. Great publicity drives called on Americans to buy as many bonds and stamps as they could.

G. Arousing Public Opinion. Though most Americans strongly supported the war effort, the Central Powers still had many sympathizers.

A pair of government posters in World War I.

The war was also opposed by two other groups. The socialists opposed the war because they saw it as a struggle between rival groups of capitalists. The pacifists were against it because they believed that all wars were evil. To sell the war to every American, the government organized the Committee on Public Information. The CPI turned out millions of posters and pamphlets. It also trained thousands of "four-minute men" to give short talks in behalf of the war anywhere they could find an audience.

In getting all Americans to support the war, the CPI taught them to hate the enemy. Unfortunately, they began to hate fellow Americans who, they thought, were friendly to the enemy. Socialists, pacifists, and people with German names were persecuted. Many lost their jobs or saw their businesses ruined by boycotts. Some were even beaten or tarred and feathered. Some places would not allow the playing of German music or the teaching of the German language in the schools. Sauerkraut was renamed "liberty cabbage." The dachshund was called the "liberty pup."

Because of these strong feelings, Congress passed the Espionage (spying) and Sedition Acts. These laws were directed more against Americans suspected of being disloyal than against enemy spies. They made it a crime 1. to interfere with the draft, war production, or the sale of war bonds; and 2. to use "disloyal, profane, or abusive language" about the American government, the Constitution, the flag, or the uniforms of the armed services. More than fifteen hundred people were jailed for breaking these laws. Some received sentences as high as twenty years in prison. Many people protested that our government could not "make the world safe for democracy" while it violated the American people's rights of free speech and a free press. The Supreme Court, however, upheld the laws. It ruled that the people's rights could legally be limited whenever there was "a clear and present danger" to the nation.

H. Winning the War. In the meantime, the war in Europe was still going badly for the Allies. Early in 1918 the Communist government of Russia signed a peace treaty with Germany. This left the Germans free to move their armies from Russia to the western front. Acting swiftly, they began a great offensive against the French and British, whom they now outnumbered. In the first eight days of their offensive, the Germans advanced more than thirty miles and took almost 100,000 prisoners. American "doughboys" (infantrymen) were thrown into the battle almost as soon as they arrived in France. Though inexperienced, they helped to stop the German advance. The sight of these fresh, well-fed, and well-equipped new troops

WORLD WAR I

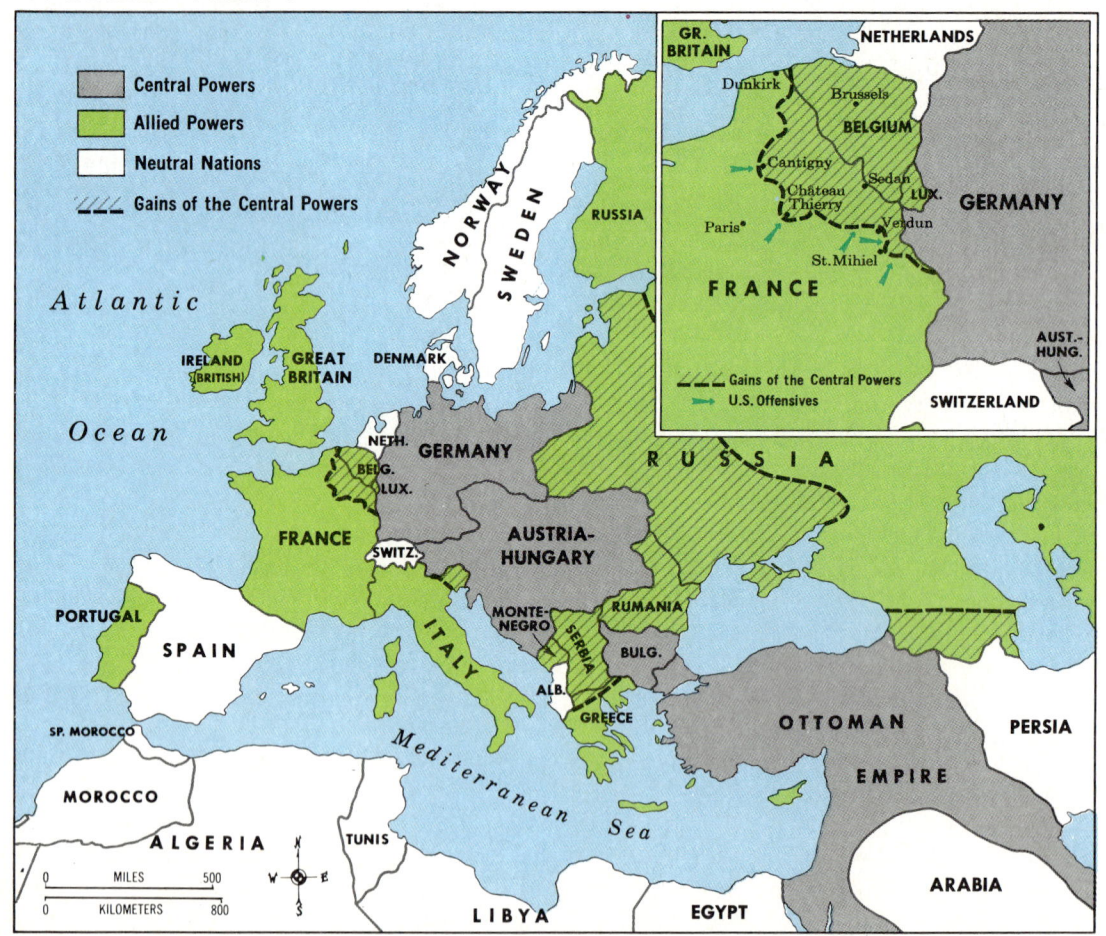

"Over the top." Before an offensive, the artillery would shell the enemy for hours to "soften him up." Then infantrymen would charge "over the top" (out of their trenches) across "No Man's Land" into the enemy's trenches.

also boosted the morale of the Allies and took the spirit out of the Germans.

By July enough Americans had arrived to turn the tables. The Allies now started a mighty counteroffensive. The American army was to advance through the Argonne Forest. This was the most difficult section of the front. It was full of swamps and ravines. The Germans were dug into trenches protected by minefields, barbed wire, machine-gun nests, and heavy artillery. The offensive lasted more than six weeks. Day after day, the Americans advanced in spite of very heavy casualties. They finally broke through the German lines, taking thousands of prisoners and capturing an important railroad junction. The British and French also made important advances.

Meanwhile, the Allies were forcing the other Central Powers to surrender. Early in November, revolts broke out in Germany and the emperor was forced to flee. The German commanders decided to surrender before the Allies could destroy their armies or invade Germany. On the morning of November 11, 1918, the powers signed an armistice and the First World War came to an end.

REVIEWING THE SECTION

A. Knowing New Terms

For each term in the first column, write in your notebook the *letter* of the best description in the second column.

Terms
1. Convoys
2. Espionage and Sedition Acts
3. Food and Fuel Administrations
4. Liberty Bonds
5. Nineteenth Amendment
6. Pacifists
7. Selective Service Act
8. War Industries Board
9. War Labor Board
10. War Shipping Board

Descriptions
a. Drafted able-bodied men into the armed forces
b. Prevented strikes in important industries
c. Gave women the right to vote
d. Increased production and limited the use of scarce products
e. Issued by the federal government to help pay for the war
f. Made plans for the production of arms and war materials
g. Opposed not only World War I but also all other wars
h. Punished spies and Americans suspected of being disloyal
i. Reduced submarine attacks on merchant ships by having them travel in groups escorted by warships
j. Stirred up the American people to hate the enemy and Americans who did not fully support the war
k. Took care of sending American troops and equipment to Europe

B. Understanding the Facts

The war had different effects on different groups of Americans. For each group below, tell whether the war "benefited" it, "harmed" it, or had "mixed effects." Give at least one fact to support your answer in each case.

1. Young men
2. Consumers
3. Women
4. Blacks
5. Organized labor
6. Unorganized workers
7. Business people
8. Socialists, pacifists, and people with German names

IMPROVING YOUR SKILLS

A. Mastering the Map

Study the map on page 476. In your notebook complete the following:

1. The four Central Powers were _____, _____, _____, and the _____ _____.
2. Seven Allied nations in Europe were _____ _____, _____, _____, _____, _____, _____, and _____.
3. On the western front, the Central Powers seized _____, _____, and part of _____.
4. On the eastern front, they conquered a large part of _____.
5. In the south, they conquered _____, _____, _____, and part of _____.
6. American troops fought important offensive battles at _____, _____ _____, and _____.

B. Telling Facts From Opinions

Write "Fact" for each statement that can be proved by getting the necessary information. Write "Opinion" if you think the answer depends on values and judgment. Be prepared to give the reasons for your answers in class.

1. The Allies would have lost the war if the United States had not come to their aid.
2. The United States Navy played a very important part in defeating German submarine warfare.
3. The United States raised and trained a large army and sent it into battle much faster than the Germans had expected.
4. The head of the War Industries Board had as much power over business as an absolute monarch or dictator.
5. American farmers and mineowners would probably have produced enough even if the government had not raised the prices they received for their products.
6. World War I changed attitudes about "women's work."
7. Employers would probably have had to recognize unions because of the shortage of labor during World War I, even if the government had not asked them to do so.
8. War taxes were fair because the government was only taking back part of the profits Americans were making because of the war.
9. In teaching hatred of the enemy, the government also stirred up hatred among Americans.

479

10. In upholding the laws under which socialists and pacifists were punished, the Supreme Court violated our democratic principles.
11. American troops in France were more valuable for their effects on Allied and German morale than for the battles they won.

MAKING HISTORY LIVE

1. Look up old newspapers and magazines or read a book about World War I. Then write a report to the class on one of these topics:
   a. Why many Americans came to hate the Germans during World War I; b. How the American people felt when Congress declared war on Germany; c. How German Americans were treated; d. How the Americans won an important battle; e. What happened to the "Lost Battalion."
2. Play songs of the First World War, such as "Over There" and "Pack Up Your Troubles." Copy the words to one song.
3. Bring in pictures or make posters and cartoons for a class display about the First World War.
4. Write a paragraph beginning with these words:
   a. "If the United States had not entered the war in 1917 . . ." or b. "If Germany had won the war . . ."
5. Write some answers that a few "typical" Americans might have given in March 1917 if an Inquiring Reporter had asked: "Should the United States declare war on Germany?"
6. Write up a discussion on one of these questions:
   a. To keep the United States out of the war, should President Wilson have forbidden Americans to travel on Allied ships or to do business with the Allies? b. Was Congress wise to give the President power over business and labor during the war? c. Should Congress have passed the Espionage and Sedition Acts?
7. Make a poster, bulletin board display, or construct a cartoon showing significant stages in the fight for women's suffrage. You could also use the Nineteenth Amendment as the basis for a display of what there is yet to do to achieve "equality of the sexes."

Chapter 28

THE FAILURE TO MAKE A LASTING PEACE

EUROPE was almost wrecked by the First World War. Some 9,000,000 people died in the war; more than 20,000,000 were wounded. Large areas were completely ruined. Governments fell deeply into debt. To meet their swollen war expenses, they printed great amounts of paper money, which fell rapidly in value. Industry and commerce were paralyzed. Millions of young men returning from the war could not find jobs. Many of them joined armed bands that offered to fight for anyone who hired them.

To make matters worse, postwar Europe was torn by new conflicts arising from old hatreds. Four large empires ruled by powerful monarchs—the Russian, Turkish, Austrian, and German empires—were broken up by the war. The subject peoples who belonged to these empires tried to set up their own independent nations. But they soon began to fight with one another over boundaries. Fighting also broke out between groups trying to gain control in each country. The Communists, for example, were encouraged by their success in Russia to start revolts in several other countries. Crops, factories, and railroads were ruined in this new fighting. Millions of Europeans faced death from hunger, cold, and disease during the first few years after the end of the war.

How did President Wilson try to help Europe? How did he try to build a peace that would last? Why did he fail? Why did the United States return to a policy of isolationism? What were the results of its actions? You will find the answers to these questions in the following chapter.

Why Did the United States Return to Isolationism?

A. American Relief in Europe. When World War I ended, President Wilson was satisfied with its results. The defeat of Germany, the fall of other undemocratic governments, and the freeing of many subject peoples—all these things pleased him. But he knew that Europe was in a bad condition. So he proposed that the United States, which had not been damaged by the war, should help Europe to deal with its new troubles. "Everything for which America fought has been accomplished," Wilson said. "It will now be our fortunate duty to assist by example, by sober counsel [advice], and by material aid in the establishment of democracy throughout the world."

The United States lent the Allied governments billions of dollars to repair war damage and restore their economies. It also established a relief organization to help needy people directly. The American Relief Administration gave food, clothing, fuel, and medicines to millions of people in a dozen countries, including even Communist Russia. Meanwhile, the President himself sailed for Europe to help write peace treaties for the defeated Central Powers.

B. Making the Peace. 1. Two Opposing Viewpoints. The peace conference met in Paris, the capital of France, early in 1919. Almost thirty nations were represented. All important decisions, however, were made by the "Big Four," the heads of the American, British, French, and Italian governments. It soon became clear that they did not all hold the same views about making the peace. President Wilson, who had a long-range view, believed in a "peace without victory." This was a peace settlement that gave nothing to the winners and took nothing from the losers. He also made fourteen suggestions, known as the Fourteen Points, for doing away with the causes of war. Among Wilson's Fourteen Points were freedom of the seas, disarmament (reduction of armies and navies), and independence for subject peoples. Most important, in Wilson's opinion, was his suggestion for a league (alliance) of nations to prevent future wars.

The three European leaders, on the other hand, felt that it was much more important to settle immediate problems. First, they wanted to make sure that they would never again be attacked by the nations they had just defeated. The French premier, in particular, wanted to crush Germany, which had invaded his country twice in his lifetime. Second, the Europeans wanted the defeated nations to pay for the damages and costs of the war. Third, the Allies wanted certain territories that belonged to the losers. Early in the war, they had signed secret agreements dividing these territories among themselves. Now they wanted the United States to accept their agreements. Wilson refused. The United States, he said, had not signed the agreements and was not bound by them. The dispute grew so bitter that at one point Wilson threatened to return to the United States.

2. The Peace Terms. As you might expect, both sides came to a compromise in the final treaties. The German peace treaty shows this very well. Germany was severely punished and greatly weakened. It lost a good deal of terri-

The "Big Four" of the Paris Peace Conference. From left to right: Premier Orlando of Italy, Prime Minister Lloyd George of Britain, Premier Clemenceau of France, and President Wilson. Why did the leaders of Italy, Britain, and France oppose Wilson's belief in a "peace without victory"?

tory in Europe to neighboring countries. All of its overseas colonies were taken away and divided among Great Britain, France, and Japan. It was allowed to have only a small army and navy, without submarines or military airplanes. It had to pay the huge sum of $33 billion as reparations (payments for the damage it had done).

On the other hand, Wilson saved Germany from being completely crushed. He made sure that Germany lost only those European territories in which mostly non-Germans lived. Far more important, he drew up the constitution for a new world organization, the League of Nations, and made it a part of the German peace treaty. Wilson thought the League his greatest achievement. To get it, he had given in to the European powers on a number of other issues.

C. The League of Nations. The League of Nations was the first organization in history formed by nations for the purpose of stopping war. It had two main bodies, the Assembly and the Council. Every member nation was represented in the Assembly. Each had one vote, regardless of its size or population. The Council had nine members. Five were the great powers—the United States, Great Britain, France, Italy, and Japan. These were to be the permanent members of the Council. The four remaining members were smaller powers that the Assembly elected. They were to serve on the Council for three-year terms. Any issue that threatened world peace could be discussed by either the Assembly or the Council. On important questions, the decision of either body had to be unanimous. If a nation refused to accept its decision, the League could call on its members to stop trading with it, or even to use force against it.

As this brief description shows, the League of Nations was a weak confederation. In fact, it was much like the United States under the old Articles of Confederation (see page 102). It depended completely on the member nations, especially on the great powers who were the permanent members of the Council. It could act only if the great powers were willing to enforce a decision that all the members of the Assembly or Council had voted for.

A number of international agencies were established to work with the League. The World Court was made up of fifteen judges. Its main job was to decide questions of international law on which member nations had disagreed. The job of the International Labor Organization was to improve conditions for workers all over the world. Other League agencies helped refugees, protected subject peoples from persecution, fought disease, and did other humanitarian work.

D. American Rejection of the Peace Treaties. President Wilson was not entirely pleased with the League's constitution or the other provisions of the peace treaties. But he felt sure that the Senate would approve them. He also felt sure that the United States would be the League's leading member. In time, he thought, the League could change the peace terms to make them fair. It could also help solve the other problems left by the war.

Most newspapers, many important organizations, and a large part of the American public supported Wilson. Four important groups, however, were opposed to the peace treaties and the League. 1. Isolationists did not want the United States to "get entangled in Europe's problems." They charged that the League was a "super-government" that would involve the United States in foreign wars against its will. 2. Another group believed that Germany had been treated too harshly. 3. Still another believed that Germany had not been treated harshly enough. 4. The most important group against ratification was a number of Republicans in Congress.

Some of these Republican Congressmen were only looking for an issue that would help them win the next election in 1920. But others, led by Senator Henry Cabot Lodge of Massachusetts, strongly disliked President Wilson and his policies. One reason for their attitude was the part the President had played in the Congressional elections of 1918. Though the Republicans had loyally supported Wilson's war program, the President had asked the American people to elect only Democrats to Congress. Nevertheless, the Republicans had won a majority in both houses. Lodge, Wilson's enemy, had become Chairman of the Senate Foreign Relations Committee. He was thus in a powerful position to stop the ratification of the treaties.

Instead of openly opposing the German peace treaty and the League of Nations, Lodge cleverly suggested a number of changes in them. President Wilson refused to accept these changes. He argued that the treaties had been made by almost thirty governments, and so

According to this cartoon, why did the Senate refuse to ratify the Treaty of Versailles and join the League of Nations?

no one nation had the right to change them. Though weakened by sickness and overwork, Wilson set out on a speaking tour to win public support for ratification without changes. The strain proved too great. The President suffered a severe stroke and lay ill for many months. From his sickbed, he ordered his loyal supporters to vote against the treaty with Lodge's changes. When the vote was taken, the treaty received a bare majority, instead of the two-thirds vote it needed for ratification. Thus it was defeated by the votes of its friends as well as its enemies.

E. The Election of 1920. A few months later, the Democrats met and nominated a candidate for President who strongly supported the League of Nations. The Republicans chose Senator Warren G. Harding of Ohio, who opposed the League. Harding's campaign slogan was "A return to normalcy"—that is, to conditions before the war. This slogan had a great appeal for the American people. They were tired of high prices, high taxes, the dispute over the peace terms, and other problems the war had created. The Republicans won a large majority, and Harding became President.

President Harding signed a separate peace treaty with Germany. The United States never joined the League of Nations. Wilson accused the Republicans of returning to isolationism, a policy that the United States had long since outgrown. He bitterly predicted that America's failure to enter the League would weaken the world organization and open the way to another war.

REVIEWING THE SECTION

A. Knowing New Terms

PART 1. In your notebook write the new terms in this section that best complete these statements.

1. The peace treaties after World War I were written by the leaders of the four great powers that won the war—____ ____ ____, ____ ____, ____, and ____.
2. President Wilson's proposals to do away with the causes of war were called the ____ ____.
3. The nations that lost the war were required to pay the winning nations for the damage they had done. Such payments were called ____.
4. The new world organization to prevent wars was called the ____ ____ ____.
5. This organization had two main bodies. All member nations were represented in the ____; the great powers controlled the ____.
6. The organization that decided questions of international law was named the ____ ____.

PART 2. Write the meaning of each term in your notebook *in your own words*.

(In **B**1) "peace without victory" (In **E**) "A return to normalcy"
(In **D**) "super-government"

B. Understanding the Facts

PART 1. For each result of the German peace treaty below, write "Wilson" in your notebook if the President wanted it; "Allies" if the leaders of the European Allies wanted it; and "Both" if both Wilson and the Allies wanted it. Be prepared to explain your answers in class.

1. Germany lost some territories in Europe to its neighbors.
2. These were territories in which mainly non-Germans lived.
3. Germany had to give up all its colonies to the winners.
4. Germany was disarmed.
5. Germany had to pay very heavy reparations.
6. The League of Nations was to be established.

Conclusion. Which side had better reason to be satisfied with the German peace treaty, Wilson or the European Allies? Why?

PART 2. Complete this chart comparing the Congress of the Confederation with the League of Nations. In your notebook write "Same" if the League resembled Congress in any of the ways listed below. If the two differed, explain how.

Congress of the Confederation	League of Nations
1. The Congress had a single house.	1.
2. Every state sent delegates to the Congress.	2.
3. Each state, regardless of size, had one vote.	3.
4. Decisions were made by nine of the thirteen states. Amendments required a unanimous vote.	4.
5. There was no executive to enforce its decisions.	5.
6. There was no court to settle disputes among the states.	6.

Conclusion. Which were more important, the ways the two organizations were alike or the ways they were different?

IMPROVING YOUR SKILLS

Looking at Both Sides

PART 1. To compare Wilson's views with those of the other Allied leaders, complete this chart in your notebook.

Wilson's Views	Views of the Other Allied Leaders

1. "A peace without victory"
2. Main proposals of the Fourteen Points
   a.
   b.
   c.
   d.
	1.
	2.
	3.
	4.

Conclusion. Which do you think had the wiser viewpoint? Explain.

PART 2. In your notebook list the arguments given by Americans for not ratifying the peace treaty with Germany, which included the constitution of the League of Nations. Then try to find an answer to each argument.

Reasons for Voting Against Ratification	Arguments for Ratification
1. The League was a "super-government." It would involve the United States in Europe's wars and other troubles.	1.
2. The peace terms were too harsh or too easy on the Germans.	2.
3. Many Republicans were opposed to Wilson and his policies.	3.

Conclusion. Which side had the stronger case? Prove your answer.

MAKING HISTORY LIVE

1. Write both sides of the debate: "Should the United States have joined the League of Nations?"
2. Write a paragraph on one of these opening phrases:
   a. "If President Wilson had not angered the Republican leaders in Congress. . . ." b. "If Wilson had been able to use the radio or TV in 1919. . . ." c. "If the United States had joined the League of Nations in 1919. . . ."
3. Draw a cartoon to show one of the following:
   a. the opposing views of President Wilson and the European leaders at the Paris Peace Conference; b. the effects of the peace terms on Germany; c. the opposing attitudes of President Wilson and the Republican leaders toward the League of Nations.

How Did the Policy of Isolationism Work?

A. Relations with the League. President Harding believed that the United States should return to its old policy of isolationism. He saw his election victory as proof that the American people thought so too. President Wilson, however, had been just as sure that the United States could not isolate itself any longer. It was too great a power in a world "shrinking" because of modern transportation and communication. Many Americans supported each point of view. The conflict between the two views went on until World War II, twenty years later. Let us try to find out which side was right.

President Harding would not allow the United States to have anything to do with the League of Nations. He even gave orders that any messages from the League should be returned unopened. When the question of joining the World Court came up, Harding said "No." The Court was the "back door to the League," he insisted. He meant that the United States would soon find itself in the League if it joined the World Court.

President Harding died suddenly in 1923. His policy toward the League was changed somewhat by his successors, Presidents Calvin Coolidge and Herbert Hoover. They began to send representatives to League meetings, provided these dealt with long-range issues rather than immediate problems. The United States took part, for example, in several talks on disarmament. It also cooperated in some other League activities. In 1926 the Senate voted to join the World Court, but it set certain conditions to protect American rights. Since the Court did not accept these conditions, our country never became a member. Nevertheless, the United States did join the International Labor Organization.

B. The Washington Conference (1921). 1. Reasons for the Meeting. Our relations with Japan created a second problem for President Harding. Japan had joined the Allied side early in World War I. It had quickly seized German holdings in the Far East, including a province of China and three groups of Pacific islands (see map, page 489). It had also tried to make China a protectorate. The United States was alarmed by Japan's growing power. A Japanese protectorate in China would violate the Open Door Policy. By building airfields on their new island possessions, moreover, the Japanese would have a number of "unsinkable aircraft carriers." From these, they could launch air attacks against American shipping to the Philippines and China in the event of war.

American foreign relations were also troubled by the danger of a naval arms race between the United States, Japan, and Great Britain. The Americans and Japanese had greatly increased the size of their fleets during the war. When it ended, both powers were still building new warships. The British were determined to keep their naval leadership by building as many ships as their rivals. But a naval race among the three great powers was bound to be very costly. It was also likely to make them fear and distrust one another. In fact, the American yellow press was already talking of the likelihood of war between the United States and Japan.

RIVALS IN THE PACIFIC, 1921

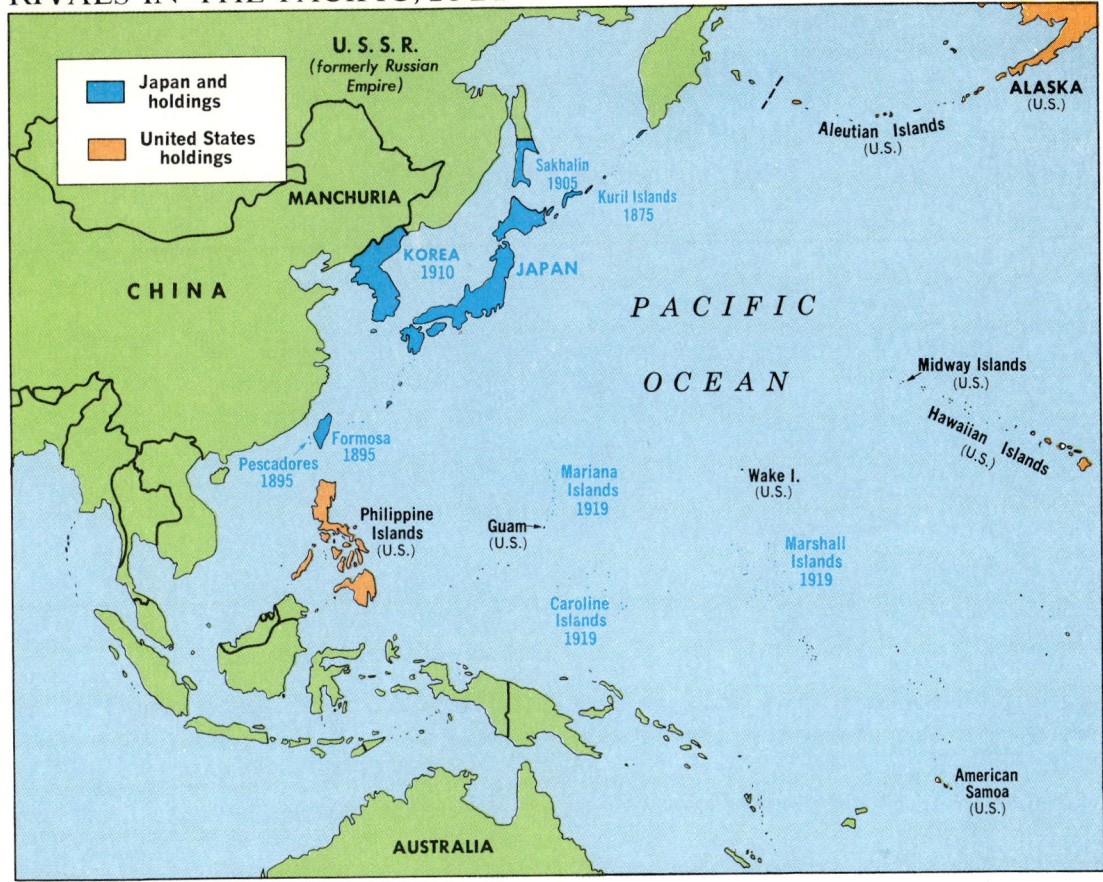

2. THE WASHINGTON TREATIES. President Harding therefore invited all the nations with interests in the Far East to send delegates to a meeting in Washington, D.C. Three agreements were worked out at this conference. 1. The great powers agreed to stop building new warships and to scrap some already in use. The American and British navies were to be equal in size; the Japanese fleet was to be three-fifths of their size. 2. The great powers agreed to settle peacefully any disputes over their Pacific possessions. 3. All the governments at the conference agreed to respect China's independence, to stop taking over its territory, and to support the Open Door Policy. What is more, Japan agreed to pull out of the Chinese province it had already taken. The Washington agreements, and especially Japan's withdrawal from China, were considered a great victory for President Harding.

C. The War Debts Problem. 1. THE AMERICAN ATTITUDE. American loans to the Allies during and after the war gave rise to still another problem. The war debts, as they were called, amounted to more than ten billion dollars. The Allies objected to paying back so large a sum. They argued that they had suffered very heavy losses during the war, while the United States had grown richer and stronger. President Harding would not listen. He insisted that the war debts had to be paid in full.

The Washington Conference, 1921. President Harding is welcoming the delegates from many foreign lands. Why did he break with his policy of isolationism in this case?

In 1922 Congress raised tariff rates to a new high. The European governments pointed out that the new rates made it very hard for them to sell enough goods in the United States to pay their debts. President Harding again ignored their protests.

Meanwhile, Germany was finding it very difficult to make the reparations payments it owed the Allies. In 1923 its money became worthless and its entire economic system came to a standstill. The German government stopped its reparations payments completely. The Allies then agreed to reduce Germany's reparations payments if the United States canceled or reduced the war debts. Once again the American government refused. These refusals aroused anger against the United States in Europe.

2. THE OUTCOME. Soon afterward an international commission studied the reparations problem. It advised a reduction in Germany's payments and large loans for rebuilding the German economy. American bankers then sold several billion dollars' worth of German bonds to the American people. The Germans used most of this money to modernize their factories. They paid out the rest as reparations to the Allies. The Allies in turn used some of the money to make payments on their war debts to the United States.

In 1929 a great depression began in the United States. American bankers stopped lending Germany money, the Germans stopped paying reparations to the Allies, and the Allies stopped paying their war debts to the United States. Since that time, nothing has been paid on either the reparations or the war debts. The Americans who bought German bonds suffered heavy losses. Their disappointment further strengthened the spirit of isolationism in the United States.

D. The Paris Peace Pact (1928). By this time, Great Britain and France had had a number of quarrels over reparations and other issues. As a result, the British established ties with Germany. This so worried the French that they appealed to the United States in 1928 to sign a treaty of friendship.

The American government was unwilling to sign such an agreement. But it did not want to refuse the French completely. So it suggested a treaty that would be open to all nations. The signers of this treaty would agree to settle all their disputes by peaceful means rather than by war.

Even the isolationists supported this international agreement, which was named the Paris Peace Pact. It was signed by most of the nations in the world and registered with the League of Nations. Many experts, however, doubted the value of the Paris Peace Pact. They said that it did not tell how the signers would be punished if they broke their promise.

E. The Manchurian Incident (1931-1932). Events soon proved that the experts were right. In 1931 Japan complained that bandits were attacking its citizens and property in China's northernmost province, Manchuria (see map, page 489). Without warning, a Japanese army invaded and conquered the entire province. Manchuria became a protectorate of Japan.

Japan's action in the "Manchurian Incident" violated the Paris Peace Pact, the Washington agreements, and the constitution of the League of Nations. It raised a storm of protest all over the world. The American government announced that it would not recognize Japan's protectorate. The League of Nations called for a hearing and invited the United States to send a delegate. President Hoover agreed, but made it clear that the American delegate would only be an observer. He would not take an active part in the talks or support any action the League might take.

League members talked about taking economic action against Japan. Cutting off its trade would probably have been effective. For Japan could support its large population only by importing raw materials and selling manufactured goods. But the member nations were afraid to act without American support. So they only criticized Japan and agreed not to recognize the conquest of Manchuria. The failure to stop Japan in Manchuria seriously weakened the League. It also encouraged other warlike governments, as we shall see later, to begin their own programs of conquest.

According to this cartoon, why was Japan's invasion of Manchuria a threat to world peace? Do you think the Japanese would have been afraid to attack if the United States had been a member of the League of Nations?

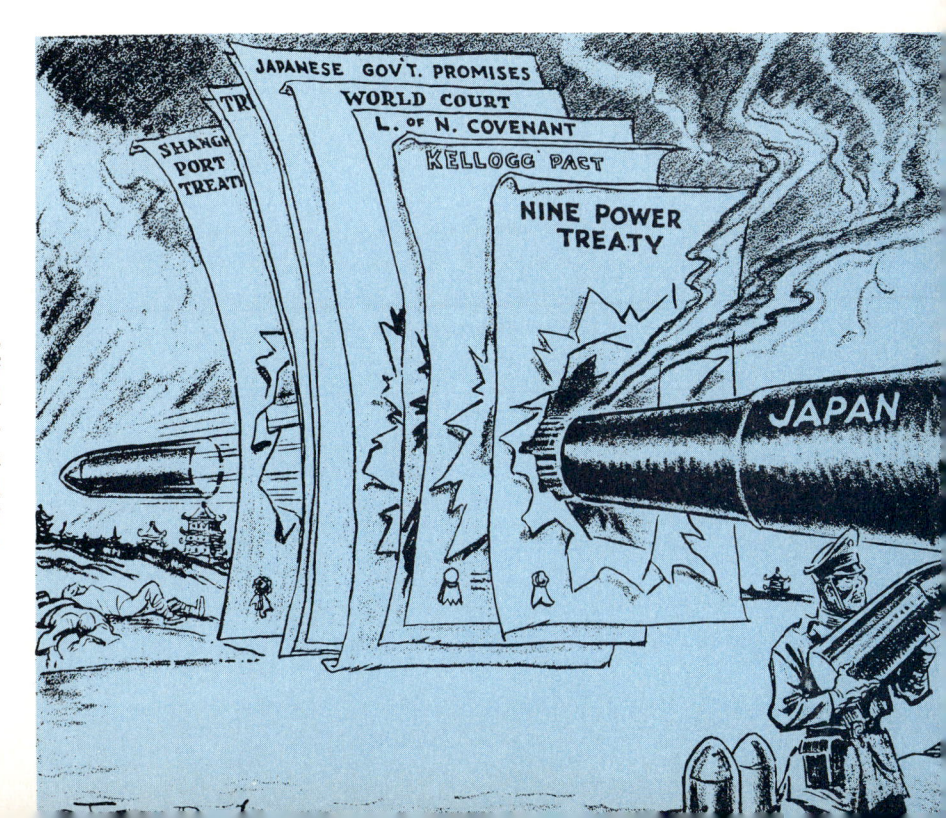

REVIEWING THE SECTION

A. Knowing New Terms

In your notebook write the *letter* of the statement that tells what each italicized term meant in the postwar period.

1. *"Back door to the League"*: a. the American peace treaty with Germany b. our membership in the World Court c. our protests against Japanese actions in China d. our Open Door Policy in China
2. *"Unsinkable aircraft carriers"*: a. large modern warships b. American bases in Europe c. Japanese-controlled islands in the Pacific d. Japanese-held territories on China's mainland
3. *Naval race:* a. rivalry among the great powers to build the largest navy b. agreement to give up war as a way of settling disputes c. experiments to develop more deadly weapons d. the British effort to remain the world's leading naval power
4. *Manchurian Incident:* a. Japan's defeat of Russia in Manchuria b. Japan's conquest of Manchuria in 1932 c. the League of Nations' criticism of Japan for taking Manchuria d. American refusal to recognize Japan's protectorate in Manchuria
5. *War debts:* a. payment for damages suffered in World War I b. money the United States owed its allies c. loans to help Germany recover from World War I d. payments the Allies owed to the United States
6. *Paris Peace Pact:* a. agreement not to use war to settle disputes among nations b. treaty of friendship between France and the United States c. the League's decision not to take action against Japan d. agreement to limit the size of the great powers' navies

B. Understanding the Facts

Write "Isolationist" in your notebook if each of the following actions is an example of isolationism; "Internationalist" if it is an example of international cooperation; and "Neither" if it is not clearly an example of either policy. Be prepared to explain your answers in class.

1. President Harding refused to deal with the League of Nations.
2. Presidents Coolidge and Hoover sent observers to League conferences.
3. The United States offered to join the World Court on special conditions intended to protect its rights.
4. The United States joined the International Labor Organization.
5. The American government called the Washington Conference.
6. The United States signed the Washington treaties on naval disarmament, Pacific possessions, and China.

7. The American government refused to reduce the war debts owed by its former allies.
8. The President refused to sign a treaty of friendship with France, but suggested instead a general treaty to outlaw war.
9. President Hoover sent a delegate to the League's hearings on the Manchurian Incident, but only as an observer.
10. The United States refused to support the League's actions on Manchuria.

Conclusions. 1. Was the United States completely isolationist during the period after World War I? 2. In which cases did our government follow a policy that was completely isolationist? 3. In which case did our government cooperate completely with other nations? 4. In which case was our policy most successful? Explain why. 5. In which case was American policy least successful? Prove your answer.

IMPROVING YOUR SKILLS

A. Telling Facts From Opinions

Write "Fact" for each statement that can be proved by getting the necessary information. Write "Opinion" if you think the answer depends on values and judgment. Be prepared to give the reasons for your answers in class.

1. It was harder for the United States to be isolationist as a great power than as a weak, undeveloped nation.
2. If the United States had joined the World Court, it would probably have become a member of the League of Nations too.
3. Japan's growing power in the Far East after World War I was a threat to American interests there.
4. If the naval race among the three great powers had continued, their distrust of one another would have increased greatly.
5. The United States won a great victory over Japan in the Washington treaties.
6. The Washington Conference ended the great-power rivalry in the Far East for a time.
7. The United States was right in insisting that the Allies pay their war debts in full.
8. Germany would have paid reparations if the amount had been smaller.
9. The way the United States handled the problem of war debts and reparations worked out badly for all the nations concerned.
10. The Paris Peace Pact did not end the use of force to settle disputes among nations.

11. If the United States had supported the League, Japan would have been forced to withdraw from Manchuria.

B. Mastering the Map

Study the map on page 489. Then complete the following statements.

1. The three groups of islands that Japan took from Germany after World War I were the _____, _____, and _____.
2. From its base in Formosa, Japan could easily attack an important American possession, the _____ _____.
3. From the Mariana Islands, the Japanese could easily reach the nearby American island of _____.
4. From the Marshall Islands, the Japanese could move eastward to attack an important American possession, the _____ Islands.
5. The Japanese army that seized Manchuria came from a neighboring Japanese possession, _____.
6. From Manchuria, the Japanese could advance either southward into _____ or northward into the _____.

SUMMING UP THE UNIT

How Was the United States Drawn Into World Affairs?

A. The First Steps. Isolationism became our country's foreign policy under our first President, George Washington. It remained our policy for more than a century. Nevertheless, the United States could not help getting involved little by little in the affairs of other nations. The turn away from isolationism began in the Far East. During the nineteenth century, the United States built a large trade with China and opened Japan to western trade. Later it took over Hawaii, Samoa, and some other Pacific islands. These gave the United States stepping stones across the Pacific to the Far East.

B. The Spanish-American War. In 1898 the United States went to war with Spain, mainly to help Cuba win its independence. Our nation won an easy victory over the weak and battle-weary Spanish forces. Cuba gained its independence, but the United States became its protector. Our nation also took the Philippines, Puerto Rico, and Guam from Spain. America's easy victory showed that it had become a world power. Theodore Roosevelt and other leaders felt the time had come for America to take an active part in world affairs.

C. Governing the New Possessions. The United States had little experience in governing foreign possessions before 1898. But it soon developed a new system of rule. This was intended to improve the people's way of life and to prepare them to govern themselves. During the next half-century, Alaska and Hawaii became states, the Philippines won their independence, and Puerto Rico became a self-governing commonwealth. In most of the smaller American possessions, the people gained a voice in government.

D. Involvement in Latin America. Under Theodore Roosevelt, the United States also became active in Latin America. Our country had first become interested in our "neighbors to the South" in 1823, soon after they won their independence from Spain. At that time President Monroe warned the European powers not to mix in the affairs of the western hemisphere or to establish new colonies there. The United States acted three times during the next eighty years to enforce the Monroe Doctrine.

Theodore Roosevelt went much further, however. He built the Panama Canal and a number of American bases to protect it. He also took control of several countries bordering on the Caribbean Sea in order to keep European powers from interfering in their affairs. Roosevelt's policy of taking strong action in Latin America was followed by Presidents Taft and Wilson. The Caribbean Sea became an "American lake" as the United States gained control of most of the nations around it.

E. The First World War. When war broke out in Europe in 1914, the United States tried to remain neutral and isolationist. It failed. President Wilson insisted on our "freedom of the seas," our right as a neutral nation to trade with Europe. As a result, American businesses built up a large trade with the Allies, who controlled the seas. This led to trouble with the leading Central Power, Germany. German submarines sank American ships and German agents damaged American factories. In the spring of 1917, the United States declared war on Germany.

The American government organized its people and industries for war with amazing speed. Its large army, strong navy, and plentiful supplies helped the Allies to defeat Germany and the other Central Powers.

F. Making the Peace. At the peace conference in France, President Wilson proposed a "peace without victory," based on his Fourteen Points. His goal was to remove the conditions that led to rivalries and wars among nations. But the European leaders were more interested in taking revenge against their defeated enemies. They wanted territory belonging to Germany and the other Central Powers as well as payments for war damages. They also wanted to keep the Central Powers from becoming strong again. The final peace terms were a compromise. The Central Powers were disarmed and weakened. The Allies gained territory and were promised reparations payments. Wilson got the League of Nations, a new international organization for keeping the peace. The Senate refused, however, to approve the peace treaties. The United States never joined the League of Nations.

In 1920 the American people elected a Republican President, Warren G. Harding. The new President called for a return to the old policy of isolationism. He refused to deal with the League of Nations or cancel the war debts owed by America's former allies. The United States could not, however, isolate itself completely from world affairs. Harding himself called a conference to deal with problems in the Pacific. His successor, President Coolidge, supported a treaty to outlaw war. In 1932 President Hoover sent a delegate to a League of Nations conference on the Manchurian Incident. But he refused to support any action the League might take. The League's failure to stop Japan encouraged other powers to attack weaker countries. This led experts to ask: "Would the United States be able to stay out of the new troubles in Europe and Asia?"

REVIEWING THE UNIT

A. Knowing Important People

For each description, write in your notebook the *letter* of the person to whom it applies. You may use the same letter more than once.

A. George Dewey
B. George W. Goethals
C. William C. Gorgas
D. Warren G. Harding
E. Henry C. Lodge
F. William McKinley
G. Matthew C. Perry
H. John J. Pershing
I. Queen Liliuokalani
J. Theodore Roosevelt
K. William H. Taft
L. Woodrow Wilson

1. I asked Congress to declare war on Spain.
2. I became a national hero by leading a charge against Spanish troops in Cuba.
3. I became a hero by sinking an entire Spanish fleet.
4. I claimed credit for starting the Panama Canal without delay.
5. I conquered yellow fever in Cuba and Panama.
6. I was the monarch of Hawaii.
7. I wanted peace, but asked Congress to declare war on Germany.
8. I helped to defeat the peace treaties after World War I by making a number of changes that the President would not accept.
9. I commanded the American armies in France.
10. I led the United States back to "normalcy" and isolationism.
11. I planned the League of Nations, but could not persuade my country to join it.
12. I showed the Japanese the advantages of trading with the West.
13. Though I was against American involvement in Latin American affairs, I twice sent troops into Mexico.
14. I increased American influence in Latin America by encouraging American bankers and businesses to invest there.
15. I was the engineer responsible for building the Panama Canal.

B. Understanding the Facts

Choose the term that does *not* belong with the others in the group.

1. *American relations with China:* a. The Opium War (which opened China to Western trade)   b. Open Door Policy   c. Boxer Uprising   d. Washington Conference
2. *American relations with Japan:* a. Perry's expedition   b. Treaty ending the Russo-Japanese War   c. Trouble over immigration and discrimina-

tion on the West Coast   d. American relief at the end of World War I
3. *American possessions in the Pacific:* a. Alaska   b. Hawaiian Islands   c. Puerto Rico   d. Samoan Islands
4. *Causes of the Spanish-American War:* a. Monroe Doctrine   b. Yellow press   c. De Lôme letter   d. Sinking of the *Maine*
5. *Government of the American possessions:* a. Protectorate in Cuba   b. Independence for the Philippines   c. Commonwealth status for Puerto Rico   d. Statehood for Alaska and Hawaii
6. *Relations between the United States and Latin America:* a. Maximilian Affair   b. Pan-American Union   c. Roosevelt's extension of the Monroe Doctrine   d. War-debts dispute
7. *Countries to which the United States sent troops:* a. Venezuela   b. Cuba   c. Dominican Republic   d. Mexico
8. *Reasons for American entry into World War I:* a. British propaganda   b. Large trade with the Central Powers   c. German sabotage   d. Desire to save democracy
9. *American actions on the "home front" in World War I:* a. Selective Service Act   b. Laws against Communists   c. Heatless and meatless days   d. Sales of Liberty Bonds
10. *Provisions of the peace treaties after World War I:* a. A peace without victory   b. Loss of territories by the Central Powers   c. Payments for war damages   d. Establishment of the League of Nations
11. *New international organizations after World War I:* a. International Labor Organization   b. League of Nations   c. World Court   d. Washington Conference
12. *America's return to isolationism after World War I:* a. Failure to ratify the peace treaties   b. Refusal to reduce the war debts   c. Signing of the Paris Peace Pact   d. Failure to stop the Japanese in Manchuria

C. *Knowing Where Things Happened*

On an outline map of the world, do the following:

1. Label the oceans and shade them in pencil or color them light blue.
2. Label the continents.
3. Write the *letter* of each of the following places on the map to show where it is located. If it is a large place, write the letter near its center.

   a. United States
   b. China
   c. Japan
   d. Alaska
   e. Philippine Islands
   f. Samoan Islands
   g. Hawaiian Islands
   h. Caribbean Sea
   i. Cuba
   j. Puerto Rico
   k. Panama Canal
   l. Mexico
   m. Central America
   n. Venezuela
   o. Great Britain
   p. France
   q. Russia
   r. Germany
   s. Austria
   t. Serbia (now part of Yugoslavia)

497

D. Knowing When Things Happened

PART 1. Arrange the events in each group in the correct order.

A

1. Open Door Policy
2. Opening of China to western trade
3. Opening of Japan to western trade

B

1. Revolution in Panama
2. Roosevelt extension of the Monroe Doctrine
3. Spanish-American War

C

1. American occupation of Veracruz
2. American pursuit of Pancho Villa
3. Start of World War I in Europe

D

1. German submarine attacks on American merchant ships
2. Sinking of the *Lusitania*
3. American declaration of war on Germany

E

1. Paris Peace Conference
2. Senate refusal to ratify the peace treaties
3. Wilson's Fourteen Points

F

1. Japan's conquest of Manchuria
2. Paris Peace Pact
3. Washington Conference

G

1. American entry into World War I
2. American involvement in Latin America
3. American involvement in the Far East

PART 2. Write the dates of these three events in your notebook without looking them up. Then check to make sure you have them right.

1. The Spanish-American War
2. The beginning of World War I
3. The end of World War I

RECOMMENDED READING

A. Historical Books

ADAMS, B. *Last Frontier: A Short History of Alaska*. New York: Hill and Wang, 1961.
APPEL, B. *The People Talk: American Voices from the Great Depression*. New York: Simon & Schuster, 1982.
BARNETT, C. *The Great War*. New York: Putnam, 1979. WWI from beginning to end.
BOWEN, E., et al. *Knights of the Air*. Alexandria, Va.: Time-Life Books, 1980. Pilots and planes of WWI.
BROWNSTONE, D. M., et al. *Island of Hope, Island of Tears*. New York: Rawson, Wade, 1979.

CHEN, J. *The Chinese of America*. New York: Harper & Row, 1980. Their struggles and contributions.
FARR, N. *America Becomes a World Power*. Eds. D. Calhoun, and L. W. Bloch. West Haven, Conn.: Pendulum Press, 1977.
———. *The Roaring Twenties and the Great Depression*. Eds. D. Calhoun, and L. W. Bloch. West Haven, Conn.: Pendulum Press, 1977.
FEJES, C. *Villagers*. New York: Random House, 1981. An artist's view of Yukon River Indians.
FISH, C. R. *Path of Empire*. Chronicles of America, vol. 46. New York: U.S. Pubs.
GOLDSTON, R. *The Great Depression*. Indianapolis, Ind.: Bobbs-Merrill, 1968.
———. *The Road Between the Wars: 1918–1941*. New York: Dial, 1978.
GREENWALD, M. W. *Women, War & Work*. Westport, Conn.: Greenwood Press, 1980.
JANTZEN, S. *Hooray for Peace, Hurrah for War*. New York: Alfred A. Knopf, 1971. Life in the U.S. during WWI.
KELLER, U., ed. *The Building of the Panama Canal in Historic Photographs*. New York: Dover, 1982.
KUYKENDALL, R., and DAY, A. *Hawaii: A History*. Englewood Cliffs, N.J.: Prentice-Hall, 1978.
LAWSON, D. *The United States in the Spanish American War*. New York: Abelard-Schuman, 1976.
MCCLELLAN, G. S., ed. *U.S. Policy in Latin America*. New York: Wilson, 1963.
PERL, L. *Puerto Rico*. New York: William Morrow, 1979. History, culture, and present problems.
SHEPHERD, W. R. *Hispanic Nations of the New World*. Chronicles of America, vol. 50. New York: U.S. Pubs.
STUMER, H. M. *This Was Klondike Fever*. Seattle, Wash.: Superior, 1979.

B. Biographies and Autobiographies

GARVER, S., and MCGUIRE, P. *Coming to North America: From Mexico, Cuba, and Puerto Rico*. New York: Delacorte Press, 1981.
GILL, B. *Lindbergh Alone*. New York: Harcourt Brace Jovanovich, 1977.
KUHN, F. *Commodore Perry and the Opening of Japan*. New York: Random House, 1955.
NORTON, A. A. *Theodore Roosevelt*. Boston: Twayne, 1980.
PANELLA, V. *The Other Side*. Garden City, N.Y.: Doubleday, 1979. Growing up Italian in America.
SULLIVAN, W. *Franklin Delano Roosevelt*. New York: Harper & Row, 1970.
WHITNEY, S. *Eleanor Roosevelt*. New York: Franklin Watts, 1982.
WOOD, L. N. *Walter Reed: Doctor in Uniform*. New York: Messner, 1943.
WRIGHT, N. *The Red Baron*. New York: McGraw-Hill, 1977.

C. Historical Fiction

BYRD, E. *I'll Get By*. New York: Viking Press, 1981. As Julie copes in N.Y.C. of the '20's.
DANK, M. *Khaki Wings*. New York: Delacorte Press, 1980. A 16-year-old pilot in World War I.
NICOL, C. W. *The White Shaman*. Boston: Little, Brown, 1979. Richard is adopted by Eskimos.
REMARQUE, E. M. *All Quiet on the Western Front*. Various editions. A very popular novel about World War I from the German viewpoint.
———. *The Road Back*. New York: Avon, 1964. Problems of the returning soldiers.
WHITEHOUSE, A. *Squadron Forty-Four*. Garden City, N.Y.: Doubleday, 1965.
YEP, L. *Dragonwings*. New York: Harper & Row, 1975. A Chinese immigrant boy's story.

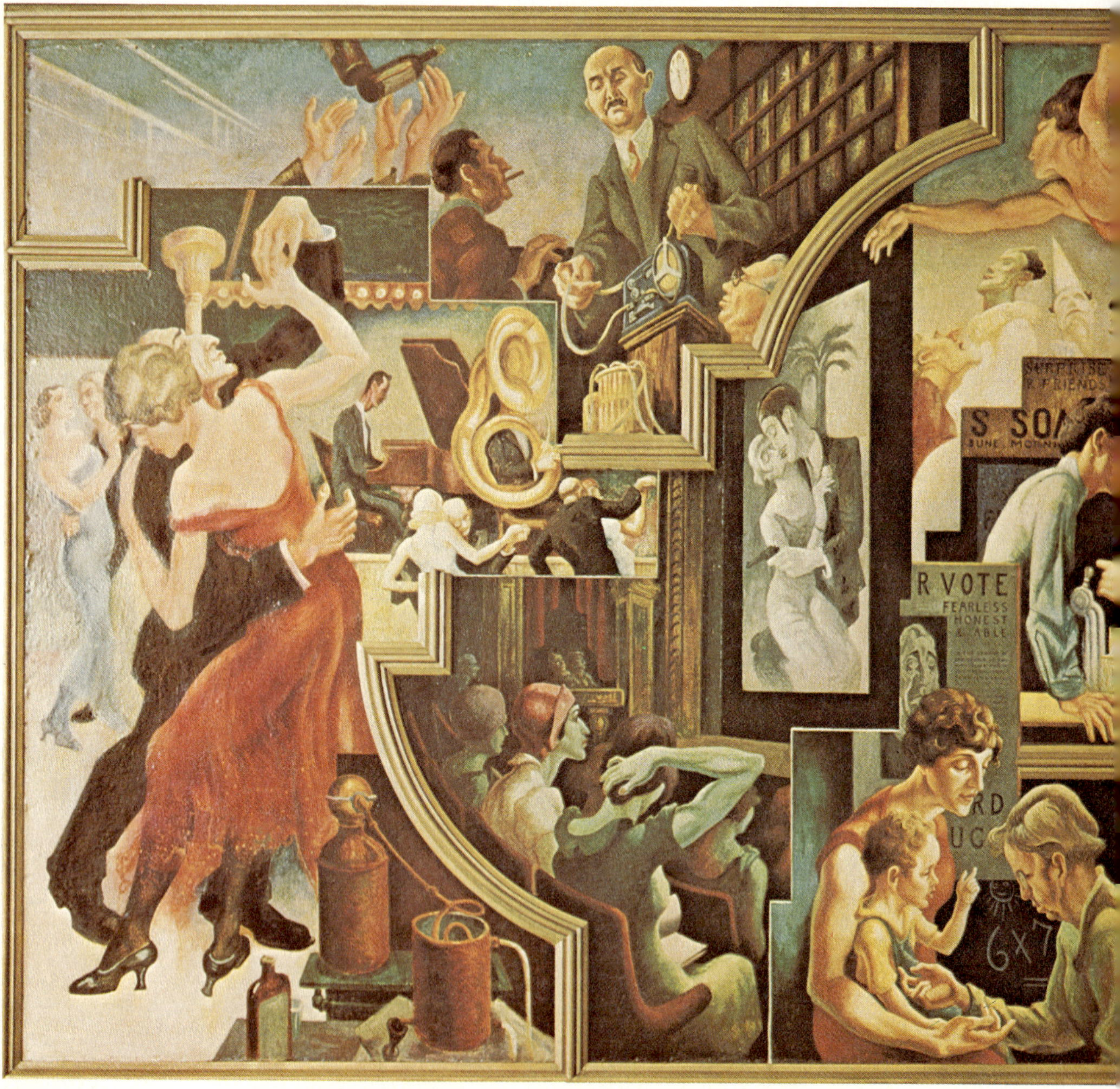
R VOTE
FEARLESS
HONEST
& ABLE

Unit Seven

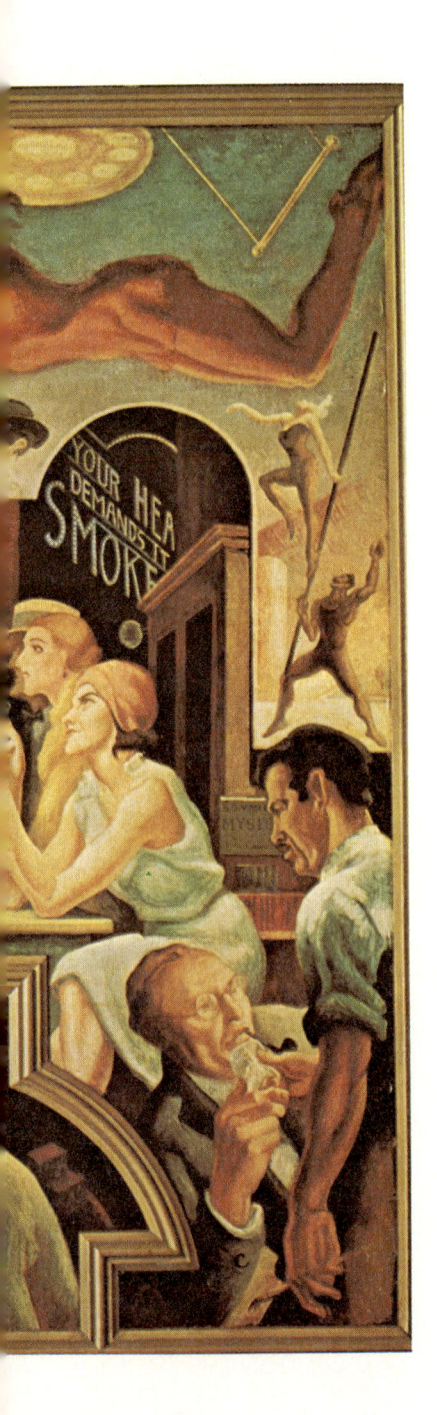

BETWEEN TWO WORLD WARS

The First World War was so costly that many people considered it "the war to end war." They felt sure that no nation would ever again be foolish enough to start a great war. As we know, events proved them wrong. Germany wanted revenge for its defeat and punishment. Two of the Allies, Italy and Japan, were dissatisfied with their gains. All three countries suffered from economic troubles because of the war. In each country, a dictator came to power by promising to lead his people to prosperity and power. The three dictatorships began a march of conquest that led to the outbreak of the Second World War in 1939, only twenty-one years after the end of "the war to end war."

In this unit we shall see the following:
1. *What changes took place in the United States between the First and Second World Wars*
2. *How the United States became involved in World War II*

This painting by Thomas Hart Benton shows some scenes from the late 1920s. How have attitudes toward the dangers of violence, alcohol, and smoking changed since then? Why?

3. How the United States and its allies won the war
4. How the victors tried, but failed, to agree on terms for a lasting peace

UNIT 7: 1918-1945

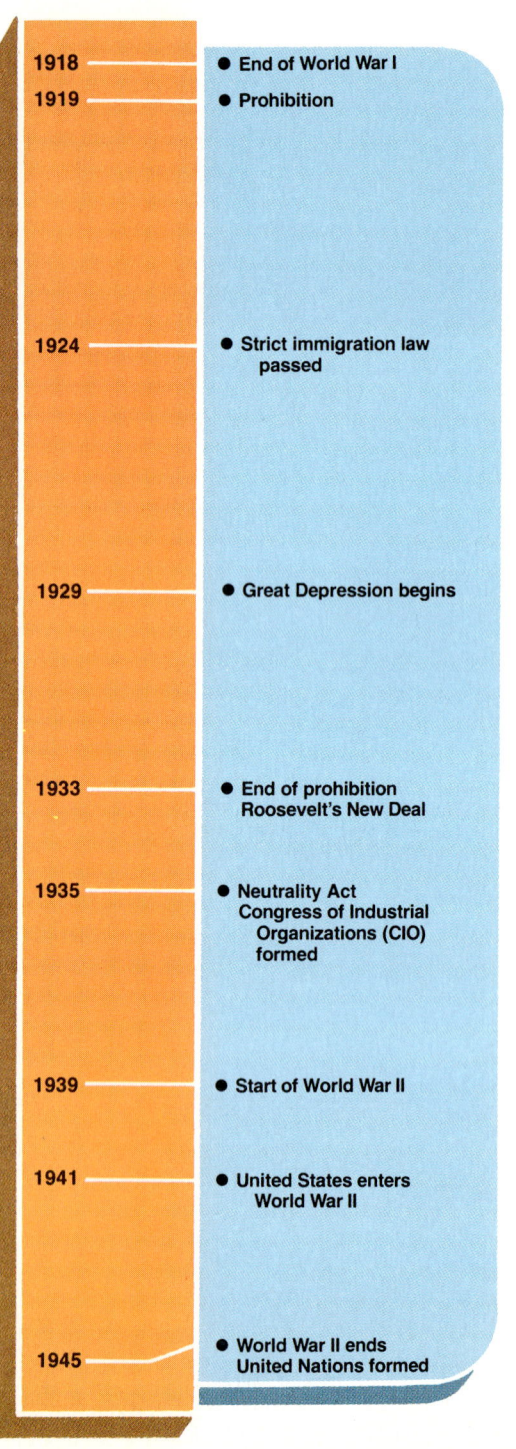

1918	End of World War I
1919	Prohibition
1924	Strict immigration law passed
1929	Great Depression begins
1933	End of prohibition; Roosevelt's New Deal
1935	Neutrality Act; Congress of Industrial Organizations (CIO) formed
1939	Start of World War II
1941	United States enters World War II
1945	World War II ends; United Nations formed

Chapter 29

THE UNITED STATES AFTER WORLD WAR I

The ten-year period after World War I has become known in American history as the "Roaring Twenties" or "Jazz Age." As these names show, it was a time of gaiety and excitement. The war, with its millions of dead, had made many people feel that life was uncertain and therefore to be enjoyed while it lasted. This feeling was especially widespread among the young. Rebelling against their parents, whom they blamed for the war, they began a headlong search for thrills. They smoked, drank, and held wild parties, at which they danced to a rhythmic new music called jazz.

Young women, even more than young men, tried to free themselves from the customs of the past. Unlike their mothers, they "bobbed" their hair (cut it short), and wore tighter dresses that ended above the knees. They worked at jobs only men had held and played games once considered "for men only." These young women, called "flappers," came to symbolize American women. But they made up only a minority of American women. Still, to many Americans, women were trying to prove their equality with men.

Except for a brief depression, the Roaring Twenties were a boom time, a period of great economic prosperity. Unfortunately, this prosperity did not last long. In 1929 the United States plunged into the worst economic depression in its history. In the first section of this chapter, you will read about the Roaring Twenties, the period of gaiety and prosperity. In the second section, you will read about the reasons for the depression that ended the period of good times.

How Did the United States Change in the 1920s?

A. Prohibition and Its Effects. One of the most striking features of the Roaring Twenties was Prohibition. The Eighteenth Amendment, ratified early in 1919, prohibited (forbade) the manufacture and sale of intoxicating liquors. Congress defined an intoxicating liquor as one that had more than one-half of one percent of alcohol. Since this included even wine and beer, the law was unpopular and was widely disobeyed. In fact, drinking became "the thing to do" just because it was forbidden. Secret drinking places called "speakeasies" flourished. "Bootleggers" smuggled in liquor from abroad or made it themselves. Since they were breaking the law and risking long prison terms, they charged very high prices. They used part of their large profits to bribe government officials to overlook their illegal activities.

In a short time bands of criminals known as "gangsters" took over the liquor business. Soon they were using their power and profits to move into other fields. They set up gambling houses, made businesses pay "protection" to keep their property from being damaged, and took over labor unions. Activities carried on by gangsters were called "rackets." "Racketeering" became a multi-million dollar industry in the Roaring Twenties. The gangsters even formed private armies of gunfighters and battled over territory, much like the nobles of Europe in the Middle Ages.

Prohibition was finally ended in 1933 by the Twenty-First Amendment, which repealed the Eighteenth Amendment. Within the next few years, the federal government sent many leading gangsters to prison—usually for not paying income taxes on their profits! But the organized crime and racketeering that started in the Roaring Twenties have continued to this day.

B. The Growth of Intolerance. 1. THE "RED SCARE." The spirit of intolerance—that is, distrust of minorities—that gripped Americans during World War I led to a "Red scare" after the war. Many Americans, frightened by the Communist takeover in Russia, persecuted people with Russian names or socialist ideas. In 1919 the Communists were blamed for a wave of strikes that really started because prices were rising much faster than wages. Union leaders were accused of being Reds. The attorney general of the United States, acting under the wartime Espionage and the Sedition Acts, arrested thousands of people. More than five hundred of them who were born in Europe were sent back to the countries they had come from. State officials arrested hundreds more who were thought to be Reds. Most of them were later proved to be innocent or were simply released. But several years passed before the American people regained their usual tolerance and respect for freedom of speech and the press.

2. THE NEW K.K.K. A second sign of intolerance was the rebirth of the Ku Klux Klan (see page 343). In its new form, this organization was still the enemy of blacks, but it now also attacked Catholics, Jews, union leaders, and foreigners. The new K.K.K. spread rapidly in the Midwest as well as in the South. It claimed more than five million members in

1925. It quickly declined, however, when its leaders were proved to be criminals.

C. A New Immigration Policy. Intolerance was also one of the reasons why Congress passed new immigration laws in the early 1920s. For the first time in our history, immigration was strictly limited. Under the immigration act of 1924, only about 150,000 people were allowed to enter the United States from Europe each year. What is more, a quota (certain number) of immigrants was set for each European country. This quota was based on the number of people in the United States in 1890 who had originated—that is, who had come or whose ancestors had come—from each country. In practice, this meant that 85 percent of the total number of immigrants had to come from Great Britain, Germany, and the other nations of northern or western Europe. Only 15 percent could be citizens of the countries of southern

An illustration of the Roaring Twenties. Flappers wore short skirts and cut their hair.

The "new K.K.K." marching in Washington, D.C. What other groups besides blacks did the new Ku Klux Klan attack? Why did the K.K.K. attract so many members in the 1920s?

IMMIGRATION TO THE UNITED STATES FROM EUROPE, 1880-1930

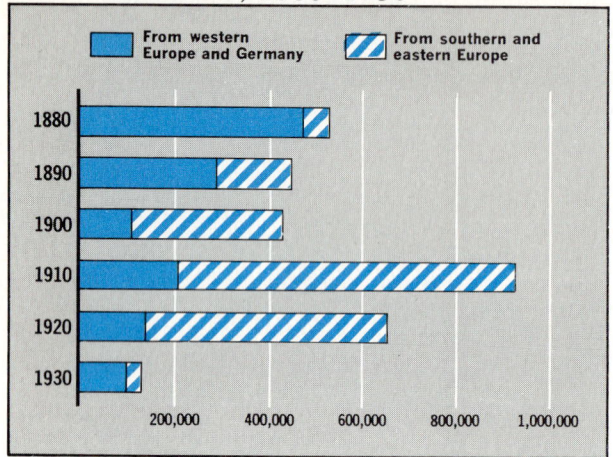

Bar chart showing immigration from western Europe and Germany, and from southern and eastern Europe, for the years 1880, 1890, 1900, 1910, 1920, and 1930. Horizontal scale: 200,000 to 1,000,000.

and eastern Europe. Immigrants from Asia were almost completely shut out. Since few northern Europeans wished to come to the United States at that time, the effect of the law was to reduce the flood of immigrants to a trickle.

Opponents of the new immigration laws pointed out how important immigration had been to our nation's development. They showed that immigrants from southern and eastern Europe had already made contributions to our country's growth. Scientists produced evidence that no race or nationality was inferior to any other. Historians reminded the American people that equality was a basic principle of both the Christian religion and democracy.

Supporters of the new policy answered that the United States no longer needed immigrant labor. They also said that the new immigrants from southern and eastern Europe were harder to "Americanize" than the old immigrants. The American Federation of Labor and other unions likewise backed the new laws. They argued that immigrants usually worked for lower wages and were often used to break strikes. Because of this difference of opinion, it took more than forty years to change the policy of limited immigration that began in the 1920s.

D. The Economic Boom. Still another feature of the Roaring Twenties was a great economic boom, or period of rapidly rising prosperity. This boom was a result of the war, which had expanded American industry and brought large profits to American businesses. Many used their profits to introduce new machines and methods of production that led to reduced costs and prices. The automobile industry made the greatest gains. So many cars were made at such low cost that the automobile ceased to be a "rich man's toy." It became instead the prized possession of the average middle-class family. Steelmaking, petroleum refining, road building, and other industries allied to automobile making expanded as automobile production increased. Still other industries—including chemicals, electrical appliances, aviation, motion pictures, and the radio—also grew swiftly as a result of the war.

Henry Ford urged business people to raise wages so that workers would be able to buy the output of the expanding industries. He set the standard by paying workers a very high wage, five dollars a day. Many firms gave their workers a share of the profits, free insurance, old-age pensions, and other benefits. Progressive businesses believed that it paid to keep workers satisfied because they would work harder and would not join unions.

To sell the huge amounts of goods produced by the factories, American businesses also developed new methods of marketing. Especially important were chain stores, large-scale advertising, and installment buying. Saving was no longer considered a virtue. Instead, Americans were urged to spend freely in order to keep the economy growing.

E. Government Policies. 1. SUPPORT OF BIG BUSINESS. The Republican party governed the nation during the Roaring Twenties. Its leaders returned to the policy of helping big business that the Republicans had followed successfully after the Civil War. Taxes on large corporations and the wealthy were reduced. Only a few antitrust cases were brought to court by the government—mostly against labor unions. Railroads were allowed to combine and raise their rates to meet the challenge of the truck and bus. Shipping and aviation companies received large sums of money from the government on the ground that they would be needed in case of another war. Tariffs were raised in 1922 and again in 1930. Most Americans believed that these government policies were the main reason for the nation's prosperity.

2. CORRUPTION UNDER HARDING (1921-1923). The Republican record was spoiled for a time by corruption. President Harding made the mistake of placing personal friends in high government posts. His attorney general took bribes for getting people government positions and contracts for public works. For a price, he even offered protection to bootleggers and pardons to criminals. The head of the veterans' bureau stole money intended for medicines and other supplies for wounded war veterans. The secretary of the interior received large payments from an oil company to which he rented government oil lands at a very low price. When these scandals were made public, Harding was heartbroken. He died soon afterward of a sudden illness.

3. THE COOLIDGE ADMINISTRATION (1923-1929). The new President, Calvin Coolidge, greatly admired business and their achievements. "The business of America is business" was one of his favorite sayings. He also favored economy in government. He was able to reduce taxes and still pay off much of the nation's war debt.

In 1924 Coolidge ran for the presidency. The Democrats nominated a candidate with much the same views as Coolidge. Reformers therefore organized a third party, which they named the Progressive Party (see page 406). Coolidge received more votes than the candidates of the other two parties combined. He was clearly the kind of President the American people wanted at that time.

4. THE ELECTION OF 1928. Coolidge refused to run again in 1928, so the Republicans nominated a very strong candidate, Herbert C. Hoover. After earning a fortune as an engineer, Hoover had entered the public service during World War I. He had an outstanding record as food administrator during the war, as head of the American Relief Administration after the war, and as secretary of commerce under Harding and Coolidge. In the last position, he had encouraged businesses to cut costs by improving methods of production and by com-

Two heroes of the 1920s. Left: Rudolph Valentino, the idol of millions of moviegoers. Right: Babe Ruth, the "Sultan of Swat," one of the greatest baseball players ever.

bining small businesses to form large ones. Hoover, like Coolidge, was a friend of big business, which he considered the foundation of the nation's prosperity. He also defended prohibition, which he called a "noble experiment."

The Democrats nominated Alfred E. Smith, who had made an excellent reputation as governor of New York State. Born and bred on the "sidewalks of New York," Smith had a strong appeal for city workers. He ran as a "wet"—that is, as an opponent of prohibition.

Smith's program and background were unpopular outside the big cities. What is more, he was the first Roman Catholic ever to run for the presidency. His enemies began a "whispering campaign" against him all over the nation. People told other people that Smith would "take orders from the Pope" if he was elected. The result was a one-sided victory for Hoover. Hoover even broke the Solid South (see page 345) by carrying four southern and two border states.

In his inaugural address, Hoover told the American people: "Given a chance to go forward with the policies of the last eight years, we shall soon with the help of God be in sight of the day when poverty will be banished from the nation." Unfortunately, the United States plunged into a terrible depression only a few months after Hoover took office.

REVIEWING THE SECTION

A. Knowing New Terms

For each term in the first column, write in your notebook the *letter* of the best description found in the second column.

Terms
1. Bootlegger
2. Economic boom
3. Bobbed hair
4. Intolerance
5. New K.K.K.
6. Prohibition
7. Quotas
8. Racketeering
9. Red scare
10. Roaring Twenties

Descriptions
a. The number of immigrants allowed to enter the United States from various countries
b. Activities carried on by well-organized bands of criminals
c. Distrust of minority groups
d. Exaggerated fear of socialism and communism
e. Symbol of women's break with the past
f. Organization that encouraged discrimination against blacks, Catholics, Jews, and foreigners
g. Outlawing of intoxicating liquors
h. Period of rapid business expansion
i. Person who sold liquor in violation of the law
j. Place where liquor was sold illegally
k. Period of pleasure seeking after the First World War

B. Knowing Important People

For each important person in the first column, write the *letter* of the best description in your notebook.

Important People

1. Calvin Coolidge
2. Warren G. Harding
3. Herbert C. Hoover
4. Alfred E. Smith

Descriptions

a. First Roman Catholic to run for the presidency
b. Leading gangster of the Prohibition Era
c. President associated with corruption in the government
d. President noted for government economy and aid to business
e. President who had helped the victims of World War I

C. Finding the Reasons

In your notebook write the letters of *all* the correct answers to each question.

1. Why is a great war usually followed by a period of pleasure seeking?
   a. People have more money to spend because of the war. b. Having lived with the thought of death for years, they want to get the most out of life. c. Governments encourage such behavior to help people forget their troubles.
2. Why did racketeering grow during the Prohibition period?
   a. Criminals organized gangs to take over the liquor business. b. Gangsters used profits they made in the liquor "racket" to corrupt government officials. c. Their profits and power made it possible for racketeers to take over lawful businesses.
3. Why did intolerance grow after World War I?
   a. The government had encouraged hatred of the Germans and other enemy peoples during the war. b. The Communists tried to seize power in the United States as they had in Russia. c. Both the federal and state governments persecuted people thought to be Communists.
4. Why did Congress limit immigration in the 1920s?
   a. Prejudice against immigrants from southern and eastern Europe had already existed before World War I. b. The war stirred up hatred of the Central Powers, which ruled much of southeastern Europe. c. Unions were afraid that immigrants would pull down the wages of their members.
5. Why was there an economic boom in the 1920s?
   a. The war had greatly helped American industry. b. American businesses weakened unions and cut wages. c. The federal government followed policies favorable to business.

6. Why was President Coolidge liked by most Americans?
a. He exposed the corruption of the Harding administration. b. He reduced government spending and taxes. c. The nation was very prosperous during his presidency.
7. Why did Herbert Hoover win a one-sided victory in 1928?
a. He had earned a reputation as a great humanitarian. b. He was even more friendly to business than Coolidge. c. Many Americans distrusted the Democratic candidate because he was a Catholic.

IMPROVING YOUR SKILLS

A. Reading the Time Line

Look at the time line on page 502. Then answer the following questions.

1. How many years of peace were there between the end of World War I and the beginning of World War II?
2. In what year were quotas set for people entering United States?
3. How long did prohibition last?
4. Why did President Roosevelt have to turn most of his attention to foreign affairs in 1939?
5. a. How long did World War II last? How long was the United States in the war?

B. Interpreting the Graph

Study the graph on page 506. Then complete the following statements.

1. The number of immigrants from northern and western Europe and Germany was much larger than the number from southern and eastern Europe in the years ____, ____, and ____.
2. The number of immigrants from southern and eastern Europe was much larger than the number from northern and western Europe in the years ____, ____, and ____.
3. The largest number of immigrants arrived in the year ____, when the total was over ____.
4. The smallest number arrived in the year ____, when the total was less than ____ thousand.
5. World War I was responsible for the drop in immigration between ____ and ____.
6. Immigration laws with a quota system were responsible for the even greater drop between ____ and ____.

MAKING HISTORY LIVE

1. a. Compare the behavior of young people today with the way they behaved after World War I. b. Why did they behave that way then? c. Do young people have the same reasons for such behavior, where it exists, today? d. What do you think of such behavior?
2. a. Why did many Americans disobey the Prohibition law? b. Do you think they were right or wrong? Explain why you think so. c. How might such disrespect for the law have been prevented?
3. a. Why was the Ku Klux Klan born in the 1860s? (See page 343.) b. Why was it reborn in the 1920s? c. The K.K.K rose a third time in the 1950s. What do you think should be done about such an undemocratic organization?
4. Prepare for a panel discussion of our immigration laws. Give the main provisions of the Immigration Act of 1924. Then give arguments for and against the law. Look up the Immigration Act of 1965 (see page 626). From what areas have most new immigrants come since 1965? Then prepare to discuss whether our immigration policy was better then or now.
5. a. Report on one case of corruption in the Harding administration. b. Report on a case of government corruption in recent years. c. Discuss what should be done to reduce government corruption.
6. Take part in a class debate on one of these questions: a. Should the government help big business? b. Should the government regulate business? c. Should average Americans spend freely or save part of their income?
7. Is there any comparison between women's break with traditions after World War I and the "women's liberation" movement in our day? In what ways are many women breaking with tradition today?

What Were the Causes of the Great Depression?

A. The Stock Market Crash. One day late in October 1929, the stock market opened for business as usual. People looked forward to another profitable day of buying and selling shares of stock (see page 183). Stock prices had been rising for years because business was booming. Within the last few months they had been shooting up, often gaining several "points" (several dollars a share) in a single day. But this day turned out very different. People who wanted to sell stocks found that there were very few buyers. A panic suddenly swept stockholders all over the country. Thousands rushed to sell their holdings. Prices fell so fast that the ticker tape could not keep up with the changes. By late afternoon the average price of stocks had fallen eighteen points. A second wave of selling a few days later brought the average price down another twenty-two points. Within a few weeks the market value of all stocks fell more than a third, for a total loss to stockholders of over thirty billion dollars. This was the great "stock market crash." It touched off the worst depression in our country's history.

Millions of Americans who thought they were rich suddenly found themselves poor when the stock market crashed. They could no longer afford to buy new houses or automobiles, take vacations, or send their children to college. When they stopped spending money, business suffered. Even more damaging was the loss of confidence in the future. Businesses dropped plans for expansion, cut back wages, and laid off workers. The result was a further drop in buying that caused still more workers to lose their jobs. This downward trend continued year after year. In 1932 production was only about half that of 1929. Some twelve million people, almost one-fourth of the total labor force, were out of work.

B. Overexpansion of Credit. Why did the stock market crash? Why did the crash touch off a terrible depression? Most experts agree that there were at least four major weaknesses in the American economic system in the 1920s. One was the overexpansion of credit—that is, too much borrowing. People could buy stock at that time by paying only 10 percent in cash. They simply borrowed the rest, using the stock as security for the loan. This meant they could buy ten times as much stock as they could actually afford. Many people did just that. As a result of their buying, stock prices and profits rose rapidly. The chance to get rich quickly attracted hordes of new investors, most of whom knew little or nothing about stocks. By 1929 most stocks cost several times as much as they were really worth. Experts, who understood the danger, quietly began to sell their stocks. When ordinary investors heard about this, they became alarmed. Many rushed to sell their holdings. The rush to sell brought on the stock market crash.

A similar boom and crash took place in real estate. The prices of land and houses rose rapidly as more and more people rushed to buy them with borrowed money. The real estate boom collapsed soon after the stock market crash, wiping out the wealth of thousands more Americans.

Buying on the installment plan was a third reason for the overexpansion of credit. During the 1920s Americans learned to buy on "easy credit" terms. But when they lost their jobs or were forced to take wage cuts, they could not meet the payments. Their homes, automobiles, radios, and furniture were taken away from them. Installment buying fell off sharply, adding to the depression.

Most credit was supplied by banks in the 1920s. When a large number of people could not repay their loans, hundreds of banks shut down for lack of funds. Millions of people who had deposited their money in banks because they were safer than stocks or real estate suddenly lost their lifetime savings.

C. An Unbalanced Economy. A second basic cause of the depression was a lack of balance in the American economy between production (the ability to manufacture products) and consumption (the ability to buy them). This weakness arose because the rich made greater gains during the 1920s than ordinary Americans. The number of millionaires and multimillionaires increased rapidly. They did not, as a rule, spend all that they earned. Instead they used part of their profits to expand their businesses, buy new machines, and improve methods of production. They also invested in stocks and real estate and deposited large sums in banks. Thus they encouraged the overexpansion of both industry and credit.

The income of the average American rose during the 1920s, but it did not keep up with the growth of industry. In other words, consumption did not keep up with production. That is why businesses encouraged installment buying, which makes it possible for people to buy more than they can pay for. But this was only a temporary solution. After a few years, many people had used up their credit and had to cut down their purchases. Early in 1929 the automobile, steel, home building, and other major industries reported a drop in sales. This

A bread line in New York City during the Great Depression. The unemployed could get "20 meals for $1." What sort of meals do you think they were? What does the length of the line tell you?

was one of the danger signals that warned wise investors to sell their stocks.

Another danger signal was unemployment, which increased as machines replaced workers. In the early 1920s, a million Americans could not find work. The number of unemployed rose to two million in 1928 and doubled again by the end of 1929.

D. "Sick Industries." Other large groups of Americans failed to share in the nation's prosperity because they worked in "sick industries." These were industries that were doing poorly because of changing conditions. Coal mining, for example, declined because people were using more oil and electricity. Trucks and buses were taking business from the railroads. In New England the textile, shoe, and leather industries were losing customers because of rising wages and other high costs. The entire region suffered as one company after another shut down or moved to the South, where costs were lower.

The most depressed industry of all was agriculture. Just as in the 1880s, the American farmer was suffering from high costs and low prices. During the First World War, the government had encouraged farmers to grow more and more. Many had borrowed heavily to buy more land and machinery. When conditions in Europe returned to normal after the war, there was a world surplus of wheat, cotton, and other farm products. Prices dropped sharply. They remained low all during the 1920s. In this era of prosperity, the average cash income of a farmer ranged from only three to five hundred dollars a year. Many people left their farms, or lost them and became tenant farmers on land taken over by banks.

E. Weakness of Labor Unions. Another reason why the income of many Americans remained low was the weakness of the union movement. Unions had made great gains during the war, but they suffered sharp setbacks after it ended. In 1919 they called thousands of strikes for higher wages to offset rapidly rising prices. This turned out to be a serious mistake. For just then two million soldiers were being discharged from the armed forces, and they needed jobs. Employers took advantage of the situation to break the unions. When the steel workers' union called a strike, for example, the steel owners shut down their plants. They reopened the plants only after they had hired and trained all the new workers they needed. The strikers had to beg to be rehired on the companies' terms. The failure of the strike destroyed the union.

Once again, as in the Gilded Age, the government sided with the employers. When the coal miners struck, the government used its wartime powers against them even though the war was over. It ordered them to return to work or else face jail sentences. The Supreme Court handed down a series of decisions against picketing and other weapons of labor. It also ruled against laws to protect women and child workers.

The union movement was further weakened by several other developments. One was the "Red scare," in which many union leaders were accused of being Communists. Another was the new business policy of treating workers well (see page 506). A third was the fact that many companies set up their own unions to keep their workers from joining outside labor organizations.

The American Federation of Labor, which had four million members in 1919, lost half of them during the next ten years. Other labor organizations likewise suffered serious losses. The large majority of American workers remained unorganized. Their wages rose more slowly than the prices of the goods they bought, especially in the late 1920s. In a period of rapid economic progress, they were standing still or even falling behind.

F. Government Policies. 1. BEFORE THE DEPRESSION. The Harding and Coolidge administrations did little to solve these problems. Almost no laws were passed to help agriculture, the other sick industries, labor unions, or the unemployed. Twice Congress passed a law to raise farm prices; twice President Coolidge vetoed it. "Farmers have never made money," he explained. "I don't believe we can do much about it."

At the same time the government favored the wealthy by reducing taxes and supported big business by raising tariff rates. The new tariff rates of 1922 were so high that Europeans turned to other countries for trade. They bought farm products from countries like Argentina and Canada that would take their manufactured goods in exchange.

2. DURING THE DEPRESSION. Herbert Hoover, like the two Presidents before him, believed that the government should help business but not interfere with it. Yet his administration was more active in fighting depression than any earlier one. The President called business people to the White House and urged them not to cut wages or lay off workers. Congress voted large sums to help businesses, workers, and farmers. One government agency lent a half-billion dollars to large companies, such as banks and railroads, to keep them from failing. The government spent several hundred million dollars more on public works to make jobs for the unemployed. It spent still another half-billion to buy up surplus crops.

These measures helped a little. However, the amounts the government spent were too small to overcome such a large depression. President Hoover was unwilling to go further. When hundreds of cities asked for federal help to feed the unemployed, Hoover refused. He felt that such aid would be a step toward socialism. In 1930 Congress raised tariff rates to the highest level in our nation's history. President Hoover signed the tariff bill, even though economists and bankers warned against it. Within the next year, twenty-five foreign nations struck back by cutting down their imports of American goods. The drop in foreign trade made the depression even worse.

In contrast to the prosperous 1920s, unemployment grew during the 1930s. One out of four workers could not find a job. How are the people shown here reacting to the economic crisis?

Isaac Soyer. *Employment Agency.* 1937. Oil on canvas. 34¼ × 45 inches. Collection of Whitney Museum of American Art.

G. The Election of 1932. President Coolidge was given the credit for the nation's prosperity; President Hoover received the blame for the depression. He was also criticized for refusing to provide federal relief for the unemployed. Nevertheless, the Republican party again nominated him for the presidency in 1932.

The Democrats nominated the governor of New York, Franklin D. Roosevelt. "FDR" promised the American people a "New Deal" if he was elected. The federal government, he told them, would see to it that no person starved. It would end the depression by taking strong action to deal with the nation's many economic problems. Roosevelt won the election by a sizable margin. But many people wondered whether he would be able to keep his bold campaign promises.

REVIEWING THE SECTION

A. Knowing New Terms

For each term in the first column, write in your notebook the *letter* of the best description in the second column.

Terms
1. New Deal
2. Overexpansion of credit
3. Sick industries
4. Stock market crash
5. Unbalanced economy

Descriptions
a. Coal mining, agriculture, and some other industries did badly even during the boom.
b. As banks and other businesses failed, millions of Americans lost their savings and jobs.
c. Consumers could not buy all the goods that industry produced.
d. FDR promised to help the needy and end the depression.
e. The prices of stocks dropped a great deal in a short time.
f. People borrowed large amounts to buy goods, stocks, and real estate.

B. Finding the Reasons

Write the letters of *all* the correct answers to each question.
1. Why did the stock market crash in October 1929?
   a. The government ordered that stocks should be sold only for cash.
   b. Big investors started false rumors that frightened ordinary investors into selling their stocks.
   c. Many ordinary investors rushed to sell their stocks when they found out that the experts were selling.
2. Why was credit overexpanded in 1929?

a. Many investors bought stocks for 10 percent cash, borrowing the other 90 percent. b. Many consumers bought more than they could afford by using the installment plan. c. Many banks lent money without carefully checking the income of the borrowers.
3. Why did unemployment rise during the 1920s?
a. People bought less because of higher prices. b. Better machinery and methods made it possible to produce more goods with fewer workers. c. Employers laid off workers because they knew that a depression was coming.
4. Why were many New England industries "sick" in the 1920s?
a. The region had used up most of its natural resources. b. Its workers were mostly uneducated and unskilled. c. Wages and other costs of production were higher than in the South.
5. Why was agriculture "sick" in the 1920s?
a. Farm prices dropped after World War I because of overproduction. b. Prices of the manufactured goods bought by farmers went up. c. Many farmers had borrowed a good deal during the war and found it hard to repay.
6. Why did the unions lose members in the 1920s?
a. Workers could not afford to pay union dues. b. Employers fired workers who refused to quit the unions. c. The unions were weakened by court decisions and other government actions.
7. Why did President Hoover fail to end the depression?
a. He was against any government action to end the depression. b. He allowed government help to businesses and farmers, but the amounts were too small to be effective. c. He approved a tariff law that reduced our nation's foreign trade.

IMPROVING YOUR SKILLS

Making an Outline

Fill in this outline to show the main causes of the Great Depression.

A. The Stock Market Crash
  1. What the crash was
  2. Its results

B. Overexpansion of Credit
  1.
  2.
  3.
  4.

C. An Unbalanced Economy

    1.
    2.
    3.

D. "Sick Industries"

    1.
    2.

E. Weakness of Labor Unions

    1.
    2.
    3.
    4.

MAKING HISTORY LIVE

1. Practice reading the stock market page of the daily newspaper. Explain it to the class.
2. What are shares of stock? Explain the advantages and disadvantages of stock ownership.
3. Discuss some of the advantages or disadvantages of installment buying.
4. After reading about economic conditions today, do you think the weaknesses of the 1920s still exist? Explain your answer.
5. a. Draw a poster for either the Republicans or the Democrats in the election of 1932; b. Draw a cartoon to show how most Americans felt before and after the stock market crash.
6. Interview people who remember the Roaring Twenties and the Great Depression. Ask them about their own experiences during these periods. Write a summary of your interviews.

Chapter 30

FDR AND THE NEW DEAL

BY INAUGURAL DAY (March 4, 1933), the United States appeared to have reached the edge of disaster. The number of unemployed had grown to thirteen or fourteen million. Many of these people had lost their homes. In the cities, the homeless lived in tiny shacks they had built on vacant lots and stood on "breadlines" for their meals. Unemployed war veterans were allowed to sell apples on street corners to earn a few cents a day. When an employer advertised for a worker, hundreds of people appeared hours before the firm opened in the morning. The job usually went to the person willing to accept the lowest wage, perhaps only eight to ten dollars a week.

Conditions in the farming areas were also very bad. The price of corn had fallen so low that farmers burned it instead of coal. Dairy farmers staged "milk strikes"—that is, refused to sell their milk unless the price was raised. Armed bands stopped the milk trucks of dairy farmers who had refused to join the strike and poured the milk on the ground. Every month thousands of farmers lost their homes and land because they could not meet their mortgage payments. In the Midwest, groups of them banded together to keep law officers from selling their farms. They often used force to stop the sales.

Still another threat to the economy was the condition of the banks. So many banks had shut down that the public had lost confidence in them. A rumor that a bank might close was enough to start a "run"—a stampede of hundreds of depositors demanding their money. A bank kept only a small part of its deposits on hand. If it was hit by a run, it quickly used up all its cash and had to shut down. In one state after another the governor closed all the banks to stop the runs. But the closing of hundreds of banks in many parts of the nation threatened to bring the economy to a standstill.

In this chapter we shall see what the new President, Franklin D. Roosevelt, did to save our nation. His program, which he had named the New Deal, had three main parts—relief, recovery, and reform. "Relief" meant that the federal government would help people in need. "Recovery" meant that it would help business to get back on its feet. "Reform" meant that it would make improvements in our economy to eliminate the weaknesses that had caused the Great Depression.

How Did the New Deal Provide Relief and Promote Recovery?

A. The New Deal Approach. In his inaugural address, President Roosevelt described the difficulties facing the United States. He admitted that it was a very dark hour. But he pointed out that our nation was still very rich. Its main problem was a lack of confidence. "The only thing we have to fear is fear itself," he told the American people. To restore their confidence, he promised "to wage a war against the emergency as great as if we were invaded by a foreign foe."

FDR gathered around him a group of college professors, lawyers, and other experts who became known as the "Brain Trust." These experts suggested a great variety of measures to solve depression problems. The President tried out many of their ideas. "It is common sense," he said, "to take a method and try it. If it fails, admit it frankly and try another. But above all, try something."

President Roosevelt began at once to send the Brain Trust's suggestions to Congress. Since the situation was desperate and the American people wanted action, Congress quickly made them into laws. In fact, more laws dealing with economic questions were passed during the first hundred days of the New Deal than in all our previous history. Most of these early New Deal laws dealt with relief and recovery rather than with reform.

FDR's inauguration, 1933.

FRANKLIN DELANO ROOSEVELT: FRIEND OF THE "FORGOTTEN MAN"

Franklin Roosevelt enjoyed even greater advantages in wealth and social position than his fifth cousin Theodore. He grew up on a beautiful country estate at Hyde Park, New York. He was educated first at home, then in a fashionable preparatory school, and finally at two of the best universities in the United States. Between the ages of seven and fourteen, he visited Europe every year with his parents. Handsome and charming, he made friends everywhere. He married a niece of Theodore Roosevelt. Eleanor was a very good wife. For many years she devoted herself entirely to making her husband and their five children happy.

Inspired by Teddy's success as President, Franklin decided to enter politics. Though a Democrat, he was elected to the state legislature by his Republican neighbors. There he soon attracted attention by fighting against the Democratic political machine, Tammany Hall. In 1912 young Roosevelt helped Wilson win the Democratic nomination. He was appointed Assistant Secretary of the Navy as a reward. In 1920 he was nominated as the Democratic candidate for Vice-President. He traveled all over the country, making hundreds of speeches in support of the League of Nations. The Democrats lost, but Roosevelt became well known. Able, popular, and the bearer of a famous name, he was clearly destined to rise high in our nation's service.

Then, in 1921, disaster struck. After a long day of boating and swimming, Roosevelt complained of a chill. The next day he was paralyzed, the victim of a dread disease, poliomyelitis or infantile paralysis. Never again was he able to stand or walk without wearing heavy braces on his legs. But he managed through constant exercise to regain his strength and health. He reentered politics. In 1928 he ran for governor of New York and won. In 1932 he won the presidential election and served as our President until his death in 1945.

As chief executive, Franklin Roosevelt was outstanding for his programs to aid the "forgotten man," the ordinary person whom the federal government had rarely helped before. His New Deal aroused a great deal of controversy. One question often discussed was why Roosevelt, who was wealthy and wellborn, "turned against his class" and helped the common people. Some historians believe that his illness was the reason. His own suffering, they think, led him to sympathize with the suffering of others. But there is a simpler explanation. Like many other great Americans before him, FDR believed in the ideals of American democracy. He believed that our government, which derives its powers from the people, should use those powers to help them.

B. Saving the Banks. FDR's most urgent task was to save the banks. He immediately ordered a "bank holiday"—that is, the closing of all banks throughout the nation. Federal examiners very quickly checked their books. The few banks that were in bad financial condition were kept closed; the rest were allowed to reopen. A new government agency, the Federal Deposit Insurance Corporation, was formed to prevent future losses to depositors. The FDIC insured savings accounts so that depositors would be paid even if a bank shut down. All these measures restored public confidence in the banks.

C. Helping the Needy. The government also acted swiftly to help the needy. Congress gave a half-billion dollars to states and cities for supporting the unemployed. It voted another three billion dollars to the Public Works Administration. PWA built large projects like dams, bridges, and highways. These public works were expected to "prime the pump." By this phrase, experts meant that large-scale government spending for wages and materials would help the economy to start working again.

The public works program was slow in getting started because large projects require a great deal of planning. Another weakness was that it offered few jobs for unskilled workers. So Congress created the Work Projects Administration. WPA's job was to start quickly a number of simple projects on which the able-bodied unemployed could work. Many of these projects had little value. But many others, such as parks and playgrounds, brought the nation lasting benefits.

The largest group of unemployed were young people. The Civilian Conservation Corps was created especially for them. Young men who joined the CCC were sent to government camps, mostly in the national parks. There they planted trees, fought forest fires, and stopped soil erosion. Their work helped to save our natural resources. It also improved the health of the young people and gave them a love for the outdoors.

CCC workers digging an irrigation ditch. By the end of 1941 over two and a half million young people had been on the CCC rolls. How did their work help both them and our nation?

Other measures were taken to help debtors. One agency helped people who could not meet the mortgage payments on their homes. It took over their mortgages and arranged for smaller payments. The payments did not start until the people could afford to pay. Another agency used the same methods to help farmers keep their farms.

D. Encouraging Business. Besides priming the pump, the New Deal tried to help business directly. The government greatly increased its loans to business, small as well as large. Firms engaged in foreign trade benefited from the Trade Agreements Act. Congress gave the President the power to cut tariff rates in half for nations that agreed to make similar cuts in their tariffs on American goods. During the next few years our nation signed thirty tariff-cutting agreements with other nations. Our foreign trade doubled. Farmers, as well as businesses, benefited as our exports increased. The Trade Agreements Act was so successful that the President was later given the power to reduce tariffs another one-fourth. The Act is still in force today.

The most important New Deal measure to help business was the National Recovery Administration. NRA's job was to stop the price cutting and other unfair business practices that had ruined many firms. The antitrust laws were suspended for two years. Businesses in each industry were encouraged to make up a list of fair practices for their industry. Those who promised to follow these fair practices were allowed to display the Blue Eagle, symbol of the NRA. The public was urged to buy only from such firms.

The NRA soon ran into serious trouble, however. Some leading businesses refused to cooperate because they felt that NRA would destroy American free enterprise. Small busi-

NRA parades like this one aroused a great deal of patriotic feeling. They influenced Americans to buy articles carrying the NRA "blue eagle" label.

nesses charged that big business benefited much more than they did from the fair practice lists. Experts pointed out that the government was helping to form monopolies, which would remain a threat long after the depression ended. Disputes over the NRA ended, however, when the Supreme Court declared it unconstitutional in 1935.

E. Aid to Farmers. The New Deal also tackled the difficult farm problem. The Agricultural Adjustment Administration was given the job of reducing the surpluses that had caused farm prices to fall. The AAA paid farmers if they reduced the amount of land planted in major crops. Another government agency bought up surplus crops. It gave large amounts of food to the needy, charitable organizations, and schools. It stored the rest in warehouses for future use.

F. Paying for the New Deal. The many activities of the government under the New Deal were very expensive. Government spending doubled in the first year and tripled in the second. Only during the First World War had the federal government spent larger sums. President Roosevelt defended the high cost by reminding the nation that it was once again fighting a war—a war against poverty.

The government met its expenses by raising taxes and borrowing. The major tax increases were on business profits and large incomes. Wealthy business people, angered by these taxes and by speeches in which FDR criticized business, became enemies of the New Deal.

REVIEWING THE SECTION

A. Knowing New Terms

PART 1. For each New Deal agency in the first column, write in your notebook the *letter* of the best description in the second column.

Agency
1. Agricultural Adjustment Administration
2. Civilian Conservation Corps
3. Federal Deposit Insurance Corporation
4. National Recovery Administration
5. Public Works Administration
6. Work Projects Administration

Description
a. Built large projects, such as dams and bridges
b. Built smaller projects, such as parks and playgrounds
c. Guaranteed accounts in savings banks against loss
d. Improved our forests and other resources
e. Lent money to farmers and homeowners
f. Protected businesses from unfair practices
g. Reduced farm surpluses

524

PART 2. Explain each term in your notebook *in your own words*.

(In the chapter introduction) run on a bank
(In **A**) "Brain Trust"
(In **B**) bank holiday
(In **C**) to "prime the pump"

B. *Finding the Reasons*

In your notebook write the letters of *all* the correct answers to each question.

1. Why did the United States seem to be on the "edge of disaster" in March 1933?
   a. Fourteen million Americans were out of work. b. Farmers could not make a living and were losing their farms. c. Many banks had shut down.
2. Why were President Roosevelt and Congress willing to try all sorts of measures to improve conditions?
   a. Most of the measures were suggested by experts. b. The federal government had little experience in dealing with economic problems. c. The American people wanted quick action.
3. Why did President Roosevelt order a bank holiday and a federal check of all banks?
   a. He thought the banks were trying to cheat the public. b. He wanted to stop the runs on banks by restoring public confidence. c. He wanted to bring the banks under government control.
4. Why was the Work Projects Administration needed?
   a. The Public Works Administration had failed. b. Public works took a long time to get started. c. Most of the unemployed did not have the skills needed for building public works.
5. How did the Civilian Conservation Corps help young people?
   a. It gave them healthful outdoor jobs. b. It trained them for trades in which there was a shortage of workers. c. It helped to save our nation's natural resources.
6. Why did most American farmers benefit from the AAA?
   a. It gave them cash payments if they planted smaller areas. b. It caused farm prices to rise by reducing overproduction. c. It gave surplus food to needy foreign nations.
7. Why did many business people turn against the New Deal?
   a. It did little or nothing to help them. b. Its taxes fell most heavily on them. c. They were against any government action affecting business.
8. Why did most Americans favor the New Deal?
   a. It took strong action to solve the nation's economic problems. b. It helped millions of people. c. It reduced government costs and taxes.

How Did the New Deal Reform the Economy?

A. Reforms to Help Workers. A notable part of the New Deal, reform, stirred up the greatest controversy. For most of our history, the government helped business but did not try to regulate it. President Roosevelt, like the Progressives before him, believed that the government should regulate business for the public good. He also wanted to reduce the power of the wealthy upper class. The government, he said, should help "the forgotten man at the bottom of the economic pyramid"—that is, the average American worker and farmer.

1. THE NATIONAL LABOR RELATIONS ACT. The New Deal included some important laws to help the workers. One of them, the National Labor Relations Act, greatly strengthened unions. The law guaranteed workers the right of collective bargaining. In practice, this meant that employers had to bargain with representatives of the workers on hours, wages, and working conditions. The workers themselves would decide, through special elections, who would bargain for them. If a majority in a firm voted for a certain union, that union would bargain for all the workers. The National Labor Relations Board was set up to enforce the law and to watch over the elections.

The union movement made great gains as a result of the Labor Relations Act. The American Federation of Labor doubled its membership during the next few years. It also helped to form a new labor organization, the Congress of Industrial Organizations. The CIO organized both skilled and unskilled workers in mass-production industries like steel and auto manufacturing. It carried on a series of successful strikes against some of the nation's largest business firms. As a result, it quickly won several million members. Since the 1930s unions have continued to grow and to bring important benefits to their members. Even so, three-fourths of our nation's workers still do not belong to unions today.

2. SOCIAL SECURITY. A second New Deal law, the Social Security Act, protected workers against the hardships of old age and unemployment. It made both workers and employers contribute to a government insurance fund. If workers lost their jobs, they received government payments until they found another job or used up their benefits. When they retired at the age of 65 after working a certain number of years, they received pension payments for the rest of their lives. Also, the Social Security Act gave federal money to the states to aid needy children, the blind, and other disadvantaged groups. It also gave funds for health services.

3. THE WAGE-HOUR LAW. A third major New Deal reform was the Fair Labor Standards Act, or wage-hour law. This act forbade employers engaged in interstate commerce to pay their workers less than a certain wage (at first 40¢ an hour). They could not force employees to work more than forty hours a week. Those who agreed to do overtime work had to be paid a much higher hourly rate. The Fair Labor Standards Act also put an end to child labor. It forbade the shipment from one state to another of products made by firms employing children under sixteen.

4. THE HOUSING PROGRAM. Getting rid of the big-city slums was the main purpose of the

United States Housing Authority. The USHA tore down slum buildings and built modern apartment houses in their place. The apartments were rented at very low rates to people with small incomes. The federal government also helped states and cities to start their own low-cost housing programs. Still another new government agency, the Federal Housing Administration, encouraged the building of small private houses.

B. The Farm Program. 1. THE SECOND AAA. The first Agriculture Adjustment Act, passed in 1933, was soon declared unconstitutional by the Supreme Court. Congress then passed a new law, which did much more to help the farmer. As before, the government asked farmers to reduce the amount of land planted in major crops and bought up surplus crops. But now it also allowed the secretary of agriculture to ask farmers not to sell more than a certain part of their crop. In return, the secretary was to guarantee the farmers a fair price for what they sold. If they received less than this price, the government made up the difference.

Soil conservation was another feature of the new AAA. The government agreed to pay farmers if they grew plants that held down and enriched the soil. It also gave them millions of young trees free of charge. They were expected to plant groups of these trees to prevent the soil from washing or blowing away, especially on the Great Plains.

A third feature of the new AAA was crop insurance. If farmers wanted this insurance, they paid the government a small part of their produce. In return, the government paid them for any damage to their crops.

2. OTHER AIDS TO FARMERS. The government also helped to improve the farmers' lives by making electricity available to them.

What was the purpose of the second Agriculture Adjustment Act?

The Rural Electrification Administration built power lines in rural areas and helped to provide electric power at low rates.

The poorest farmers of all, the tenant farmers, suffered as a result of the A A A. A million of them were driven from their farms in a few years because smaller areas of farmland were being planted. The New Deal tried to help them. It lent them money to start their own farms and taught them better farming methods. But many became farm laborers or went to the cities in search of new jobs.

C. Remaking the Tennessee River Valley. The boldest of all the New Deal experiments was the Tennessee Valley Authority. T V A was given control over the valley of the Tennessee River, which includes large parts of seven southeastern states (see map below). In 1933 this region was one of the poorest in the nation. T V A built more than twenty dams along the river to stop floods, improve navigation, and produce electric power. It also reduced soil erosion by planting trees on steep hillsides and by teaching farmers better methods of plowing. Many industries were attracted to the Tennessee Valley by the low-cost electric power and shipping the T V A provided. As a result, the region became one of the most prosperous parts of the United States.

D. Financial Reforms. Early in the New Deal, a Senate investigation had revealed bad practices by bankers and stock brokers (firms that bought and sold stocks for the public). These practices had helped bring on the stock market crash and depression. To prevent such evils in the future, Congress changed the Federal Reserve Act (see page 420). It gave the Federal Reserve Board greater control over the member banks and their loans. It also created still another government agency, the Securities and

THE TENNESSEE VALLEY AUTHORITY

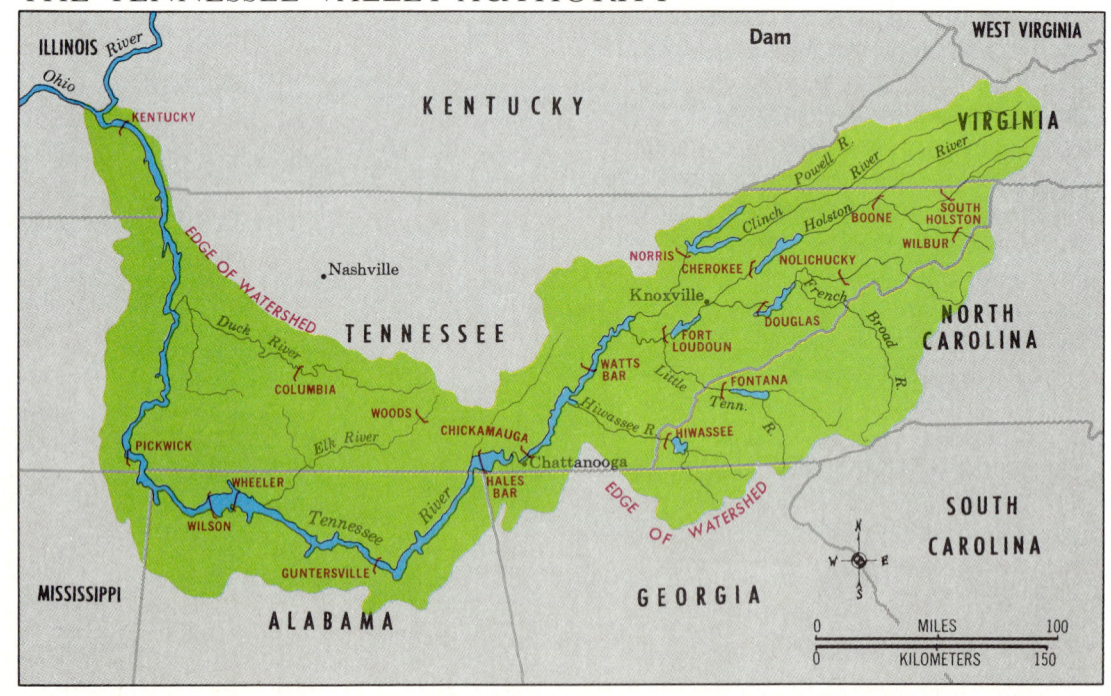

Exchange Commission. Companies that wanted to issue new securities (stocks and bonds) had to get the SEC's approval. Another job of the SEC was to police the exchanges where stocks were bought and sold.

E. The Election of 1936. When President Roosevelt ran for reelection in 1936, most of his New Deal program had already been passed. In the election campaign, he pointed with pride to his many achievements. He also promised to continue his fight to end poverty and help the "forgotten man." The Republican candidate attacked the New Deal because it was getting the nation ever deeper into debt. He also charged that it was interfering with the people's liberties and opening the way for socialism.

The election was a one-sided victory for the Democrats. Roosevelt carried forty-six of the forty-eight states. The Democrats also won large majorities in both houses of Congress.

F. Changing the Supreme Court. This great victory encouraged Franklin D. Roosevelt to make changes in the Supreme Court. Most of the judges were opposed to the reforms the New Deal was making. They had already declared several New Deal laws unconstitutional and were expected to kill others as cases reached them. Since six of the nine justices were over seventy years of age, the President proposed that they should be asked to retire. If they refused, he wanted the power to appoint a new justice to "assist" each man over seventy.

This plan aroused a storm of protest. FDR was accused of plotting to "pack the court" with his own judges and of seeking to upset the balance of powers under the Constitution. The strong protest forced the President to drop his plan. But when other cases involving New Deal laws reached the Supreme Court, the justices now found them constitutional. Then two justices who opposed the New Deal retired and FDR filled their places with New Dealers. So the President won in the end.

G. End of the New Deal. The Supreme Court struggle showed that many members of Congress started to rebel against the New Deal and the increased power given the President. FDR's position was further weakened by a mild depression that began in 1937. In the election of 1938, Republicans won back a number of seats in Congress. They joined forces with many southern Democrats who had turned against the New Deal. The "Republicrats," as the combined group was called, were able to prevent the passing of other New Deal reforms. In 1939 FDR, like Woodrow Wilson before him, found himself deeply involved in troubles overseas. These quickly brought an end to the period of reform.

H. Results of the New Deal. The active period of the New Deal lasted only five years, from 1933 to 1938. During those few years, our government made a large number of changes

Which of FDR's plans does this cartoon describe? Is it accurate?

THE INGENIOUS QUARTERBACK!

affecting all Americans. At the time there was a great deal of controversy about many of these New Deal changes. But today, a generation later, it is easier to examine them calmly.

A few New Deal measures, like the NRA, were clearly unsuccessful and were allowed to die. Others, like the WPA and CCC, were temporary measures that came to an end when conditions improved. Most of the New Deal reforms, however, are still in force today. They have become a permanent part of the American way of life. What is more, both major parties have accepted the basic idea of the New Deal—that the federal government is responsible for supporting the needy, helping the common people, and dealing with economic problems.

REVIEWING THE SECTION

A. Knowing New Terms

Here are some names of New Deal laws and agencies. Below them is a list of things they did. In your notebook write the *letter* of the law or organization next to what it did. (You may use a letter more than once.)

New Deal Laws and Agencies

A. Agricultural Adjustment Administration
B. Fair Labor Standards Act
C. National Labor Relations Act
D. Securities and Exchange Commission
E. Social Security Act
F. Tennessee Valley Authority
G. United States Housing Authority

What They Did

1. Built dams to control floods, improve navigation, and produce electric power
2. Built low-cost houses for the poor
3. Bought up farm surpluses
4. Controlled the sale of new stocks and bonds
5. Gave pensions to retired workers
6. Guaranteed farmers a fair price for their crops
7. Guaranteed workers the right of collective bargaining
8. Provided for elections to decide who would bargain for the workers in a certain firm
9. Improved the living conditions in a whole region of the United States
10. Insured farmers against damage to their crops
11. Outlawed child labor
12. Paid farmers to grow soil-conserving plants
13. Made weekly payments to workers when they lost their jobs
14. Set minimum wages and maximum hours for workers
15. Watched over the stock market

B. Understanding the Facts

Write "True" in your notebook if the statement is correct. If the statement contains an error, rewrite it so that it is correct.

1. Franklin D. Roosevelt's attitude toward government regulation of business was like Theodore Roosevelt's and William H. Taft's.
2. The number of American workers belonging to labor unions more than doubled after the Labor Relations Act was passed.
3. The A.F. of L. was made up of skilled workers, the C I O of unskilled workers.
4. The Social Security Act provided payments for farmers when they retired because of old age.
5. For workers in interstate commerce, the Fair Labor Standards Act set a "floor" under which their wages could not fall and a "ceiling" above which their weekly hours of work could not rise.
6. The first A A A could order farmers to plant less land in certain crops; the new A A A could also tell them how much of a certain crop they should sell.
7. Under the new A A A, the government insured farmers against damage to their homes and equipment.
8. The A A A put many tenant farmers and farm laborers to work.
9. T V A is generally considered the most successful New Deal reform because it brought prosperity to one of the poorest regions in the United States.
10. The Securities and Exchange Commission and the improved Federal Reserve System both helped to prevent another stock market crash and severe depression.

IMPROVING YOUR SKILLS

A. Mastering the Map

Study the map on page 528. Then answer the following questions.

1. In which three southern states do the tributaries (branches) of the Tennessee River rise?
2. In which two states have most of the T V A dams been built?
3. Into what river does the Tennessee flow?
4. In what state do the two rivers meet?
5. Which seven states are affected by the T V A?

B. Getting Different Viewpoints

Complete this chart on the effects of the major New Deal reforms. Write "For" in your notebook if the group at the top of the column was clearly helped by a reform. Write "Against" if the group had good reason to oppose the reform. Write "Not sure" if the effects on the group were not important or not clear.

	Business Leaders	Farmers	Workers
1. Agricultural Adjustment Act			
2. Civilian Conservation Corps			
3. Federal deposit insurance			
4. Higher taxes on business profits and large incomes			
5. Low-cost housing			
6. National Labor Relations Act			
7. Public works			
8. Rural electrification			
9. Social security			
10. Wage-hour law			

Conclusions. 1. Which group benefited most from these New Deal reforms?
2. Which group had the most reasons for being dissatisfied?

C. Looking at Both Sides

1. Make a list of the New Deal activities (in both sections of this chapter) that you think were good for the United States.
2. Make a list of the New Deal activities that you think were mistakes.
3. On the whole, was the New Deal a success or a failure? Give reasons for your answer.

Chapter 31

FDR'S FOREIGN POLICY

WHEN Franklin D. Roosevelt ran for Vice-President in 1920, he insisted that the United States should join the League of Nations. But when he ran for President in 1932, he spoke against joining the League. Roosevelt's change showed how isolationist the United States had become during the 1920s. A candidate for President who spoke for close cooperation between the United States and foreign nations would have lost millions of votes.

On the other hand, changing conditions were making it harder for a great power like the United States to isolate itself. Presidents Coolidge and Hoover both tried to improve our troubled relations with Latin America (see page 463). President Roosevelt went much further. He adopted a policy of friendship between the United States and the twenty republics to the south. The United States was also worried by developments in Europe and Asia. Most serious was the rise to power of dictators in Italy, Japan, and Germany. These dictators followed a policy of conquest that threatened to bring on another world war. Would the United States remain isolationist and do nothing? Or would it join with other peace-loving nations to stop the dictators? The future of mankind might depend on our government's answer.

In the first section of this chapter, we shall study our nation's new policy in Latin America. In the second section, we shall see how the United States tried to stay out of the troubles in Europe and Asia and why, once again, it failed.

How Did FDR Improve Relations With Latin America?

A. The Good Neighbor Policy. In his first inaugural address, President Roosevelt said, "I would dedicate this nation to the policy of the good neighbor—the neighbor who respects the rights of others." These words announced a new policy toward Latin America. The Good Neighbor Policy, as it was quickly named, had three main features. First, our government stopped "policing" Latin America. Shortly after he took office, FDR withdrew the marines from Nicaragua and Haiti. He also announced that the United States was giving up its right to police Cuba. From that time on, troubles in the Western Hemisphere would be considered by all twenty-one members of the Pan-American Union (see page 457). The United States would step in only if the Union agreed it should.

Economic cooperation was a second feature of the Good Neighbor Policy. The United States signed agreements to reduce tariffs with most of the Latin American nations. It also set up a special government bank that lent money to Latin American nations to help their economic development. Such government-to-government loans, it was hoped, would avoid the troubles that had often resulted when Latin American countries failed to repay loans by private bankers. In addition, the United States sent experts to Latin America to increase production and to improve living standards. These experts taught modern methods of farming and mining, road building, education, disease control, and medical care.

A third feature of the Good Neighbor Policy was cultural cooperation. Latin American writers, artists, musicians, and dancers came to the United States. Cultural leaders and entertainers from our nation visited Latin America. Teachers and students were encouraged to attend each other's universities. Books, pamphlets, and other educational materials were sent to schools and newspapers. In many parts of the United States, units on Latin America were added to courses in history and geography.

B. Early Tests of the Good Neighbor Policy. Latin Americans doubted at first that the United States would really carry out its new policy. But our government soon passed several severe tests. In 1933 the dictator ruling Cuba was overthrown. Power changed hands several times before a strong government was finally established; yet the United States refused to step in. The small Caribbean republics continued to suffer from economic troubles. The United States gave them aid, but did not send troops. In 1938 the Mexican government took over oil fields and other valuable lands held by both American and European companies. The companies appealed to the American government for help. President Roosevelt only asked the Mexican government to pay for the properties it had taken. He persuaded the companies to accept the payments Mexico offered, even though these were much less than the companies wanted. These developments helped to convince Latin Americans that the United States really meant to be a "good neighbor." The wall of distrust built by a generation of American police actions began to crumble.

C. Benefits of the Good Neighbor Policy. The Good Neighbor Policy also had other important results. American corporations now felt sure that Latin American governments would protect them. So they invested large sums in Latin American mines, plantations, and railroads. These investments helped provide the United States with tropical foods, minerals, and other raw materials it needed. They also provided jobs for Latin Americans and helped raise their living standards. As a result, they bought larger amounts of manufactured goods from the United States.

Still another benefit of the Good Neighbor Policy was a stronger defense for the western hemisphere. The United States no longer had to protect the entire hemisphere single-handed. It could now count on the help of the other members of the Pan-American Union. This new cooperation for defense was soon tested by the dictators of Italy, Germany, and Japan.

D. The Axis Threat to Latin America. Mussolini and his Fascist party came to power in Italy in 1922. Ten years later a group of military leaders gained control of the Japanese government. In the next year Adolf Hitler, leader of the National Socialist (Nazi) party, became dictator of Germany.

The three dictatorships signed a military agreement, popularly known as the Rome-Berlin-Tokyo Axis. The Axis Powers, as they came to be called, all had similar ideas. They insisted that they were "have-not" nations. They meant that they were poor because they lacked land and other natural resources. They also said that their people were better than the people of other nations. They claimed the right to conquer inferior peoples and make them slaves.

The Axis Powers looked to Latin America as a good place to expand because it had rich natural resources and a small population for its

How did the Good Neighbor Policy affect United States businesses and Latin Americans such as these tin miners and farmers?

size. They sent special agents there to organize armed groups like their own Fascist or Nazi parties. These agents had some success, especially among settlers who had come from Italy, Germany, or Japan. The Axis Powers also started many important companies in Latin America, including airlines with fields near the

535

Left: Benito Mussolini, who turned Italy into a dictatorship ruled by his Fascist party. Right: Adolph Hitler, leader of the Nazi party and dictator of Germany from 1933 to 1945. What was the third country that joined their Axis alliance?

Panama Canal. In addition, they sold arms to Latin American governments at special low prices. Then they sent in military advisers, supposedly to teach the armed forces how to use the new equipment. The real purpose of these advisers, however, was to influence the governments of the nations that had bought the arms.

E. Common Defense of the Western Hemisphere. The Pan-American Union called several conferences to deal with the growing influence of the Axis Powers. President Roosevelt himself attended the first meeting, held in Argentina in 1936. There the member nations announced that a threat to any one of them would be considered a threat to all. They agreed to meet and work out a plan of action if such a threat arose.

This agreement came into effect after World War II broke out. Since the war sharply reduced Latin America's trade with Europe, the United States increased its aid. In return, Latin American nations increased their output of raw materials the United States needed to make war equipment. In 1940 Hitler conquered Holland and France. The members of the Pan-American Union warned the German dictator against trying to take over the Dutch or French colonies in the Western Hemisphere.

The United States entered the war late in 1941. All of the Latin American nations except Argentina declared war on the Axis Powers or broke off relations with them. Latin American governments also arrested Axis agents, took over Axis airlines, and allowed the United States to build military bases on their territories. Thus the Good Neighbor Policy proved especially valuable when it was the United States that needed help.

REVIEWING THE SECTION

A. Knowing New Terms

In your notebook write the terms in this section that best complete these statements.

1. The policy of cooperation between the United States and Latin America adopted by FDR was called the _____ _____ Policy.
2. Two warlike dictators who came to power after World War I were the head of the Fascist party in Italy, _____, and the head of the Nazi party in Germany, _____.
3. Italy, Germany, and Japan signed an alliance known as the _____ _____ _____ _____.
4. The three warlike dictatorships became known as the _____ _____.
5. The three powers claimed the right to conquer other peoples because they were poor or "_____" nations.

B. Understanding the Facts

In your notebook write the *letter* of the correct choice.

1. In the 1930s the United States did *not* follow a policy of isolationism toward:
   a. Africa and Australia   b. Europe and Asia   c. Latin America   d. all other nations.
2. Under the Good Neighbor Policy, the United States would send troops into a Latin American nation only if:
   a. the American government found it necessary to act   b. a special treaty allowed it to do so   c. the government of the Latin American nation asked for the troops   d. the members of the Pan-American Union thought it necessary.
3. The settlements arranged by FDR between the Mexican government and the foreign companies in 1938 pleased:
   a. the Mexican government   b. the American companies   c. the European companies   d. all of them.
4. The Good Neighbor Policy succeeded in:
   a. building up Latin America's industries   b. ending poverty and illiteracy in Latin America   c. increasing trade between Latin America and the United States   d. doing all these things.
5. In their dealings with Latin America, the Axis Powers succeeded in:
   a. establishing many companies there   b. greatly increasing their trade   c. gaining control of Latin America's natural resources   d. winning the friendship of most Latin American governments.

IMPROVING YOUR SKILLS

Making an Outline

In your notebook complete this outline of the section by filling in the missing items.

A. The Good Neighbor Policy (Give a definition.)
  1. End of American police action in Latin America
     a.
     b.
     c.
  2. Economic cooperation
     a.
     b.
     c.
  3. Cultural cooperation

B. Early Tests of the Good Neighbor Policy (not interfering in Cuba, other small Caribbean countries, and Mexico)

C. Benefits of the Good Neighbor Policy
  1. Economic benefits
     a.
     b.
     c.
  2. Stronger defense of the western hemisphere

D. The Axis Threat to Latin America
  1. Rise of dictators in Europe and Asia
  2. Their warlike ideas
  3. Axis activity in Latin America
     a.
     b.
     c.

E. Common Defense of the Western Hemisphere
  1. Agreement to plan actions together
  2. Actions during World War II
     a.
     b.
     c.
     d.
     e.

How Did the United States Get Into World War II?

A. The Beginning of World War II. The Axis dictators began their march of conquest when Japan seized Manchuria in 1931 (see page 491). A few years later Mussolini conquered the large African nation of Ethiopia. Soon afterwards Hitler annexed Germany's neighbors, Austria and Czechoslovakia (see map, page 555). The British and French, alarmed by Hitler's actions, warned him not to attack Poland. Nevertheless, he invaded that country in the fall of 1939. Great Britain and France then declared war on Germany. That was how the Second World War began.

Canada, Australia, and other former British colonies soon joined Great Britain and France in the war. Their side became known as the Allies or, later, the United Nations. Germany was supported by Italy and several smaller nations—Hungary, Rumania, Bulgaria, and Finland. The name "Axis Powers" was applied to all of them. The Soviet Union, which had signed an agreement with Hitler a few days before he invaded Poland, stayed neutral. But it gave raw materials and other aid to the Axis side.

B. American Isolationism. The Axis march of conquest had presented a difficult problem for the American government. "Should the United States cooperate with the League of Nations to stop the dictators, or should it continue its policy of isolationism?" In the early 1930s our nation was still strongly isolationist. Most Americans believed that the United States had become involved in earlier wars by doing business with the warring nations. To stay out of another war, they were ready to give up the "freedom of the seas" for which Americans had fought in the War of 1812 and World War I. This attitude led Congress to pass the Neutrality Acts of 1935, 1936, and 1937. The laws forbade Americans to sell arms and war materials to nations at war, to lend them money, or to sail on their ships except at their own risk. President Roosevelt applied the Neutrality Acts in two conflicts, the Ethiopian War and the Spanish Civil War.

C. Weakness of the Neutrality Acts. FDR did not, however, apply the Neutrality Acts when fighting broke out between Japan and China in 1937. He pointed out that the law worked to the advantage of Japan, even though it had started the war by invading China. If the United States refused to sell Japan arms, it could buy them elsewhere or make them from raw materials bought in the United States. China, on the other hand, could not afford to buy American materials and had few arms factories. It needed American aid, which it would not be able to get if the Neutrality Acts were applied.

The President asked Congress to change the laws so that he could refuse aid to the aggressor (attacking nation) and give it to the victim. He also called on all peace-loving nations to cooperate in refusing help to aggressors. "The epidemic of world lawlessness is spreading," the President warned. He predicted that this "epidemic" would continue, if no action was taken, until the entire world was involved.

FDR did not succeed in arousing the American people and gaining their support. Congress refused to change the Neutrality Acts. The President, however, did not apply the laws. (He was able to do this because Japan and China had not declared war on each other.) The American government helped China by sending medical supplies and other military aid. But it also had to let Japan buy large amounts of war materials from American businesses. A noted humorist pointed out that our nation was, in effect, supplying the Japanese with bombs and supplying the Chinese with bandages.

D. The "Great Debate." After Hitler seized Czechoslovakia, the President again asked Congress to change the Neutrality Acts. If Germany attacked Great Britain and France, he pointed out, the Neutrality Acts would be helping Germany, the aggressor. Germany was fully prepared for war: It neither needed nor expected American help. But Great Britain and France were not prepared. They needed American help, but the Neutrality Acts would prevent them from getting it.

The President's request touched off a bitter debate between the isolationists and those who wanted to stop the aggressors. After weeks of discussion, Congress put off the decision. When it met again, World War II had already begun.

E. Changes in the American Position.
1. "CASH-AND-CARRY." Once the war was on, Congress changed the Neutrality Acts. Warring nations were allowed to buy American arms, provided that they paid cash and carried them away in their own ships. This "cash-and-carry" provision made it possible for Great Britain and France to obtain American arms. At the same time, it kept American bankers and shippers from getting deeply involved and dragging the nation into the war.

American aid almost came too late. Using thousands of planes and tanks, the Germans conquered Poland in a few weeks. They rested over the winter. When spring came, they quickly took over four small neutral nations— Denmark, Norway, Holland, and Belgium. They also attacked France and, to the world's surprise, conquered that great power in only seven weeks. Next they prepared to invade the British Isles. To "soften up" the British for the invasion, the German air force launched raid after raid on British cities. German submarines also took a heavy toll of British shipping.

2. THE DEFENSE PROGRAM. Hitler's victories alarmed the American people. If he conquered Great Britain, he might gain possession of the British fleet. Then he would be able to take over Canada and other European possessions in the western hemisphere. What would the United States do then?

To meet this danger, the United States strengthened the defenses of the western hemisphere in four ways: 1. Congress voted billions of dollars to build up the American armed forces. It also began, for the first time in our history, to draft men in peacetime. 2. President Roosevelt gave the British fifty destroyers and thousands of guns made during World War I. In return, Great Britain gave the United States eight naval and air bases along the Atlantic coast. 3. The President assured Canada that the United States would protect it from invasion. The two nations set up a military board to plan a common defense. 4. The United States joined with Latin America against possible Axis attacks (see page 536).

3. "LEND-LEASE." Because of the dangerous world situation, FDR decided to run for the presidency a third time in 1940. He won, and so became the first President to serve more than two terms. At his inauguration, he announced that the United States would greatly increase its aid to the Allies. "We must become the arsenal [supplier of weapons] for democracy," he said, "to keep the war away from our country and our people."

In the spring of 1941, Congress passed the Lend-Lease Act. This allowed the President to lend or lease weapons and other materials to foreign nations. They no longer had to pay cash. Instead, they could get help just by promising to return the materials or to pay part of their cost after the war. Under Lend-Lease, the United States supplied Great Britain and the other Allies with about fifty billion dollars' worth of aid before the war ended.

F. New Axis Victories. By this time, Hitler had suffered his first setback. The British air force, though outnumbered, had inflicted such heavy losses on the Germans that Hitler had to give up his plan to invade Great Britain. He decided to advance eastward instead. This plan proved successful. In the spring of 1941, the Germans quickly conquered Yugoslavia, Greece, and Crete. A combined German-Italian army defeated the British in North Africa and invaded Egypt. It looked as though the Axis planned to take Great Britain's most valuable possessions, the oil-rich Middle East and India (see map, page 543).

In June, 1941, however, Hitler suddenly invaded the Soviet Union. His powerful armies, reinforced by troops from other Axis countries, advanced rapidly during the next five months. They took over an area several times the size of France and destroyed entire Russian armies. But the Soviet Union is a vast country with a very large population. The Russians raised new armies and continued to resist. Winter stopped the Germans' drive before they could take the two leading Russian cities, Moscow and Leningrad.

G. "All Aid Short of War." The new series of German victories frightened the American people. They were also shocked by Hitler's brutal policies. Millions of people in the conquered countries, they learned, were being sent to Germany as slave laborers. Millions more were being thrown into terrible concentration camps, where they were killed or worked to

Repeated German bombing raids on London and other British cities left great destruction and thousands dead. Yet the people's morale remained high.

death. Most Americans now agreed that the United States could not allow Hitler and his followers to win. If Nazi Germany took over the Soviet Union, it would become the strongest nation in the world. Together with its Axis partners, it would threaten the freedom of every other nation.

The most urgent problem in the summer of 1941 was to deliver American Lend-Lease supplies to Great Britain and the Soviet Union. To avoid German submarines, the United States began to ship supplies to Iceland. There they were picked up by British ships. Our navy also established an air and sea patrol to warn the British when German submarines were nearby. The Germans struck back by torpedoing American destroyers and merchant ships. FDR then ordered American warships to sink the "rattlesnakes of the deep" (German submarines) on sight. Congress gave American merchant ships the right to arm themselves. In effect, the United States was already fighting an undeclared naval war with Germany.

H. The Attack on Pearl Harbor. Meanwhile, the United States was also becoming deeply involved in the Far East. The Japanese, taking advantage of Hitler's victory over France, occupied French Indochina in 1940. They gathered armed forces there to take over the British and Dutch possessions nearby (see map, page 543). The American government objected to Japan's expansion. To show its displeasure, it increased its aid to China and cut down its trade with the Japanese. (American businesses were forbidden to sell Japan various war materials—first airplanes and airplane parts, then aviation gasoline, and finally scrap iron and steel.) In the summer of 1941, our government forbade Japan to buy anything in the United States on credit. It also threatened to cut off all trade if Japan did not give up its plans for further conquests. The Japanese government sent over a "peace mission" to change the

In death camps and other organized places of murder, the Nazis systematically killed millions of people including six million Jews.

The bombing of Hawaii. The Japanese knocked out this airfield near Pearl Harbor, as well as the naval base. The clouds of smoke in the background are rising from burning American battleships.

HIGH TIDE OF AXIS CONQUEST, 1942

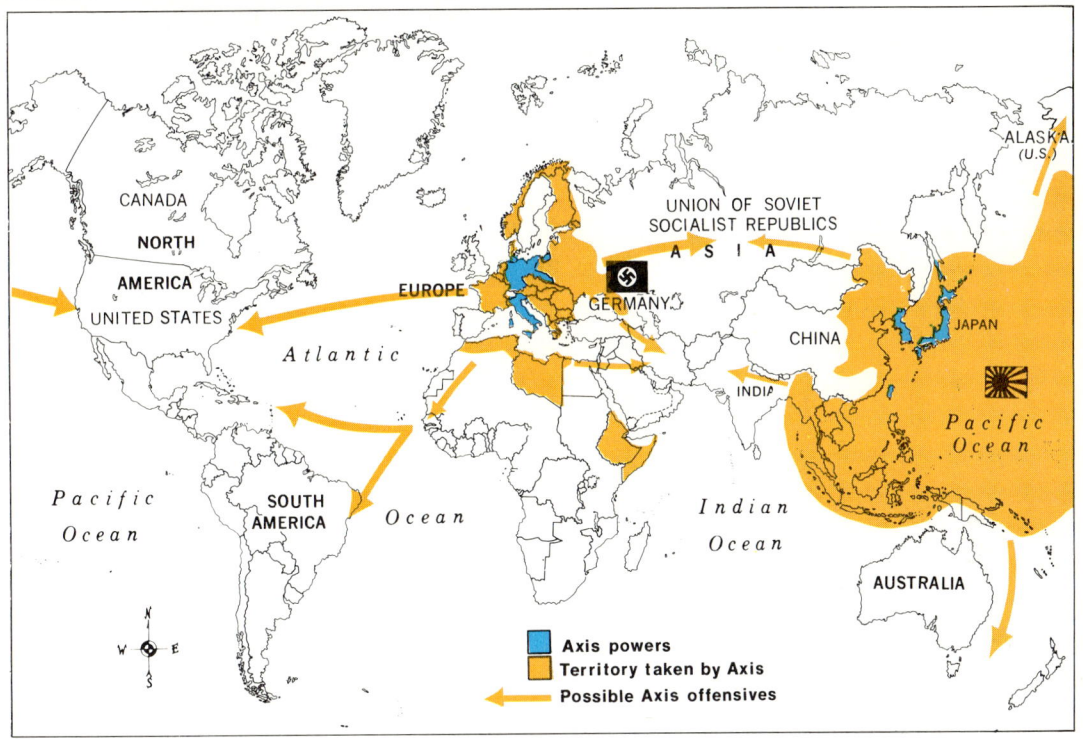

Axis powers
Territory taken by Axis
Possible Axis offensives

American attitude. But its fleet prepared to attack the United States if the mission failed.

On a Sunday morning—December 7, 1941—the people of Hawaii were awakened by the sound of explosions and gunfire. They could see wave after wave of Japanese planes, launched from aircraft carriers, bombing the great naval base at Pearl Harbor. The Japanese "sneak attack" brought the United States into World War II. The next day Congress declared war on Japan. A few days later Germany and Italy declared war on the United States. Once again our nation had failed to stay out of a great war overseas.

REVIEWING THE SECTION

A. Knowing New Terms

In your notebook write the terms in this section that best complete these statements.
1. A nation that attacks another nation is called an _____.
2. Americans were forbidden to sell war materials or lend money to warring nations under the _____ Act.

3. Foreign nations were allowed to get war materials in the United States provided they paid in full and took them away in their own ships under the "_____" amendment to this law.
4. Enemies of the Axis could get American war materials simply by promising to return them or pay for them at some future date under the _____ Act.

B. Understanding the Facts

In your notebook write the *letter* of the correct choice.
1. World War II started when:
   a. Japan attacked Manchuria   b. Italy invaded Ethiopia   c. Germany took over Austria and Czechoslovakia   d. Germany invaded Poland.
2. During the early part of World War II, the Soviet Union was:
   a. one of the Allies   b. a completely neutral nation   c. a neutral nation helping the Axis Powers   d. one of the Axis Powers.
3. To keep the United States out of an overseas war, the Neutrality Acts of 1935, 1936, and 1937 forbade:
   a. American bankers to make loans to warring nations   b. American manufacturers to sell them war materials   c. American travelers to sail on their ships   d. all these ways of getting involved.
4. President Roosevelt objected to the Neutrality Acts because they:
   a. treated both the aggressor and the victim alike   b. encouraged aggressors to attack weaker nations   c. actually helped the aggressor in some cases   d. had all these faults.
5. When war broke out between Japan and China in 1937, America:
   a. applied the Neutrality Acts   b. helped China, but not Japan   c. helped China, but sold war materials to Japan   d. helped Japan, but not China.
6. When President Roosevelt asked Congress to change the Neutrality Acts in the summer of 1939, Congress:
   a. quickly did so   b. delayed action   c. refused to consider the matter   d. voted to help the Axis Powers.
7. The American Defense Program, begun in 1940, was intended to:
   a. frighten the Axis Powers   b. help the Allies win the war   c. strengthen the defenses of the western hemisphere   d. accomplish all these purposes.
8. As the war continued, Congress increased American aid to the Allies because it was:
   a. alarmed by Germany's military successes   b. angered by Hitler's agreement with the Soviet Union   c. impressed by President Roosevelt's arguments   d. influenced by British propaganda.
9. The Japanese attacked Pearl Harbor because:
   a. Hitler had asked them to do so   b. they had plans for invading the United States   c. the United States was trying to keep them from con-

quering Southeast Asia and the East Indies   d. the United States was planning to attack Japan.

IMPROVING YOUR SKILLS

A. Mastering the Map

Study the map on page 543. Then answer the following questions.
1. On which continents were Germany's conquests located?
2. On which continent did Japan make most of its conquests?
3. Which important countries in North America were threatened by possible Axis offensives? Which important countries in northern Asia were threatened? Which in southern Asia?

B. Looking at Both Sides

1. Why did FDR want Congress to change the Neutrality Acts?
2. Why did Congress refuse to do so until after World War II began?
3. Which side do you think was right? Why?

MAKING HISTORY LIVE

1. Pretend that you are the "inquiring photographer" in 1939. Interview people from different Latin American countries to find out what they think of the Good Neighbor Policy. Write their answers down.
2. Complete *one* of these statements:
   a. "If the United States had cooperated with the League of Nations in the 1930s . . ." b. "If Congress had changed the Neutrality Acts in the 1930s . . ." c. "If Congresss had *not* changed the Neutrality Acts in 1940 and 1941 . . ."
3. Draw a cartoon to show the American attitude toward the Axis march of conquest: a. In the 1930s; b. In 1940 and 1941.
4. Draw a poster for or against amending the Neutrality Acts in the summer of 1939.
5. Prepare for a debate on the question: "Judging by what happened during the 1920s and 1930s, can a great nation like the United States isolate itself in the modern world?" Write points for each side.
6. Talk to people who remember what happened in the 1930s and early 1940s. Ask them to tell you how Germany and the other Axis Powers treated the peoples they had conquered. Write their replies down.

Chapter 32

THE UNITED STATES IN WORLD WAR II

THE JAPANESE destroyed a large part of the American Pacific fleet in their surprise attack on Pearl Harbor. As a result, they were free to advance wherever they wished. Within the next few months they conquered a large and valuable empire in Southeast Asia and the western Pacific. They stood ready to invade India, Australia, and Alaska (see map, page 543).

During the same period, the Germans renewed their offensive in Soviet Russia. This time they advanced toward the southeast. Their goal was to force Russia's surrender by capturing its main oil fields. Another Axis army prepared to invade the Middle East, the main source of oil for Great Britain (see map, page 543). In the war at sea, German submarines became even bolder and more destructive than before. Daring to operate right off the coast of the United States, they were sinking more than thirty Allied ships a week. In the summer of 1942, it looked as though the Axis Powers might win the war. In this chapter we shall see how the Allies stopped their advance and then went on to victory.

How Did the United States Organize for War?

A. The Opposing Sides. In the early part of the war, the Axis Powers had two great advantages. First, they were fully prepared for war. Second, they were taking the offensive. As a result, their armies often caught the enemy by surprise. If they failed to surprise the enemy, they could still break through enemy lines by concentrating their forces at a single important point.

In other ways, however, the Allies—Great Britain, China, the Soviet Union, the United States, and their many smaller allies—had the advantage. They had large populations, vast territories, and rich natural resources. They also had many more factories to turn out war goods. Their superiority in these ways told more and more heavily against the Axis as the war went on.

B. The American Armed Forces. Thanks to the defense program begun in 1940, the United States was partly prepared by the time it entered the war. It had already set up the Selective Service System and had taken more than 1,500,000 men into the armed forces. Before the war ended, some three and a half years later, our government had armed and trained more than 15,000,000 Americans. This included most young men, many older men, and 200,000 women volunteers. For the first time, women served actively in all branches of the armed forces. They also released men for fighting by filling important civilian jobs.

C. The "Miracle of Production." 1. THE PRESIDENT'S PLAN. World War II has been called a "war of machines." By using planes and tanks to smash the Allies' lines, the Ger-

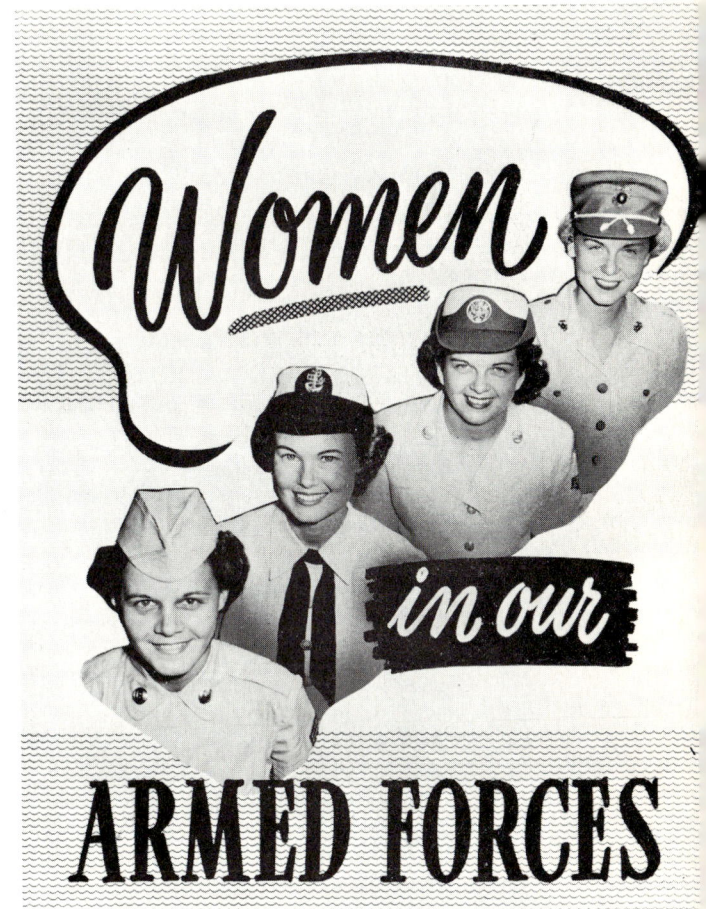

A recruiting poster. During World War II, women served in the armed forces and in industry. What did most of them do after the war?

547

mans had shown how important "machines" are in modern war. President Roosevelt therefore called for a "miracle of production." He announced that the United States would try to make about 50,000 planes and tanks a year and equally large amounts of other weapons. He also promised to build a "bridge of ships" to carry American supplies across the Atlantic Ocean. "Impossible," said many experts. In actual fact, however, American industry went far beyond the President's goals. American war production in 1942 was larger than that of all the Axis Powers combined. It increased greatly in 1943 and again in 1944. The United States became the "arsenal of democracy," as the President had promised. It equipped its own huge army and built the largest navy and air force the world had ever seen. It also supplied much of the equipment used by its allies. Its ships carried millions of American troops and mountains of war materials to the battlefronts overseas.

2. ORGANIZING WAR PRODUCTION. This "miracle of production" was achieved by private business under the government's direction. A government agency, the War Production Board, planned new factories, changed others to war production, and assigned scarce materials to the most important users. After the Japanese seized Southeast Asia, the world's main source of natural rubber, the War Production Board helped to find new sources. It also started an entirely new industry to make synthetic (artificial) rubber. An important part in war production was played by America's largest peacetime industry, automobile manufacturing. Auto plants stopped producing cars to make tanks, jeeps, and other kinds of military equipment. For example, the Ford Motor Company built an aircraft assembly plant a half-mile long, equipped it, and started production—all in less than a year!

3. THE IMPORTANCE OF SCIENTIFIC RESEARCH. Scientists were also part of the "mir-

The Willow Run bomber plant. Here giant four-engined bombers were assembled by the mass production methods developed in the automobile industry. Why was the United States called the "arsenal of democracy"?

acle of production." American university experts joined with British scientists and Germans who had fled from the Nazis to do important war work. They invented radar, which could spot enemy planes hundreds of miles away, and sonar for tracking down enemy submarines. They also developed synthetic rubber and other substitutes for scarce materials. Their most important invention, however, was the atomic bomb (see page 558).

D. The Labor Force. To increase production, our factories needed more and more workers. But the armed forces were taking away millions of men. Women, young people, retired workers, and even partly disabled were called on to help. New methods were used to train workers quickly. The regular work week was lengthened to forty-five hours. Workers with special skills were asked to put in even longer hours.

The labor shortage gave unions a strong bargaining position. Nevertheless, both the A.F. of L. and the CIO agreed not to strike until the end of the war. In return, the government helped workers to get higher wages and better working conditions. The patriotism of the unions won the public's respect. Their membership almost doubled during the war.

E. The Farmers' Achievement. As in the First World War, the government called on farmers to produce extra food for our armed forces and allies. It guaranteed them high prices for as long as the war lasted and for two years afterward. By using more fertilizer and the latest machinery and methods, the farmers were able to increase their output with fewer workers.

F. Regulating the Consumer. Most Americans enjoyed larger incomes because of the war. But the supply of goods for civilians was smaller. If the government had allowed people to buy freely, prices would have gone up very fast. The Office of Price Administration was set up to prevent inflation (high prices). OPA fixed the

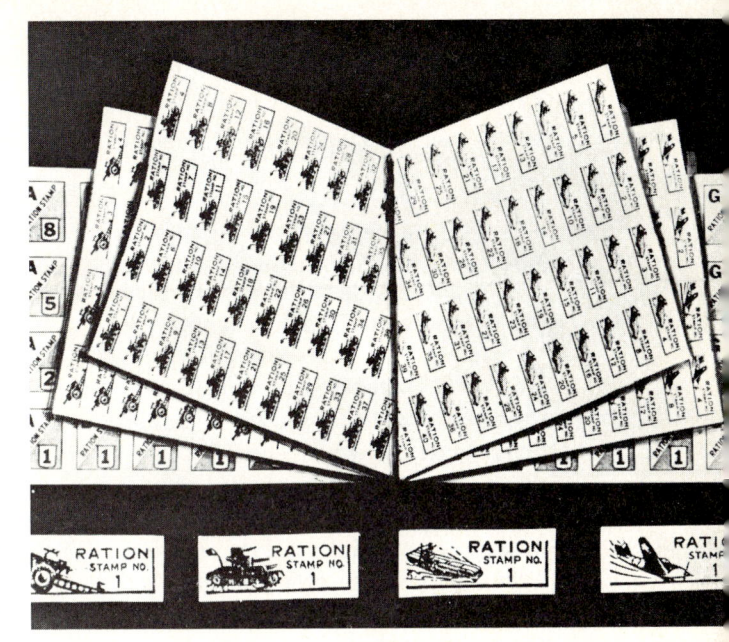

A book of ration stamps. Different kinds of stamps were needed to buy different kinds of scarce articles, such as meat, butter, and soap. Do you think rationing is the best way to control high prices brought about by war shortages? Why?

prices of most products, controlled rents, and set up a system of rationing. All Americans received a certain number of ration stamps, which they had to use to buy goods in short supply. Among these were meats and fats, coffee and sugar, butter and cheese, canned goods, shoes, and tires. Though there was some cheating, most Americans were able to obtain a fair share of scarce goods because of rationing. Prices rose only 30 percent in five years.

G. Paying for the War. Because World War II was a "war of machines," it was even more costly than the First World War. The United States alone spent $330 billion in five years, or well over $100,000 a minute! Part of this huge sum was raised through taxes. Even ordinary workers now had to pay income taxes, which were deducted from their wages. Taxes on large incomes and business profits were higher than ever. Taxes were also placed on amusements and luxury articles like luggage and cosmetics.

The government borrowed most of the money it needed, mainly by selling bonds to the American people. The government debt rose from $50 billion in 1939 to $250 billion in 1945. It was hoped that the debt would be paid off by the American people after the war.

H. Public Opinion. The American people accepted the sacrifices of war with little grumbling. Their morale was high because they saw the war as a struggle of free peoples against terrible dictatorships. Many people volunteered to serve as air raid wardens or blood donors. They also saved fats and tin cans and planted "victory gardens" of vegetables in their backyards to help the war effort.

Because of the high public morale, the American government did not have to take extreme measures like those used in World War I. Only secret agents and active supporters of the enemy were arrested. Censorship was not needed because the newspapers agreed not to print news that might help the enemy.

This democratic spirit was spoiled by a single major incident. On the West Coast, the bombing of Pearl Harbor had aroused strong feelings against Japanese Americans. Many people regarded anyone who looked Japanese as a possible enemy agent. To avoid trouble, the government sent more than a hundred thousand Japanese immigrants and Americans of Japanese origin to special camps. This action has been called "the worst single wholesale violation of the civil rights of American citizens in our history."

In spite of their mistreatment, thousands of Japanese Americans enlisted in the armed forces. They won many honors for their courage and patriotism. Their behavior proved once again that immigrants, whatever their national origin, usually become loyal citizens. Thanks to the united support of the American people, our nation was soon able to play a leading part in winning the war.

REVIEWING THE SECTION

A. Knowing New Terms

Explain each of these terms in your notebook *in your own words.*

(In **C1**) "war of machines"
"miracle of production"
"bridge of ships"

(In **C2**) War Production Board
(In **F**) OPA
rationing

B. Understanding the Facts

Complete this chart comparing conditions in the United States during the two world wars. If conditions in the second conflict were like those in the first, write "Same." If not, explain how they were different. Use a notebook.

The Home Front in World War I	The Home Front in World War II
1. The Selective Service System was set up soon after the United States entered the war.	1.
2. Most able-bodied, unmarried young men served in the armed forces.	2.
3. The government set up several boards to regulate war production.	3.
4. Unions grew much stronger. In return for their no-strike pledge, the government helped them to get better wages and conditions for the workers.	4.
5. Farmers raised larger crops with fewer workers.	5.
6. Consumers were asked to use less of scarce goods.	6.
7. Prices rose rapidly.	7.
8. To pay for the war, the government greatly increased taxes and sold large amounts of bonds.	8.
9. Government propaganda stirred up hatred of the enemy. The press was censored.	9.
10. Thousands of Americans were arrested for criticizing the government and the war.	10.

Conclusion. In which war was the home front better organized? Why do you think this was so?

C. Finding the Reasons

Write the letters of *all* the correct answers to each question.
1. Why did the Axis Powers almost win the war in the summer of 1942?
    a. The Japanese conquered a large empire in the western Pacific. b. The Germans almost gained control of Russia's main oil fields. c. The Germans threatened to cut off British supplies by sinking large numbers of allied ships and taking the British oil fields in the Middle East.
2. Why did the Allies eventually win the war?
    a. They had many more people and much more land than their enemies. b. They had much larger industries and more natural resources. c. Their soldiers had more experience and better training.

3. Why was the United States able to produce huge quantities of war equipment?
   a. Its great mass-production industries were used to make war goods.
   b. Many large new factories were built to make war equipment.
   c. American businesses were used to taking orders from the government.
4. Why were scientists important in World War II?
   a. They invented important new weapons. b. They developed new methods of fighting. c. They found substitutes for rubber and other scarce materials.
5. How did World War II help to change the role of women in American life?
   a. Women performed factory jobs. b. Women served in the armed forces. c. Women headed the largest wartime government agencies.
6. Why was the American government able to hold prices down during World War II?
   a. The OPA fixed prices and rationed scarce goods. b. The output of civilian goods was greatly increased. c. American consumers managed to get along with less.
7. Why was American morale high in World War II?
   a. People did not have to make many sacrifices. b. They saw that they were fighting for a very good cause. c. The government put out a great deal of propaganda against the Axis Powers.
8. Why was the treatment of Japanese Americans during World War II a violation of democratic ideals?
   a. They were deprived of liberty and property without a trial. b. They were treated in this way because of their nationality and race. c. Most of them had not done anything wrong.

IMPROVING YOUR SKILLS

Interpreting the Graph

Study the two graphs on the next page. Then complete the following statements.

GRAPH 1. Spending by the United States War Department

1. Our War Department spent the smallest amount, less than $_____ billion, in the year _____.
2. It spent the largest amount, over $_____ billion, in _____.
3. The largest increase in spending was in the year _____, when spending rose from about $_____ billion to more than $_____ billion.
4. The smallest increase, only about $_____ billion, came in _____.

SPENDING BY THE UNITED STATES WAR DEPARTMENT, 1940-1945

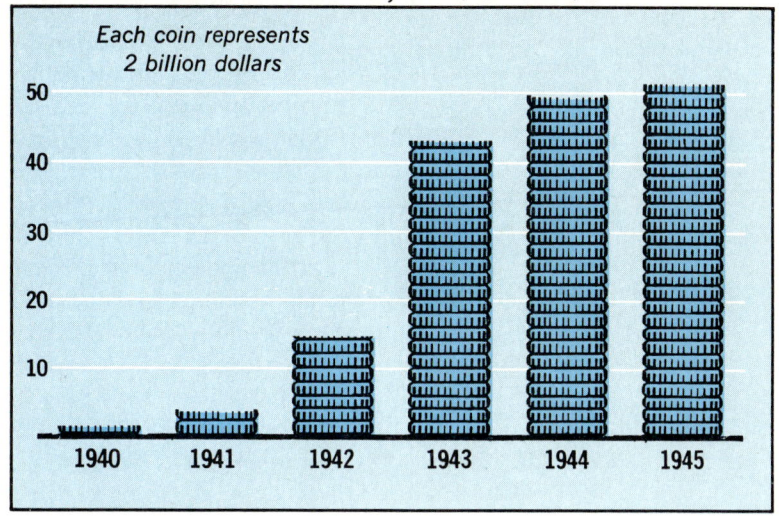

GRAPH 2. Naval Construction

1. The tonnage of naval vessels built in American shipyards more than doubled in the years ____, ____, and ____.
2. Tonnage declined in the years ____ and ____.
3. The total amount built while the United States was at war (1942-1945) was about ____ million tons.

UNITED STATES NAVAL CONSTRUCTION, 1940-1945

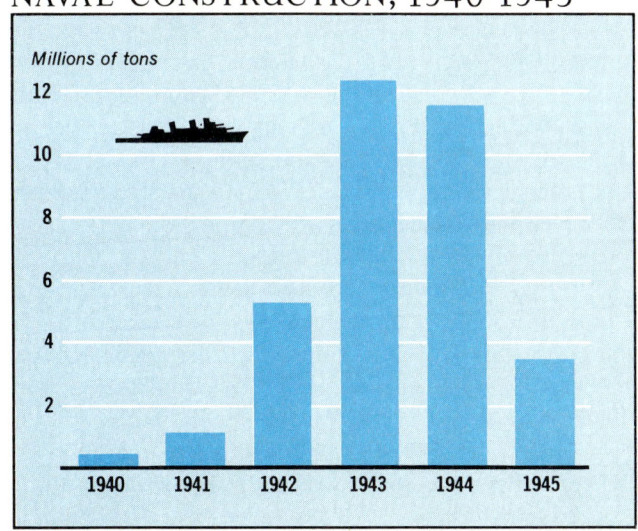

How Did the Allies Win the War?

A. The Plan for Victory. President Roosevelt had to make a very difficult decision in 1942. The United States had to fight powerful enemies who had conquered large territories and were advancing on many battlefronts. "How should our nation divide its efforts?" the President had to decide. "How much of our strength should we send to each battlefront?"

The Russian leader, Joseph Stalin, wanted the Americans and British to begin a large-scale invasion of France as soon as possible. This would be a great help to Russia because Hitler would have to split his forces between two fronts. American generals also favored a "second front" in France as the shortest road to Germany and victory. However, Winston Churchill, the British prime minister, opposed an invasion of France. The German defenses along the French coast were very strong. It would take years, Churchill said, to gather forces strong enough to break through them. He wanted instead to attack the Axis by way of North Africa and southern Europe. This would be an easier, though slower, way to weaken Germany and win the war. Many Americans, chiefly on the West Coast, favored a third plan. They wanted the United States to concentrate on beating Japan instead of sending large forces to Europe.

The final plan was a compromise. President Roosevelt decided to send two-thirds of America's strength to Europe because the Nazis were stronger and more dangerous than the Japanese. He also agreed to a second front in North Africa and southern Europe. At the same time, however, forces would be massed in England for an attack on Germany through France at some later date. In the Pacific, the Americans would build up chiefly their navy and air forces. They would try to free the territories taken by the Japanese and then advance on Japan itself. It was expected, however, that Germany would be defeated before Japan. After Germany fell, the United States would be free to turn its full strength on its enemy in Asia.

B. The War in the West. 1. TURNING THE TIDE. In the fall of 1942, the Western Allies were already strong enough to take the offensive against the European Axis powers. The British won the first victory. They began a powerful drive against the Germans and Italians in Egypt. They defeated the enemy forces and pushed them westward across Libya (#1 on the map on page 555). Then an Allied force, made up mainly of British and Americans, landed in Morocco and Algeria. The Allies drove the Axis troops eastward (#2 on the map). In May, 1943, the entire German-Italian army in North Africa was trapped in Tunisia and forced to surrender (#3 on the map).

In the meantime, the Russians had won a great victory at Stalingrad (#4 on the map). In the fall of 1942, the Germans and their allies had entered this important industrial city on the Volga River. Their purpose was to cut off oil shipments that passed through Stalingrad to Russian forces in the north. But the Russians resisted in stubborn house-to-house fighting. When winter came, Russian reinforcements suddenly poured across the frozen Volga and surrounded the Axis forces. After a savage

ALLIED OFFENSIVES IN THE WEST

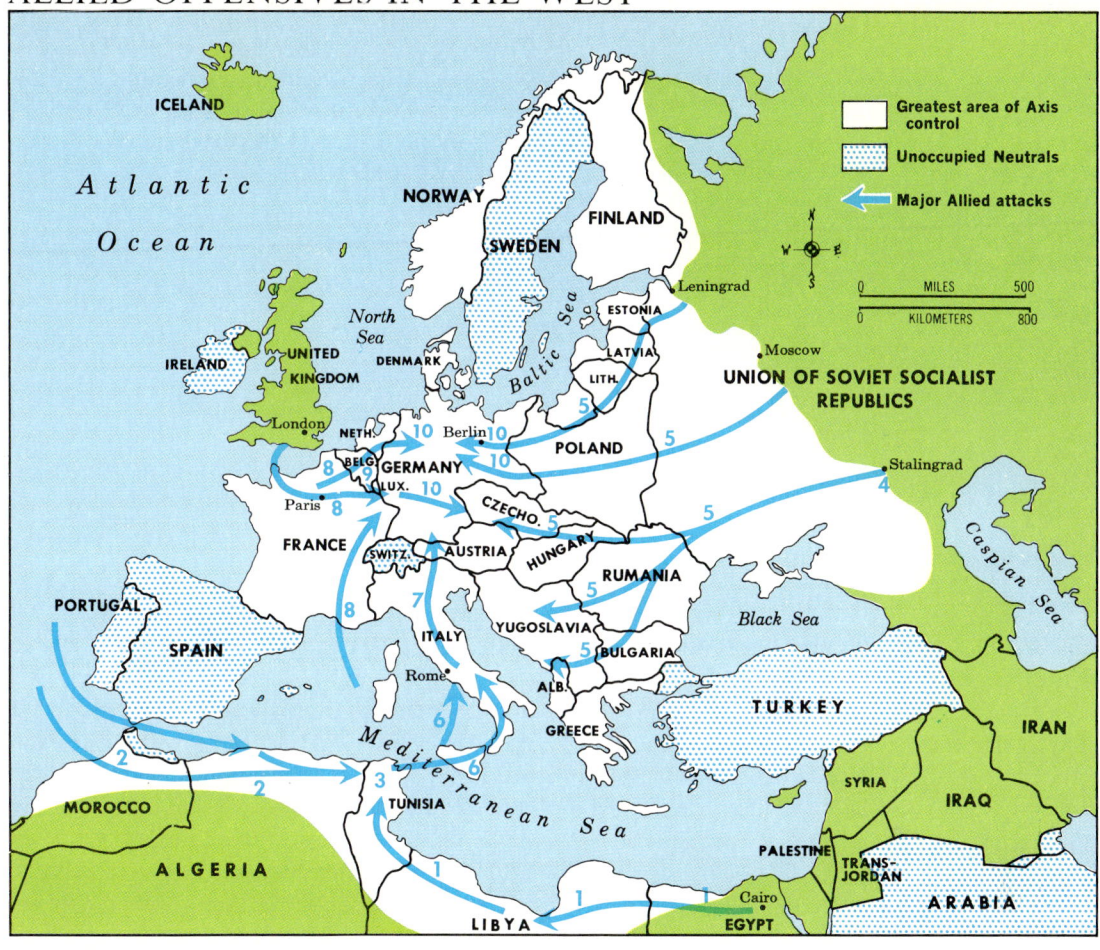

struggle, they captured what was left of a once-mighty Axis army.

2. EARLY ALLIED OFFENSIVES. From that time on, the Russians took the offensive against their enemies. Their great manpower made it possible for them to fight on a battlefront almost two thousand miles long. By striking first in one place and then in another, they drove the Axis forces back slowly but steadily. During the next two years they freed all Russian soil, then advanced across the Balkan Peninsula and eastern Europe (#5 on the map). Finally, in the spring of 1945, they invaded Germany itself.

Meanwhile, the Western Allies carried the war from North Africa into southern Europe. In the summer of 1943, they invaded first Sicily and then southern Italy (#6 on the map). The Italian government dismissed Mussolini and surrendered to the Allies. A few months later, Italy actually joined the Allies against the Germans. However, the fighting in Italy did not stop. The Germans used the mountains of the Italian Peninsula to set up one strong defense line after another. The Allies had to fight their way up these mountains against heavy enemy fire. But each time they broke through the Germans' defenses, they found

555

American landing craft in an English harbor. The ships were being prepared to carry soldiers and materials for the Allied landing in France on "D-Day" (June 6, 1944).

that the Germans had retreated to the next defense line. The slow and costly Allied advance in Italy (#7 on the map) continued until the end of the war.

The Germans, already weakened by the war on two fronts, also suffered heavy losses on a third front, in the air. British bombers blasted German industrial areas by night. American bombers returned to the same places by day to destroy buildings missed in the night bombings. They also hit targets of special importance to the German war effort, such as gasoline refineries, synthetic rubber plants, and railroad lines.

In the "Battle of the Atlantic," the tide began to turn against the Axis in 1943. American ships and planes, equipped with sonar and radar, hunted down and sank dozens of German submarines. American shipyards were now able to turn out ships much faster than the submarines could sink them.

3. FINAL OFFENSIVES. Early in June 1944, the greatest seaborne offensive in history began. This was the Allied invasion of France from England. First thousands of Allied planes and warships bombarded the German defenses along the English Channel. Then Allied troops poured ashore from landing craft. They had to fight their way through strong defenses, and their losses were very heavy. By nightfall, however, they had won a strong beachhead. When enough reinforcements had been landed, the Allies let loose a powerful land offensive. They smashed through the German lines, freed Paris, and raced toward the German frontier (#8 on the map).

The Western Allies were forced by strong defenses to slow down when they reached the German border. They were even driven back for a time in the Battle of the Bulge (#9 on the map). There Hitler threw his remaining forces into a desperate attempt to smash the Allied advance. He also bombed Great Britain with a new weapon, the ballistic missile or flying bomb. These last-ditch efforts failed. The Allies crushed the Germans' offensive and broke through their fortifications. They pushed forward to meet the Russians, who were advancing from the east (#10 on the map). The German capital of Berlin fell to the Russians. Hitler, who was hiding in an underground shelter in

Berlin, killed himself. On May 7, 1945, the German commander surrendered and the war in Europe came to an end.

C. The War in the East. 1. THE TURNING POINT. Though Australia and New Zealand helped, the war in the East was mainly an American affair. Our first task was to stop the Japanese advance. In May 1942, the Japanese sent a large force to invade Australia by way of the Coral Sea. In June they started another offensive against the island of Midway (#1 and 2 on the map on page 558). Each time the American Pacific fleet, though outnumbered, sailed out to stop the Japanese. But the two fleets did not meet. Instead, their planes fought the battles. Both times American pilots forced the Japanese to retreat by sinking or damaging most of their aircraft carriers. The Battles of the Coral Sea and Midway were the turning point of the war in the Pacific.

2. "ISLAND HOPPING." The Americans now went over to the attack. To advance across the broad Pacific, they used "island hopping." They would pick a target several hundred miles away, but within range of their planes. After bombing it heavily, they would send a force by sea to capture it. Then they would quickly build new airfields there and start bombing the next target.

The Americans used this method to advance along two routes—in the southwest Pacific and in the central Pacific. In the southwest Pacific, they first captured the little island of Guadalcanal after a long and costly struggle. Then they "hopped" along the Solomon Islands and the coast of New Guinea toward the Philippines (#3 on the map). The Japanese sent almost their entire navy to stop the invasion of the Philippines. They were met by the American Pacific fleet, which had been strengthened with dozens of new aircraft carriers and other warships. In the largest naval battle in history, the Battle of Leyte Gulf, the Americans nearly wiped out the Japanese navy.

The second American offensive drove across the central Pacific toward Japan. Our forces "hopped" from the Gilbert Islands to the Marshalls, and then to the Marianas (#4 on the

United States commanders in World War II. From left to right: George C. Marshall, chief of staff; Dwight D. Eisenhower, commander of Allied forces in Europe; Douglas A. MacArthur, commander of Allied forces in the southwest Pacific; Chester A. Nimitz, commander of the Pacific fleet.

map). From bases in the Marianas, long-range American bombers carried the war to Japan itself. Their fire-bombs destroyed one industrial center after another. But the Japanese still refused to surrender. Instead, they fought more and more desperately as the Americans neared their shores. Capturing the little island of Iwo Jima, 750 miles from Japan, cost the Americans over twenty thousand in dead and wounded. The conquest of Okinawa, 300 miles from Japan, cost them eighty thousand more (#5 and 6 on the map).

3. THE JAPANESE SURRENDER. When the war in Europe ended, the United States began to move its armies to the Pacific. It was preparing to invade Japan. Experts believed that the invasion would cost a million casualties. At this point, the President of the United States had to make a fateful decision. In July 1945, Allied scientists had exploded a terrible new weapon, the atomic bomb. A single A-bomb had the power of twenty thousand tons of T.N.T., or as much as several thousand ordinary bombs. The President had to decide whether this destructive new weapon should be used against the Japanese to shorten the war and save American lives.

President Roosevelt, who had been elected to a fourth term in 1944, had died suddenly a few months later. His successor, Harry S Truman,

OFFENSIVES IN THE PACIFIC

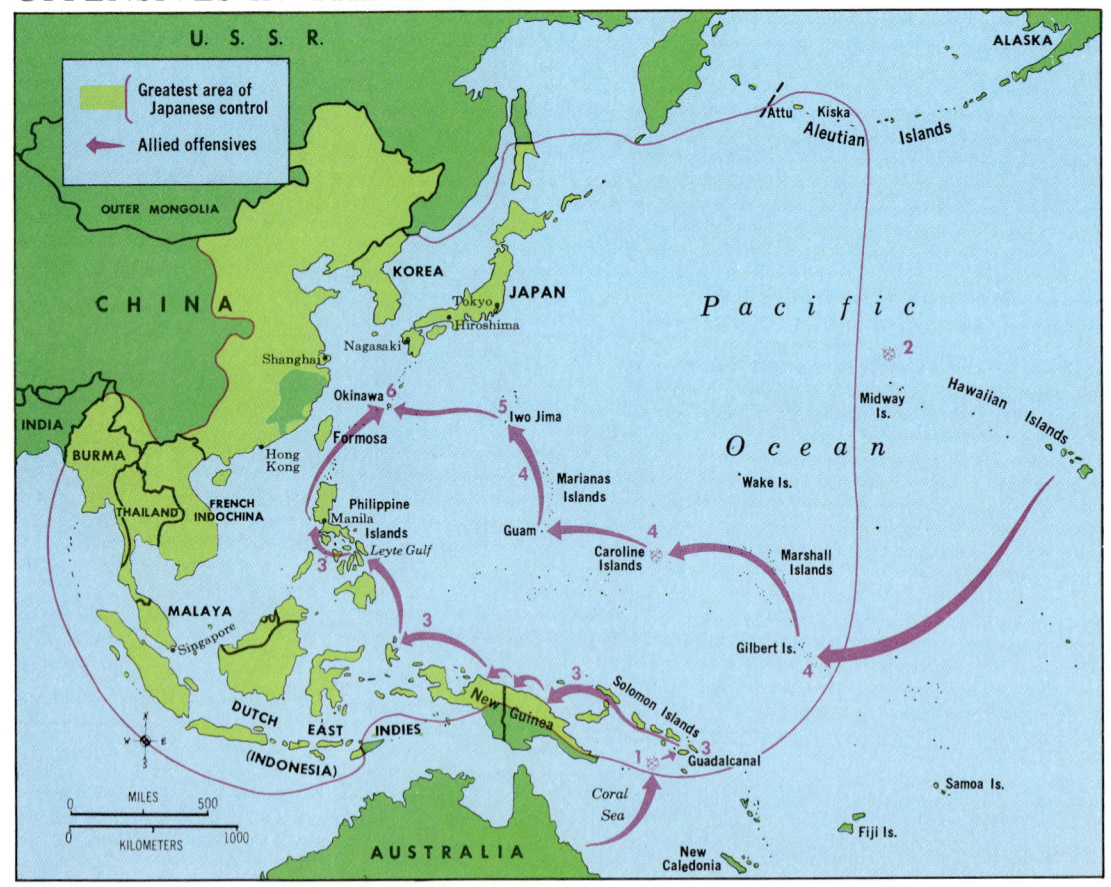

HIGHLIGHTS OF WORLD WAR II

September 1, 1939 Start of World War II
June 22, 1940 French surrender to Germany
June 22, 1941 Axis invasion of the Soviet Union
December 7, 1941 Japan's bombing of Pearl Harbor
September 3, 1943 Italy's surrender to the Allies
June 6, 1944 D-Day, Allied invasion of France
May 7, 1945 V-E (victory in Europe) Day, German surrender
August 6, 1945 A-bomb dropped on Hiroshima
August 15, 1945 V-J (victory over Japan) Day, Japan's surrender

Hiroshima after the A-bomb.

had to make the decision. Truman decided to use the bomb. But first he warned the Japanese to surrender or face "prompt and utter destruction." The Japanese government, not knowing about the A-bomb, paid no attention to the warning.

On August 6, a lone American plane dropped a single bomb on the industrial city of Hiroshima. The city was wiped out, with a loss of some eighty thousand lives. Two days later Russia declared war on Japan and invaded Manchuria. The next day the city of Nagasaki was destroyed by a second American A-bomb. The Japanese surrendered at last. On August 15, 1945, six years after it started, the Second World War came to an end.

D. Costs of the War. Fifty-six nations took part in World War II. More than 20,000,000 soldiers were killed in battle, and an even larger number were wounded. Millions of civilians also died—in bombings, in Hitler's concentration camps, and from hunger and disease. The economic cost of the war was probably more than a trillion dollars ($1,000,000,000,-000)! Europe had never fully recovered from the First World War; the second war left it in ruins. The war also caused heavy damage in other parts of the world. Clearly, humanity could not bear another great conflict, especially if it were fought with missiles carrying atomic warheads. It was now more important than ever to build a strong and lasting peace.

REVIEWING THE SECTION

A. Knowing New Terms

Explain each of these terms in your notebook *in your own words*.

(In **A**) second front
(In **B2**) Battle of the Atlantic
(In **C2**) island hopping

B. Knowing Important Persons

In your notebook write the *names* that complete each sentence correctly.

1. The prime minister of Great Britain in World War II was _____ _____.
2. The ruler of the Soviet Union was _____ _____.
3. The President of the United States at the end of the war was _____ _____.
4. The supreme commander of the Allied forces in Western Europe was General _____.
5. The commander of the Allied armies in the Pacific was General _____.
6. The commander of the American Pacific fleet was Admiral _____.

C. Knowing the Facts

PART 1. Here are six battles of World War II. In your notebook write where each took place (in Europe or the Pacific) and who won it (America, Britain, Russia, or any combination of these nations).

1. Battle of the Atlantic
2. Battle of the Bulge
3. Battle of the Coral Sea
4. Battle of Leyte Gulf
5. Battle of Midway
6. Battle of Stalingrad

PART 2. Which nation or nations won back these places from the Axis?

1. Balkan Peninsula
2. Eastern Europe
3. Egypt
4. France
5. Germany
6. Italy
7. North Africa
8. Sicily
9. Tunisia

D. Summing Up the Chapter

In your notebook write the correct order for each group of events.

PART 1. *Axis Offensives*

1. The fall of France
2. German bombing of Great Britain
3. German invasion of Poland
4. German invasion of Russia
5. Japanese attack on Pearl Harbor

PART 2. *Allied Victories in the West*

1. Invasion of Italy
2. Freeing of France
3. Victories in North Africa
4. Freeing of the Balkan Peninsula and Eastern Europe
5. Final defeat of Germany

PART 3. *Allied Victories in the Pacific*

1. Battles of the Coral Sea and Midway
2. Bombing of Japan
3. Capture of Iwo Jima and Okinawa
4. Island hopping in the southwest and central Pacific
5. Japan's surrender

IMPROVING YOUR SKILLS

A. *Interpreting the Graph*

Study the graph below. Then answer the following questions.

1. The least costly conflict was the _____-_____ War. Our total casualties (killed and wounded) were only about _____ men.
2. The most costly conflict was _____ _____ _____, in which almost _____ men were killed in battle.
3. Compare this chart with the one on page 327. The most costly conflict in our history was the _____ _____ _____.

AMERICAN CASUALTIES IN WARS
Each symbol represents 25,000 men

† Killed in battle
† Other deaths
🛏 Wounded

Spanish-American War
World War I
World War II
Korean War
Vietnam War

561

B. Mastering the Map

Study the maps on pages 555 and 558. Then do the following exercise.

MAP 1. Allied Offensives in the West

1. List the places freed from the Axis by the Americans and British.
2. List the countries freed by the Soviet Union.
3. Which freed a larger part of Europe, the western Allies or the Soviet Union?

MAP 2. Offensives in the Pacific

1. Trace the steps in the American advance toward Japan in the southwest Pacific. Are these steps and those in the next #2 the best? Explain.
2. Do the same for the American advance in the central Pacific.

MAKING HISTORY LIVE

1. Explain why you would agree or disagree with each of these military decisions:
   a. To start a second front in North Africa and Italy instead of France;
   b. To send two-thirds of American strength to Europe, one-third to the Pacific.
2. Bring in drawings, pictures, and souvenirs for a class display on World War II.
3. Talk to someone who fought in World War II. Write about one or two war experiences.
4. On the basis of your outside reading, report on one important battle of World War II.
5. Prepare for a panel discussion on the winning of World War II. Represent one of the victorious powers and tell what this country did to win the war. Also try to determine which nation did the most.

Chapter 33

MAKING THE PEACE AFTER WORLD WAR II

Both President Roosevelt and Prime Minister Churchill had held high government posts during the First World War. They had followed closely the Allies' peace efforts and had seen them fail. They had learned an important truth from this failure. Allies have to cooperate during a war in order to defeat their common enemies. But they find it much harder to work together after the war ends. Once the danger is over, they usually become rivals for territory, wealth, and power.

The Allied leaders of World War I did not meet for peace talks until several months after the war's end. Roosevelt and Churchill decided that they would not make the same mistake. So they met several times during World War II. Churchill also met a few times with the Russian dictator, Joseph Stalin. Most important, all three leaders met twice during the war. At these meetings they made plans both to win the war and to make the peace. As a result, they had already laid the foundations for peace by the time the war ended.

In this chapter we shall learn what agreements the Big Three—Roosevelt, Churchill, and Stalin—reached. We shall also study the new world organization they created to replace the League of Nations. Finally, we shall see why cracks soon appeared in the foundation they had built so carefully.

What Agreements Did the Big Three Reach?

A. Principles of the Peace. Roosevelt and Churchill met for the first time in the summer of 1941 aboard a warship off the Atlantic coast of Canada. Here the two leaders drew up the Atlantic Charter, a statement of principles to guide the making of the peace. These were much like the Fourteen Points of President Wilson in World War I (see page 482). The Atlantic Charter promised the peoples of the world that Great Britain and the United States would: 1. take no territory for themselves at the end of the war; 2. restore self-government to all the countries that had been conquered; 3. work to improve economic conditions so that people everywhere might "live out their lives in freedom from fear and want"; 4. set up a new world organization to take the place of the League of Nations. These principles were later put into a statement that all of the Allies, including the Soviet Union, signed.

The Atlantic Charter had important effects on the warring nations. It raised the morale of the Allies by showing them that they were fighting for freedom and a better life for all peoples. It weakened the Axis by encouraging the conquered peoples to form "underground" (secret) forces to fight for freedom.

B. The Yalta Agreements. The first meeting of the Big Three dealt mainly with military matters. The second meeting, however, had an important bearing on the peace. This meeting took place at Yalta in southern Russia as the war was nearing its end.

Since the Allied armies were about to conquer Germany, the Big Three had to decide how to govern it until a peace treaty could be made. They agreed to divide Germany into four zones. Each zone was to be occupied and ruled by the military forces of one of the great powers —the United States, the Soviet Union, Great Britain, and France (see map, page 566). The Germans were to be completely disarmed. Their war industries were to be taken over as part payment for all the damage they had done. Their leaders were to be tried as war criminals.

The Big Three also decided at Yalta how the nations freed from German rule were to be governed. Governments representing "all democratic elements" were to be set up in these nations. "Fair and free elections" were to be held as soon as possible.

A third agreement dealt with the war against Japan. Stalin agreed to declare war on Japan a few weeks after Germany surrendered. In return, he was to receive some northern Japanese islands and special rights in the rich Chinese province of Manchuria. This part of the Yalta agreements was kept secret at the time for military reasons. But when it was made public, it created a stir. Many people criticized it for violating both the territorial rights of our ally China and the principles of the Atlantic Charter. Others defended the agreement on the ground that it could save the lives of thousands of American soldiers by speeding Japan's surrender. Nobody knew at the time the Yalta agreements were made that the atomic bomb would soon be perfected.

C. Establishment of the United Nations Organization. The three great powers also reached two other important agreements before the end of the war. They set up a system for making the peace treaties. They also wrote the charter (constitution) of a new world organization named the United Nations. The UN's charter was approved by delegates from fifty nations at a meeting held in San Francisco shortly before the end of the war.

The United States became the first nation to join the UN. The Senate voted 89 to 2 for ratification. This vote showed how weak isolationism had become in the United States because it had not kept our country out of World War II. Most Americans now wanted our government to cooperate with other nations.

The UN was set up very quickly. The members decided to use the League of Nations' buildings in Switzerland for some of their activities, but to set up their main headquarters in New York City. They began to meet in temporary quarters before the end of 1945. The UN's permanent buildings were completed a few years later (see photo, page 579).

D. The Spread of Communism. By the time the UN began to meet, the Soviet Union and the Western powers were already quarreling. The main cause of disagreement was the rapid spread of Communist influence. In spite of strong protests by the Western powers, Stalin again and again violated the Atlantic Charter and the Yalta agreements. He kept under Soviet control three small republics along the Baltic Sea, a large slice of Poland, and parts of several other neighboring nations. He also set up Communist governments in Poland and all the other countries of Eastern Europe taken over by the Soviet army (see map, page 567). These countries became known as "satellites" (protectorates) of the Soviet Union.

In the words of Winston Churchill, the Communists lowered an "iron curtain" to cut off their new territories from contact with the outside world. They kept people from coming into their countries or leaving them. They carefully censored all their radio broadcasts, books, and

OURS...to fight for

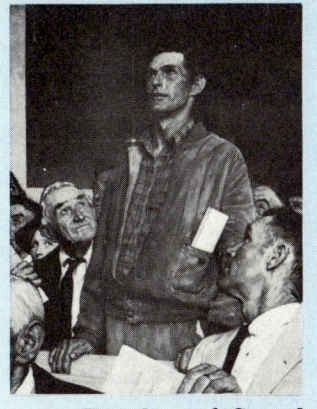

Freedom of Speech

Freedom of Worship

Freedom from Want

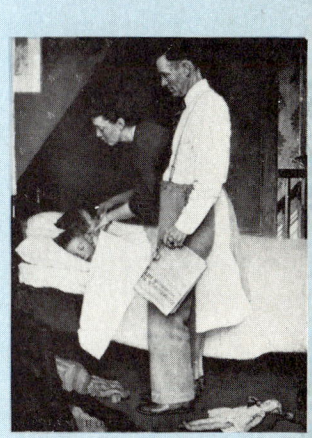

Freedom from Fear

This poster shows the "Four Freedoms" that President Roosevelt promised the American people and their allies early in the war. How did his promise help raise their morale? Which of these freedoms can be found in the U.S. Constitution?

newspapers. They especially forbade their subjects to read Western writings or listen to Western radio programs. The "iron curtain" had two purposes. First, the Communists did not want their former allies to know what they were doing to the people under their control. Second, they did not want their subjects to know what was happening in the democratic nations.

565

THE DIVISION OF GERMANY

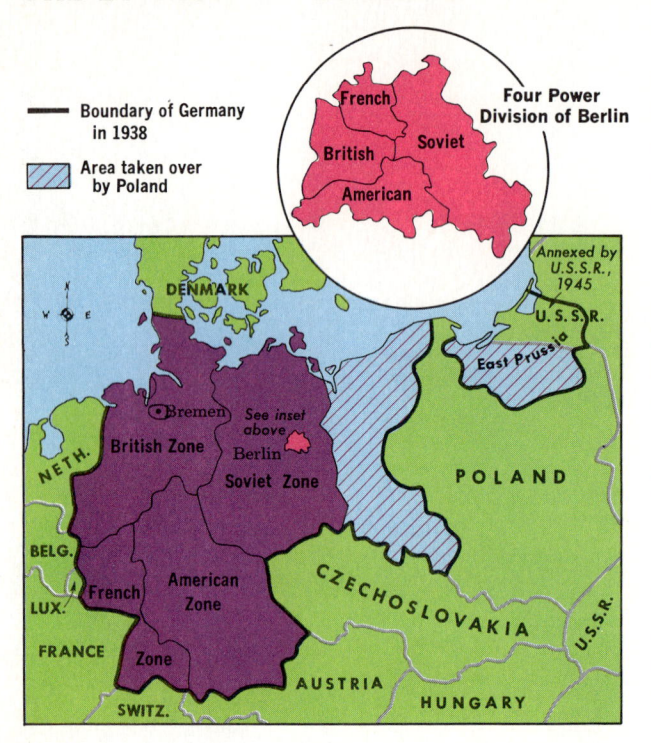

The Big Three at Yalta early in 1945. President Roosevelt, who looked ill when this picture was taken, died a few weeks later.

Even these large gains did not satisfy Stalin. He ordered Communist parties all over the world to take advantage of the economic troubles resulting from the war. In each country, Communists blamed the postwar troubles on the capitalist system (see page 670). Communism, they promised, would end the troubles and bring peace and prosperity. Many people were won over by the Communist promises. In France and Italy, the Communists gained so much power that they nearly won control of both governments. In Asia and Africa, the Communists encouraged the people of the colonies to rebel against their European rulers. The Soviet Union and its satellites promised to support such "wars of liberation" from the "imperialist powers."

The United States was alarmed by the Communist gains. President Truman, as we shall see later, took strong action to stop communism from spreading further. Meanwhile, however, the great powers went on with their efforts to write peace treaties.

E. An Unusual Peace. 1. THE TREATIES FOR THE SMALLER AXIS NATIONS. The peace talks were marked by bitter disputes between the Soviet Union and the Western powers. It took two years for them to agree on peace terms for Italy and the smaller Axis nations—Hungary, Rumania, Bulgaria, and Finland. Each of the defeated nations except Bulgaria lost some territory. Each was disarmed and had to pay for war damages. The Soviet Union got most of the territory and most of the payments. Hungary, Rumania, and Bulgaria became Soviet satellites. Stalin allowed them to violate the disarmament clause of the peace treaties by building up new armies. These forces had Russian uniforms, Russian equipment, and even Russian officers!

2. THE DIVISION OF GERMANY. How to treat Germany was a still more difficult problem for the victorious powers. Under the Yalta agreements, the country was divided into four occupation zones. A council of the four Allied

COMMUNIST GAINS AS A RESULT OF WORLD WAR II

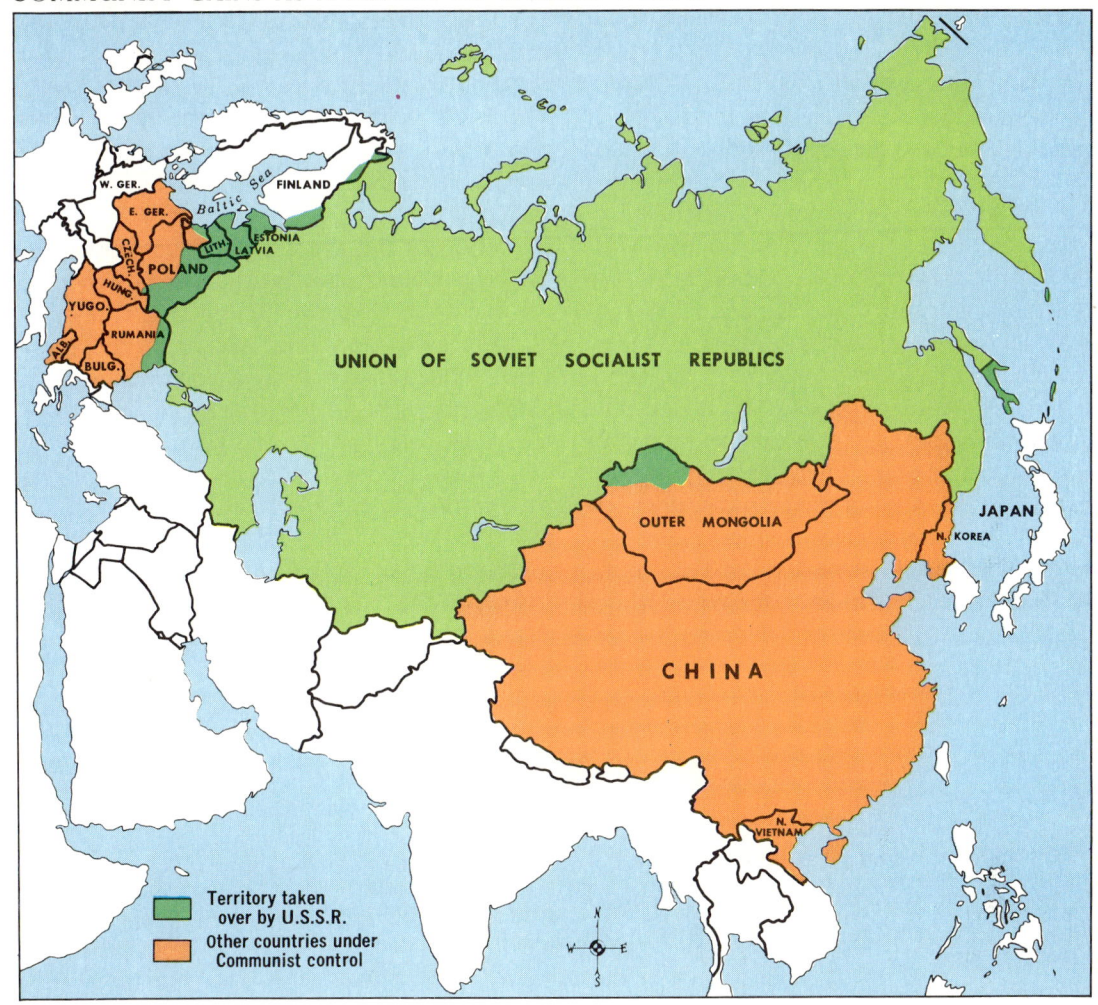

Territory taken over by U.S.S.R.
Other countries under Communist control

commanders was supposed to work out a single set of rules for the entire nation and enforce them. But the Soviet commander and the three other members of the council soon began to quarrel. Since the council could act only by unanimous agreement, it could get nothing done. Germany was, in effect, four separate countries. Its trade and industry were ruined. Instead of recovering from the war, it sank into a depression. The United States and Great Britain had to ship in food and other necessities for the people in their zones.

Representatives of the four powers met several times to work out a peace treaty for Germany. Each time they failed. In 1948 the three Western powers decided to unite their zones and set up a democratic German government to rule over them. Stalin tried hard to keep them from doing so. The result was a dangerous clash known as the Berlin crisis (see page 671). In 1952 the Western powers finally signed a separate agreement with the West German Republic. Meanwhile, the Russians had set up a Communist government in eastern Germany, making it another of their satellites. Germany is still divided into two separate countries today.

3. THE JAPANESE PEACE TREATY. Japan, like Germany, was occupied by the troops of several nations. But the country was not divided into occupation zones. Instead, control rested with the American forces under General MacArthur. Ignoring Soviet protests, General MacArthur went ahead to "democratize" Japan. He dismissed its military leaders, made many economic and social reforms, and drew up a new democratic constitution.

In Japan's case, as in Germany's, the four powers could not agree on peace terms. In 1951 the United States finally drew up a peace treaty that almost all of the wartime allies approved. Under this treaty, Japan lost all the territories it had taken since 1895. (The Pacific islands taken from Germany after World War I were placed under American protection.) Japan also had to pay damages to the nations it had attacked in World War II. In a separate treaty with the United States, it gave our government the right to keep troops and bases on its soil. The Soviet Union refused to sign the Japanese peace treaty. It made a separate agreement with Japan a few years later.

F. Results of the Peacemaking. On the whole, the peacemaking after World War II was even less successful than after World War I. In spite of their early start, the leaders of the great powers failed to agree on peace terms for Germany and Japan. They also failed to enforce the peace treaties they had written for the other Axis nations. Their only success was the new world organization, the UN. People all over the world hoped that the UN would be able to heal the growing split between the great powers so that the world might have peace at last.

REVIEWING THE SECTION

A. Knowing New Terms

In your notebook write the new terms in this section that best complete these statements.

1. The leaders who shaped the peace—President Roosevelt, Prime Minister Churchill, and Premier Stalin—were known as the "____ ____."
2. The statement of principles drafted by Roosevelt and Churchill and signed by all the United Nations was named the ____ ____.
3. The most important wartime agreements were made at the ____ meeting.
4. The world organization to replace the League of Nations was named the ____ ____.
5. The nations that fell under Communist control as a result of World War II were called the Soviet Union's ____.
6. Severe Communist limits on contact between Eastern Europe and the rest of the world were called the "____ ____."

B. Finding the Reasons

In your notebook write the letters of *all* the correct answers to each question.

1. Why did the Big Three meet during the war?
   a. They had to make plans for defeating their enemies. b. They wanted to become personal friends. c. They thought it would be easier to plan the peace while they were still fighting together.
2. Why did the Atlantic Charter help the Allies win the war?
   a. It raised the morale of their troops by telling them what they were fighting for. b. It encouraged the peoples conquered by the Axis to fight for their freedom. c. It kept Stalin from taking over foreign territories and taking away their peoples' freedom.
3. Why were the Yalta agreements criticized?
   a. They provided that Germany should be divided into four occupation zones. b. They gave Stalin the right to set up Communist governments in eastern Europe. c. They gave the Soviet Union control of territory belonging to an ally, China.
4. Why did our Senate ratify the U N Charter?
   a. The U N was very different from the League of Nations. b. Isolationism had become very weak in the United States because it had failed to keep our nation out of World War II. c. Most Americans were now willing to cooperate with foreign nations.
5. Why did the American and British governments object to Stalin's actions during and after World War II?
   a. He took over foreign territory in violation of the Atlantic Charter. b. He violated the Yalta agreements by setting up Communist governments in eastern Europe. c. He stirred up discontent and revolts in many parts of the world.
6. Why was the peacemaking after World War II unsuccessful?
   a. The Communists violated the treaties made for the smaller Axis nations. b. The three great powers could not agree on peace treaties for Germany and Japan. c. Not a single wartime agreement was actually carried out.

IMPROVING YOUR SKILLS

A. Mastering the Map

Study the maps on pages 566 and 567. Then do the following exercise.

MAP 1. Division of Germany

1. Which nation occupied the smallest zone of Germany?

2. In whose zone was the former German capital, Berlin?
3. Who ruled over Berlin?

MAP 2. Communist Gains as a Result of World War II

1. Name the countries that the Soviet Union took over completely as a result of World War II.
2. Name the countries from which the Soviet Union took some territory.
3. Name the countries that became Soviet satellites.

B. *Looking at Both Sides*

For each of these wartime and postwar decisions, write "Good" if you think it helped make a lasting peace; write "Bad" if you think it had a harmful effect; and write "Not sure" if its effects were not clearly good or bad. Be prepared to explain the reasons for your opinions in class.

1. *The Atlantic Charter*
   a. To forbid the victors to take territory
   b. To assure self-government for all freed nations
   c. To assure higher living standards for all peoples
2. *The Yalta agreements*
   a. To divide Germany into four occupation zones
   b. To disarm Germany
   c. To seize German industries as payment for war damages
   d. To punish war criminals
   e. To set up democratic governments in the freed nations
   f. To give Russia some Japanese islands and control of Manchuria in return for entering the war against Japan
3. *Agreement to establish the U N.*
4. *Treaties for Italy and the smaller Axis nations*
   a. To disarm these nations
   b. To take territory from them
   c. To make them pay for war damages
5. *Treatment of Germany*
   a. To unite the three zones of western Germany under a democratic government
   b. To make a separate peace treaty with West Germany
6. *Treatment of Japan*
   a. To democratize Japan
   b. To make a peace treaty without the Soviet Union
   c. To make a defense treaty between Japan and the United States

How Does the UN Work to Keep World Peace?

A. Purposes of the UN. The League of Nations came to an end during World War II. It had failed in its main purpose, preventing another world war. Would the new world organization, the United Nations, be more successful? Only time would tell. But the UN had several important advantages over the League. First, it had the world's strongest power, the United States, as a member. Second, it had the League's experience to profit from. Third, it was given responsibilities and powers that the League did not have.

The preamble (introduction) to the UN's Charter gives the organization the following important aims or purposes: 1. "to save succeeding generations from the scourge [evil] of war"; 2. "to promote social progress and better standards of life"; and 3. "to reaffirm faith in fundamental human rights, in the dignity and worth of the human person, in the equal rights of men and women and of nations large and small."

B. Machinery of the UN. To achieve these aims, the UN has six major parts or bodies. 1. The *General Assembly* is made up of delegates from all of the member nations. Each member, regardless of its size or power, has one vote in the Assembly. The task of this body is to talk over any problem affecting world peace and recommend what action should be taken. The old League of Nations Assembly needed a unanimous vote—that is, the vote of all its members—for any important decisions. The UN General Assembly needs the votes of only two-thirds of its members.

2. The *Security Council* has five permanent members. These are the United States, the Soviet Union, Great Britain, France, and the People's Republic of China. There are also nonpermanent members elected by the General Assembly for two-year terms. (There were six nonpermanent members at first. The number has since been raised to ten.)

The Security Council is the UN body that takes action. It is supposed to meet whenever a threat to world peace arises. After looking into the situation, it can do one of two things. It can ask all the nations involved to work out an agreement, or it can work out an agreement itself. To enforce its decisions, the Council can act against a nation it finds to be at fault. It can ask the UN's members to break relations with the nation, to stop trading with it, or even to use force against it. The UN Charter provides for a body called the Military Staff Committee to plan any military action that may be needed.

The UN does not have its own army to keep order among nations. It was hoped that the members would organize such an "international police force." Unfortunately, the split among the great powers has kept this from being done. But member nations have lent troops to the UN for special purposes, like patrolling the borders between hostile nations.

Action by the Security Council requires a two-thirds vote. However, any of the five permanent members can prevent action by voting against it. This "great-power" veto was widely criticized when the charter was written, but both the United States and the Soviet Union insisted on it. They gave two reasons for their position: First, they would be chiefly responsible for carrying out any UN decision. Second, no action would be effective anyway unless they supported it. In practice, however, the Soviet Union has used the veto over a hundred times since the UN began its work. Its vetoes have often paralyzed the Security Council. In such cases, the Assembly has often had to step in to try to settle the dispute.

3. The *International Court of Justice,* or World Court, decides questions of international law. The Court has changed very little since the League's time, yet it is stronger than it was. It was never a part of the League, but it is now a part of the UN. More important, the UN's member nations have agreed to accept the Court's decisions; formerly nations did not have to do so.

4. The League of Nations was most successful when it helped people all over the world to solve their problems. So this kind of work has been greatly expanded in the UN. A new body, the *Economic and Social Council,* has been created for this purpose. This body also checks on the work of more than a dozen special groups, known as the specialized agencies. These include the International Labor Organization (see page 484), the International Bank for Reconstruction and Development, the World Health Organization, the Food and Agriculture Organization, and the United Nations Educational, Scientific, and Cultural Organization (UNESCO). The name of each specialized agency tells what sort of work it does.

5. The *Trusteeship Council* watches over the way nations rule their colonies. It is chiefly responsible for the colonies taken from the nations defeated in the First and Second World Wars. These colonies were named trusteeships. The governing power or trustee was required to help the colonial peoples and to train them for self-government. Most of the trusteeships have gained their independence since 1945.

6. The UN needs thousands of workers to take care of its correspondence, arrange for meetings, publish information, and carry on other activities. These workers are known as the *Secretariat*. They are directed by the *secretary general,* who is the UN's highest officer.

The secretary general is nominated by the Security Council and elected by the General Assembly. The secretary general directs the Secretariat and carries out the requests of the different UN bodies. At times, the secretary has been called on by the General Assembly and Security Council to help settle disputes among member nations.

C. The UN's Achievements. The UN's main task is to keep peace. During the first few decades of its life, it was able to stop more than a dozen serious world disputes. In Korea, a UN army drove back the aggressor. (For details, see page 681.) UN troops helped to restore peace

Javier Perez de Cuellar, the current secretary general of the United Nations.

in the Suez Canal dispute, in the Congo, in Cyprus, and in Lebanon.

The UN has carried on many other important activities. It has, for example, issued the Universal Declaration of Human Rights, which is based on our Bill of Rights. It has held successful meetings for lowering tariffs and developing peaceful uses for atomic energy. The Trusteeship Council has helped colonial peoples to win self-government. The specialized agencies have stamped out disease, extended educational opportunities, increased food production, and helped start industries in less-developed (poor) nations.

The UN is also important as a meeting place for delegates from all over the world. Here they can express their own views and listen to those of other peoples. Through such discussions they can learn to understand one another. Delegates can also meet privately at the UN to talk over differences between their governments and try to settle them. This is what American and Russian delegates did at the time of the Berlin crisis. In short, the UN works for better understanding among all peoples.

D. Weaknesses of the UN. The UN, like the League of Nations, is a confederation—that is, an alliance of independent nations. It depends on its member nations, chiefly the permanent members of the Security Council, to make decisions and to carry them out. That is why it has been weakened by the rivalry between the two leading world powers, the United States and the Soviet Union. As a result of this rivalry, the Soviet Union has used the veto very often to keep the Security Council from taking action. Though the General Assembly can take over in such cases, it cannot act. It can only make recommendations for action by the member nations.

A second problem has been the rapid increase in the UN's membership. Since the end of World War II, colony after colony had gained its freedom and become a new nation. The total number of UN members has grown from fifty

UN peace-keeping troops in Cyprus. UN troops were stationed on the island for several years to prevent a civil war between islanders of Greek and Turkish descent. Why hasn't the UN been able to prevent wars in other parts of the world?

A doctor (right) and a UN volunteer examine a child suffering from malnutrition. Their work is part of a UN health project in Upper Volta in Africa.

in 1945 to 157 in 1983. Several objections have been raised to this state of affairs. 1. It is much harder to get things done, especially in the General Assembly. 2. Many of the new nations are very small, yet they have the same vote in the General Assembly as the great powers. 3. Most of the new nations were formerly colonies of the western powers. So they often tend to oppose the West and to side with the Communist members. There are so many of them that their votes can often decide an important question.

A third serious problem of the UN has been a lack of funds. Many nations either do not have the money to pay their share of the dues or refuse to pay. Communist nations and France have often withheld payments when the UN has acted in ways they disapproved. These countries, for example, opposed the UN's use of troops to restore order in the Congo. So they did not pay their share of the cost. The US pays one-fourth of the regular budget of the UN. But the United States paid only part of its share to education programs to protest UNESCO actions against Israel.

E. The Over-All Picture. It has been suggested that the UN Charter should be changed to eliminate these weaknesses. It would, however, be almost impossible to do this. Any change would have to be approved by both the General Assembly and the Security Council. This would mean getting the support of every permanent member of the Council. But it is doubtful if the large nations would vote for changes that reduced their power.

Because of its weaknesses, the UN has not been able to fulfill the high hopes once held for it. Still, it has done a great deal to promote world peace. It will be able to do much more if the United States and the Soviet Union end their rivalry. This rivalry, known as the Cold War, will be studied in the next unit. We shall see how the rivalry developed and what steps have been taken to try and end it.

REVIEWING THE SECTION

A. Knowing New Terms

In your notebook write the new terms in this section that best complete these statements.

1. The UN body that discusses questions affecting world peace is the _____.
2. The main body in the UN for taking action is the _____.
3. The specialized agencies are directed by the _____ Council.
4. Questions of international law are decided by the International Court of Justice or _____.
5. The UN's correspondence and other day-to-day work are handled by the _____.
6. The highest officer of the UN is the _____.
7. The conflict between the United States and the Soviet Union after World War II has been named the _____.

B. Understanding the Facts

PART 1. Write the *letter* of the UN body that fits each description. (You may use the same letter more than once.)

A. General Assembly
B. Security Council
C. Economic and Social Council
D. Trusteeship Council
E. World Court
F. International Labor Organization
G. World Health Organization
H. Food and Agriculture Organization
I. UNESCO
J. Secretariat

Descriptions

1. Can discuss any matter affecting world peace.
2. Can recommend a course of action to be taken by the member nations.
3. Is made up of representatives from every member nation.
4. Decides questions of international law.
5. Encourages colonial powers to give their subjects independence.
6. Encourages cultural exchanges among different nations.
7. Has often been paralyzed by the great-power veto.
8. Helps to stamp out disease.
9. Is composed of secretaries and clerks, as well as higher officials.
10. Looks for ways to improve conditions for workers all over the world.
11. Strives to increase food production.
12. Carries on many kinds of activities to help underdeveloped nations.

PART 2. Complete this chart comparing the League of Nations and the UN. Write "Same" if the UN is like the League in any of the ways listed. If it differs, tell what the difference is. Write in your notebook.

League of Nations	United Nations
1. It was an alliance of independent nations.	1.
2. Its Assembly was made up of delegates from all the member nations.	2.
3. Each member nation, whether large or small, had one vote in the Assembly.	3.
4. The Assembly made important decisions by unanimous vote.	4.
5. The Council was made up of the great powers, which were permanent members, and other member nations, which were elected for short terms.	5.
6. Council decisions were made by unanimous vote.	6.
7. The Assembly and the Council had much the same powers.	7.
8. The World Court was not a part of the League. Member nations did not have to accept its decisions.	8.
9. A few special agencies were set up to deal with special problems.	9.
10. A special body, the Mandates Commission, watched over the colonies taken from the nations defeated in World War I.	10.

IMPROVING YOUR SKILLS

Telling Facts From Opinions

Write "Fact" for each statement that can be proved by getting the necessary information. Write "Opinion" if you think the answer depends on values and judgment.

1. The UN's General Assembly is stronger than the Assembly of the League because it is easier to get a two-thirds vote than a unanimous vote.
2. Both the United States and the Soviet Union wanted the great-power veto.
3. The UN could do much more if the great-power veto were ended.
4. An international police force could have settled many of the disputes brought before the UN.
5. The World Court is stronger now than it was in the League's time.
6. The UN carries on many more activities to help needy peoples than the League did.
7. Important features of the UN were borrowed from the League.
8. The main weakness of the UN is the conflict between the Soviet Union and the United States.
9. The new nations of Asia and Africa should not have been allowed to enter the UN until their governments became stronger and more experienced.
10. The UN should move its headquarters from the United States to a nation that is neutral in the Cold War.

MAKING HISTORY LIVE

1. Some people think that President Truman should have kept the Russians from taking control of eastern Europe in violation of the Atlantic Charter and Yalta agreements. If you agree with them, write a paragraph beginning with the words, "If I had been President of the United States in 1945, I would have . . ."
2. If you have visited the UN or seen a film or TV program or read a newspaper or magazine about the UN, tell what you learned.
3. On the basis of outside reading, report on the work done by *one* major UN body or specialized agency.
4. Tell why you would be for or against *one* of these suggestions for strengthening the UN:
a. Giving extra votes to the larger, richer, and stronger nations in the General Assembly. b. Ending the great-power veto. c. Allowing the General Assembly to take action whenever the Security Council is paralyzed by a great-power veto. d. Organizing an international police force under the UN.
5. a. Compare the UN today with the government of the United States under the Articles of Confederation (see page 102). b. Some people think that the world needs a government as strong as that of the United States under the Constitution. Explain why you would favor or oppose such a "United States of the World."

6. Help make a class display of posters, cartoons, and pictures on the UN and its activities. Use magazines or newspapers from home or be original.

SUMMING UP THE UNIT

How Was Our Nation Affected by Two World Wars?

A. The "Roaring Twenties." After the First World War, the United States entered a period of gay good times known as the "Roaring Twenties." American industry, which had grown greatly during the war, continued to expand. Businesses made fortunes, and the living standards of the common people rose. But the prosperity was built on weak foundations. Many Americans, especially workers in "sick industries" and farmers, did not share in the country's prosperity. Trade unions lost members. Millions of people bought more than they could afford on the installment plan. Many others borrowed heavily to buy stocks or real estate. The result was a "boom" period, followed by the stock market crash and the worst depression in our history.

B. The New Deal. Under President Hoover, Congress took some steps to end the depression, but these were not enough. When Franklin D. Roosevelt became President in 1933, he began the "New Deal." This was a three-part program of "relief, recovery, and reform." New Deal relief measures helped millions of needy Americans. Recovery measures, largely through government spending, helped business make a start again. (Production did not, however, reach the level of 1929 until the Second World War.) Most important in the long run were the New Deal reforms. These were based on the Progressives' idea that government should help the common people and regulate business in the public interest. Many of the reforms, such as social security and the minimum wage law, have become a permanent part of our way of life.

C. Foreign Policy Under FDR. The Roosevelt administration also made far-reaching changes in our foreign policy. The Good Neighbor Policy changed our way of dealing with Latin America. Our government turned from "policing" our neighbors to the south to cooperating with them in solving common problems. The United States also gave the Latin Americans a great deal of help during the 1930s. In return, they helped the United States in World War II.

In its attitude toward Europe, the United States remained isolationist from 1920 to 1940. When dictators came to power and began to conquer weaker nations, Congress passed the Neutrality Acts. They forbade Americans to do business with any nations at war. In effect, the laws helped the aggressors because their victims could not get American military aid.

Our government changed its policy, one step at a time, after World War II began. First Congress allowed Great Britain and other warring nations to buy arms in the United States, provided that they paid cash and came to get them. Then it passed the Lend-Lease Act, under which the United States supplied enemies of the Axis Powers with arms on their promise to pay later. Next, American ships were permitted to carry war materials as far as Iceland. As a result, American ships were soon fighting an undeclared naval war with German submarines. Meanwhile, the United States was also trying to keep Japan from taking over Southeast Asia. This led to the Japanese "sneak" attack on Pearl Harbor, which brought the United States into World War II.

D. Winning the War. The American people did not want to change Presidents during the war. So they elected FDR to a third, and then to a fourth, term of office. Under his direction, the United States prepared for war with amazing speed. Our nation raised a tremendous army and built the largest and most powerful navy and air force the world had ever seen. We supplied both our own armed forces and those of our allies with huge amounts of war equipment.

The United States joined Britain, the Soviet Union, and the smaller Allies to turn the tide against the Axis Powers in 1942. The western Allies freed North Africa and most of Italy. Then, in June 1944, they invaded France. Meanwhile, the Russians drove all Axis forces from their own soil, most of the Balkan Peninsula, and eastern Europe. Finally, in the spring of 1945, the Allies invaded Germany from east and west and forced it to surrender.

In the east, the American navy and air force had the main responsibility. After turning back a Japanese attack on Australia, they began offensives in two areas of the Pacific. In the southwest Pacific, they took the Solomon Islands, then New Guinea, and finally the Philippines. In the central Pacific, they conquered bases within bombing range of Japan. Then they began a heavy bombing of the enemy's homeland in preparation for an invasion. But Japan's leaders still refused to surrender. In August, 1945, American planes dropped two A-bombs and destroyed two Japanese cities. Japan surrendered and the Second World War finally came to an end.

United Nations headquarters in New York City. The 39-story building houses the Secretariat.

E. Making the Peace. In talks held before the war's end, the Big Three decided a number of questions bearing on the peace. They agreed to divide Germany into four occupation zones, to establish democratic governments in the nations freed from Axis rule, and to set up a new world organization, the UN. But as soon as the war was over, the Soviet Union began to break

579

these agreements. It took territory from its neighbors, set up Communist governments in more than a half-dozen nations, and stirred up trouble in many parts of the globe.

American efforts to stop Communist expansion led to a conflict between the two great powers known as the Cold War. In the next unit we shall learn what disputes arose between them and how they were settled. We shall also see how the United States has continued to advance in domestic affairs since the end of World War II.

REVIEWING THE UNIT

A. Knowing Where Things Happened

On an outline map of the world, do the following:

1. Shade in the oceans or color them light blue.
2. Label: a. the oceans and continents; b. the United States, Canada, Alaska, Mexico, and Central America; c. Great Britain, France, Germany, Italy, North Africa, the Soviet Union, and the Balkan Peninsula; d. Japan, China, the Philippine Islands, New Guinea, the Solomon Islands, the Mariana Islands, and the Hawaiian Islands.
3. Use color or shading to show the main German and Japanese conquests.
4. Draw arrows to show the offensives by which the Allies drove back the Axis Powers and won the war.

B. Knowing When Things Happened

PART 1. For each date in the first column, write the *letter* of the important event in the second column with which it is associated.

Dates
1. 1918
2. 1929
3. 1933
4. 1939
5. 1941
6. 1945

Events
a. Beginning of the Great Depression
b. Beginning of World War I
c. Beginning of World War II
d. Beginning of the New Deal
e. End of World War I
f. End of World War II
g. American entry into World War II

PART 2. Arrange the names of these Presidents in the correct order.

1. Calvin Coolidge
2. Warren G. Harding
3. Herbert C. Hoover
4. Franklin D. Roosevelt
5. Harry S Truman

C. Knowing Important People

Write the *names* of the important people that best complete these statements in your notebook.

1. The Big Three of the peacemaking after World War II were _____, _____, and _____.
2. The dictators of Italy and Germany in the 1930s were _____ and _____.
3. The only President of the United States who served more than two terms was _____.
4. The President who had to decide whether to use the A-bomb on Japan was _____.
5. Three American military leaders in World War II were Generals _____ and _____ and Admiral _____.
6. The secretary general of the UN today is _____.

D. Knowing Important Terms

PART 1. Choose the term that does *not* belong with the others in the group.

1. *Highlights of the Roaring Twenties:* a. Women break with some customs of the past b. Ku Klux Klan revived c. A.F. of L. established
2. *Basic causes of the Great Depression:* a. Overexpansion of credit b. Runs on the banks c. Sick industries d. An unbalanced economy
3. *New Deal measures:* a. Bank holiday b. Higher tariffs c. Insuring of bank deposits d. Work projects for the unemployed
4. *Permanent reforms of the New Deal:* a. Fair Labor Standards Act b. Labor Relations Act c. National Recovery Act d. Social Security Act
5. *Basic causes of World War II:* a. Rise to power of the Fascists and Nazis b. Conquests of the dictators c. Formation of the Rome-Berlin-Tokyo Axis d. Good Neighbor Policy
6. *American policy toward the aggressors:* a. Alliance with Great Britain and France b. Neutrality Acts c. "Cash-and-carry" amendment d. Lend-Lease Act
7. *American achievements in World War II:* a. Arsenal of democracy b. Bridge of ships c. Guns instead of butter d. Miracle of production
8. *Allied successes in World War II:* a. Battle of the Atlantic b. Use of ballistic missiles c. Invasions of Italy and France d. Island hopping in the Pacific
9. *Plans for peace after World War II:* a. Atlantic Charter b. Establishing the UN c. Iron Curtain d. Yalta agreements
10. *Parts of the UN:* a. Economic and Social Council b. General Assembly c. Security Council d. War Production Board

PART 2. For each government agency in the first column, write the *letter* of the best description in the second column.

Government Agency

1. Agricultural Adjustment Administration
2. Civilian Conservation Corps
3. Federal Deposit Insurance Corporation
4. National Recovery Administration
5. Public Works Administration
6. Securities and Exchange Commission
7. Tennessee Valley Authority
8. United States Housing Authority

Description

a. Built bridges, highways, and other large government projects
b. Built tenement houses for the poor
c. Worked to save our forests and other natural resources
d. Guaranteed the safety of bank deposits
e. Tried to end unfair practices by businesses
f. Improved economic conditions in a large region
g. Limited production of farm crops to raise prices
h. Policed the issue and sale of stocks
i. Provided loans for needy homeowners

RECOMMENDED READING

A. *Historical Books*

ALLEN, F. L. *The Big Change.* New York: Bantam, 1961. Developments in the United States between 1900–1950.

BAILEY, R. *The Home Front: U.S.A.* Ed. Time-Life Books. Alexandria, Va.: Time-Life, 1978.

BUCHANAN, A. R. *Black Americans in World War II.* Santa Barbara, Calif.: American Bibliographical Center-Clio Press, 1977.

DANIELS, J. *The Time Between the Wars: Armistice to Pearl Harbor.* Ed. F. Freidel. New York: Garland, 1979.

DIVINE, R. A. *Roosevelt and World War II.* New York: Penguin, 1970.

DORNBERG, J. *The Two Germanys.* New York: Dial Press, 1974.

EISENHOWER, D. D. *Crusade in Europe.* Garden City, N.Y.: Doubleday, 1948. The war in North Africa and western Europe, described by the Allied commander.

ELLIS, C. *Famous Ships of World War Two.* New York: Arco, 1977. From all the countries involved.

FAULKNER, H. U. *From Versailles to the New Deal.* Chronicles of America, vol. 51. New York: U.S. Pubs.

FRANK, A. *Anne Frank: The Diary of a Young Girl.* Garden City, N.Y.: Doubleday, 1952.

HERSEY, J. *Hiroshima.* New York: Alfred A. Knopf, 1968. Six who survived the atom bomb.

HOLMES, W. J. *Underseas Victory II, 1943–1945: The Tide Turns.* New York: Zebra Books, 1979.

JABLONSKI, E. *A Pictorial History of the World War II Years*. Garden City, N.Y.: Doubleday, 1978.

LAWSON, D. *An Album of World War II Home Fronts*. New York: Franklin Watts, 1980.

LEASOR, J. *Boarding Party*. Boston: Houghton Mifflin, 1979. The Calcutta Light Horse's last action.

LEWIS, D. L. *When Harlem Was in Vogue*. New York: Alfred A. Knopf, 1981.

LUCARD, E. *The United Nations: How It Works and What It Does*. New York: St. Martin, 1979.

MELTZER, M. *Never to Forget*. New York: Harper & Row, 1976. The horrors of the Holocaust, Nazi Germany.

MERILLAT, H. C. *Guadalcanal Remembered*. New York: Dodd, Mead, 1982.

NEVINS, A. *The New Deal and World Affairs*. Chronicles of America, vol. 56. New York: U.S. Pubs.

OSADA, A., ed. *Children of the A-Bomb*. New York: Putnam, 1963. Stories of boys and girls in Hiroshima when the bomb exploded.

SALOUTOS, T. *The American Farmer and the New Deal*. Ames, Iowa: Iowa State Univ. Press, 1982.

B. *Biographies and Autobiographies*

FINKE, B. F. *General Patton: Fearless Military Leader*. Ed. D. S. Rahmas. Charlotteville, N.Y.: SamHar Press, 1972.

GIES, J. *Franklin D. Roosevelt: Portrait of a President*. Garden City, N.Y.: Doubleday, 1971.

HELLMAN, P. *Avenue of the Righteous*. New York: Atheneum, 1981. Christians who saved Jews from Hitler.

ROTHCHILD, S., ed. *Voices from the Holocaust*. New York: New American Library, 1981. Recollections before, during, and after.

SCHULKE, F., ed. *Martin Luther King, Jr*. New York: Norton, 1976. His life in pictures.

TOLAND, J. *Hitler*. New York: Ballantine, 1976. A pictorial documentary of his life.

TREGASKIS, R. *John F. Kennedy and PT-109*. New York: Random House, 1962. Brave deeds of the young naval officer who became President of the United States.

WOJCIECHOWSKA, M. *Till the Break of Day*. New York: Harcourt Brace Jovanovich, 1972. Adolescence of a unique Polish girl.

ZASSENHAUS, H. *Walls: Resisting the Third Reich*. Boston: Beacon Press, 1974. Women who led Norwegian and Danish refugees to safety in Hitler years.

C. *Historical Fiction*

DEMETZ, H. *The House on Prague Street*. Trans. H. Demetz. New York: St. Martin, 1980. A half-Jewish Czech girl during World War II.

HOLMAN, F. *The Murderer*. New York: Scribner, 1978. Hershy's troubles with anti-Semitism.

LEFFLAND, E. *Rumors of Peace*. New York: Harper & Row, 1979. Suse's trauma on Pearl Harbor day.

LINGARD, J. *The File on Fraulein Berg*. New York: Elsevier/Norton, 1980. Is the new German teacher a spy?

MAZER, H. *The Last Mission*. New York: Delacorte Press, 1979. Jack's 24 bomber missions at age 15 in World War II.

PRISING, R. *Manila, Goodbye*. Boston: Houghton Mifflin, 1975. A boy's life as a P.O.W. in WWII.

VONNEGUT, K., JR. *Slaughterhouse Five*. New York: Delacorte Press, 1969. Billy Pilgrim from World War II to Tralfamadore.

WUORIO, E. L. *Detour to Danger*. New York: Delacorte Press, 1981. As Nando finds Nazis in Spain.

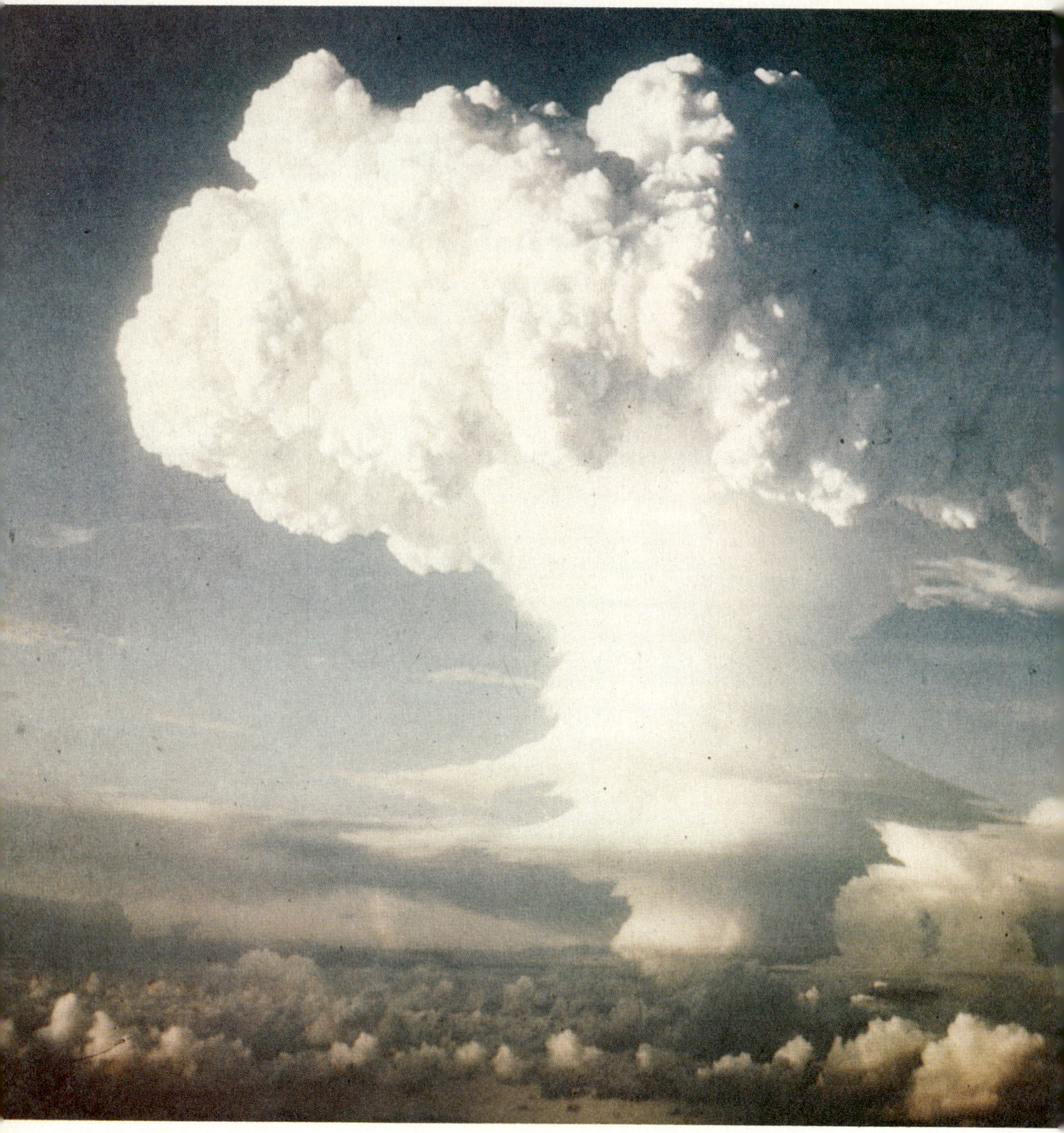

Unit Eight

AFTER WORLD WAR II

World War II was even bigger and deadlier than World War I. Once again, however, the United States was lucky enough to escape the worst effects of the war. The American mainland was not touched. American industry, already the most productive in the world, doubled its output between 1941 and 1945. Thanks to new advances in science and industry, this huge production continued to increase after the war. Our nation entered the greatest period of prosperity in its history.

One might think that such wealth would make Americans a satisfied and happy people. But our country's rapid growth during and after World War II has given rise to serious problems at home. There is poverty in the midst of plenty; there are millions of people without jobs; prejudice and discrimination still exist; our rich resources are declining; our dependence upon other peoples in the world increases. In foreign relations, the United States has been involved in troubles all over the world. Twice since 1945, young Americans have gone off to fight in other lands. Crises have several times threatened to engulf our nation in a nuclear (atomic) war.

Some nuclear weapons are thousands of times as powerful as the A-bombs that destroyed the Japanese cities of Hiroshima and Nagasaki. The mushroom-shaped cloud has become a symbol of our time, often called the atomic or nuclear age.

In this unit we shall see the following:
1. How our nation made progress and overcame crises at home from the 1940s to the present
2. How our government has tried to solve the problems of poverty and discrimination
3. In what ways our people have tried to improve the quality of their lives
4. How the United States has tried to stop the spread of communism and work for peace in the world
5. What the outlook is for the future of the United States and the world

UNIT 8: 1945 - Present

1946	Full Employment Act
1947	Taft-Hartley Act
1948	Truman Doctrine and Marshall Plan
	Berlin airlift
1950	Korean War
1954	School integration decision
1956	Suez crisis
1957	Sputnick launched
1961	New Frontier begins
1962	Cuban missile crisis
1963	President Kennedy assassinated
1964	Civil Rights Act
	U.S. at war in Vietnam
1967	Arab-Israeli War
1969	First person walks on the moon
1972	Nixon visits China and the Soviet Union
1973	Cease-fire in Vietnam
1974	Watergate scandal
	Gasoline shortages
	Nixon resigns
	Camp David agreement
1978	Iran seizes American hostages
1979	
1981	American hostages released

Chapter 34

DEVELOPMENTS IN THE GENERATION AFTER WORLD WAR II

ON THE DAY Harry S Truman became President of the United States, he said to reporters, "Boys, pray for me." He had good reason to want their prayers. He had been Vice-President only a few short months when President Roosevelt died. Though inexperienced and unprepared, he suddenly had to make a number of far-reaching decisions. He had to decide how to end the war, make the peace, and change a wartime economy to peacetime production.

The Presidents who followed President Truman in the 40 years after World War II had to deal with problems of wars and near-wars involving the United States. At the same time, problems at home continued to occupy their time and energy. Our modern world has given rise to series of problems that are very complex. Sometimes it is difficult to understand how Presidents are able to handle the variety of problems and programs that require their attention. Most would agree with a later judgment of President Truman's that the job of President of the United States is a "man-killer."

How did President Truman deal with postwar problems? How did succeeding Presidents manage to handle domestic problems while our country was involved in Far Eastern conflicts? How did the presidency withstand one of the most severe challenges in its history? You will find the answers to these questions in this chapter.

How Did Presidents Handle Problems at Home in Midcentury, 1945–1968?

A. The Change from War to Peace. "Bring the boys back home" became the cry of the American people as soon as Japan surrendered. Within a few months almost every man and woman in the armed forces received discharge papers. Our armed forces, the strongest in the world, decreased rapidly in size and strength.

Under President Truman, most wartime controls on prices and goods were ended. Then there was a great demand for articles that had been hard to get during the war. Industry changed from war production to the manufacture of civilian goods with amazing speed. The changeover provided jobs for returning soldiers. Instead of the depression that had followed past wars, our nation enjoyed an economic boom.

Four administration measures encouraged the boom. 1. Congress passed the Full Employment Act. The law set up the Council of Economic Advisers to help the President in finding ways to keep Americans fully employed. 2. Congress also passed the "GI Bill of Rights." This law gave money to veterans who continued their education or bought a business, farm, or home. 3. Once again the armed forces were built up to meet the Communist threat. Selective service was restored. The government's spending for the armed forces was a great help to business. 4. The government spent billions of dollars to rebuild Japan and the war-damaged countries of Europe. They in turn bought most of the machinery and other materials they needed from the United States.

B. Inflation. The postwar boom touched off a rise in prices. As soon as government controls were lifted prices increased. Unions then organized strikes for higher wages. Wage increases caused businesses to raise prices again. This in turn brought more strikes for still higher wages. Prices rose sharply once more when the United States went to war in Korea in 1950. The government then decided to restore wage and price controls. But prices at the end of the war in 1953 were more than double the prices in 1939.

Postwar boom. What were some of the reasons for the great increase in consumer spending in the late 1940s and early 1950s?

C. Labor Problems. 1. THE TAFT-HARTLEY ACT. Frequent strikes—chiefly in major industries like coal, steel, and railroads—turned the public against labor unions. Unions were also blamed for high prices. As a result, Congress passed the Taft-Hartley Act in 1947 over President Truman's veto. The Taft-Hartley Act did the following four things. 1. Unions were forbidden to put pressure on workers and employers and to force employers to hire unnecessary workers. 2. States could pass "right-to-work" laws. These laws allow companies with union contracts to hire nonunion workers. 3. Union officers had to give the government information about the income and expenses of the union. 4. The President could delay strikes in important industries for 80 days—a "cooling-off" period to work out a peaceful settlement.

Supporters of the Taft-Hartley Act said the law restored the balance of power between labor and management. But unions condemned it as a "slave-labor law."

2. LABOR'S GAINS. Nevertheless, labor made some important gains in the postwar period. In 1955, the American Federation of Labor and the Congress of Industrial Organizations joined to form a single giant labor organization with 15 million members. Wages rose steadily, and hours of work were reduced. Unions now found themselves bargaining for "fringe benefits"—vacations with pay, health insurance, retirement pensions, and the like. Many business people began to see that production increased as working conditions improved. Workers evidently worked faster when they were treated better.

D. The "Red Menace." Another postwar problem was the fear of communism. Soviet influence was spreading rapidly in Europe and Asia. The American Communist party, though small, was very active. Several spy rings were uncovered in the United States and Great Britain. One ring gave the Soviet Union important information about the atomic bomb.

The Truman administration took several steps

Senator Joseph McCarthy testifying during the investigation of his charges of Communist influence in the army. What did the Senate do to curb his power?

to deal with the "Red Menace." The attorney general made public a list of organizations believed to be disloyal to our government. The Central Intelligence Agency (CIA) was formed to deal with Communist activities in other countries. The FBI (Federal Bureau of Investigation) was expanded to check on Communists within the United States. Several hundred government workers were dismissed for disloyalty. Others gave up their jobs rather than face questioning. Dozens of people were accused of being Communists. They were tried and sent to prison under wartime laws. Congress then passed the Internal Security Act, forcing all Communists to register with the government. Finally, in 1954, Congress outlawed the Communist party.

The fear of communism was shown in other ways. Workers for government and business firms who were believed to have Communist leanings were dismissed. Books believed to contain Communist ideas were removed from schools and libraries. Committees of Congress called in hundreds of people for questioning. Some admitted they had supported Communist-

One Chicago newspaper, certain that President Truman had lost the election, printed this headline before the balloting was over. As you can see, the President had the last laugh.

led movements by mistake. Others refused to talk about their activities under the Fifth Amendment. Some of them lost their jobs. Many Americans felt the treatment they received was unfair and undemocratic.

One of the leading anti-Communists was Senator Joseph R. McCarthy of Wisconsin. He won a large following by making charges of communism in high places. His charges became more extreme as time went on. Finally, he accused the President, the secretary of the army, and several generals of "coddling (being kind to) Communists." After a long public hearing the Senate censured (criticized) McCarthy for conduct unbecoming a senator. He lost his influence, and the fear of communism began to die down. The Supreme Court also found that parts of some anti-Communist laws were unconstitutional and some people had been treated unjustly.

E. The Election of 1948. The Democrats chose Truman to run for President in 1948. Some groups in the Democratic party opposed him and formed their own parties. A group of southern members of Congress formed the States' Rights party. Another group wanted to get rid of the atomic bomb and seek friendship with the Russians. This group formed the Progressive party. With the Democrats split, many experts thought Truman had little chance of winning.

The President faced a strong rival in Governor Thomas E. Dewey of New York. But Truman was a fighter. He traveled all over the country, stopping in hundreds of towns to speak to crowds. To the experts' surprise, he was elected by a good majority. The States' Rights party carried only a few southern states.

F. Truman's Fair Deal. As President in his own right, Truman announced that he would expand FDR's New Deal. He asked Congress for new reforms, which he called the "Fair Deal." Congress approved only a few of his proposals: raising the minimum wage, increasing social security benefits, and providing low-cost housing. Far more important, however, were Truman's efforts to combat communism in Europe and Asia. We shall see what these were in a later section.

590

G. The Election of 1952. "We like Ike" was the main Republican slogan in the election of 1952. "Ike" was the war hero, General Dwight D. Eisenhower. He was the strongest Republican candidate in many years. As commander of the Allied armies in Europe in World War II, Ike had won the affection of officers and enlisted soldiers. His great popularity proved to be too much of a handicap for the Democratic candidate, Adlai Stevenson. In addition, many Americans blamed the Democrats for the costly Korean War. As a result, General Eisenhower won by a large majority. The Republicans gained control of the federal government after twenty years of Democratic rule.

H. Eisenhower's Policies. 1. THE PRESIDENT'S VIEWPOINT. The new President called himself a "middle-of-the-roader." He meant to follow a course that avoided extremes. He believed that the federal government should help the common people. So he accepted many New Deal reforms. On the other hand, he believed the federal government had become too powerful. So he promised to return some of its powers to the states and private businesses. Congress passed almost every bill that Eisenhower wanted.

President Eisenhower did not like large government projects that competed with private business. He opposed the building of new power plants by TVA. Instead, he encouraged a private company to build them. He also turned over valuable oil lands off our coasts, which had been under federal control, to the states closest to them.

2. SOME EXCEPTIONS. One important exception to the President's policy of reducing federal power was the St. Lawrence Seaway. In 1955, the American and Canadian governments agreed to make a number of improvements in the Great Lakes and St. Lawrence River. The new seaway made it possible for ocean-going vessels to carry grain and other goods from the Midwest to the Atlantic Ocean at low cost. It also increased the trade between the United States and Canada and produced large amounts of hydroelectric power for both countries.

Other exceptions were in the fields of transportation and education. The President approved of a government program to build a network of highways connecting all parts of the United States. And, after the Soviet Union sent a space satellite into orbit in 1957, Congress quickly voted money for new scientific laboratories with modern equipment. It also created scholarship programs to help bright and needy students get a college education.

"I Sure Wish Us the Best of Luck." According to this cartoon, what dangers does a "middle-of-the-roader" like President Eisenhower face?

I. Growing Discontent. In the campaign of 1956, the Republican party claimed that President Eisenhower had brought the nation "Peace, Progress, and Prosperity." Most Americans agreed. Ike's election by a larger margin than before was not a surprise.

Like some earlier Presidents, however, Eisenhower lost much popularity during his second term. Our nation spent more money for arms and space research. Several million people lost their jobs during two periods of lower prices and decreased sales. Federal income from taxes dropped and the government went deeper into debt.

Farmers objected to the cuts in price supports. To increase their income, they planted more crops. The government then bought up the surplus. Now it had the added cost of storing these crops. Labor was angered when the President signed a bill requiring unions to give the government reports on their leaders and finances.

J. The Presidency of John F. Kennedy. The Democratic candidate, Senator John F. Kennedy of Massachusetts, won the presidency in 1960. His election was unusual in several ways. He was the youngest man and the first Roman Catholic to be elected President. His margin of victory over Richard M. Nixon was also one of the narrowest in our history. Although Kennedy had a 303–219 margin over Nixon in electoral votes, the two candidates were separated by only 100,000 votes from the 68 million votes cast for both of them.

The new President quickly captured the imagi-

President Dwight D. Eisenhower poses with our youngest elected President, John F. Kennedy, on inauguration day, 1960.

JOHN F. KENNEDY:
HERO IN WAR AND PEACE

During the battle for the Solomon Islands in World War II, a small motor torpedo boat was sunk by a Japanese destroyer. The commander, though badly injured, towed one of his men three miles to a nearby island by holding the strap of the man's life jacket in his teeth. Then he swam long distances to other islands, risking death by sharks and capture by the Japanese, to find help for his shipwrecked crew. Thanks to his efforts, his men were saved. A popular book, *PT-109*, was written about this remarkable example of heroism. It brought fame to the young hero, John F. Kennedy.

What made Kennedy so brave and determined? His family background and upbringing were certainly important factors. Both of his grandfathers, though the sons of poor Irish immigrants, rose to high positions in Massachusetts politics. His father made a fortune and then became an important federal official. His mother too was an unusual person. Though busy as the wife of an important man and the mother of nine children, she was active in politics. The Kennedys always fought to win. "Once you say that you're going to settle for second place," John explained to a friend, "that's what happens to you in life, I find."

It was not easy for John to be first. Like Theodore Roosevelt, he was a weak and sickly child who built up his body through exercise. He made the swimming team in college. He also played football until he suffered a back injury. This was made much worse in the sinking of the PT boat. Though navy surgeons operated on his spine in 1944, his condition slowly grew worse. Ten years later he had a second operation. For weeks he lay close to death. For many months more he had to lie still in bed. He was never completely cured. Until the day of his death, he was in almost constant pain, both from his back and other ailments.

Kennedy did not let his physical suffering interfere with his activities. He entered politics soon after the war and served fourteen years in Congress before being elected President. At first he knew little about ordinary Americans and their problems. But he read a great deal, traveled widely, and listened to people wherever he went. His sympathy for the victims of poverty and prejudice grew out of what he learned for himself, not just from what he read in books.

John F. Kennedy was President for only a thousand days. Judged by his achievements, he may not be considered a great President. Yet the American people loved him and mourned deeply when he was killed. For he was a young, handsome, and vigorous man, with a charming family. His speeches, calling for a better nation and a better world, stirred the nation. Above all, his courage in the face of danger, hardship, and pain earned him respect. John F. Kennedy was a hero both in war and in peace.

nation of the American people by his appeals for a better world. He accused the Republicans of letting things drift. There were too many Americans out of work and American industry was moving too slowly. He proposed to "get America moving again." His plan was to step up government spending and to lower taxes. As more money was spent, he explained, business would expand and provide jobs for the unemployed. President Kennedy also worked for reforms to help minority groups and the poor. He called his program the "New Frontier." He asked Americans to become pioneers again, to make the country a better place for all people. Only a few of his measures were passed by Congress. These helped improve poor areas of the nation. They also aided men and women who had been out of work for a long time.

In November 1963, President Kennedy took time from his official duties to visit some important cities. As his party drove slowly through the city of Dallas, gun shots rang out. The President, shot in the head, died a short time later. The presidency passed to Vice-President Lyndon B. Johnson of Texas.

K. Lyndon B. Johnson Becomes President. The new President was unusually well qualified for his position. Johnson had served in Congress for almost 25 years. As Senate leader of his party, he had shown great ability to get laws passed. Johnson soon showed the same skill in dealing with Congress. He persuaded Congress to pass laws they had refused to pass while Kennedy was President.

In the election of 1964, Johnson won a smashing victory. At his inauguration, he promised to make America the "Great Society"—that is, a richer, more progressive, and better country. Since the Democrats had won large majorities in both houses of Congress, President Johnson was able to put his program into effect quickly.

L. The "War on Poverty." In his inaugural address, President Johnson announced, "This administration today, here and now, declares war on poverty in America." Soon after his speech, he asked Congress to help "that one-fifth of all American families with incomes too small to meet their needs." These laws, which Congress quickly passed, have become known as the Johnson "War on Poverty."

1. ANTIPOVERTY LAWS. A new government agency was established to help the poor. First, it set up a Job Corps to train unemployed young people for skilled jobs. Second, it established a program where educated Americans lived among the poor and helped teach them needed skills. This program was known as VISTA, Volunteers in Service to America. "Community Action Programs" encouraged people in poor neighborhoods to develop programs to meet their particular needs. These programs offered such services as day care centers, advice on loans and business practices, and legal help.

In 1965, Congress extended social security benefits to seven million workers who had not been covered by social security laws before.

Lyndon B. Johnson taking the oath as President a few hours after the assassination of President John Kennedy. Mrs. Johnson is on the new President's right, Mrs. Kennedy on his left.

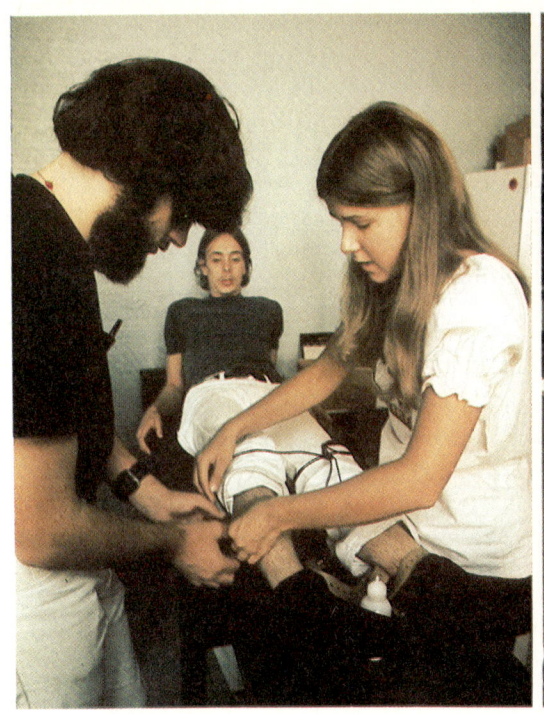

The lives of many people were affected by President Johnson's War on Poverty. The woman on the left is a VISTA volunteer who works in a health clinic. The woman on the right is learning new skills.

Farm laborers and workers in small stores and hospitals now received the benefits of social security. Congress also provided hospital and medical care for elderly and poor people at little or no cost. (See page 662.)

Congress also voted funds for housing projects. Many of these projects became areas where only the poor lived. Congress, therefore, provided special rent payments for poor families who moved into middle-class neighborhoods. It also established a "Model Cities" program to rebuild slums in a number of cities.

2. EDUCATION. Automation had cut the number of jobs for unskilled people. The War on Poverty provided for vocational and job training to retrain unemployed adults for skilled work. Especially popular was Operation Head Start. Here, teachers worked with children only three or four years old to give them a better start in their regular schooling. For poor but able students, the government also offered part-time work and college scholarships.

3. CRITICISMS OF THE WAR ON POVERTY. Conservatives (people who want to keep things as they are) pointed out that the poverty programs were being run by inexperienced people. Money was being spent on administration of the programs rather than for help to the poor. They also felt that the programs cost huge sums of money at the same time the nation was involved in a costly war in Vietnam. Conservatives also argued that the War on Poverty weakened the character of the poor by encouraging them to depend on the government.

Liberals (people who want reform) criticized the President's program for opposite reasons—it

595

was too small and moved too slowly, they said. They urged the federal government to spend at least $5 billion a year for housing and education. They said our nation could eliminate poverty by spending more for these purposes than for arms. In so doing, our nation could save the billions of dollars spent each year on welfare and on fighting disease and crime.

M. Civil Rights Laws. Because Johnson was a southerner, his position on the rights of minorities was questioned at the time he came into office. But laws passed with Johnson's support erased any doubt about his belief in equal treatment for all people. More important civil rights laws were passed during President Johnson's terms of office than at any time since the end of the Civil War.

1. THE CIVIL RIGHTS ACT OF 1964. This law was directed against discrimination in several areas. It forbade discrimination in voting requirements. It banned job discrimination by employers in hiring, firing, and promotions. Hotels, restaurants, and other interstate businesses were forbidden to discriminate against any customer because of his or her race, color, religion, or national origin. It also prohibited discrimination in any program receiving federal funds. This meant that schools practicing racial segregation could not receive federal money.

2. THE VOTING RIGHTS ACT OF 1965. The Twenty-fourth Amendment to the Constitution, adopted in 1964, abolished the use of the poll tax as a qualification for voting. Yet, several states used a literacy test (a test of a person's ability to read and write) to determine a person's qualification for voting. The Voting Rights Act allowed the federal government to register voters in these states, when less than half the eligible voters were registered.

3. FAIR HOUSING ACT OF 1968. This law forbade racial and religious discrimination by real-estate agents in the renting or selling of houses and apartments.

N. The Election of 1968. In his full term in office, President Johnson was under severe criticism from a growing number of Americans who opposed the war in Vietnam. Johnson was a proud man who felt he had done much to reduce poverty and promote civil rights. The President was hurt by the growing opposition to his policies in Vietnam. Thus, he declined to run for reelection in 1968. Vice-President Hubert H. Humphrey became the Democratic candidate. He promised to continue Johnson's policies. In a close election, Humphrey was defeated by the Republican candidate, Richard M. Nixon, former Vice-President under President Eisenhower. Nixon promised to end the war in Vietnam and "bring the nation together."

REVIEWING THE SECTION

A. Knowing New Terms

For each term in the first column, write in your notebook the *letter* of the best description in the second column.

Terms	Descriptions

1. Central Intelligence Agency
2. Middle-of-the-roader
3. Cooling-off period
4. Fair Deal
5. GI Bill of Rights
6. War on Poverty
7. VISTA
8. Right-to-work law
9. Civil Rights Act of 1964

a. Paid war veterans who continued their education
b. Tried to improve on reforms of the New Deal
c. Forbade discrimination in voting requirements
d. Allowed employers with union contracts to hire nonunion workers instead of union workers
e. Dealt with Communist activities in foreign countries
f. Gave labor and management time to reach agreement before a strike started
g. Name given to the Johnson program to help the poor
h. Program in which volunteers work with the poor
i. A person who follows a moderate policy between two extremes

B. Knowing Important Facts

For each action in the first column, write in your notebook the *letter* of the important person in the second column who performed it. (You may use a letter more than once, and you may have more than one letter for each answer.)

Actions

1. Reduced the power of the federal government
2. Guided the changeover from war to peace
3. Succeeded to the presidency when the President died
4. Led an extreme attack on communism in the United States
5. Responsible for the passage of several civil rights laws
6. Signed a bill strongly opposed by labor unions
7. Approved federal funds to build highways across the country
8. Promoted laws to provide housing for the poor

Important People

A. Harry S Truman
B. Joseph R. McCarthy
C. Dwight D. Eisenhower
D. John F. Kennedy
E. Lyndon B. Johnson

C. Finding the Reasons

Write in your notebook the letters of *all* the correct answers to each question.

1. Why did President Truman ask the reporters to pray for him?
   a. He had to face many difficult problems.   b. He had little of the experience a President needs.   c. He had to deal with a Republican majority in Congress.
2. Why was there an economic boom after World War II instead of the usual postwar depression?
   a. The government closely regulated business.   b. Consumers greatly increased their spending.   c. The government soon began to spend large amounts on arms and aid to foreign nations.
3. What harmful effects did the quick ending of rationing and price controls have?
   a. Prices rose.   b. High prices caused a large number of strikes.   c. It caused many Americans to turn to communism.
4. Why did labor unions dislike the Taft-Hartley Act?
   a. It forbade strikes in important industries.   b. It caused a drop in union membership.   c. Companies with union contracts were allowed to hire nonunion workers.
5. Why were the American people afraid of communism after World War II?
   a. Communist influence was growing in Europe and Asia.   b. The American Communist party was growing fast.   c. Communist spy rings were discovered in the United States and Great Britain.
6. Why did the American people elect Eisenhower as President in 1952?
   a. He had more experience in politics than his rival.   b. He had won a great reputation as a general in World War II.   c. Most Americans usually voted for Republicans.   d. The Democrats nominated a very weak candidate.
7. In what area(s) was President Kennedy most successful?
   a. He did away with unemployment.   b. He created a feeling among Americans that our nation could be a better place in which to live.   c. He increased the output of American industry.   d. He convinced Congress to vote in favor of almost all the measures in the New Frontier program.
8. Why did President Johnson call his program a "War on Poverty"?
   a. He wanted to show that it would cost as much as a war.   b. He wanted the American people to know it would be a hard fight.   c. He wanted to create the feeling that the government would work hard to solve the problem.
9. Why was education made an important part of the War on Poverty?
   a. Automation had increased the need for educated workers who were able to learn difficult skills.   b. Our economy was changing fast, and educated workers could adjust faster than the uneducated.   c. A democratic government like ours needed educated citizens.

10. Why was the administration of President Johnson an important period in progress toward civil rights for all Americans?
   a. During the Johnson administration, the Supreme Court ruled that segregated public schools were unconstitutional. b. Congress forbade discrimination in voting requirements because of race, color, religion, or national origin. c. Real-estate agents were forbidden to discriminate in renting or selling housing.

IMPROVING YOUR SKILLS

A. Reading the Time Line

Study the time line, page 586, as well as the information in this section. Then answer the following questions:

1. Which President, in the period from 1945 to 1968, could boast of a large number of domestic reforms?
2. Which President made the most foreign policy decisions?
3. Was President Eisenhower more active in dealing with domestic or foreign affairs?
4. Did President Kennedy accomplish more in domestic or foreign affairs?

B. Looking at Both Sides

Complete the following list in your notebook. List four achievements of the War on Poverty and four criticisms offered against the War on Poverty.

For	Against
1.	1.
2.	2.
3.	3.
4.	4.

Conclusion: Who do you think was right, President Johnson or his critics? Why?

How Did Presidents Meet Problems as the Republic Began Its Third Century, 1969 to the Present?

A. The Nixon Policies. Like Dwight D. Eisenhower, President Nixon believed that the power of the federal government should be reduced. During his terms of office, many of the reforms of President Johnson's War on Poverty were reduced or eliminated. Some Community Action programs received no federal support. Nixon believed that many antipoverty programs had failed. He said that government spending for such programs tended to cause an increase in prices.

President Nixon offered his own plan for fighting poverty. He proposed that state and local governments should plan their own antipoverty programs. As a result, Congress passed the first "revenue-sharing" plan in 1972. Six billion dollars were distributed to states and local governments to use for their own programs.

In 1972, President Nixon was reelected in a landslide victory. This was the first election in which 18-year-olds could vote for President. The Twenty-sixth Amendment to the Constitution had been passed by Congress in 1971. Only a few weeks before the election, the President announced that an agreement had been reached for ending the war in Vietnam. This effort, and the President's attempt to gain an understanding with the Communist governments of the Soviet Union and China, will be studied in a later section.

B. The Watergate Scandal. The troubles of "Watergate" began soon after President Nixon began his second term. In June 1972, during the election campaign, five members of the President's campaign team had been arrested. They had broken into the headquarters of the Democratic party in the Watergate Building in Washington, D.C. They were trying to install equipment to tap phones and gain information about Democratic campaign plans.

According to evidence brought into the open a year later, there were efforts by the President and his staff to stop an investigation of the incident by the FBI. The captured burglars received heavy sentences at their trial. One of the convicted men admitted that he had lied in court and had been under pressure to "keep quiet." President Nixon denied that he knew anything about the break-in beforehand or about any attempts to prevent an investigation of it. In his denial, he told the American people that he accepted the responsibility for actions by his staff, and he accepted the resignations of three top aides and advisers.

However, the problem would not go away. It was revealed that since 1960, Presidents had taped their White House conversations. President Nixon steadfastly refused to make public the tapes of conversations in his office about the break-in and possible "cover-up" of an investigation. Finally, the Supreme Court ordered him to turn over the tapes to the Senate committee investigating the whole affair. The tapes revealed that the President had previous knowledge of the "cover-up." The House of Representatives began the legal steps to impeach the President. During the last week of July 1974, the House Judiciary Committee reported grounds for the

600

Members of the Senate Watergate Committee listening to one of President Nixon's former aides. Why was the scandal they were investigating called the Watergate scandal?

impeachment of President Nixon. These included the charges of obstructing justice and failure to carry out his oath of office.

Rather than face an impeachment trial before the Senate, President Nixon resigned his office on August 9, 1974—the first President to do so. In his final statement to his staff, and in statements in later years, President Nixon admitted no wrongdoing. He said simply that he "made some mistakes."

Almost one year before the President's resignation, Vice-President Spiro G. Agnew had resigned his office. A jury had indicted him on charges of failure to pay income taxes in past years. Following the procedures of the Twenty-fifth Amendment, President Nixon then appointed Gerald R. Ford, a member of the House of Representatives from Michigan, as Vice-President. The appointment was approved by both houses of Congress. On August 9, 1974, Vice-President Ford was sworn in as the 38th President of the United States.

This was a trying period for American democracy. Our form of government under the Constitution passed the test with flying colors. A change in government was made under the most extreme circumstances—without disorder or bloodshed.

C. President Gerald R. Ford. 1. THE NEW ADMINISTRATION. President Ford had served in the House of Representatives for 25 years before he became Vice-President in 1973. He became the first person to serve as President without being chosen by the people in a national election. Following the procedures of the Twenty-fifth Amendment, Ford appointed the former governor of New York, Nelson A. Rockefeller, to the office of Vice-President. Now, for the first time in American history, the nation was led by a President and a Vice-President who had not been chosen as the result of a national election.

2. THE FORD POLICIES. President Ford continued President Nixon's policies in domestic and foreign affairs. But he made it clear that he would have an "open government." He would speak frankly to the American people and have

President Ford holding his first cabinet meeting in the White House. What problems did the new President face after Nixon's resignation?

601

no secrets. Ford promised to restore the people's confidence in the honesty of their leaders and "heal the wounds" caused by Watergate.

A month after taking office, he announced that he was granting a pardon to former President Nixon for all federal crimes he "committed or may have committed" while serving as President. The intent of the pardon, according to President Ford, was to spare the nation any further distress caused by the Watergate scandal. This action caused much debate throughout the nation. Those who supported the pardon believed that President Nixon had suffered enough through the disgrace of resignation. Other people felt the former President should be brought to trial if he had committed crimes while in office.

3. FURTHER INVESTIGATIONS. Following the shock of the Watergate scandal, Congress looked into the activities of other government agencies. Newspapers reported that the CIA had abused its power by carrying out illegal actions against American citizens. The Senate Intelligence Committee investigated these and other charges. After more than a year of the inquiry, the committee reported the CIA had engaged in spying activities on citizens in all walks of life. No section of our society had been safe from being spied on in one way or another, in the name of national security. Both the CIA and the FBI were involved in the report. As a result, Congress prepared to pass laws setting up committees to become "watchdogs" over these and other governmental agencies.

D. The Election of 1976. The important issues in the campaign were those of unemployment, inflation, and government spending for defense. When people are out of work and there is a smaller demand for goods, prices usually drop. But such was not the case in the early 1970s. Unemployment had reached its highest point since the Great Depression of the 1930s, and prices had continued to rise. President Ford had been unable to find the answer to these problems in his two years in office. The Watergate scandal, without a doubt, also hurt the Republican cause. In one of the closest elections in our his-

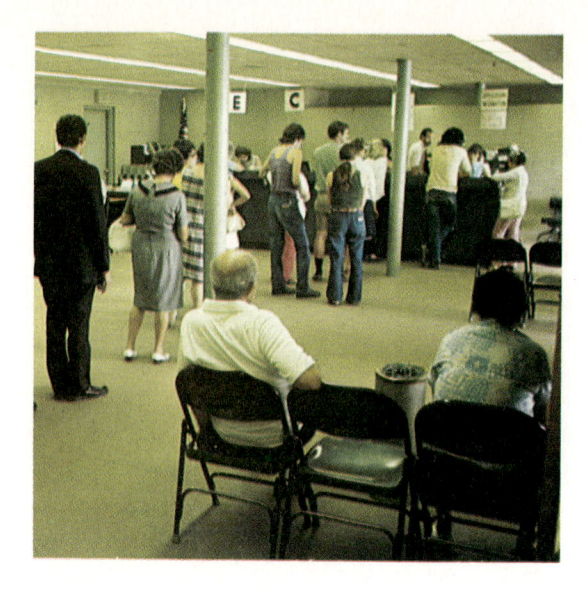

Unemployed workers lining up at a state employment office during the 1970s. How can unemployment and inflation affect the way people vote?

tory, Jimmy (James E.) Carter, former governor of Georgia and the Democratic candidate, defeated President Ford. A change of only a few thousand votes in a few states would have changed the election result.

E. President Carter's Program. 1. THE NEW ADMINISTRATION. President Carter had campaigned as a Washington "outsider." He had never been elected to a national office. Nor was he the favorite of Washington politicians. As President, however, Carter found that he needed the support and experience of those he had campaigned against. Although the Democrats controlled both houses of Congress, few of Carter's domestic programs were approved. His years in office were marked by history-making events in foreign matters. There were few notable achievements in caring for problems at home.

One of the President's goals was to prepare an energy plan for the country's future. The Department of Energy was approved as a part of the President's Cabinet in 1977. Early in his term, Carter asked Congress to pass laws to reduce the nation's use of oil and gas. He recommended greater use of coal and nuclear and solar energy. Congress debated his suggestions for more than a year. Its final action contained only a small part of the President's requests. Later in his term, Congress passed the Energy Security Act. This law created a new government agency to develop the use of fuels other than coal and gas.

2. ECONOMIC PROBLEMS. Unemployment and inflation had been major issues in the campaign of 1976. They did not disappear after Carter was elected. The problems were unusual—high unemployment as well as rising prices. Economists called this condition "stagflation." If the President asked for higher taxes to provide government help for the unemployed, inflation might become worse. If measures were taken to fight inflation, greater unemployment might result. President Carter therefore asked businesses and labor unions to cooperate willingly to control wages and the prices of goods. However, this effort had little effect in solving the troublesome economic problems of the day. President Carter left office facing many of the same problems he had come up against when he took office four years earlier.

President Carter in the White House. What were some of the programs he wanted to put into effect?

F. The Election of 1980. Americans seemed ready for a change in government policies in 1980. The issues in the campaign were similar to those in 1976—inflation, unemployment, and national defense. The Democrats nominated President Carter for a second term. The President was still highly respected by the American people. However, many people seemed to feel he did not have the leadership ability to solve difficult problems at home.

The Republicans named as their candidate Ronald Reagan, a well-known actor and former governor of California. Reagan proposed to reduce taxes and the size of the federal government. He also wanted to greatly increase America's military strength. Reagan's ideas reflected a growing concern among Americans that their country had lost respect abroad. During Carter's administration, Americans had been held hostage in Iran for over a year (page 686). At the time of the election, no action by Carter had secured their release. In 1979, the Soviet Union had invaded the nation of Afghanistan. Although the White House strongly protested, Soviet troops remained. Soviet strength in Cuba had also increased during this period. With these events in mind, the Republicans claimed that the country's prestige had been damaged under the Carter administration.

The voter turnout may have shown the mood of the country. Only slightly more than half the eligible voters bothered to go to the polls. In the election, the Republicans won a smashing victory. Ronald Reagan won a majority of votes in 44 of the 50 states. In addition, the Republicans gained a majority in the Senate for the first time since the election of President Eisenhower.

G. President Reagan's Goals. Right after taking office, President Reagan took steps to begin his program. Before Reagan became president, he had promised to lower government spending and the size of the federal government. He also planned to lower taxes and balance the budget. Reagan promised to watch over a build-up of America's military strength. These goals could be reached only by changing policies that the government had followed for 35 years.

Ronald Reagan being sworn in as President of the United States. Why do you think Reagan was elected President in 1980?

H. "Reaganomics": The Economic Program.

President Reagan believed the government had grown "too big." Social programs, such as welfare, food stamps, and school lunches, were costly. The federal government, said Reagan, was doing what private businesses and individuals should be doing. These social programs were costing the taxpayers billions of dollars a year. These expenses had to be cut if the budget was to be balanced. What revenues the government received could be put to use in other areas. The money could be spent to build up our nation's military strength. Such a buildup would create new jobs and thus help the nation's economy.

Hand in hand with a reduction in spending for social programs, was a cut in business and personal income taxes. If taxes were lower, people would have more money to spend. Thus, they would be able to buy more goods. To meet this need industry would have to produce more products. More people would be put to work. Since more people would be working and receiving wages, more taxes would be paid. Thus, the government would receive greater revenues and the budget would be balanced.

In 1981, Congress passed a bill reducing income taxes. Within two years, interest rates (the amount people must pay when they borrow money) dropped by more than half. At the same time, the rate of inflation was slowed down. Nevertheless, unemployment continued to rise, reaching a high of more than ten percent in 1982. Those people without work were unable to pay taxes. As a result, revenues received from taxes dropped lower and lower. The budget could not be balanced. The federal debt in a single year reached its highest point in history. President Reagan urged the American people to "stay the course." He said the program would take time to succeed. Critics of the program argued that the proposed cure for our federal debt was worse than the debt itself.

I. The New Federalism.

In the past, argued President Reagan, the federal government had been given too much power. The trend toward

Opposite views of the best size of the federal budget.

bigger and bigger federal programs had to be halted. Accordingly, the President proposed that many programs run by the federal government be turned over to state and local governments. Many social programs, including welfare and food stamps, should be run by the states. These governments, said Reagan, are closer to the people. Citizens in each state know their needs better than the leaders in Washington. However, opponents of the plan argued that since some states were richer than others, aid to the needy would differ from state to state. A majority of Congress agreed with President Reagan and adopted part of his program. States began receiving funds to spend on some social programs. States also received greater freedom in deciding how such funds were to be spent.

THE FEDERAL DEBT

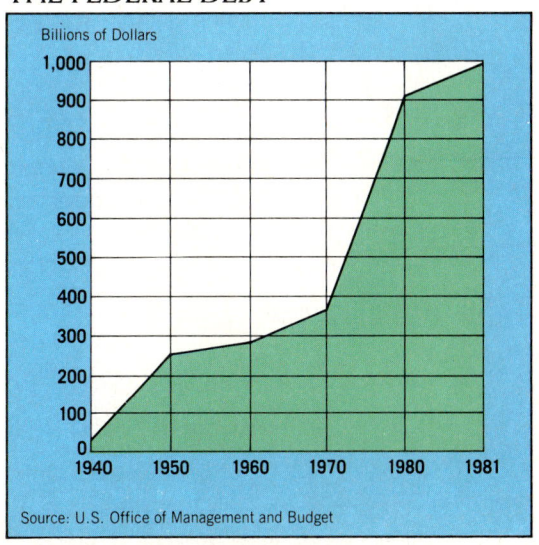

Source: U.S. Office of Management and Budget

REVIEWING THE SECTION

A. Knowing New Terms

Explain the following terms in your notebook *in your own words*.

(In **A**) "revenue-sharing"
(In **A**) Twenty-sixth Amendment
(In **B**) Watergate scandal
(In **B**) "cover-up"
(In **C**) "open government"
(In **C**) Twenty-fifth Amendment
(In **E2**) "stagflation"
(In **H**) "Reaganomics"

B. Knowing Important Facts

For each action in the first column, write in your notebook the letter of the person in the second column who performed it. (You may use a letter more than once and you may have more than one letter for each answer.)

Actions	Important People
1. Believed that states and local governments should plan programs to reduce poverty	A. Richard M. Nixon
2. Became President after a close election vote	B. Gerald R. Ford
3. Started the "revenue-sharing" plan	C. Jimmy Carter
4. Resigned when accused of nonpayment of income taxes	D. Nelson A. Rockefeller
5. Served less than one full term as President	E. Spiro T. Agnew
6. Pardoned a former President	F. Ronald W. Reagan
7. Had impeachment charges considered against him	
8. Recommended federal tax cuts	
9. Appointed as Vice-President	
10. President during hostage crisis in Iran	

C. Finding the Reasons

In your notebook write the letters of *all* the correct answers to each question that follows.

1. President Nixon did not favor President Johnson's plans to relieve poverty in the United States because he believed:

   a. the Johnson programs were failures   b. there was less poverty in America than people believed   c. spending for such programs was a cause of inflation.

2. Some of the taped White House conversations about the Watergate scandal were released by President Nixon because:

   a. he wanted to make sure the public knew all the facts   b. his advisers urged him to do so   c. he was ordered to do so by the Supreme Court.

3. Historians have said that our form of government "passed the test" in the Watergate scandal because:

   a. through it all, our people had confidence in their leaders   b. the Twenty-fifth Amendment worked as planned   c. the change in government that followed the crisis took place without violence or disorder.

4. The confidence of the American people in their leaders was shaken during the 1970s because of:

   a. the results of an investigation of the CIA   b. the Watergate scandal   c. the War on Poverty.

5. The administration of President Ford and Vice-President Rockefeller was unusual in American history because:

   a. neither man had been chosen as a result of a national election   b. both men had been long-time members of the House of Representatives   c. both men held office as a result of the Twenty-fifth Amendment.

6. President Ford probably failed to be elected in 1976 because he:

   a. represented the party of the Watergate scandal   b. had been unable to stop inflation and rising unemployment in his years in office   c. would not end the war in Vietnam.

7. President Carter faced difficulty in solving the nation's economic problems because:

   a. the Republican party controlled both houses of Congress   b. there was a condition of high prices and high unemployment at the same time   c. Congress spent years debating his plans to reduce unemployment.

8. One reason Ronald Reagan succeeded in the campaign of 1980 was that:

   a. the problems of the nation were completely different from those four years earlier   b. President Carter had placed strict controls on wages and prices   c. many Americans felt the nation's strength had been weakened by foreign events.

9. President Reagan's program to reduce unemployment and balance the budget was different from the approach of earlier Presidents in that he:

   a. planned to increase spending for social programs   b. suggested the federal government increase the amount of its grants to the states   c. proposed to reduce personal income taxes.

10. High unemployment generally causes:

    a. reduced government revenues from taxes   b. additional government programs to help the poor and needy   c. a reduction in the size of government agencies.

IMPROVING YOUR SKILLS

Looking at Both Sides

Complete each of the following lists in your notebook.

PART 1. Compare the arguments for and against President Ford's decision to pardon President Nixon.

	For		*Against*
1.		1.	
2.		2.	
3.		3.	

Conclusion: With which side do you agree? Why?

PART 2. Compare the arguments for and against President Reagan's plan to give the states control over some social programs and to let them make their own decisions on how to use these funds.

	For		*Against*
1.		1.	
2.		2.	
3.		3.	

Conclusion: With which point of view do you agree? Why?

MAKING HISTORY LIVE

1. Interview people or read accounts about one of the following events. Then report on your findings.
   a. President Eisenhower's trip to Korea in 1952 b. The Senate hearings of Senator Joseph McCarthy c. President Kennedy's assassination d. Former President Carter's greeting of the hostages released from Iran
2. Begin a classroom display of newspaper clippings about actions by the government, private businesses, or individuals to reduce poverty in the United States.
3. Research the details of the election campaigns mentioned in this chapter. Give a report to the class on the topic, "If I had been 18 in 19____, I would have voted for _____."
4. Research materials in your school library. Make a display of the headlines of the important events in the Watergate scandal.
5. Research cartoons from a variety of newspapers and magazines that show opposite points of view about a program proposed by President Reagan.

Chapter 35

POVERTY, PREJUDICE, AND DISCRIMINATION

"ALL MEN ARE CREATED EQUAL," states our Declaration of Independence. Equality is certainly one of the great ideals of our democracy. Yet it has been very hard to achieve. Prejudice (dislike of those who are "different") is still alive in the United States. The reason is simple. People like to think that the way they look and act is the way others should look and act. That is why they feel that people who act differently or do not look the same are inferior to them. Prejudiced opinions are formed without taking time and care to reason and judge fairly. Prejudice is hard to stamp out. What is worse, it often leads to discrimination—that is, actions that deprive some people of the rights most other people enjoy.

Blacks are one group of Americans who have suffered greatly from prejudice and discrimination. Millions of blacks were kept as slaves by force. Even blacks who won their freedom were not immediately given rights as American citizens. It is only since the historic Supreme Court decision of 1954 that blacks have made great progress toward obtaining the rights that belong to all Americans.

The struggle by blacks for equal rights has put the spotlight on other groups in our society who have suffered from discrimination—American Indians, Hispanics (Spanish Americans), and Asian Americans, for example. Women, too, have often been placed in positions of inferiority because society has been oriented toward male leadership.

In this chapter, we shall see how black Americans have suffered in the past and how they have made progress toward equality. We shall also see how other minorities have benefited from their fight for equal rights. And we shall see why there are poor in America and how there is a link between poverty and minority position.

How Have Black People Been Denied Equal Rights?

A. Discrimination in the South. 1. POLITICAL DISCRIMINATION. When Reconstruction ended in 1877, southern whites were determined to put blacks "in their place" again. They began by taking away the right to vote. At first, blacks who tried to vote were beaten or their ballots were not counted. Soon, however, southern states passed laws to keep blacks from voting at all.

Four kinds of laws were especially important. 1. The "grandfather clause" allowed the vote only to people whose grandfathers had voted. 2. Any person who wanted to vote had to pay a poll tax each year. Few blacks could afford the tax. Since many poor whites also could not pay, the poll tax greatly reduced the number of voters in southern states. This made it easier for a small but powerful group of whites to control elections. 3. All new voters had to pass a literacy (reading and writing) test. But voting officials asked blacks to recite long sections of the state constitution, explain complicated laws, or answer very hard questions. Even college graduates could not pass such "literacy tests." 4. Blacks were not allowed to vote in the Democratic party elections in which the party's candidates were picked. Since the Democrats almost always won in the South, these "primary" elections were actually more important than the regular elections. The "white primary" kept blacks from choosing officials who would help them.

Blacks were also denied other civil rights. They were not allowed to serve on juries. If they dared to become witnesses against a white person, what they said in court carried little weight. If a black person and a white person broke the same law, the black received the harsher punishment. Yet, despite these violations of a person's equal rights as a citizen, the federal government took no action.

2. SOCIAL DISCRIMINATION. Blacks were kept down by southern whites through segregation (separation). Special laws, known as "Jim Crow" laws, were passed for this purpose. These laws punished blacks if they used the same facilities—such as hotels, restaurants, libraries, and parks—as whites used. They were also forced to sit in a separate section, usually at the rear, in theaters, trains, and buses. Their children were required to go to separate schools.

Facilities for blacks were inferior to those for whites. Black schools were often poor shacks, and they were open for only a few months of the

From the days of "Jim Crow" laws. What forms of discrimination against black Americans are shown in this picture?

year. The teachers were poorly paid and poorly prepared. Many were not even high school graduates. Yet only about half of the black children in the South were attending even these schools in 1900.

3. ECONOMIC DISCRIMINATION. Blacks were also denied the chance to earn a good living. Most became sharecroppers or laborers on land owned by whites. Those who had learned skilled trades were usually forced to do simple, low-paid physical work instead.

4. A REIGN OF TERROR. Blacks were severely punished for breaking the laws and customs of white southerners. White juries almost always found them guilty as charged, and white judges put heavy penalties on them. But white people who beat or even killed blacks were seldom punished. Several hundred blacks were lynched (murdered by lawless mobs) each year. Sometimes white mobs attacked the black section of a town just to "teach the blacks a lesson."

B. The Southern Attitude. Discrimination in the South against blacks was based mainly on racial prejudice. Since most white southerners believed that blacks were an inferior people, they claimed that blacks had to be kept down. Whites especially feared marriage between the races. They believed it led to "race pollution"—that is, to a spoiling of the qualities that, according to them, made the white race superior.

Southern whites gained some benefits from discrimination. Landowners and business people enjoyed a supply of cheap, obedient labor. Poor whites were protected from black competition for their jobs. They also had the pleasure of feeling superior because they could "boss" blacks around. Political leaders found it easy to keep control of the government. Even corrupt and less-qualified leaders could win elections by posing as champions of "white supremacy."

C. Disadvantages of the Southern Policy. The southern policy was not only terribly unfair to black people. In the long run, it also hurt the South. It is hard to build a prosperous society when so many people are kept poor and ignorant. Since blacks were not allowed to do skilled work, southern industry did not have a large supply of skilled labor. The low wages received by black workers tended to keep wages of southern whites low. Business people suffered too because they could not sell many goods to people with small incomes. The region also had to bear another burden. This was the extra cost of keeping up separate schools and other facilities for both races.

The slow development of the South held our nation back. The southern treatment of blacks also had important effects abroad. Because it clearly violated democratic ideals, it spoiled our nation's reputation as a leader of democracy.

D. The Northern Attitude. Until World War I, most northerners accepted this state of affairs with little protest. Reconstruction had proved such a failure that reformers were afraid to interfere in the South again. So they turned their attention to other problems in the North brought about by the changes in industry. Most important, many white northerners had the same preju-

Slum in a northern city. How do you think discrimination might affect the lives of these children?

611

dice against blacks as did white southerners. Northern states did not pass "Jim Crow" laws or keep blacks from voting. But they did discriminate in other ways. Blacks, for example, found it almost impossible to join unions of skilled workers or to move into good neighborhoods. In most northern cities, blacks lived in a segregated neighborhood, or ghetto, usually in the worst part of town. White northerners, too, wanted blacks kept "in their place."

E. The "Separate but Equal" Decision. Prejudice also seemed to be behind a series of Supreme Court decisions that supported the South's "Jim Crow" laws. In a famous decision of 1896, the highest court in our nation held, "If one race be inferior to the other socially, the Constitution of the United States cannot put them on the same plane [level]." Separate facilities for whites and blacks, it ruled, were legal as long as they were equally good. This ruling became known as the "separate but equal" doctrine. In practice, as we have seen, facilities in the South were indeed separate, but they were certainly not equal. Many years passed before the efforts to change this situation began to be successful.

REVIEWING THE SECTION

A. Knowing New Terms

For each term in the first column, write in your notebook the *letter* of the best description in the second column.

Terms

1. Civil rights
2. Prejudice
3. Discrimination
4. "Grandfather clause"
5. "Jim Crow" laws
6. Literacy test
7. Poll tax
8. "Separate but equal" decision

Descriptions

a. Actions that are unfair to groups or to individuals because they belong to certain groups
b. Supreme Court ruling that allowed segregation
c. Dislike of individuals who are different
d. Test to determine whether a person can read or write well enough to be able to vote
e. Laws that forbade blacks in the South to use the same facilities as whites
f. Legal provision that a person could vote only if his grandfather had the right to vote
g. Payment required before a person could vote
h. Legal action to keep blacks off southern juries
i. Rights to which all American citizens are entitled by law

B. Understanding the Facts

PART 1. Tell whether the following statements show forms of political, economic, or social discrimination. (Some of the statements involve more than one form of discrimination.)

In the South

1. Blacks were kept from voting.
2. Blacks could not serve on a jury.
3. Blacks were given heavier penalties than whites for the same offenses.
4. Blacks were not allowed to hold skilled jobs.
5. Black children had to attend separate schools.
6. Blacks had to use separate restaurants.
7. Whites committing crimes against blacks were often found not guilty.
8. Hundreds of blacks were lynched by white mobs.

In the North

1. Blacks were kept out of unions of skilled workers.
2. People would not sell them houses or rent them apartments in white neighborhoods.

Conclusion. What were the main differences between discrimination in the North and in the South?

PART 2. In your notebook, write the *letter* of the correct choice.

1. The main difference between *prejudice* and *discrimination* is that:
   a. prejudice is based on facts; discrimination is based on opinions   b. prejudice is a feeling of dislike of other people; discrimination consists of actions against them   c. prejudice is practiced by the majority against a minority; discrimination is practiced by a minority against the majority   d. prejudice is illegal; discrimination is legal.
2. Blacks who took literacy tests for voting in the South usually failed because they:
   a. could not read and write   b. made many careless mistakes   c. were asked very difficult questions   d. suffered from all of these handicaps.
3. Segregation in the South was unfair to blacks because they:
   a. were made to feel inferior   b. were denied the chance to learn in good schools if whites went to such schools   c. were usually given worse facilities than the whites   d. suffered from all these disadvantages.
4. Southern whites who benefited from discrimination included:
   a. business people   b. politicians   c. workers   d. all these groups.
5. In the long run, race discrimination has hurt:
   a. blacks   b. southern whites   c. northern whites   d. all these groups.
6. Many northerners discriminated against blacks mainly because they:
   a. did not want blacks to have skilled union jobs   b. considered blacks inferior   c. did not want blacks to live in their neighborhoods   d. were influenced by all these reasons.

7. Which of the following describes the "separate but equal" decision of the Supreme Court?
a. It allowed segregation to continue in the South. b. It immediately resulted in making blacks' facilities equal to those of whites. c. It made it easier for southern blacks to progress. d. It upheld the spirit of the Fourteenth Amendment.

IMPROVING YOUR SKILLS

A. Telling Facts From Opinions

Write "Fact" for each statement that can be proved by getting the necessary information. Write "Opinion" if you think the answer depends on values and judgement. (For a review, see pages 237–238.)

1. Jim Crow laws were used to separate blacks from whites.
2. The "separate but equal" doctrine paved the way for equal rights for blacks.
3. Only about half of the black children in 1900 attended public schools.
4. After the period of Reconstruction, southern whites were right in putting blacks "in their place" again.
5. The poll tax prevented many blacks from voting.

B. Interpreting the Graph

Study graph 1 and graph 2. Then write "True" in your notebook if each statement is correct according to the graphs. If it is wrong, rewrite the statement so that it is correct.

BLACK AND WHITE UNEMPLOYMENT IN THE U.S., 1954-1982

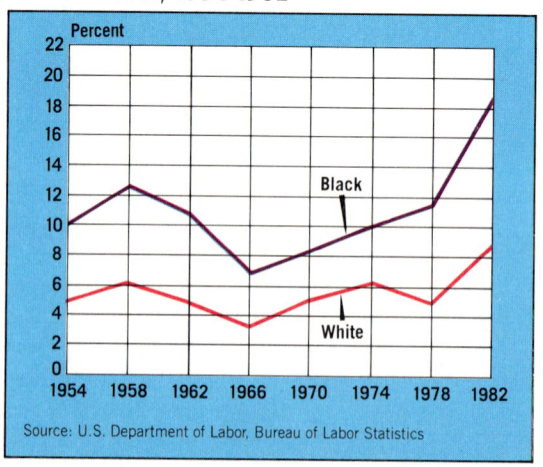

Source: U.S. Department of Labor, Bureau of Labor Statistics

GRAPH 1. Black and White Unemployment

1. Blacks have had a higher percentage of unemployment than whites in each year shown since 1954.
2. In 1982, the percentage of blacks unemployed was twice that of whites unemployed in the same period.
3. Every time there was a drop in white unemployment, black unemployment also dropped.
4. From 1974 to 1982, the percentage of blacks unemployed increased, but the increase was less than that of white unemployment.

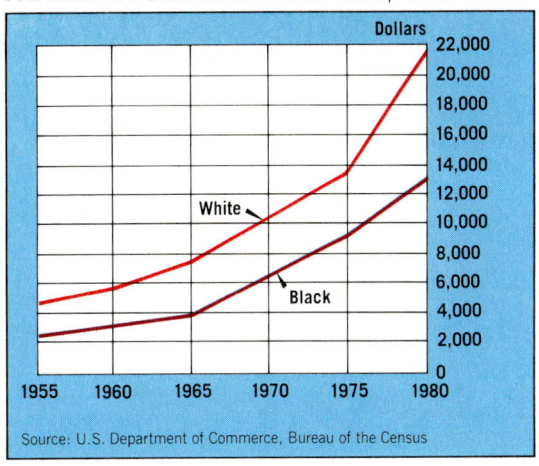

THE GAP BETWEEN BLACK AND WHITE FAMILY INCOME IN THE U.S., 1955-1980

Source: U.S. Department of Commerce, Bureau of the Census

GRAPH 2. The Gap Between Black and White Family Income

1. In 1955, the income of the average white family was over a thousand dollars a year higher than the income of the average black family.
2. In 1980, the difference in income between white and black families was less than five thousand dollars a year.
3. The graph shows that as white families earn more and more, black families are earning less and less.
4. Between 1955 and 1980, both white and black families more than doubled their incomes.

How Have Blacks Advanced Toward Equality?

A. The First Steps. Even during the difficult period after Reconstruction, blacks improved their condition bit by bit. The new schools, poor though they were, taught thousands to read and write. Outstanding students went on to colleges that reformers, both black and white, had helped to start. In time the graduates of these schools began to form a new class of ministers, teachers, and business people. Blacks like the educator Booker T. Washington and the scientist George Washington Carver became famous. Their achievements showed once again that blacks could excel if they were given the chance.

Two important black organizations—the National Association for the Advancement of Colored People and the National Urban League—were formed shortly before World War I. The NAACP took action in the courts to win the rights guaranteed to blacks by the Fourteenth and Fifteenth amendments. As a result of its work, the Supreme Court ruled that the "grandfather clause" and all-white party elections were illegal. The National Urban League helped blacks who moved into the cities from the countryside. It found housing for the newcomers, trained them for factory work, and helped them to get jobs.

B. Effects of World War I. Unfortunately, during President Wilson's administration the federal departments of the Post Office, Treasury, and Interior segregated their facilities, restaurants, and offices. So did the Senate and the Library of Congress. But black Americans did make important advances as a result of World War I. At first, black soldiers were kept in segregated units and were used mainly as cooks and attendants. But then they were allowed to fight in all-black combat units. When these won high honors for courage, many Americans began to change their opinion of blacks. To them it seemed to be wrong to deny equal rights to people who had fought bravely in the defense of their country.

Even more important, the great demand for war supplies created many jobs in northern industry. Thousands of blacks left the South to fill these jobs. New York, Philadelphia, Washington, and Chicago became the American cities with the largest black populations. Blacks succeeded in many types of work, both skilled and unskilled. Their children received a better education in northern schools. The black section of New York City, known as Harlem, became the center for many black writers, musicians, singers, and athletes. Like the earlier black leaders, they helped to weaken old prejudices.

C. The New Deal and Blacks. Blacks, even more than other unskilled workers, were usually "the last to be hired and the first to be fired." As a result, they suffered severe hardships during the Great Depression. But they also benefited greatly from the New Deal. The federal government put many unemployed blacks to work and paid them higher wages than they had ever earned before. It also helped needy sharecroppers and farm laborers, many of whom were black. At the same time the CIO, which had just been formed, began to organize the mass production industries. Since it took in unskilled as well as skilled workers, it soon had more than a million black members. They received the same wages, hours, working conditions, and fringe benefits as other union members.

Both President and Mrs. Roosevelt were interested in helping black people gain opportunities in our society. In fact, Eleanor Roosevelt was a champion of the cause of human rights for all people throughout the world. The Roosevelts often invited black leaders to the White House. The President also appointed hundreds of blacks to important positions in the government.

D. Blacks in World War II. World War II did more to further equality for blacks than did World War I. The German dictator, Adolf Hitler, believed the Germans were a "master race," destined to make slaves of "inferior races." Many Americans saw how foolish racist ideas were. They also saw they could not attack such ideas strongly as long as race prejudice existed in our own country.

When the United States entered the war, the armed forces were still segregated. During the war, President Roosevelt ordered that practice to be gradually ended. Blacks also found many jobs in industry, just as they had during World War I. The President helped black workers by starting the Fair Employment Practice Committee. Its function was to make sure that companies did not discriminate against any minority group. The committee was abolished when the war ended. However, many states adopted the idea and set up committees to prevent any discrimination in hiring.

After World War II, American treatment of blacks received a good deal of attention from other countries. The Communists tried to turn world opinion against the United States. Their newspapers carried headlines of events in the United States that showed discrimination against blacks. They charged that our country was not a real democracy. These attacks were aimed at creating anti-American feeling in the new nations of Asia and Africa where nonwhite peoples were struggling for independence from white rule.

In the early post-World War II period President Truman made important contributions in the area of civil rights. He ordered an end to all discrimination in the armed forces and the federal civil service. He also urged the passage of a stronger civil rights law. However, southern senators used the filibuster (giving long speeches) to kill the measure.

E. New Supreme Court Decisions. In the 1950s the Supreme Court took the center of the stage in the fight against discrimination. Its most impor-

Some noted blacks: from left to right, Marian Anderson, opera and concert singer; Langston Hughes, author and poet; Malcolm X, minister and fighter for the rights of blacks.

617

tant decision came in 1954, when it reversed the 1896 "separate but equal" ruling. "In the field of public education," the Court now said, "the doctrine of 'separate but equal' has no place. Separate educational facilities are inherently [in themselves] unequal." The Supreme Court ordered all public schools to integrate—that is, to enroll pupils without discriminating on the basis of race. During the next few years, the Court also ordered the end of segregation in all types of public facilities.

F. "Massive Resistance" by Southern Whites. Most of the southern states strongly resisted the Supreme Court's decisions. Virginia, for example, allowed its public schools to close and supported private schools open only to white children. In Little Rock, Arkansas, President Eisenhower had to use federal troops to guard the first black students entering that city's all-white high school. President Kennedy had to use federal troops to guard the first black students entering the universities of Mississippi and Alabama.

Southern whites also turned to violence, just as they had done in the Reconstruction period. The Ku Klux Klan was revived and joined with other groups in favor of white supremacy. Many black leaders and whites who sided with blacks lost their jobs. Black store owners were forced to close their doors because whites would no longer shop there. Dozens of blacks were beaten and killed. Black churches, schools, and homes were bombed or set on fire. Local police made little effort to find those who had committed these crimes. In a few cases, the President sent FBI agents to find the criminals. But all-white juries usually either freed those who were caught or found them guilty of a lesser offense.

G. Passive Resistance by Blacks. Blacks in turn organized to fight against segregation. With the support of white members of the clergy, college students, and other reformers, blacks started a drive to change the situation in the South. The tactic they most often used was passive (nonviolent) resistance. This included all sorts of peaceful demonstrations, such as parades, boycotts, "freedom rides," "sit-ins," and "pray-ins." These demonstrations brought public attention to the black demand for equality. But the police often answered nonviolence with violence. They used clubs and guns, horses and police dogs, and tear gas and fire hoses to break up demonstrations. The protestors were not supposed to fight back and rarely did so. When their leaders were arrested, dozens of followers often insisted on being arrested too.

The violence of the police and other southern whites turned many white northerners against them. The peaceful behavior of the demonstrators, on the other hand, won their sympathy. It also helped to change the viewpoint of many white southerners. Besides, the troubles were bad for business. It was often southern business people who led the way in working out compromises. In one southern city after another, segregation began to crumble.

H. New Laws and Their Effects. Under President Johnson, the federal government also took strong action to help blacks in their struggle. The Twenty-fourth Amendment abolishing the poll tax, the broad Civil Rights Law of 1964, and the Voting Rights Act of 1965 were all passed within a two-year period. (See page 596.)

These legal actions by the federal government had far-reaching results. Almost all of the public school systems in the South promised to integrate, and most of them began to do so. Both public and privately owned hotels and restaurants in southern cities opened their doors to blacks. With the help of federal officials, thousands of new black voters registered in the election of 1966. For the first time since Reconstruction, blacks were elected to public office in the South.

Three other steps toward black equality were taken at this time. The War on Poverty helped some blacks to become skilled workers. At the same time, the AFL–CIO started a drive to end discrimination in its member unions. Finally, a number of states and cities passed laws to end discrimination in housing.

Mary McLeod Bethune talking with Eleanor Roosevelt.

MARY McLEOD BETHUNE: A BLACK EDUCATOR

Mary McLeod was the seventeenth child of a poor black cotton farmer in South Carolina. She did not start school until she was eleven years old. Yet she had a dream that one day she would become a leader of her fellow black Americans. The first sign that her dream might come true was the scholarship she won when she was fourteen. In faraway Colorado, a hard-working white woman had set up a small fund to educate a black girl, one who was "sure to make good." Mary, a star pupil, was the girl chosen.

For the next seven years, she worked very hard to get a good education. After graduating from college, she became a teacher. Then she got married and had a son. Yet she did not give up her dream of helping her people. One day Mary McLeod Bethune learned that there was no school for the children of thousands of black laborers who were building a hotel and railroad in Florida. With only $1.50 in her purse, she went to Florida with her young son. She rented a little cottage and opened a school for girls. She and her pupils built the furniture themselves and planted a vegetable garden. They made money by baking sweet potato pies and singing for the wealthy northerners at the hotel. A hotel guest, impressed by Mary's little school, raised money for a large new building. She named it Faith Hall because she felt that her faith in her future had brought it about.

During World War I, Mary Bethune joined a women's suffrage group. She also set up special classes to teach blacks, men as well as women, how to pass the literacy test for voting. The Ku Klux Klan threatened to set fire to her school. The night before the election, she bravely faced the Klan's night riders. If they burned down her school, she told them, she would build it again—and again and again, if need be. The next day she led a hundred blacks to the polls. The incident made her famous.

During the New Deal period, Mary Bethune served with the National Youth Administration. She traveled throughout the United States, setting up projects to help her people. In 1935 she won the Spingarn Medal, for the black "who had made the noblest achievement during the year." This was a high point of her career. In that same year, she established the National Council of Negro Women.

When World War II came, she was old and ill. Nevertheless, she accepted a post with the War Department to help end segregation in the armed forces. In 1945 she attended the talks that started the UN, which promised equal rights for all people. She lived to hear the Supreme Court's 1954 decision outlawing segregation in the public schools. Mary McLeod Bethune knew that the black's fight for equal rights was far from over. But she had faith in a future without discrimination or prejudice, in which blacks would at last enjoy full equality with other Americans.

I. A Critical Situation. As usual, however, the road to success was not a smooth one. In the summer of 1964, race riots broke out in the black sections of a few northern cities. The riots showed that many blacks were becoming impatient. The nation had reached new heights of prosperity, but the rate of black unemployment was very high. Almost one-third of black youths who had left school could not find jobs. In farm areas, new machines were still replacing black sharecroppers and farm laborers. Many of them went North and were forced to live in the slums of large cities.

In the years after 1964, riots broke out in several large northern cities. New black organizations began teaching their followers to hate whites and to use violence to gain their rights. Though only a small percentage of blacks followed these groups, they had a great influence. Their strong language, together with the riots, angered many people who had sympathized with the black cause. Some people began to think it was not possible to satisfy black demands. A "white backlash"—strong opposition to reforms for blacks—developed.

In 1968, the National Advisory Commission on Civil Disorders, appointed by the President, made its report to the nation. In its report, the commission stated that ". . . certain fundamental matters are clear. . . . The most fundamental is the racial attitude and behavior of white Americans toward black Americans. Race prejudice has shaped our history decisively in the past; it now threatens to do so again. White racism is

A Detroit block after the 1967 riot. Twenty-three people were killed, more than a thousand injured, and millions of dollars' worth of property destroyed. Did such riots solve the racial problems of the 1960s and 1970s?

essentially responsible for the explosive mixture which has been accumulating [growing] in our cities. . . . Our nation is moving toward two societies, one black, one white—separate and unequal. . . ." Congress quickly passed a new civil rights law to strengthen the earlier laws. At the same time, steps were taken to find more jobs for young blacks.

J. The Years That Followed. Although blacks have not yet reached complete equality in America's economic, social, and political life, progress toward this goal continues. Blacks are attending college in increasing numbers. There are more black professionals than ever before. The number of blacks entering politics has increased steadily. For example, blacks have served as mayor in the cities of Los Angeles, Detroit, Atlanta, Newark, Chicago, and New Orleans. In the end, Americans across the nation have come to realize that the rights of blacks and other minorities must no longer be ignored.

From left to right, Shirley Chisholm, politician and educator; Thurgood Marshall, associate justice of the Supreme Court; Jackie Robinson, baseball player and businessman.

March on Washington, 1963. Dr. King looks out over the thousands of people who took part in the march.

MARTIN LUTHER KING: THE MAN WHO WOULD NOT HATE

When Martin Luther King was struck down by an assassin's bullet in April 1968, people all over the United States mourned his death. The pope and other foreign leaders paid tribute to his memory. At President Johnson's request, Congress quickly passed a strong civil rights bill.

The black leader whom they honored was born in Atlanta, Georgia, in 1929. A minister's son and a brilliant student, he received a good education in both southern and northern colleges. In 1955 Dr. King was appointed minister of a small church in Montgomery, Alabama. Montgomery's blacks were planning to boycott the city's bus line because it was segregated. (Blacks had to sit at the back of buses and to give up their seats to white riders when there were no seats in the front.) Dr. King was chosen to lead the boycott. He won a great victory. After a year-long struggle, the buses were integrated.

During the next ten years, Dr. King won other important victories. He took an active part in the "sit-ins," the "freedom rides," and the great march on Washington in 1963. His efforts influenced Congress to pass the Civil Rights Act of 1964 and the Voting Rights Act of 1965. He also became known abroad when he was awarded the famous Nobel Peace Prize in Sweden in 1964.

Dr. King's successes showed that his ideas appealed to whites as well as blacks. These ideas were based on Christian and democratic ideals of equality, brotherhood, and love. "I have a dream," he said, "that my four children will one day live in a nation where they will not be judged by the color of their skin but by the content of their character." He tried to achieve his dream by nonviolence—that is, by peaceful methods like parades and demonstrations. "We must use the weapon of love," he explained. "We must have compassion [pity] and understanding for those who hate us."

Too often, however, nonviolence was answered with violence. Some of King's followers were murdered. Thousands were beaten and imprisoned. King himself was beaten and jailed, and his home was bombed. Yet his faith in nonviolence never weakened.

After 1965 he shifted his efforts to the North. He tried to get more jobs and better housing for northern blacks. But he had little success. More and more blacks, especially young people, became impatient and turned to violence. Even while millions of Americans were mourning Dr. King's death, angry young blacks rioted in more than a hundred cities. Their behavior showed that time was running out. America would have to solve its race problem soon or face the danger of even greater violence.

REVIEWING THE SECTION

A. Knowing New Terms

For each new term in the first column, write in your notebook the *letter* of the best description in the second column.

Terms	*Descriptions*
1. Integration	a. Methods used by southern whites to preserve discrimination
2. NAACP	b. Peaceful tactics used by blacks to end discrimination
3. National Urban League	c. Unfavorable reaction of whites, angered by black violence, to black demands for equal rights
4. Passive resistance	d. Sharing of schools and other facilities by both whites and blacks
5. "White backlash"	e. Organization that helps blacks from rural areas get used to life in the city
	f. Organization that has helped blacks to get their rights through action of the courts

B. Knowing Important Facts

For each form of discrimination given below, list in your notebook two or three measures that have been taken to end it.

Forms of Discrimination	*Measures to End Discrimination*
1. Denial of the right to vote	1. a. _____ b. _____ c. _____
2. Segregation in private and public facilities	2. a. _____ b. _____ c. _____
3. Discrimination in employment	3. a. _____ b. _____ c. _____

C. Understanding the Facts

1. Explain why blacks have usually been "the last to be hired and the first to be fired."

2. Explain how the ideas in the following statements helped blacks in the United States.
   a. We fought World War I "to make the world safe for democracy."
   b. We fought World War II to keep those Germans who considered themselves a "master race" from enslaving other peoples, whom they regarded as "inferior races."

IMPROVING YOUR SKILLS

A. Looking at Both Sides

1. List the major gains made by blacks in the United States since 1915.
2. List the difficulties and problems they still face.
3. On the whole, do you think that our nation is solving the problem of discrimination against blacks fast enough? Explain your point of view.

B. Interpreting the Graph

Study graph 1 and graph 2. Then write "True" in your notebook if each statement that follows is correct according to the information given. If it is wrong, rewrite it so that it is correct.

Graph 1

AVERAGE INCOME, 1981

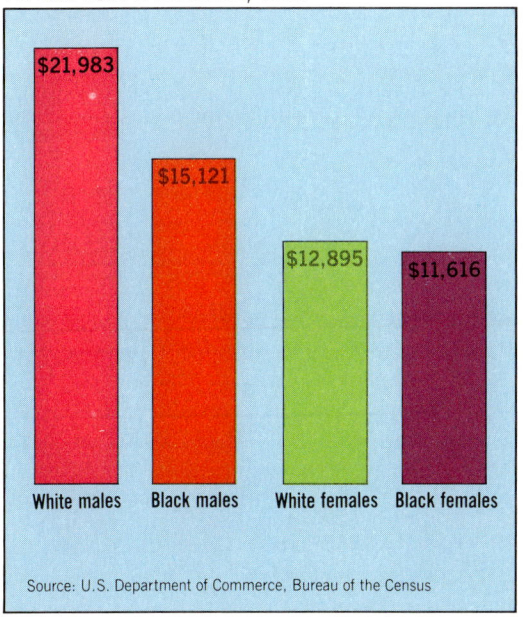

White males	Black males	White females	Black females
$21,983	$15,121	$12,895	$11,616

Source: U.S. Department of Commerce, Bureau of the Census

Graph 2

PERCENTAGE, ALL WORKERS WITH $10,000 YEARLY INCOME OR MORE

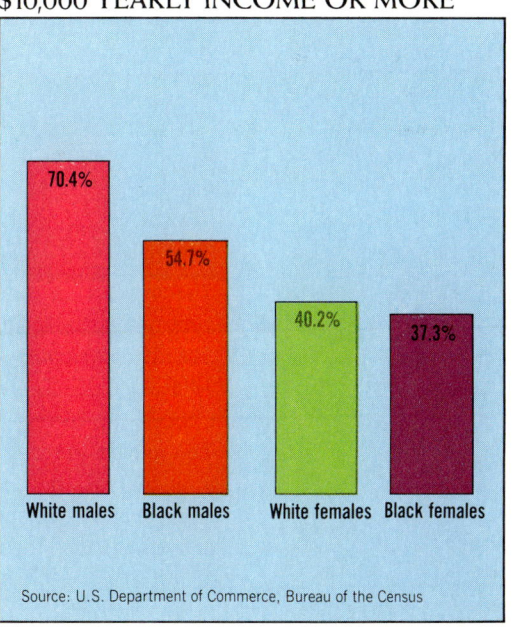

White males	Black males	White females	Black females
70.4%	54.7%	40.2%	37.3%

Source: U.S. Department of Commerce, Bureau of the Census

1. White males have a higher average income than any other group.
2. Black females have a higher average income than white females.
3. There is a greater percentage of blacks, male and female, earning incomes of $10,000 a year than of white males making the same amount.
4. A black female in 1981 had less than one chance in ten of having an income of $10,000 a year.

GRAPH 3. Study graph 3, which shows life expectancy, that is, the number of years a person can expect to live. Complete the following statements by writing the correct answer in your notebook.

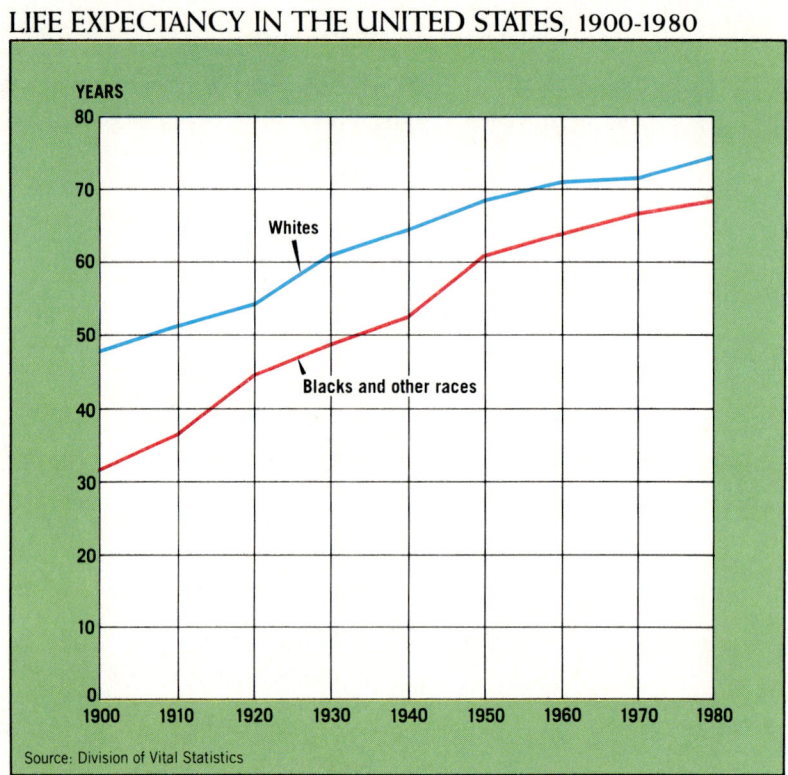

LIFE EXPECTANCY IN THE UNITED STATES, 1900-1980

Source: Division of Vital Statistics

1. The number of years whites could expect to live rose from _____ in 1900 to _____ in 1979, a gain of _____ years.
2. The life expectancy of blacks and other races rose from _____ years in 1900 to _____ years in 1979, a gain of _____ years.
3. Choose the correct answer.
   The gap in life expectancy between whites and blacks and other races has
   a. increased   b. decreased   c. remained the same.
4. The greatest difference between the life expectancy of whites and blacks and other races took place in:
   a. 1900   b. 1920   c. 1940.

624

What Other Groups Have Suffered From Discrimination?

A. Spanish Americans (Hispanics). Today there are almost 15 million Americans who are of Spanish-speaking origins. They or their ancestors came to the United States from a variety of nations. Many of these Hispanics came from Mexico or what was once Mexican-owned territory. Others are from Puerto Rico, Cuba, and Central and South American countries.

Mexican Americans make up the largest group of Hispanics in the United States. Many prefer to be called Chicanos. Mexican Americans are proud of their culture, which is much older than the United States. Some trace their families back to the original Spanish settlers. When Spain conquered much of the New World over 450 years ago, the Spanish mixed with the Indians of Mexico and, to a lesser degree, with the African slaves the Spanish had brought to Mexico. Long before the Pilgrims landed on the East Coast, these Spanish-speaking people were living in what became northern Mexico and is now part of the United States. They lived under the rule of Spain and then of Mexico. They were the original founders of many of the cities in what is now the southwestern part of the United States. This region includes much of California, New Mexico, Texas, Nevada, Utah, Arizona, and Colorado. The area became part of the United States as a result of the annexation of Texas and the conquests resulting from the Mexican War of 1846–1848 (land from Texas to the Pacific coast).

Mexican Americans provided many of the skills needed for the growth of our country's cattle industry and sheep raising. By the early 1900s, there was a shortage of cheap labor in the western part of the United States. Business people and farmers offered low-paying jobs to thousands of Mexicans who moved into the United States from Mexico. In the early part of this century most of the mine workers and railroad workers in the western states were Chicanos. Today, two-thirds of the Mexican Americans live in cities. Some are now successful business people, land owners, and professionals.

Mexican-American migrant workers harvesting the tomato crop in California. Why do such farm workers have to travel from one section of the country to another?

625

Many Mexican Americans have suffered from discrimination in housing, education, and jobs. At times, they have suffered from violence, such as the riots against Chicanos in Los Angeles in 1943. But Mexican Americans have a long history of struggling against discrimination.

Probably the best-known Chicano leader is Cesar Chavez. He organized farm workers in California in an attempt to get better wages and working conditions. At first, most large farm owners would not deal with his union, the United Farm Workers. Chavez believed in peaceful protest against the terrible conditions in the fruit orchards and vegetable fields. However, he had to call many strikes to achieve his goals. After many strikes and arrests, Chavez's United Farm Workers won better conditions for vegetable and fruit pickers. His leadership inspired a movement throughout the nation to improve the living conditions of all Hispanics.

The second largest group of Spanish-speaking Americans has come from the Commonwealth of Puerto Rico. Many came to the United States because of the lack of jobs in Puerto Rico. Almost a million have settled in New York City. Puerto Ricans are American citizens, whether they are among the one and a half million living in the United States or the over 3 million in Puerto Rico. English is taught as a second language in schools in Puerto Rico. But most Puerto Ricans who come to the United States have had little schooling. Many prefer to speak Spanish to show they are proud of their Spanish background.

Puerto Rican leaders helped convince Congress that people should not be denied the right to vote simply because they could not read and write English. They could become well-informed citizens by reading Spanish-language newspapers. In 1974, the 1965 Voting Rights Act was finally changed. The law was broadened to include Spanish-speaking Americans and other "language minorities." Spanish was becoming almost an official second language. Now the federal government supports and sometimes requires bilingual (two-language) courses to be taught in public schools.

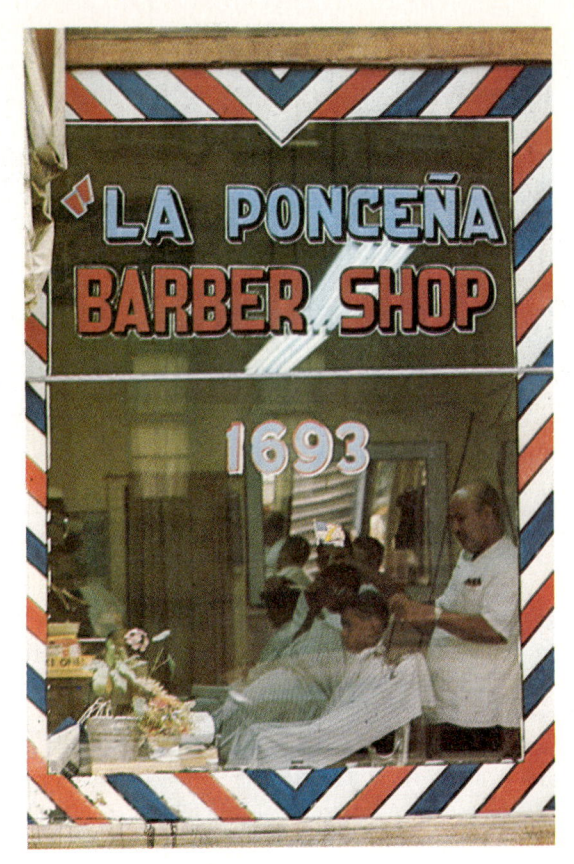

Thousands of Spanish-speaking people have prospered in a variety of occupations despite suffering from prejudice and discrimination.

Like other minority groups, Puerto Ricans have suffered from discrimination when trying to get good jobs and decent housing. Many Puerto Ricans have found work in the clothing industry in New York City. Others work in hospitals and small manufacturing plants. Puerto Ricans are now entering other occupational fields. More and more are becoming business people, teachers, doctors, lawyers, police officers, fire fighters, and political leaders.

A third Spanish-American group, the Cubans, began to arrive in the United States in the early 1960s. They were fleeing from a Communist dictator, Fidel Castro, who had taken control of Cuba. Within fifteen years, Cubans made up more than half the population of Miami, Florida.

Almost all Spanish-speaking immigrants have suffered from the prejudices of their American neighbors. However, the Cubans have probably suffered less because many have been well educated and light-skinned. While some of the Mexicans and Puerto Ricans who came to the United States have been educated, many have been poor with little schooling. They have had to take low-paying, unskilled jobs and live in the poorest sections of our cities. Those with dark skins have often been regarded as black. They have suffered from a double prejudice—prejudice against their skin color and prejudice against their different culture and language.

Like earlier immigrants, Spanish Americans have been working their way up into the middle class. Laws against discrimination and new programs to fight poverty promised to help them as well as blacks. Many have taken part in programs to train them for better jobs. Others have formed organizations to guide and provide assistance to young Hispanics who wish to go to college. Although the conditions of Hispanic people have improved, progress for many has been slow. During the 1970s, thousands of discouraged Puerto Ricans left New York City to return to Puerto Rico.

B. Immigration Since 1965. When Congress passed the Immigration Act of 1965, our nation took another step toward achieving our democratic ideal of equality. This act ended the quota system that had discriminated against immigrants of certain nationalities and races (see page 505). Now a person can enter the United States if that person meets one of these special qualifications. 1. The person has close relatives in this country. 2. The person has a profession such as science or law. 3. The person has a skill that American industry can use. 4. The person is a refugee.

The new law also increased the number of immigrants allowed to enter the United States. Up to 170,000 immigrants can now be admitted from the Eastern Hemisphere, and 120,000 from the Western Hemisphere. Those people meeting the special qualifications are given preference.

They are the first ones to be selected from among the thousands wanting to immigrate. The new law has resulted in a change in the source of newcomers to the United States. In 1980, fifteen years after the passage of the new law, there were six times the number of immigrants from Asian countries as there were in 1965. (For a picture of the change in immigration, see the chart on page 634.)

C. Asian Americans. Most of the million and a half Americans of Asian descent live in Hawaii or on the West Coast. There was little feeling against people from the Far East in Hawaii, where they made up almost half the population. But prejudice against Asians was strong in California and other western states. These states discriminated against them in education, jobs, and housing. The Chinese were the first group of immigrants to suffer discrimination by the federal government. Alarmed by the large numbers of Chinese laborers coming into the United States, Congress in the 1880s forbade Chinese people to enter the country or become citizens. Later it barred the Japanese and other Asian people.

Like other ethnic groups, Chinese Americans were discriminated against because they were different. Yet, Chinese Americans have accomplished much to be proud of. For example, in the nineteenth century, Chinese immigrants helped build the nation's railroads. Today, Chinese Americans are business people, doctors, lawyers, teachers, and scientists. In 1974, the Supreme Court ruled that they had been discriminated against in American schools. Bilingual instruction for Chinese students was ordered in San Francisco schools.

The most shocking instance of discrimination against Asians took place during World War II. More than 100,000 Americans of Japanese descent living in the West Coast area were forced to move inland to special camps. Many of these people were American citizens. But some suspected they would not be loyal to the United States in the war with Japan. Japanese Americans who owned homes and businesses had to sell

Interning Japanese Americans on the West Coast. An official is examining the few possessions these two families were able to bring with them.

them at once for whatever they could get. The camps were surrounded by barbed wire. Most of the people in the camps had to live in wooden sheds until the end of the war. Years later, the United States government admitted it had made a terrible mistake. Today Japanese Americans are more prosperous than ever. Many own businesses and farms. A large percentage of Japanese American children have graduated from college.

Another Asian group, the Filipinos, settled mainly on the West Coast. Many Filipinos recruited by businesses began to arrive from the Philippines in the early 1900s. Many worked in low-paying jobs, such as fruit and vegetable picking and dishwashing. Others worked in the canning and fishing industries. There was much housing and job discrimination against them. Congress was pressured into passing a law in 1934 limiting Filipino immigration to only 50 persons a year. But since the new immigration law was passed in 1965, thousands of Filipinos again are coming to the United States. Many of them are college-educated professionals and business people (see the chart on page 634).

D. The American Indian. 1. A LONG HISTORY OF MISTREATMENT. No group has suffered as much from prejudice and discrimination as the Indians, or Native Americans. Ever since colonial days, most whites have looked down on them. In only two colonies, Rhode Island and Pennsylvania, were they treated as equals. Elsewhere, especially in Virginia and Massachusetts, colonists persecuted even those tribes that had helped them.

This entire country once belonged to the American Indians. But time and again white people forced them from their villages to lands farther west. In treaty after treaty, our government promised that the new lands the Indians received would be theirs forever. Each time, however, our government eventually broke the treaty and drove the Indians out. Most Americans approved of the government's actions because they believed Indians were inferior. Many whites wanted to settle on Indian lands. Some people argued that attacks by Indians on white settlements were reason enough to kill them. "The only good Indian is a dead Indian!" was a widespread saying on the frontier.

2. WARDS OF THE GOVERNMENT. The Indians fought their last battles in the Far West in the 20-year period after the Civil War. They won a few victories. The most famous was their defeat of General Custer's force at the Little Big Horn in 1876. But they could not hope to win in the end. The railroads were bringing more and more troops and settlers to the West. Moreover, the bison herds on which many Indian tribes depended for food and clothing were being killed off rapidly. In the 1880s, the last resisting tribes—the Sioux, Nez Percés, and Apaches—were finally forced to make peace and to settle on reservations. They became wards (people under the protection or control of others) of the federal government.

In 1887, Congress passed the Dawes Act. Under the act, any Indian head of a household who left the tribe and tried farming received a homestead of 160 acres. Any adult single person who did the same received 80 acres. This land was part of the reservation. If the land was worked for 25 years, it became the personal property of the Indian family and they could become American citizens. After all the Indians received their land, the rest of the reservation could be sold by the government to homesteaders, industrialists, and ranchers.

Most Indians were used to living and working in tribes. Nevertheless, half of them decided to try the government's plan. A small number succeeded. A few even became wealthy when oil was discovered on their land. But most preferred their Indian traditions. And 25 years was a long time to wait. They either gave up their farms or were cheated out of them. Indians who stayed with their tribes on the reservations lived mainly by herding sheep, goats, and other livestock. Most reservation lands were dry and poor. In addition, many Indians died of the "white people's diseases." By the end of the nineteenth century, their numbers were falling fast. That is why the Indian was often referred to as the "vanishing American."

3. TWENTIETH-CENTURY POLICIES. During World Wars I and II, thousands of Indians served in the armed forces. In 1924, a law gave citizenship to all Indians born in the United States. Some had already become citizens through laws passed years before. Yet some states held out against allowing Indians to vote. Not until 1948 were Indians permitted to vote in Arizona.

President Franklin D. Roosevelt began a "new deal" for the Indians in 1934. They were encouraged to keep their tribal life, their customs, and their old languages. Individual Indians were not urged to take land for private farms as had been done under the Dawes Act. Instead, the government tried to help tribes keep their reservation lands. Many Indians set up tribal councils, a new form of government, to help run the reservations.

At the same time, Indians were taught to make better use of their lands for grazing and farming. The federal government also worked to improve their health and education. As a result, the Indian population rose steadily from one-third million in the 1930s to about a million and a half today.

In the 1950s, however, President Eisenhower withdrew the federal government's support. He persuaded many Indians to leave the reservations. Those who would not go became wards of the states in which they lived. The states could then gain control of any of the reservations' natural resources such as oil and timber. This change led to a good deal of suffering. Presidents Kennedy and Johnson decided to return to the Roosevelt policy.

The Indian problem is still not solved, however. About half the Indians in the United States today live on or near reservations, chiefly in the Southwest. The average income of the Indian family is much less than that of blacks. Indians are the poorest Americans. Their white neighbors almost always look down on them. But many young Indians have received an education and have found work in the cities. Some have obtained skilled jobs. And a group of educated leaders has developed. These leaders will not allow other Americans to forget the white people's treatment of Native Americans. They also

American Indians are organized in a variety of groups to protect their rights. Why do you think it took the U.S. government until 1924 to make Indians American citizens?

believe that it is very important for American Indians to preserve and maintain their rich cultural traditions.

Indians today are neither "forgotten" nor "vanishing" Americans. The movement for Indian equality increased in strength in the 1970s. A group called the American Indian Movement (AIM) took the lead in attempts to force the government to return land taken in the nineteenth century. At Wounded Knee, South Dakota, in 1973, 200 Indians occupied the town and held out against United States marshals for ten weeks before surrendering. There was some bloodshed during that occupation. But American attention was directed to Indian claims to right the wrongs of the past. The Indian group gave up only when the government promised to discuss ways of providing Indians with land and of paying for land taken from them. In later incidents, Indian groups have gone to court in attempts to recover their land. The settlement of these cases will have a great deal to do with the future independence of the American Indian.

E. Equality for Women. There are more women than men in the United States. There are more women than men at voting age. Because women live longer than men the difference in numbers is likely to become even greater. Thus, the problem of discrimination against women is a serious one. Women now have almost the same rights as men. Nevertheless, in the past, women have been shut out of certain occupations and, in general, still receive less pay than men doing the same work.

The demands for complete equality for women in American society increased in the 1960s. There are several reasons why this was so. Women took jobs in business and industry during World War II. In addition, American families became smaller in size. Women did not have to spend as much time at home as before. The increase in home conveniences and labor-saving discoveries allowed some women more time for work outside the home.

In 1966, the National Organization for Women (NOW) was formed to promote equal treatment

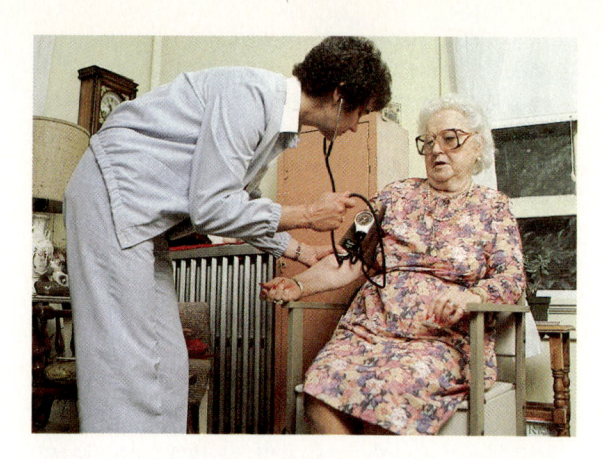

Why are more and more women now choosing to become doctors, police officers, lawyers, and business executives?

for women. Under the leadership of Betty Friedan, NOW and other "women's liberation" organizations have stressed that women are individuals, with their own abilities and goals.

The women's liberation movement, which includes the support of some male leaders of business and government, seeks to destroy the old ideas that "a woman's place is in the home," or "it's a man's world." Leaders of the movement point out that discrimination against women has been practiced throughout much of our history. On the average, a woman's pay is only about 60 percent of what a man receives for the same work. Women have seldom been selected over men as office managers. Women have been shut out of occupations in police, fire, and sanitation departments. Women have been discouraged from being lawyers, doctors, or scientists. Despite the majority of women voters, women make up only a small percentage of the elected officials across the nation. Some textbooks in the past described women only in terms of homemakers, nurses, and secretaries. They seldom showed women as professional people. Even our language has been geared to men in certain positions and occupations—mailman, policeman, chairman, congressman—as if women were not expected to hold such positions.

Congress proposed an Equal Rights Amendment (ERA) in 1972. This proposal guaranteed complete equality for women. Opponents of ERA carried on an active and successful campaign against the proposed amendment. They feared women might lose some of the advantages they already had if the amendment were approved. Those favoring the proposed amendment argued that women needed a written guarantee of their rights. To become an amendment to the Constitution, the ERA needed the approval of 38 state legislatures. However, it failed to win the backing of enough states. Thus, it never became the accepted law.

The position of women has improved in the years since 1960. The percentage of women who are nurses, librarians, and elementary school teachers (once considered to be "women's work") has declined. The percentage of women in professional studies—dentistry, medicine, law, pharmacy—has tripled. In such professions as psychology, college teaching, accounting, medicine, the law, and chemistry, there is a growing percentage of women. In 1981, President Reagan appointed Sandra Day O'Connor as the first woman Supreme Court justice. The Army, Navy, and Air Force academies have opened their doors to women training to become officers in the armed forces. Women made up 43 percent of the working force in the nation by 1981. There is no doubt that Americans are changing their attitudes toward women's role in American society.

Chief Justice Warren Earl Burger swears in Sandra Day O'Connor as an associate justice of the Supreme Court. Why do you think her appointment was important to the cause of women's rights?

Marching for women's rights. What are some of the demands for women's rights besides that of equal pay for equal work?

F. Other Special Groups. There is probably no group living in the United States whose religion, language, or race has not placed it in a minority position. Catholics, Jews, and certain Protestant groups have suffered from those who would not accept their beliefs. The election of a Catholic, John F. Kennedy, to the presidency showed that religious prejudice was on the decline. In spite of trouble now and then, religious prejudice is no longer thought to be a serious problem in our nation.

REVIEWING THE SECTION

A. Knowing New Terms

PART 1. For each group listed in the first column, write in your notebook the *letter* of the larger class in the second column to which it belongs. (You may use the same letter more than once.)

Groups

1. American Indians
2. Catholics
3. Chinese
4. Cubans
5. Filipinos
6. Japanese
7. Jews
8. Mexicans
9. Protestants
10. Puerto Ricans

Classes

A. Native Americans
B. Asians
C. Religious groups
D. Spanish-speaking groups

PART 2. Explain the meaning of each term in your own words.

(A) Chicano
(A) Hispanic
(A) bilingual
(A) double prejudice
(D) AIM
(E) NOW
(E) ERA

B. Understanding the Facts

In your notebook write the *letter* of the correct choice.

1. The Voting Rights Act of 1965 gave the right to vote to:
   a. foreign citizens   b. people who could read and write Spanish   c. women   d. all these groups.
2. The largest group of Spanish-speaking Americans is from:
   a. Cuba   b. Mexico   c. Puerto Rico   d. the Philippines.
3. Puerto Ricans are different from other Spanish-speaking groups coming to the mainland of the United States because they:
   a. are already American citizens   b. are mostly well educated   c. include many professional people   d. usually speak English.
4. The minority group denied the right to enter the United States and become American citizens were:
   a. American Indians   b. blacks   c. Asians   d. Spanish Americans.
5. During the nineteenth century, the federal government:
   a. defeated the Indians in battle   b. took away their lands   c. forced them to live on reservations   d. did all these things.

632

6. In the twentieth century, the federal government had a policy toward the Indians of:
   a. training them to make better use of their lands   b. improving their education and health conditions   c. getting them to leave the reservations   d. carrying on all these policies.
7. The Civil Rights Act of 1964 helped:
   a. racial minorities like blacks and Asians   b. people with different national origins like Spanish-speaking immigrants   c. women   d. all these groups.
8. The Immigration Act of 1965 is more democratic than the immigration laws of the 1920s because it:
   a. allows no immigrants from Asia to enter the United States   b. has ended all restrictions on the number of immigrants that can enter each year   c. gives preference to individuals with special qualifications, not to certain nationalities and races   d. has made all these changes.
9. The women's liberation movement has made gains toward its goals in that:
   a. women get higher pay than men today   b. the Twenty-seventh Amendment was added to the Constitution   c. there are more women who are becoming nurses and librarians   d. there are more women in professions like law, medicine, and chemistry.
10. Cesar Chavez is best known for:
    a. influencing Congress to pass the Voting Rights Act   b. the organization of the California farm workers   c. his fight for bilingual education   d. the publication of Spanish-language newspapers.
11. Present studies show that:
    a. thousands of Hispanics have gotten jobs that pay high wages   b. discrimination against Mexican Americans has ended   c. Cubans by the thousands are returning to their homeland   d. Spanish-speaking people make up half the population of several eastern cities.
12. "Moved from their homes, forced to sell homes and businesses, placed in special camps. . . ." This is a description of an act of discrimination against the:
    a. Filipinos   b. Chinese Americans   c. Japanese Americans   d. Cuban Americans.
13. The events at Wounded Knee, South Dakota, in 1973:
    a. directed Americans' attention to Indian claims of wrongs done to them in the past   b. caused a change in immigration laws   c. resulted in the organization of the United Farm Workers   d. started a return of Indians to the cities.
14. An example of discrimination claimed by women's groups is that:
    a. books in schools have pictured women only as homemakers   b. men are usually given positions of authority over equally qualified women   c. our language has referred only to men in certain occupations   d. all of these are examples.

IMPROVING YOUR SKILLS

Study the chart below. Write "True" in your notebook if each statement is correct according to the chart. If it is wrong, rewrite it so that it is correct.

The Ten Leading Sources of Immigrants to the United States

1965		1970		1980	
1. Canada	38,327	1. Mexico	44,469	1. Mexico	56,680
2. Mexico	37,969	2. Philippines	31,203	2. Vietnam	43,483
3. United Kingdom	27,358	3. Italy	24,973	3. Philippines	42,316
4. Germany	24,045	4. Greece	14,464	4. South Korea	32,320
5. Cuba	19,760	5. Cuba	16,334	5. China, Taiwan	27,651
6. Colombia	10,885	6. Jamaica	15,033	6. India	22,607
7. Italy	10,821	7. United Kingdom	14,158	7. Jamaica	18,970
8. Dominican Republic	9,504	8. China	14,093	8. Dominican Republic	17,245
9. Poland	8,465	9. Canada	13,804	9. United Kingdom	15,485
10. Argentina	8,465	10. Portugal	13,195	10. Cuba	15,054

Source: U.S. Immigration and Naturalization Service

1. Canada, leading in the number of immigrants in 1965, does not appear in the "top ten" in 1980.
2. The United Kingdom is the only European country from which a large number of immigrants came in all the years listed.
3. In 1970, over 17,000 immigrants came from Cuba to the United States.
4. In 1965, over 75,000 immigrants came to the United States from Mexico and Canada.
5. In 1965, no Asian country was a major source of immigrants.
6. In 1980, the majority of immigrants came from Asian countries.

Conclusions: How has the picture of immigration to the United States changed in the 15-year period? From which regions of the world are most newcomers coming? How do you account for the change in the 15-year period?

MAKING HISTORY LIVE

1. On the basis of outside reading, report on an outstanding American belonging to one of the minorities discussed in this chapter. Discuss her or his achievements. Be sure to tell about the problems that person had to overcome.
2. a. Explain the statement, "The United States is a nation of minorities."
   b. Select one of these minorities and tell how its members have helped our nation's progress.

3. Imagine that you are traveling abroad and have met someone who dislikes the United States. She insists that our country is not a real democracy because of the prejudice and discrimination against minority groups. How would you answer her?
4. Prepare to take part in a debate on the question, Are women in an inferior position in the United States today?
5. If your community has a large minority group, report on how it is treated.
6. a. Draw a cartoon showing how all groups of Americans have contributed to our nation's greatness; or b. Draw a poster urging Americans to work together, regardless of differences in race or national origin.
7. Gather materials for a scrapbook of achievements by members of one of the minority groups discussed in this chapter.
8. Contribute to a class display on the achievements of racial and religious minorities.

What Problems Do Americans Face?

A. Automation and Its Effects. It was not very long ago that readers of science fiction were amazed by stories about robots, machines with almost human intelligence. These stories do not impress us today because we already have such machines. They are known as computers. Computers can perform some jobs faster and more accurately than humans. They can even control other machines.

Many companies in the United States now depend on robots to improve production. Robots perform many of the tiresome and dangerous jobs once done by human workers. Computers are used in some factories to watch over the flow of materials on the assembly line. Some computers even check pollution levels. As a result, only a few workers are needed to check whether the work is done properly. The use of machines to perform work is called *automation*. It is changing our economic life, solving some problems, and creating new ones.

This new industrial revolution has brought some advantages. Wages are higher. Hours of work are shorter. There are new industries and new jobs. Some difficult and dangerous jobs have been eliminated. However, there is a price that is being paid for such progress. Some workers are losing their jobs because of automation.

635

A modern office. With the help of electronic computers, work can be done with great speed and accuracy.

At the same time, workers in other countries often are paid lower wages than in the United States. Thus many foreign products can be sold for less than the same product made in America. Consumers often prefer to buy the lower-priced foreign products. So fewer American goods are made and American workers lose their jobs. Without jobs, workers face hard times.

B. Appalachia and Other "Depressed Areas." The story of coal-mining towns in the hills of West Virginia gives us a picture of what unemployment is like. Much of this region, known as Appalachia, has needed special help from the federal government. Because of its widespread poverty, it has been called a "depressed area."

Some of the reasons for the poverty of Appalachia can be traced to automation. During the last thirty years, workers in the coal mines have been gradually replaced by machines. When people moved away to look for work, other businesses were forced to close. They didn't have enough customers. Left behind were the handicapped, people afraid to move, and older people who did not want to leave their friends. There were no new jobs to be found. People lived for a time on government, company, and union benefits. Then they dug into their life savings. Finally, most of them had to seek public assistance.

Many towns all over the United States have gone through similar experiences. They have suffered for various reasons. Sometimes workers have been replaced by machines. Or employers found it cheaper to move to new locations. Other times people bought less expensive foreign goods rather than American products. So stores or factories were forced to close their doors. But whatever the reason, these towns are facing difficult economic times.

C. Troubles in Large Industries. In the 1980s, many industrial cities in the country were approaching the title of "depressed areas." Plants

The "face of poverty." What makes places such as parts of Appalachia depressed areas?

636

that once appeared to be the source of our industrial strength—steel, autos, and rubber companies—were closing down. In the Midwest, workers were laid off and plants shut down in such steel cities as Youngstown, Ohio, and Gary, Indiana. Automobile plants, also, had to lay off a large part of their labor force because of a drop in sales. One car company received huge loans from the federal government just to stay in business. The state of Michigan, home of the largest auto manufacturers, had one of the highest unemployment rates in the nation in 1983.

What caused the troubles in our leading industries? Automation was one cause. Another was competition from foreign manufacturers. Their goods could be sold more cheaply because their expenses were less. Another was the growing practice of American companies to produce their goods abroad. In many foreign nations, workers receive much lower salaries than people doing the same kind of work in the United States. Thus, it is profitable for American companies to produce their goods in foreign factories.

D. Victims of the Agricultural Revolution. Much the same thing has happened in farming. Because of modern machinery and methods, farmers can produce larger and better crops. Big companies and wealthy farmers who can afford to buy new machines have benefited greatly. But small farmers who compete with them have suffered. Several million small owners and tenant farmers (those who rent their farmland) have left their farms for the cities. There they hope for a new job and a new life. Those who remain find their costs rising and their income falling.

Even worse off are those men and women who work on other people's farms. Most of them are migrants who "follow the harvests." They travel from place to place to pick the crops as they ripen. Farm laborers are usually paid by the amount of fruit or vegetables gathered in one day. But the work is seasonal, and they are unemployed much of the year. Now automatic pickers and harvesting machines are replacing these low-paid workers.

Harvesting wheat. In what ways has the introduction of modern farm machinery changed the lives of Americans?

E. The Unskilled and Undereducated. What happens to the miners, farmers, and other people who move to the cities? If their education has been limited, they most likely do not have the skills that industries need. But machines have reduced the number of jobs available to unskilled workers. The newcomers find their best chances for jobs in service occupations as salespeople in small stores and restaurants, and as workers in hospitals. In these occupations, wages are usually low, and the hours long. What is more, there are thousands of other people who can fill the same jobs.

The ranks of unskilled workers are also filled by another group of people, the high school dropouts. Employers naturally prefer to hire those who have graduated from high school. "If a student couldn't do well in school," they ask, "why should I expect that person to do well in my business?" When dropouts find work, it is almost always a low-paying job.

F. The Young and the Old. A high rate of unemployment has troubled the nation in recent years. From 1977 to 1982, the rate of unemployment jumped from 7 percent to over 10 percent—about 11 million workers. The jobless rate among the 15- to 20-year-old group was espe-

637

cially high. (Among black youths, the rate was over 40 percent.)

In the youth group were those who did not finish high school. However, high school graduates also found it hard to get jobs that paid well. Since employers prefer those with experience, they hire few people right out of high school. And they tend to pay them very low wages. (See chart on this page.)

Older people, too, are facing difficult times. In some industries, older people have lost their jobs. They then have a difficult time finding new work. It is often hard to acquire a new skill later in life. Many companies prefer to hire young people and train them, instead of retraining older people. As a result, some unemployed Americans find themselves "too old" to get a decent job even though they still are able to work hard.

G. The Poor in the 1980s. There were about 32 million people in our nation who were living at or below poverty level in 1981. (See chart on page 639.) This is a huge number for the richest country in the world—nearly 15 percent of the total population of the United States. The Bureau of the Census also tells us that the number of poor among Hispanics and blacks is two and three times that of whites.

HOW EDUCATION RAISES INCOME

Heads of Family (age 25 or older)	Average Family Income, 1981
5 years or more of college	$38,785
Finished college	$32,720
1 to 3 years of college	$26,873
Finished high school	$23,003
1 to 3 years of high school	$16,810
Finished grade school	$14,568
Did not finish grade school	$11,998

Source: U.S. Department of Commerce

Gray Panthers demanding improvements in the Social Security system. Many older people have joined groups such as the Gray Panthers. They seek improved conditions for the elderly.

H. People with Special Problems. The rest of the poor are hindered in other ways. Women almost always receive lower pay than men, even for the same work. This means hardship in homes where the mother is the family breadwinner. Sick people are another disadvantaged group. Employers want their workers on the job every day. They do not like to hire a person who has had a history of illness or suffers from a physical or emotional handicap. People who have been alcoholics, drug addicts, or those with prison records also find it hard to get work.

I. Effects of Poverty. "The curse of the poor is their poverty," wrote a well-known scholar more than a century ago. He meant that the poor found it hard to better themselves because poverty is a great handicap. Many poor are caught in a cycle that never seems to end. Lack of education means an unskilled job at low pay. Unskilled workers are the first to lose jobs. Since their education is poor, it is hard to find another job. Poor people live in the worst homes and apartments and probably do not eat well. They are more likely to be sick and unable to obtain proper medical care. Problems pile up. Then people lose hope that conditions will improve. This feeling of hopelessness often grips people in poverty. It affects parents and children alike. Children inherit the conditions of the poor, and those conditions tend to be passed on from one generation to the next.

J. Assistance for Those in Need. Until the New Deal of the 1930s, assistance to those in need was a problem to be solved by state and local governments. Before that time, the poor were put in county homes, working at meaningless jobs with little pay. But the Great Depression increased the number of poor so rapidly that local governments could not handle the problem.

Under the leadership of President Franklin Roosevelt, Congress began programs to care for the poor (see page 522). This help was thought to be only for the emergency of the 1930s. Few thought that aid to the needy would grow as it has in the half-century since then. President Roosevelt himself told the nation that "to dole out relief in this way is to administer a narcotic, a destroyer of the human spirit. . . ." But the Social Security Act and other New Deal legislation continued "help" programs. Step-by-step increases in assistance to the poor have been approved during the terms of almost every President since Roosevelt.

Increased concern for people living in poverty meant greater expenses for the government. In cases involving claims for assistance, courts have usually ruled that in a wealthy society such as ours, a decent living is the right of every person. As a result, such plans as Medicaid and the food stamp program were expanded both in numbers of people covered and the amount of aid given. (For more about Medicaid, see page 662.)

Most Americans would agree that government should assist those in need—that no person should be without the necessities of life. At the same time, there is a fear that the nation cannot afford to pay these costs of assistance. Some people believe that the money should be spent on our defense program or on more explorations into space.

President Carter promised to look into the welfare program when he took office. But he

---

Who Are the Poor?

In the United States in 1981, based on estimates by the Census Bureau of poverty income, almost 32 million Americans were poor (non-farm family of four with an income of less than $9,300). These include the following:

14.0 percent of all Americans are poor.
11.1 percent of whites are poor.
34.2 percent of blacks are poor.
26.5 percent of Hispanic people are poor.
15.3 percent of people 65 years and older are poor.
18.0 percent of the poor live in central cities.
23.0 percent of the poor live on farms.

Source: U.S. Department of Commerce, Bureau of the Census

Since the early 1960s, the federal Food Stamp Program has enabled millions of low-income Americans to buy more food. In what ways do you think the program has affected these people's diet and health?

quickly realized that such a task would require a tremendous amount of time and energy. In the end, few changes were made. President Reagan also was dissatisfied with our welfare system. He believed that taxpayers could not afford to spend so much on social programs. He argued that the best way to help the poor was to provide them with jobs. These jobs, he said, should come from private industry, not government. (See page 605.) As a result, Reagan requested less money for food stamps, school lunches, Medicaid, and other social programs. He proposed a New Federalism. Under this plan, several of these programs were to be turned over to the states.

REVIEWING THE SECTION

A. Knowing New Terms

In your notebook write the new terms in this section that best complete these statements.

1. Electronic machines that can do work similar to that of the human brain are known as _____.
2. The kind of production in which workers are eliminated by using machines to control other machines is known as _____.
3. Machines that perform some of the dangerous jobs once performed by workers are called _____.
4. A region that needs special help because so many people are unemployed is called a _____ _____.
5. Those who travel from place to place to pick crops are _____ farm workers.
6. A young man or woman who fails to graduate from high school is called a high school _____.
7. President Reagan's plan for turning social programs over to the states is called the _____ _____.

B. Understanding the Facts

In your notebook, write the *letter* of the correct choice.

1. A result of the new industrial revolution is that:
   a. the problem of unemployment has been reduced   b. workers are receiving higher wages and working fewer hours   c. skilled jobs are more difficult and dangerous.

2. Which of these is an example of discrimination?
    a. School dropouts find it difficult to get good jobs. b. Women are often paid less than men for the same work. c. Goods produced by lower-paid workers in a foreign country may be cheaper than American-made goods.
3. Which of these would most likely be seen in a "depressed area"?
    a. Farming with crop-picking machinery b. People working in service occupations c. Empty factory buildings d. Computers in stores and businesses.
4. A reason why some people are able to get only low-paying jobs is:
    a. lack of education b. poor health c. lack of a skill or trade d. all of these reasons.
5. When did the federal government begin programs to help poor people?
    a. In the late nineteenth century b. Under the New Deal c. After World War II d. With the War on Poverty.
6. In addition to automation, a cause of large unemployment at present is that:
    a. some workers are asked to take dangerous jobs b. foreign manufacturers are producing goods more cheaply than American manufacturers c. more goods are being produced than people can buy.
7. President Reagan's policy regarding poverty programs was to:
    a. increase research in automation for large industries b. depend more heavily on private industry for help c. increase the food stamp program to include more people in need.
8. Which of the following statements best describes how our nation tried to deal with poverty from 1930 to 1980?
    a. The federal government has reduced the amount of assistance to older people. b. Courts have ruled that there are only a few cases in which the government can give medical assistance. c. Government assistance programs have helped an increasing number of people. d. The government has stopped its aid to poor people, except for medical benefits.

IMPROVING YOUR SKILLS

Interpreting Tables and Graphs

A. The Table. Study the table on page 638. Then tell which of these statements best expresses the main idea of the table.

1. All heads of families who have finished high school are guaranteed an income of over $30,000.
2. A person who finishes high school will probably make as much money as a person who has finished college.
3. The greater the amount of education a person receives, the greater will be his or her income.

B. The Graph. Study the graph below (The Increasing Cost of Public Assistance). Then complete the following statements in your notebook.

THE INCREASING COST OF PUBLIC ASSISTANCE*

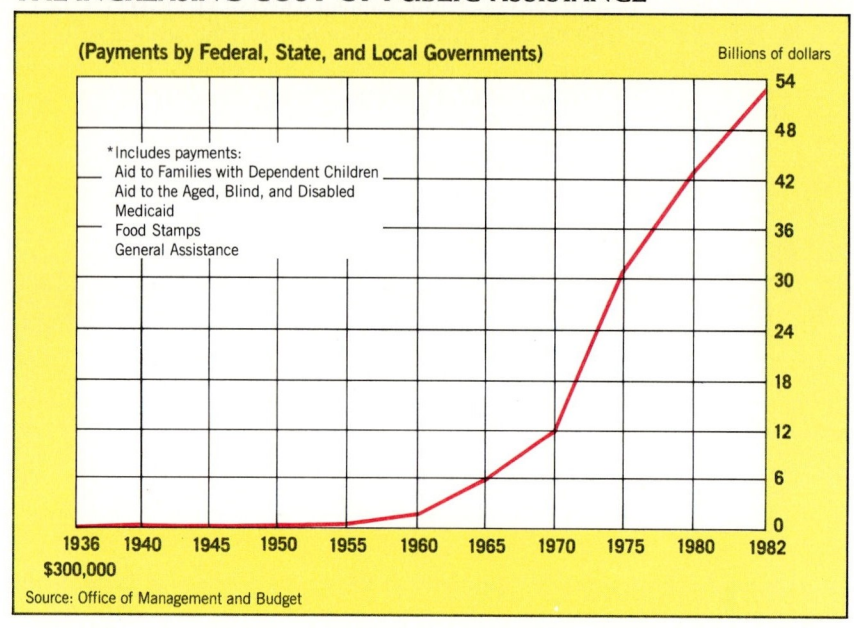

(Payments by Federal, State, and Local Governments) — Billions of dollars

*Includes payments:
— Aid to Families with Dependent Children
— Aid to the Aged, Blind, and Disabled
— Medicaid
— Food Stamps
— General Assistance

1936 $300,000 — 1940 — 1945 — 1950 — 1955 — 1960 — 1965 — 1970 — 1975 — 1980 — 1982

Source: Office of Management and Budget

1. The cost of public assistance programs (increased, dropped, changed very little) _____ in the years 1940–1945.
2. The total cost of public assistance programs in 1950 was about $_____.
3. Between 1965 and 1970, public assistance costs increased by about $_____ billion.
4. The cost of public assistance programs in 1980 was about $_____ billion.
5. The greatest five-year increase in public assistance costs took place between the years _____ and _____, a total of $_____ billion.

Chapter 36

IMPROVING THE QUALITY OF AMERICAN LIFE

WE AMERICANS LIKE TO THINK that we enjoy one of the highest standards of living in the world. Many people of other countries disagree. They admit that we have the most automobiles, TV sets, telephones, and household conveniences. But they point out that our way of life has some serious defects. Many Americans are victims of poverty and prejudice. Millions suffer the effects of polluted (dirt-filled) air and water, crowded cities, crime, and unemployment. Over the years, these problems have been handled in different ways.

In this chapter, you will find answers to these five questions:

1. What special problems do American city dwellers face?
2. Why has conservation of our natural resources become more and more important?
3. How is our nation meeting the crisis in energy needs?
4. How has our way of life affected our people, our human resources?
5. What measures have been taken by the government and public to solve these problems?

What Problems Do Cities Face?

A. Growth of Cities. "Would you rather live in a big city or in the country?" Ask the average American this question and he or she may well answer, "I prefer the country. A big city may be a good place to visit, but I wouldn't want to live there." In spite of this attitude, the United States has become a nation of city dwellers during the past hundred years or so. In 1880, most Americans lived in the country. In 1980, the United States Bureau of the Census reported that nearly 75 percent of Americans lived in an urban environment—that is, in or near a city. At the same time, only 2.4 percent of the population lived on farms. The movement of people to the city has been called the "urban revolution." It has greatly changed the American way of life. Like other revolutions we have studied, the urban revolution has brought important benefits but also has created serious problems.

B. The City's Attractions. Why did millions of Americans leave the country, which they say they prefer, to live in the cities? The answer is the great change in industry and agriculture that took place after the Civil War. Thanks to modern methods of farming, a small part of our population can feed all the rest. Jobs in farming have been disappearing. At the same time the number of jobs in or near cities had grown because of the expansion of industry and trade there. People who could not find work in the country came to the city. The chance to improve one's economic standing has been the city's strongest attraction. Cities often offered better public and private schools than the small rural districts.

Because of its large population, the city offers a number of other advantages. It is easy for almost any kind of person to find friends there. It is also easy to buy any kind of merchandise because city stores are usually nearby and well stocked. The city offers greater opportunity for health and medical care, including hospitals and clinics for special illnesses. Cities are the centers of the news media—television, radio, newspapers, magazines, and books of every kind. The city is especially good for entertainment. City people have their pick of plays, movies, concerts, and sports events.

C. Drawbacks of City Life. 1. CROWDS. One reason why some Americans dislike the city is crowding. So many people are trying to live in comfort in one small area. Yet, even with the crowds, people can feel very lonely in the city because they are surrounded by strangers.

New York City at night. What are some of the advantages of living in a large city?

2. POLLUTION. Waters around our nation's cities have become more and more polluted because of the waste matter from factories and homes. In some cities, getting good drinking water or finding a safe place to swim has become a major problem.

Air pollution is another serious problem. Many industrial cities suffer from smog (a smoky fog). Smog is caused by tons of waste matter that gasoline-burning motors, coal-burning or oil-burning furnaces, and some industrial plants pour into the air every day. Smog not only dirties everything in the city, it hurts the eyes, throat, and lungs. Some chemicals in smog can turn into acid and eat away the stone and metal walls of buildings. Fortunately, some cities have made progress in their efforts to solve the smog problem. Pittsburgh, Pennsylvania, and Chattanooga, Tennessee, once considered to be among the dirtiest cities in the nation, are outstanding examples of how smog can be reduced, if not eliminated entirely.

3. NOISE. Noise can also be a polluter. Visitors are more likely to notice city noise than the people of the city themselves. Some experts feel that the noise level of our cities is too high and is a health hazard. Noise levels may be especially high near airports. Our modern airports, in most cases, have been located several miles from the edge of the city. But spreading suburbs now surround many of them.

4. CRIME. When people of several large cities were asked what they thought was their own city's greatest problem, crime was usually the answer. The rate of crimes in large cities is over four times that of rural areas, and nearly twice that of surburbs. (Crime rate is the number of serious crimes per 100,000 people.) The crime rate is highest in the poorer sections of cities. In these areas, crimes like murder and assault are often committed by poor people against other poor people.

5. OTHER PROBLEMS. Because they are so large and so complex, modern cities have other difficult problems. A heavy snowstorm, a strike, or a power failure can stop normal activities for days at a time. With many people living together, disease epidemics are a constant threat. Fires can spread quickly from one building to another. To deal with these problems, cities have large police and fire departments, public health services, and other costly facilities.

D. The Flight to the Suburbs. To escape these disadvantages, millions of Americans have moved to the suburbs, the smaller towns around big cities. Suburbs often have been called "bedroom towns" because their inhabitants sleep there but make their living in the nearby city. This has changed somewhat, however, as industry, jobs, sports complexes, and shopping centers have moved to the suburbs, too. Many families moved to the suburbs so that the children could attend the new suburban public schools.

From 1960 to 1980, the movement out of the cities into the suburbs continued at a strong pace. The suburbs have spread so fast that they have swallowed up the open countryside. Along the highways outside any of the largest cities of our country, there is one suburb after another. A large part of the Atlantic Coast from Massachusetts to Virginia has become one long city. This "supercity" or "strip city" contains one-fifth of the nation's total population. Other supercities have developed in almost every part of the nation. (See map on page 646.)

Suburban America. What are some of the advantages of living in a suburb?

The 1980 census reveals that people are now moving even farther away from large cities. In the 1970s, smaller towns and rural areas grew faster than large urban areas for the first time since 1820. Americans are also moving from the Northeast and Midwest to the newer cities of the South and West—the "Sunbelt." Five Sunbelt cities—Los Angeles, Dallas, San Diego, Houston, and San Antonio—now rank among the nation's ten largest cities.

E. Effects on the City. The growth of suburbs has caused problems for the big city. The city has the expense of providing trains, buses, roads, and parking spaces for many thousands of commuters. These are the people who travel from their homes in the suburbs to their jobs in the city. Commuters often pay little or no tax to the city government. As many middle-class or upper middle-class families have moved to the suburbs, people who are poorer have no choice but to stay in the cities. Yet the cities have less money to spend on helping these people. As a result, cities now have a higher poverty rate than rural areas.

Industries have fled from the city to the suburbs to escape high rents or transportation costs. This means a loss of jobs for people who remain in the city. People without jobs cannot pay taxes. But the expense of services in the city is rising each year. Thus the tax burden falls heavily on people and industries that stay in the city. With income falling and costs rising, many cities are in danger of financial collapse.

Perhaps a worse danger for cities is the growing separation of society—a class of middle-income whites living in suburbs and small towns, and a class of low-income blacks and other minorities living in our cities. One recalls the prediction of the National Commission on Civil Disorders (see page 620), "Our nation is moving

GIANT URBAN AREAS OF THE UNITED STATES

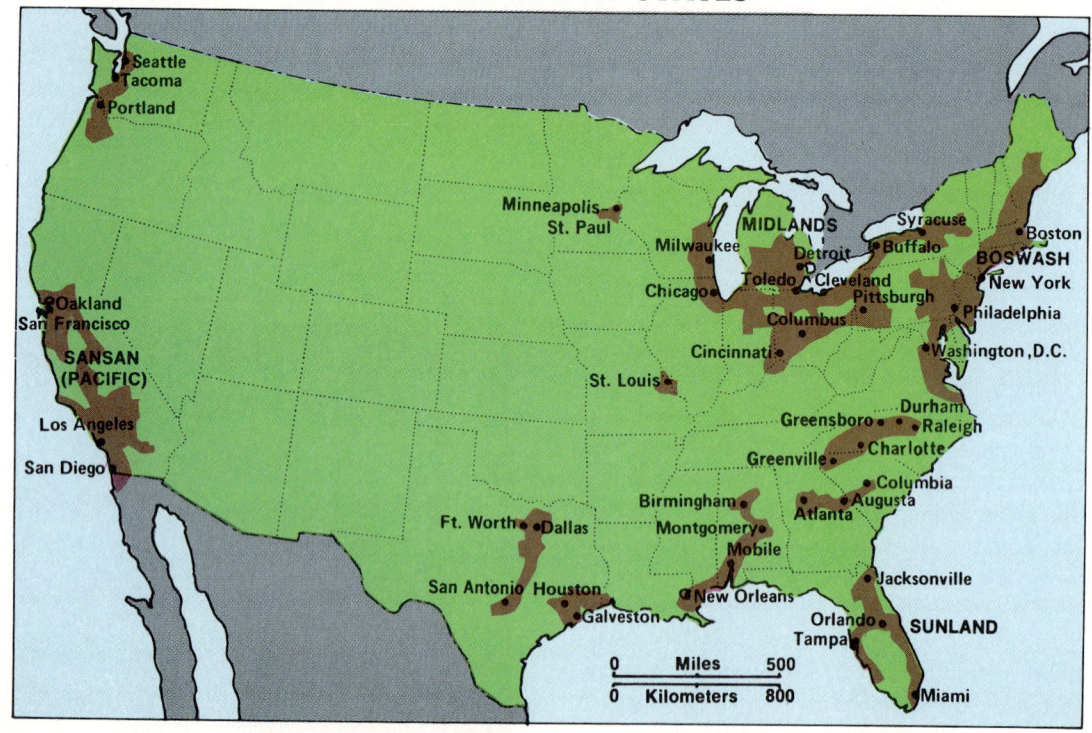

toward two societies, one black, one white—separate and unequal. . . ." Blacks make up 12 percent of our population. They are now in the majority in Cleveland, Newark, Baltimore, Washington, Richmond, Detroit, and Atlanta.

F. Solving Urban Problems. How have American cities been trying to solve their problems? To bring back businesses and the well-to-do taxpayers, many cities have tried "urban renewal" programs. Slums and older buildings in the central part of the city are torn down. New office buildings, large shopping centers, and expensive apartment houses are built in their places. In this way, the city's most valuable land is used to attract businesses and people with high incomes. But the people whose homes were torn down cannot afford to live in the new apartments. They are moved to low-cost housing in outlying areas or crowded into substandard housing elsewhere in the city.

To solve the traffic problem, some cities have blocked off large sections of the downtown area for convenient shopping. Parking spaces are provided on the outskirts of the city. Mass transportation facilities (trains and buses) also have been improved. The plan is to have people from the suburbs drive to the outskirts of the city, park their cars there, and take fast trains or buses into the city. San Francisco and Washington have recently completed modern, rapid train systems that speed passengers in and out of the downtown area.

Steps to control air and water pollution have not been completely successful. There are several reasons for this. First, the cost is high—much higher than any city can afford by itself. Second, the city can control only the land within its borders. But pollution involves the surrounding suburbs as well. These areas have their own local governments. Most people living in the suburbs do not want to become involved with city problems. In many cases, they moved to the suburbs to avoid these problems. As a result, the problems of urban and suburban living have become the concern of state and federal governments.

A Bay Area Rapid Transit train in San Francisco. Why do many cities need modern mass transportation systems such as trains, subways, and buses?

G. The Federal Role. Many of the programs of President Lyndon Johnson's Great Society dealt with urban problems. But the billions of dollars spent on these programs did not solve urban problems. In 1965, Congress created a new executive department, the Department of Housing and Urban Development (HUD). HUD has provided funds for communities to build housing units for senior citizens and low-income families. Another new department concerned with city problems, the Department of Transportation, was created in 1966. Its purpose was to supervise federal aid to our nation's highways. The first secretary of the department was Robert C. Weaver, the first black to hold a cabinet position.

Under President Gerald Ford, most programs to aid cities were combined into the Community Development Program. However, decisions about how to spend this aid were left up to the local governments. As President, Jimmy Carter also put into effect a limited federal program to aid urban areas.

By 1980, almost one-fourth of the income of cities came from federal grants. Over the years, cities came to depend on federal monies to provide a variety of services. Under President Reagan, however, such aid to cities was greatly reduced. The administration believed that cities should take better charge of their financial affairs. Throughout the country, cities felt the pinch of reduced funds. To make up for the loss in federal aid, cities had to raise taxes, reduce services, or eliminate some jobs.

H. One Person—One Vote. Until the 1960s, the number of people included in state legislative districts varied greatly. In some states, state representatives had been elected from districts established years before. According to plan, each district was supposed to have about the same number of people. But as cities grew in population, the old districts remained.

As a result of these population changes, people in cities did not have representatives on the same basis as less-populated districts. In Connecticut, for example, a rural district of 800 people and a city of 15,000 each had one representative. In Georgia, rural districts with 200,000 people had the same representation as Atlanta with almost 500,000 people.

In 1962, the Supreme Court, in considering a case about the problem of representation, decided that every American citizen is entitled to equal treatment under the law. This means that districts should be as equal in population as a state can make them. And such districts must have equal representation. In some states, urban lawmakers now outnumber representatives from rural districts. In those states there are more city people than rural residents. It would seem that urban problems now have a much better chance of receiving a fair hearing from state lawmakers.

REVIEWING THE SECTION

A. Knowing New Terms

PART 1. In your notebook write the new terms in this section that best complete the statements.

1. The shift in population from the country to the city in the past century is called the _____ revolution.
2. One of the biggest problems of modern city life is the dirtying or _____ of the air and water.
3. Unless the wind is blowing, some cities are covered with a blanket of foul air known as _____ .
4. The smaller towns around a big city are called its _____ .
5. Many people are eager to live in the South and West in an area called the _____ .
6. People who live in suburbs but travel daily to work in the city are called _____ .

PART 2. Explain each statement *in your own words*.

(In **A**) "A big city may be a good place to visit, but I wouldn't want to live there."
(In **C2**) "If the water we drink doesn't kill us, the air we breathe will."
(In **D**) Suburbs are often called "bedroom towns."

B. Knowing Important Facts

Complete this chart by listing in your notebook the measures being taken to solve each problem.

Problems of the Cities   *Remedies*

1. Traffic jams   1. a. _____
                                                b. _____
                                                c. _____

2. Water and air pollution   2. a. _____
                                                b. _____
                                                c. _____

3. Flight of the well-to-do   3. a. _____
   to the suburbs   b. _____
                                                c. _____

4. Large number of poor people   4. a. _____
                                                b. _____
                                                c. _____

C. Finding the Reasons

In your notebook write the letters of *all* the correct answers to each question.
1. Why do people in some countries think that the United States does *not* have one of the highest standards of living in the world?
   a. They have more autos, TV sets, and telephones than we do.
   b. Millions of Americans are poor.   c. Many Americans suffer disadvantages because they live in big cities.
2. Why did millions of Americans move from the country to the city during the past century?
   a. The cities offer better health care, entertainment, and education than rural areas.   b. Fewer and fewer people were needed for farming.
   c. More and more people were needed for industry and commerce.
3. Why has air pollution become an important problem for cities?
   a. The number of autos, trucks, and buses is increasing.   b. Our factories keep growing in number and size.   c. Changes in climate have resulted in fewer windy days.
4. Why have millions of Americans moved from the cities to the suburbs during the past 30 years?
   a. They hoped to escape the disadvantages of city life.   b. They liked living in places with more space.   c. They did not like to travel to work.
5. Why are many cities short of money in the 1980s?
   a. The cost of providing needed services has gone up.   b. Most commuters pay little or no tax to the city government.   c. Funds from the federal government have been reduced.

6. Why do cities need the help of state and federal governments?
   a. They cannot afford the cost of solving their problems.   b. Many of their problems involve the surrounding areas.   c. City governments are usually dishonest and badly run.
7. Why was the Supreme Court's decision concerning "One person—one vote" so important to cities?
   a. It reduced dishonesty in city governments.   b. It insisted that cities should have fair representation in the state legislatures.   c. It made the federal government more democratic.

IMPROVING YOUR SKILLS

A. Mastering the Map

Study the map on page 646. Then answer the following questions.
1. Which strip cities extend along the east and west coasts?
2. What are the major cities in BosWash?
3. Which strip cities are not near large bodies of water?

B. Looking at Both Sides

1. List in your notebook the advantages of city life given in this section, and others you may think of.
2. List the disadvantages of city life in this section and any others you may think of.
3. On the whole, where would you prefer to live—in the city, in the country, or in a suburb? Explain why.

MAKING HISTORY LIVE

1. Draw a cartoon showing the advantages or problems of city life.
2. Prepare for a class debate on the question, Should people who live in the suburbs pay taxes in the city where they work?
3. People in a community want a playground built on a vacant lot. Some city officials want an office building there in order to bring more money to the city. What arguments can you offer for or against one of these positions?
4. Research current magazines, newspapers, and reports for classroom displays. Among the topics you can choose are (1) crime rates—a comparison of rates in large cities and in suburban and rural areas; (2) local and ethnic populations of your city or community; (3) where your community gets its income and how it is spent; or (4) news items and reports of federal programs to aid cities.
5. Make a report on air or water pollution in your community. Find out what the main causes of pollution are and what is being done about them.

How Can We Conserve Our Natural Resources?

A. The Nature of the Problem. "From shirt-sleeves to shirt-sleeves in three generations" has been the sad experience of many an American family. The first generation was poor to start with, but worked hard and saved. The second generation used the savings to build a future. The third spent the fortune carelessly and ended up poor.

Some experts fear the United States is following the same path. Our early ancestors worked hard to lay the foundations for our nation's wealth. The generations that followed made the United States rich and powerful. Are we now wasting our wealth with the result that the next generation will be poor?

Natural resources are the basis of our nation's wealth. Our nation has been using its resources at an unbelievable rate. We have already taken from the earth as much coal, petroleum, iron ore, and other resources as the entire human race in all previous history. Even now, we are using as much as the rest of the world combined. And the amount continues to increase as our production of goods and our use of automobiles and home conveniences increase. Can we continue to use our resources at this rate? Let us look at the situation in our country today.

B. The Water Problem. Water is a resource no one can do without. According to some experts, however, the United States is running out of clear, usable water. For example, one expert on the water situation writes that, "unless we learn very quickly how to trap it [water], conserve it, share it, keep it unpolluted . . . and move it from one place to another, we are going to be in desperate straits [a difficult position]."

Dams, channels, and reservoirs trap water over thousands of square miles for use by the millions of people in large urban areas. Yet some of our largest cities have faced water shortages when there has been less than normal rainfall over a period of a few years. Many of the water systems that supply our older cities are a hundred years old. They are badly in need of repair. Some leak as much water as they deliver. One northeastern city estimates that its water lines leak two gallons of water for every gallon delivered to homes and industry.

Over the years there have been several periods of drought in the Southwest. In dry western states, water has been pumped from underground lakes or pools to irrigate farm lands. For many years, farmers have managed to make the desert bloom with crops, by flooding fields with cheap water. Those days appear to be coming to an end. Irrigated crop lands now use more than 80 percent of the water used in the nation. Water is being taken from underground lakes faster than nature can restore it.

New Jersey Girl Scouts, U.S.A., assisted by Boy Scouts, remove trash from the Hackensack River. What are community groups in your area doing to fight pollution?

Industry use has also grown rapidly. It requires 100,000 gallons of water, for example, to manufacture a single automobile. Individual use has been growing by leaps and bounds. In 1900, the average American used about 6 gallons of water a day. Now the amount is 150 gallons. At the present rate of growth, by the year 2000, our nation could be using 50 times as much water as it did in 1900.

At the same time that our need for fresh water has increased, damage to our supply of water has reached a serious level. In 1971, the Council on Environmental Quality announced that nearly all of our rivers were polluted to some degree. As a result of this and other reports, Congress passed the Water Pollution Control Act in 1972. This act provided for the spending of billions of dollars in the construction of sewage treatment plants. These plants contain equipment to treat, or clean up, the raw sewage (untreated waste matter) in the water. The law aimed at stopping the dumping of raw sewage in the nation's water by 1985. Heavy fines were to be imposed on industries that violated the law. Many large industries have opposed the enforcement of the law, pointing to the increased cost of changing their factories and equipment to meet the requirements set by Congress.

In 1977, the purity of our drinking water came under the supervision of the federal government for the first time. Until that year, only a few water systems were regulated directly by the federal government. The Safe Drinking Water Act of 1974 provides that the water in our 240,000 water systems has to meet federal drinking water safety standards.

C. Proposed Solutions. One of the ways to meet any problem of scarcity is to increase the supply. The United States has a plentiful supply of rainfall—greater than the amount of water we use. Much more water could be saved by the building of dams by the federal, state, and local governments. Old water systems can be repaired or replaced. The value of these solutions has to be measured against the cost of such construction.

Much water is also wasted through the pollution of waterways by cities and industries that have used them as sewers. Discoveries of ways to make sewage and factory wastes harmless can be put to use. Another way to increase the water supply is by desalting seawater. This is expensive, but it is being done in other countries where water is scarce.

These proposals will cost billions of dollars and take many years to carry out. For the present, the best way to deal with scarcity is to reduce use of water. Farmers can cut down on water for irrigation where possible. In some areas they can use better methods of dry farming—the production of crops on dry land without irrigation. Dry farmers plant crops that can endure drought. They use methods that allow the soil to receive and hold water and prevent it from evaporating. Industries can use the same water over and over again if it is not polluted. The average American can be aware of the need for saving water, and can practice water saving in homes in daily use. That this can be done was demonstrated by people in California cities in the drought of the spring of 1977. Within a few weeks, people had reduced their use of water by one-third when the emergency arose.

Irrigation canal in the Palo Verde Valley in California. Who else besides farmers benefits from irrigation projects?

D. Forests and Soil. By 1900, careless logging methods and forest fires had destroyed half the forests that once covered so much of the nation. Our country began to import large amounts of timber from other countries. Today, the future is much brighter. Timber is a resource that can be renewed. Improved cutting methods, replanting, and faster-maturing trees have actually increased our total acreage of forests in the last generation.

The waste of our soil became a matter of great concern in the 1930s. Millions of tons of topsoil were being washed away by floods or blown away by winds each year. Experts feared that large areas of our nation would become desert unless strong measures were taken to reduce erosion (wearing away) of the soil.

The situation has improved a great deal since that time, thanks largely to New Deal measures like the AAA and TVA (see pages 527 and 528). Farmers have learned to plow in ways that reduce erosion. They have also learned to plant trees and grasses on unused farmland to enrich the soil and protect it from erosion. Yet the danger of loss of precious soil in periods of drought remains. Despite the increased use of new fertilizers and improved seeds, the increasing population of the nation demands that our valuable soils be saved.

Measures taken to conserve our soils have proved to be a benefit for the American people. Our vast areas of fertile farmland have been able to produce more food than our people need. The rising standard of living in some foreign countries has created new markets for American farm products. The nation's production of grain has caused a problem of overabundance. What should be done with surplus food? How much should be saved for possible lean years? How much should be sold or given to poorer nations of the world? How much help should the federal government give when surplus crops cause a drop in food prices?

E. Our Metal Resources. Once the United States seemed to have an unlimited supply of some metal resources. The region near Lake Superior held large and rich deposits of iron ore. Today, most of these rich ores have been exhausted. Large deposits still remain, but they are mostly low-grade and costly to refine. Today, imports of iron ore provide almost one-third of the demand by our nation's industries. The farther the nation must look for imports in the future, the higher will be the cost of producing iron and steel.

The United States is still one of the world's largest producers of copper. But tin, tungsten, manganese, and chromite, all important in industrial production, must be imported. It is clear that our resources can no longer be used as freely as in the past. It is almost certain that the United States will have to import more and more from other countries if our standard of living is to be maintained. The dependence of our nation on other peoples of the world is a reality.

Using a computer to study a tree. How do Americans benefit from scientific methods of forest management and conservation?

REVIEWING THE SECTION

A. Knowing Important Facts

For each problem in the first column, write the solutions mentioned in the text.

Problems of Conservation	Proposed Solutions
1. Water shortage	1. a. _____ b. _____ c. _____
2. Destruction of forests	2. a. _____ b. _____ c. _____
3. Soil erosion	3. a. _____ b. _____ c. _____
4. Shortages of iron ore and other minerals	4. a. _____ b. _____ c. _____

B. Understanding the Facts

In your notebook write the *letter* of the correct choice.

1. A nation's natural resources are important because:
   a. it is sure to become great if it has a large supply of them   b. it is certain to remain poor if it does not have rich resources   c. its businesses can produce goods at lower cost if resources are plentiful and cheap   d. all these statements are true.
2. During the nineteenth century, the United States used up a large part of its natural resources because:
   a. the American people thought the supply was almost unlimited   b. farmers and business people were very careless in using them   c. the federal government was not interested in conserving them   d. all these things happened.
3. During the twentieth century, efforts have been made to conserve our natural resources through:
   a. government control of their use   b. better ways of farming, logging, and mining   c. the discovery of new sources and substitutes   d. all these approaches.
4. Our water problem can be helped by:
   a. cutting down the use of water by agriculture, industry, and the public   b. reducing the runoff of rain water   c. treating sewage and industrial wastes to reduce water pollution   d. all of these solutions.

5. In dealing with soil erosion, our nation has:
   a. failed to take effective action   b. made some progress in recent years   c. made great progress in the last 40 years   d. completely solved the problem.
6. In the case of metal resources, our nation has:
   a. plenty of every important metal   b. large supplies of all metal resources except iron ore   c. many metals in lower-grade ores and the need for some imported ones   d. severe shortages of every important metal.
7. The Water Pollution Control Act:
   a. guaranteed the purity of drinking water   b. provided for fines to be imposed on families that dumped sewage into rivers and streams   c. limited the amount of water an individual can use daily   d. provided funds for the construction of sewage treatment plants.
8. In the United States, the greatest amount of water is used:
   a. in individual bathing   b. in the manufacture of aluminum   c. as a result of leaks in older water systems   d. in the irrigation of crop lands.

MAKING HISTORY LIVE

1. Report on one of our nation's natural resources. Tell how it is taken from the earth and processed and what its main uses are.
2. Make a list of common daily activities. Show how each activity depends upon natural resources. Note which of these resources were probably imported from abroad.
3. a. Draw a poster urging conservation of one of our natural resources.
   b. Draw a cartoon to show how we have wasted our resources in the past.
4. Contribute to a class display on our nation's natural resources. Show how we use each resource, what we are doing to conserve it, and what else we should be doing.

How Can the Nation Meet Its Energy Needs?

A. The Energy Crisis. When the Arab-Israeli war began in the fall of 1973, Americans had little idea that it would reveal the crisis in energy resources in the United States. But it did just that. The Arab countries together are the world's largest producers of crude oil (see chart, page 657). Shortly after the outbreak of war in the Middle East, the Arab nations announced that no oil would be shipped to countries supporting Israel in the conflict. This refusal to sell a product to certain areas is called an embargo. At that time, about one of every five barrels of oil used in the United States came from Arab nations. The loss of this vital supply of oil changed America's view of its energy resources. Americans began to realize that their supply of fuel for cars, homes, and factories was not endless.

In the next few months, oil companies nearly doubled the price of gasoline and fuel oil for homes. Cars formed lines blocks long to get their supply of valuable gasoline at filling stations. The number of car pools increased dramatically. President Nixon asked for emergency measures from Congress. A speed limit of 55 miles an hour was set for the nation's highways. Outdoor lighting was limited and gasoline rationing was authorized. Congress later passed laws requiring auto manufacturers to increase the production of cars that would travel farther on a gallon of fuel.

In March 1974, the Arab countries ended their embargo of oil to the United States. But the Arab countries belonged to a special organization of oil-producing countries. This Organization of Petroleum (oil) Exporting Countries (OPEC) raised the price of the oil that its members were exporting to the rest of the world. So the United States had to pay very high prices for oil from OPEC members.

During the crisis, Congress approved the building of an Alaskan oil pipeline. This 800-mile pipeline was completed in the summer of 1977. Since that time, the Alaskan pipeline has delivered over a million barrels of oil a day. However, the success of the pipeline did not eliminate our need to import oil. Today the United States imports nearly two billion barrels of the crude oil it needs for business and personal use (see chart, page 658). Our nation has learned some lessons from the embargo of 1973. Americans now use much less oil than they did in the early 1970s.

It had been known for some time that our supply of petroleum was running low. One solution

Long lines of cars waiting for gasoline during the oil embargo of late 1973 and early 1974. Is the United States now less dependent on foreign oil?

THE LARGEST OIL-PRODUCING NATIONS

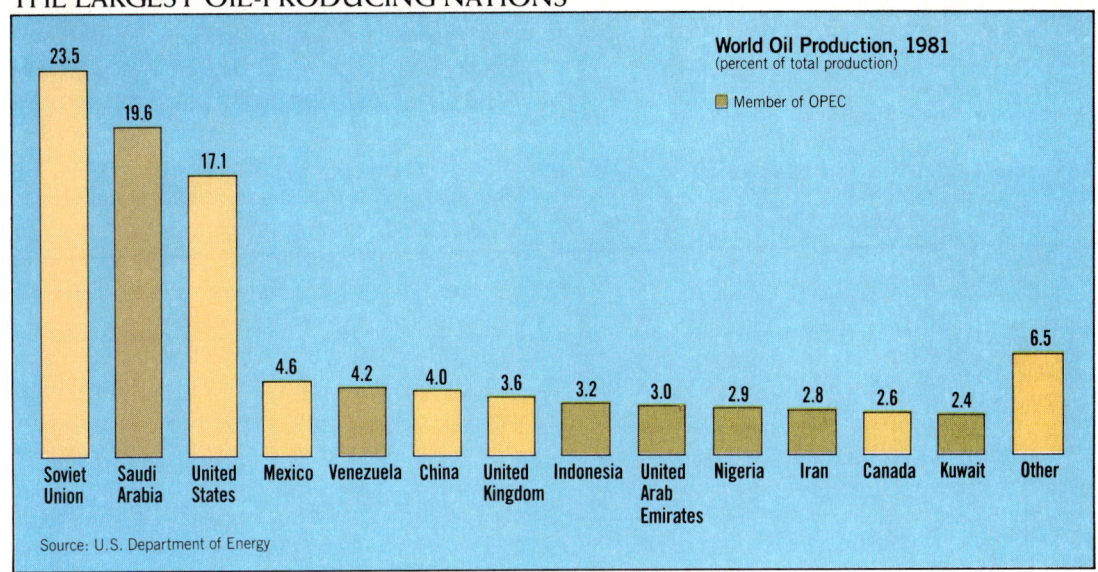

World Oil Production, 1981
(percent of total production)
■ Member of OPEC

Country	Percent
Soviet Union	23.5
Saudi Arabia	19.6
United States	17.1
Mexico	4.6
Venezuela	4.2
China	4.0
United Kingdom	3.6
Indonesia	3.2
United Arab Emirates	3.0
Nigeria	2.9
Iran	2.8
Canada	2.6
Kuwait	2.4
Other	6.5

Source: U.S. Department of Energy

was to dig deeper wells on land and beneath the seas along our shores. This "offshore" drilling has increased greatly since the oil shortages of 1973. It was also discovered that petroleum can be gotten from shale (a kind of rock) in the Rocky Mountains. Thus far, this source of energy has proved expensive to develop.

Early in his term of office, President Carter proposed an energy plan to cut United States energy demands. He suggested an increase in oil and gas prices, better insulation for homes, and a tax on cars that are "gas-guzzlers." In response to our energy needs, Congress, in 1977, approved the establishment of a new executive department, the Department of Energy. This new department helps develop our nation's energy policy. It also promotes the conservation of energy and controls the use of nuclear power.

B. Other Energy Sources. 1. COAL. Our nation's main fuel, other than petroleum, is coal. Neither of these fuel resources can be replaced. Unlike petroleum, however, our coal supply should last for hundreds of years. Because of these large amounts of coal, scientists and energy experts have been looking for ways to increase its use. For example, the Energy Security Act of 1980 called for new power and industrial plants to use fuels other than oil or natural gas. There have been problems, however, with increasing coal production. First, creating new kinds of

The Alaska pipe line carries oil across Alaska, from its northern source at Prudhoe Bay to the port of Valdez in the south. Why was the United States willing to pay billions of dollars for it?

SHARE OF TOTAL U.S. OIL USE FROM IMPORTS

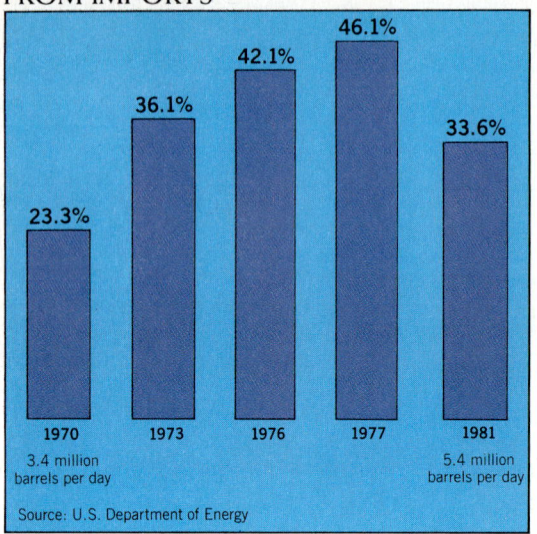

Year	Percentage
1970	23.3%
1973	36.1%
1976	42.1%
1977	46.1%
1981	33.6%

1970: 3.4 million barrels per day
1981: 5.4 million barrels per day
Source: U.S. Department of Energy

fuels from coal can be expensive. Second, some people claim that additional mining will ruin the beauty of our landscape. Finally, burning coal often pollutes the air.

2. NATURAL GAS AND WATER. Oil reserves can be saved by using substitutes. Our large deposits of natural gas have been put to use in the past generation. Even now, however, the supply of natural gas has been reduced dangerously. Much of this fuel has been imported. Some producers say that the price of natural gas must be increased to make it worthwhile for them to search for new gas fields. Water power is a second substitute. It has an important advantage. It can never be used up. Many hydroelectric plants, which use water to make electricity, now dot our nation. But hydroelectric plants can supply only a small part of our energy needs because the number of good sites is limited. At present, only about 3 percent of our power needs are satisfied by the use of hydroelectric power.

3. NUCLEAR POWER. By the early 1980s, nuclear power plants were set up in many parts of the country. At present, only about 12 percent of our total energy source comes from nuclear power. Some experts believe that nuclear reactors can meet most of our energy needs in the future. But plans to expand the use of nuclear energy have met with some problems.

The most serious problem took place in 1979. In that year, there was a breakdown in the cooling system of the Three Mile Island nuclear power plant near Harrisburg, Pennsylvania. This caused some radioactive gas to escape into the air. Fortunately, experts were able to correct the problem and no lives were lost.

The problems at Three Mile Island gave support to people who claimed that nuclear power plants are dangerous and ought to be closed down. The greatest objection to nuclear power is that reactors produce radioactive wastes. That is, they give off rays that are dangerous to health. These wastes can remain radioactive for thousands of years. Where can the wastes be safely stored? Not surprisingly, many states have objected to the use of their land as dumping sites for radioactive materials.

Presidents Carter and Reagan believed in the value of nuclear power in our nation's future. They pointed out that the danger at Three Mile Island was the result of poor training of employees, not the reactor itself. Under President Rea-

A nuclear power plant. Many people believe that nuclear power offers a good source of energy for our nation. Others say that the dangers from atomic radiation outweigh any advantages.

gan, the federal government spent billions of dollars to clean up sites where nuclear waste materials had been stored.

C. New Sources of Energy. Can we find new energy from old sources? Some scientists and engineers believe there are other sources of energy that can replace our present fuels. The idea of heating homes with the warm rays of the sun (solar energy) is gaining in popularity. Schools in several large cities are experimenting with solar units to provide classroom warmth. The National Science Foundation is experimenting with the idea of producing electricity from solar heat in desert areas. The federal government is spending 50 times what was once spent for research in solar energy. But, even with success in such research, it will be many years before the sun can become a major source of usable energy.

Geothermal energy (heat from within the earth) is also the basis of research. Hot springs called geysers send up fountains or jets of hot water or steam. The steam or hot water can be used to provide electricity and heat. Areas of some states in the Far West have been marked as "known geothermal resource areas" by the federal government. One such area in northern California produces energy from geysers that equals the energy production of a nuclear power plant.

REVIEWING THE SECTION

A. Knowing New Terms

Explain each term in your notebook *in your own words.*

(In **A**) embargo
(In **A**) "offshore" drilling
(In **A**) "gas-guzzler"
(In **A**) OPEC
(In **B**) hydroelectric
(In **C**) geothermal

B. Understanding the Facts

Write in your notebook all the letters of *all* the correct answers to each question.

1. What did the federal government do in response to the oil embargo by Arab states?
   a. It doubled the price of gasoline. b. It set a speed limit of 55 miles an hour on the nation's highways. c. It placed a heavy tax on the purchase of new cars. d. It did all of these.

2. The growing shortage of petroleum resources has led to:
   a. the use of natural gas as a substitute in home heating   b. the digging of deeper wells   c. the drilling under the seas near our coasts   d. all of these.
3. The Alaskan oil pipeline:
   a. made the United States the leading oil producer in the world   b. ended the nation's dependence on foreign oil   c. was speeded up by the oil embargo of 1973   d. caused a sharp decline in gasoline prices.
4. Opponents of the use of nuclear power plants would argue that:
   a. nuclear reactors ruin the beauty of the landscape   b. there have been serious accidents at nuclear power plants   c. our supply of uranium will soon be used up   d. radioactive wastes remain dangerous for years.
5. The natural resource that presents the *least* problem in conservation at present is:
   a. coal   b. petroleum   c. iron ore   d. natural gas.
6. Hydroelectric power supplies only a small part of our total power needs at present because:
   a. it is expensive   b. the number of good sites is limited   c. the water supply is easily used up   d. there is opposition to its use because of the dangers involved.
7. The shortage of petroleum might be overcome by:
   a. increasing the use of solar energy   b. developing other energy sources within the earth   c. doing research to uncover new sources of oil   d. all of these.
8. Sources of geothermal energy thus far have been discovered:
   a. in the states of the Atlantic coast   b. in areas of the Far West   c. off the shores of the Gulf of Mexico   d. along the Great Lakes.

IMPROVING YOUR SKILLS

Interpreting the Graphs

Study the graphs on pages 657 and 658. Then do the following exercise:

1. How many countries produce more oil than the United States?
2. What African countries are major oil producers? Which are members of OPEC?
3. From which country or countries in the Americas might the United States find a source of oil for import?
4. In which period was there the greatest increase in the import of oil?
5. How many more barrels of oil did the United States import in 1981 than in 1970?
6. What conclusions can you draw from the information on the graphs?

How Can We Conserve Our Human Resources?

A. The Sputnik Scare. In 1957, the Russians launched Sputnik I, the first space satellite launched into space. Americans were shocked: "How could a backward nation like Russia," they wondered, "beat the United States in exploring outer space?" This development, among others, raised questions about the quality of education in our nation's schools. The American school system is the largest and most expensive in the world. It has the highest percentage of students attending high school and college. How was it that our nation was not able to produce engineers and scientists equal to those of the Soviet Union—or so it seemed to many?

B. Improving Our Educational Resources.

1. THE PROBLEMS. A survey of our youth at the time of Sputnik revealed that thousands of young Americans could not read or write at all. Several million were so weak in basic skills that they could not get or hold decent jobs. For many, inferior education was largely the result of poverty. The most poorly educated people were found in areas where the amount spent on schools was low, and in the slums of large cities.

American education was weak in another way. Not enough young people were choosing difficult fields of study like science, mathematics, and engineering. In these fields, the Soviet Union was graduating twice as many young people as the United States. In Russia, however, only the best students went on to high school and college. Americans are not willing, of course, to follow the practice of the Soviet Union and some other European countries. We believe that more young people, not fewer, should have the advantages of a higher education. But this belief presents problems. Can we educate "all the children of all the people" and at the same time hold high educational standards?

2. FEDERAL AID TO EDUCATION. After Sputnik, the federal government took the lead in an effort to improve the quality of education. It voted funds for study and research in mathematics, science, and engineering. Grants were given to improve classrooms, laboratories, libraries, and equipment. The federal government supplied textbooks and equipment to schools in poorer areas. Federal scholarships and loans helped millions of students whose parents could not afford the cost of an education. The loan program suffered under President Reagan's budget plans, however, which called for cuts in student aid.

A modern classroom. How is the educational equipment like, or different from, that in your own school?

As a result of the national effort to provide the most and best education for all, more Americans are completing high school and college than ever before—double the number in 1960. Today, about one percent of Americans can be called illiterate (unable to read and write their own language) compared with three times that number at the end of World War II.

C. Better Medical Care. Like our educational system, our system of medical care is the largest and, in many ways, the best in the world. Yet, in the 1960s, many Americans were learning that proper medical care was too expensive. Poor people and older people with small incomes could not afford the best medical care. Even middle-class Americans might use up a lifetime of savings from one serious illness.

Another weakness was the shortage of medical schools and doctors. Though the number of doctors had increased since 1900, they had to treat too many people. Doctors tend to have their offices in wealthy neighborhoods and cities. So people in poor neighborhoods and farm areas suffer the most from a shortage of doctors. Dentists and nurses were also too few in number to meet the needs of a growing population.

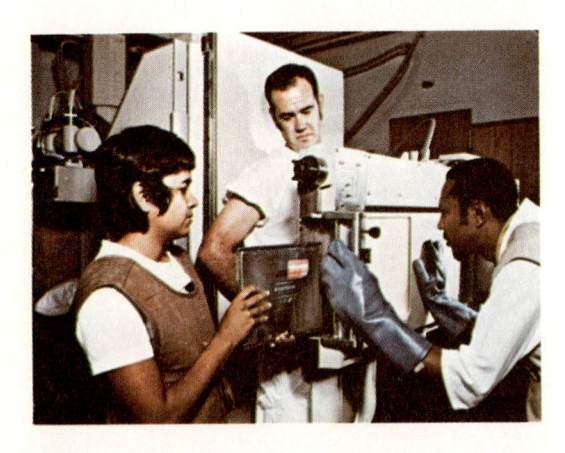

Modern health-care facilities. What do you think can be done to slow the skyrocketing costs of health care?

The federal government therefore began in 1965 to provide funds for training doctors, dentists, and nurses. It also set up medical centers for the study and treatment of such illnesses as cancer, heart disease, mental illness, and mental retardation. Most important, it put through the Medicare program to help the aged. Under the Medicare program, the government pays for care—in hospitals, in nursing homes, and at home by visiting nurses—for nearly all Americans over the age of 65 and for some disabled people under 65. By paying a few dollars a month, older people can also have most of their medical bills paid by the government.

Medicare was designed mainly for older people. But there is a different program, called Medicaid, which also provides people with better health care. Medicaid helps needy and low-income people, including those who are blind, disabled, aged, or members of low-income families with children. Medicaid provides payments for hospital and nursing home care and for various other health-care services.

The costs of the Medicare and Medicaid programs have risen sharply since their beginnings. One reason is a gradual increase in the number of Americans over 65 years of age. These people make up about 11 percent of the population. Also inflation (the high cost of goods and services) has caused the cost of hospital and medical care to increase.

D. Protecting Our Environment. 1. THE POLLUTION PROBLEM. Another threat to the quality of American life became clear in the 1970s. Slowly but surely, Americans began to realize that pollution of our air, land, and water resources creates a danger to our health.

Pollution was most serious in large cities and the suburbs and towns that surround them. In 1970, President Nixon signed the National Environmental Policy Act. This law provided for a group of advisers to prepare plans for the President and Congress concerning the problem of pollution, the use of national parks, and the saving of our wildlife. To carry out the new law, the

Environmental Protection Agency (EPA) was created. The EPA was given the power to enforce standards for pollution control of all kinds.

The automobile was the chief target of our lawmakers. Most air pollution is caused by cars, buses, and trucks. Several "clean air" laws have been passed by Congress. Auto makers have been forced to equip cars with devices to control pollution. The Clean Air Act of 1970 required that cars be equipped with exhausts that give off less carbon monoxide and nitrogen into the air we breathe. Auto makers objected to these laws. They asked Congress to delay enforcement for several years. They pointed out that the regulations passed by Congress would mean that cars with special antipollution equipment would use more gasoline. This, in turn, would make the energy crisis worse. Although the laws eventually went into effect with only slight delays, they were criticized by both the Reagan administration and business as being too costly.

Smoke and fumes from industries and power plants also pollute the air. But, some industries have "on-the-job" pollutants, too. In plants where steel is manufactured in coke ovens, workers have ten times the danger of getting cancer than other steel workers. Workers handling asbestos have about one chance in five of getting cancer. Lead poisoning is a danger in lead mines and battery plants. Even a few plastics and food additives have been found to be dangerous to health. Congress has attempted to provide for stricter testing of new chemicals by passing the Toxic Substances Control Act in 1976.

What will it take to solve our pollution problem? What will these measures cost? The Council on Environmental Quality gives us some idea of the costs involved. To "clean up America" by the year 1990 would require about $200 billion—nearly all of it spent by private industry. Americans have to make a decision about how much they are willing to spend and sacrifice to improve our nation's health.

2. RECREATION AND LEISURE. Our people work fewer hours per week than Americans did 100 years ago. As a result, there is a greater need for facilities for recreation. The national park system started over 100 years ago has been enlarged and improved. In recent years, the government has bought up historic sites, lands bordering on oceans and lakes, and park lands near large cities. During the summer months, Americans travel to parks all over the nation. Bicycling, fishing, swimming, and camping have become the sports in which most Americans participate.

Smoke from factories and power plants can make the air we breathe unhealthful. In what ways can this air pollution be stopped?

Americans are spending over $200 billion a year in the search for enjoyment through leisure-time activities. Television watching is probably the most popular form of leisure activity. The average American home has the TV set turned on for six hours each day. Video games also have become a multibillion dollar industry.

Hundreds of millions of Americans are spectators at various sporting events. Horse and auto racing, baseball, football, and basketball are the favorite spectator sports. More and more people are going to museums, the theater, or musical concerts. In addition, our nation spends more money on the printing of books than any other country in the world. People in the United States are now spending over $10 billion a year on reading materials.

Colorado's Rocky Mountain National Park. Why should regions such as this one with its superb scenery be part of the national park system?

E. Our Senior Citizens. Americans are living longer than ever before. An estimate of the population of the United States in another 20 years shows that there will be more people over 65 and fewer people under 19. Even now, about 11 percent of our people are 65 years of age or older. Almost 10 million people are at least 75 years old. Some Americans are retiring from their work earlier. Thus, many of our older people, "senior citizens," are not working and are living off savings and pensions from government and private industry.

What senior citizens are able to do with their leisure time is only one problem to be faced. Many have not wanted to retire from work. They used to be forced to retire by laws and company rules that made age 65 the final year of full-time work. Since most retired people live on fixed incomes, they suffer when the cost of living rises. One out of six Americans over age 65 is living in poverty. There is no doubt that millions of older people can still do productive work. In the interests of using all our human resources, lawmakers increased the retirement age in 1978 from 65 to 70.

F. Unemployment. There is no greater waste of human resources than to have people out of work. Although our nation has more people working than ever before, unemployment increased to over 10 percent in 1982. The problem was the worst in the large eastern cities. Unemployment among blacks and other races was nearly twice that of the white population. Forty-five percent of young black people were unable to find jobs.

There are several reasons for high unemployment in our nation's cities. One is that industries have moved from urban areas to other parts of the country. Another reason is that many more people are looking for jobs. More women have joined the work force in recent years. Because of the high cost of living, there are more families in which both parents have full-time jobs. Not the least important reason is the number of tasks now being performed by machines. As a result, people are not needed in industrial tasks as they once were.

How should unemployment be reduced? Should the federal government create jobs through a program of necessary public works? Should industry be encouraged to expand by reducing taxes on its earnings? Should personal income taxes be reduced, so people will have more money to spend on goods and services? Should the hours of present workers be reduced, thus creating the need for additional workers? Thus far, there seems to be no simple answer to the problem. Unemployment remains high. The most valuable resource of our nation, its people, is still not being fully used.

REVIEWING THE SECTION

A. Knowing New Terms

Explain each term in your notebook *in your own words*.

(In **A**) "Sputnik scare"
(In **B**) illiterate
(In **C**) Medicare
(In **D**) EPA
(In **D**) "clean air" laws
(In **D**) "on-the-job" pollutants
(In **E**) senior citizens

B. Knowing Important Facts

For each problem in the first column, write in your notebook the action taken to solve it.

Problems	Actions
1. Illiteracy and inferior education	1. a. _____ b. _____ c. _____
2. Lack of adequate medical care	2. a. _____ b. _____ c. _____
3. Pollution of our environment	3. a. _____ b. _____ c. _____

Conclusions: In your opinion, which problem has the federal government done the most to solve? For which problem has it done the least?

C. Finding the Reasons

In your notebook write the letters of *all* the correct answers to each question.

1. Why did many Americans begin to worry about our nation's educational system in 1957?
   a. Russian scientists were ahead of ours in exploring space. b. Millions of young Americans could not read or write. c. Fewer young people had chosen to follow careers in science and engineering.
2. Why is it harder for American high schools to set high standards than for European high schools?
   a. We spend less on education. b. We provide a high school education for all children, not just for those with ability and money. c. We have older school buildings.

665

3. Why has medical care become a serious problem?
   a. The cost of good medical care has risen rapidly.   b. Our nation has a growing number of older people.   c. The health of American people has been getting worse.
4. Why has unemployment become a major problem?
   a. People out of work are a waste of human resources.   b. Modern machines have done away with the need for many kinds of jobs.   c. Fewer families now need more than one worker just to make ends meet.
5. Why has early retirement from work caused serious problems for many Americans?
   a. Early retirement has caused unemployment among young people.   b. Older people may find it hard to live on a small fixed income as the cost of living rises.   c. Older people require more medical care than younger people.
6. Why did Congress pass the National Environmental Policy Act?
   a. To set standards for control of air pollution   b. To provide the President with advice concerning conservation of our wildlife   c. To set standards for estimating the cost of new cars.

IMPROVING YOUR SKILLS

Looking at Both Sides

1. List in separate columns in your notebook the arguments for and against the law requiring people to retire from their jobs, public and private, at age 70. How might this law affect workers and job seekers?
2. On the whole, with which side of the question do you agree? Explain why.

MAKING HISTORY LIVE

1. Some experts say that production could increase so much in the next 20 years that the average American will be able to earn twice as much, work only 20 hours a week, or retire at the age of 40. If you were given a choice, which of these three benefits would you pick? Tell why.
2. Join a committee to study and report on one of the problems in one of the following areas: education, medical care, pollution control, recreation, old age, or unemployment. Tell what is already being done and what more could be done to solve it.

Chapter 37

THE NEW AMERICAN FOREIGN POLICY

AFTER WORLD WAR II, the United States followed a policy of cooperation with other nations. It played a leading part in the United Nations. It also formed military alliances, signed treaties, and made other agreements with foreign nations. The old policy of isolationism, of keeping out of world affairs, seemed dead.

There are three main reasons for this change in American foreign policy. First, the world continues to shrink as means of transportation and communication are further improved. No place in the world is more than a day's travel away by plane. News travels even faster by radio, television, and satellite communications. Second, the United States is one of the strongest powers in the world. The American people came to understand that a powerful nation has great responsibilities. Third, stopping the spread of communism became a major goal of our nation's foreign policy.

In this chapter we shall study the highlights of the Cold War. We shall learn what gains the Communists have made and what successes our government has had in stopping them. We shall examine some of the conflicts—such as the Vietnam War—that have threatened world peace.

We shall also examine how our government has tried to ease tensions and improve relations between the United States and Communist nations. In addition, we will see how the United States has been working for peace in many parts of the world.

How Did a "Cold War" Develop and Deepen?

A. The Communist Challenge. Communism is a system in which the government owns the land and all types of business. Under the capitalist system, on the other hand, most businesses and land are owned by individuals. Over the years Communists have called on people around the world to put an end to capitalism and establish

"Diplomatic Exchange." What does this cartoon tell you about the Cold War?

communism. So Communists were very pleased when Stalin brought a number of countries under Communist control after World War II.

Most Americans, on the other hand, did not want to see communism spread. They had just fought a great war against dictators who threatened their way of life. Now they found themselves facing another threat to their freedom. They were determined to stop this threat before it became too powerful. They strongly supported our government's policy of "containing communism"—that is, of stopping its spread anywhere in the world.

B. President Truman's Policies. 1. THE TRUMAN DOCTRINE. The United States started its policy of containment in 1947 to prevent Communists from taking over Greece and Turkey. When Greek Communists stirred up a revolt in Greece, Stalin supported the revolt. He also demanded that Turkey give him some important territories. If the Communists took over these two countries, they would gain control of the eastern end of the Mediterranean Sea (see map, pages 670 and 671).

President Truman told Congress: "It must be the policy of the United States to support free peoples who are resisting attempted subjugation [conquest] by armed minorities or outside pressure." This statement of our responsibility to nations threatened by communism has become known as the Truman Doctrine. It became an important part of our foreign policy.

Congress quickly voted large sums of money to help Greece and Turkey. The United States sent the two countries arms, advisers, and economic aid. As a result, the Greek government crushed the Communist-led revolt and Turkey turned down Stalin's demands. Both nations became allies of the United States.

2. THE EUROPEAN RECOVERY PROGRAM (ERP). In France, Italy, and other countries of Western Europe, unemployment and prices were high. Many people blamed these troubles on capitalism. At the same time, they were attracted by Communist promises of peace and prosperity.

Our secretary of state, George C. Marshall, promised to help these people rebuild their homes, factories, and transportation systems. The result was the European Recovery Program, or Marshall Plan. ERP was the largest program of economic aid in history. From 1948 to 1952, the United States sent more than 12 billion dollars' worth of machinery, raw materials, and other supplies to the war-torn countries of Western Europe. These countries made a remarkable recovery. As conditions improved, their Communist parties lost strength.

C. The Berlin Crisis. Germany—because of its size, location, and large industries—was the key to the recovery of Western Europe. However, it was divided into four occupation zones after World War II. This division held back its recovery from the war. To solve this problem, the United States, Great Britain, and France decided in 1948 to unite their zones into one.

This action angered Stalin who had expected the Germans to turn to communism if they remained hungry and without hope. Stalin, therefore, decided to drive the Western powers out of Berlin, the capital of Germany. Berlin was located over a hundred miles inside the Soviet zone. Therefore, it was easy for Stalin simply to order his troops to stop all traffic to the city's Western sections. Because of this blockade, two million people of West Berlin faced starvation unless the Western powers gave in and left the city.

However, the United States found a way to defeat Stalin. It supplied West Berlin by air—every few minutes, day and night, in good weather or bad. Giant American and British cargo planes brought food, fuel, and other necessities to the isolated western part of Berlin. The Russians tried to stop the airlift. They fired antiaircraft guns and flew fighter planes near the lanes used by the allied planes. A single accident might have led to war, but the airlift continued. After a year, the Russians called off the blockade of West Berlin. The people of West Berlin, grateful for the help they received, became

An American plane airlifting food and supplies to West Berliners. How do you think these Berliners felt about the air lift?

strong friends of the United States and enemies of communism. People all over the world gained new respect for American courage and power.

D. A System of Alliances. 1. THE NORTH ATLANTIC TREATY ORGANIZATION (NATO). The Berlin crisis had shown how weak the defenses of Western Europe were. As a result, the United States asked the Western nations to form a military alliance against possible Communist moves into Western Europe. The North Atlantic Treaty was signed in 1949. West Germany joined the alliance in 1955. NATO had fifteen members—the United States and Canada, most of the nations of Western Europe, and Greece and Turkey. Each member gave some of its armed forces to the alliance. An overall military command was set up in France. General Eisenhower became NATO's first commander. NATO directed the forces supplied by its members and made plans for using them in case of a Soviet attack.

2. THE ORGANIZATION OF AMERICAN STATES (OAS). At about the same time, the United States helped organize most nations of Latin America into one alliance. This was called the Organization of American States. It was organized like the United Nations and had a similar

MILITARY ALLIANCES IN 1982

- NATO nations
- WARSAW PACT nations
- Other

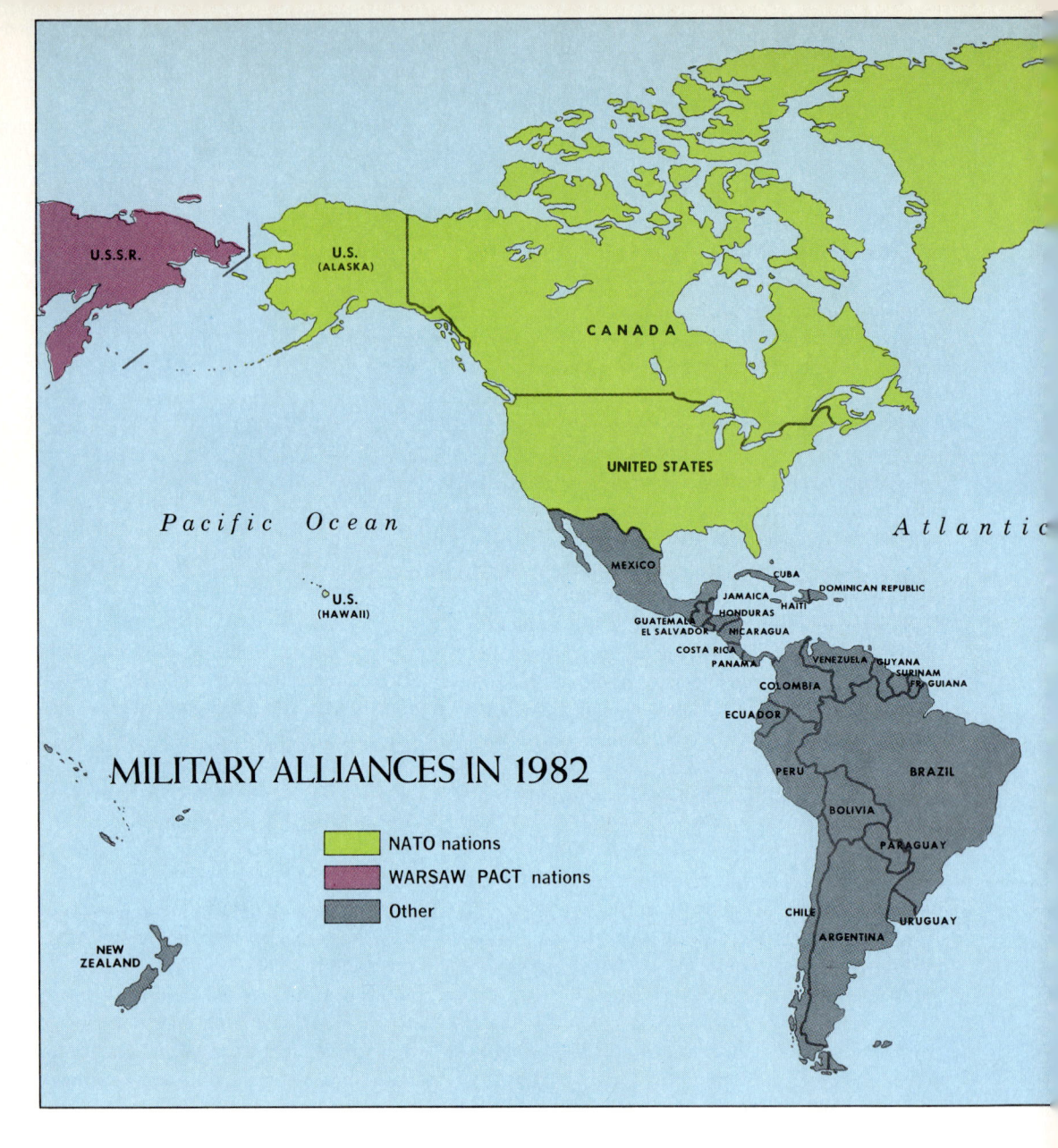

purpose—to keep peace in the Western Hemisphere. Its members agreed to defend each other and to work for peace.

In the next few years, the United States also formed alliances with a number of Pacific nations. These included China, the Philippines, Australia, New Zealand, and even our former enemy, Japan. These alliances were necessary because of Communist gains in Asia.

3. THE WARSAW PACT NATIONS. The Soviet Union decided to form an alliance of Communist-controlled nations in Eastern Europe. These nations included Poland, Hungary, East Germany, Albania, Romania, Bulgaria, and Czechoslovakia. All of these nations had come under Soviet influence after World War II. In 1955, at a meeting in Warsaw, Poland, these nations agreed to defend each other in the event of an

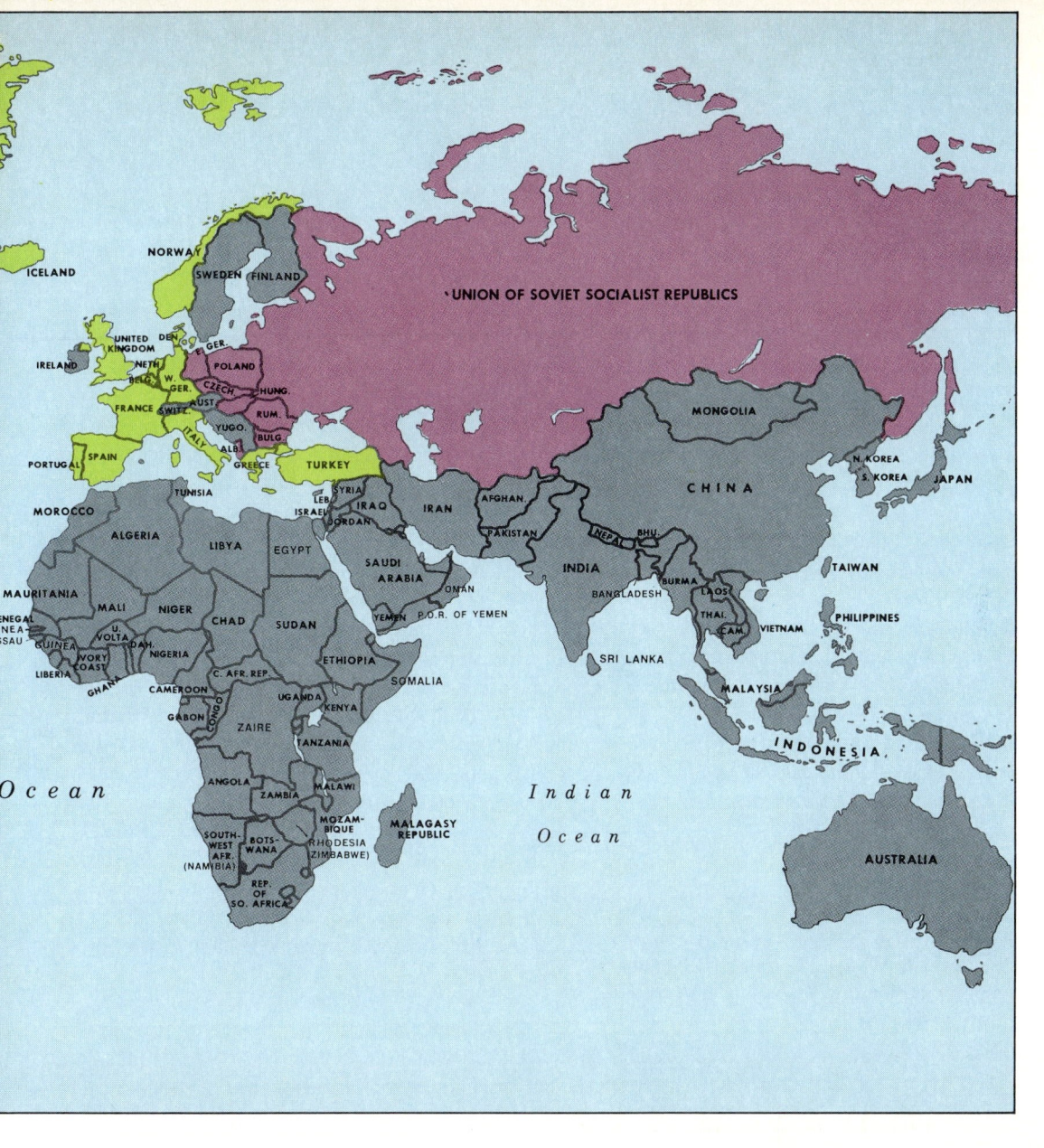

attack from outside Eastern Europe. There was no doubt that the Warsaw Pact was an answer to the formation of NATO in Western Europe.

E. The Spread of National Communism. In 1948, a quarrel developed between the Communist nation of Yugoslavia and the Soviet Union. As a result, the Soviet Union tried to overthrow the ruler of Yugoslavia, Marshal Tito. Tito asked the West for help. Though he was a Communist, the United States sent him military and economic aid. This aid helped Yugoslavia to keep its independence from direct orders from the Soviet Union. Yugoslavia is an example of national communism—that is, communism free from Soviet control.

In 1956, the Soviet Union sent a powerful army into Hungary and crushed a revolution in

671

that country. Thousands of Hungarians fled to other countries, including the United States. The United Nations and the United States condemned the Soviet use of force in Hungary. But neither the United Nations nor the United States became involved. Both feared that any action might touch off another world war.

In 1956, riots in Poland were handled differently. Workers there had protested against Communist police terror. They demanded "bread and freedom." This time, the Soviet Union did not send its armies to stop the riots. Instead, Poland's Communist leaders were given more freedom of action. Soon afterward, Poland received economic aid from the United States. Over a period of years, then, Poland, Yugoslavia, Czechoslovakia, and later Hungary adopted a system of national communism.

In 1968, Soviet leaders said Czechoslovakia had gone too far with national communism. Communist leaders in that country had promised the people greater democracy. To stop this trend, the Soviet Union and its Warsaw Pact allies invaded Czechoslovakia with 600,000 troops. The protesters were jailed and a more pro-Soviet government was set up.

Czechs battling Russian tanks in Prague, the capital of Czechoslovakia. Why do you think the United States did not try to stop this Warsaw Pact invasion of Czechoslovakia in 1968?

F. The Nuclear Arms Race. In 1949 the Soviet Union exploded its first atomic bomb (A-bomb). The United States developed a second type of nuclear weapon, the hydrogen bomb (H-bomb), in 1952. The Soviet Union followed by exploding an H-bomb less than a year later. Great Britain soon built its own A-bombs and H-bombs. These nations were now members of a "nuclear club." (By 1977, three other nations—China, France, and India—had developed their own nuclear weapons.)

In testing nuclear weapons a great deal of pollution was created. Radioactive dust from nuclear explosions polluted soil, water, plants, and animals. The rays of these radioactive materials remain deadly for years.

To make matters worse, it looked as though the Soviet Union might take the lead from the United States in the development of giant rockets and ballistic missiles. These weapons can carry bombs to targets in another country within minutes. To deal with this threat, the United States built up its own collection of missiles. Each power soon had enough nuclear missiles to destroy each other with the press of a button. To ease this situation the United States started talks with the Soviet Union. They hoped to stop the testing of nuclear weapons and keep other nations from making them. The talks failed at first because the two great powers did not trust each other.

G. Nikita Khrushchev's "Peaceful Coexistence." 1. NEW SOVIET POLICY. Soon after President Eisenhower took office in 1953, Joseph Stalin died. Nikita Khrushchev won the struggle for power and became premier (head) of the Soviet Union. He promised the Russian people that in foreign affairs, the Soviet Union would follow a policy of "peaceful coexistence." By this he meant that his country would try to live in peace with the capitalist nations. They would be rivals only in economic matters, such as the production of food and manufactured goods and aid to poor nations. He boasted that the Soviet Union would soon prove that communism was better than capitalism by producing and giving more than the United States.

The new policy of "peaceful coexistence" brought about some changes in the Cold War. Khrushchev held meetings with President Eisenhower and other Western leaders. The "iron curtain" was partly lifted. Trade and tourism between the Soviet Union and the West increased. Cultural exchanges between Eastern and Western countries were arranged.

2. THE U-2 INCIDENT. "Peaceful coexistence" did not last long. President Eisenhower had agreed to meet with Premier Khrushchev in Paris in May 1960. However, just before the meeting, it was revealed that the U-2, an American spy plane, had been shot down over the Soviet Union. Soviet leaders attacked the President for "spying on the Soviet Union." The meeting was called off. Before the incident, President Eisenhower had been invited to visit the Soviet Union. That, too, was canceled. American experts agreed that these strong Soviet actions marked the end of "peaceful coexistence."

3. THE SECOND BERLIN CRISIS. A divided Germany had proved to be a failure for Communism. West Germany and West Berlin had become prosperous under capitalism. East Germany and East Berlin, on the other hand, had stayed poor under Communist rule. Thousands of East Germans came to Berlin to escape Communist rule. They crossed from the eastern to the western part of the city—and to freedom. To stop the flow of East Germans to the West, Khrushchev threatened to drive the Western powers out of Berlin.

In 1961, the Communists suddenly built a wall—with barbed wire, minefields, and armed guards—to separate the two parts of Berlin. This made it difficult for East Germans to escape as easily as they had before. But hundreds still risked their lives to get across the barrier to democracy and prosperity. The Berlin Wall became a real part of the "iron curtain" around Communist territory.

4. THE CUBAN MISSILE CRISIS. Khrushchev's worst setback took place in Cuba. Cuba underwent a revolution in 1959. The leader of the new government, Fidel Castro, had won the support of the Cuban people in overthrowing a corrupt dictator. Once in power, Castro introduced communism to the island. He crushed all opposition and took away the property of wealthy Cubans. He also signed military agreements with the Soviet Union and Communist China. President Eisenhower, after trying to reach an agreement with Castro, cut off all trade with Cuba. After a while, he ordered a complete boycott of Cuba's main crops, sugar and tobacco. This did not change Castro's policies. In fact, he became even more opposed to the United States than before.

In 1961, President Kennedy approved an invasion of the island by Cuban refugees who had fled to the United States. Without help from the American navy and air force, however, they never had a chance. Castro's Soviet-built tanks and planes quickly smashed the invasion. Almost all the men involved were either killed or captured.

To Khrushchev, President Kennedy's failure to support the invasion was a sign of weakness. This led him to a very bold step. He secretly sent Castro a large number of bombers and missiles, together with Soviet workers to build missile-launching sites. But Khrushchev misjudged our young President. When Kennedy learned about the missile sites, he declared a state of national emergency. The new Soviet weapons in Cuba, he pointed out, could destroy almost every city in the Western Hemisphere. He demanded that they be removed at once. To back up his statement, the President ordered the navy to blockade Cuba. Every ship approaching the island was to be stopped and searched. If a ship refused to stop, it would be sunk.

The entire world rested on the edge of war for six days. If Khrushchev did not give in, the result might be a nuclear war that could destroy the world. But the Soviet premier gave in. He agreed to withdraw the bombers and missiles and take down the launching sites. In return, President Kennedy lifted the blockade and promised not to invade Cuba. The missile crisis was over.

This photograph, taken by one of our airplanes, proved that the Russians were setting up missile bases in Cuba.

But Cuba still remained a Communist country "on our doorstep" and a base for the spread of communism in the Western Hemisphere.

Seventeen years after the end of the most terrible war in the history of the world, a Cold War still threatened to turn into a shooting war between the world's two most powerful nations. How the relations between the United States and the Soviet Union affected events elsewhere in the world will be discussed in the next sections.

REVIEWING THE SECTION

A. Knowing New Terms

On the following page, for each new term in the first column, write in your notebook the *letter* of the best description in the second column.

New Terms

1. Berlin crisis
2. European Recovery Program
3. National communism
4. NATO
5. OAS
6. Truman Doctrine
7. Peaceful coexistence
8. Warsaw Pact

Descriptions

a. Statement of our nation's responsibility to help nations threatened by communism
b. Clash between the Soviet Union and Western powers over Germany's former capital
c. Khrushchev's policy of living in peace with capitalistic nations
d. Military alliance formed by the United States, Canada, and thirteen European nations as a defense against communism
e. Nations able to destroy one another in a matter of minutes by launching guided missiles
f. Program of large-scale American aid to the nations of Western Europe
g. New American policies of alliances with other nations
h. Agreement among Communist nations of Eastern Europe to support one another in case of attack
i. Type of communism free from control by the Soviet Union
j. Alliance of nations of the Western Hemisphere against war and communism

B. *Understanding the Facts*

Match the events in the left column with the President, in the right column, in whose administration the event took place. You may use the same President more than once. Write the letters for the correct answers in your notebook.

Event

1. The Soviet Union exploded its first atomic bomb.
2. Fidel Castro established a Communist government in Cuba.
3. The United States began a naval blockade of Cuba.
4. The Marshall Plan helped in the recovery of nations of Western Europe.

President

A. Harry S Truman
B. Dwight D. Eisenhower
C. John F. Kennedy

(*continued*)

5. Allied planes carried out the airlift to save West Berlin.
6. Hungary revolted against the control of the Soviet Union.
7. Nikita Khrushchev became premier of the Soviet Union.
8. A United States spy plane, the U-2, was shot down over the Soviet Union.
9. NATO was formed to halt Communist aggression in Europe.
10. Joseph Stalin began his post-World War II aggressive foreign policy.

IMPROVING YOUR SKILLS

Telling Facts From Opinions

Write "Fact" in your notebook if the statement can be either proved or disproved by getting the necessary information. Write "Opinion" if the answer depends upon values and judgment.

1. The American government gave up its policy of isolation from foreign affairs after World War II.
2. Communism teaches that revolutions against capitalism are a good thing.
3. The American government was right in changing its foreign policy after World War II.
4. The spread of communism is a greater threat to the United States today than the conquests of dictators in the 1930s.
5. The European Recovery Program was designed to keep the Communists from gaining control of France and Italy.
6. If the United States had not helped Greece and Turkey, the Soviet Union would have gained control of the eastern Mediterranean.
7. The American system of alliances was designed to keep the Soviet Union from using military force to spread communism.
8. The American policy toward the revolt in Hungary was a correct one under the circumstances.
9. The American boycott of Cuba's chief crops hurt the Cuban economy.
10. If President Kennedy's actions in the Cuban crisis had not succeeded, all the large nations of the world would have expected war.

How Did Communist Expansion Lead to Wars in Asia?

A. The Communist Victory in China. The American policy of "containing" communism had met with success in Europe. Although Communists had taken over several nations of Europe after World War II, communism had not spread further in the decades after 1948. But, while the United States had given a great deal of attention to Europe, changes were taking place in Asia. These changes presented a severe test of the American policy of containment.

The Communists won their greatest victory of the post–World War II period when Communist military forces took over China. For many years the United States had been helping the Chinese government of Chiang Kai-shek. The Soviet Union had been helping his rival, Mao Tse-tung. Chiang was head of the Chinese Nationalist party. Mao was the leader of the Chinese Communist party. As soon as Japan surrendered in 1945, civil war broke out between the two parties. In spite of large-scale American aid, the Nationalists lost. Early in 1949, Chiang Kai-shek was forced to retreat to the island of Taiwan (Formosa) off the coast of China (see map, pages 670 and 671). Mao Tse-tung became ruler of mainland China, called the People's Republic of China. To protect Taiwan from a Communist invasion, the United States sent ships there and signed an alliance with Chiang Kai-shek. His government was called the Republic of China.

Mao's government in China had the appearance of the Soviet Union under Stalin. Opponents of his rule were thrown into jail or put to death. The Chinese were expected to follow Mao's orders and give up their personal freedoms and wants for the good of the Chinese nation. Close cooperation developed between the Soviet Union and China. Russian experts went to China to give advice on the building of industries. Mao's dislike of the United States was a deep one. The United States had opposed his drive to power and voted against the admission of mainland China to the United Nations.

B. The Korean War. The United States lost a great deal of power in Asia when Chiang Kai-shek was driven to Taiwan. Eagerly, the Communists pushed further into Asia. In 1950, another Cold War crisis arose in Korea, a neighbor of China (see map, pages 670 and 671).

At the end of World War II, Korea had been freed from Japanese rule by Soviet and American armies. The country was divided into two occupation zones. The United States set up a government in South Korea. The Soviet Union established a Communist dictatorship in the North. Both major powers then withdrew their forces.

A few months later a powerful North Korean army, trained and equipped by the Soviet Union, invaded the South. The United States immediately brought the situation before the United Nations. The Security Council (with the Soviet delegate absent) condemned North Korea's action and called on its members to help South Korea. The troops of sixteen nations, the first "international police force" in history, were sent to restore the peace. The United States supplied the largest army, together with a strong navy and air force. General MacArthur, head of the Allied occupation of Japan, was placed in command of all the United Nations forces, including the South Koreans.

After a few weeks of fighting, the United Na-

U.S. soldiers attacking an enemy position in Korea. Do you think it was wise for the U.S. to join the UN war effort against North Korea? Why?

tions forces took the offensive. They smashed the North Korean armies and advanced swiftly northward. As they neared Chinese territory, a large Chinese army suddenly swept across the border from Manchuria. The United Nations forces retreated southward. When reinforcements arrived, the United Nations army started a new offensive. But this advance was slow. For almost two years, United Nations forces held a line north of the 38th parallel (the boundary between North and South Korea).

The Korean War was finally ended by a truce in 1953. Korea remained divided as before. Yet the war had important results. It showed that the United States would fight to keep Communists from conquering other countries. The policy of containment was successful. The action in Korea also showed that the United Nations would act quickly to halt aggression when it was not blocked from such action by the Soviet Union.

C. Troubles in Southeast Asia. 1. THE FRENCH ARE DEFEATED. Trouble started in Indochina soon after the Japanese surrender in 1945. Indochina, which belonged to France before World War II, did not want to return to French rule. As might have been expected, fighting broke out between the French and their colonies who wanted independence. The leader of the independence movement in Indochina was a Communist named Ho Chi Minh. His forces received help from the Soviet Union. In 1954, they won a great victory over the French. Both sides then agreed to hold peace talks at Geneva, Switzerland—the home of the old League of Nations.

2. THE GENEVA AGREEMENT, 1954. The agreement worked out at Geneva divided Indochina into four parts—Laos, Cambodia, North Vietnam, and South Vietnam. Free elections were supposed to be held in order to reunite the north and south. They were never held. North Vietnam became a Communist nation under Ho Chi Minh. With the help of the giant Communist nations, the Soviet Union and China, North Vietnam began an attempt to control all the other nations created by the Geneva agreement.

3. THE UNITED STATES AIDS SOUTH VIETNAM. As pressure was placed on South Vietnam by the North Vietnamese, the government of South Vietnam asked the United States for help. President Eisenhower agreed to send military and economic aid. In South Vietnam, Communist guerrillas (bands of soldiers who carry out surprise attacks) were supported with weapons and supplies from North Vietnam and China. This occurred because the government of South Vietnam had failed to make reforms and win the people's support. As the guerrilla raids grew in number and strength, President Kennedy increased aid to South Vietnam to include military supplies and advisers. He did not want Southeast Asia to fall to the Communists.

4. THE UNITED STATES AT WAR. The government of South Vietnam grew weaker. In 1964, President Lyndon Johnson decided that stronger action by the United States was needed. He charged that North Vietnam had secretly sent troops into South Vietnam. He announced that the United States would stop this hidden Com-

munist aggression as it had stopped open aggression in South Korea. The President sent hundreds of thousands of American troops to Vietnam and ordered American planes to bomb North Vietnam. American allies—South Korea, Australia, New Zealand, the Philippines, and Thailand—also sent troops to help South Vietnam.

President Johnson stated that his aim in Vietnam was to stop Communist aggression. He offered to meet with Ho Chi Minh and other Communist leaders to talk over peace terms. But the North Vietnamese insisted that peace talks would begin only when the bombing of North Vietnam was stopped and all foreign troops had left South Vietnam. Meanwhile air raids in the North continued. Both sides continued to escalate (step up) the fighting. President Johnson hoped that continued pressure on North Vietnam would bring them to the peace table.

As the struggle wore on, American opposition to the war grew stronger and louder. Protest demonstrations were held throughout the nation. Many young men refused to be drafted if it meant fighting in Vietnam. As the number of American troops in Vietnam reached half a million, some members of Congress called for a halt to the bombing of the North. They argued that if America stopped the bombing, the North Vietnamese might agree to begin peace talks. But all hopes for a quick end to the war were dashed in 1968. A giant offensive by North Vietnam and the Vietcong (South Vietnamese Communist guerrillas) recovered much of the ground that had been taken by Americans and South Vietnamese.

In March 1968, President Johnson limited the bombing of the North to a few named targets. He also announced that he would not run for reelection as President that same year. North Vietnam then appeared willing to begin peace talks. In 1968, open meetings of representatives of the opposing nations were begun in Paris.

When President Nixon took office in 1969, he asked the American representatives in Paris to work toward a quick end to the war. Protests against the continuation of the war were increasing. Faced with a daily rising death toll, President Nixon announced a plan of "Vietnamization" of the war. American troops would be withdrawn gradually, and the South Vietnamese would continue the fight. The withdrawal of troops by the United States was increased in 1971 and 1972. The Air Force carried out most of the American effort with continued raids on targets in North Vietnam.

5. THE WAR ENDS FOR THE UNITED STATES. Shortly before election day in 1972, President Nixon told the nation that peace talks were successful. A cease-fire would be arranged in a matter of weeks. A settlement was signed in January 1973. In the next few months, North Vietnam released almost 600 American prisoners of war, leaving more than 1,000 not accounted for. The last American troops left Vietnam in March, and the longest war in our history was over. More than 46,000 Americans had died in the attempt to contain communism in Southeast Asia. In the months following the departure of the United States forces, Communist forces made steady advances against the South Vietnamese. Early in

A wounded American soldier being carried onto a helicopter by South Vietnamese troops. Why didn't the American policy of stopping the Communist takeover of South Vietnam succeed?

1975, a Communist government was established in South Vietnam. A year later, North and South Vietnam were reunited into one nation. Hanoi, in North Vietnam, became the capital. The former North Vietnamese flag and national anthem became the symbols of the reunited people.

6. AFTER VIETNAM. Many Americans wanted to forget the experience of Vietnam. The war had caused much bitterness. Few parades or welcoming demonstrations greeted returning veterans. This lack of support severely hurt many of them. They felt the nation did not appreciate the sacrifices they had made. Others found that the experiences in Vietnam made it difficult to return to civilian life. Still the United States had not completely forgotten its experience in Vietnam. Late in 1982, a memorial to the veterans of the Vietnam War was dedicated in Washington, D.C.

D. Improving Relations With Communist Leaders. 1. THE SOVIET UNION. During the course of the long conflict in Vietnam, several events took place that helped to improve relations between the United States and the Soviet Union. President Nixon had a long record as a strong anti-Communist. Yet as President, Nixon showed a willingness to strive for better relations between the United States and Communist nations. This policy of easing tensions became known as *détente*.

In May 1972, President Nixon traveled to Moscow for a meeting with leader Leonid Brezhnev of the Soviet Union. Out of the meeting came an agreement that limited the number of American and Soviet strategic missiles and missile launchers. Leonid Brezhnev welcomed Nixon's visit for a number of reasons. He hoped to obtain technical information from American scientists and engineers to help Soviet industry. He also had hopes of purchasing American grain to ease shortages in the Soviet Union caused by failing wheat crops.

Also, Leonid Brezhnev was interested in improving relations with the United States because of the Soviet Union's growing fear of Communist China. The cooperation between the two

President and Mrs. Nixon with Chinese officials during their visit to China in 1972. How did this visit mark a change in U.S. foreign policy?

large Communist powers had come to an end. Under Chairman Mao Tse-tung, China had become a rival of the Soviet Union for leadership in the Communist world. Mao had accused the Soviet Union of not doing enough to encourage "wars of liberation." China now had developed nuclear weapons. It had attacked India in 1962 and helped Castro start revolts in Latin America. It repeatedly had charged that the Soviet Union's policies were not those of the founder of communism, Karl Marx. Mao claimed to be the true representative of Communist teaching. As a result of Chinese announcements and actions, the Soviet Union had gathered a half million troops on the Chinese border. Some clashes between Soviet troops and Chinese border guards had taken place as a result.

2. CHINA. Earlier in 1972, during the Vietnam War, President Nixon visited China for meetings with Mao Tse-tung. This was the first visit of an American President to China. The talks went smoothly. No agreements were reached but the talks helped pave the way for better feeling between the two nations. Shortly afterward, Communist China was admitted to the United Nations and the Security Council. In 1976 Mao died. In 1979, the United States and China established full diplomatic relations. Since 1949, the United States had recognized and supported the Republic of China or Taiwan. In 1979, the United States broke diplomatic relations with Taiwan, but it still maintains close trade ties with that country.

REVIEWING THE SECTION

A. Knowing New Terms

Explain each term in your notebook *in your own words*.

(In **B**) "international police force"
(In **C3**) guerrilla
(In **C4**) Vietcong
(In **C4**) Vietnamization
(In **D**) détente

B. Knowing Important People

For each description listed below, write in your notebook the *letter* of the person to whom it applies. (You may use the same letter more than once.)

Description

1. Agreed with President Nixon on limiting number of strategic missiles
2. Defeated on mainland China by Communist forces
3. Became Communist ruler of mainland China
4. Leader of North Vietnam
5. Ally of the United States on island of Taiwan
6. Led China to rival Soviet Union as leader among Communist nations
7. Hoped to ease grain shortage by buying wheat from the United States
8. Sent Chinese armies into Korea

Important People

A. Chiang Kai-shek
B. Mao Tse-tung
C. Ho Chi Minh
D. Leonid Brezhnev

C. Understanding the Facts

PART 1. Arrange the events in each group in the order in which they happened. Write the numbers of the events in correct order in your notebook.

   A. 1. China supports revolutions in Latin America.
      2. Chinese Nationalist government driven to Taiwan.
      3. Civil war breaks out in China.

B. 1. United States and Soviet Union withdraw forces from Korea.
   2. Korea is divided into two parts.
   3. United Nations forces sent to Korea.
C. 1. Agreement is made at Geneva on future of Indochina.
   2. Vietcong begins raids in South Vietnam.
   3. President Johnson orders bombing of North Vietnam.
D. 1. President Nixon meets with Mao Tse-tung.
   2. North Vietnam releases prisoners of war.
   3. Protests against American involvement in Vietnam spread in the United States.

PART 2. In your notebook, write the *letter* of the correct answer.
1. A reason why the United States supported the Chinese Nationalists on Taiwan is that:
   a. it expected the Nationalists to invade mainland China   b. the Nationalist government opposed the spread of communism   c. the Nationalist government and the Soviet Union have had friendly relations.
2. The friendship between the Soviet Union and Communist China changed considerably because:
   a. Mao had accused the Soviets of being traitors to the true teachings of communism   b. they were on different sides in the Vietnam War   c. the Soviet Union supported Cuba's Fidel Castro and China did not.
3. A final result of the years of war in Vietnam is that:
   a. American troops will be stationed in Southeast Asia for many years
   b. North Vietnam remains Communist and South Vietnam is a democracy
   c. a Communist government rules a reunited North and South Vietnam.
4. One of the reasons the United Nations was able to send a force into Korea was that:
   a. every large nation agreed that force was necessary   b. the Soviet Union did not take part in the decision to use force   c. it was the United Nations that had divided Korea in the first place.
5. A reason why President Johnson continued to order the bombing of North Vietnam despite protests throughout the United States is that:
   a. North Vietnam had shown signs of giving up the fight   b. the bombings were weakening the strength of the Vietcong   c. he hoped to force North Vietnam into talks of peace.
6. President Nixon announced a plan of "Vietnamization" of the war in order to:
   a. withdraw American forces over a period of time   b. end United States participation in the war at once   c. spend more time at important meetings in Paris.
7. Leonid Brezhnev welcomed a meeting with President Nixon in 1972 because:
   a. he wanted to get North Vietnam to withdraw from the war   b. President Nixon had a record for being anti-Communist   c. he had become fearful of the growing power of Communist China.

IMPROVING YOUR SKILLS

Interpreting the Graph

Study the graph. Then write "True" in your notebook if the statement is correct according to the graph. If the statement is wrong, rewrite it so that it is correct.

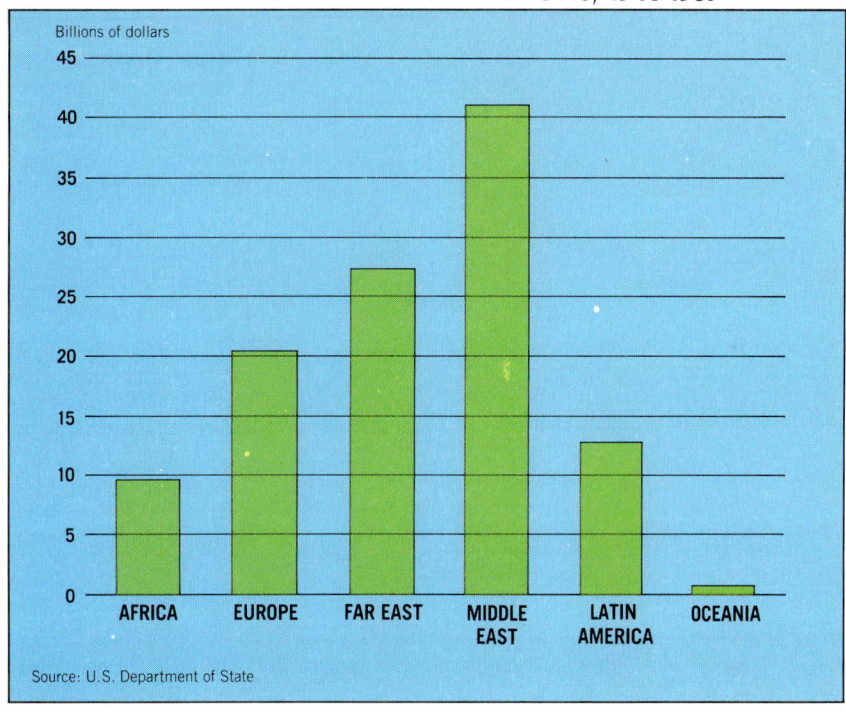

U.S. ECONOMIC AID TO FOREIGN NATIONS, 1946-1981

Billions of dollars

Africa	~9.5
Europe	~20.5
Far East	~27
Middle East	~41
Latin America	~13
Oceania	~1

Source: U.S. Department of State

1. The countries of Europe have received the largest amounts of American aid.
2. The countries of Latin America have received the least aid.
3. All aid to Latin America and African countries does not equal the amount of aid to countries of the Far East.
4. Total American aid in the 36 years after the end of World War II amounted to more than $100 billion.

How Has the United States Been Working for Peace?

A. A Change in Outlook. At the end of World War II, the United States no longer tried to keep out of world affairs. Our nation took an active part in the workings of the United Nations. It used its power to try to contain communism in Europe, Asia, and Latin America. For this reason, Americans were involved in two bloody wars in Asia. But, as the 1970s began, there were signs that a change in policy was taking place. America was trying to end its role in the war in Vietnam. The United States adopted a policy of détente toward the Soviet Union. Efforts were made to end the nuclear arms race. Our government tried to establish normal relations with mainland China. Americans seemed to desire relief from wars and conflicts that could lead to war.

B. The Middle East. 1. THE NATION OF ISRAEL. American policy in the Middle East has always supported the state of Israel. This tiny, democratic nation was established in 1948. After World War II, Great Britain had withdrawn from Palestine. The United Nations then recommended the area be divided into Jewish and Arab states. Jews living in Palestine formed the state of Israel, fulfilling a dream of hundreds of years. President Truman quickly recognized Israel's independence. However, the surrounding Arab states did not. War then broke out in the Middle East. Peace was restored through the efforts of the United Nations. It was an uneasy peace. The violence of 1948 was a sign of events to come.

2. MORE ARAB–ISRAELI WARS. a. *The War of 1956*. Since 1948 every President has supported Israel with military and economic aid. The United States has also aided various Arab nations in an effort to contain communism. At the same time, the Soviet Union has provided Arab nations with military aid. One of these nations was Egypt.

In 1956, Egypt launched a series of attacks against Israel. The United States cut off its aid to Egypt in an effort to halt the raids. However, Egypt went boldly forward and seized the Suez Canal, thus shutting off Israeli shipping. The Suez Canal was owned largely by the French and British governments. These nations, with Israel, invaded Egypt. They easily defeated the Egyptian forces. The United Nations, led by the United States and the Soviet Union, ordered a halt to the invasion. A United Nations force took up buffer positions between Egyptian and Israeli armies.

b. *The Six-Day War*. The years that followed were marked by frequent raids by Arab and Israeli forces across their borders. In 1967, Egypt unexpectedly ordered the United Nations forces to leave. It then moved its own troops toward Israel. Despite bitter fighting, Israel won a victory in only six days. After the war, Israel kept part of the territory it had occupied in Egypt, Syria, and Jordan.

c. *The War of 1973*. In 1973, Egypt and Syria launched a surprise attack against Israel. Again, the power of the United States and the Soviet Union was successful in arranging a cease-fire. In the fall of 1973, the Arab states decided to stop shipping oil to the United States and other nations that had supported Israel. As you recall, this caused an oil shortage in the United States (see page 656).

3. PEACE EFFORTS. a. *Camp David*. Both Israel and the Arab nations looked to the United

States for leadership in establishing a lasting peace in the Middle East. However, a terrorist group, the Palestine Liberation Organization (PLO) publicly stated that it wanted to destroy Israel. The PLO denied Israel's right to exist.

Leadership in a peace movement then came from an unexpected source. In 1975, Egypt canceled its friendship treaty with the Soviet Union. The Arab nation hoped to establish friendlier relations with the United States. Then, in late 1977, President Anwar Sadat of Egypt defied the wishes of other Arab states and met with Israeli leaders. Going further, Egypt became the first Arab state to recognize Israel's right to exist.

Discussions for a peaceful settlement were soon begun. However, when the negotiations seemed headed for failure, President Carter intervened. He invited President Sadat and Prime Minister Menachem Begin, of Israel, to come to the United States. In 1978, the two leaders met with President Carter at the President's retreat at Camp David, Maryland. After 13 days of meetings, they hammered out an agreement. The doc-

THE MIDDLE EAST

An Israeli military position under Syrian military attack during the 1973 war. Why did the United States and the Soviet Union want the Arab-Israeli wars to end quickly?

ument became a plan for peace in the Middle East.

b. *President Reagan's Plan for Peace.* War returned to the Middle East in 1982 when Israel invaded Lebanon. The PLO guerrillas, who had their base in Lebanon, were defeated. A multinational force was created to keep peace while order in the war-torn nation was restored. President Reagan sent over 1,000 U.S. Marines to assist in that effort. He then offered his own plan for peace in the Middle East. He asked that Arab nations accept the right of Israel to exist. In turn, Israel would return some of the occupied land it had held from previous wars. For its part, the United States would give an "ironclad" guarantee of Israel's security.

4. THE HOSTAGE CRISIS IN IRAN. In 1979, a revolution in Iran forced out the nation's ruler, the Shah. Under the Shah, Iran had been a friend

and ally. However, many people of Iran had a deep dislike for the Shah and his methods. His attempts to modernize Iran were not accepted by those with deep religious beliefs in Islam. Furthermore, his secret police became known for its cruel methods. Several forces carried out the revolution in Iran. But the most important was the Islamic clergy under the leadership of the Ayatollah Khomeini. For him and his followers, the United States was to blame for all of Iran's troubles.

In the summer of 1979, President Carter allowed the Shah to enter the United States for medical treatment. This action set off violent demonstrations in Iran against the United States.

The former hostages return safely home to the United States. Why did some people think that events in Iran showed America's growing weakness around the world?

In November 1979, supporters of Iran's new Islamic leaders seized the American embassy and held 52 American embassy personnel hostage. They remained prisoners of the Iranians for the next 14 months.

The United States hesitated to use force to release the hostages. Violence might only lead to more violence. An attempt to free the 52 Americans four months later ended in failure. It also resulted in the deaths of eight Americans when their rescue helicopters crashed in the desert.

The hostages were finally released in January 1981, a few minutes after Ronald Reagan took the oath of office as President of the United States. Few events in recent years have united the American people as their concern did for the safety of "our hostages." But for some it was a sign of America's growing weakness. They argued for increased military strength so that such an event could not happen again. Others agreed with President Carter's attempts to bring about a peaceful settlement of the crisis. They feared that military action might have brought on another world war.

5. THE SOVIETS INVADE AFGHANISTAN. While the United States was busy trying to free its hostages in Iran, the Soviet Union invaded Afghanistan. Afghanistan is a landlocked country bordering Iran. Its population is mostly herders, nomads, and farmers. In a short time, a pro-Communist government took control of the country. The invasion brought the Soviet Union one step closer to the oil-rich Middle East.

The United States protested the Soviet invasion. All grain shipments to the Soviet Union were halted. President Carter announced that United States athletes would not take part in the Olympic Games scheduled for Moscow in the summer of 1980. A planned agreement to limit strategic weapons was dropped by the Congress. Despite this pressure, Soviet troops, tanks, and planes did not leave Afghanistan. The sturdy mountain and desert fighters of Afghanistan continued to hold out against the invaders. In the minds of some, the Cold War had returned.

The Peace Corp in action. A young woman from Minnesota teaches special education in a school in Malaysia.

C. Latin America. 1. PRESIDENT KENNEDY'S PROGRAM. For some years Latin Americans had felt neglected by the United States. After World War II, European nations had received a great deal of American aid in an effort to halt the spread of communism. For Latin America, which has some of the poorest nations in the world, little help had been offered.

As President, Kennedy offered Latin America a program for economic development. He called it an Alliance for Progress. The United States would spend billions of dollars to speed up Latin America's economic growth. The governments of Latin America would spend an equal amount to carry out needed reforms. One reform, for example, would be to divide large estates among poor peasants.

Another of President Kennedy's programs was the Peace Corps. This program was started to help developing nations everywhere—in Asia and Africa as well as the Middle East and Latin America. Peace Corps officials enlisted thousands of Americans with special talents. Their job was to live among poor people and teach them needed skills—building roads, preventing the spread of disease, improving farming methods. The Peace Corps grew in size, and its members were praised wherever they worked throughout the world.

2. TROUBLE IN THE DOMINICAN REPUBLIC. In 1965, a revolt broke out in the Dominican Republic, a tiny nation near Cuba. At that time, Castro was training revolutionaries to be sent to other Latin American countries. President Lyndon Johnson feared that Communist-trained people were among the leaders of the revolt. He sent

U. S. Marines to the republic. They were withdrawn when a new government was elected. But many Latin Americans felt that President Johnson had violated the Good Neighbor Policy (see page 534).

3. PRESIDENT CARTER'S POLICIES. a. *Human Rights*. When he took office in January 1977, President Carter told Americans that he would press for respect of human rights throughout the world. In speaking before the United Nations, he declared, "No member of the United Nations can claim that mistreatment of its citizens is solely its own business." In support of this policy, the United States reduced aid to Argentina, Brazil, and Uruguay—where citizens had been jailed because of their political beliefs. Chile was also denied aid for the same reason.

Some Latin Americans felt they had been singled out for punishment by the United States. They claimed the United States continued to carry on normal relations with other nations where human rights were abused.

b. *The Panama Canal Treaties*. Carter's human rights policy may have concerned some Latin Americans. However, there was general approval of the agreements reached in 1977 between the United States and the Republic of Panama over the future of the Panama Canal. The United States agreed to gradually give up control of the canal to Panama. Administrative control of the canal would pass completely to Panama by the year 2000. The United States also agreed to protect the canal, which would stay open to all ships in times of peace. The warships of the United States would have special rights in times of war.

The people of Panama celebrated the announcement of the treaties with a national holiday. A month later, they approved the treaties with a national vote. The United States Senate ratified (approved) the treaties by a two-thirds vote before they went into effect in 1978.

4. PRESIDENT REAGAN'S POLICIES. The Caribbean countries are "next door" to the United States. A large share of United States trade and more than half its imports of oil pass through the Panama Canal and the Gulf of Mexico. Early in his term, President Reagan sought to stop Cuba's influence in this region.

Attention was centered on unrest in El Salvador. The State Department charged that Salvadorean guerrillas were armed and trained by Cuba and the Soviet Union. Others argued that the government of El Salvador had so oppressed its people that a revolt was bound to happen. The President believed that the unrest in the tiny nation was a serious Communist threat. He announced that the United States "would do whatever is prudent and necessary to block foreign aggression in the Caribbean."

Late in 1982, President Reagan visited several Latin American countries. Relations between the United States and Latin America had been strained during the war between Britain and Argentina over the Falkland Islands earlier that year. The United States had supported its old ally, Britain. However, many Latin Americans felt that our nation should have supported Argentina.

One nation visited by President Reagan was Brazil. Earlier, President Carter had criticized Brazil for violations of human rights. In 1982, however, the nation held its first elections in 17 years. Many political prisoners were freed. As a result of these changes, President Reagan announced that the United States would grant Brazil a loan to help it reduce its huge foreign debt.

D. Europe 1. THE NATO ALLIANCE. In 1949, the United States and Western European nations had formed NATO to combat the spread of communism in Europe (see page 669). However, over the years, the United States and European powers have not always agreed on policies toward the Soviet Union.

The Reagan administration viewed the years of détente with the Soviet Union as a failure. It claimed that détente allowed the Russians to gain a superiority in weapons. It also enabled the Soviet Union to receive technology developed in the West. Détente did not keep the Soviet Union out of Afghanistan. Secretary of state Caspar Weinberger summed up the administration's position: "The Soviet Union poses a greater danger to the American people than any other foreign power in our history."

Europeans live with the Soviet Union "on their doorstep." They are not eager to arouse the "Russian bear." It has been said that Europeans have come to look on the Soviet Union not as an enemy but as an unfriendly neighbor.

Western European nations did little when Iran held 52 Americans hostage. Nor did they take strong measures against the Soviet Union after its invasion of Afghanistan. In addition, they were unwilling to follow the United States in imposing sanctions (penalties) against the Polish government for its suppression of human rights (see below). The American plan to place nuclear weapons in Western Europe met with antinuclear demonstrations in France, Britain, and West Germany.

2. POLAND. In 1981, the Polish government imposed martial law on the nation (no free press, no free speech or assembly, imprisonment of objectors). This action was a response to growing and outspoken dissatisfaction with 30 years of Communist rule. The antigovernment movement was led by the workers' union, Solidarity. As strikes continued to disrupt the nation, Soviet forces gathered on the Polish border. The Polish Prime Minister then imposed martial law (military rule). The Solidarity leader, Lech Walesa, was placed under arrest. At that point, President Reagan decided to impose economic sanctions against the Polish government. But the sanctions did little to influence events in Poland. Martial law continued for a year. Shortly before martial law was lifted, Walesa was freed. But the power of Solidarity had been broken.

Could greater military power on the part of the United States have influenced events in Poland? In Afghanistan? Could any changes have been made short of war? These are questions political and military leaders are trying to answer.

E. Dealing With Nuclear Weapons. 1. THE NUCLEAR TEST BAN TREATY. In 1963, the United States, the Soviet Union, and Great Britain signed the Nuclear Test Ban Treaty. The three powers agreed not to test nuclear weapons in the air, on the ground, in outer space, or under water. Underground tests were not included in the treaty. By the end of 1963, 113 nations had signed the Test Ban Treaty. In 1968 another agreement to stop the spread of nuclear weapons was signed. Unfortunately, China and France, who had already built their own nuclear bombs, refused to sign the agreement.

2. THE SALT AGREEMENTS. When President Nixon visited Moscow in 1972, he came to an agreement with Brezhnev limiting the size of underground nuclear tests. He also took part in the Strategic Arms Limitation Talks—known as SALT. Strategic weapons have the power to destroy an enemy's weapons, missiles, war materials, factories, and population. The SALT agreement limited the number of strategic weapons to those already in existence or then being manufactured.

This U.S. submarine-launched missile is capable of carrying a nuclear weapon to a target thousands of miles away. What is the advantage of launching such missiles from submarines?

In June 1979, President Carter and Premier Brezhnev signed a second agreement, SALT II. This treaty limited the number and type of missiles that could be delivered from one nation to another. The treaty met with opposition in the Senate. Many felt it favored the Soviet Union because it failed to limit Soviet production of certain weapons. Events in Iran and Afghanistan took place while the debate went on. As a result, the treaty was never approved by the Senate.

3. PRESIDENTIAL POLICIES. President Carter argued that all nuclear testing should be stopped. He opposed the building of nuclear reactors called breeder reactors. Such plants, he claimed, encouraged the production of nuclear weapons.

As President, Ronald Reagan maintained that the Soviet Union's nuclear arsenal was superior to that of the United States. He called for increased spending for the development and production of new weapons. He asked for modern bombers, new ships, and an advanced missile system. He further proposed that missiles be placed in the nations of Western Europe.

In the meantime, there was a growing movement for a "nuclear freeze" in both the United States and Europe. Supporters of the "freeze" wanted to put an end to all nuclear weapons. In 1982, the General Assembly of the United Nations passed two resolutions calling for the major powers around the world to stop their production of nuclear weapons. Supporters pointed out that both the United States and the Soviet Union could destroy each other several times over. Critics of the "freeze" claimed that such a plan would give the Soviet Union a position of superiority. They argued that in the last several years, the Soviet Union has built and stored huge stockpiles of nuclear weapons. To agree to a "freeze" now would give the Soviet Union a permanent advantage over the United States in nuclear weapons. Furthermore, a balance of such weapons by each nation would insure that neither side would attack the other. The Reagan administration announced that it wanted to put an end to the "arms race," but on a basis of equality with the Soviet Union.

F. The Space Exploration Program. In 1957, Soviet scientists won great glory for their nation—and a Cold War victory—by the first successful launching of a space satellite, Sputnik I (see page 661). As a result of this success, our government speeded up its efforts to equal the Russian feat. The Soviet Union went forward with space exploration, sending a rocket to the moon and putting the first man and later the first woman into space orbit. Soon, the United States took over the lead in the "space race." In 1968, the first flight to the moon was made by United States astronauts. In the following year, an excited world watched television as Neil Armstrong and Edwin Aldrin became the first humans to set foot on the moon's surface. In 1971, United States astronauts drove a motor vehicle 17 miles across the surface of the moon.

Another significant event in space exploration took place in July 1975. American and Soviet crews met in space, crossed into each other's space ship, shared meals, and carried out experiments together. In 1976, a United States space vehicle, Viking I, landed on the planet Mars. Directed from the earth, it took pictures, sampled soil, and searched for life on the planet.

Great achievements in space exploration continue. Distant planets have been photographed by both United States and Soviet space vehicles. Voyager II expects to pass Uranus in 1986 and Neptune in 1989. Soviet cosmonauts have remained in space for 175 days. In 1981, the United States successfully launched and returned the first reusable space craft, Columbia. It has repeated its round trip four times.

Americans are proud of their space program and its achievements. In addition to the heroic deeds performed by our astronauts, there are other benefits from the space program. Satellites now carry millions of phone calls and television programs around the world. Satellites are our eyes in space for locating important changes in weather conditions. Thousands of inventions used in space exploration have been applied for use by the public. Of course, the space program is also very important for the nation's defense.

An astronaut in training for the Space Shuttle Program. The space shuttle will carry astronauts between earth and an orbiting space platform. How does the exploration of space benefit Americans?

Space satellites are used to observe other countries' military preparations. Rockets and equipment developed for space exploration can also be used for carrying nuclear weapons or for attacking enemy missiles or spy satellites.

Space exploration has cost our nation billions of dollars. In the 1970s, the United States decided to reduce the amount of money that it spends on space exploration. How important is the space program to the future development and security of our nation and the world? How much time and money should be spent in continuing it? These are issues which the American people must decide.

REVIEWING THE SECTION

A. Knowing New Terms

In your notebook write the new terms in this section that best complete the statements in the following exercise.

691

1. Persons who are held as prisoners until certain terms are met are called _____.
2. President Kennedy's program to help Latin America was named the _____ _____ _____.
3. President Carter announced a _____ _____ policy that has reduced aid to some countries that have political prisoners.
4. The agreement between the United States and the Soviet Union to limit the number of strategic weapons is known as _____.
5. _____ is the name of the workers' union in Poland that put pressure on the Communist government to carry out reforms.
6. Groups that want a _____ _____ demand that nations stop the production of nuclear weapons at once.

B. Knowing Important Places

For each description in the left column, write in your notebook the *letter* of the country to which it applies. You may use the same letter more than once.

Descriptions

1. Made treaty with the United States giving it greater control over a canal
2. Fought wars with Israel in 1948, 1956, 1967, and 1973
3. Communist-supported revolt in this nation put down by U.S. Marines
4. Revolution in this country led to taking 52 American hostages
5. Revolution in this country was considered a Communist threat in Latin America
6. Its citizens were the victims of terrorist attacks by the PLO
7. Base for training revolutionaries in Latin America
8. Signed the Camp David agreement with Israel
9. Carried out an invasion of Afghanistan
10. Headquarters of the PLO, invaded by Israel
11. Arab neighbors have refused to recognize it as a sovereign state

Countries

A. Israel
B. Soviet Union
C. Iran
D. Poland
E. Dominican Republic
F. Panama
G. Cuba
H. Egypt
I. El Salvador
J. Lebanon

C. Knowing Important Facts

Complete the chart in your notebook. Choose two of the issues listed in the left column. Then list arguments for and against each issue.

Issues	Arguments	
	For	Against

1. Human rights policy
2. SALT agreements
3. "Nuclear freeze"

Conclusion: Which policies do you favor? Which do you oppose? Why?

IMPROVING YOUR SKILLS

Mastering the Map

Study the map on pages 670 and 671. Then answer the following questions.

1. Which NATO countries have borders touching Warsaw Pact countries?
2. Locate the following countries on the map: the United States, the Soviet Union, France, China, the United Kingdom, and India. Each of these countries has nuclear weapons. Which belong to neither NATO nor the Warsaw Pact?

MAKING HISTORY LIVE

1. Gather information for a classroom display or construct a time line showing achievements in the exploration of space.
2. Give reasons for approving or disapproving two of the following: a. The Peace Corps b. President Johnson's use of U.S. Marines in the Dominican Republic c. The Nuclear Test Ban Treaty d. Expenditures for space exploration e. United States aid to both Israel and the Arab nations f. President Reagan's plans for an arms build-up.
3. Construct a chart or draw a cartoon showing ways in which the United States and the Soviet Union have opposed each other and ways in which they have cooperated since World War II.
4. Research headlines and photos from newspapers and magazines concerning American attitudes during the 14-month hostage crisis. Make a display for the classroom.
5. Make a chart showing the reactions of Presidents Carter and Reagan to specific problems in foreign relations studied in this chapter.

SUMMING UP THE UNIT

How Have Conditions Changed Since World War II?

A. Domestic Developments Since World War II. The United States came out of World War II the richest and most powerful nation in history. Our great industries turned quickly to peacetime production. Instead of the usual postwar depression, the economy entered a long period of prosperity and growth. This continued, with only a few exceptions, for the next thirty years. After the end of the Vietnam War in 1973, an unusual period both of inflation of prices and wages and of prolonged high unemployment puzzled our economic planners.

In spite of our nation's prosperity after World War II, our government faced some difficult problems. During President Truman's term of office, rapidly rising prices caused waves of strikes. This led Congress to pass laws requiring a "cooling-off" period before a strike could start in an important industry. Another problem was the "Red Menace," the fear of communism in the United States. Because of these difficulties, the Truman reform program, with a few exceptions, was buried by Congress.

Eisenhower was a "middle-of-the-road" President. He believed that the power of the federal government should be reduced. Only a few important measures were passed during his administration. However, during this period, there were major Supreme Court decisions outlawing segregation in schools and other public facilities.

President Kennedy wanted to "get our nation moving again," but his reform program, like Truman's, was defeated in Congress. It was only when Lyndon Johnson became President that our government again began to work at economic and social reform. With his long experience in Congress and great popular support, Johnson was able to push his Great Society program through Congress.

This program had many parts. The War on Poverty aimed at providing a decent living for every American. The Civil Rights Act of 1964 and the Voting Rights Act of 1965 attempted to end economic and political discrimination against blacks and other minority groups. The Immigration Act of 1965 ended discrimination against people seeking to enter our country. Greater attention was given to the government's role in improving education and medical care. Protests against the nation's continued presence in Vietnam sometimes hid the importance of reforms passed in the period from 1963 to 1968.

The victory of Richard M. Nixon in the election of 1968 showed that Americans wanted a change from "rapid reform and big government." As President, Nixon reduced or eliminated many of the programs started by Johnson. Nixon also faced continual pressure to get the United States out of the war in Vietnam. The United States finally did end its part in the war in 1973. In that year, Arab nations placed an embargo on shipments of oil to the United States, for months drying up our chief source of foreign oil. Americans became aware of the shortage of our own oil reserves. All events of the Nixon years were clouded by the Watergate scandal, which finally involved the President himself. Faced with the preparation of impeachment charges by the House of Representatives, the President resigned in 1974.

Americans survived the crisis of Watergate in a peaceful, orderly fashion. Gerald Ford, who had been appointed Vice-President earlier by President Nixon, became President. His administration may best be remembered for the manner in which the new President was able to restore the confidence of the American people in the honesty of their government. President Ford followed most of the policies established by Nixon. Shortly after taking office, he pardoned former President Nixon for offenses he "committed or may have committed." The Watergate scandal and the presidential pardon may have been major

694

reasons for the defeat of the Republican party in the election of 1976. James E. Carter (Jimmy Carter), former governor of Georgia, won the election.

President Carter also faced the problems of inflation and high unemployment. These conditions, together with high interest rates, held back economic progress during his term of office. In the campaign of 1980, the Republicans repeatedly asked the question, "Are you better off today than you were four years ago?" The American people answered the question with a smashing victory for the Republican candidate, Ronald W. Reagan.

In his first few months in office, President Reagan was able to get much of his economic program approved by Congress. Taxes on incomes were lowered. Military spending was increased. Spending for social programs was reduced. In the following months, inflation slowed down and interest rates dropped markedly. But the unemployment rate rose to the highest point since the Great Depression of the 1930s. In addition, the federal budget faced its greatest deficit in history.

B. Postwar Developments in Foreign Affairs. Our government faced even more difficult problems abroad than at home. In 1945 and 1946, Stalin took over most of Eastern Europe and tried to spread communism in many other places. Our government was determined to stop this new threat to our way of life. The result was a great struggle between the United States and the Soviet Union, which was known as the Cold War.

In Europe, the United States was very successful. Greece and Turkey, with our help, stopped the Communist threat. A huge program of economic aid helped Western Europe recover from the war. When Stalin tried to drive the Western powers out of Berlin, we supplied the city by air. We then formed NATO, a Western alliance to prevent the further spread of communism in Europe. Soon afterward, Soviet satellite countries, led by Yugoslavia, began to follow an independent policy called national communism.

In Asia, however, the United States was much less successful. Communists gained control of North Korea, China, and Vietnam. Their attempts to expand their holdings led to wars in Korea and Vietnam. America was involved in Vietnam during the administrations of four Presidents. Our part in the war seriously divided feelings in our own nation in the 1960s and early 1970s. The Soviet Union also gained a foothold in the Middle East by supplying arms and military equipment to several Arab nations.

Latin America had been considered safe from communism since the Good Neighbor Policy. So Americans were shocked when Cuba set up a Communist government and tried to start revolutions elsewhere. Stalin's successor, Khrushchev, encouraged Fidel Castro and sent bombers and missiles to Cuba. President Kennedy forced the Soviet dictator to remove them. But Cuba remained a center for spreading communism in the Western Hemisphere. President Kennedy offered programs of economic aid to Latin America that were only partly successful. In 1978, the United States signed new canal treaties with Panama. Both actions were welcomed in Latin America. Later, some Latin American countries were offended by President Carter's statements on human rights. They claimed they were being unfairly accused of suppressing opposing points of view. President Reagan's 1982 trip to Latin America, with promises of aid to Caribbean nations, attempted to heal some of these wounds.

The Middle East remains one of the trouble spots of the world. Arab nations surround and threaten Israel as they have done for more than 35 years. Throughout, the United States has supported the independence of Israel. No positive steps toward a lasting peace in the Middle East were taken until the Camp David agreement between Israel and Egypt in 1978. President Carter played a crucial role in bringing about this important agreement.

Terrorist raids and killings by the PLO led Israel to invade Lebanon in 1982. The PLO guerrillas were driven out of Lebanon and scattered among several Arab countries. President Reagan sent U.S. Marines as part of a peacekeeping force in Lebanon, and offered a peace plan for the nations involved.

In Iran, Islamic leaders led a revolt against the Shah. His admission into the United States for medical treatment touched off a wave of hatred in Iran toward our nation. Americans in the embassy in Teheran were seized and held hostage for 14 months. Failure to secure their release for so long may have influenced the election of 1980.

At one time, there were signs of hope in easing tensions between the United States and the Soviet Union. A period of détente led to agreements regarding the testing of nuclear arms and the production of strategic weapons. A split between the Soviet Union and China divided the two largest Communist powers. Hope that better relations might continue was dashed by the Soviet invasion of Afghanistan and its influence in the suppression of basic rights in Poland. Furthermore, there were signs of Soviet influence in training revolutionaries in Latin America. Sanctions imposed by Presidents Carter and Reagan had little effect on Soviet policies.

Egyptian President Anwar Sadat, President Jimmy Carter, and Israeli President Menachem Begin all shake hands after the signing of the historic Middle East peace treaty.

C. The Future of America.
The greatness of America is found in its people. No period in our history has been without its problems, and our people have been able to solve them. Those qualities that Americans possess have given our nation a prosperity and standard of living such as no other people have ever enjoyed. We have learned to overcome many problems. These include the problems involved in settling the continent and in founding a new kind of government in which the people rule. Our nation overcame a division in our land that resulted in a brutal war among our own citizens. The United States had to deal with the problems of its expanding power and influence in lands outside North America. We participated in global wars against serious threats to our way of life. In addition, the United States met the Communist challenges to our economic and political system. And our nation successfully overcame the problems created by crime and disgrace in our highest government officials.

The United States has been able to meet changing conditions throughout its history. No nation has ever had such a mixture of people of varied cultures and backgrounds sharing in the government of a country. Discrimination against some groups has been a national shame, but unlike some other governments in the world, ours has taken historic steps to reduce and, hopefully, eliminate discrimination entirely.

Our modern technological age is far removed from the farming age of our founding as a nation. The problems we have today are more complex than those faced by our ancestors of over 200 years ago. In our modern life, we have instant communication and rapid transportation, a greater amount of scientific knowledge, better health care, and better opportunities for education. Our citizens are better informed than ever in history. Our democracy depends on these informed and educated citizens to act wisely and to guide our nation in solving future problems. Our nation was never in a better position to fulfill its destiny—a truly democratic society recognizing the worth and dignity of each individual.

In what ways have Americans fulfilled the goals that past generations have sought to achieve?

REVIEWING THE UNIT

A. Knowing When Things Happened

For each development listed below, write in your notebook the *letter* or *letters* from the time line that show when it happened. (You may use two, or even three, letters for some developments.)

Truman	Eisenhower	Kennedy	Johnson	Nixon	Ford	Carter	Reagan
A	B	C	D	E	F	G	H
1945	1953	1961	1963	1969	1974	1977	1981

697

PART 1. *Domestic Developments*

1. Two strong civil rights laws passed
2. School integration case decided by Supreme Court
3. GI Bill of Rights passed
4. St. Lawrence Seaway Treaty signed
5. New immigration law passed
6. The New Federalism
7. A former President is pardoned
8. War on Poverty waged
9. Taft-Hartley law passed
10. Watergate scandal exposed
11. Vice-President appointed
12. Anti-Vietnam War protests occurred

PART 2. *Foreign Policy Developments*

1. Alliance for Progress
2. Human rights policy
3. End of Vietnam War for the United States
4. Visits to Soviet Union
5. Civil war in Greece
6. Communist victory in China
7. Camp David agreement
8. European Recovery Program
9. Nuclear Test Ban Treaty
10. Peace Corps begun
11. North Atlantic Treaty
12. Korean War
13. Panama Canal Treaty
14. First presidential visit to China
15. Sanctions against Poland
16. Berlin airlift
17. Launching of first space satellite
18. SALT agreement talks
19. United States arms build-up
20. Cuban missile crisis

B. *Knowing Where Things Happened*

On an outline map of the world, do the following:

1. Use light pencil shading or blue crayon to show all large bodies of water.
2. Label the continents, the oceans, and the Mediterranean Sea.
3. Label very large countries, such as the United States, Canada, Brazil, the Soviet Union, China, and Australia.

4. Write the *letters* of the following events in the places where they happened:
   a. Building the St. Lawrence Seaway
   b. Berlin crisis
   c. Aid to Greece and Turkey
   d. U.S. Marines in Lebanon
   e. Iranian hostage crisis
   f. Korean War
   g. Independence of Israel
   h. Martial law in Poland
   i. Soviet invasion of Afghanistan
   j. Cuban missile crisis
   k. War in Vietnam
   l. Trouble in the Dominican Republic

C. Knowing Important People

For each person in the first column, write in your notebook the *letter* of the country in the second column that he governs or governed. You may use the same letter more than once and may use two letters for the same person.

Important People

1. Leonid Brezhnev
2. Fidel Castro
3. Chiang Kai-shek
4. Anwar Sadat
5. Nikita Khrushchev
6. Mao Tse-tung
7. Joseph Stalin
8. Menachem Begin
9. Marshal Tito
10. Ayatollah Khomeini

Countries

a. Cuba
b. Israel
c. Mainland China
d. Egypt
e. Soviet Union
f. Taiwan
g. Yugoslavia
h. Iran

D. Knowing Important Terms

In your notebook, write the *letter* of the item in each group that does *not* belong with the others.

1. *President Truman's achievements:*
   a. Full Employment Act   b. Policy of containing communism   c. building of the St. Lawrence Seaway   d. ending price controls and rationing
2. *"Red Menace":*
   a. Central Intelligence Agency   b. Federal Bureau of Investigation   c. Senator Joseph McCarthy's charges   d. States' Rights party
3. *Measures to keep blacks from voting:*
   a. grandfather clause   b. literacy test   c. poll tax   d. white supremacy

4. *Federal aid to education:*
   a. GI bill of Rights b. Medicare c. Operation Head Start d. college scholarships
5. *Crises for Americans in the Cold War:*
   a. Berlin Wall b. Cuban missiles c. South Africa d. guerrilla warfare in Vietnam
6. *Watergate scandal:*
   a. investigation "cover-up" b. impeachment charges c. price inflation d. taping conversations
7. *Twenty-fifth Amendment:*
   a. Jimmy Carter elected as President b. President Ford appointed as Vice-President c. Gerald Ford becomes President d. Nelson Rockefeller appointed as Vice-President
8. *Antidiscrimination movement:*
   a. "separate but equal decision" b. passive resistance c. "sit-ins" d. federal troops at Little Rock High School
9. *Increased immigration to the United States from 1965 through 1980:*
   a. Chicanos b. Filipinos c. Koreans d. Canadians
10. *Indian affairs:*
    a. Dawes Act b. OPEC c. Demonstration at Wounded Knee d. AIM
11. *Equal rights for women:*
    a. NOW b. Women in armed forces academies c. Twenty-fifth Amendment d. proposed Equal Rights Amendment
12. *Saving our resources:*
    a. geothermal energy b. solar energy c. Pollution Control Act d. Community Development Program
13. *Senior citizens:*
    a. early retirement age b. 11 percent of our population c. illiteracy d. social security benefits
14. *Peaceful coexistence:*
    a. Berlin Wall b. Korean truce c. Khrushchev-Eisenhower meetings d. cultural exchanges
15. *Trends in large cities:*
    a. high unemployment rate b. decaying water systems c. movement of people to the Sunbelt d. increased federal aid under President Reagan
16. *President Carter's policies:*
    a. prepare an energy program for the future b. deny aid to countries that hold political prisoners c. step up nuclear testing d. limit strategic weapons
17. *Domestic policies of President Reagan:*
    a. support of social programs b. reduced size of government c. lower income taxes d. increased military spending
18. *Presidents who had more than one administration:*
    a. Eisenhower b. Carter c. Truman d. Johnson

RECOMMENDED READING

A. Historical Books

CHAFE, W. H. *The American Woman*. New York: Oxford Univ. Press, 1972. Changing roles and status of women, 1920–1970.

CLARK, L. E., ed. *Through African Eyes*. New York: Praeger/Holt, Rinehart & Winston, 1971. Cultures in change, written by Africans.

DELORIA, V., JR. *Behind the Trail of Broken Treaties*. New York: Delacorte Press, 1974. An Indian Declaration of Independence.

DORNBERG, J. *The Soviet Union Today*. New York: Dial Press, 1976. How it works.

FARR, N. *America Today: 1945–1981*. Eds. D. Calhoun, and L. W. Bloch. West Haven, Conn.: Pendulum Press, 1977.

FORMAN, J. D. *That Mad Game*. New York: Scribner, 1980. War and the chances for peace.

GOLDSTON, R. *The Cuban Revolution*. Indianapolis, Ind.: Bobbs-Merrill, 1970.

GRAHAM, F., JR. *Since Silent Spring*. Boston: Houghton Mifflin, 1970. What have we done about pollution warnings.

HALACY, D. S. *The Energy Trap*. New York: Four Winds Press, 1975.

HARRINGTON, M. *The Other America*. New York: Macmillan, 1962. Poverty in America.

HODGSON, G. *America in Our Time: From World War II to Nixon—What Happened and Why*. New York: Random House, 1978.

KAISER, R. G. *Russia*. New York: Atheneum, 1976. The people and power of Russia.

KING, M. L., JR. *Why We Can't Wait*. New York: Harper & Row, 1964. A famous black leader explains his position.

LAWSON, D. *The United States in the Vietnam War*. New York: Crowell, 1981.

SKURZYNSKI, G. *Safeguarding the Land*. New York: Harcourt Brace Jovanovich, 1981.

B. Biographies and Autobiographies

COHEN, D. *Undefeated: The Life of Hubert H. Humphrey*. Minneapolis, Minn.: Lerner, 1978.

COMPLING, E. *Kennedy*. North Pomfret, Vt.: David & Charles, 1980.

DAVID, L., and DAVID, I. *Ike & Mamie: The Story of the General and His Lady*. New York: Putnam, 1981.

FITZPATRICK, J. P. *Puerto Rican Americans*. Englewood Cliffs, N.J.: Prentice-Hall, 1971.

FORD, G. R. *A Time to Heal: The Autobiography of Gerald R. Ford*. New York: Harper & Row, 1979.

HYATT, R. *The Carters of Plains*. Huntsville, Ala.: Strode, 1977.

KING, M. L., SR., and RILEY, C. *Daddy King*. New York: William Morrow, 1980. His inspiring life in his own words.

MANN, P. *Golda*. New York: Coward, McCann & Geoghegan, 1971. Life of the Milwaukee girl who became prime minister of Israel.

MARTINEZ, E. S., and VASQUEZ, E. *Viva La Raza*. Garden City, N.Y.: Doubleday, 1974. The struggle for Mexican Americans.

MITCHELL, E. B., and ALLEN, T. D. *Miracle Hill*. Norman, Okla.: Univ. of Oklahoma Press, 1967. A Navaho boy's story of his life and education.

SACHEN, J. *Movers and Shakers*. New York: Quadrangle/Times Books, 1973. American women thinkers and activists.

C A N
Columbia R.
Seattle
Olympia
WASHINGTON
Spokane
Portland
Columbia R.
Salem
OREGON
Missouri
R.
MONTANA
Helena
Yellowstone
R.
NORTH DAKOTA
Bismarck
SOUTH DAKOTA
Pierre
Missouri
IDAHO
Boise
Snake R.
WYOMING
Cheyenne
NEBRASKA
Platte R.
P A C I F I C O C E A N
Sacramento R.
Humboldt R.
NEVADA
Carson City
Great Salt Lake
Salt Lake City
UTAH
San Francisco
Oakland
Sacramento
CALIFORNIA
Colorado R.
COLORADO
Denver
KANSAS
Arkansas R.
Wichita
Los Angeles
San Diego
Colorado R.
ARIZONA
Phoenix
Gila R.
Tucson
Santa Fe
Rio Grande
Albuquerque
NEW MEXICO
Canadian R.
OKLAH
Oklahoma City
Red
El Paso
Pecos R.
Colorado R.
Fort Worth
TEXAS
Austin
San Antonio
Rio Grande
M E X I C O
Honolulu
Pacific Ocean
Hilo
0 Miles 200
0 Kilometers 300
USSR
Arctic Circle
Nome
Yukon R.
Fairbanks
Bering Sea
Anchorage
CANADA
ALASKA
Juneau
0 Miles 500
0 Kilometers 800

THE UNITED STATES

★ National capital   ○ State capital

0 — 500 Miles
0 — 800 Kilometers

THE PRESIDENTS OF THE UNITED STATES

NAME	STATE	YEARS IN OFFICE
1. George Washington	Virginia	1789-1797
2. John Adams	Massachusetts	1797-1801
3. Thomas Jefferson	Virginia	1801-1809
4. James Madison	Virginia	1809-1817
5. James Monroe	Virginia	1817-1825
6. John Quincy Adams	Massachusetts	1825-1829
7. Andrew Jackson	Tennessee	1829-1837
8. Martin Van Buren	New York	1837-1841
9. William Henry Harrison	Ohio	1841
10. John Tyler	Virginia	1841-1845
11. James K. Polk	Tennessee	1845-1849
12. Zachary Taylor	Louisiana	1849-1850
13. Millard Fillmore	New York	1850-1953
14. Franklin Pierce	New Hampshire	1853-1857
15. James Buchanan	Pennsylvania	1857-1861
16. Abraham Lincoln	Illinois	1861-1865
17. Andrew Johnson	Tennessee	1865-1869
18. Ulysses S. Grant	Illinois	1869-1877
19. Rutherford B. Hayes	Ohio	1877-1881
20. James A. Garfield	Ohio	1881
21. Chester A. Arthur	New York	1881-1885
22. Grover Cleveland	New York	1885-1889
23. Benjamin Harrison	Indiana	1889-1893
24. Grover Cleveland	New York	1893-1897
25. William McKinley	Ohio	1897-1901
26. Theodore Roosevelt	New York	1901-1909
27. William Howard Taft	Ohio	1909-1913
28. Woodrow Wilson	New Jersey	1913-1921
29. Warren G. Harding	Ohio	1921-1923
30. Calvin Coolidge	Massachusetts	1923-1929
31. Herbert Hoover	Iowa	1929-1933
32. Franklin D. Roosevelt	New York	1933-1945
33. Harry S. Truman	Missouri	1945-1953
34. Dwight D. Eisenhower	Texas	1953-1961
35. John F. Kennedy	Massachusetts	1961-1963
36. Lyndon B. Johnson	Texas	1963-1969
37. Richard M. Nixon	California	1969-1974
38. Gerald R. Ford	Michigan	1974-1977
39. Jimmy Carter	Georgia	1977-1981
40. Ronald Reagan	California	1981-

705

THE DECLARATION OF INDEPENDENCE
The Unanimous Declaration of the Thirteen United States of America, July 4, 1776

When in the Course of human events, it becomes necessary for one people to dissolve the political bands which have connected them with another, and to assume among the powers of the earth, the separate and equal station to which the Laws of Nature and of Nature's God entitle them, a decent respect to the opinions of mankind requires that they should declare the causes which impel them to the separation.
—We hold these truths to be self-evident, that all men are created equal, that they are endowed by their Creator with certain unalienable Rights, that among these are Life, Liberty and the pursuit of Happiness.—That to secure these rights, Governments are instituted among Men, deriving their just powers from the consent of the governed,—That whenever any Form of Government becomes destructive of these ends, it is the Right of the People to alter or to abolish it, and to institute a new Government, laying its foundation on such principles and organizing its powers in such form, as to them shall seem most likely to effect their Safety and Happiness. Prudence, indeed, will dictate that Governments long established should not be changed for light and transient causes; and accordingly all experience hath shewn, that mankind are more disposed to suffer, while evils are sufferable, than to right themselves by abolishing the forms to which they are accustomed. But when a long train of abuses and usurpations, pursuing invariably the same Object evinces a design to reduce them under absolute Despotism, it is their right, it is their duty, to throw off such Government, and to provide new Guards for their future security.—Such has been the patient sufferance of these Colonies; and such is now the necessity which constrains them to alter their former Systems of Government. The history of the present King of Great Britain is a history of repeated injuries and usurpations, all having in direct object the establishment of an absolute Tyranny over these States. To prove this, let Facts be submitted to a candid world.—He has refused his Assent to Laws, the most wholesome and necessary for the public good.—He has forbidden his Governors to pass Laws of immediate and pressing importance, unless suspended in their operation till his Assent should be obtained; and when so suspended, he has utterly neglected to attend to them.—He has refused to pass other Laws for the accommodation of large districts of people, unless those people would relinquish the right of Representation in the Legislature, a right inestimable to them and formidable to tyrants only.—He has called together legislative bodies at places unusual, uncomfortable, and distant from the depository of their public Records, for the sole purpose of fatiguing them into compliance with his measures.—He has dissolved Representative Houses repeatedly, for opposing with manly firmness his invasion on the rights of the people.—He has refused for a long time, after such dissolutions, to cause others to be elected; whereby the Legislative powers, incapable of Annihilation, have returned to the People at large for their exercise; the State remaining in the mean time exposed to all the dangers of invasion from without, and convulsions within.—He has endeavoured to prevent the population of these States; for that purpose obstructing the Laws of Naturalization of Foreigners; refusing to pass others to encourage their migration hither, and raising the conditions of new Appropriations of Lands.—He has obstructed the Administration of Justice, by refusing his Assent to Laws for establishing Judiciary powers.—He has made Judges dependent on his Will alone, for the tenure of their offices, and the amount and payment of their salaries.—He has erected a multitude of New Offices, and sent hither swarms of Officers to harass our people, and eat out their substance.—He has kept among us, in times of peace, Standing Armies without the Consent

of our legislatures.—He has affected to render the Military independent of and superior to the Civil power.—He has combined with others to subject us to a jurisdiction foreign to our constitution, and unacknowledged by our laws; giving his Assent to their Acts of pretended Legislation:—For quartering large bodies of armed troops among us:—For protecting them, by a mock Trial, from punishment for any Murders which they should commit on the Inhabitants of these States:—For cutting off our Trade with all parts of the world:—For imposing Taxes on us without our Consent:—For depriving us, in many cases, of the benefits of Trial by jury:—For transporting us beyond Seas to be tried for pretended offences:—For abolishing the free System of English Laws in a neighbouring Province, establishing therein an Arbitrary government, and enlarging its Boundaries so as to render it at once an example and fit instrument for introducing the same absolute rule into these Colonies:—For taking away our Charters, abolishing our most valuable Laws, and altering fundamentally the Forms of our Governments:—For suspending our own Legislatures, and declaring themselves invested with power to legislate for us in all cases whatsoever.—He has abdicated Government here, by declaring us out of his Protection and waging War against us.—He has plundered our seas, ravaged our Coasts, burnt our towns, and destroyed the lives of our people.—He is at this time transporting large Armies of foreign Mercenaries to complete the works of death, desolation and tyranny, already begun with circumstances of Cruelty & perfidy scarcely paralleled in the most barbarous ages, and totally unworthy the Head of a civilized nation.—He has constrained our fellow citizens taken Captive on the high Seas to bear Arms against their Country, to become the executioners of their friends and Brethren, or to fall themselves by their Hands.—He has excited domestic insurrections amongst us, and has endeavoured to bring on the inhabitants of our frontiers, the merciless Indian Savages, whose known rule of warfare, is an undistinguished destruction of all ages, sexes and conditions. In every stage of these Oppressions We have Petitioned for Redress in the most humble terms: Our repeated Petitions have been answered only by repeated injury. A Prince, whose character is thus marked by every act which may define a Tyrant, is unfit to be the ruler of a free people. Nor have We been wanting in attentions to our British brethren. We have warned them from time to time of attempts by their legislature to extend an unwarrantable jurisdiction over us. We have reminded them of the circumstances of our emigration and settlement here. We have appealed to their native justice and magnanimity, and we have conjured them by the ties of our common kindred to disavow these usurpations, which would inevitably interrupt our connections and correspondence. They too have been deaf to the voice of justice and of consanguinity. We must, therefore, acquiesce in the necessity, which denounces our Separation, and hold them, as we hold the rest of mankind, Enemies in War, in Peace Friends.—

WE, THEREFORE, THE REPRESENTATIVES OF THE UNITED STATES OF AMERICA, in General Congress, Assembled, appealing to the Supreme Judge of the world for the rectitude of our intentions, do, in the Name, and by authority of the good People of these Colonies, solemnly publish and declare, That these United Colonies are, and of Right ought to be FREE and INDEPENDENT STATES; that they are Absolved from all Allegiance to the British Crown, and that all political connection between them and the State of Great Britain, is and ought to be totally dissolved; and that as Free and Independent States, they have full Power to levy War, conclude Peace, contract Alliances, establish Commerce, and to do all other Acts and Things which Independent States may of right do.—And for the support of this Declaration, with a firm reliance on the protection of divine Providence, we mutually pledge to each other our Lives, our Fortunes and our sacred Honor.

THE CONSTITUTION

The exact text of the Constitution is given in the

PREAMBLE

The preamble, or introduction, to the Constitution lists the goals which the Founding Fathers hoped it would achieve. (For details, see page 130.)

ARTICLE I. THE LEGISLATIVE BRANCH

Section 1. *The Two Houses of Congress.* Congress is the legislature, or lawmaking body, of our federal government. It consists of two houses, the House of Representatives and the Senate.

Section 2. *The House of Representatives.* Representatives are elected by the people for a two-year term. In each state, people eligible to vote for the lower house of the state legislature are also eligible to vote for representatives. (In effect, each state decides the qualifications for voting in federal elections within its borders.)

To be a representative, a person must be at least 25 years old, a citizen of the United States for at least 7 years, and an inhabitant of the state that elects him or her.

The number of representatives from a state depends on its population. This includes all free persons and three-fifths of "all other persons"—that is, slaves. (See the three-

---

WE, the people of the United States, in order to form a more perfect Union, establish justice, insure domestic tranquillity, provide for the common defence, promote the general welfare, and secure the blessings of liberty to ourselves and our posterity, do ordain and establish this Constitution for the United States of America.

ARTICLE I.

Section 1. All legislative powers herein granted, shall be vested in a Congress of the United States, which shall consist of a Senate and House of Representatives.

Section 2. The House of Representatives shall be composed of members chosen every second year by the people of the several States; and the electors in each State shall have the qualifications requisite for electors of the most numerous branch of the State Legislature.

No person shall be a representative who shall not have attained the age of twenty-five years, and been seven years a citizen of the United States, and who shall not, when elected, be an inhabitant of that State in which he shall be chosen.

Representatives and direct taxes shall be apportioned among the several States which may be included within this Union, according to their respective numbers, which shall be determined by adding to the whole number of free persons, including those bound to service for a term of years,

OF THE UNITED STATES

inner, colored area and explained in the outer.

and excluding Indians not taxed, three fifths of all other persons. The actual enumeration shall be made within three years after the first meeting of the Congress of the United States, and within every subsequent term of ten years, in such manner as they shall by law direct. The number of representatives shall not exceed one for every thirty thousand, but each State shall have at least one representative, and until such enumeration shall be made, the state of New Hampshire shall be entitled to choose three, Massachusetts eight, Rhode Island and Providence Plantations one, Connecticut five, New York six, New Jersey four, Pennsylvania eight, Delaware one, Maryland six, Virginia ten, North Carolina five, South Carolina five, and Georgia three.

When vacancies happen in the representation from any State, the Executive authority thereof shall issue writs of election to fill such vacancies.

The House of Representatives shall choose their Speaker and other officers; and shall have the sole power of impeachment.

Section 3. The Senate of the United States shall be composed of two Senators from each State, chosen by the Legislature thereof, for six years; and each Senator shall have one vote.

Immediately after they shall be assembled, in consequence of the first election, they shall be divided equally as may be into three classes. The seats of the Senators of the first class shall be vacated at the expiration of the second year, of

fifths compromise, on pages 124–125.) A census (count of the population) is to be taken every ten years. But each state, no matter how small its population, must have at least one representative.

If a seat in the House becomes vacant (usually through the death of a representative), the governor of the state may appoint a substitute.

The House of Representatives chooses its Speaker and other officers. It has the special power to impeach federal officials. (For details, see page 133.)

Section 3. *The Senate.* The Senate consists of two senators from each state. Senators are chosen by the state legislature. (This was changed by the Seventeenth Amendment, on page 418.) A senator's term of office is six years.

One-third of the Senate is elected every two years. (This makes the Senate a continuous body, as described on page 132.)

A senator must be at least thirty years old, a citizen for at least nine years, and an inhabitant of the state that elects him or her.

The Vice-President of the United States serves as the presiding officer of the Senate. He or she may vote only in case of a tie.

The Senate chooses its other officers, including the President *pro tempore,* who serves as the presiding officer when the Vice-President is absent.

The Senate tries impeachments. When the President is impeached, the chief justice of the Supreme Court serves as presiding officer. A two-thirds vote is needed for conviction.

Convicted persons are removed from office and may not hold any other federal office. They may also be tried for their offenses in the usual way.

Section 4. *Election and Meeting of Congress.* Each state regulates its own elections, but Congress may make rules for electing representatives. (Thus Election Day, set by Congress, is the same throughout the United States.)

Congress must meet at least once a year. (The date was changed by the Twentieth Amendment, on page 132.)

710

the second class at the expiration of the fourth year, and of the third class at the expiration of the sixth year, so that one third may be chosen every second year; and if vacancies happen by resignation, or otherwise, during the recess of the Legislature of any State, the Executive thereof may make temporary appointments until the next meeting of the Legislature, which shall then fill such vacancies.

No person shall be a Senator who shall not have attained the age of thirty years, and been nine years a citizen of the United States, and who shall not, when elected, be an inhabitant of that State for which he shall be chosen.

The Vice President of the United States shall be president of the Senate, but shall have no vote, unless they be equally divided.

The Senate shall choose their other officers, and also a president *pro tempore,* in the absence of the Vice President, or when he shall exercise the office of President of the United States.

The Senate shall have the sole power to try all impeachments. When sitting for that purpose, they shall be on oath or affirmation. When the President of the United States is tried, the Chief Justice shall preside; and no person shall be convicted without the concurrence of two thirds of the members present.

Judgment in cases of impeachment shall not extend further than to removal from office, and disqualification to hold and enjoy any office of honour, trust or profit, under the United States; but the party convicted shall nevertheless be liable and subject to indictment, trial, judgment, and punishment according to law.

Section 4. The times, places and manner of holding elections for Senators and Representatives, shall be prescribed in each State by the Legislature thereof; but the Congress may at any time by law make or alter such regulations, except as to the places of choosing Senators.

The Congress shall assemble at least once in every year, and such meeting shall be on the first Monday in December, unless they shall by law appoint a different day.

Section 5. Each House shall be the judge of the elections, returns, and qualifications of its own members, and a majority of each shall constitute a quorum to do business; but a smaller number may adjourn from day to day, and may be authorized to compel the attendance of absent members, in such manner, and under such penalties, as each House may provide.

Each House may determine the rules of its proceedings, punish its members for disorderly behaviour, and, with the concurrence of two thirds, expel a member.

Each House shall keep a journal of its proceedings, and from time to time publish the same, excepting such parts as may, in their judgment, require secrecy; and the yeas and nays of the members of either House on any question, shall, at the desire of one fifth of those present, be entered on the journal.

Neither House, during the session of Congress, shall, without the consent of the other, adjourn for more than three days, nor to any other place than that in which the two Houses shall be sitting.

Section 6. The Senators and Representatives shall receive a compensation for their services, to be ascertained by law, and paid out of the Treasury of the United States. They shall, in all cases, except treason, felony, and breach of the peace, be privileged from arrest during their attendance at the session of their respective Houses, and in going to, and returning from, the same; and for any speech or debate in either House, they shall not be questioned in any other place.

No Senator or Representative shall, during the time for which he was elected, be appointed to any civil office under the authority of the United States, which shall have been created, or the emoluments whereof shall have been increased during such time; and no person holding any office under the United States, shall be a member of either House during his continuance in office.

Section 7. All bills for raising revenue shall originate in the House of Representatives; but the

Section 5. *Rules of Congress.* Each house of Congress decides whether its members have the necessary qualifications and have been fairly elected (see page 132). A majority of the members must be present to do business. Absent members may be forced to attend.

Each house makes its own rules. It may punish a member for bad conduct. It may expel a member by a two-thirds vote.

Each house keeps a journal (the *Congressional Record*). How the members have voted on a certain bill is put into the record whenever one-fifth of the members ask that this be done.

Neither house may adjourn for more than three days or move to a different place without the consent of the other house.

Section 6. *Rights of Members of Congress.* Senators and representatives are paid by the federal government. Their salaries are fixed by law. They may not be arrested while Congress is in session, except for three offenses—"treason, felony, and breach of the peace." They may not be questioned (by the executive, the courts, or state officials) about anything they have said in Congress.

No senators or representatives may be appointed during their term of office to any position that was created or given a higher salary while they were in Congress. No federal officials may hold their position and serve in Congress at the same time.

Section 7. *The President's Veto.* Tax bills must start in the House of Representatives,

711

but the Senate may change them.

After a bill has passed both houses, it is sent to the President. The President may either sign the bill or veto it ("return it with objections"). Congress may pass the bill over a veto by a two-thirds vote of each house. The vote must be recorded in its journal. If the President holds a bill for ten days (not counting Sundays), it becomes a law without the President's signature unless Congress has adjourned meanwhile. If Congress has adjourned, the bill dies after ten days (the "pocket veto").

The same procedure applies to any other action that requires the approval of both Congress and the President.

Section 8. *Powers of Congress.* To collect taxes, pay the government's debts, and provide for the defense and welfare of the nation;

To borrow money;

To regulate trade with foreign nations,

712

Senate may propose or concur with amendments as on other bills.

Every bill which shall have passed the House of Representatives and the Senate, shall, before it become a law, be presented to the President of the United States; if he approve he shall sign it, but if not he shall return it, with his objections, to that House in which it shall have originated, who shall enter the objections at large on their journal, and proceed to reconsider it. If after such reconsideration two thirds of that House agree to pass the bill, it shall be sent, together with the objections, to the other House, by which it shall likewise be reconsidered, and if approved by two thirds of that House, it shall become a law. But in all cases the votes of both Houses shall be determined by yeas and nays, and the names of the persons voting for and against the bill shall be entered on the journal of each House respectively. If any bill shall not be returned by the President within ten days, (Sundays excepted), after it shall have been presented to him, the same shall be a law, in like manner as if he had signed it, unless the Congress by their adjournment prevent its return, in which case it shall not be a law.

Every order, resolution, or vote, to which the concurrence of the Senate and House of Representatives may be necessary, (except on a question of adjournment), shall be presented to the President of the United States; and before the same shall take effect, shall be approved by him, or being disapproved by him, shall be re-passed by two thirds of the Senate and House of Representatives, according to the rules and limitations prescribed in the case of a bill.

Section 8. The Congress shall have power

To lay and collect taxes, duties, imposts and excises, to pay the debts, and provide for the common defence and general welfare of the United States; but all duties, imposts, and excises shall be uniform throughout the United States:

To borrow money on the credit of the United States:

To regulate commerce with foreign nations, and

among the several States, and with the Indian tribes:

To establish an uniform rule of naturalization, and uniform laws on the subject of bankruptcies throughout the United States:

To coin money, regulate the value thereof, and of foreign coin, and fix the standard of weights and measures:

To provide for the punishment of counterfeiting the securities and current coin of the United States:

To establish post offices and post roads:

To promote the progress of science and useful arts, by securing, for limited times, to authors and inventors, the exclusive right to their respective writings and discoveries:

To constitute tribunals inferior to the Supreme Court:

To define and punish piracies and felonies committed on the high seas, and offences against the law of nations:

To declare war, grant letters of marque and reprisal, and make rules concerning captures on land and water:

To raise and support armies: but no appropriation of money to that use shall be for a longer term than two years:

To provide and maintain a navy:

To make rules for the government and regulation of the land and naval forces:

To provide for calling forth the militia to execute the laws of the Union, suppress insurrections and repel invasions:

To provide for organizing, arming, and disciplining the militia, and for governing such part of them as may be employed in the service of the United States, reserving to the States respectively, the appointment of the officers, and the authority of training the militia according to the discipline prescribed by Congress:

To exercise exclusive legislation, in all cases whatsoever, over such district (not exceeding ten miles square) as may by cession of particular States, and the acceptance of Congress, become the seat of the government of the United States,

among the states (interstate commerce), and with the Indian tribes;

To make rules for naturalization (citizenship for foreigners) and for bankruptcy (business failure);

To coin money and regulate its value; to set standards for the weights and measures used in the United States;

To punish counterfeiters;

To establish post offices and build post roads;

To protect authors and inventors (by issuing copyrights and patents);

To set up a system of federal courts;

To punish piracy, other crimes committed on the high seas, and offenses against the law of nations (international law);

To declare war and give permission to privately-owned ships to seize enemy vessels; (Such private ships were known as privateers, and the permission was called a "letter of marque and reprisal.")

To raise and support armies; (The two-year limit on funds for the army was intended to keep the President or a general from becoming a dictator.)

To support a navy;

To make rules for the armed forces;

To call up the militia (state troops) to carry out federal laws, put down uprisings, and stop foreign invasions;

To make rules for the militia, when called into federal service;

To rule the District of Columbia and other federal holdings;

To make all laws needed to carry out these powers. (This is the very important "elastic clause" discussed on page 160.)

Section 9. *Limits to Congress' Powers.* Congress may not end the slave trade until the year 1808.

The right of *habeas corpus* may be suspended only in case of rebellion or invasion. This is an order, signed by a judge, either to arrange a prisoner's early hearing or to set the prisoner free at once.

Bills of attainder and *ex post facto* laws are forbidden. (A bill of attainder is a law punishing a person without a regular trial in court. An *ex post facto* law makes certain actions illegal even if they were performed before the law was passed. Both kinds of laws had been passed by the British Parliament.)

Any direct tax must be based on the census. (This provision prevented Congress from taxing people more heavily in one state than in another. The income tax became an exception as a result of the Sixteenth Amendment.)

No tax may be put on exports, no port may be given an advantage over another, and ships going from one state to another may not be taxed.

The treasury can spend money only with Congress' permission. A statement of federal receipts and spending must be issued regularly. (This is our federal budget.)

No titles of nobility may be granted by the federal government. No federal official may accept a gift or title from a foreign nation without the consent of Congress.

Section 10. *Powers Forbidden to the*

and to exercise like authority over all places purchased by the consent of the legislature of the State in which the same shall be, for the erection of forts, magazines, arsenals, dock-yards, and other needful buildings. And,

To make all laws which shall be necessary and proper for carrying into execution the foregoing powers, and all other powers vested by this Constitution in the government of the United States, or in any department or officer thereof.

Section 9. The migration or importation of such persons as any of the States now existing shall think proper to admit, shall not be prohibited by the Congress prior to the year one thousand eight hundred and eight; but a tax or duty may be imposed on such importation, not exceeding ten dollars for each person.

The privilege of the writ of *habeas corpus* shall not be suspended, unless when in cases of rebellion or invasion the public safety may require it.

No bill of attainder or *ex post facto* law shall be passed.

No capitation, or other direct tax, shall be laid, unless in proportion to the *census* or enumeration herein before directed to be taken.

No tax or duty shall be laid on articles exported from any State. No preference shall be given by any regulation of commerce or revenue to the ports of one State over those of another; nor shall vessels bound to, or from, one State be obliged to enter, clear, or pay duties in another.

No money shall be drawn from the treasury, but in consequence of appropriations made by law; and a regular statement and account of the receipts and expenditures of all public money shall be published from time to time.

No title of nobility shall be granted by the United States; and no person holding any office of profit or trust under them, shall, without the consent of the Congress, accept of any present, emolument, office, or title of any kind whatever, from any king, prince, or foreign state.

Section 10. No State shall enter into any treaty, alliance, or confederation; grant letters of marque and reprisal; coin money; emit bills of credit;

make any thing but gold and silver coin a tender in payment of debts; pass any bill of attainder, *ex post facto* law, or law impairing the obligation of contracts, or grant any title of nobility.

No State shall, without the consent of the Congress, lay any imposts or duties on imports or exports, except what may be absolutely necessary for executing its inspection laws; and the net produce of all duties and imposts, laid by any State on imports or exports, shall be for the use of the treasury of the United States; and all such laws shall be subject to the revision and control of the Congress. No State shall, without the consent of Congress, lay any duty of tonnage, keep troops, or ships of war, in time of peace, enter into any agreement or compact with another State, or with a foreign power, or engage in war, unless actually invaded, or in such imminent danger as will not admit of delay.

ARTICLE II.

Section 1. The executive power shall be vested in a President of the United States of America. He shall hold his office during the term of four years, and together with the Vice President, chosen for the same term, be elected as follows:

Each State shall appoint, in such manner as the legislature thereof may direct, a number of electors equal to the whole number of Senators and Representatives to which the State may be entitled in the Congress; but no Senator or Representative, or person holding an office of trust or profit under the United States, shall be appointed an elector.

The electors shall meet in their respective States, and vote by ballot for two persons, of whom one at least shall not be an inhabitant of the same State with themselves. And they shall make a list of all the persons voted for, and of the number of votes for each; which list they shall sign and certify, and transmit sealed to the seat of the government of the United States, directed to the President of the Senate. The President of the Senate shall, in the presence of the Senate and House of Representatives, open all the certificates, and

States. The states may not make treaties, given permission to privateers, coin money, issue bills of credit (a kind of paper money), pass a bill of attainder or *ex post facto* law, impair a contract, or grant a title of nobility.

A state may tax imports or exports only with the consent of Congress and for purposes of inspection (to keep out infected plants and animals, for example).

A state may not keep troops or warships in peacetime, make agreements with other states or foreign nations, or wage war without the consent of Congress. It may, however, defend itself from a foreign invasion or other danger.

ARTICLE II. THE EXECUTIVE BRANCH

Section 1. *The Presidency.* Both the President, our chief executive, and the Vice-President are elected for four-year terms.

Each state decides how its electors for President and Vice-President are to be chosen. The number of electors from each state is equal to the number of its senators and representatives combined. Members of Congress and other federal officials may not serve as electors.

The electors meet in their own states (usually in the state capital) and vote for two persons. The votes are counted and the results are sent to the presiding officer of the Senate in a sealed envelope. These envelopes are opened and the electoral votes are counted before both houses of Congress. The person with the highest number of votes becomes President. The person with the second highest number of votes becomes Vice-President. (This was changed by the Twelfth Amendment, under which electors cast separate ballots for President and Vice-President.) In case of a tie or the lack of a majority for any candidate, the House of Representatives chooses the President; the Senate chooses the Vice-President. In such elections, each state casts only one vote.

Congress may set the dates on which electors are chosen and cast their ballots. (They are chosen on Election Day, but cast their ballots several weeks later.)

A candidate for President must be at least thirty-five years old and a citizen of the United States by birth. The President must have lived in the United States for at least fourteen years.

If the President dies, is unable to work, or is removed from office, the Vice-President becomes President. Congress shall take care of cases in which no Vice-President is available. (This has been changed by the Twenty-Fifth Amendment, on page 146.)

The President's salary may not be changed.

the votes shall then be counted. The person having the greatest number of votes shall be the President, if such number be a majority of the whole number of electors appointed; and if there be more than one who have such majority, and have an equal number of votes, then the House of Representatives shall immediately choose by ballot one of them for President; and if no person have a majority, then from the five highest on the list the said House shall in like manner choose the President. But in choosing the President, the votes shall be taken by States, the representation from each State having one vote; a quorum for this purpose shall consist of a member or members from two thirds of the States, and a majority of all the States shall be necessary to a choice. In every case, after the choice of the President, the person having the greatest number of votes of the electors shall be the Vice President. But if there should remain two or more who have equal votes, the Senate shall choose from them by ballot the Vice President.

The Congress may determine the time of choosing the electors, and the day on which they shall give their votes; which day shall be the same throughout the United States.

No person except a natural born citizen, or a citizen of the United States, at the time of the adoption of this Constitution, shall be eligible to the office of President; neither shall any person be eligible to that office who shall not have attained the age of thirty-five years, and been fourteen years a resident within the United States.

In case of the removal of the President from office, or of his death, resignation, or inability to discharge the powers and duties of the said office, the same shall devolve on the Vice President, and the Congress may by law provide for the case of removal, death, resignation, or inability, both of the President and Vice President, declaring what officer shall then act as President, and such officer shall act accordingly until the disability be removed, or a President shall be elected.

The President shall at stated times, receive

for his services, a compensation, which shall neither be increased nor diminished during the period for which he shall have been elected, and he shall not receive within that period any other emolument from the United States or any of them.

Before he enter on the execution of his office, he shall take the following oath or affirmation:

"I do solemnly swear, (or affirm,) that I will faithfully execute the office of President of the United States, and will, to the best of my ability, preserve, protect, and defend the Constitution of the United States."

Section 2. The President shall be commander-in-chief of the army and navy of the United States, and of the militia of the several States, when called into the actual service of the United States; he may require the opinion, in writing, of the principal officer in each of the executive departments, upon any subject relating to the duties of their respective offices, and he shall have power to grant reprieves and pardons for offences against the United States, except in cases of impeachment.

He shall have power, by and with the advice and consent of the Senate, to make treaties, provided two thirds of the Senators present concur; and he shall nominate, and by and with the advice and consent of the Senate, shall appoint ambassadors, other public ministers and consuls, judges of the Supreme Court, and all other officers of the United States, whose appointments are not herein otherwise provided for, and which shall be established by law. But the Congress may by law vest the appointment of such inferior officers, as they think proper, in the President alone, in the courts of law, or in the heads of departments.

The President shall have power to fill up all vacancies that may happen during the recess of the Senate, by granting commissions which shall expire at the end of their session.

Section 3. He shall, from time to time, give to the Congress information of the state of the Union, and recommend to their consideration such meas-

The President may not receive any other payment from the federal government or any state during the term of office.

At the inauguration, the President takes an oath to perform the duties of the President and to defend the Constitution.

Section 2. *Powers of the President*. The President is commander in chief of the armed forces and of the state militia when called into federal service. The heads of the executive departments have to report to the President on the work of their departments. The President has the power to grant reprieves (delays of punishment) and pardons for offenses against the federal government.

The President makes treaties, with the consent of two-thirds of the Senate. The President appoints ambassadors, judges, and other high federal officials, with the consent of a majority of the Senate.

When the Senate is not in session, the President may make temporary appointments to these positions.

Section 3. *Powers of the President* (continued). The President gives Congress "information on the state of the Union" (see photo, page 147) and asks it to pass laws thought necessary. The President may call Congress together for special sessions. If the two houses cannot agree on when to adjourn, the President may set the date. The President receives ministers from foreign nations, takes care that the laws are "faithfully executed," and grants commissions to all officers in the armed forces.

Section 4. *Removal.* The President, Vice-President, and other federal officials can be removed through impeachment and conviction on three charges—"treason, bribery, or other high crimes and misdemeanors."

ARTICLE III. THE JUDICIAL BRANCH

Section 1. *Protection of Judges.* The judicial department is made up of the Supreme Court and lower courts established by Congress. The judges hold office "during good behavior" (see page 152). Their pay may not be reduced while they are in office.

Section 2. *Jurisdiction of the Federal Courts.* Federal courts hear all cases 1. arising under the Constitution, laws, and treaties of the United States; 2. affecting foreign ministers; 3. occurring at sea; 4. in which the United States is a party; 5. between two or more states; 6. between a state and the citizen of another state; 7. between citizens of different states; 8. between citizens of the same state about land given them by different states; and 9. between a state and foreign states or people. (However, the Eleventh Amendment protects the states from being sued in a federal court by citizens of another state or by foreigners.)

Cases involving foreign ministers and state governments go directly to the Supreme Court. In other cases the Supreme Court may hear appeals if it wishes. Congress may,

ures as he shall judge necessary and expedient. He may on extraordinary occasions, convene both Houses, or either of them; and in case of disagreement between them, with respect to the time of adjournment, he may adjourn them to such time as he shall think proper. He shall receive ambassadors and other public ministers. He shall take care that the laws be faithfully executed; and shall commission all the officers of the United States.

Section 4. The President, Vice President, and all civil officers of the United States, shall be removed from office on impeachment for, and conviction of, treason, bribery, or other high crimes and misdemeanors.

ARTICLE III.

Section 1. The judicial power of the United States shall be vested in one Supreme Court, and in such inferior courts as the Congress may, from time to time, ordain and establish. The judges, both of the Supreme and inferior courts, shall hold their offices during good behaviour; and shall, at stated times, receive for their services, a compensation, which shall not be diminished during their continuance in office.

Section 2. The judicial power shall extend to all cases, in law and equity, arising under this Constitution, the laws of the United States, and treaties made, or which shall be made under their authority; to all cases affecting ambassadors, other public ministers, and consuls; to all cases of admiralty and maritime jurisdiction; to controversies to which the United States shall be a party; to controversies between two or more States, between a State and citizens of another State, between citizens of different States, between citizens of the same State claiming lands under grants of different States, and between a State, or the citizens thereof, and foreign States, citizens or subjects.

In all cases affecting ambassadors, other public ministers and consuls, and those in which a State shall be party, the Supreme Court shall have original jurisdiction. In all the other cases before mentioned, the Supreme Court shall have appellate jurisdiction, both as to law and fact, with such exceptions, and under such regulations, as the Congress shall make.

The trial of all crimes, except in cases of impeachment, shall be by jury; and such trial shall be held in the State where the said crimes shall have been committed; but when not committed within any State, the trial shall be at such place or places as the Congress may by law have directed.

Section 3. Treason against the United States, shall consist only in levying war against them, or in adhering to their enemies, giving them aid and comfort. No person shall be convicted of treason unless on the testimony of two witnesses to the same overt act, or on confession in open court.

The Congress shall have power to declare the punishment of treason, but no attainder of treason shall work corruption of blood, for forfeiture, except during the life of the person attainted.

ARTICLE IV.

Section 1. Full faith and credit shall be given in each State to the public acts, records, and judicial proceedings of every other State. And the Congress may by general laws prescribe the manner in which such acts, records, and proceedings shall be proved, and the effect thereof.

Section 2. The citizens of each State shall be entitled to all privileges and immunities of citizens in the several States.

A person charged in any State with treason, felony, or other crime, who shall flee from justice, and be found in another State, shall, on demand of the executive authority of the State from which he fled, be delivered up, to be removed to the State having jurisdiction of the crime.

No person held to service or labour in one State, under the laws thereof, escaping into another, shall, in consequence of any laws or regulation therein, be discharged from such service or labour, but shall be delivered up on claim of the

however, make regulations for such appeals.

All federal crimes are tried by a jury in the state in which they have been committed. Congress decides where a crime should be tried if it was not committed inside any state.

Section 3. *Treason.* Treason consists only of making war against the United States or giving "aid and comfort" to its enemies. A person can be convicted of treason only on the testimony of two witnesses or on his or her own confession in open court.

Congress can set the penalties for treason, but only the accused person may be punished. (In England, a traitor's entire family was often punished.)

ARTICLE IV. COOPERATION AMONG THE STATES

Section 1. *Acceptance of All State Actions.* Every state must accept the legal actions and records of the other states. (Marriages and divorces are the most common examples.)

Section 2. *Return of Fugitives.* A citizen of one state is entitled to equal treatment in the other states.

When a person charged with a serious crime has fled from one state to another, he or she must be returned at the governor's request.

A runaway slave or indentured servant must likewise be returned on demand.

Section 3. *Admission of New States.* Congress admits new states. It may not, however, form a new state from the territory of another state without that state's consent.

Congress governs the federal territories (see page 103).

Section 4. *Protection of the States.* The United States guarantees every state a republican form of government. (That is, it must act to keep a monarchy or dictatorship from being set up.) It must protect a state from invasion and from "domestic violence" (an uprising) at the request of the state's legislature or governor.

ARTICLE V. AMENDING THE CONSTITUTION. Congress may propose amendments by a two-thirds vote of both houses. If two-thirds of the states so request, Congress must call a special convention to propose amendments. Proposed amendments go into effect when they have been ratified by the legislatures or by special conventions in three-fourths of the states.

ARTICLE VI. SUPREMACY OF THE FED-

party to whom such service or labour may be due.

Section 3. New States may be admitted by the Congress into this Union; but no new State shall be formed or erected within the jurisdiction of any other State; nor any State be formed by the junction of two or more States, or parts of States, without the consent of the legislatures of the States concerned, as well as of the Congress.

The Congress shall have power to dispose of and make all needful rules and regulations respecting the territory or other property belonging to the United States; and nothing in this Constitution shall be so construed as to prejudice any claims of the United States, or of any particular State.

Section 4. The United States shall guarantee to every State in this Union a republican form of government, and shall protect each of them against invasion; and on application of the legislature, or of the executive, (when the legislature cannot be convened) against domestic violence.

ARTICLE V.

The Congress, whenever two thirds of both Houses shall deem it necessary, shall propose amendments to this Constitution, or, on the application of the legislatures of two thirds of the several States, shall call a convention for proposing amendments, which, in either case, shall be valid to all intents and purposes, as part of this Constitution, when ratified by the legislatures of three fourths of the several States, or by conventions in three fourths thereof, as the one or the other mode of ratification may be proposed by the Congress; provided, that no amendment, which may be made prior to the year one thousand eight hundred and eight, shall in any manner affect the first and fourth clauses in the ninth section of the first article; and that no State, without its consent, shall be deprived of its equal suffrage in the Senate.

ARTICLE VI.

All debts contracted, and engagements entered

into, before the adoption of this Constitution, shall be as valid against the United States, under this Constitution, as under the confederation.

This Constitution, and the laws of the United States which shall be made in pursuance thereof, and all treaties made, or which shall be made, under the authority of the United States, shall be the supreme law of the land: and the judges, in every State, shall be bound thereby, any thing in the Constitution or laws of any State to the contrary notwithstanding.

The Senators and Representatives before mentioned, and the members of the several State legislatures, and all executive and judicial officers, both of the United States and of the several States, shall be bound, by oath or affirmation, to support this Constitution; but no religious test shall ever be required as a qualification to any office or public trust under the United States.

ARTICLE VII.

The ratification of the conventions of nine States, shall be sufficient for the establishment of this Constitution between the States so ratifying the same.

Done in Convention, by the unanimous consent of the States present, the seventeenth day of September, in the year of our Lord one thousand seven hundred and eighty-seven, and of the independence of the United States of America the twelfth. In witness whereof we have hereunto subscribed our names.

GEORGE WASHINGTON, PRESIDENT
and Deputy from Virginia.

(Following Washington's signature are those of the delegates from the states represented at the Convention.)

(On September 13, 1788, Congress certified that a sufficient number of states had ratified and that the Constitution should be put into operation.)

ERAL GOVERNMENT. The federal government accepts all debts and other obligations of the Confederation.

The Constitution and law or treaties made under it are the supreme law of the land. Judges in every state must recognize this fact.

Senators and representatives, members of the state legislatures, and other federal and state officials must take an oath to support the Constitution. But no religious test shall ever be required for any federal office.

ARTICLE VII. ADOPTING THE CONSTITUTION

The Constitution shall go into effect as soon as nine states have ratified it.

AMENDMENTS

Amendments One through Ten, known as the Bill of Rights, took effect in 1791.

ARTICLE I. *Freedom of Religion, Speech, Press, Assembly, and Petition.* Congress is forbidden to make laws about an "establishment of religion," or to prevent freedom of religion, freedom of speech and the press, the right of peaceful assembly, or the right of petition.

ARTICLE I. Congress shall make no law respecting an establishment of religion, or prohibiting the free exercise thereof; or abridging the freedom of speech, or of the press; or the right of the people peaceably to assemble, and to petition the government for a redress of grievances.

ARTICLE II. *The Right to Bear Arms.* A free country needs a "well regulated militia." So the government may not interfere with the people's right to bear arms.

ARTICLE II. A well regulated militia being necessary to the security of a free State, the right of the people to keep and bear arms shall not be infringed.

ARTICLE III. *Security of the Home.* A soldier may not be stationed in a private home in peacetime without the owner's consent. This may be done in wartime, but only if Congress passes a law saying so.

ARTICLE III. No soldier shall, in time of peace, be quartered in any house without the consent of the owner; nor in time of war, but in a manner to be prescribed by law.

ARTICLE IV. *Security of the Home* (continued). The people, their homes, and their possessions shall be safe from unreasonable searches and seizures. A search warrant may be issued only if witnesses give good reasons under oath. The warrant must describe the place to be searched and the persons or things to be seized.

ARTICLE IV. The right of the people to be secure in their persons, houses, papers, and effects, against unreasonable searches and seizures, shall not be violated; and no warrants shall issue, but upon probable cause, supported by oath or affirmation, and particularly describing the place to be searched, and the persons or things to be seized.

ARTICLE V. *Rights of an Accused Person.* In serious crimes, a person must be indicted by a grand jury before being tried. The accused person may not be tried twice for the same offense. The accused person may not be forced to be a witness against himself or herself. The accused person may not have his or her life, liberty, or property taken away without due process of law (see page 166). Private property may not be taken for public use without fair payment.

ARTICLE V. No person shall be held to answer for a capital or otherwise infamous crime, unless on a presentment or indictment of a grand jury, except in cases arising in the land or naval forces, or in the militia, when in actual service, in time of war or public danger; nor shall any person be subject for the same offence to be twice put in jeopardy of life or limb; nor shall be compelled, in any criminal case, to be witness against himself; nor be deprived of life, liberty, or property, without due process of law; nor shall private property be taken for public use without just compensation.

ARTICLE VI. In all criminal prosecutions the accused shall enjoy the right to a speedy and public trial, by an impartial jury of the State and district wherein the crime shall have been committed, which district shall have been previously ascertained by law, and to be informed of the nature and cause of the accusation; to be confronted with the witnesses against him; to have compulsory process for obtaining witnesses in his favour; and to have the assistance of counsel for his defence.

ARTICLE VII. In suits at common law, where the value in controversy shall exceed twenty dollars, the right of trial by jury shall be preserved; and no fact tried by a jury shall be otherwise re-examined in any court of the United States than according to the rules of the common law.

ARTICLE VIII. Excessive bail shall not be required, nor excessive fines imposed, nor cruel and unusual punishments inflicted.

ARTICLE IX. The enumeration in the Constitution of certain rights, shall not be construed to deny or disparage others retained by the people.

ARTICLE X. The powers not delegated to the United States by the Constitution, nor prohibited by it to the States, are reserved to the States respectively or to the people.

ARTICLE XI. The Judicial power of the United States shall not be construed to extend to any suit in law or equity, commenced or prosecuted against one of the United States by Citizens of another State, or by Citizens or Subjects of any Foreign State.

ARTICLE VI. *Rights of an Accused Person* (continued). A person accused of a crime has the right to a speedy and public trial by a fair (impartial) jury in the district where the crime was committed. The accused person must be informed of the charges against him or her. The accused person has the right to know the witnesses against him or her, to summon witnesses in his or her favor, and to have a lawyer.

ARTICLE VII. *Rights of an Accused Person* (continued). A jury must be used in any lawsuit involving more than twenty dollars.

ARTICLE VIII. *Rights of an Accused Person* (concluded). Excessive bail, excessive fines, and cruel and unusual punishments are forbidden.

ARTICLE IX. *Reserved Rights.* The people have other rights besides those listed here.

ARTICLE X. *Reserved Rights* (continued). Powers not delegated to the federal government or forbidden to the states are reserved to the states and the people.

ARTICLE XI. *Jurisdiction of the Federal Courts* (1798). A case may not be brought against a state in a federal court by citizens of another state or a foreign nation.

ARTICLE XII. *Election of the President and Vice-President* (1804). The electors shall cast separate ballots for President and Vice-President. If no person has a majority, the House of Representatives chooses the President from the three highest candidates. Each state casts a single vote in this election. The Senate follows a similar procedure to choose the Vice-President when no candidate has a majority of the electoral votes.

ARTICLE XII. The electors shall meet in their respective States, and vote by ballot for President and Vice President, one of whom, at least, shall not be an inhabitant of the same State with themselves; they shall name in their ballots the person voted for as President, and in distinct ballots the person voted for as Vice President; and they shall make distinct lists of all persons voted for as President, and of all persons voted for as Vice President, and of the number of votes for each, which list they shall sign and certify, and transmit sealed to the seat of the government of the United States, directed to the President of the Senate; the President of the Senate shall, in the presence of the Senate and House of Representatives, open all the certificates, and the votes shall then be counted: the person having the greatest number of votes for President shall be the President, if such number be a majority of the whole number of electors appointed; and if no person have such majority, then from the persons having the highest numbers, not exceeding three, on the list of those voted for as President, the House of Representatives shall choose immediately by ballot the President. But in choosing the President, the vote shall be taken by States, the representation from each State having one vote; a quorum for this purpose shall consist of a member or members from two thirds of the States, and a majority of all the States shall be necessary to a choice. And if the House of Representatives shall not choose a President whenever the right of choice shall devolve upon them, before the fourth day of March next following, then the Vice President shall act as President, as in the case of the death or other constitutional disability of the President.

The person having the greatest number of votes as Vice President shall be the Vice President, if such number be a majority of the whole number of electors appointed; and if no person have a majority, then from the two highest numbers on the list the Senate shall choose the Vice President: a quorum for that purpose shall consist of two thirds of the whole number of Senators, and a majority of the whole number shall be necessary to a choice.

But no person constitutionally ineligible to the office of President shall be eligible to that of Vice President of the United States.

ARTICLE XIII. Section 1. Neither slavery nor involuntary servitude, except as a punishment for crime whereof the party shall have been duly convicted, shall exist within the United States, or any place subject to their jurisdiction.

Section 2. Congress shall have power to enforce this article by appropriate legislation.

ARTICLE XIV. Section 1. All persons born or naturalized in the United States, and subject to the jurisdiction thereof, are citizens of the United States and of the State wherein they reside. No State shall make or enforce any law which shall abridge the privileges or immunities of citizens of the United States; nor shall any State deprive any person of life, liberty, or property, without due process of law, nor deny to any person within its jurisdiction the equal protection of the laws.

Section 2. Representatives shall be apportioned among the several States according to their respective numbers, counting the whole number of persons in each State, excluding Indians not taxed. But when the right to vote at any election for the choice of electors for President and Vice President of the United States, representatives in Congress, the executive and judicial officers of a State, or the members of the legislature thereof, is denied to any of the male inhabitants of such State, being twenty-one years of age, and citizens of the United States, or in any way abridged, except for participation in rebellion or other crime, the basis of representation

ARTICLE XIII. *End of Slavery* (1865). Slavery or forced service is forbidden, except as punishment for a crime.

ARTICLE XIV. *Equal Rights for All Americans* (1868). All persons born or naturalized (granted citizenship) in the United States are citizens of the United States and of the state where they live. No state can take away their rights as citizens; deprive them of life, liberty, or property without due process of law; or deny them the equal protection of the laws.

The number of representatives from a state depends on the number of inhabitants it has. (This ends the three-fifths rule, in Section 2 of Article I). If a state denies the vote to citizens over twenty-one years of age, except for rebellion or crimes, the number of its representatives is to be reduced.

Anyone who took an oath, as a federal or state official, to support the Constitution and then supported a rebellion (the Confederacy) is forbidden to hold federal or state office. Congress may restore such rights by a two-thirds vote of both houses.

The debts of the United States in ending the rebellion (the Civil War) are legal. But debts arising from the rebellion against the United States and payments for the loss or emancipation of slaves are illegal. They may not be paid by the federal government or any state.

ARTICLE XV. *Right to Vote for Former Slaves* (1870). Citizens of the United States may not be denied the right to vote because of their race or color or because they were once slaves.

ARTICLE XVI. *Income Tax* (1913). Congress may collect taxes on incomes without regard to a state's population.

therein shall be reduced in the proportion which the number of such male citizens shall bear to the whole number of male citizens twenty-one years of age in such State.

Section 3. No person shall be a senator or representative in Congress, or elector of President and Vice President, or hold any office, civil or military, under the United States, or under any State, who having previously taken an oath, as a member of Congress, or as an officer of the United States, or as a member of any State legislature, or as an executive or judicial officer of any State to support the Constitution of the United States shall have engaged in insurrection or rebellion against the same, or given aid or comfort to the enemies thereof. But Congress may by a vote of two-thirds of each house remove such disability.

Section 4. The validity of the public debt of the United States, authorized by law, including debts incurred for payment of pensions and bounties for services in suppressing insurrection or rebellion, shall not be questioned. But neither the United States nor any State shall assume or pay any debt or obligation incurred in aid of insurrection or rebellion against the United States, or any claim for the loss or emancipation of any slave; but all such debts, obligations, and claims shall be held illegal and void.

Section 5. The Congress shall have power to enforce, by appropriate legislation the provisions of this article.

ARTICLE XV. Section 1. The right of citizens of the United States to vote shall not be denied or abridged by the United States or by any State on account of race, color, or previous condition of servitude.

Section 2. The Congress shall have power to enforce this article by appropriate legislation.

ARTICLE XVI. The Congress shall have power to lay and collect taxes on incomes, from whatever source derived, without apportionment among the several States, and without regard to any census or enumeration.

ARTICLE XVII. The Senate of the United States shall be composed of two Senators from each State, elected by the people thereof, for six years; and each Senator shall have one vote. The electors in each State shall have the qualifications requisite for electors of the most numerous branch of the State legislatures.

When vacancies happen in the representation of any State in the Senate, the executive authority of such State shall issue writs of election to fill such vacancies: *Provided,* That the legislature of any State may empower the executive thereof to make temporary appointments until the people fill the vacancies by election as the legislature may direct.

This amendment shall not be so construed as to affect the election or term of any Senator chosen before it becomes valid as part of the Constitution.

ARTICLE XVIII. Section 1. After one year from the ratification of this article the manufacture, sale, or transportation of intoxicating liquors within, the importation thereof into, or the exportation thereof from the United States and all territory subject to the jurisdiction thereof for beverage purposes is hereby prohibited.

Section 2. The Congress and the several States shall have concurrent power to enforce this article by appropriate legislation.

Section 3. This article shall be inoperative unless it shall have been ratified as an amendment to the Constitution by the legislatures of the several States, as provided in the Constitution, within seven years from the date of the submission hereof to the States by the Congress.

ARTICLE XIX. The right of citizens of the United States to vote shall not be denied or abridged by the United States or by any

ARTICLE XVII. *Direct Election of Senators* (1913). Senators are to be elected by the voters in each state—that is, by people eligible to vote for the lower house of the state legislature.

When a seat in the Senate becomes vacant, the governor of the state may appoint a Senator to fill it. This person is to hold office either for the rest of the Senator's term or until the next election, as the state legislature decides.

ARTICLE XVIII. *Prohibition* (1919). It is forbidden to make, sell, and transport intoxicating liquors within the United States, to import them, or to export them.

Congress and the states may pass laws to enforce this prohibition.

A seven-year limit is set for ratifying this amendment. (Several later amendments also included such a provision.)

ARTICLE XIX. *Voting for Women* (1920). A citizen of the United States may not be denied the right to vote on account of sex.

ARTICLE XX. *End of the "Lame Ducks"* (1933). The President and Vice-President take office on January 20 (instead of March 4). The newly elected Congress meets on January 3, three months after Election Day. (It used to meet in December, more than a year after the election! During that year, the old Congress continued to meet and pass laws, even though it contained many "lame ducks," members of Congress who had lost the election.)

If the President-elect dies before the inauguration, the Vice-President becomes President. If neither is available, Congress will choose someone to act as President.

State on account of sex.

Congress shall have power to enforce this article by appropriate legislation.

ARTICLE XX. Section 1. The terms of the President and Vice President shall end at noon on the 20th day of January, and the terms of Senators and Representatives at noon on the 3rd day of January, of the years in which such terms would have ended if this article had not been ratified; and the terms of their successors shall then begin.

Section 2. The Congress shall assemble at least once in every year, and such meeting shall begin at noon on the 3d day of January, unless they shall by law appoint a different day.

Section 3. If, at the time fixed for the beginning of the term of the President, the President elect shall have died, the Vice President elect shall become President. If a President shall not have been chosen before the time fixed for the beginning of his term, or if the President elect shall have failed to qualify, then the Vice President elect shall act as President until a President shall have qualified; and the Congress may by law provide for the case wherein neither a President elect nor a Vice President elect shall have qualified, declaring who shall then act as President, or the manner in which one who is to act shall be selected, and such person shall act accordingly until a President or Vice President shall have qualified.

Section 4. The Congress may by law provide for the case of the death of any of the persons from whom the House of Representatives may choose a President whenever the right of choice shall have devolved upon them, and for the case of the death of any of the persons from whom the Senate may choose a Vice President whenever the right of choice shall have devolved upon them.

Section 5. Sections 1 and 2 shall take effect on the 15th day of October following the ratification of this article.

Section 6. This article shall be inoperative unless it shall have been ratified as an amendment to the Constitution by the legislatures of three-fourths of the several States within seven years from the date of its submission.

ARTICLE XXI. Section 1. The eighteenth article of amendment to the Constitution of the United States is hereby repealed.

Section 2. The transportation or importation into any State, Territory, or possession of the United States for delivery or use therein of intoxicating liquors, in violation of the laws thereof, is hereby prohibited.

Section 3. This article shall be inoperative unless it shall have been ratified as an amendment to the Constitution by conventions in the several States, as provided in the Constitution, within seven years from the date of the submission hereof to the States by the Congress.

ARTICLE XXII. Section 1. No person shall be elected to the office of the President more than twice, and no person who has held the office of President, or acted as President, for more than two years of a term to which some other person was elected President shall be elected to the office of the President more than once. But this Article shall not apply to any person holding the office of President when this Article was proposed by the Congress, and shall not prevent any person who may be holding the office of President, or acting as President, during the term within which this Article becomes operative from holding the office of President or acting as President during the remainder of such term.

ARTICLE XXIII. Section 1. The District constituting the seat of Government of the United States shall appoint in such manner as the Congress may direct: A number of electors of President and Vice President equal to the whole number of Senators and Representatives in Congress to which the

ARTICLE XXI. *Repeal of Prohibition* (1933). The Eighteenth Amendment is repealed (ended).

Bringing intoxicating liquor into any state, territory, or possession where it is prohibited is illegal. (This is to protect those parts of the country that still have their own prohibition laws.)

ARTICLE XXII. *Two Terms for President* (1951). A person may be elected President for only two terms; or for only one term if the person has served as President for more than two years. (This happens when the President dies and the Vice-President takes the elected President's place in the first two years of the term.)

ARTICLE XXIII. *Voting in the District of Columbia* (1961). The District of Columbia is to choose electors for President and Vice-President. The number of electors is to be the same as if it were a state, except that it may not have more electors than the state with the least population.

ARTICLE XXIV. *Against the Poll Tax* (1964). No citizen of the United States may be denied the right to vote for presidential electors or members of Congress because he or she has failed to pay a poll tax or any other tax.

ARTICLE XXV. *Presidential Disability and Succession* (1967). If the President is removed from office, dies, or resigns, the Vice-President becomes President.

When there is no Vice-President, the President will nominate a Vice-President, with the consent of more than half the votes of both houses of Congress.

If the President tells Congress in writing that the President is unable to perform the presidential duties, then the Vice-President will take over as Acting President.

Whenever the Vice-President and a majority of the President's cabinet, or another body chosen by Congress, decide that the President can-

730

District would be entitled if it were a State, but in no event more than the least populous State; they shall be in addition to those appointed by the States, but they shall be considered, for the purposes of the election of President and Vice President, to be electors appointed by a State; and they shall meet in the District and perform such duties as provided by the twelfth article of amendment.

Section 2. The Congress shall have power to enforce this article by appropriate legislation.

ARTICLE XXIV. Section 1. The right of citizens of the United States to vote in any primary or other election for President or Vice President, for electors for President or Vice President, or for Senator or Representative in Congress, shall not be denied or abridged by the United States or any State by reason of failure to pay any poll tax or other tax.

Section 2. The Congress shall have the power to enforce this article by appropriate legislation.

ARTICLE XXV. Section 1. In case of the removal of the President from office or his death or resignation, the Vice President shall become President.

Section 2. Whenever there is a vacancy in the office of the Vice President, the President shall nominate a Vice President who shall take the office upon confirmation by a majority vote of both houses of Congress.

Section 3. Whenever the President transmits to the President pro tempore of the Senate and the Speaker of the House of Representatives his written declaration that he is unable to discharge the powers and duties of his office, and until he transmits to them a written declaration to the contrary, such powers and duties shall be discharged by the Vice President as Acting President.

Section 4. Whenever the Vice President and a majority of either the principal officers of the executive departments, or of such other body as Congress may by law provide, transmit to the President pro tempore of the Senate and the Speaker of the House of Representatives their written declaration that the President is unable to discharge the powers and duties of his office, the Vice President shall immediately assume the powers and duties of the office as Acting President.

Thereafter, when the President transmits to the President pro tempore of the Senate and the Speaker of the House of Representatives his written declaration that no inability exists, he shall resume the powers and duties of his office unless the Vice President and a majority of either the principal officers of the executive department, or of such other body as Congress may by law provide, transmit within four days to the President pro tempore of the Senate and the Speaker of the House of Representatives their written declaration that the President is unable to discharge the powers and duties of his office. Thereupon Congress shall decide the issue, assembling within 48 hours for that purpose if not in session. If the Congress, within 21 days after receipt of the latter written declaration, or, if Congress is not in session, within 21 days after Congress is required to assemble, determines by two-thirds vote of both houses that the President is unable to discharge the powers and duties of his office, the Vice President shall continue to discharge the same as Acting President; otherwise, the President shall resume the powers and duties of his office.

ARTICLE XXVI. Section 1. The right of citizens of the United States, who are 18 years of age or older, to vote shall not be denied or abridged by the United States or by any state on account of age.

Section 2. The Congress shall have power to enforce this article by appropriate legislation.

not discharge presidential duties, the Vice-President will take over as Acting President.

The President may begin working again after telling Congress of the ability to do so. If the Vice-President and a majority of the President's cabinet or the body chosen by Congress disagree with the President, Congress will decide the issue. If it decides by a two-thirds vote that the President is unable to take up presidential duties, the Vice-President will continue as Acting President. Otherwise the President will return to office.

ARTICLE XXVI. *Voting Age Lowered to 18* (1971). Eighteen is the legal voting age for citizens in local, state, and federal elections.

Glossary of Historical Terms

ABOLITIONISTS: Americans in the 1800s who worked to end slavery.

ABSOLUTE MONARCHY: A form of government that gives a hereditary ruler complete control.

AFL-CIO: A labor organization made up of the American Federation of Labor and the Congress of Industrial Organizations.

AGGRESSOR: A nation that attacks another nation first; an invader.

AGRICULTURAL ADJUSTMENT ADMINISTRATION: The government agency that regulates farm production to help farmers.

AGRICULTURAL REVOLUTION: The great change in American farming that began after the Civil War.

ALIEN: A foreigner.

ALIEN AND SEDITION ACTS: Laws passed by the Federalists in the late eighteenth century to weaken their enemies, the Republicans.

ALLIANCE: An agreement by two or more nations to cooperate in certain ways.

ALLIED POWERS (ALLIES): Great Britain, France, and the other nations on their side in World Wars I and II.

ALL-WATER ROUTE: A way to sail directly from Europe to the Far East.

AMENDMENTS: Changes in the Constitution.

AMERICAN FEDERATION OF LABOR (A.F.L.): A large workers' organization, formed in the late nineteenth century, that joined together a number of unions of skilled workers.

AMERICAN REVOLUTION (REVOLUTIONARY WAR): The war in which the United States won its independence from Great Britain.

ANTI-FEDERALISTS: Group that opposed the ratification of the Constitution because it gave too much power to the central government.

ANTITRUST ACT: A law to prevent trusts (monopolies).

ARTICLES OF CONFEDERATION: The unsuccessful first constitution of the United States, that lasted from 1781 to 1789.

ASSEMBLY: A lawmaking body.

ATLANTIC CHARTER: Proposals for a just peace, issued by President Franklin Delano Roosevelt and Prime Minister Churchill early in World War II.

AUTOMATION: The use of machines to control the work of other machines.

AXIS POWERS: Germany, Italy, Japan, and their allies in World War II.

BANK OF THE UNITED STATES: The bank handling the finances of our nation in its early years.

BILL OF RIGHTS: The first ten amendments to the Constitution, which guarantee a number of important freedoms to all Americans.

BLACK CODES: Southern laws passed before and after the Civil War to limit the rights of blacks.

BLOCKADE: The use of warships to keep a nation from trading with other nations by sea.

BOOM: A period of rapid business expansion.

BOSS: A politician whose organization can turn out a large vote for his or her party.

BOYCOTT: A means of influencing an unfriendly nation or business firm by refusing to buy its goods.

CABINET: The heads of the executive departments of the federal government when they serve as the President's advisers.

CAPITALISTS: People who own a business or other property.

CAPTAINS OF INDUSTRY: Businessmen who built our great industries in the period after the Civil War.

CARPETBAGGERS: Northerners who became officials in the South after the Civil War.

CENSUS: The count of our nation's population, taken every ten years; called for in the Constitution to determine the number of representatives each state should have in Congress.

CENTRAL POWERS: Germany and its allies in World War I.

CHARTER: A document issued by the king, giving certain people permission to start a colony in America.

CHEAP MONEY: Money without sufficient backing to give it real value. In times when the value of money falls, prices go up and money buys less ("inflation").

CHECKS AND BALANCES: A system set up by our Constitution which gives each branch of the federal government powers to limit (check) the other two.

CIVIL RIGHTS: The rights and freedoms to which all American citizens are entitled by law.

CIVIL SERVICE: The government's employees.

CIVIL WAR: A war between two groups of people within a nation.

CIVIL WAR (WAR BETWEEN THE STATES): The conflict between the North and the South (the Union and the Confederacy) from 1861 to 1865.

CLAYTON ANTITRUST ACT: The law forbidding business practices that interfere with free competition.

COLD WAR: The rivalry between the United States and the Soviet Union for world leadership after World War II.

COLLECTIVE BARGAINING: A means of reaching agreement on wages, hours, and working conditions through talks between representatives of the employer and workers.

COLONY: A settlement in a new land which keeps its ties with the country from which the settlers came.

COMMITTEE (OF CONGRESS): A group of members of Congress who study all bills on a certain subject.

COMMITTEES OF CORRESPONDENCE: Before the Revolutionary War, groups of Patriots in the colonies who kept in touch with one another by post.

COMMUNISM: The economic system of the Soviet Union, China, and other countries in which almost all business is owned by the government.

COMPROMISE: An agreement in which each side gains a part of what it wants.

CONCURRENT POWERS: Powers exercised by both the federal government and the states, such as the power to tax.

CONFEDERACY: The government of the southern states during the Civil War.

CONGRESS: The lawmaking branch of our federal government.

CONGRESS OF INDUSTRIAL ORGANIZATIONS (C.I.O.): A workers' organization made up of unions, each of which takes in all the workers, both skilled and unskilled, in an industry.

CONSERVATION: The saving of natural resources.

CONSTITUTION: A document laying down the rules for running a government.

CONSTITUTIONAL CONVENTION: The meeting of delegates from the various states that drew up our Constitution.

CONSUMER: A person who buys goods for his or her own use.

CONTINENTAL CONGRESS: The first government of the American states; it led the country during the Revolutionary War.

"COOLING-OFF" PERIOD: Under the Taft-Hartley Act, the eighty-day period for working out a settlement before a strike can be called.

COPPERHEADS: Northerners who wanted to end the Civil War by allowing the South to win.

COTTON BELT ("COTTON KINGDOM"): The row of southern states where cotton was the main crop.

COTTON GIN: Whitney's invention for removing the seeds in cotton quickly; it made cotton growing a profitable industry.

CREDITORS: People who have lent money.
CRITICAL PERIOD: The years after the American Revolution when the future of our country was uncertain.
CRUSADES: The "Wars of the Cross," in which the Christian knights of western Europe tried to take the holy land of Palestine from the Moslems.
CURRENCY: Paper money.
"CUT-THROAT COMPETITION": Unfair practices by business people to drive their rivals out of business.

DAUGHTERS OF LIBERTY: An organization of Patriots that tried to protect the rights of colonists from attack by the British.
DEBTORS: People who have borrowed money.
DECLARATION OF INDEPENDENCE: The official announcement, drafted chiefly by Thomas Jefferson, of the thirteen colonies' independence from Great Britain. The new nation called itself the United States of America.
DELEGATED POWERS: Powers given to the federal government by the Constitution.
DEMOCRACY: A form of government in which the people rule.
DEMOCRATIC PARTY: The political party, formed by Andrew Jackson in the 1830s, that is still one of our two major parties.
DEMOCRATIC-REPUBLICAN PARTY (REPUBLICANS): The political party formed by Jefferson to fight against a strong federal government.
DEPRESSION: A period of hard times, when many people are unemployed.
DETENTE: The relaxing or easing of international tensions and hostility.
DICTATORSHIP: A government run by one person who has seized power.
DISCRIMINATION: The singling out of a person or a group for unfair treatment.

ECONOMIC REVOLUTION: The great advances in American industry, transportation, and farming that took place after the Civil War.

ELASTIC CLAUSE: The Constitutional provision that allows the federal government to exercise powers not listed in the Constitution.
ELECTORAL COLLEGE: A body of people from each state which our Constitution set up to elect the President and Vice-President.
EMANCIPATE: To free, especially to free persons from slavery.
EMANCIPATION PROCLAMATION: President Lincoln's order during the Civil War declaring that slaves in enemy territory were free.
EMBARGO ACT: Jefferson's law forbidding Americans to trade with foreign nations.
EMPIRE: A group of countries ruled over by one powerful nation.
ERA OF GOOD FEELING: The period after the War of 1812 when the Republicans were the only political party.
ESTABLISHED CHURCH: The religious organization (and teaching) approved by the government; the people have to pay for its support.
EUROPEAN RECOVERY PROGRAM (MARSHALL PLAN): Large-scale American aid to western Europe after World War II.
EXCISE TAX: A tax on goods made and sold within a country.
EXECUTIVE: The branch of government that enforces the laws.
EXPORTS: Goods sent out of a country.

FAIR DEAL: President Truman's reform program.
FAIR LABOR STANDARDS ACT (WAGE-HOUR LAW): The federal law setting minimum wages and maximum hours for workers in interstate commerce.
FAR EAST: The part of Asia farthest east from Europe.
FARMERS' ALLIANCES: Organizations formed by farmers in the late nineteenth century to fight for economic and political reforms.
FASCISM: The type of dictatorship set up by Mussolini in Italy after World War I.
FEDERAL RESERVE SYSTEM: A reform in banking procedures initiated by the federal gov-

ernment in the early 1900's. The new system made our banks safer and more efficient.

FEDERAL SYSTEM OF GOVERNMENT: The system under which both the central (federal) and the state governments have important powers.

FEDERAL TRADE COMMISSION: The government agency that tries to stop unfair practices by business.

FEDERALISTS: Group that supported the adoption of the Constitution and wanted a strong federal government.

FEMINISTS: Women who fought for equal rights with men.

FILIBUSTER: In the Senate, an attempt by opponents of a bill to kill its chances of passing by holding the floor for days.

FOOD AND DRUG ADMINISTRATION: The federal agency that protects the public from harmful foods and drugs.

FOREIGN POLICY: A nation's relations with other nations.

FOURTEEN POINTS: President Wilson's proposals for a just peace after World War I.

FREE ENTERPRISE: Motto of Americans who believe that business people should be free to do as they think best without government interference.

FREEDPEOPLE: The blacks freed from slavery as a result of the Civil War.

FREEDOM OF THE SEAS: The right of a neutral nation to trade with other nations in time of war.

FREE SOIL PARTY: The political party formed to stop the spread of slavery in the federal territories.

FRENCH AND INDIAN WAR: The war from 1754 to 1763 of the French and their Indian allies against the British and their American colonists.

FRONTIER: The place where settlements ended and the wilderness began.

FUGITIVE SLAVE LAW: The law requiring northerners to return runaway slaves to the South.

FUNDAMENTAL ORDERS OF CONNECTICUT: The first written constitution in America.

GHETTO: The part of a city inhabited mainly by members of a minority group.

GILDED AGE: The period from 1865 to 1900, so called because a few extremely wealthy Americans lived lavishly while many others were poor.

GOOD NEIGHBOR POLICY: President Franklin Delano Roosevelt's program to improve our relations with Latin America.

GRANGES: Organizations formed by farmers after the Civil War to improve farm life and help farmers economically and politically.

GREAT COMPROMISE: The agreement arrived at by the Constitutional Convention to set up a Congress with two houses.

GREAT SOCIETY: President Johnson's program to end poverty and improve the quality of American life.

GREENBACKS: Paper money not backed by gold or silver.

HABEAS CORPUS: The right of an arrested person to be set free if not brought quickly to trial.

HARD-CORE UNEMPLOYED: People who cannot find jobs without special help.

HAVE-NOT NATIONS: Countries that do not have enough natural resources to support their people.

HOMESTEAD ACT: The law, passed during the Civil War, giving people a farm free of charge if they worked it for five years.

HOUSE OF REPRESENTATIVES: The lower house of our Congress, in which the number of representatives a state has depends on its population.

IMMIGRANT: People who come into a country to settle.

IMPEACHMENT: The procedure for removing high federal officials.

IMPORTS: Goods brought into a country.

IMPRESSMENT (OF SEAMEN): The practice of seizing young men to serve as sailors on warships.

INAUGURAL ADDRESS: The speech made by the President upon taking office.

INCOME TAX (GRADUATED): A tax that increases as a person's income rises.

INDENTURED SERVANTS: People who agreed to work a certain number of years without pay in exchange for passage money and other benefits.

INITIATIVE: A procedure which permits voters to force their legislature to introduce a certain bill.

INJUNCTION: An order issued by a judge, for example, one forbidding workers to perform certain actions that may damage their employer's property.

INTEGRATION: The bringing together of whites and blacks in schools and other facilities open to the public.

INTERNAL IMPROVEMENTS: Roads, canals, and other public works.

INTERSTATE COMMERCE COMMISSION: The government agency that regulates the railroads and other facilities that do business across state lines.

INTOLERABLE ACTS: A number of British moves aimed at punishing the people of Massachusetts for the Boston Tea Party.

"IRON CURTAIN": A term coined by Prime Minister Churchill of Britain to describe the efforts of Communist governments to close off their lands from contact with the rest of the world.

ISLAM: The great religion founded by the Prophet Mohammed in the seventh century.

ISOLATIONISM: The American policy of avoiding alliances with foreign nations.

"JIM CROW" LAWS: Southern laws forbidding blacks to use the same public facilities as whites.

JUDICIARY: The branch of government that interprets (explains) the exact meaning of disputed laws.

KNIGHTS OF LABOR: A late nineteenth-century labor organization that took in all workers, skilled or unskilled.

KNOW-NOTHINGS: Americans who disliked foreigners and wanted to stop immigration.

KOREAN WAR: A three-year war (1950-1953) that pitted American and U.N. forces against North Korean and Chinese Communists over South Korea.

KU KLUX KLAN: A secret organization formed by southern whites after the Civil War to keep blacks and their white allies from holding power.

LABOR RELATIONS ACT: A New Deal law that required employers to recognize unions and bargain with them.

LABOR UNION: An organization formed by workers to improve working conditions and increase wages.

LATIN AMERICA: The lands in the Western Hemisphere south of the Rio Grande, called Latin America because most of the people speak languages derived from Latin.

LEAGUE OF NATIONS: The first international organization to prevent war, established after World War I.

LEGISLATURE: The branch of government that makes the laws.

LEND-LEASE ACT: A law, passed early in World War II, permitting the United States to lend or lease war supplies to Great Britain and the other Allies to help them in their struggle against the Axis powers.

LIMITED MONARCHY: A government headed by a king or queen whose powers have been reduced.

LOCKOUT: The tactic, used by an employer against striking workers, of shutting down a factory until the workers agree to come back on the employer's terms.

LOUISIANA: The part of the Mississippi River Valley claimed by France in the seventeenth and eighteenth centuries.

LOYALISTS (TORIES): Americans who sided with the British in the Revolutionary War.

MANIFEST DESTINY: Slogan of many Americans in the early part of the nineteenth century who wanted the United States to expand westward to the Pacific.

MARTIAL LAW: Military rule—that is, a government enforced by soldiers, which often deprives citizens of their normal rights.

MASS PRODUCTION: A method of manufacturing that turns out large amounts of goods at low cost.

MAYFLOWER COMPACT: An agreement by the Pilgrims to set up a government of their own.

MEDICARE AND MEDICAID: Government payments for hospital and medical care for the old and poor.

MERIT SYSTEM: Choosing government employees by means of tests that measure their ability.

MEXICAN CESSION: The lands taken from Mexico by the United States as a result of the Mexican War.

MIDDLE COLONIES: The English colonies in America between New England and the southern colonies.

"MIDDLE-OF-THE-ROADER": A person who pursues moderate policies.

MINUTEMEN: An organization of Patriots who were ready to fight the British at a moment's notice.

MODERATES: People who try to solve problems gradually and peacefully.

MONOPOLY (TRUST): Control of an industry by a single company or by several companies working together.

MONROE DOCTRINE: President Monroe's policy statement of America's determination to keep European powers out of the western hemisphere.

MOSLEMS (MUSLIMS): Followers of the relligion of Islam, founded by the Prophet Mohammed.

MUCKRACKERS: Writers of the early 1900s who aroused the public to political and economic corruption ("muck") in the United States.

NATIONAL BANKS: Banks chartered by the federal government during the Civil War to increase the sale of government bonds.

NATIONAL COMMUNISM: Communist rule in countries no longer under Soviet control.

NATIONAL GUARD: The militia (troops) of the different states, now under federal control.

NATIONALISM: A feeling, widely shared by the people of a country, of great loyalty to and pride in their nation.

NAZISM (NATIONAL SOCIALISM): The brutal dictatorship established by Hitler in Germany in the 1930s.

NEAR EAST: The part of Asia nearest Europe.

NEUTRAL: Not taking sides in a dispute.

NEW DEAL: President Franklin Delano Roosevelt's program to end the Great Depression and help the common people.

NEW ENGLAND: The English colonies in America northeast of New York.

NEW FRANCE: The lands along the St. Lawrence River and Great Lakes, first settled by the French.

NEW FREEDOM: President Wilson's reform program.

NEW FRONTIER: President Kennedy's reform program.

NEW IMMIGRANTS: The people who came to America in the late nineteenth and early twentieth centuries, largely Catholics and Jews from southern and eastern Europe.

NOMINATING CONVENTION: The meeting at which delegates of a political party choose their candidates for President and Vice-President.

NORTH ATLANTIC TREATY ORGANIZATION (NATO): An alliance of the United States,

Canada, and many European nations to stop the spread of communism in Europe.

NORTHWEST TERRITORY: In our early history, the territory north of the Ohio River and west of the Appalachian Mountains.

NUCLEAR WEAPONS (A-BOMBS AND H-BOMBS): Very powerful bombs that release the tremendous energy locked inside the atom.

NULLIFICATION: A doctrine that a state can kill a federal law it considers unconstitutional.

OFFICE OF ECONOMIC OPPORTUNITY: Government agency in charge of President Johnson's War on Poverty.

OPEN DOOR POLICY: A policy recognizing the right of all nations to trade with China on equal terms.

ORGANIZATION OF AMERICAN STATES: An organization of the United States and the Latin American nations to stop the spread of communism in the Western Hemisphere.

PACIFISTS: People who are against war.

PAN-AMERICAN UNION: An organization to promote trade and friendship between the United States and Latin America.

PARLIAMENT: The English legislature.

PASSIVE RESISTANCE (NONVIOLENCE): Peaceful methods used by blacks and other groups to gain their rights.

PATRIOTS: Colonists who wanted America to break free of British rule.

PEACEFUL COEXISTENCE: Belief that the United States and the Soviet Union can live together in peace despite their differences.

PEASANT: A poor farmer.

PILGRIMS: A small Protestant sect that settled in New England to escape religious persecution.

PIONEERS (FRONTIERS PEOPLE): The first white people to enter regions inhabited only by Indians.

PLANTATION: A very large farm, usually worked by slaves.

POCKET VETO: One way the President can kill a bill. If the President holds the bill for ten days, and Congress adjourns during that time, the bill is dead.

POLITICAL PARTY: A group of people with similar views who work to elect candidates who will represent their views.

POLL TAX: A tax on voters; used in a few states in the past to keep blacks from voting.

POLLUTION: The dirtying of our water and air by waste products from homes and industry.

POPULIST (PEOPLE'S) PARTY: A political party formed in the late nineteenth century to help farmers and city workers.

PREAMBLE: The introduction to the Constitution.

PRECEDENT: An action taken to meet a new situation that sets an example for future generations to follow.

PREJUDICE: Dislike of those who are different.

PRESIDENT: The chief executive of the United States.

PRIMARY ELECTION: An election held before the regular election, in which the voters choose their party's candidates.

PRIVILEGED CLASS: A group that can command special treatment from the rest of society.

PROCLAMATION OF NEUTRALITY: President Washington's announcement that the United States would not take part in Europe's wars.

PROGRESSIVE ERA: A period, from 1900 to 1916, of important reforms in American government and industry.

PROGRESSIVES: A group that brought about many reforms during the Progressive Era.

PROHIBITION ACT: The law forbidding the manufacture and sale of intoxicating liquors.

PROPAGANDA: Information that is spread widely to help or harm a person, group, or nation.

PROTECTIVE TARIFF: A high tax on imports, usually effective in keeping out the products of foreign manufacturers.

PROTECTORATE: A weak country, watched over and partly controlled by a stronger one.

PROTESTANTS: Christian groups that do not recognize the pope as their leader.
PUBLIC WORKS: Government projects to improve conditions and provide jobs.
PURITANS: A large group of Protestants that settled in New England.
"PUSH-BUTTON WAR": A war in which powerful nations would cause great destruction to each other in a short time by launching hundreds of missiles with nuclear warheads.

QUAKERS: A Protestant sect often persecuted for its extreme views.

RADICALS: People who want to make great and rapid changes in government.
RATIONING: A system for sharing scarce goods fairly, chiefly in wartime.
REAPPORTIONMENT: The setting up of election districts so that all of them have about the same population.
RECALL: A reform of the Progressives which gives voters power to remove an official before his or her term of office has ended.
RECONSTRUCTION: Program of the federal government for dealing with the defeated southern states after the Civil War.
REDCOATS: Red-uniformed soldiers of the British army in the eighteenth century.
RED SCARE: Exaggerated fear of socialism and communism after the first and second world wars.
REFERENDUM: Progressive reform in which voters decide whether a bill should be passed or defeated.
REFORMERS: People who seek to eliminate evils and improve living conditions.
RELIGIOUS TOLERATION: Recognition of the right of people of a different faith to practice their religion.
REPRESENTATIVE: A person chosen to act for a group of people.
REPRESENTATIVE GOVERNMENT: A government in which the laws are made by a representative assembly, elected by the voters.

REPUBLIC: A country in which the head of government does not inherit his or her position.
REPUBLICAN PARTY: One of our two major parties formed before the Civil War.
RESERVED POWERS: The powers left to the states under the Constitution, such as control of education and elections.
ROMAN CATHOLIC CHURCH: The Christian church headed by the pope in Rome.

SABOTAGE: Planned destruction of property.
SATELLITE NATIONS: The countries of eastern and central Europe that came under Russian control after World War II.
SECESSION: Withdrawal of a state from the nation, as the southern states from the Union in 1860.
SECRET BALLOT: A voting method in which a citizen can vote as he or she pleases because nobody can tell how he or she voted.
SECRETARY GENERAL: The highest official of the United Nations.
SECTIONALISM: A feeling of loyalty to a section, or part, of the nation.
SEDITION: Any action which aims at weakening or overthrowing the lawful government.
SEGREGATION: To set one group of people apart from other people, especially in housing, schools, and other public facilities.
SELECTIVE SERVICE ACT: A law setting up a system of drafting men for the armed forces.
SENATE: The upper house of our Congress, made up of two representatives from each state.
SENATORIAL COURTESY: The custom of letting the senator from a state name the high federal officials whom the President appoints to serve there.
SENIORITY: The practice of choosing as the chairperson of a congressional committee the committee member belonging to the majority party who has served in that house of Congress for the longest time.
SEPARATION OF POWERS: Division of the powers of the federal government among the

739

three branches; a Constitutional safeguard against dictatorship.

SERF: Farm workers in Europe during the Middle Ages. They owed their lord a part of their crop and certain services in return for the use of a piece of land.

SETTLEMENT HOUSE: A place where slum dwellers can get help, training, and recreation.

SHARECROPPER: A farm worker in the South after the Civil War, who paid for the use of a piece of land with a share of the crop.

SHERMAN ANTITRUST ACT: A law of 1890 forbidding businesses to form trusts (monopolies).

SLAVERY: A system under which human beings were considered the property of their masters.

SMUGGLING: Bringing goods into a country secretly to avoid paying taxes.

SOCIAL SECURITY: A system of government insurance for the old, unemployed, and others who cannot support themselves.

SOCIALISTS: People who believe that business should be owned by the government.

SOLID SOUTH: Nickname for the South since the Civil War, because it usually elected Democrats to office.

SONS OF LIBERTY: An organization of Patriots that tried to protect the rights of colonists from attack by the British.

SOUTHEAST ASIA TREATY ORGANIZATION (SEATO): An alliance of the United States, Great Britain, and nations of Southeast Asia to prevent the spread of communism in that region.

SPANISH-AMERICAN WAR: The war from 1898 to 1899 between the United States and Spain over Cuba.

SPEAKER: The one elected by the House of Representatives to serve as its chairperson.

SPOILS SYSTEM: The practice of politicians who have won an election of giving their followers jobs held by members of the party that has lost.

STATES' RIGHTS: Catchword of groups that claim the federal government is trying to take away Constitutional rights belonging to the states.

STOCK MARKET: A place where shares of stock in corporations are bought and sold.

STRIKE: Refusal of a group of employees to work until the employer meets their terms.

SUBMARINE WARFARE: The practice, used by German submarines in the first and second world wars, of torpedoing enemy ships without warning.

SUBURBS: The smaller towns around a big city.

SWEATSHOP: A factory that employed workers at low wages, for long hours, and under unsanitary conditions.

TAFT-HARTLEY ACT: A law passed after World War II to limit the power of unions.

TARIFFS (CUSTOMS DUTIES): Taxes on goods imported into a country.

TECHNOLOGICAL UNEMPLOYMENT: Loss of jobs as a result of new machines.

TEMPERANCE MOVEMENT: Effort of reformers to make the public aware of the evils of drink, and to fight for laws to limit its manufacture and sale.

TENNESSEE VALLEY AUTHORITY: The government agency that brought the Tennessee River under control and improved the river valley.

TERRITORY: A part of the United States ruled by the federal government through a governor appointed by the President.

TOWN MEETING: A form of direct democracy, in which the citizens of a town make its laws.

TRADE ACTS: British laws regulating the colonies' trade with Great Britain and other nations.

TRANSCONTINENTAL RAILROAD: A railroad that made coast-to-coast travel by rail possible.

TREATY: An agreement between nations.

TRUMAN DOCTRINE: The American policy of stopping the spread of communism.

Unanimous: In complete agreement.

Underdeveloped nations: Countries (mainly in Asia, Africa, and Latin America) that have not yet reached the level of development of the advanced industrial nations.

Underground Railroad: The network of hiding places by which slaves escaped from the South in the years before the Civil War.

United Nations (Organization): The international organization formed after World War II to prevent a third world war.

Unwritten constitution: The practices and customs outside of the Constitution that have become an important part of our government machinery.

Urban Revolution: The rapid change that has brought the large majority of Americans from the countryside into the cities.

Vice-President: The person elected to take over as President when the President dies or is unable to work.

Vietnamese War: The war won by North Vietnam and its Communist allies against U.S.-supported South Vietnam.

War Hawks: Congressmen who wanted war with Great Britain in 1812.

War of 1812: The war between the United States and Great Britain over British seizures of American ships and sailors.

War on Poverty: President Johnson's program to end poverty in the United States.

Warrant: A document issued by a judge, givin officials the right to search a certain place.

Western Hemisphere: The half of the globe west of Europe; the two continents of North and South America.

Whig party: A political party formed in the 1830s to oppose Jackson and the Democrats.

White Supremacy: The belief that whites are superior to blacks; used by white racists to justify white control of government.

Wild West: The newly settled Far West in the last half of the nineteenth century, the scene of much lawless violence.

Workers Compensation: Payments to a worker hurt on the job.

Yalta Conference: The meeting of President Roosevelt, British Prime Minister Churchill, and Russian Premier Stalin to plan the peace after World War II.

Yellow press: Newspapers that attracted many readers by printing sensational and often misleading stories.

Zenger trial: The case in which a New York printer's acquittal on a charge of libel resulted in a great victory for freedom of the press.

Index

A

Abolitionists, 261, 296–98, 304, 310. *See also* Slavery
Adams, John, 187, 194–95, 200, 220, 278
Adams, John Quincy, 226, 243
Adams, Samuel, 70–71, 116
Addams, Jane, 399–400
Afghanistan, 604, 686, 688–89, 696
Africa, 541, 554–55. *See also specific countries*
Agassiz, Louis, 273
Agnew, Spiro, 601
Agricultural Adjustment Administration (AAA), 524, 527–28, 653
Agriculture, 3, 514, 524, 527–28, 549, 592, 616, 626, 637, 651-52
Agriculture Department, U.S., 147
Alabama, 241, 330, 618
Alamo, battle of, 266, 267
Alaska, 124, 267, 328–29, 446–47, 495
Alaskan oil pipeline, 656
Alcott, Louisa May, 401
Aldrin, Edwin, 690
Algeria, 554
Alien and Sedition Acts (1798), 195, 200, 278
Alliance for Progress, 687
Allies: in World War I, 467–69, 473–74, 476–77; after World War I, 482–83, 489–90; in World War II, 539, 546–47, 554, 564
Amazon River, 455
Amendments to the Constitution, 132, 146, 159, 328, 337–38. *See also specific amendments by number*
American Communist party, 589
American Federation of Labor (AFL), 372–73, 506, 549, 589, 618
American Indian Movement (AIM), 630
American party, 275–76
American Red Cross, 330
American Relief Administration, 482, 507
American Revolution (1775–83): battles, 39, 57, 60, 64–65, 71, 76–78; results of, 85–87; and slavery, 116, 209, 212–13, 220, 294
Anderson, Marian, 617
Antietam Creek, battle of, 322
Anti-Federalists, 125–26, 164, 191
Appalachia, 636
Appalachian Mountains, 39, 60, 62–63, 80, 85, 103–4, 110, 381
Appomattox, surrender at, 324
Arabs, 656, 684–85, 694, 696
Argentina, 462, 515, 536, 688
Argonne Forest, battle of, 477
Arizona, 380, 629

Arkansas, 242, 618
Armada, Spanish, 24
Armstrong, Neil, 696
Army, U.S. *See* United States Army
"Arsenal of democracy," 540, 548
Arthur, Chester A., 393–94
Articles of Confederation, 102, 108–11, 117–19, 123, 125, 130, 132, 152, 164, 172
Asia. *See specific countries*
Atlanta, Ga., 620, 647
Atlantic, battle of, 556
Atlantic Charter, 564–65
Atlantic Coastal Plain, 30
Atomic bomb, 549, 558–59, 564, 672. *See also* Nuclear arms race; Nuclear weapons
Audubon, John James, 273
Austin, Moses, 266
Australia, 539, 546, 557
Austria, 481, 539
Austria-Hungary, 466–67
Automation, 635–36
Automobiles, 359, 637, 656–57, 663
Aviation, 547–48, 556–58
Axis Powers, 535–36, 539, 541, 547, 564
Aztecs, 22

B

Balkan Peninsula, 555
Ballot, secret, 407
Baltimore, Lord, 37
Baltimore, Md., 214, 647
Bank Holiday, 522
Bank of the United States: first, 160, 182–83; second, 194, 219, 221, 230, 236, 243, 251–52, 298, 302
Banking, 384–85, 514, 519–20, 522, 528–29, 540
Banneker, Benjamin, 294
Barbary states, war with, 202–3
Barton, Clara, 330
Bases, U.S., 435, 442, 446–47, 460, 462, 495, 536, 540
Begin, Menachem, 685
Belgium, 540
Bell, Alexander Graham, 357
Bellamy, Edward, 401
Berlin crisis, 669, 695
Berlin Wall, 673
Bethune, Mary McLeod, 619
Big Four, 482
Big Three, 564
Bill of Rights: English, 48; state, 85; U.S., 159, 164–67, 172
Bingham, George Caleb, 274
Black codes, 295, 336–37, 343

Blacks, 5, 23, 33, 36, 86, 124, 455, 474, 504, 596, 610–12, 616–21, 638, 646–47, 664, 694. *See also* Civil War; Slavery
Blackwell, Elizabeth, 375
Bleeding Kansas, 310
Bloomer, Amelia, 259
Boone, Daniel, 104
Booth, John Wilkes, 335–36
Bootleggers, 504, 507
Boston, Mass., 39, 69, 71, 77, 79
Boston Massacre, 69–71
Boston Tea Party, 69–71
Boxer Rebellion, 436
Braddock, Edward, 60, 62–63
Brain Trust, 520
Brazil, 3, 18, 22, 24, 119, 462, 688
Brezhnev, Leonid, 680, 690
"Bridge of ships," 548
Britain. *See* Great Britain
Brown, John, 310, 312
Bryan, William Jennings, 395–96, 445, 469
Bryant, William Cullen, 273
Buchanan, James, 310–11, 313
Budget cuts, 605, 695
Bulgaria, 566
Bulge, battle of, 556
Bull Run, battles of, 317–18, 322
Bunker Hill, battle of, 77
Burgoyne, John, 79
Burr, Aaron, 192
Business, 364, 505–7

C

Cabinet, 146–47, 161, 180
Cabot, John, 18
Cabral, Pedro, 18
Calhoun, John C., 243–44, 250–51
California, 124, 146, 236, 267, 304–5, 377, 436, 626–27
Cambodia, 678–79
Camp David peace accords, 684–85, 696
Canada, 3, 26, 63, 68, 78, 85–86, 119, 207–9, 213, 221, 515, 539–40, 591
Canals, 229–30
Cape Horn, 455, 460
Caribbean islands. *See* West Indies
Carnegie, Andrew, 363, 372
Carpetbaggers, 343
Carter, Jimmy, 602–4, 639–40, 647, 657, 685–86, 688, 690, 695–96
Cartier, Jacques, 18
Carver, George Washington, 616
Cash-and-carry policy, 540
Castro, Fidel, 673, 687, 695
Catholicism. *See* Roman Catholicism

742

Cattle Kingdom, 377–78
Census Bureau, 124, 638, 644
Central America. *See* Latin America; *specific countries*
Central Intelligence Agency (CIA), 589, 602
Central Pacific Railroad, 378–79
Central Powers, 467–68
Charles I, 37, 47
Charles II, 37, 39–40
Charleston, S.C., 37
Charters, royal, 35, 62, 68, 85, 103
Chattanooga, Tenn., 645
Chavez, Cesar, 626
Cheap money movement, 386, 395–96
Checks and balances concept, 153–55, 164
Chesapeake affair, 207, 209
Chiang Kai-shek, 677
Chicago, Ill., 213, 616
Chicanos, 625–26
Child labor, 409, 420, 514, 526
Chile, 455, 462
China, 3, 13, 16, 111, 434–36, 488–89, 491, 494, 539–40, 564, 677–78, 680, 689, 695–96
Chinese Americans, 5, 378, 627
Christianity, 14, 22–23, 288. *See also specific denominations*
Churchill, Winston, 554, 563–65
Church of England, 37, 53–54
Cities, 644–48
Civilian Conservation Corps (CCC), 522, 530
Civil rights, 550, 596, 610–12, 616–21, 694
Civil Rights Act (1964), 596, 618, 694
Civil service, 146, 393–94
Civil War (1861–65): battles, 317–24; causes, 285–90, 294–98, 302–6, 310–14; results, 327–30, 355. *See also* Blacks; slavery
Clark, George Rogers, 80
Clark, William, 202
Clay, Henry, 226, 243, 251–52, 267, 303–4
Clayton Antitrust Act (1914), 420
Clean Air Act (1970), 663
Cleveland, Grover, 394, 439, 457
Cleveland, Ohio, 647
Clipper ships, 434
Coal industry, 414, 657–58
Cold War, 574, 668–74, 695
Collective bargaining, 526
Colombia, 460–61
Colonial period, 11, 29–33, 35–40, 49, 52–57, 61–65, 68–72
Colorado, 377
Columbia, 690
Columbus, Christopher, 13, 17, 91

Committee on Public Information (CPI), 475
Committees, congressional, 137–39
Committees of Correspondence, 70, 193
Communism, 473, 476, 481–82, 504, 565–66, 574, 589–90, 617, 669–74, 677–80, 684, 687, 694–96. *See also* China; Soviet Union
Community Action Programs, 594, 600
Community Development Program, 647
Compromise of 1850, 304–6, 310
Computers, 635
Comstock Lode, 377
Concentration camps, 541, 627–28
Concord, battle of, 70–71, 77
Confederacy, 313–14, 317–24, 328, 334, 338
Conference committees, congressional, 139–40
Congo, 574
Congress, U.S.: under Articles of Confederation, 102, 108–11, 192; under Constitution, 123–26, 131–34, 137–40, 148; recent proceedings, 435, 440, 446–47, 457, 461, 469–70, 473, 484, 490, 520, 522, 529, 539–40, 588–90, 594–95, 694–95. *See also* House of Representatives; Senate
Congressional Record, 132, 139
Congress of Industrial Organizations (CIO), 526, 549, 589, 618
Connecticut, 39, 55, 110, 123
Conservation, 364, 381, 415, 653
Constitution, U.S., 54, 64, 100, 475; amendments, 132, 146, 159, 328, 337–38 (*see also specific amendments by number*); changes, 158–61; checks and balances, 153–55; compromises, 123–25; drafting, 115–19; executive branch, 144–48; federal system, 116–19; judicial branch, 152–53; legislative branch, 131–34, 137–40; as model, 456; and protection of rights, 164–67; ratification, 125; text, 130–31, 708–731. *See also* Bill of Rights, U.S.
Constitutional Convention, 111, 116–19, 123–26, 192
Continental Army, 77, 79, 109
Continental Congress, 71, 77–78, 102, 193, 294
Coolidge, Calvin, 488, 495, 507–8, 514, 516, 533
Cooling-off period, 589
Cooper, James Fenimore, 273
Copper, 653
Copperheads, 319–20
Coral Sea, battle of, 557
Cornwallis, Charles, 80
Coronado, Francisco de, 22
Corruption, in government, 344, 507, 600–2

Cortés, Hernando, 22
Cotton belt, 241
Cotton Kingdom, 295
Council of Economic Advisers, 588
Council on Environmental Quality, 652, 663
Court of Appeals, 153
Courts. *See* Judicial branch
Crane, Stephen, 401
Crawford, William H., 226
Credit, overexpansion of, 512–13
Crime, 504, 645
Critical Period, 100–5, 108–11, 118–19, 171
Crowds, 644
Crop insurance, 527
Cuba, 236, 439–42, 460–61, 494, 534, 604, 625–27, 673–74, 687–88, 695
Currency controversy, 109
Custer, George A., 628
Custom duties, 69–70, 109. *See also* Tariffs
Czechoslovakia, 539–40, 672

D

Da Gama, Vasco, 16
Dallas, Texas, 646
Daughters of Liberty, 69
Dawes Act (1887), 629
Debs, Eugene V., 419
Decatur, Stephen, 218
Declaration of Independence, 64, 78, 86–87, 91, 130, 193, 294; text, 706–7
Declaration of the Rights of Man, 186
Deere, John, 274
Delaware, 39–40, 319
Delegated powers, 116, 118, 160
De Lôme letter, 440
Democracy, 45–47, 52–53, 87, 91, 99, 105, 116, 696
Democratic party, 138, 244, 267, 304, 306, 312, 345, 391–96, 445–46, 469, 508, 516, 529, 590–96, 600–5, 694–95
Democratic-Republican party. *See* Republican party
Denmark, 462, 540
Depression (economic), 109, 369, 371, 394–95, 448, 490, 503, 508, 512–16, 520, 528–29. *See also* New Deal
De Soto, Hernando, 22
Détente, 680, 688–89, 696
Detroit, Mich., 213–14, 620, 647
Dewey, George, 441
Dewey, Thomas E., 590
Disarmament, 488, 690
Discrimination, 6, 345, 436, 610–12, 617–18, 694, 696
District of Columbia, 181, 214
Dix, Dorothea, 259, 261

743

Dominican Republic, 461–62, 687–88
"Don't haul down the flag," 445
Doughboys, 476
Douglas, Stephen A., 310–12
Douglas, William O., 167
Douglass, Frederick, 296
Draft, 473, 540, 547, 588

E

East Germany, 673
East Indies, 13, 16, 69
Eastern Europe. *See specific countries*
Economic and Social Council (UN), 572
Economic boom, 506
Economic depression. *See* Depression
Economic revolution period, 353–59, 363–66, 368–73, 376–81, 384–87, 393, 433
Edison, Thomas A., 357–58
Education, 55, 260, 400–1, 588, 591, 595, 610–11, 618, 637, 661–62, 694, 696
Education Department, U.S., 147
Egypt, 554, 684–85, 696
Eighteenth Amendment, 400, 504
Eighth Amendment, 166–67
Eisenhower, Dwight D., 146–47, 591–92, 618, 629, 669, 673, 678, 694
El Salvador, 688
Elastic clause, 160, 172, 182, 220
Elderly, 637–38, 664
Electoral college, 145–46, 161, 226
Electricity, 357
Emancipation Proclamation (1862), 328
Embargo Act (1807), 207–8
Employment. *See* Labor; Unemployment
Energy crisis, 603, 656–59
Energy Security Act (1980), 603, 657
England. *See* Great Britain
Environmental protection, 662–63
Environmental Protection Agency, 663
Equal Rights Amendment, 631
Era of Good Feeling, 218
Erie Canal, 229–30, 242
Espionage and Sedition Acts (1917), 475–76, 504
Established church, 32, 53, 86. *See also* Religion
Ethiopia, 539
Europe. *See* Cold War; World War I; World War II; *specific countries*
European Recovery Program (ERP), 668–69
Executive branch, 131, 144–48, 153–55, 161, 171–72

F

Fair Deal, 590

Fair Employment Practices Committee, 617
Fair Housing Act (1968), 596
Fair Labor Standards Act (1938), 161, 526
Falkland Islands, 688
Far East, 15, 18, 24, 91. *See also specific countries*
Farewell Address, Washington's, 191
Farmers' Alliances, 386–87
Farming. *See* Agriculture
Federal Aviation Administration, 161
Federal Bureau of Investigation (FBI), 589, 600, 602, 618
Federal Communications Commission (FCC), 161
Federal Deposit Insurance Corporation (FDIC), 522
Federalism, 116–19
Federalist Papers, 192
Federalist party, 125–26, 191–95, 199–202, 207, 215, 218–20
Federal Reserve Act (1913), 420
Federal Reserve System, 420, 528
Ferdinand, 16
Feudalism, 288
Fifteenth Amendment, 616
Filibusters, 133, 139, 617
Filipino Americans, 5, 628
Fillmore, Millard, 304
Finland, 539
Flappers, 503
Florida, 22, 26, 62–63, 188, 208–9, 221, 236
Food Administration, 474
Food and Agriculture Organization (UN), 572
Food and Drug Administration (FDA), 415
Ford, Gerald R., 601–2, 647, 694
Ford, Henry, 359, 506
Ford Motor Company, 548
Foreign policy, 186–88, 194–95, 202–3, 206–9, 267, 320, 431, 433–34, 436, 442, 457, 461–62, 467, 488–89, 494–95, 533–36, 578–79, 668–74, 677–80, 684–91
Forests, 653
Fort Sumter, battle of, 313
Foster, Stephen, 274
Fourteen Points, 482, 495, 616
Fourteenth Amendment, 337–38
France, 3, 11, 24, 26, 62–64, 78, 80–81, 109, 111, 180, 186–87, 193–95, 206–8, 222, 320, 431, 456–57, 466–67, 536, 539–40, 554, 556, 564, 574, 678, 689
Franklin, Benjamin, 53, 56, 64, 116
Freedmen's Bureau, 336
"Freedom of the seas," 468, 539
Freedom rides, 618
Free Soil party, 304, 306, 310

Frémont, John C., 268, 311
French and Indian War (1754–63), 60, 62–63, 68, 72, 78, 91
French Revolution, 186–87, 191
Friedan, Betty, 630
Friends, Society of, 40, 54, 294
Frontier. *See* West
Fuel Administration, 474
Fugitive Slave Law, 305
Full Employment Act (1946), 588
Fuller, Margaret, 273
Fulton, Robert, 229
Fundamental Orders of Connecticut, 55
Fur trade, 434

G

Gadsden Purchase (1853), 269
Garfield, James A., 146, 393
Garrison, William Lloyd, 296–97
Gary, Ind., 637
General Assembly (UN), 571, 574
Geneva Agreement (1954), 678
George II, 37
George III, 68, 77, 80, 87
Georgia, 250
Geothermal energy, 659
Germany, 3, 4, 32, 37, 435, 457, 466–67, 481, 490, 501, 533, 535–36, 539, 554–57, 564, 566–68, 669, 673, 689
Gettysburg, battle of, 322
Gettysburg Address, 323
Ghettos, 526–27, 612, 647
G.I. Bill of Rights, 588
Gilbert Islands, 557
Gilded Age, 366, 369–71, 391–96, 399–402, 406
Glorious Revolution (1688), 47
Godey's Lady's Book, 273
Goethals, George W., 461
Gold rush, 269, 377, 460
Gompers, Samuel, 372–73
Good Neighbor Policy, 534–36, 688, 695
Gorgas, William C., 442, 461
Grandfather clauses, 345, 610, 616
Granger movement, 385–86
Grant, Ulysses S., 322, 324, 344, 375, 391
Gray, Asa, 273
Great American Desert, 377, 380
Great Britain, 4, 11, 24, 30–32, 60–61, 63, 76, 80, 124, 186–87, 191, 200, 206–9, 212–15, 218, 221–22, 228, 265, 320, 433, 435–36, 457, 466–67, 539–41, 554, 564, 567, 688–89
Great Compromise, 123, 126
Great Depression. *See* Depression
Great Lakes, 3
Great Plains, 377–80

Great Society programs, 594–96, 694
Greece, 47, 116, 541, 668, 695
Greenback party, 386
Guam, 435, 442, 445, 494
Guantanamo Bay base, 442
Guerillas, 439–40
Guiana, British, 457

H

Habeas corpus, 164, 328
Haiti, 295, 462, 534
Hale, Sarah Josepha, 273
Hamilton, Alexander, 180–83, 186–87, 191–92, 194
Hancock, John, 71
Harding, Warren G., 485, 488–90, 495, 507, 514
Harlem (New York City), 616
Harrison, Benjamin, 394
Harrison, William Henry, 214, 218, 267
Harvard College, 56, 70
Hawaii, 435, 446–47, 494–95, 543
Hayes, Rutherford B., 344, 393
Head Start programs, 595
Health care. *See* Medical and health care
Henry, Joseph, 273
Henry, Patrick, 116, 144
Hessian soldiers, 79
Highways, interstate, 591
Hiroshima, and atomic bomb, 559
Hispanic Americans, 625–27, 638, 694
Hitler, Adolph, 535–36, 539, 542, 556–57, 617
Ho Chi Minh, 678–79
Holland. *See* Netherlands
Homestead Act (1862), 242, 378
Honduras, 462
Honolulu, Hi., 435
Hooker, Thomas, 39
Hoover, Herbert, 488, 491, 495, 507–8, 514–16, 533
House of Representatives, 123–26, 131–34, 137–40, 145, 226, 600–1
Housing and Urban Development Department (HUD), 647
Housing programs, 526–27, 596, 618
Houston, Sam, 266
Houston, Texas, 646
Howe, William, 79
Hudson, Henry, 18
Hudson River School (painting), 274
Huerta, Victoriano, 462
Hughes, Langston, 617
Humanitarian movement, 399–401
Human rights, 573, 617, 688, 696
Humphrey, Hubert H., 596
Hungary, 466–67, 539, 566, 671–72
Hutchinson, Anne, 54

I

Iceland, 542
Illinois, 80, 241
Immigrants, 4–5, 30–33, 230, 236, 243, 275–76, 370–71, 436, 505–6, 625–28, 694
Immigration Act (1965), 626, 694
Impeachment, 133–34, 153, 342, 600–1, 694
Incas, 22
India, 4, 16, 63
Indiana, 80
Indians, 5, 13, 22–23, 29, 36, 38–40, 54, 60, 62–63, 68, 71, 80, 85, 104, 110–11, 187–88, 208–9, 215, 221, 240, 250, 267, 377, 379–80, 456, 628–30
Indies. *See* East Indies; West Indies
Industrialization, 356–59, 363–66, 369–73, 652
Inflation, 588, 603–5, 694–95
Initiatives, 407
Integration, 610–12, 618, 694
Intelligence Committee (Senate), 602
Internal Security Act (1951), 589
International Bank for Reconstruction and Development, 572
International Court of Justice (UN), 572
International Labor Organization, 484, 488, 572
Interstate commerce, and Constitution, 117, 153, 160–62, 172, 203, 220–21
Interstate Commerce Act (1887), 386, 418
Interstate Commerce Commission (ICC), 162, 386, 414, 418
Intolerable Acts, 71, 77
Iowa, 242
Iran, 604, 685–86, 689, 696
Ireland, 467
Irish Americans, 378, 467
Iron, 653
Iron and steel industry, 363
Iron curtain, 673
Irrigation and dams, 415, 651
Irving, Washington, 273
Isabella, 16
Islam, 14
"Island hopping," 557–58
Isolationism, 431, 433, 467, 484–85, 488, 490–91, 494–95, 533, 539–40
Israel, 684–85, 696
Italy, 5, 457, 501, 533, 535, 539, 543, 555–56, 566
Iwo Jima, battle of, 558

J

Jackson, Andrew, 215, 218, 221, 226, 243, 248–54, 257–58, 266, 279
James I, 35

James II, 39
Jamestown, Va., 35–36, 38, 40
Japan, 434, 436, 446, 488–89, 491, 494–95, 501, 533, 535, 539–40, 546, 554, 557–59, 564, 568, 588, 627
Japanese Americans, 5, 436, 447, 550, 627–28
Jay, John, 187–88, 194, 207
Jazz Age, 503–4, 578
Jefferson, Thomas, 78, 118, 193, 219, 248, 257, 278; attitude toward slavery, 294; and Democratic-Republican party, 191, 194; as President, 199–203, 206–8, 466; as secretary of state, 180, 186–87
Jews, 54, 504
Jim Crow laws, 610, 612
Job Corps, 594
Johnson, Andrew, 336–37, 342
Johnson, Lyndon, 594–96, 618, 629, 647, 678–79, 687–88, 694
Johnstown, Pa., 637
Jordan, 684
Judaism, 54, 504, 631
Judicial branch, 131, 152–55, 172
Judiciary Committee (House), 600–1

K

Kansas, 310
Kansas-Nebraska Act (1854), 310–12
Kelley, Oliver H., 385
Kennedy, John F., 147, 592–94, 618, 629, 631, 673, 678, 687, 694–95
Kentucky, 104, 241, 319
Key, Francis Scott, 214
Khomeini, Ruhollah, 686
Khrushchev, Nikita, 672–73
King, Martin Luther, Jr., 621
Knights of Labor, 372
Know-Nothings, 275–76
Knox, Henry, 180
Korea, 677–78, 695
Korean War (1950–53), 147, 588, 591, 677–78, 695
Ku Klux Klan, 343–44, 504–5, 618

L

Labor, 369–70, 474, 579, 592, 616. *See also* Unemployment; Unions
Labor, Department of, 414
Labor Relations Act (1935), 526
Lafayette, Marquis de, 78, 80
Lake Champlain, battle of, 79
Land Ordinance (1785), 103, 105
Laos, 542, 678–80
Latin America, 23, 87, 288–89, 445, 453–57, 460–63, 495, 533–36, 540, 625–27, 669–70, 687–88, 695–96. *See also specific countries*

League of Nations, 482–85, 488, 491, 495, 533, 539, 564–65, 571–73
Lebanon, 573, 685, 696
Lee, Robert E., 318, 322, 324
Legislative branch, 130–34, 154–55, 171
Lend-Lease Act (1941), 540–42,
Lewis, Meriwether, 202
Lexington, battle of, 70–71, 77
Leyte Gulf, battle of, 557
Liberia, 295
Liberty Bonds, 474
Libya, 554
Lincoln, Abraham, 147, 311–14, 319–21, 335–36; debate with Douglas, 311–12; reconstruction plan, 335–37
Literacy tests, 610
Little Big Horn, battle of, 628
Little Rock, Ark., 618
Lockwood, Belva, 375
Lodge, Henry Cabot, 484–85
London Company, 35
Lone Star Republic, 266
Long drive, 377–78
Long Island, battle of, 79
Longfellow, Henry Wadsworth, 273
Los Angeles, Calif., 620, 646
Louis XIV, 26
Louisiana, 26, 188, 200, 241
Louisiana Purchase, 200–1
Louisiana Territory, 104, 200–2, 209, 215, 303, 310
Lovejoy, Elijah, 297
Loyalists, 77–78, 86, 191
Lusitania, 468
Lynchings, 611
Lyon, Mary, 261

M

MacArthur, Douglas, 147, 568, 677
McCarthy, Joseph R., 590
McClellan, George B., 322, 324
McCormick, Cyrus, 274
McDowell, Edward, 402
Machine politics, 392
McKinley, William, 395–96, 413, 436, 439–40, 445, 447
Madison, James, 116, 208–10, 213–15, 219, 466
Magellan, Ferdinand, 18
Maine, 39, 78, 214, 261, 303
Maine, 440
Malcolm X, 617
Manchuria, 491, 495, 539, 559, 564
Manifest Destiny, 265
Manilla Bay, battle of, 441
Mann, Horace, 260–61
Mao Tse-tung, 678, 680
Marbury v. Madison, 153
Mariana Islands, 557–58

Marines, U.S. *See* United States Marines
Marshall, George C., 669
Marshall, John, 219–20, 250
Marshall Islands, 557
Marshall Plan, 669
Marx, Karl, 680
Maryland, 37, 40, 53, 118, 233, 294, 319
Mason-Dixon Line, 40
Massachusetts, 37, 39, 53, 55–56, 69–71, 86, 109–11, 126, 260–61, 628
Maury, Matthew F., 274
Maximilian, 457
Mayflower, 37, 53
Mayflower Compact, 53
Medical and health care, 595, 639, 662, 694, 696
Medicare and Medicaid programs, 639–40, 662
Mediterranean Sea, 15, 24
Melville, Herman, 273
Metals, 653
Mexican Americans, 625–26
Mexican War (1846–48), 267–69, 303–4
Mexico, 3, 22–23, 265, 267–69, 455, 457, 462–63, 470, 534
Miami, Fla., 626
Middle East, 541, 546, 684–86, 694–96
Midway, battle of, 557
Migrant workers, 637
Milk industry, 519
Mineral resources, 653
Mining, 377
Minorities. *See specific groups*
Minutemen, 70–71, 78
Mississippi, 241, 618
Mississippi River, 3, 22, 26, 62–63, 85, 110–11, 201, 241, 384
Missouri, 242, 303, 319
Missouri Compromise (1820), 303, 310–11
Model Cities program, 595
Mohammed, 14
Monitor and *Merrimac*, battle between 324
Monopolies, 364–65, 414–15
Monroe, James, 218–22, 279, 456–57, 495
Monroe Doctrine, 221–22, 457, 461–62, 495
Monticello, 193
Moon, space flights to, 690
Morgan, J. P., 364, 414
Morocco, 554
Morse, Samuel, 274, 357
Moslems, 14–15, 22, 24. *See also* Arabs
Mott, Lucretia, 259
Mount Vernon, 118, 186, 188
Muckrakers, 401, 409, 415
Mussolini, Benito, 536, 539, 555

N

Nagasaki, and atomic bomb, 559
Napoleon Bonaparte, 195, 200–1, 206, 208, 214, 215
Napoleon III, 457
National Advisory Commission on Civil Disorders, 620, 646–47
National Association for the Advancement of Colored People (NAACP), 616
National Association for Woman Suffrage, 400
National Council of Negro Women, 619
National Environmental Policy Act (1970), 662
National Equal Rights Party, 375
National Guard, 119, 147
Nationalism, 218, 273
National Labor Relations Act (1935), 526
National Organization for Women (NOW), 630
National Recovery Administration (NRA), 523–24, 530
National Republican party. *See* Whig party
National Road, 203, 219, 241
National Urban League, 616
Native Americans. *See* Indians
Natural gas, 658
Natural resources, 364, 381, 415, 651–53
Navy, U.S. *See* United States Navy
Nazis, 535
Near East. *See* Middle East
Nebraska, 310
Negroes. *See* Blacks
Netherlands, 18, 80, 81, 109, 111, 180, 536, 540
Neutrality, 186–7, 206–7, 467–68
Neutrality, Proclamation of (1793), 186–87
Neutrality Acts (1935), 539–40
Nevada, 377
Newark, N.J., 620, 647
New Deal, 516, 519–24, 526–30, 578, 616, 629, 639. *See also* Depression; Roosevelt, Franklin D.
New England, 35, 37–38, 40, 62, 207, 213, 228–29, 268
New Federalism, 605, 640
New France, 26, 63
New Freedom, 420
New Frontier programs, 594
New Guinea, 557
New Hampshire, 39, 110
New Jersey, 39, 79, 80, 110, 119, 123, 230, 419
New Mexico, 266–67, 304–5, 380
New Netherlands, 39
New Orleans, La., 111, 188, 200, 215, 620

746

New South, 329–30
New York, 39, 69, 79, 80, 110, 126, 146, 213, 230
New York City, 40, 177, 207, 230, 616, 626–27
New York Journal, 440
New York Sun, 273
New Zealand, 557
Nicaragua, 462, 534
Nineteenth Amendment, 400, 474
Nixon, Richard M., 596, 600–2, 656, 662, 679–80, 689, 694
Noise, 645
Nonviolent resistance, 618
Norteamericanos, 453, 462
North, 40, 124, 296–97, 304, 306, 312, 344–45, 399. *See also* Civil War; South
North Atlantic Treaty Organization (NATO), 669, 688–89, 695
North Carolina, 37, 78, 104, 109, 233
North Korea, 677–78
North Vietnam, 678–80
Northwest Ordinance, 103, 105, 294, 303
Northwest Territory, 105, 187, 208, 213, 230, 294, 446
Norway, 540
Nuclear arms race, 672, 691
Nuclear energy, 658–59
Nuclear freeze, 691
Nuclear Test Ban Treaty (1963), 689
Nuclear weapons, 673, 689, 691

O

O'Connor, Sandra Day, 631
Office of Price Administration (OPA), 549
Ohio River, 60, 62, 103
Oil. *See* Petroleum
Okinawa, battle of, 558
Oklahoma, 380
Old age programs, 637–38, 664
Olympic Games, 686
"One person, one vote" ruling, 648
Open Door policy, 436, 488–89
Opium War, 434
Oregon, 202, 267
Organization of American States (OAS), 457, 669–70
Organization of Petroleum Exporting Countries (OPEC), 656

P

Pacific Ocean, battles in, 557–59
Pacifists, 475
Palestine, 14
Palestine Liberation Organization (PLO), 685, 696
Panama, 460–61, 688, 695

Panama Canal, 460–61, 495, 536, 688, 695
Pan-American Union, 457, 534–36
Panic of 1837, 252
Paris, Treaty of (1783), 81, 110, 187
Paris Peace Conference (1919), 482–85, 495
Paris Peace Pact, 490–91
Parliament (Great Britain), 32–33, 47–49, 61, 69–70, 77, 87, 91
Passive resistance, 618
Patriotism, 77–78, 191
Peace, 571–74
Peace Corps, 687
"Peaceful coexistence," 672–73
Peace treaties: Revolutionary War, 81, 110, 187; World War I, 482–85, 491, 495; World War II, 566–68
Pearl Harbor, attack on, 447, 542–43, 546
Peninsular Campaign, 322
Penn, William, 39–40
Pennsylvania, 39–40, 53, 56, 60, 64, 104, 110, 126, 628
Pennsylvania Gazette, 64
Perry, Matthew C., 434
Perry, Oliver H., 213–14
Pershing, John J., 473
Petroleum, 357, 591, 603, 656–57, 694
Philadelphia, Pa., 40, 56, 64, 71, 77, 79, 111, 116, 616
Philippines, 18, 435, 441–42, 445, 447–48, 488, 494–95, 557, 628
Pierce, Franklin, 306
Pilgrims, 37, 53, 55
Pittsburgh, Pa., 645
Pizarro, Francisco, 22
Plantation system, 35–36, 118, 233, 329
Plymouth, Mass., 37–39, 53
Pocahontas, 38
Pocket veto, 140
Poe, Edgar Allan, 273
Poland, 5, 539–40, 565, 672, 689, 696
Police power, 119
Political parties, 137–38, 148, 191–95. *See also specific parties*
Polk, James Knox, 267
Poll taxes, 345, 610, 618
Pollution, 645, 647, 662–63
Ponce de León, Luis, 22
Poor Richard's Almanack, 64
Populist party, 387, 395
Portugal, 11, 23–24, 87, 456
Poverty, 594–96, 600, 612, 636, 638–40
Presidency, U.S., 117–18, 126, 133, 140, 144–48, 152–54, 161, 171–72, 434, 436, 446, 508. *See also specific Presidents*
Presidents *pro tempore* (of Senate), 132
Primary elections, 407, 610, 616

Princeton, battle of, 79
Progressive Era, 406–9, 413–16, 418–20
Progressive party, 419, 507, 590
Prohibition, 400, 504, 508
Propaganda, during WWI, 467, 475
Protectorates, U.S., 442
Protestantism, 32, 37, 40, 55, 631
Public education, 55–56, 260, 400–1
Public Works Administration, 522
Puerto Rico, 441–42, 445, 448–49, 460, 463, 494–95, 625–27
Pulaski, Casimir, 78
Puritans, 37, 39, 53–55

Q

Quakers, 40, 54, 294
Quebec, 63, 68
Quotas, immigration, 505–6, 627

R

Racism, 6, 345, 436, 611–12, 617, 620
Radical Republicans, 337, 342
Radicals. *See* Communism; Socialism
Railroads, 356, 371, 378–79, 384–86, 414, 418, 507
Randolph, Edmund, 180
Rationing, during WWII, 549, 588
Reagan, Ronald, 604–5, 631, 640, 647, 661, 663, 685, 688, 690, 695–96
"Reaganomics," 605
Realism (literature), 401
Recalls, 408–9
Reconstruction period, 334–39, 342–45, 610–12
Recreational activities, 662
Red Cross, 330
"Red menace," 589–90, 694
"Red scare," 504, 514
Reed, Walter, 442
Referendum, 407–8
Religion, 32, 39–40, 46, 53–56, 86, 164, 631. *See also specific faiths*
"Remember the *Maine,*" 440
Republican party, 191, 193–95, 218–22, 226, 310–13, 345, 392–96, 416, 445, 506–7, 516, 529, 590–96, 600–5, 694–95
Reserved powers, 117, 119
Revenue-sharing legislation, 600
Revere, Paul, 71
Revolutionary War. *See* American Revolution
Rhode Island, 39, 53–54, 109, 116, 126, 228, 628
Richmond, Va., 647
"Rights of Englishmen," 48–49, 78, 85, 91, 164

747

Rio Grande, 455, 457
Riots, 620, 672
Roaring Twenties, 503–4, 578
Rockefeller, John D., 364–65
Rockefeller, Nelson A., 601
Roman Catholicism, 23, 26, 31–32, 37, 289, 400, 456, 504, 508, 631
Rome, 14, 288
Roosevelt, Eleanor, 617
Roosevelt, Franklin D., 154, 516, 520–21, 524, 529, 533, 536, 539–40, 542, 548, 558, 563–64, 616–17, 629, 639. *See also* New Deal
Roosevelt, Theodore, 413–16, 418–19, 433–34, 436, 441, 445–46, 460–62, 468, 494–95, 520
Rough Riders, 413, 441
Rubber industry, 548–49, 556, 636
Rules Committee (House), 139
Rumania, 539, 566
Rural Electrification Administration, 528
Russia, 5, 222, 329, 436, 446, 456–57, 466, 473, 481. *See also* Soviet Union
Russo-Japanese War, 436

S

Sabotage, 469
Sadat, Anwar, 685
Safe Drinking Water Act (1974), 652
St. Lawrence River, 18, 26, 63, 591
St. Louis, Mo., 202
Salvation Army, 400
Samoa, 435, 494
San Antonio, Texas, 646
San Diego, Calif., 646
San Francisco, Calif., 436
Sanitary Commission (Civil War), 330, 399
San Juan Hill, battle of, 441
Santa Anna, Antonio López de, 266
Santo Domingo, 200
Saratoga, battle of, 80
Satellites, space, 591, 661, 691
Scalawags, 343
Science and technology, 548–49
Scotland, 4, 60–61
Secretariat (UN), 572
Secretary general (UN), 572
Securities and Exchange Commission (SEC), 529
Security Council (UN), 571, 574, 677, 680
Sedition Act. *See* Alien and Sedition Acts
Segregation, 345, 610–12, 618, 694
Selective Service, 473, 540, 547, 588
Senate, 123–26, 131–34, 137, 140, 145, 147, 152, 172, 418, 484–85, 488, 495, 590, 601
Senatorial courtesy, 134

"Separate but equal" court decision, 612, 618
Separation of powers, 131, 171
Seventeenth Amendment, 418
Seward, William, 329
Shah of Iran, 685–86, 696
Shale, 657
Sharecroppers, 329, 611
Shays's Rebellion, 109–11, 131
Sherman, William T., 324
Sherman Antitrust Act (1890), 365, 387, 414–15, 418, 420
Shipping industry, 228, 434–35, 507, 540, 548, 556
Silk trade, 434
Silver purchase acts, 386–87, 395
Sinclair, Upton, 415
Sit-ins, 618
Sixteenth Amendment, 418
Sixth Amendment, 166
Slater, Samuel, 228
Slavery: abolition of, 328; in ancient times, 288; and Civil War, 294–98, 302–6, 310–14; in colonies, 36, 52, 56, 287–90; in Constitution, 124; in Northwest Ordinance, 105; during Revolution, 86; treatment of, 234–35. *See also* Abolitionists; Blacks; Civil War
Slums, 526–27, 612, 647
Smith, Alfred E., 508
Smith, John, 36, 38
Smog, 645
Smuggling, 62, 68
Socialism, 401–2, 419, 473, 475, 504, 515
Social Security, 526, 594–95, 639
Soil conservation, 527–28, 653
Sojourner Truth, 296
Solar energy, 659
Solidarity, 689
Solid South, 345, 392, 508
Solomon Islands, 557
Sons of Liberty, 69–70
South, 39, 53, 80, 124, 233–36, 250, 297–98, 304, 306, 312–13, 335–38, 342–45, 381, 392, 399–400. *See also* Civil War; North
South America. *See* Latin America; *specific countries*
South Carolina, 37, 80, 233, 250–51, 313–14
South Dakota, 630
South Korea, 677–78
South Vietnam, 678–80
Soviet Union, 3, 119, 539, 541–42, 546, 554–56, 559, 564–68, 574, 661, 668–74, 677, 680, 684, 686, 688–90, 695–96. *See also* Communism; Russia
Space program, 591, 661, 691

Spain, 11, 13, 17, 22, 24, 62–63, 80–81, 104, 109, 111, 180, 188, 221–22, 435, 439–42, 445, 447, 456, 460, 494, 539
Spanish-Americans. *See* Hispanic Americans
Spanish-American War (1898), 409, 439–42, 447, 460, 494
Spargo, John, 401
Speakeasies, 504
Speakers (of House), 131
Spoils system, 249–50, 392
Sports, 663
Sputnik, 591, 661, 691
Square Deal, 413–14
Stalin, Joseph, 555, 563, 566–67, 668–69, 695
Stamp Act, 68–71
Stamp Act Congress, 69
Standard Oil Company, 364, 401, 414
Statehood, for territories, 446
States' rights, 119, 236, 250–51
States' Rights party, 590
Steam locomotives and ships, 229, 433
Steel industry, 636
Steffens, Lincoln, 401
Stephens, Uriah, 372
Stephenson, George, 229
Steuben, Baron von, 78
Stevens, Thaddeus, 337
Stevenson, Adlai, 591
Stock market crash, 512–13, 528–29. *See also* Depression
Stowe, Harriet Beecher, 306
Strategic Arms Limitation Talks (SALT), 689–90
Strikes, 371–72, 414, 474, 694
Strip city, 645
Submarines, 468–70, 473, 540, 542, 546, 556
Suburbs, 645–46
Suez Canal, 684
Sugar plantations, 435, 439, 442, 448
Sunbelt, 646
Supercity, 645
Supremacy clause, 119, 153
Supreme Court, U.S., 99, 140, 147, 152–54, 160–61, 164–66, 171–72, 219–21, 250, 258, 311, 342, 409, 414–15, 420, 446, 476, 514, 529, 600, 612, 616–18, 648, 694
Sweatshops, 369
Syria, 684

T

Taft, William Howard, 416, 418–19, 447–48, 460, 462, 495
Taft-Hartley Act (1947), 589
Taiwan, 677, 680
Tarbell, Ida, 401
Tariffs, 109–10, 117, 124, 230, 235–36,

243, 250–51, 298, 302, 312, 394–95, 418, 439, 442, 448, 490, 507, 512, 514–15, 522–23. *See also* Customs duties
Taxes, 345, 474, 514, 524, 549, 605, 640
Taylor, Zachary, 268, 304
Tea trade, 434
Television, 663
Temperance movement, 261, 400
Tenant farmers, 637
Tenement laws, 409
Tennessee, 241, 253
Tennessee Valley Authority (TVA), 528, 591, 653
Territories, U.S., 103, 105, 435, 442, 446, 449, 494–95
Texas, 236, 242, 266–67, 377, 470
Thirteenth Amendment, 328
Three-fifths compromise, 125
Tito, Marshall, 671
Toleration Act (Md.), 37
Tories. *See* Loyalists
Town meetings, 53, 91
Toxic Substances Control Act (1976), 663
Trade, 186, 206–8, 230, 433, 514–15, 522–23; with China, 434–36; during colonial period, 36–37, 39–40, 62, 68–69; with Cuba, 439; with Europe, 433; with Hawaii, 435; with Japan, 434; with Philippines, 448
Trade Acts, 61–62, 68, 109
Trade Agreements Act (1934), 522–23
Trade unions. *See* Unions
Traffic problems, 647
Transcontinental railroads, 378–79
Transportation Department, U.S., 647
Treaties. *See* Peace treaties
Trenton, battle of, 79
Trial by jury, 48, 85, 166
Tripoli, war with, 202–3
Truman, Harry S, 144, 147–48, 153–54, 558–59, 566, 587–590, 617, 668, 684, 694
Truman Doctrine, 668
Trusteeship Council (UN), 572
Trusts, 364–65, 414–15
Tubman, Harriet, 297
Tunisia, 554
Turkey, 481, 668, 695
Turner, Nat, 295
Twain, Mark (Samuel Clemens), 401
Tweed, William M. (Boss), 391
Twentieth Amendment, 132
Twenty-fifth Amendment, 146
Twenty-first Amendment, 159, 504
Twenty-fourth Amendment, 618
Twenty-sixth Amendment, 600
Tyler, John, 267
Typhoid, 442

U

U-2 incident, 673
Uncle Tom's Cabin (Stowe), 306
Underground Railroad, 297
Unemployment, 513, 522, 603–5, 620, 664, 694–95. *See also* Depression; New Deal
UNESCO (United Nations Educational, Scientific, and Cultural Organization), 572
Union of Soviet Socialist Republics. *See* Soviet Union
Union Pacific Railroad, 378–79
Unions, 258, 371–73, 474, 504, 507, 514, 526, 549, 578, 588–89, 592, 618, 626. *See also* Labor
United Farm Workers, 626
United Kingdom. *See* Great Britain
United Nations (UN), 564–65, 568, 571–74, 677–78, 680, 684, 691
United Nations Charter, 565, 571, 574
United Nations Educational, Scientific, and Cultural Organization (UNESCO), 572
United States Army, 440–42, 446, 461–62, 473, 476–77
United States Marines, 461–62, 685, 688, 696
United States Navy, 440–42, 447, 460, 462, 473, 488–89, 542
Universal Declaration of Human Rights, 573
"Unwritten" Constitution, 161
Urban renewal programs. *See* Cities; Slums
Uruguay, 456, 688
Utah, 304–5, 379

V

Valley Forge, Pa., 81
Van Buren, Martin, 254, 258, 266, 279, 304
Vassa, Gustavus, 294
Venezuela, 457, 461
Vermont, 39
Vespucci, Amerigo, 17
Veto power, 56, 140
Vice-Presidency, U.S., 132, 145–46, 148
Video games, 663
Vietcong, 679
Vietnam, 542, 678–80, 695
Vietnam War, 147, 595–96, 678–80, 694–95
Viking I, 692
Vikings, 13
Villa, Pancho, 462
Virginia, 35–36, 60, 69, 80, 104, 118, 123, 126, 180–81, 193, 233, 241, 294–95, 312, 618, 628

Virgin Islands, 462
Volunteers in Service to America (VISTA), 594
Voting, 53, 407, 600, 610, 618, 648, 694
Voting Rights Act (1965), 596, 618, 626, 694
Voyager II, 690

W

Wage-price controls, 549, 588
Wake Island, 435
Walesa, Lech, 689
War debts, 489–90
War Hawks, 208–9, 213, 226, 279
War Industries Board, 474
War Labor Board, 474
War of 1812 (1812–15), 206–9, 212–15, 218–22, 253, 279, 466, 539
War on Poverty, 594–96, 600, 618
War Production Board, 548
War Shipping Board, 474
Warsaw Pact, 670–71
Washington, Booker T., 400–1, 616
Washington, D.C., 180, 214, 547, 616, 647
Washington, George, 118, 200, 206–7, 278; at Constitutional Convention, 111, 116; during French and Indian War, 50; as President, 147–48, 161, 179–83, 186–88, 191–95, 431, 433, 494; during Revolutionary War, 77, 81
Water, 651–52, 658
Water Pollution Control Act (1972), 652
Watergate scandal, 600–2, 694–95
Wayne, Anthony, 187
Weaver, Robert C., 647
Webster, Daniel, 250
Weinberger, Caspar, 688–89
Welfare programs, 522. *See also* Social Security
West, 110, 240–44, 287, 376, 380–81, 433
West Germany, 567, 669, 673, 689
West Indies, 23–24, 26, 36, 62, 109, 187, 455, 462, 495, 534
West Virginia, 636
Western Europe. *See specific countries*
Whaling industry, 435
Wheatley, Phillis, 294
Whig party, 244, 254, 267, 304, 310
Whiskey Rebellion, 182, 194
Whiskey tax, 181, 194, 200
White backlash, 620
White House, 214, 515
White Plains, battle of, 79
White primaries, 610, 616
White supremacy attitude, 611–12, 618
Whitney, Eli, 233, 274, 295
Whittier, John Greenleaf, 273

749

Wildcat currency, 252
Wilderness Campaign, 324
Wilderness Road, 104, 241
Williams, Roger, 39, 54
Wilson, Woodrow, 146, 419–20, 460, 462, 466–70, 473–74, 481–85, 488, 495, 529, 564, 616
Women, 30, 52, 56, 119, 230, 240–41, 243, 258–59, 261, 330, 369–70, 372, 375, 390, 399, 409, 474, 503, 547, 549, 630–1
Women's Medical College, 375
Women's rights movement, 258–59, 330, 400, 409, 474, 630–1
Workers. *See* Labor; Unions
Worker's compensation, 409, 414
Works Project Administration (WPA), 522, 530

World, 401
World Court (UN), 484, 488
World Health Organization (UN), 572
World War I, 462, 466–70, 473–77, 481–85, 490, 495, 501, 503, 514, 539, 563, 568, 616, 629
World War II, 446, 448, 501, 536, 539–43, 546–50, 554–59, 563–68, 573, 579, 588, 591, 617, 627–30
Wounded Knee, S.D., 630
Wright, Frances, 259
Wyoming, 259

X

XYZ affair, 194–95

Y

Yalta agreement, 564–67
Yankee clippers, 228, 434
Yellow fever, 442, 460–61
Yellow journalism, 439–40, 488
Yorktown, battle of, 80
Youngstown, Ohio, 637
Youth, 503, 522, 526, 549, 637–38
Yugoslavia, 541, 671, 695

Z

Zenger, John Peter, 55
Zimmermann Note, 470

Acknowledgments

For permission to reprint "This Land Is Your Land" by Woody Guthrie, which appears on page one, acknowledgment is made to TRO—© 1956, 1958, 1970 Ludlow Music, Inc. New York, N.Y. Used by permission.

Photographs

United Press International: Page 1; Maine State Development Office: 4 (top); Coronet Instructional Media: 4 (center); Union Pacific Railroad: 4 (bottom); United Airlines: 5 (top); H. Armstrong Roberts: 5 (center); Union Pacific Railroad: 5 (bottom); United States Department of the Interior, Bureau of Reclamation: 6 (top); Arthur Mina: 6 (bottom); The Bettmann Archive: 10–11; The Granger Collection: 15 (top); New York Public Library: 15 (bottom); American Museum of Natural History: 18 (Photo by Janet Chernela, Courtesy of The American Museum of Natural History; James M. McLean: 23 (top); American Airlines Photo: 23 (bottom); Coronet Instructional Media: 24 (top); British Museum: 24 (bottom); Black Star © Edward Pieratt: 31 (left); Library of Congress: 31 (right), 32; Coronet Instructional Media: 37; Historical Picture Service, Chicago: 38; The Bettmann Archive: 39; Library of Congress: 40; Coronet Instructional Media: 47; Historical Pictures Service, Chicago: 48; Colonial Williamsburg Foundation: 49; Smithsonian Institution: 53; New York Public Library: 54 (top); The Bettmann Archive: 54 (bottom); Standard Oil Company, N.J.: 55; The Bettmann Archive: 56; National Archives: 63; Library of Congress: 64; New York Public Library: 69; Library of Congress: 70; The Bettmann Archive: 71, 72, 79 (center), 80; New York Public Library: 79 (left); United States Department of the Interior, National Park Service: 79 (right); Valley Forge Historical Society: 81; Indiana Historical Society Library: 85; Coronet Instructional Media: 87; United States Department of the Interior, National Park Service: 88; H. Armstrong Roberts: 97, 98–99 (left, center, and right), 103; John Hancock Mutual Life Insurance Company: 104; The Bettmann Archive: 110, 111; Eastern National Park and Monument Association: 117; National Gallery of Art: 118; Historical Picture Service, Chicago: 125, 126; Coronet Instructional Media: 133 (left and right); The Bettmann Archive: 134; Editorial Photocolor Archives: 138 (top); Coronet Instructional Media: 138 (bottom); United Press International: 140, 147, 148; White House Photo Office: 153; Department of the Treasury, U.S. Customs Service: 160; American Airlines Photo: 161; United Press International: 166; H. Armstrong Roberts: 167; Coronet Instructional Media: 171; The Historic New Orleans Collection: 176–177 (top and bottom); Museum of the City of New York: 181; The Granger Collection: 182 (top); Library of Congress: 182 (bottom), 187; Coronet Instructional Media: 188; New York Public Library: 193; The Bettmann Archive: 194; Library of Congress: 202 (top); The Bettmann Archive: 202 (bottom); The Granger Collection: 207; Library of Congress: 208; The Bettmann Archive: 212; Library of Congress: 214; The Bettmann Archive: 215; Library of Congress: 219; Historical Pictures Service, Chicago: 220; The Bettmann Archive: 221, 222; Library of Congress: 228; The Bettmann Archive: 230; H. Armstrong Roberts: 234; The Granger Collection: 235; Maryland Historical Society, Baltimore: 241; International Harvester: 243; The Bettmann Archive: 249; Woolaroc Museum, Bartlesville, Oklahoma: 250; The Bettmann Archive: 251; Library of Congress: 252, 259 (left); New York Public Library: 259 (center); Historical Pictures Service, Chicago: 259 (right); The Bettmann Archive: 260 (top); John Hancock Mutual Life Insurance Company: 260 (bottom); Mount Holyoke College: 261; Library of Congress: 267, 268 (left and right); New York Public Library: 268 (center); The Granger Collection: 269; The New York Public Library/Art Resource: 273; The Granger Collection: 275; The Bettmann Archive: 284–285; The New York Historical Society: 287; New York Public Library: 289; The Granger Collection: 290 (top); Scala/Art Resource: 290 (bottom); New York Public Library: 296 (left); His-

751

torical Pictures Service, Chicago: 296 (center); Library of Congress: 296 (right); Boston Society, Old State House: 297 (top); Cincinnati Art Museum: 297 (bottom); Library of Congress: 304; New York Public Library: 305; Library of Congress: 306; Historical Pictures Service, Chicago: 311; The Bettmann Archive: 313; Chicago Historical Society: 319; Library of Congress: 321; United States Department of the Interior, National Park Service: 323, 324; The Bettmann Archive: 328; The New York Historical Society: 329; The Bettmann Archive: 336; Library of Congress: 337 (top and bottom), 338 (left and right), 342, 343; Historical Pictures Service, Chicago: 344; The Bettmann Archive: 352–353; United States Steel: 357 (top); Historical Pictures Service, Chicago: 357 (bottom); The Granger Collection: 358; Historical Pictures Service, Chicago: 359; Carnegie Institute: 363 (left); Historical Pictures Service, Chicago: 363 (center left); Morgan Guaranty Trust Company: 363 (center right); Ford Motor Company: 363 (right); Library of Congress: 365; Shostal Associates: 366; Historical Pictures Service, Chicago: 370 (left); St. Louis Post Dispatch: 370 (center left); Library of Congress: 370 (center right); RCA Victor Records: 370 (right); The Bettmann Archive: 371, 372; New York Infirmary: 375 (top); Brown Brothers: 375 (bottom); Denver Public Library, Western History Department: 378 (left and center); Solomon D. Butcher Collection/Nebraska State Historical Society: 378 (right); The Granger Collection: 379; Library of Congress: 380, 385; New York Public Library: 387 (left and right), 393, 395; Historical Pictures Service, Chicago: 400; National Archives: 401; Wide World Photos: 408 (top); United Press International: 408 (top); Library of Congress: 413; Theodore Roosevelt Association: 415; Culver: 419 (top); Library of Congress: 419 (bottom); Vermont Agency of Development and Community Affairs: 430–431; Brown Brothers: 435; New York Public Library: 440; Theodore Roosevelt Association: 441; H. Armstrong Roberts: 447; Puerto Rico Economic Development Administration: 449 (left and right); *Manchete:* 455 (left); United Nations: 455 (right); Wide World Photos: 456; United Nations, Y. Nagata/ARA: 461; Theodore Roosevelt Association: 462; National Archives: 463 (left and right); New York Public Library: 468; Chicago Historical Society: 469; Library of Congress: 475 (left); Museum of the City of New York: 475 (right); United States Army Photograph: 477; National Archives: 483; Library of Congress: 484; Library of Congress: 490; Jerry Doyle: 491; The New School for Social Research: 500–501; The Granger Collection: 505 (top); National Archives: 505 (bottom); Stephen Sally: 507 (left); Library of Congress: 507 (right); F.D.R. Library, Hyde Park, New York: 513; Whitney Museum of American Art: 515 (Isaac Soyer, *Employment Agency*. 1937. Oil on canvas. 34¼ × 45 inches. Collection of the Whitney Museum of American Art.); National Archives: 521; F.D.R. Library, Hyde Park, N.Y.: 522; National Archives: 523 (top); New York Public Library: 523 (bottom); Frederic Lewis, Inc.: 527 (top and bottom); Library of Congress: 529; United Nations: 535 (top); United Press International: 536 (left); Hugo Jaeger, Time/Life Picture Agency and © Time/Life, Inc.: 536 (right); United States Army Photograph: 541; National Archives: 542 (left); United States Army Photograph: 542 (right), 547; Library of Congress: 548; National Archives: 549; United Press International: 556; United States Navy Photograph: 557; United States Army Photograph: 559; National Archives: 565; United Press International: 566; United Nations: 572, 573, 574, 579; Wide World Photos: 584–585; Balterman/Freelance Photographers Guild: 588; United Press International: 589, 590; Greensboro Daily News: 591; United Press International: 592; Wide World Photos: 594; Vista/Emma Rodriguez: 595 (left and right); Wide World Photos: 601 (left); United Press International: 601 (right), 602, 603; The White House Photo Office: 604; Van Bucher/Photo Researchers: 610; Y. Beller/Freelance Photographers Guild: 611; United Press International: 617 (left, center, and right), 619, 620 (top, left, center, and right), 621; John Running/Stock, Boston: 626; Wide World Photos: 628; Coronet Instructional Media: 629; Ann Chwatsky/Leo De Wys: 630; Michael Evans/White House Photo Office: 631 (top); Wide World Photos: 631 (bottom); International Business Machines: 636 (top); Sanderling/Freelance Photographers Guild: 636 (bottom); Allis-Chalmers Corp.: 637; Diana Walker/Liaison Agency: 638; Arthur Mina: 640; Harold M. Lambert Studios: 644; Adelaide Garvin Ungerland © 1978: 645; Jack Albertson/Stock, Boston: 647; Girl Scouts of the United States of America: 651; Coronet Instructional Media: 652; © Earl Roberge/Photo Researchers: 653; United Press International: 656; Wide World Photos: 657; Coronet Instructional Media: 658; Langley/Alpha Photo Associates: 661; Coronet Instructional Media: 662, 663; Michael Meadows/Editorial Photocolor Archives: 664; The Bettmann Archive: 668; United Press International: 672, 674; United States Army Photograph: 678, 679; Wide World Photos: 680, 685; © Gamma Liaison: 686; Action Photo by Leroy Woodson: 687; H. Armstrong Roberts: 689; United Press International: 695; H. Armstrong Roberts: 697.